Russian Research Center Studies, 59

Soviet-Polish Relations, 1917-1921

Soviet-Polish Relations, 1917-1921

Piotr S. Wandycz

Harvard University Press

Cambridge, Massachusetts 1969

The Russian Research Center of Harvard University is supported by a grant from the Ford Foundation. The Center carries out interdisciplinary study of Russian institutions and behavior and related subjects.

Library of Congress Catalog Card Number 69-18047
SBN 674-82780-5
Printed in the United States of America

For my Father

Preface

During the formative years following the October Revolution of 1917, antagonism and complexity characterized Soviet-Polish relations. The very word "relations" may seem inappropriate, because for the entire period none officially existed. But irrespective of the legal situation the Soviet Russian problem was paramount for the Poles, the Polish question was important for the Bolsheviks, and there was a considerable play of negotiations along with armed conflict.

The relations between the two countries may be examined from different perspectives. They may be studied in terms of ideology and social revolution, or one may concentrate on territorial issues and become drawn into the labyrinth of Ukrainian, Lithuanian, and Belorussian affairs. Whatever the view, one must recognize ideological, socio-political, and territorial problems. Domestic developments in Poland, the Civil War in Russia, and the changing international scene are pertinent. To examine all these issues without being absorbed by any single problem; to preserve some clarity in the midst of confusion; to draw a comprehensive yet not an oversimplified picture: these have been the greatest chal lenges and difficulties of this study.

By concentrating on Soviet-Polish relations this book only touches on the cooperation or lack thereof between Poland and the Russian Whites. Polish Communists receive greater attention than their importance in the politics of the country otherwise would warrant. Military affairs appear only when necessary for an understanding of the general situation. The international background is not treated in detail. A more extensive analysis of Poland than of Russia results partly from an imbalance in documentation, and partly because Polish politics more decisively influenced the country's foreign policy than politics within Soviet Russia influenced the moves of the Lenin regime.

This study attempts to present Soviet-Polish relations against the background of past centuries. Irrespective of one's view of continuity in Russian history, it is evident that in 1917 neither country could start with a clean slate. Many aspects of their relations were new but few were divorced from the past. The four years discussed here were only a phase in the long history of

Russo-Polish relations. Still, they were crucial years. They inaugurated a quarter of a century during which a Bolshevik Russia faced a non-Communist Poland—a period which came to an abrupt end with the Second World War. Much of it was determined by events from the October Revolution of 1917 to the Treaty of Riga of 1921. These events were not merely of local importance; they affected Eastern Europe and indeed the entire European continent.

In the preparation of this book I encountered some technical problems connected with transliteration from the Cyrillic alphabet and with the rendition of geographic names. While adhering to the prevailing rules of transliteration I found it necessary to make certain exceptions. I retained the more familiar form of Kerensky, Zinoviev, Trotsky, and a few others. I used the original spelling of Polish names, for instance Dzierżyński (though Dzerzhinsky is better known) and gave both the original form and the transliterated one in the case of Latvian names such as Vatsetis (Vaciētis). As a rule I used the official geographic names in existence after the Treaty of Riga, except for those which have an anglicized form: Warsaw, Brest, Danzig, Moscow, and others.

The generous support of many institutions and individuals made this book possible. The bulk of research and writing was accomplished while I was a Research Fellow at the Russian Research Center at Harvard, and I would like to thank the Center, and Merle Fainsod, Abram Bergson, Richard Pipes, Adam Ulam, and Mrs. Helen Parsons. The typing of the manuscript was kindly arranged by Miss Loueva F. Pflueger, executive secretary of the department of history at Yale. I am grateful for the financial assistance received from Indiana University under the Ford International Program; the Rockefeller Foundation; the American Philosophical Society in Philadelphia; and the Yale University Stimson Fund. The expert help of librarians, archivists, and scholars in the field greatly facilitated my labors. I would like to specifically thank Paul Depta of the Widener Library, Harvard University, Fritz T. Epstein and Andrew Turchyn of the Indiana University Library, Oktawian Jastrzębski from Montreal, Wacław Jędrzejewicz and Adam Koc of the Józef Piłsudski Institute of America, Lev F. Magerovsky of the Archive of Russian and East European History and Culture of Columbia University, and Wiktor Sukiennicki and Witold Sworakowski of the Hoover Institution at Stanford. I am grateful to Anna M. Cienciala of the University of Kansas, and to Betty Jo Winchester, for assistance with material from the Public Record Office in London and the National Archives in Washington.

The material from the Trotsky and Smolensk Archives and from the Moffat Papers is cited here by permission of the Harvard College Library; citations from Crown-copyright records in the Public Record Office appear by permission of the Controller of H.M. Stationary Office. I would like to thank the Hoover Institution on War, Revolution, and Peace; the Archive of Russian and East European History and Culture at Columbia University; the Historical Manuscripts Division of Yale University Library; the National Archives in Washington; the Józef Piłsudski Institute of America; and the Polish Institute of Arts and Sciences in New York for allowing me to cite or quote from their archival holdings. I want to thank the Polish Academy of Sciences, the National Library in Warsaw, and the Institute of Polish-Soviet Relations for microfilms of the Kossakowski and Osmołowski manuscripts and select copies of documents from the Paderewski Archive.

I am indebted to colleagues in this country and in Poland who kept me informed of recent publications and assisted in numerous other ways: Henryk Batowski and Henryk Wereszycki of Jagiellonian University, Cracow; Tadeusz Cieślak of the Institute for the History of Soviet-Polish Relations, Warsaw; Robert Tucker and Richard H. Ullman of Princeton University; and Wiktor Weintraub of Harvard University. Dr. Karol Poznański, perhaps the last surviving member of the secretariat of the Polish peace delegation at Riga, kindly commented on various aspects of the conference. I owe a special dept of gratitude to my friend Robert H. Ferrell of Indiana University for reading the entire manuscript and improving it stylistically and otherwise. My family's constant interest in the progress of this study was most inspiring.

Having received so much help and encouragement, I am nonetheless solely responsible for the presentation and interpretation of the material in this book. No one is more aware than I of its imperfections.

P. S. W.

New Haven, Connecticut
September 1968

Contents

Maps

Contents

Soviet-Polish Relations, 1917-1921

Some Abbreviations Used in the Text

glavkom (glavnokomanduiush-chii) — supreme commander

KPRP (Komunistyczna Partia Robotnicza Polski) — Communist Workers' Party of Poland

Narkomindel (Narodnyi Komissariat Inostrannykh Del) — National Commissariat for Foreign Affairs

POW (Polska Organizacja Wojskowa) — Polish Military Organization

PPS (Polska Partia Socjalistyczna) — Polish Socialist Party

revkom (revoliutsionnyi komitet) — revolutionary committee

revvoensovet (revoliutsionnyi voennyi sovet) — revolutionary war council

RKP (b) (Rossiiskaia Kommunisticheskaia Partiia) (bolshevikov) — Russian Communist Party (bolsheviks)

SDKPiL (Socjaldemokracja Królestwa Polskiego i Litwy) — Social Democracy of the Kingdom of Poland and Lithuania

Tsentroplenbezh (Tsentralnaia Kollegiia o Plennykh i Bezhentsakh) — Central College for Prisoners of War and Refugees

VTsIK (Vserossiiskii Tsentralnyi Ispolnitelnyi Komitet) — All-Russian Central Executive Committee

1

The Heritage of the Past

The October Revolution of 1917 opened a new era of Russian-Polish relations. The Bolsheviks proclaimed a break with the tsarist past. The Poles, recovering their independence after almost a century and a half, were in many respects a different nation from the *Respublica* of nobles which went down in the partitions. But as subsequent years were to tell, it was hardly possible to discard the past. It weighed too heavily on Russians and Poles, influencing their ways of thinking and acting. Even Lenin had to admit late in 1920 that the war then being fought between the two countries resulted from Poland's historic position of a great power opposing another great power, Russia. "Poland," he said, "cannot abandon this old perennial struggle even now."[1]

For hundreds of years antagonism and strife had characterized relations between the two countries. It was no series of petty antagonisms, but a clash between two civilizations—a conflict between Eastern and Western historical trends. The Catholic church had drawn Poland into the Western European stream of life. The Poles became part of a universal tradition with all it implied: an international language (Latin), which remained the second tongue of the elite for centuries; Western scholarship and philosophy; Western art; Western-type politics and socio-economic relations. Acceptance of Christianity from Rome opened large perspectives for the Poles and indicated the broad lines of their development.

The influence of Greek Orthodoxy on Russia was of a different nature. Not only was the outlook of the Eastern church in striking contrast to that of the church of Rome, but the Russians took over Byzantine theology without acquiring Hellenism. Greek never played the part in Russia which Latin took in the West. The fall of Byzantium, coinciding with the rise of Moscow, diminished the chance that Orthodoxy might become a channel through which universal ideas would enter Russia. The result was cultural self-centrism and increased separation. As Petr Chaadayev wrote: "we Russians have nothing in common with Homer, the Greeks, the Romans, and the Germans; all this is completely foreign to us."[2]

The consequences of this state of affairs were important, and a Russian scholar, analyzing the historic enmity between Poland

and Russia, saw its cause primarily in Polish Catholicism. The Roman church, K. N. Iarosh said, had become an instrument of Poland's subjugation by the West. All the ideas which had come through Catholicism were alien to Russia and Slavdom.[3] Other influences also worked to further separate the two countries. Byzantine autocracy, reinforced by Mongol despotism, made relations in Russia between the government and the governed resemble those between the conqueror and the conquered. Michael Florinsky summed it up succinctly: "notions of legality, constitutionality, and democracy were alien to the Russian historical tradition."[4] In Poland the opposite was true. Influenced by Western thought, Polish theories of power, law, and liberty developed along native lines with an emphasis on liberties and privileges. A sixteenth-century law book asserted that the king and the estates should be subject to the law; the Polish constitution of 1791 proclaimed that all authority originated from the will of the nation.[5] Even if the term "nation" had a narrow definition, its use limited the executive power.

Striking differences between Russia and Poland existed in social and economic affairs. While an agrarian aristocratic regime accompanied by serfdom prevailed in both countries, the Russian regime always denied the absolute nature of private property, and until the late eighteenth century the nobility held its land in exchange for services. Communal land ownership was a typical feature of peasant holdings. Such things were practically unknown in Poland. Serfdom continued in Russia largely because the dependence of serfs on lords completed the dependence of the nobility on the tsar—a foundation on which rested the autocratic system. In Poland serfdom endured because the nobility was strong enough to oppose any reform attempted by a ruler—for instance John Casimir. The very character of Polish nobility, egalitarian and antimonarchical, contrasted with the Russian, state-made and state-controlled.

Differences in domestic developments found expression in the foreign policies of the two countries. In Poland the diet (sejm) influenced matters of war and peace, and the nobles preferred negotiations and unions to outright conquests which might strengthen the royal power. The state expanded by contracting acts of union—as with Lithuania and Livonia—and in the new lands wide autonomy prevailed. The phenomenal Russian expansion was largely by sword and was often followed by leveling of differences. Diplomacy was a sacred domain of the tsar, and it changed from one reign to another. Justifications for expansion seldom corresponded to reality. Moscow began to "gather Russian lands" as the successor of Kiev but soon conquered the non-Russian Kazan and moved east. The Third Rome idea, later the Panslavic creed, did not have a consistent application, but the theme that Providence had "placed upon us the charge of humanity" periodically reappeared.[6] On the whole, opportunities rather than theories determined Russian expansion. The drive to the Baltic and Black seas, even if part of a plan, started when states that barred Russian access to these waters began to decline. Conquests in Asia had a grounding in geopolitics, and with the control of the vast hinterland the Russian position became almost unassailable. As for the expansion of Poland, far from systematic and bearing a clear imprint of the vested interests of the nobility, it proved less than successful. After the collapse of the plans of the Piast rulers to gather western Slavs in opposition to Germany, the Poles turned eastward—a policy that was to bring them up against Russia. By union with Lithuania, completed in 1569, Poland acquired huge territories, but although the state stretched from the Baltic to the Black Sea it never established itself on either litoral. Prussia remained a thorn in the northwest, the unconquered Crimea in the southeast. Once Russia installed herself on the Baltic and outmaneuvered Poland in the south she gained a superior position.[7]

The Poles rationalized their eastern expansion in terms of a mission undertaken on behalf of the Christian West. Poland was the shield against the Moslems and the Orthodox, and her task was Westernization and civilization. As Mickiewicz put it, Poland was "the embodiment of the idea totally opposite to that of Russia." It was the idea of a union of equals as contrasted with expansion by conquest, of spreading Western civilization against Eastern despotism and barbarism, of liberty versus oppression.

Divergent ideas and values swayed the minds of Russians and Poles. But while the two peoples reacted to each other with suspicion, there was also a feeling of common Slav background. Two treaties signed during the reign of John Casimir in the late seventeenth century described the Russians respectively as hereditary enemies and people of the same Slav blood. Nicholas I allegedly said that he knew only two sorts of Poles, those whom he hated and those whom he despised; but the same tsar reminded Russian troops departing for war against Poland in 1830 that Poles were brethren.[8] Many Russians considered the Poles superficial, treacherous, and sly, but were simultaneously impressed by Western features of Polish life. Many Poles viewed the Russians as uncouth, primitive, unpredictable, and treacherous, but Russian culture fascinated them. The Russians resented Polish insistence on representing the West against them. Polish hopes for Western support of Poland as the "bulwark of the West" were often vain, but the Russians did not realize it and constantly suspected a Polish-Western conspiracy.

The history of relations between Poland and Russia falls into two periods, divided by the Polish partitions. During the first the chief cause of conflict was the vast borderland area which roughly corresponds to present-day Belorussia and the Ukraine. During the second phase, Polish independence was the main issue, but the problem of borderlands also continued for a long time because the Poles could conceive of a Polish state only in its old partition frontiers. Attempts at Russo-Polish reconciliation occurred both before and after the partitions, though their character was naturally different prior to or after 1795. All these attempts failed.

The origins of the political and territorial conflict go back to the formation of the Polish-Lithuanian union in the late fourteenth century. Through association with the Lithuanian state, which controlled large territories of old Kievan Rus, Poland was drawn into the duel between Lithuania and Moscow which had become unavoidable once Lithuania failed to add to her possessions the emerging state of Muscovy. From that time on Moscow and Wilno appeared as rival centers for all the Russias. A Lithuanian-Russian symbiosis would perhaps have been possible had pagan Lithuania become Orthodox. Francis Dvornik, for one, believes that had this happened it might have accelerated the union of Russian lands, prevented the subsequent Russian antagonism against the Latins, and given the Poles an opportunity to act as a friendly transmitter of Western culture to the Orthodox Russians.[9] Pressed in the west by the Germans, the Poles needed a breathing space in the east—politically and economically—and there was no guarantee that a huge Russo-Lithuanian state might not engulf the small Polish kingdom. Nor was there much reason to suppose that an Orthodox Russo-Lithuanian empire would have been more friendly to Poland than Muscovy. These are speculations, and the Polish-Lithuanian union accompanied by Lithuania's conversion to Catholicism set the course of history.

The tightening of the union involved Poland in Eastern questions. Transfer of the Ukraine from Lithuanian to Polish rule, and attempts to resolve the religious question by the Union of Brest brought Poland face to face with Muscovy. The sixteenth-century strife under Sigismund Augustus and Ivan the Terrible proved inconclusive, and the Polish king suggested on his deathbed the candidacy of Ivan, his bitter foe, to the crown of Poland. This bold idea aimed at the continuation of the policy of unions initiated by Poland and Lithuania. It failed because of the incompatibility of Poland and Muscovy. Under King Stephen Batory and his immediate successors the Poles moved over to the offensive, and their activities reached a peak in the Times of Trouble and the attempt to install the son of the Polish king, the future Władysław IV, on the throne of the tsars. Had the king been a great statesman instead of a champion of Catholicism, the plan of joining Russia and Poland under the same dynasty might have worked. Nikolai M. Karamzin remarked that although only the city of Moscow had elected Władysław, he could have remained tsar and changed Russia's fate by weakening autocracy. Perhaps, he added, "the fate of Europe would also have changed for many centuries."[10]

It seemed logical that once Poland had entered the path of extreme expansion she had no business to stop halfway on the Dnieper. Controlling Kiev and multitudes of Orthodox people, she "should have reached the Kremlin, the patriarchate of all the Russians and solved the problem there."[11] Neither the king nor the gentry seemed to have realized this, and Polish intervention in Russia in the early seventeenth century, during which the Poles occupied Moscow and garrisoned the Kremlin, engendered only a new bitterneses and hatred. The Russians saw in it a Western-Jesuit plot. Anti-Catholic and anti-Western reaction swept Russia. For years the occupation of Moscow in 1610 would stand as a symbol of Poland's imperialism and hostility toward Russia. Despite this background of hostility, Polish cultural influences cleared the path for the Petrine reforms of the next century.

From the mid-seventeenth century the political situation began to change to Poland's disadvantage. Bohdan Khmelnitskyi's uprising in the Ukraine led to that country's secession from Poland and acceptance of the overlordship of the tsar. This did not bring peace and freedom to the Ukraine, but war and political decline. A new struggle began in which the Ukraine was the main object. While a Russo-Polish compromise treaty of Andrusovo in 1667 split the Ukraine along the Dnieper, the Russians were now on the offensive. Under Peter the Great, Muscovy replaced the old policy of territorial pressure by attempts to dominate the weakening Polish-Lithuanian Commonwealth. The method of corrupting Poland's elite, preventing reforms, and interfering in domestic affairs reached perfection under Catherine II. The use of the Greek Orthodox issue in Poland was tactically excellent and enjoyed popularity in Russia. Under these conditions, a pro-Russian policy attempted by the king and the Czartoryski "familia" stood little chance of success. Eventually difficulties in Poland, together with international complications, made St. Petersburg adopt in 1772 the scheme of partitions.

The story of the Polish Partitions is too well known to dwell on, but two aspects require a brief comment. Were the lands taken by Russia considered Russian? What was the impact of the partitions on Russo-Polish relations and on the population?

After the second partition Catherine II had a commemorative medal struck with the inscription *ottorzhennaiia vozvratikh* ("I regained what had been torn away"), recalling Russian claims to the old Kievan patrimony. Her contemporaries and immediate successors did not take this assertion too seriously.[12] Such terms as "Polish provinces," "provinces detached from Poland," or simply "Polish lands" described the new acquisitions, and the expression "western provinces" appeared sporadically only after 1819. The Russians had no feeling of ethnic identity with the Belorussians, long referred to as Lithuanians, and they called Ukrainians the "Cherkassian nation."[13] In religious composition, the absolute majority of the population in the new provinces was not Orthodox, but Uniate, Catholic, and Jewish. While the Poles were in a minority in areas annexed during the partitions, they were not a mere handful of magnates but a large group comprising small gentry and burghers. They represented the nationally conscious strata of the population, the only segment recognized in eighteenth-century politics. They had left their cultural imprint on most of the territory, and the old Polish frontier was perceptible as a line dividing two different civilizations. As a British general who accompanied the Russian armies in 1812 observed upon crossing it, the country westward looked "more European."[14]

The partitions left a permanent scar on Russo-Polish relations. Catherine II had carried them out by methods both unscrupulous and ruthless. Memories of the massacre of the inhabitants of Warsaw's suburb of Praga long survived. Violation of solemn pledges, and the use of a handful of Polish reactionaries (Targowica confederation) as a Russian instrument provided examples of the cynicism of the *tsaritsa*. No wonder the partitions appeared a crime, not only to Poles but to liberal-minded Russians. The population of the annexed territories suffered under measures designed to diminish Polish influence and integrate them with Russia. The Uniate church came under attack; small gentry unable to prove its noble status was reduced to the level of the peasantry; peasants in turn were caught in the net of the harsh Russian serfdom. Though many of these policies were temporarily reversed to Polish advantage, they were indeed a token of more to come.

The period of partitions merged imperceptibly into that of the Napoleonic wars, which for Poland brought new hopes and new divisions. A change in Russo-Polish relations took place under Alexander I and his Polish adviser, Prince Adam Czartoryski. The tsar confided to the prince that he considered the partitions a crime, and Czartoryski attempted to win Alexander to the plan of rebuilding Poland under the Romanovs. The tsar called this project "his favorite idea" and examined it in many variations under the changing conditions of the Napoleonic wars. At one point the Russian ruler expressed a willingness to cede to the re-created Poland (linked forever with Russia) the lands taken in the second and third partitions. While tactical motives—a desire to detach the Poles from Napoleon—undoubtedly affected the thinking of the tsar, his interest in a Russo-Polish settlement was genuine. At the Congress of Vienna in 1815 Alexander appeared as a champion of the cause of resurrected Poland—joined to Russia by dynastic ties—and he compromised only before the opposition of the other great powers, who feared such an extension of Russian might. A large part of the Duchy of Warsaw, created by Napoleon was now renamed the Kingdom of Poland, and linked with Russia under the rule of the tsar. Alexander granted a liberal constitution and reserved the right to an "internal extension," understood as a promise to increase the kingdom's size by the addition of the "Polish provinces."

The Vienna settlement brought a territorial stabilization which was to endure for a hundred years. The bulk of pre-1772 Poland, i.e., the Kingdom of Poland with its capital of Warsaw and the "Polish provinces," found itself under Russian rule. The former was largely a self-governing unit. The latter were not. The Russo-Polish problem began to center around two interconnected questions: would the Kingdom of Poland remain a truly constitutional state influencing Russia toward liberalism? Would the former eastern territories become part of the kingdom or be absorbed into the Russian empire? Tadeusz Kościuszko best expressed Polish patriotic sentiment when he said that only restoration of Polish unity up to the Dvina and Dnieper would create "an equilibrium and a genuine friendship with the Russians."[15] It appeared that Alexander believed this too.

Alexander's hope that the Kingdom of Poland might affect decisively Russia's transformation into a constitutionally governed state—the "Polish provinces" becoming a bridge between the kingdom and the empire—produced a series of moves which raised Polish hopes. The founding of a Wilno educational district under the authority of Czartoryski, comprising most of the Belorussian and Ukrainian lands, led to a renaissance of Polish culture in these provinces. The tsar in 1817 established a separate Lithuanian army corps recruited from five "Polish gubernia," and placed it under the command of Grand Duke Constantine, who already commanded the army of the Kingdom of Poland. Two years later he extended the authority of the grand duke to civil administration; governors and officials of the five gubernia, mostly Poles, were to refer to Warsaw for instructions. The tsar emphasized the connection between these measures and his constitutional and federative plans for Russia by telling Polish deputies that, "You have also offered me the means to show my country what I have been preparing for her for a long time."[16]

These great plans of Alexander, which would have introduced a new era in the Russo-Polish relations, foundered on two rocks: the tsar's inability to understand constitutionalism, and Russian resistance to any territorial cessions to the Poles. The constitutionalism of Alexander was an intellectual mood which he could not easily reconcile with his authoritarian leanings.[17] As for the opposition of conservative Russian circles, it was symbolized by the historian Karamzin who already in 1811 had warned Alexander that Russia's interests demanded that "there be no Poland under any shape or name."[18] In another memorandum of 1819 Karamzin argued that the Poles could never become trustworthy allies. Any cessions of territory gained during the partitions would be a betrayal of Russia's *raison d'état*. His point of view coincided with that of other prominent figures to whom "destruction of the political existence of Poland" formed "the entire modern history of Russia," and who asserted that conquest of Poland had been "principally for the sake of multiplying the relations of Russia with the other nations of Europe."[19]

Harassed by the conservatives, annoyed by the friction between Russians and Poles in the Congress Kingdom (popularly so-called to stress that the Kingdom of Poland had been a creation of the Congress of Vienna), and disenchanted with liberalism, Alexander gave up his policy. Russia received no constitution; interference with the Kingdom of Poland assumed threatening proportions; Polish hopes for reunification with the eastern provinces fell to the ground.

Russian-Polish cooperation had failed on the official level. Did it have any better chance through collaboration of liberal and revolutionary circles? Polish contacts with the Decembrists showed that this was not necessarily the case, for the Decembrists aimed at a republican form of government and preached radical reforms. Anxious to enlist Polish support, they were far from unanimous on territorial cessions to Poland. Pavel I. Pestel went further than others in his willingness to return to the Poles the gubernia of Grodno, Minsk, Volhynia, and part of Wilno.[20] The Poles were primarily interested in reuniting "Polish provinces," and they rejected dictation on the form of their future political and social system. Contacts with the Decembrists yielded no concrete political result, but they did produce a tradition and legend of cooperation between Polish and Russian liberals and revolutionaries, symbolized in the literary field by the friendship between Mickiewicz and Pushkin.

Whatever the chances for a normalization of Russo-Polish relations after 1815—given the anomalous union of a constitutional kingdom with an autocratic empire, and the problem of the "Polish provinces"—the 1830 insurrection put an end to them. The outbreak came suddenly. The Poles started it without any unity of purpose. The Right saw in the revolution a protest in favor of constitutional liberties. To the Left the insurrection was an attempt to break all links with Russia, reunite with the lost provinces, and become a social as well as national revolution. Under the influence of the Left, the sejm attempted to draw a distinction between the autocratic Russian regime and the Russian nation, and assert that the struggle was against the former and not the latter. In a manifesto drafted by the historian Joachim Lelewel and addressed "To the Russian Brethren," the Poles presented the past as a common struggle against tsarist despotism. The slogan in Warsaw (attributed to Lelewel), "For Our Freedom and Yours," became the watchword.

The slogan was not absolutely convincing. Even to a prominent radical such as Maurycy Mochnacki the struggle was not a war between the fiction of constitutionalism and autocracy but between the Polish nation and "the Muscovite horde with a mark of the Tatar yoke on its forehead"—the perennial struggle between the civilized Poles and the Eastern barbarians.[21] On the Russian side the war with Poland appeared primarily as a national struggle, and a liberal like Pushkin joined those who openly attacked the Poles. While he met with criticism from some Russian intellectuals for debasing his talent for an unworthy cause, few indeed were the liberals whose sympathies were unreservedly on the Polish side.

The 1830 revolution extended to the "western gubernia," but popular support there fell below Polish expectations. The ever widening gap between the Polish privileged classes and the Belorussian, and Ukrainian peasantry could only have been bridged by sweeping reforms and the abolition of serfdom. For this the government in Warsaw, which had not emancipated the peasants in the kingdom, was not prepared. Besides, divergences on the nature and aims of the insurrection precluded energetic action in the eastern territories. In 1831 the sejm passed a decree for reunification with the Kingdom of Poland of any province in which the revolution had gained a foothold, but paper resolutions were no substitute for bold policy.

The defeat of the badly led Polish troops put the Congress Kingdom at the mercy of the Russians. The Poles, whom Alexander had regarded as a positive element in the empire, appeared to Nicholas as rebels. The kingdom lost its constitution and the tsar made perfectly clear that if the Poles persisted in their dreams about a distinct nationality and independence, they could only bring new tragedies upon themselves. A Russian-garrisoned citadel was built in the center of Warsaw, and the emperor warned that he would not hesitate to use its guns to destroy the city at the slightest sign of rebellion. The Russian government began to depolonize the Ukrainian, Belorussian, and Lithuanian territories, liquidating universities and schools, eliminating the Polish language from courts and administration, and substituting nominations for elections in local government. Deportations of small gentry, the base of the Polish element in those provinces, assumed large proportions. The idea of reuniting the "Polish gubernia" with the Kingdom disappeared; the population was meant to become and to stay Russian.

After the insurrection collapsed, the Polish political center shifted to the West, mainly to Paris. Two principal trends emerged which in one form or another were to dominate Polish political life for a generation. The Right, grouped around Czartoryski, saw the main cause of defeat in the disparity between Polish and Russian forces, and strove to make the cause of Poland truly international. Seeking the support of European cabinets, Czartoryski's agents waged a relentless diplomatic duel with tsarist diplomacy in the Balkans, in Turkey, and in the Habsburg monarchy. The Left considered that the insurrection had failed because the nobles had negated its democratic and radical program. Only a social revolution could have turned the struggle for the borderlands and gained the support of the Russian peasantry. The Democratic Manifesto issued in France in 1836 proclaimed the mission of the Poles "to break the alliance of absolutism" and to "spread democratic ideas among the Slavs."[22]

Polish democrats, while bitterly critical of the noble-dominated *Respublica,* shared with the conservatives the view that all inhabitants of prepartition Poland were Poles, though of differing local descent, and it was only in the late 1840's that isolated voices asserted that Poland could be reborn as "a federation of all these heterogeneous lands."[23] Such an attitude made genuine cooperation with Russians very difficult, even with such radicals as Aleksandr Herzen and Mikhail Bakunin. In addition, the whole outlook of the Polish and Russian exiles was radically different.

Russian revolutionaries reproached the Poles for their attachment to the past, which interfered with revolutionary élan. The Poles in turn saw in radicalism the destructive Russian spirit, and suspected that universalism implied denial of Polish national rights. Herzen brilliantly diagnosed the Russo-Polish differences when he explained that unlike the Russians the Poles had to turn to the past to move forward. They "had many shrines," he wrote; "we have only empty cradles." The Poles "await the resurrection of the dead, we want to bury ours as soon as possible. The forms of our thinking, of our hopes are different, our whole genius, our whole contribution have nothing in common with one another."[24] The extreme pessimism of Herzen concerning the Russian past mingled with disillusionment about the West. He wrote that a new world in which a revolutionary Russia could find an outlet for her genius could only emerge on the ruins of Western civilization. These were prophetic thoughts. But the Poles could hardly share them.

Nor did a common Slav background provide a basis for understanding. The Slavophilism of Poles stood in direct opposition to the incipient Panslavism of the Russians. Czartoryski defined the aim of the former as "independence and equal dignity . . . of all branches of this great [Slav] tribe," and Poland's mission as bringing it about.[25] Panslavism, understood as the flowing of all Slav rivers into the Russian sea (that was Pushkin's famous phrasing) was a completely different idea, and only a feeling of despair would make some Poles subscribe to it.

Neither the revolutions of 1848 nor the Crimean War advanced the cause of Poland, though the Polish question had figured in both, but the shock Russia sustained as a result of her military defeats opened new possibilities for liberalizing the empire of the tsars. Had Alexander II granted real concessions to the Poles upon ascending the throne he could have won over the aristocracy and the upper classes, both worried by the specter of a social revolution. He chose to admonish the Poles by using the famous phrase "no daydreaming, gentlemen" (*point de rêveries, messieurs*), and adding "what my father had done was well done, and I will maintain it."[26]

The old regime, however, could not easily be maintained given the reforming policies in Russia and a Russo-French rapprochement. The government made advances to the Poles and relaxed controls in the kingdom and even in the western provinces. These moves met with a cool reception. The leader and idol of the gentry, Andrzej Zamoyski, responded with the formula: take what the Russians offer you, but make no commitments. This ambiguous policy stemmed partly from the fear of appearing less patriotic than the more radical masses. The Zamoyski camp, the "Whites," antagonized the government by speaking of a united and constitutional Poland and by solemnly renewing pledges of a Polish-Lithuanian union. An irritated Alexander told Bismarck that "there was not a gentleman in Poland who did not aim not only at the re-establishment of the independence of his country in the limits of 1772, but even at the recovery of the old provinces" lost to Russia even earlier.[27]

There was, however, such a gentleman in Poland—Marquis Aleksander Wielopolski—and he took it upon himself to begin a program of autonomy for the kingdom in close cooperation with St. Petersburg. Profoundly aristocratic and conservative, Wielopolski sought to resolve domestic problems through a Polish administration of the kingdom. He appealed to the class interests of the Whites, especially in the peasant question, and was prepared to break mercilessly all radical and patriotic opposition. Some of his reforms, particularly in education and in introducing equality for the Jews were large accomplishments, but he realized them at a high cost. His own class did not remain indifferent to patriotic aspirations and resented the marquis' high-handed methods. The democrats accused Wielopolski of abandoning Polish independence and preventing the emancipation of the peasantry. Isolated at home, mistrusted by some Russian circles which were ever fearful that autonomy in the kingdom would be "unthinkable without that of Lithuania, Volhynia, Kiev, and perhaps even Smolensk, Little Russia or Odessa,"[28] Wielopolski moved in a political vacuum. His "realism" and his autocratic techniques were out of tune with Polish attachments to an emotional patriotism influenced by the Romantics and their traditional opposition to tyranny.

The democrats, the "Reds," favored a revolution which, unlike that of 1830, was to be both national and social. They saw their natural allies among the Russian radicals. Cooperation between Polish and Russian revolutionaries gained momentum. Russian manifestoes to the "Young Generation" appeared; appeals to the army stationed in Poland; fiery articles in Herzen's *Kolokol* favoring a Polish struggle for independence and social justice, and calling on the Russians not to lend support to Poland's oppressors. Negotiations between Polish and Russian revolutionaries resulted in two agreements in 1862; one with the nascent Zemlia i Volia, which gave vague promises to create a diversion in Russia to assist the Polish fighters, the second signed on the Russian side by Herzen and N. P. Ogarev and published in the *Kolokol*. The Poles declared that while they strove to rebuild their prepartition country they would leave to the Lithuanians and Ruthenians "complete freedom to remain in union with Poland or to determine their own fate otherwise." This was a compromise criticized by the prominent Polish democratic emigré, Ludwik Mieros-ławski, and by most Russians. Even the most consistently pro-Polish Herzen expressed hope that the Ukraine would not secede and that a liberal Poland might retain a federal link with a liberal Russia.

The January 1863 revolution started by the Reds in response to the military conscription plan devised by Wielopolski has remained ever since subject of bitter controversy.[29] Its chances of success were almost nil, and it destroyed all the achievements of Wielopolski and the hopes for a more permanent Russo-Polish settlement. It resulted in harsh reprisals which shook the foundations of Polish society and inflicted a fatal blow to the Polish position in the western provinces. In a sense both the Reds who began the insurrection and the Whites who joined later had been placed in a situation in which they had no real choice. Whatever the important differences between the two groups were they could not accept a forced reconciliation with Russia within a narrow frame of administrative concessions imposed from above by Wielopolski.

The revolution of 1863 had to end tragically. If hundreds of Russians fought bravely in the Polish ranks, the tsarist army remained loyal to the regime. The revolutionary central committee cut the Gordian knot of the peasant question by decreeing a complete emancipation—a great achievement—but this could not decide the issue. Liberal and progressive Russians who had sympathized with Polish aspirations gave vent to feelings of extreme nationalism. To an ex-liberal such as Mikhail Katkov the insurrection threatened the sacred interests of Russia. Herzen, one of the few who did not abandon his pro-Polish stand, lost

much of his popularity. The Poles made attempts to internation-
alize the revolution, thereby strengthening old Russian suspicions of collusion with the West. The appeal which the revolutionary committee directed to the Russians spoke of a common
struggle for freedom but contained also the ill-chosen phrase
about a battle between European civilization and Asian barbarism. The Poles called on the Lithuanians and Ruthenians and
promised emancipation and equality of rights in a reborn Polish
state. But the peasant masses, with the exception of those in
Lithuania, remained indifferent. To counter Polish appeals the
tsarist government enlarged the scope of its emancipation decree
of 1861 by granting more land to the peasantry of Lithuania,
Belorussia, and the Ukraine. The heroic and unequal struggle
went on until late 1864. The outcome was a total defeat. The
price the Russians exacted from the Poles was heavy. Prior to the
partitions the Polish-Russian contest had been on a basis of
equality; after 1815 the Congress Kingdom at least possessed a
separate identity; and after the collapse of the 1830 revolution
there remained a slender chance for autonomy within the Russian
empire. The 1863 catastrophe, however, posed a grave threat to
the most cherished traditions of Polish national life.

The
Background

More than fifty years separated the January Insurrection from the victorious Bolshevik revolution, and these years constitute the last chapter of the old Russo-Polish relations, as well as the background of the Soviet-Polish story. This period saw the appearance of leaders who were to affect decisively the destinies of their respective countries and the growth of processes and ideas that shaped the future. The post-1863 generation included Vladimir Ilich Lenin, born seven years after the event, and Józef Piłsudski who was three years his senior. The industrialization of Poland and Russia led to the emergence of socialist movements in both countries—the Polish Socialist Party appearing in 1892, the Russian Social Democrat Party six years later. In 1864 the First International was born, protesting tsarist suppression of Polish freedom. Political evolution engendered modern nationalism in Poland, leaving an imprint on the generations to come. Developments in Russia accelerated the decay of the old tsarist regime. The peasant question was largely resolved in the Congress Kingdom, but not so in the tsarist empire. In the vast borderlands—Lithuania, the Ukraine, and Belorussia—forces of native nationalism began to introduce new elements into Russo-Polish relations. The future importance of these long-range processes was not apparent to contemporaries, and the might of the tsarist empire never appeared greater than in those first post-revolutionary years.

Russian revenge for the January Insurrection was very harsh. Alexander II and the government accused the Poles of ingratitude and treason; Westerners and liberals blamed them for having provoked the conservative reaction which set in Russia after 1863. Such Slavophiles as Iurii F. Samarin, Ivan Aksakov, or Nikolai Danilevskii gained amunition for their anti-Polish campaign. As Sergei Solovev remarked, if "the Slavophiles wish to stress the existing abnormal relationship between Russia and Poland, then the Poles are called renegades and traitors" who had "lost all right to participate in the future greatness of the Slavs."[1] At the ethnographic congress in Moscow in 1867 the absent Poles were apostrophized collectively as "the Judas of Slavdom."

The best theoretical explanation of the Russian program toward

Poland appeared in a statement by a Russian journalist who said, "There will be no Polish question at the moment when, first, the Polish nationality will lose not only its material but also its moral sway over the Ruthenian and Lithuanian nationality in the western lands, and secondly, when the solid power of the peasant communes in the Kingdom of Poland will destroy by its influence the old ideals of the Polish nobility."[2] The government of Alexander II did its best to put this program into practice. Confiscations of estates of nobles linked in any way with the Insurrection were accompanied by heavy taxation of others. Thousands of revolutionaries were deported or imprisoned. Schools became completely russified, and in 1865 Russian became the sole language of administration in the kingdom. Polish names of districts disappeared, and some towns received Russian names. Five years after the Insurrection the very term Kingdom of Poland yielded unofficially to "Vistula Land." A new administration composed of "colonialists," attracted by higher pay and other privileges, established itself as a caste completely divided from the Polish population[3]

Persecution of the Catholic clergy went together with forcible conversion of the Uniates; the Union of Brest was formally abolished in 1875. The peasant emancipation decree passed in 1864—far more radical than the *ukaz* of 1861 which applied to Russia—was expressly designed to win over the peasantry and separate it from the landowning gentry.

The policy of integrating the western lands received new impetus. Rationalized subsequently in terms of the need to defend the native peasantry against the Polish landowners, and to protect Slavdom and Orthodoxy against Western corruption and Catholicism, this policy sought to russify Lithuania, Belorussia, and the Ukraine. The notorious governor of Lithuania, Mikhail Muraviev, declared that "Lithuania is Russia and the inhabitants of Lithuania are Russians," and he promoted this idea through a ruthless regime. The use of Polish was forbidden and Lithuanian could only appear in print via the Cyrillic alphabet. Mass arrests of the gentry, deportations, crushing reparations, restrictions on acquisition of land by non-Russians—all aimed at the destruction of the Polish or polonized class which had provided leadership in 1863.[4]

The success of this policy, pursued less rigidly in later years, was not complete. In spite of reprisals, the town councils in the Wilno, Kovno, and Grodno gubernia still contained Polish majorities in 1892; on the eve of the First World War the Poles controlled the larger part of the landed estates. Nothing could change the fact

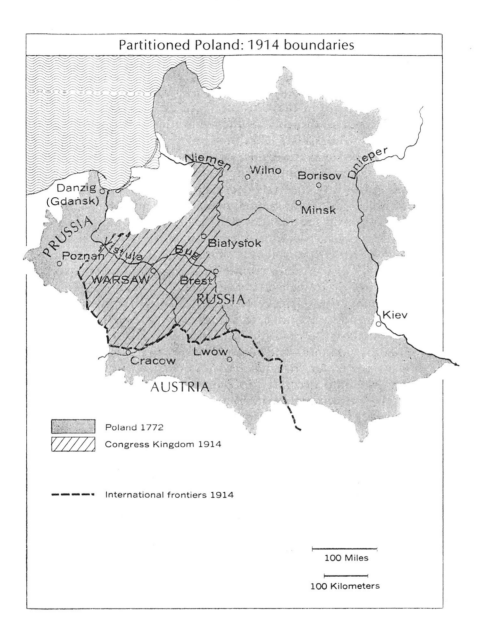

Partitioned Poland: 1914 boundaries

Danzig (Gdańsk)

PRUSSIA

Niemen

Wilno

Borisov

Dnieper

Minsk

Poznań

Vistula

Białystok

Bug

WARSAW

Brest

RUSSIA

Kiev

Cracow

Lwów

AUSTRIA

Poland 1772
Congress Kingdom 1914

- - - - International frontiers 1914

100 Miles

100 Kilometers

that the Great Russians were a small minority in the Lithuanian-Belorussian gubernia (the so-called northwestern land). At the same time the links between Poland and Lithuania were weakening. The anti-Russian opposition more and more took the form of a national Lithuanian and Belorussian revival, and, although the Poles contributed to it, they became isolated from the masses of the native population.

Russian measures in the Ukraine exhibited features similar to those in the north. Printing in the Ukrainian language was forbidden during the 1870's, Ukrainian, together with Belorussian, being considered a mere dialect of Russian. Russification made inroads, and growth of industry brought many Russians into the Ukraine. Polish influence was decreasing, and, although the majority of Poles in the Ukraine belonged to the proletariat, a Pole was still a synonym for a landowner. Social and religious reasons, reinforced by old antagonisms, largely explain why Ukrainian nationalism was not only anti-Russian but anti-Polish.

The policies of the tsarist regime in the borderlands brought a decline of Polish influence, but measures in the Kingdom of Poland did not achieve the results sought by the Russian administration. The assumption that Polish society consisted of two elements—the hostile nobility (plus the clergy) and the potentially friendly peasants—and that one could break the former by relying on the latter, did not prove correct. The government failed to take into account the economic and social trends to which it had unwittingly contributed. Poland had entered the stage of industrialization prior to 1863, and Russian blows against the gentry drove them into the towns where they assumed the leadership of a rising intelligentsia. The rapid growth of industries absorbed some of the landless peasantry and created a sizable proletariat. These new classes became centers of opposition to the tsarist regime. Nor did the emancipation decree bring the peasants to the Russian side. The policy of the government destroyed the argument that the Russian bureaucracy protected the peasants from the gentry.[5] The peasantry, brought face to face with the oppressive tsarist administration and irked by forcible russification and attacks on the church, gained political maturity and a national solidarity. Within three decades after 1863 the old Polish society which had excluded the peasants gave way to a fairly cohesive modern nation.

What was the Polish political response to the new situation? A collapse of national morale found expression in criticism of insurrections and of the Romantic outlook. The "positivist" school advocated abandonment of hopeless struggles and offered

the slogan of "organic labor"—economic and cultural activity—
to improve the status of Poles in the kingdom and borderlands.
The bourgeoisie found the slogan a justification of their desire
for economic relations with Russia, and they eagerly embraced
positivism. Hoping for a relaxation of the harsh tsarist regime,
the aristocracy adopted an attitude of loyalism. But neither
positivism nor loyalism helped slow the policies of oppression and
russification. Attempts to reopen a Polish-Russian dialogue on an
intellectual level in the early 1880's proved a little more fruitful.
The Polish periodical *Kraj* (The Homeland), founded in St.
Petersburg by Włodzimierz Spasowicz and Erazm Piltz, tried to
convince Russian progressive intelligentsia that the Poles wanted
only "a recognition of [their] national, ethnic, and cultural distinctiveness" and equal rights within the tsarist empire.[6] Though
unable to achieve any political results, *Kraj* was a symbol of
endeavors to find a *modus vivendi* with Russia.

Signs of a *détente* appeared in the 1890's. New governors such
as Count Pavel Shuvalov and Prince Aleksandr Imeretinskii, both
cultured aristocrats, offered a telling contrast to their predecessors. Polish hopes rose. Many people wanted reconciliation with
Russia; hence they believed in it. But the new governors gave
little attention to the loyalist gestures of the aristocracy.[7] Gone
were the days when Russians treated Poles as partners in negotiations. The Russian citadel and the huge Orthodox church in the
center of Warsaw proclaimed to the world that the "Vistula land"
was a tsarist colony. Only clandestine movements in Poland could
produce a political program and seek contact with their opposite
political number in Russia.

Operating in a rapidly changing economic and social context, positivism engendered two forces—the National Democratic
movement and Socialism—which became a reaction to its loyalist
and bourgeois features. The former grew out of the Democratic
Society in Paris, and was called first the Polish League and later
the National League. "The founders of the League," wrote one
of its leaders, "took the empirical method from the Positivists,
they recognized the dictates of organic labor, and they completed
them by politics. As for the idea of the nation and the aims of
political action, they [the Leaguers] were the successors of the
Romantics."[8] Moving away from the program of Polish democracy
with its stress on insurrection and the re-creation of a prepartition
Poland based on federalism, the Polish League evolved toward
clear-cut nationalism. Retaining the demand for national independence, it did not seek independence through new revolutions.
It concentrated on integrating the nation, educating the lower

classes in a national spirit, and creating greater cohesion of the Polish people. The central dogma of the National Democrats was that national egoism determined political tactics. The latter changed, but the nationalist core remained. Socially moderate— supporters of the league were the middle class and the gentry— and anti-Semitic, the movement shaped the mentality of an entire generation at the turn of the nineteenth and twentieth centuries. It was the real creator of modern Polish nationalism, and the most influential force in Polish society. Its power, character, and outstanding leaders—to mention only Roman Dmowski—disposed it to become a partner in Russo-Polish negotiations should the time for such talks come.

The emergence of socialist movements in Poland and Russia seemed to offer possibilities for a new departure in relations between these two nations. The community of proletarian class interests cut across national boundaries; proletarian solidarity could overcome national antagonism. The old Russo-Polish dilemma could be solved along entirely new lines.

The first Polish Socialist groups, inspired by Marxism and the intellectual ferment in Russia, faced the question of patriotism versus internationalism—a question of more than academic importance. What was the greater object: national independence of an oppressed people or revolution of an oppressed class? The early Socialists who in the 1880's set up the first political organization, the Proletariat, leaned toward internationalism. Socialism, they believed, was a bigger and loftier idea than the nation. Tactical considerations also influenced their thinking, for should the Socialists engage in a struggle for Polish independence the likely result would be a bourgeois state that would sacrifice socialism on the altar of national solidarity.

The internationalists did not gain monopoly of the Socialist movement and from the beginning there was a national trend.* It marked the Polish Socialist Party's program of 1892. The new party (PPS) proclaimed as its aim an "independent democratic Polish republic" based on a voluntary federation of nationalities enjoying equal rights. The fusion of national and socialist ideas in the PPS resulted largely from the old Polish revolutionary heritage. Foreign oppression and class exploitation were inextricably linked, and strife for socialism and democracy appeared unthinkable without national independence.† One of the Socialist leaders stated: "Placing the independence of Poland on top of

---

* Its chief exponent was Bolesław Limanowski.

† Leading theoreticians of Polish socialism, such as Kazimierz Kelles-Krauz, Feliks Perl, and others, pointed it out clearly.

revolutionary demands will force the Polish proletariat to take stock of its own forces," and others shared this view.[9] The PPS invoked the authority of Marx and Engels, and, indeed, the fathers of "scientific socialism" endorsed the Polish struggle for independence.[10] During the 1848 revolution Marx and Engels had insisted on Poland's rebirth within the prepartition frontiers.[11] Engels explained that their advocacy of a free Poland did not stem from a principle of nationality ("a Russian invention concocted to destroy Poland") but "the right of national existence for the historic peoples of Europe."[12] Both writers made abundantly clear that only an independent Poland could play a proper role in the social transformation of Europe. To Engels the Poles not only had "the right but the duty to be nationalistic before they became internationalists," and he viewed the "internationalist" trend as a temporary "deviation." "In order to be able to fight one needs first a soil to stand on, air, light and space," Engels declared, and he reiterated this point as late as 1892 in a preface to the Polish edition of the *Communist Manifesto*.[13]

The Polish "internationalists" were far from convinced, and the unity of the socialist movement ended with the appearance of a rival to the PPS—a social democratic group which in 1910 assumed the name of Social Democracy of Poland and Lithuania (SDKPiL). While not denying the need for struggle against national oppression, SDKPiL asserted that under the existing conditions a program of reconstructing Poland meant a retreat from and abandoning of the "immediate as well as long-range aims of the proletariat."[14]

The Social Democrats rejected, or, as they put it, modified the views of Marx and Engels on the Polish question. They emphasized that the founders of socialism had singled out Poland because that country had been the standard bearer of revolution in the nineteenth century. This was no longer true. The bourgeoisie and peasants, far from being a revolutionary force, cooperated with the partitioning powers. Only the proletariat was a vehicle of revolution. The theoretician of the Social Democrats, Rosa Luxemburg, came forward with the theory of "organic absorption" of the Kingdom of Poland by Russia, and she concluded that the former could no longer exist economically without the latter. Hence, secession from Russia could only mean collapse of Polish industry and the misery of the proletariat.[15]

The PPS and SDKPiL very soon came to grips over the question of Polish independence. They clashed at international conferences, as in 1896, and engaged in acrimonious polemics. The Socialists viewed SDKPiL as traitors to the national cause and to

Marxist teachings on Poland. The latter dubbed the PPS "social patriots" and chauvinists. Differences in temperament sharpened the conflict. Several leading Social Democrats later transferred to German or Russian socialist movements with an ease that emphasized their internationalism. Such individuals as Rosa Luxemburg, Leo Jogiches (Tyszko), Julian Marchlewski (Karski), Józef Unszlicht, Karl Radek, or Feliks Dzierżyński (better known as Dzerzhinskii), viewed Poland as only one theater of their revolutionary operations. They had little in common with most PPS leaders who followed their radical and revolutionary Polish predecessors. One could hardly imagine such people as Bolesław Limanowski, Witold Jodko-Narkiewicz, Feliks Perl, Józef Piłsudski, or Ignacy Daszyński outside the Polish scene. To some of them, socialism and the Polish cause were inseparable; to others, like Piłsudski, who was hardly a Marxist, socialism appeared as new means of the struggle for independence. The character of Polish socialism and its split over the national question are crucial for Russo-Polish relations as they appeared to the Socialists of both countries. Before attempting this question, a few words must be said about socialism in Russia.

The traditional features of Russian society—economically backward, predominantly agrarian, and hardly affected by Western political developments—explain why socialism found its first expression in the populist movement. Zemlia i volia, revived in the 1870's and later called Narodnaia Volia, saw the path to socialism through the Russian peasant communes. Inspired by Herzen's call "go to the people," the populists placed their revolutionary hopes in the peasantry and in political terrorism. Their program also postulated national self-determination. Marxian socialism born out of and in opposition to populism had a strong admixture of native radical thinking. The radicalism of Herzen and of Nikolai Chernyshevskii, the anarchism of Bakunin, and Petr Tkachev's theories of revolutionary activity all left their mark on Russian socialism. Under the influence of the pioneer of Marxism, Georgii Plekhanov, Russian Marxists founded the "Liberation of Labor" in 1883. After splits, divisions, and much discussion the Russian Social Democratic Labor Party emerged at the conference in Minsk in 1898. Lenin, Plekhanov, Pavel B. Akselrod, and Iulii Martov were among its leaders.* The program of the new party was adopted at the London and Brussels congress of 1903, at which there occurred the later famous split between the Bolsheviks and Mensheviks. After a new phase of

* None of them were present at Minsk.

divisions and perfunctory reconciliations the split became permanent in 1912. The Russian Social Democratic Labor Party (bolsheviks), abbreviated to RSDRP(b), had established itself.

Clearly, the national issue which occupied a central place in Polish socialism was of no immediate concern to the Russians, but they could not ignore Poland's rights and aspirations. The pronouncements of Marx and Engels and the championship of the Poles by Herzen and Bakunin showed the way to approach the Polish question. Chernyshevskii said the Russian nation would not lose anything if the Kingdom of Poland and even the western provinces became separate.[16] The Russian section of the First International declared that the tsarist yoke prevented a political and social liberation of the Russian and Polish nations.[17] In 1884 Proletariat and Narodnaia Volia signed an agreement which was almost an international treaty on revolutionary action. The Russian organization recognized Poland's right to independence not on ethnic or historic grounds but because the Polish people wanted it. Both organizations were to start a revolution in their respective territories (the Poles in the kingdom) at a signal from Narodnaia Volia.[18] Intervention of the tsarist police put an end to this short-lived cooperation, the first after 1863.

How did the Russian Marxists view the question of Polish independence? The problem was not simple. It had to be approached within the context of a broad theoretical issue—proletarian internationalism versus nationalism—and as a concrete matter affecting Russo-Polish relations. On both counts the teachings of Marx and Engels were not clear. Engels did not base his championship of the Polish cause on the principle of nationality. As for Russo-Polish relations one can find statements of Marx and Engels to the effect that the main task of Russian Socialists "is to work for the cause of Poland";[19] and others which indicate that once revolution progressed in Russia, Poland would lose its unique position in favor of the eastern neighbor.[20] The strong anti-Russian pronouncements of Marx raise doubts whether he applied them to the tsarist regime alone or to the Russian nation. In the last statement by Engels on the subject, the "independence of Poland and revolution in Russia mutually determine each other," and there is no subordination of Polish interests to the Russian revolutionary movements.[21] Still, possibilities of divergent interpretation remain.

The most logically consistent answer to the dilemma of nationalism versus proletarian solidarity was that of Rosa Luxemburg and her followers, who rejected national aspirations as harmful to the cause of socialist revolution. According to them, the triumph of socialism would automatically solve the question of oppressed nationalities. But if the logic of this position, shared by many Russian Socialists, was almost unassailable, such a dogmatic position was utterly unrealistic. Lenin perceived this and came forth with his own theory of nationality which ultimately prevailed among the Bolsheviks and determined their stand on the Polish question.[22]

Lenin's views on national issues evolved over many years. Prior to 1903 he saw dissatisfied nationalities as temporary allies against autocracy. The Socialists promised them nothing, although they were glad to see them as a useful diversion.[23] In 1903 Lenin agreed with Martov's phrasing of point 9 (originally 7) of the party program, which stated that a democratic republic ought to safeguard "the right to self-determination of all nations making part of the state."[24] He felt that such a clause was needed because the party must reckon with all possibile developments—nationalism being one of them. The Bolshevik leader emphasized that recognition of the right of national self-determination was not tantamount to supporting it in practice. "Social democracy as the party of the proletariat," he wrote, "has as its fundamental and main task to assist self-determination not of peoples and nations, but of the proletariat of each nationality. We must always and unconditionally strive after the closest unification of all nationalities and we can advance and support actively demands for the creation of a new class state only in individual and exceptional cases."[25]

Lenin's main consideration here, as in most of his theories, was of a practical nature.[26] His objective was to undermine, by a general and elastic formula, his opponents' use of nationalism, while making the principle of self-determination an instrument of socialism. Thus he could attack Great Russian chauvinists as pillars of reaction, and oppose the demands of oppressed nationalities for cultural and political autonomy and federalism, claiming that they endangered proletarian solidarity.[27]

In 1913 Lenin went one step further by defining self-determination in political terms. Observing the "orgy" of Russian nationalism, the growth of national tendencies among the liberal bourgeoisie and Socialists (Jewish Bund and the Caucasians), which "at the present moment bring out the national question into the open," he sought a formula "in the spirit of consistent internationalism and the unity of the proletariat of all nations."[28] He found it by defining self-determination as "the right to separate and create an independent state."

At first glance this formula was astonishing. Did Lenin imply that he was ready to recognize and support the formation of bourgeois national states? Was he in favor of breaking up the multinational Russian empire? Did he reconcile all this with proletarian internationalism? The formula as he interpreted it was a masterpiece of dialectics. He repeated again that recognition of a right, in this case the right of secession, did not imply the obligation to support it always and everywhere. Support depended on many factors and above all on the interest "of the class struggle of the proletariat for socialism."[29] For tactical reasons— to detach nationalities from the side of reaction—the Great Russian Social Democrats must "agitate for the *freedom* of separation," while simultaneously opposing actual separation.[30] As a Marxist and an internationalist Lenin did not favor the disintegration of a large state such as Russia. "Bigger states are always preferable to small," he wrote.[31] He rejected federalism and advocated what he called democratic centralism. "We are for the Jacobins against the Girondists," he declared.[32] His formula of self-determination sought to reconcile the seemingly irreconcilable: nationalism and proletarian internationalism. The object was unification and the merging of nations, but he believed it unattainable without first granting the freedom of secession. Socialism was to master the forces of nationalism and while seemingly leaving them free to move in separate directions it would guide them into internationalist unity.

Lenin's attitude toward the Polish question and Polish Socialist programs stemmed from his general theory. He argued that Marx's views on Poland required reinterpretation. Even Kautsky, who took the Polish side in the dispute, admitted that St. Petersburg was a more important revolutionary center than Warsaw. The Bolshevik leader castigated the PPS when it used such terms as "we" for the Poles and "they" for the partitioning powers, instead of reserving the "we" for the proletariat and "they" for the oppressors of any nationality. He opposed the thesis that Polish Socialists should weaken the tsarist empire by tearing Poland away from Russia, while Russian comrades concentrated on overthrowing the regime. Only the overthrow of tsardom could bring freedom and socialism to Poland; hence Poles should act in unison with Russians and not set up separate national goals. The last point contained the essence of Lenin's criticism of the PPS. He considered that the Polish propertied classes were using national slogans to avert revolution, and that Socialists, by stressing patriotic ideals, were becoming their victims.[33] Did Lenin favor an independent Poland *after* the victory of socialism in Russia? True to his idea that the right of secession would bring ultimate unification, he did not. He assumed that Poland might break away temporarily from Russia but would reunify.[34] International consciousness and economic needs would prove stronger than separatist tendencies.

What did the Poles think of Lenin's interpretation? The PPS estimated that his concept did not imply assistance to the cause of Polish independence. They were willing to cooperate with Russian Social Democrats only when the latter would unequivocally recognize Polish national aspirations, acknowledge the right of non-Russian peoples in the empire to resolve freely the question of their relationship to Russia, and coordinate revolutionary activity in the borderlands with the Poles.[35] The PPS, or more exactly its wing, PPS-Frakcja, declared that while Polish Socialists wanted an alliance with Russian Social Democrats they did not desire to merge or become "an addition to a foreign organism."[36] In these circumstances genuine cooperation was impossible.

While Lenin castigated the PPS for its nationalist outlook, he criticized the Polish Social Democrats (SDKPiL) for dismissal of nationalism as a force in politics. The Bolshevik leader refused to reject a priori the possibility that a Polish state would emerge before the collapse of capitalism, though he deemed it a slight possibility.[37] Consequently he clashed with Rosa Luxemburg, Adolf Warski (Warszawski), and Jakub Fürstenberg-Hanecki over point 9 of the party program. Lenin could not stand the rigidity of Social Democrats who asserted that "the attempt to reconcile the social democratic program of struggle for the overthrow of autocracy . . . with the nationalist program of reconstruction of Poland [was] unthinkable both from a theoretical and practical point of view." He accused Rosa Luxemburg of dogmatism and "opportunism," and wrote that she was committing a "funny error" when, fearing to intensify the "bourgeois nationalism" of oppressed nations, she played into the hands of the oppressors.[38]

The disagreement between Lenin and Luxemburg was over tactics, but it reached into the heart of Lenin's theory of nationality. The Bolshevik leader agreed that Poland no longer occupied a leading place in the revolutionary movement, and he too subordinated nationalism to proletarian internationalism. But he was angered by the inability of his opponent to understand that one could not ignore nationalism as a factor in politics. He explained that the right of self-determination in the program meant that the Socialists recognized it as a fact, but one ought to interpret it differently in Russia and Poland. In the former one must stress the right of nations to secede; in the latter their right to remain united. In each case one had to maintain the principle.[39]

Differences between Lenin and SDKPiL over self-determination and other issues, which need not be discussed here, did not prevent their cooperation. Polish Social Democrats became the only Polish organization affiliated with the Russian Social Democracy and they received financial support from their Russian comrades.[40] But the usefulness of SDKPiL was limited. In a country like Poland, where national aspirations had a profound influence on the life of the people, Social Democrats who rejected them were going against the current. That these die-hard internationalists were the sole Polish allies of Russian socialism lessened the chances of genuine cooperation between the Russian and the Polish Left.

The Russo-Japanese war and the revolution of 1905 shook the tsarist empire and brought all opposition forces into the open. The Polish question and the issue of Russo-Polish relations returned to practical politics. In Russia political movements mushroomed, and for the first time a Soviet of Workers' Deputies appeared. Among the Poles, Socialists and National Democrats came to a dramatic confrontation of ideas and policies.

The PPS took up the old revolutionary banner of Polish independence. It stood for a free Poland and for socialism, and revived the tradition of armed insurrection.* But it had hardly any allies on the Russian side. True, in 1901 the Social Revolutionaries had recognized the Poles' right "to dispose of their country," but given the differences between the PPS and the SR's, there were only friendly relations, no permanent agreements.[41] Things looked different with regard to non-Russian parties, and here the PPS favored and promoted close contacts. By cooperating with the nationalities of the tsarist empire the Polish Socialists had a double purpose. They strove to undermine Russia, hastening its disintegration, and they hoped to bring the nations of the borderlands closer to Poland. To farsighted Polish observers it was clear that "historic Poland had really disintegrated."[42] The Lithuanian, Ukrainian, and Belorussian masses had not signed the old union with Poland, and the only hope of gaining them lay in encouraging national aspirations and directing them against Russia. This the PPS was fully prepared to do.

The borderlands were seething with political activity. Within

---

* The first Polish-Russian clash since 1863 took place in Warsaw on November 13, 1904 when the PPS militia exchanged shots with Russian gendarmes and soldiers.

historic Lithuania the PPS, the SDKPiL, the Jewish Bund, Social Revolutionaries, Russian Social Democrats, Lithuanian Social Democrats, the National Lithuanian Party, the Belorussian Hromada, and others competed for power. In the Ukraine, Russian Social Democrats and Social Revolutionaries vied with Ukrainian and Polish parties. The Ukrainians were divided between Socialist, moderate, and nationalist movements. The PPS had aided the Belorussian Hromada and the Ukrainian Socialist Party, and tried to influence them "in the spirit of separation from Russia and federation with us."[43] The Polish Socialists felt that their activity in the western provinces could not be called imperialist because they were "not concerned with Polish interests but with the interests of the revolution which would liberate the peoples." Nor did they propose any future borders, leaving this to the peoples.

The policy of the PPS showed itself in a series of moves. Together with Lithuanian, Latvian, and Belorussian Socialists the Poles published a manifesto opposing war against Japan and attacking the tsarist regime. They called a conference of nationalities in Paris in which eventually the Russian Cadets, the SR's, and the Polish National Democrats participated. Another meeting followed which brought together the delegates of the PPS, the SR's, the Latvian Social Democrats, and the Georgians. It accepted the principle of national independence of peoples "demanded now by the Poles."[44]

The program of overthrowing tsarist autocracy, through disintegration of the multinational Russian empire was dear to Piłsudski, who in 1904 went to Tokyo to discuss it with the Japanese. Speaking on behalf of the PPS he suggested the creation of a Polish legion in Japan, spoke of an anti-Russian uprising in the Kingdom of Poland, and demanded Japanese support of the Polish cause at the future peace conference. In Tokyo he met the leader of the National Democrats, Roman Dmowski, who came to warn the Japanese against any diversion in Poland. The views of the two outstanding Poles were irreconcilable; their ideas on Russo-Polish relations stood miles apart.

What did the National Democrats propose? Rightists and moderates in Poland saw in the Russo-Japanese war and the turmoil which followed an analogy to the situation after the Crimean War. Military defeats and domestic pressures would lead to a more liberal course in Russia and force the government to listen to Polish overtures. Around 1904 Russian liberals began to call for reconciliation with Poland, and toward the end of the year informal conferences in Moscow united leading Russian

Cadets with such Polish moderates as Aleksander Lednicki and Ludwik Straszewicz.[45] To facilitate more formal understanding a Polish Democratic Progressive party emerged in 1905, and its leaders, joined by some National Democrats and individual members of the PPS, commenced talks with the Cadets. The results on the whole were disappointing. The Cadets were unwilling to commit themselves to anything concrete, even though Lednicki spoke only of autonomy and disclaimed any Polish ambitions to the western lands.[46] Still, a few months later the Cadets defined their point of view by declaring support for an autonomous kingdom with its own parliament (Sejm) and its own deputies in the Russian Duma. As for the Russo-Polish border they admitted the possibility of correcting the frontier "in accordance with the national composition and the desires of the local population."[47] They did not go beyond these generalities.

The National Democrats cooperated with the progressive party in attempts to gain the sympathy of the Cadets, and they participated in the above-mentioned Paris conference sponsored by the PPS. But they also pursued their own policy set out by Dmowski: to obtain concessions for the Kingdom of Poland in exchange for loyal cooperation with the government. Dmowski tried to play the part of a new Wielopolski, and his struggle against the Socialist "anarchy"—strikes and demonstrations—was reminiscent of Wielopolski's strife against the insurrectionists. When clashes between the National Democrats and the Socialists reached the dimensions of a fratricidal struggle. Dmowski argued that only a Polish administration could master the revolutionary situation in the kingdom. Such was the gist of the conversation which Dmowski held with the newly appointed president of the council of ministers, Sergei Witte, in November 1905. The Russian statesman was not prepared to talk about autonomy; Dmowski's initiative failed.[48]

Meanwhile, reaction in Russia was reasserting itself. The liberal October Manifesto of 1905 gave place to the Fundamental Laws of the Empire, which restricted the constitutional change. The Duma was to be less than an effective parliamentary body, and Dmowski's efforts to gain concessions through the Duma became unlikely. In the first Duma the National Democrats, who monopolized the Polish delegation, tried to cultivate the Cadets; in the second, in which they held the balance between Russian parties, they attempted to bargain. This policy was unsuccessful. Russian nationalism as expressed in the Fundamental Laws—"The Russian state is one and indivisible"—could not permit the Poles to become a decisive factor in domestic politics. The government dissolved the second Duma and curtailed representation of non-Russian nationalities. Dmowski admitted that his tactics did not work. The result was an increase of Russo-Polish friction.[49] Yet the National Democratic leader did not want to abandon his effort to improve relations with Russia. In 1908 he published a book entitled "Germany, Russia, and the Polish Question," in which he argued that since the main threat to Polish national survival came from Germany, the Poles had to lean on Russia. All he demanded of the latter was recognition of Polish distinctiveness and existence within ethnic borders. He tried to reinforce his case by espousal of Neoslavism, and loudly affirmed his belief in Russo-Polish reconciliation at the congress held in Prague in 1908.

The overtures of National Democracy produced no tangible result. The days of Wielopolski were over and Polish bargaining power had greatly diminished. Dmowski and his followers were contributing to illusions—prevalent among the Polish propertied classes and reinforced by the fear of a Socialist revolution—about the chances of cooperation with tsarist Russia.

The revolution of 1905 emphasized the division of political life in the Kingdom of Poland. The two main trends, National Democratic and Socialist, had clashed violently but neither could claim its approach had produced results. The watchword of Polish independence used by the PPS, and its terrorist activity against tsarist officials, led to an internal crisis. In 1906 the PPS split into a right wing (Frakcja Rewolucyjna) and the PPS-Left, which steered in the direction of the Social Democrats. Since SDKPiL throughout the entire crisis had modeled its policies on those of the Russian Socialists and rejected national demands, the split meant a reinforcement of the "internationalist" trend.[50] The dynamism of Polish socialism was further weakened when Piłsudski and several of his collaborators who had played an important part in the PPS began to move away from it. Interested primarily in preparing military cadres for a future uprising. Piłsudski saw greater scope for his talents and activities outside of party life. Continuing to influence the PPS, he began an evolution which in the long run would put him in opposition to the Socialists and the Left.[51]

If the decline of the PPS corresponded to an increased influence of the Right and Center groups that believed in an understanding with Russia, during the decade which preceded the First World War there was nonetheless little inclination in St. Petersburg to resolve the Polish question. It is true that the government granted concessions which ended religious and linguistic oppression, especially in the western lands, and brought relaxation of anti-Polish measures in education. But it was not prepared to discuss autonomy or meet halfway those Poles who in the name of political "realism" made overtures to Russia. The excuse put forward by St. Petersburg that the kingdom as a whole was striving to break away from the empire did not correspond to reality. Except for the PPS and circles close to it no Poles talked in terms of independence.

The First World War confronted the Polish leaders with the need for a choice: should they support or oppose Russia? This choice sharpened the divisions between the Right and the Left. Subordinating its ideological aims to the demand for Polish independence, the PPS, together with other leftist groups, lent support to Piłsudski, and his policy.[52] Piłsudski believed that the war would exhaust the main combatants and create favorable conditions for the re-emergence of the Polish question. Although he mentioned that an ideal denouement would be the victory of the Central Powers over Russia, and then their defeat at the hands of the Allies, he did not treat such speculations too seriously.[53] Nor did he place all his hopes on a revolution in Russia, though he considered that once it occurred it would have great significance for Europe and "above all for Poland."[54] He was clear about two things: Russia was enemy number one, and the final aim was Poland's independence.

At the beginning of the war Piłsudski attempted an independent Polish military action, but when the entry of his legionaries in the kingdom failed to kindle a revolution he fell back on a policy of cooperation with Austria. It was hardly a cordial collaboration, but there was no alternative. The strongly anti-Russian line excluded the possibility of finding sympathy even among leftist groups in Russia; the break between the PPS and the Socialist Revolutionaries had become final.[55]

The patriotic Left sided with Piłsudski, but SDKPiL and its allies spent more time and energy in attacking the PPS than in trying to counteract the influence of National Democrats on the working class.[56] With unwavering dogmatism Social Democratic leaders asserted that the period of formation of national states had gone, never to return, and that the "Polish proletariat has never striven after national independence."[57] Lenin perceived that the "imperialist war" made the principle of national self-determination even more universally applicable—he thought here of colonies—and attacked them bitterly. Blind to Polish realities, SDKPiL fought Lenin, the PPS, and even its ally, the PPS Left, which "shyly murmured about emancipation of Poland."[58]

In contrast to Piłsudski's efforts, which seemed based on quicksand, and in contrast to internal contradictions within the Left, the policy of Dmowski and his supporters appeared logical and realistic. Dmowski believed that irrespective of which side won the war the result would not be Poland's independence. But unification of Polish lands was possible, and since Germany was more dangerous the Poles had to pin their faith on Russia. Renunciation of territories in the east would be compensated by more secure borders in the west. A unified, large Poland linked with Russia could not be denied autonomy or self-government.[59] Such views appeared reasonable to many Poles in the kingdom, and National Democratic deputies in the Duma made declarations of loyalty to the empire. St. Petersburg had a unique chance of satisfying Polish demands without sacrificing Russian interests. It also could have improved its standing within the Entente by linking, as Dmowski put it, the Polish question with the cause of Franco-Russian alliance.

There were circles and individuals on the Russian side who perceived that "there was only one rational policy to adopt, and that was to make reparations as fully as lay in her [Russia's] power."[60] Liberals such as the Princes Trubetskoi, Nikolai Lvov, Petr Struve, and P. N. Miliukov favored Polish autonomy. Russian Social Revolutionaries and most Social Democrats spoke of autonomy or self-determination. Neoslavists such as Fedor Samarin and A. A. Kornilov suggested independence, probably to save Russia once and for all from Polish influences. In 1916 there emerged a Circle of the Friends of Polish Independence presided over by Professor V. D. Kuzmin-Karayev. Russian public opinion did not seem unduly concerned with the Polish question. Nor did the government at St. Petersburg.

The policy of the tsarist regime toward Poland went through several stages, determined mainly by military considerations and fear of being outbid by the Central Powers. On August 14, 1914 there appeared a manifesto to the Poles signed by the commander-in-chief, Grand Duke Nikolai Nikolaievich. Cleverly phrased and appealing to Polish sentiments, the document promised the unification of all Polish lands under the scepter of the Romanovs. It offered freedom of religion, of language, and self-government. It was hardly more than a propaganda move, comparable to simultaneous appeals by the Germans and Austrians. The Polish leaders who had provoked it, and the leading Russians, were skeptical in private about the promises in the manifesto. Neither the tsar nor the government had signed it, and a governmental instruction explained that self-government measures were to apply to Polish territories won in the course of the war, and not to the kingdom.

There was no sequel to the manifesto for some time. Proposals to establish an autonomous, ethnic Poland ruled by a viceroy—in fact a return to the 1815 situation—were discussed at the council of ministers and failed to gain unanimous approval. Nikolai Maklakov expressed the guiding thought of these deliberations when he said that "our aim is not to satisfy the Poles but to keep them from separating."[61] Dmowski and Zygmunt Wielopolski, as leaders of the Polish National Committee, found it increasingly hard to deal with the government. The creation of a Polish legion in Russia proceeded amidst innumerable difficulties. Chauvinism in Russian-occupied Galicia and intense russification and conversions to Orthodoxy alarmed both Poles and Ukrainians. An ultra-loyalist gesture of a leading National Democrat, Stanisław Grabski, who expressed willingness to abandon the province to Russia, did not enhance the Polish position. Wielopolski's pleading in St. Petersburg (Petrograd since late 1914) for concessions to bring about the reconciliation of "fraternal nations within the borders of a single state" fell on deaf ears.

Russia's military defeats brought the Polish question again to the fore. The imminent fall of Lwów caused the decision to set up a Russian-Polish commission to discuss autonomy. The evacuation of Warsaw led Premier I. L. Goremykin to issue a statement on August 1, 1915. But even the most pro-Russian Poles participating in the commission found it impossible to accept the meager offers. By the end of 1915 a disillusioned Dmowski transferred his activity to the West. The only Russian acts in the kingdom were brutal and senseless measures of mass evacuation, ordered by the High Command and inflicting misery on the Poles.

Meanwhile, the loss of the kingdom to the victorious armies of the Central Powers and the fear that they might gain Polish volunteers for their war effort had a sobering effect on Petrograd. The new premier, Boris Stürmer, and Foreign Minister Sergei Sazonov issued statements promising autonomy to the kingdom. These offers were met with derision by the Menshevik Nikolai Chkheidze and the Cadet Vasilii Maklakov, as coming at a time when the monarchy no longer controlled Polish territories. The word "independence" began to appear. Dmowski dared at last to mention Polish independence in a memorandum for the Russian ambassador in Paris, Aleksandr Izvolskii.

Aware of the need for a solution of the Polish question, Sazonov pressed for the adoption of a program of autonomy. Fearful of German and Austrian plans concerning Poland, worried by Allied representations and Polish pressures, the foreign minister urged haste lest the initiative slip from Russian hands. He met with opposition from Stürmer and the empress, who felt that "one cannot trust those Poles." The wife of Nicholas insisted that after all "we are their enemies and the Catholics must hate us."[62] Nothing was done, and Sazonov had to resign.

The fears of the Russian foreign minister proved justified, and on November 5, 1916 the emperors of Germany and Austria jointly proclaimed the creation of a hereditary and constitutional Kingdom of Poland. Irrespective of their real intentions toward the Poles, their move internationalized the Polish question—precisely what Petrograd had worked to avoid. Russia could no longer remain silent. Premier Stürmer declared on December 2, 1916, and his successor Aleksandr Trepov repeated, that a Poland comprised within ethnic borders would be free and remain in indivisible union with Russia. The vagueness of this statement was obvious, especially as there was no agreement on the nature of the internal Polish regime. Then the tsar, urged by the High Command, especially General Vasilii Gurko, in an order to the armies of December 1916, stated that Russian war aims included "the creation of a free Poland composed of all three now divided parts." What did he mean? The tsar told Wielopolski that he had in mind a Poland with her own parliament, army, and government, but even if he was sincere it was a long way from an idea to realization. Until early 1917 the Russo-Polish Commission continued to argue without ever formulating a clear program.[63]

There was little to show that the Russian government was intent on a solution acceptable to the Poles. The secret pact with France, on the eve of the fall of the tsarist regime, secured for Russia a free hand in fixing her western borders and showed Petrograd's continuing determination to deal with the Poles without interference.

In March 1917 the old empire of the tsars fell before the victorious revolution. When appraising its policy toward the Poles one can hardly improve on Dallin's epitaph for the fallen regime: "The tsarist government passed from the stage of history without having fulfilled its modest promises to Poland, without having satisfied the aspirations of those Poles who had been favorably inclined toward it, without having succeeded in keeping the Polish issue an internal Russian problem and without having made use of the issue to its own political advantage."[64]

The "February Revolution" was a victory of the liberal,

democratic, and moderate Socialist orientations. The first Provisional Government had a Cadet character, and Socialists frowned on Alexander Kerensky for participating in it. The government looked upon itself as a trustee of the people, a caretaker regime, which was to preserve order and unity until a constituent assembly would prepare a democratic constitution for the country. Honoring the international obligations of the tsarist regime, the new government adhered to the war aims of its predecessor. By pursuing a legalistic approach it limited its freedom of action, giving powerful weapons to the truly revolutionary forces in the country.[65]

In contrast to the Provisional Government, the Soviet of Workers' and Soldiers' Deputies labored under no such disadvantages. Yet, its composition—the Mensheviks and Social Revolutionaries constituted the majority—at first delayed an open competition for power. Even the Bolsheviks, until Lenin's return to Russia, favored coexistence with the Provisional Government. But a duality in Russian politics was a fact, and this fact implied a potential showdown between the government and the Soviet from the very beginning of the Revolution.

The overthrow of the tsarist regime had evoked Polish enthusiasm. As an Austrian intelligence report astutely observed, the Poles warmly greeted the Revolution not only for political and national reasons but as a victory of the idea of freedom over the hated tsarist oppression.[66] Polish leaders in Russia saw of course that the new situation created favorable conditions for the cause of Poland, and they addressed themselves to this task. Intense activity began, in the course of which the democrat Lednicki (also a member of the Cadets) concentrated on the government, and the Socialist veteran Aleksander Więckowski on the Petrograd Soviet. On March 20, 1917 Kerensky assured the Polish Democratic Club that he would strive for official recognition of Poland's independence, and three days later the club received a telegram from the commissar of the Provisional Government telling the Poles that "only democracy can assure the long desired alliance between a revived independent Poland and a great free Russia."[67]

During the last week of March the Poles showed much skill in trying to provoke binding Russian statements. The deputies to the legislative chambers, and the National Committee, after welcoming "the emancipation of our Russian brothers," stressed that the fallen regime had systematically thwarted Polish efforts. "Now," they declared, "when freedom has triumphed in Russia," the new government would realize complete unity between Russian and Polish war aims and contribute to the goal of a unified and independent Poland.[68] The Polish Right thus sought to realize at last Dmowski's idea of linking the Polish question with the Russo-French alliance, and they saw that a pro-Polish declaration of the Provisional Government would enable Paris to support officially the cause of Poland's independence. Cleverly exploiting the Allied fear of a German-recruited Polish force, Dmowski made representations in London, and his associates talked to the British envoy in Switzerland. Lord Balfour then decided to instruct the ambassador, Sir George Buchanan, to sound out the Provisional Government. This he did, and it is likely that British interest, although cautiously expressed in a Russian declaration on Poland's independence, had a part in persuading Petrograd to proceed with an official statement.* Simultaneously other Polish groups in Russia were active and it fell to Lednicki to play a decisive role in securing such a declaration.

Kerensky summoned the Polish democrat to Petersburg on March 24, and Lednicki entered into talks with principal members of the government. Two questions were on the agenda: a declaration on Polish independence and the creation of a joint Russo-Polish body to work out practical ways of separating Poland from Russia. Establishment of an organ, called the Liquidation Commission and presided over by Lednicki, gained approval at the council of ministers on March 28.[69] Its tasks were vaguely defined, and indeed given the magnitude of issues involved it could have been hardly otherwise. As the premier, Prince Georgii Lvov, put it at the first meeting of the commission, "Not only are we proceeding to the liquidation of old institutions and old affairs, but we are proceeding to the liquidation of all age-old strifes and misunderstandings between the Polish and Russian nations."[70]

The question of a government declaration on Poland, discussed at the same meeting of March 28, raised difficulties. The cabinet instructed the minister of foreign affairs, P. N. Miliukov, to prepare a draft and submit it to the next session. The document, in the drafting of which Kerensky and F. F. Kokoshkin also took part, met with Lednicki's objections. The Polish democrat took exception to leaving final decisions to the Russian constituent assembly and to the planned Russo-Polish military alli-

---

* The question of British intervention, a controversial issue in historical literature, can be now properly appraised through the Foreign Office documents. See Foreign Office to Buchanan, March 22; Buchanan to Foreign Office, March 25; Foreign Office to Buchanan, March 28; and Buchanan to Foreign Office, March 29, 1917. Public Record Office, Foreign Office, 371. 3000, file 7684, p.c. 62097, 62107, 63340, 66637 (hereafter cited as PRO, F.O.).

ance. There was a danger that the declaration might be delayed or issued in a form unacceptable to the Poles.

While Lednicki negotiated, Więckowski was busy discussing the Polish question with the Menshevik chairman of the Soviet, Chkheidze, the nonfaction Social Democrat N. D. Sokolov, and Kerensky. After talks concerning the nature of the manifesto to be issued by the Soviet—there was allegedly a proposal to insist on republican system of government in Poland—the Petrograd Soviet unanimously passed the text drafted by Sokolov.[71] This took place in the late evening of March 27, and the next day the manifesto to the Poles appeared in *Izvestia*. It was a brief document. Notifying the Polish people of the "victory of freedom" in Russia, it declared that "Russian democracy stands for the recognition of national-political self-determination of peoples, and proclaims that Poland has a right to complete independence in national and international affairs." The Soviet sent fraternal greetings to the Poles and wished them success "in the forthcoming struggle for the establishment of a democratic, republican order in independent Poland."[72]

The manifesto appeared on March 28, i.e., before the evening session of the council of ministers which instructed Miliukov to prepare a declaration on Poland. Several contemporaries and certain historians deduced that the Soviet had forced the hand of the Provisional Government and made it impossible for the latter to avoid any commitment to the Poles.[73] Soviet historians go further. Not only do they take for granted that the Soviet determined the decision of the Provisional Government, but conveniently overlooking that it was a "Menshevik Soviet" they claim all credit for the Bolsheviks.[74]

Miliukov explicitly denied that the government had been influenced by the manifesto of the Soviet, of which he had no knowledge at the time.[75] Some historians have accepted his testimony as final.[76] Yet it is hard to imagine that the activity of the Soviet, sitting almost next door in the Tauride palace, could be completely ignored by the Provisional Government. A few days earlier the council of ministers had decided to appoint a special delegation to maintain contact with the Soviet.[77] Kerensky was active in both institutions, and he was one of those persons most closely concerned with drafting the declaration. Could he have been unaware of the meeting of March 27?

It is likely that the Soviet had made no official representations at the council of ministers; there is no evidence that it did. In that sense one can say that the government did not act under direct pressure. But indirect influence could hardly be denied, and even if the manifesto and the declaration of the Provisional

Government, which followed two days later, were independent acts, they were "closely interrelated."[78]

The Provisional Government adopted its declaration on Poland shortly before midnight on March 29 and announced it the next day.[79] The document opened with the statement that the old regime which had made false promises to the Poles was gone, and the new Russia was calling Poland to life and liberty. Warning against the treacherous intentions of the Central Powers, the declaration affirmed that the Russian nation recognized "the full right of the fraternal Polish people to decide their fate . . . by their own free will." The Provisional Government "considers that the creation of an independent Polish state, comprised of all the lands in which the Polish people constitute the majority of the population, would be a reliable guarantee for lasting peace in the new Europe of the future." The Polish state would be "united with Russia by a free military alliance." The declaration labored this last point, speaking of a "new fraternal alliance," of a "union of our hearts and feeling," and a "future union of our states." The Polish nation, the document went on, would decide its own form of government through a constituent assembly in Warsaw elected on the basis of universal suffrage. The government expressed its conviction that "people tied to Poland by centuries of common history" would "be firmly guaranteed their civil and national existence." It stated that the Russian Constituent Assembly would give "its consent to those territorial changes of the Russian State which are necessary for the creation of a free Poland out of all her three, now separated parts." Appeal for cooperation, and the old Polish slogan "For your freedom and for ours," concluded the declaration.

The official pronouncement of the Russian government was an act of tremendous political and international significance. It overshadowed the manifesto of the Petrograd Soviet, created a profound impression in Poland, and affected the diplomacy of the Entente.[80] But it did not offer a final and satisfactory solution to the old Polish-Russian problem.

The Provisional State Council in Warsaw set up under the German occupation responded with sharp criticism. The council protested a "compulsory and imposed union" with Russia, and stated that "the age-long Polish-Russian conflict over the vast areas placed between ethnic Poland and Russia, and linked with the fate of Poland for centuries, has not been ended by the declaration of the Russian government."[81] Here again was the question of the borderlands. Although the central committee of the PPS upbraided the State Council for its negative stand and reminded the council that it was not an executive organ of a free nation, the Socialists, together with all Polish political parties except for the extreme Left, favored a revival of the old Polish-Lithuanian union.[82] The PPS sent a message to the Russian Socialists, which, while praising the achievements of the revolution expressed the hope that new Russia would break with old tsarist policies. What should the Russians fight for now, the message asked? Surely not to recover by force Polish and Lithuanian lands. The PPS advocated self-determination of the borderlands through their constituent assemblies, and considered that the interests of Lithuania, Belorussia, and Poland dictated close unity.[83] Such ideas stood in contrast to the Provisional Government's emphasis on ethnic Poland and on borders determined ultimately by the Russian Constituent Assembly.

A noted Polish historian, Szymon Askenazy, who stood close to the Piłsudski orientation critically analyzed the Russian declaration. "There is no independent Poland as yet," he wrote. "Russia had still not given her anything. She neither liberated her from Austro-Germans nor from herself. And already in one single declaration she speaks of four kinds of 'alliances' with her."[84] Askenazy recalled the alliances imposed on Poland by Catherine II, and saw in references to the Russian Constituent Assembly, protection of minorities, and mode of electing the constituent assembly in Warsaw another indication of the old Russian spirit of interference with internal Polish affairs. Even the Soviet manifesto, by wishing the Poles success in their struggle for a democratic and republican regime, evidenced the same tendency, he said.

There is little doubt that the Provisional Government which continued the foreign policy of its predecessor was not prepared to break entirely with the past. Nor was it willing to preside over a decomposition of the Russian state, if only for military reasons. Concessions to nationalities were limited to ethnic Poland and to a lesser extent to Finland, but no one in the government thought about self-determination of the borderlands. Welcoming the declaration on Poland, *Den* voiced hopes for a future voluntary Russo-Polish federation, and stressed that the question of Lithuanian independence did not arise. *Russkiia Vedomosti* emphasized the military alliance. A little later this newspaper urged that internal reorganization of Russia ought to proceed "on the basis of national freedom but not a governmental breakdown." It must not undermine the military might of the country in war. "The interests of the parts" must harmonize "with those of the whole at the forthcoming Constituent Assembly."[85]

It appears that Kerensky and the SR's thought of transforming Russia into a vast federation of which Poland might be a part.[86]

Some Russian papers allegedly spoke not only of Wilno but also of Lwów as "Russian cities awaiting their return to the Russian fatherland."[87] Miliukov, the main author of the Provisional Government's declaration, made clear as late as June 1918 that he contemplated an independent Poland but not an independent Lithuania or Belorussia.[88]

The equivocal stand of the Provisional Government and of its supporters on the question of nationalities gave Lenin a chance to expound his views. The World War had strengthened Lenin's championship of the principle of national self-determination. Opposing those Socialists who insisted that a class rather than a nation was the vehicle of revolution, the Bolshevik leader pointed to the different stages of development reached by Western Europe, Eastern Europe, and the colonial and semicolonial countries. While in the nationally homogeneous and industrially advanced West the emphasis ought to be on class, nationalism was likely to prove the most valuable ally of revolution in the other two areas. Lenin tried to allay the fears of his supporters that national self-determination would mean the disintegration of Russia, by stressing again that the "recognition of the right of secession *diminishes* the danger of disintegration of the state."[89] When the Ukrainians would see "that we have a republic of the soviets, they will not secede."[90] But even if secessions occurred and national bourgeois states emerged, the sequel would be a proletarian revolution within them, and then reunion with the Communist fatherland.

Lenin's determination prevailed over a strong opposition in the Bolshevik party, and the Seventh Conference in May 1917 solemnly reaffirmed the principle of national self-determination.[91] Lenin was thus in an excellent position to castigate the Provisional Government's declaration on Poland, and he made ample use of this opportunity. After mercilessly exposing its "meaningless phrases," the Bolshevik leader asserted that the authors were only sincere in one single instance, namely, when they spoke of the "free military alliance." Such an alliance, Lenin wrote, between "small Poland and huge Russia amounts in fact to a complete military subjugation of Poland."[92] The point was well taken, but when Lenin made it the chances of his party ever gaining control over Russia seemed remote. Who could have foreseen that within a few months the Bolsheviks would be in power and would have to face the Polish issue themselves? But events moved rapidly. The Provisional Government lost its feeble hold over Russia; Lenin and his supporters triumphed. The story of Soviet-Polish relations was about to begin.

The
Bolshevik
Revolution

When the Bolsheviks seized power in Petrograd on that memorable day, November 7, 1917, Russia was in a condition bordering on chaos and anarchy. The old order—political, social, economic—had broken. The Russians clearly had lost the war against the Central Powers, and relations with former allies soon changed from concealed to open hostility. The multiplicity of problems which beset the Bolsheviks was staggering, their ultimate success far from certain. The Soviet leaders faced the Polish question against this background of disintegration. And the Polish question was no longer a domestic Russian issue. France had recognized Dmowski's National Committee in Paris as Poland's spokesman in the Allied camp. Woodrow Wilson spoke on January 22, 1917 of a general consensus on the need to recreate a Polish state. Britain's interest in Poland had increased. The Polish question loomed large in Russia's attitude toward the Central Powers in actual control of the kingdom. It was inextricably linked with the problem of nationalities in the former tsarist empire. Finally, the presence of a large Polish element in Russia —evacuees from the kingdom and natives of the western provinces—raised additional political and military problems. To understand Bolshevik policy toward Poland one must treat it first in conjunction with two interrelated issues: peace and the question of nationalities. The destiny of the revolution hinged on the solution of these problems.

Lenin and his followers stood resolutely for peace, though not for humanitarian reasons. The great Bolshevik leader spoke contemptuously about pacifism and considered war waged by the proletariat against bourgeois states "rightful and holy."[1] Aside from the fact that Russia was incapable of even a defensive war, there was more to his reasoning. By demanding peace the Bolsheviks planned to end the World War through an overthrow of the regimes of Europe. Peace equaled the European revolution without which Bolshevism was not expected to prevail. No one yet imagined the possibility of communism in one country.[2]

The day after the seizure of power the Bolsheviks passed their famous Peace Decree—termination of war through an openly negotiated peace, without indemnities and annexations. They called on the working classes of England, France and Germany to help bring such a peace.[3] All this did not mean a return to the status quo of 1914; the decree provided a definition of annexation, according to which annexation meant forcible incorporation into a large state of a small or weak nationality, irrespective of when it took place and whether the nationality was in Europe or elsewhere.

The Peace Decree was clearly based on Lenin's principle of national self-determination, and it preceded by a few days the Declaration of the Rights of the Peoples of Russia, a document affirming the right of the nationalities "to free self-determination including secession and formation of an independent state."[4] It added that only recognition of this right could lead to a close union of nationalities. The Bolsheviks thus went on record that they were willing to apply at home what they preached abroad. They established the Commissariat for Nationality Affairs, presided over by J. V. Stalin as a visible sign of their desire to solve the problem of non-Russian peoples of the old empire.

The stand taken by the Bolsheviks put them in a favorable light at the peace negotiations with the Central Powers which began—after the preliminary phase concerning an armistice—on December 22, 1917. The Soviet delegation was in a particularly advantageous position since all annexations were on German side, and the principle of national self-determination would be discussed with regard to territories already detached from Russian control. The Kingdom of Poland fell within this category. The Brest-Litovsk negotiations provided the Bolsheviks with an excellent opportunity for voicing their views on the Polish question—an opportunity they used to the full. One of the chief Soviet delegates at Brest, Lev B. Kamenev, indicated the general approach when he declared that the Soviets were not claiming a restoration of the old imperial frontiers "formed by acts of violence and crime against peoples, especially against the Polish people." They were interested in "safeguarding real freedom of self-determination as to the internal State organization and the international position of such territories."[5] The Soviet delegation answered the question of what constituted expression of self-determination in practice by demanding that areas occupied by Germans be evacuated, local militia introduced, and "*all* the inhabitants of the given territory" given the chance to declare through a referendum whether they wanted to join another state or establish independent states.[6]

The Soviet formula naturally embarrassed their opponents. The German argument that the Kingdom of Poland had already

expressed its desire to be free of Russia—while basically correct—
did not mean that the country was sovereign or independent. It
was well known that the government headed by Jan Kucharzewski, appointed by the German-created Regency Council, had
sought admission to the Brest-Litovsk conference and met with
a veto of Berlin. It was also known that Polish democratic parties
did not consider Kucharzewski's government free and representative, and echoed Bolshevik demands for a referendum or elections
to a constituent assembly.[7]

Soviet Russia appeared as a true friend of the Poles. At the
Seventh Party Conference in May 1917 the Bolsheviks had spoken
of the evacuation of all parts of Poland by the occupants and of a
referendum, but then they were not in power.[8] Now their pronouncements had the ring of authority. *Izvestia* ran a series of
articles on Poland in which the authors insisted on the need for
an independent, democratic, and peace-loving Polish state. Poland, one article asserted, should not serve the interests of either
German or Russian imperialism. Polish workers and peasants
in all parts of the partitioned country must determine the nation's
fate.[9]

In the protracted verbal duel fought at Brest, Trotsky and the
other Soviet delegates fenced admirably with their opponents,
gaining much attention abroad. They repeatedly made the point
that they rejected German arguments "not because we want to
keep Poland for Russia, but because we want the Polish people
themselves to say what their political destiny is to be."[10] Trotsky
inquired what were the free institutions that the Germans had
introduced into the Polish Kingdom. Drawing a distinction between recognizing Poland and granting recognition to her existing regime, he said he had nothing against Kucharzewski's
presence at Brest, provided that the premier could appear there
together with other Polish representatives. The chief Soviet delegate declared that "it would be possible immediately to create a
provisional representation of independent Poland for the participation in the peace negotiations by a free agreement of the Polish
political parties which have the support of the masses of the
people, particularly of the working classes. We, on our side are
ready to recognize completely, without any restriction, such
representation."[11]

Several Polish historians have asserted that the Bolsheviks suggested Piłsudski's name as one of the Polish representatives to be
invited.[12] If they did so—and there is no real evidence—it would
have been a clever move. Piłsudski at that time was a German
prisoner in Magdeburg, and Soviet interest in him could have

been offered as proof of genuine concern for even non-Communist Poles. It would also have exposed German duplicity in Polish affairs.

During this early phase of the Brest-Litovsk negotiations the Bolshevik stand on Poland differed greatly from that of the previous Russian governments. The Soviet delegates appeared as champions of genuine self-determination. Even if the press emphasized the class aspect,[13] Trotsky explicitly spoke of the right of *all* Poles to determine their own fate. Was he sincere, for Poland was out of Russian reach, and the main purpose of the Bolsheviks at Brest was to use the conference for propaganda? To answer this question one must look at the Soviet government's application of the much advertised principle of self-determination to territories not occupied by the Germans, and consider how democracy was being realized at home.

The former Russian empire had gone far toward decomposition by the end of 1917, and the rule of Peoples' Commissars prevailed over only a relatively small area.[14] The Baltic countries had proclaimed their independence. The Belorussian Congress and the Ukrainian Central Rada showed separatist tendencies. In the elections to the All-Russian Constituent Assembly the Mensheviks and Right Social Revolutionaries heavily outnumbered the Bolsheviks. The Bolsheviks had no hesitation in going back on Lenin's promise of November 8, 1917 that they would bow to the will of the people, and they dissolved the Assembly. The Belorussian Congress was dispersed; Red troops began an invasion of the Ukraine.

How did the Bolsheviks reconcile these moves with their position at Brest-Litovsk? Between January 23 and 31, 1918, the Third Congress of the Soviets met, and Stalin as Commissar for Nationality Affairs delivered the main speech concerning self-determination. Although at Lenin's request he had written an essay on "Marxism and the National Question" in 1913—which was neither profound nor original—his views were not identical with those of Vladimir Ilich. On the eve of the Bolshevik revolution he stressed the right of nationalities to choose freely "the form of their political regime." After the victory he adopted a less liberal interpretation.[15] Writing about the Ukrainian problem he asserted that the Council of Peoples' Commissars would strive to give all power in the Ukraine to the workers and soldiers, and that the council was "ready to recognize the republic of any national area of Russia upon the demand of *the working population* of such an area."[16]

Stalin now reiterated his point at the Third Congress of the

Soviets. The conflict in the Ukraine had nothing to do with national self-determination, and the chauvinist bourgeoisie, he said, merely exploited the slogan for class purposes. "All this," he explained, "indicates the necessity to interpret the principle of self-determination as a right to self-determination not of the bourgeoisie but of the working masses of the given nation."[17] This was an important qualification, and it met with criticism from individual Bolsheviks, SR's, and Mensheviks. According to them, Stalin's attitude was "imbued with a centralist policy" not unlike that of the old Russian governments. He seemed to reject Lenin's theory of three stages: separation, revolution, and unification. Martov declared that "you want the nations of Russia to create everywhere not democratic but exclusively Soviet republics," and he pointed to the inconsistency between this attitude and the stand of the Bolsheviks at Brest-Litovsk. Stalin replied in a crude manner. Using the old expression "western lands," he said that there were soviets in the Ukraine but none in Poland or Lithuania; thus it was consistent for the Bolsheviks to speak of self-determination of the proletariat in the former case and demand a national referendum in the latter.[18]

Self-determination as a revolutionary weapon appeared in all clarity. The Bolsheviks were to use it in one manner when dealing with territories beyond their control, and another when confronted with the disintegration of the Russian state. The Congress of the Soviets gave its approval to such an interpretation by a resolution which confirmed the principle "understood in the sense of self-determination of the working masses of all nationalities of Russia." The congress crossed the t's and dotted the i's by expressing its conviction that by putting this resolution into practice the government would contribute to remaking "the former Russian empire . . . into a brotherly union of freely united Soviet Republics of Russia based on federal principles."[19]

Resolutions of the Third Congress of the Soviets, which modified Leninist theory on self-determination and federalism, raised doubts about whether Poland would have a different treatment from other nationalities of the old Russia. Stalin's use of the term "western lands," and the resolution's insistence on recreating the former empire as a federal Soviet republic indicated that Poland might become part of the federation. The first constitution of the Russian Socialist Federated Soviet Republic, adopted a few months later, spoke of the union of *all* the nations of Russia, and recognized expressly only the independence of Finland and the self-determination of Armenia.[20] Speaking on the federal structure of Russia, Stalin mentioned as its components Poland, the

Ukraine, and Finland. He also made clear that federalism in Russia was "destined to serve as a means of transition to the Socialist unitarism of the future."[21] Far from rejecting these views, Lenin foresaw the "closest unification of the various nationalities of Russia into one democratically centralized Soviet state."[22] Finally, the new constitution made crystal clear, by depriving all nonworkers of the right to vote, that the right of self-determination did not extend to every citizen of the state.

The meaning of all this was not lost on the Poles. One of the Socialist leaders in Russia, Kazimierz Pużak, declared that the Bolshevik insistence on self-determination, being not national but revolutionary, had a bearing on the Polish issue at Brest-Litovsk. "By demanding the evacuation of territories occupied by German troops, the Bolsheviks aimed at an intervention of the Soviets in Lithuania and in the kingdom. Such interference we cannot allow." In the Bolshevik thinking the Pole saw "remnants of the tsarist heritage." Pużak accused the Bolsheviks of having abandoned the spirit of the Petrograd Soviet manifesto on Poland.[23] Rosa Luxemburg offered a different criticism. After noting the "cool contempt" of the Bolsheviks for the Constituent Assembly, universal suffrage, freedom of press, and all other democratic liberties at home, she contrasted it with demands for referenda made at Brest-Litovsk. She realized that the latter were propaganda, but they appeared dangerous since plebiscites in the borderlands, even after German withdrawal, could not favor the Bolsheviks.[24] As on so many occasions she underestimated the Bolsheviks' ability to twist an idea to their advantage.

The Third Congress of the Soviets devoted much attention to the matter of peace, and the question of Poland reappeared during the sessions. Attempting to convince his opponents that peace was necessary to save Communism in Russia, Lenin rejected the notion of a struggle for liberation of Poland, Lithuania, or Courland. The interests of socialism, he said, "are higher than the interests of nations to self-determination." Nor could the Bolsheviks insist on a peace that would tally with their territorial demands. "Peace on the condition of the liberation of Poland, Lithuania, and Courland would be a 'patriotic' peace from *the point of view of Russia,* but would nonetheless be a peace with the *annexationists,* with the German imperialists."[25] As usual, Lenin's arguments won approval of the Soviets.

The principal debate on Poland at Brest-Litovsk took place after the Third Congress, and Trotsky's slogans about national rights contrasted strangely with the hardboiled views at the congress. When Trotsky asserted that the Ukrainian question had been settled, the delegate of the Ukrainian Rada mercilessly exposed Soviet contradictions between theory and practice, and accused the Bolsheviks of trampling upon self-determination. Trotsky riposted by striking at the most vulnerable point of the Germans—the Polish question—and just as the Germans had put forward Ukrainian delegates, he made use of pro-Soviet Poles.

The idea of having Poles within the Bolshevik delegation had originated earlier, and the Commissariat for Nationality Affairs had asked the Commissariat for Polish Affairs to send a delegate. The PPS members of the Commissariat opposed this request because "such a delegation would be part of the Russian delegation and make the Polish question appear as a domestic Russian issue."[26] They suggested that the Central Powers allow Polish representatives from the Congress Kingdom to participate in the peace conference. The Bolsheviks followed this idea but scored only a propaganda point. This time they needed something more, and two leading figures of SDKPiL appeared at the February 7 session; that is, at the first opportunity after the Ukrainian attack on the Bolsheviks. Karl Radek and Stanisław Bobiński were officially designated as members of the Soviet delegation but they addressed the conference—in Trotsky's words—as "representatives of the laboring masses of Poland." This was hardly true.*

The two Social Democrats delivered a memorandum which denounced the German occupation of the Kingdom, mentioned Piłsudski's arrest, and asserted that all major Polish parties opposed German plans regarding Poland. The Poles wanted genuine self-determination and the end of military occupation. So far the two delegates were on sure ground, but they turned then to open propaganda. They stated that "only revolutionary Russia stands guard over the genuine interests and freedom of the Polish people, and were Poland not occupied she would enjoy at present the same liberty as [enjoyed by] the other nations of Russia."[27]

The situation was not devoid of irony. Here were two representatives of a party which steadfastly rejected the principle of self-determination and opposed Polish independence, appearing as champions of both.[28] Radek and Bobiński avoided, it is true, explicit demands for Poland's independence, and included the Poles among the "nations of Russia," but they justified their presence by a desire that "the voice of Poland" be heard at Brest-

---

* SDKPiL's real strength could be gauged from its performance at municipal elections in the kingdom held in 1916. SDKPiL gained 3,200 votes out of 42,090 cast for all workers' parties. See Józef Kowalski "Z zagadnień rozwoju ideologicznego KPRP w latach 1918-1923," in *Ruch robotniczy i ludowy w Polsce w latach 1914-1923* (Warsaw, 1961), p. 265n.

Litovsk.[29] This was not very convincing, and in their subsequent opposition to the treaty, SDKPiL made clear that their stand had nothing to do with the Polish question.[30]

Soviet Russia signed the dictated treaty of Brest-Litovsk on March 3, 1918. She renounced all sovereign rights to territories including Poland, parts of Belorussia, Lithuania, and the Ukraine. According to Article 3: "No obligation whatever toward Russia," shall "devolve upon the territories referred to, arising from the fact that they formerly belonged to Russia. Russia refrains from all interference in the internal relations of these territories." Did these provisions establish legal foundations for the future Polish state? Such an interpretation hardly withstands scrutiny. The Russians considered the treaty as signed under duress, and the Party Congress which ratified it secretly empowered the Central Executive Committee to abrogate it at first opportunity.[31] Under Lenin's leadership the Bolsheviks viewed Brest-Litovsk as a temporary evil. They were willing to sign anything as long as Communism would remain unimpaired. "I want to yield space to the actual victor in order to gain time," Lenin declared.[32] The treaty lost validity in late 1918 when denounced by the Soviet government and abrogated by Germany in the Armistice.

To sum up the Bolshevik attitude toward the Polish question during this early period—as indicated by the Peace Decree, the Declaration of the Rights of the Nations of Russia, and negotiation at Brest-Litovsk—it is evident that the interests of the revolution determined the interpretation of national self-determination. Soviet Russia insisted loudly on Polish rights vis-à-vis Germany but did not treat Poland's independence as an overriding consideration. Lenin sacrificed Poland to gain time for revolutionary Russia because he had no other choice, but many Bolsheviks deplored the cession of the kingdom, not because it violated the freedom of the Poles but because it diminished Russia's state territory. If all this is clear from a historical perspective, Soviet insistence on the Polish right to independence—tactical as it was—impressed contemporaries. Wilson's Fourteen Points, one of which spoke of an independent Polish state, came out during the Brest negotiations, and the chances of an Allied-Bolshevik front against Germany did not appear hopeless. Nor could one dismiss the possibility that the Poles, especially those living in Russia, might establish some modus vivendi with the new regime. Hence, Polish reaction to the Bolsheviks and the actual relations between the Poles and the Soviet government, need now to be considered.

The Russian revolutions greatly affected Polish political trends in the kingdom and in Russia. Piłsudski and his followers concluded that Germany rather than the new Russia represented the greatest danger for Poland,[33] and Piłsudski's conflict with occupation authorities resulted in his imprisonment on July 21, 1917. The Regency Council tried in vain to assert its position as a semi-independent government, but hopes that cooperation with the Central Powers would open possibilities for eastward Polish expansion came to naught at the time of Brest-Litovsk. The conservative character of the Regency Council deprived it of support from the Left; its German association complicated its relations with the pro-Entente Right. The council began to move in a political vacuum.

The National Democrats centered their activities on the Entente. To them Bolshevik Russia was anathema, but the weakening of Russia allowed Dmowski to give up his previous position on Polish ethnic borders in the east and advocate a line which came roughly halfway between them and the old prepartition frontiers.[34] The National Democrats and their allies had no plans to dismember the Russian state, and they opposed a separate Ukraine or Belorussia. Not so the Polish Socialist Party, which favored genuine self-determination in the borderlands by way of plebiscites, and hoped that Russia under its new regime would not revert to tsarist policies of domination over Lithuania or Poland.[35]

The friendly attitude of Polish Socialists in the kingdom and in Galicia toward the Bolsheviks resulted from the latter's insistence on national self-determination. "The Poles," wrote the party organ in Cracow, "cannot trust anyone among the Russians as unreservedly as Lenin." He knew the Polish nation "and came to the conclusion that there is no reason for Poland and Russia to be bound together; Poland must be independent."[36] This was wishful thinking. During his two years' stay in Galicia Lenin had not bothered to learn Polish and showed only a slight interest in Poland's culture. He despised the Polish Socialists in Galicia, though their assistance had proved valuable when war broke out in 1914. Still, the PPS greeted enthusiastically the Peace Decree and derived great hope from the Bolshevik approach to the Polish question.[37]

While the PPS considered Lenin's insistence on the Polish right to independence as the touchstone of the new regime, support of SDKPiL for the revolution came from class and not national considerations. When, after the treaty of Brest-Litovsk a wave of strikes occurred in the kingdom, those organized by the PPS demanded Poland's independence; those led by SDKPiL, however, urged alliance with the international revolutionary movement.[38] In their January 1918 appeal, "With revolutionary Russia," the Social Democrats launched the slogan, "long live the unification of Poland with the proletarian Russian republic."[39] The gulf within the Polish Socialist camp was as deep as ever.

Trends in the kingdom, Galicia, and abroad were reflected among the Poles in Russia, though difficulties of communication and the specific Russian situation colored Polish thinking. Poles in Russia, numbering some three million people, looked upon themselves as part of a nation which, although split between occupying powers, represented a living national body. Caught in the revolutionary whirlpool they became involved in establishing new foundations for Russian-Polish relations. In turn, Soviet policy toward them indicated the future lines of the Bolshevik relationship to Poland.

National Democrats and their allies grouped in the Interparty Circle could hardly be expected to collaborate with the new regime, nor would they have been welcome if they tried. Committed to a pro-Allied stand, the Polish Right put its hopes on the Entente's Russian policy. In time, the National Democrats became involved in intervention schemes, and attempted to exploit them to enhance Polish standing with the Allies.

The Center, consisting of liberals, democrats, and some moderate Socialists, was represented by the Democratic Committee under Lednicki's leadership. The important part it began to assume under the Provisional Government ended with the October Revolution. Lednicki's Liquidation Commission, which previously had been the leading Polish institution in Russia, could hardly continue its existence. Refusing to recognize the Bolshevik government and work under its auspices, it was officially disbanded in late December 1917.[40] The Center groups out of touch with the shifting political situation in the kingdom linked their fate with the Regency Council, which on January 15, 1918 authorized Lednicki to continue his activities among Polish refugees in Russia—activities which by that time were unofficial. Because of the domestic and international position of the Regency Council this association proved a liability to democrats and liberals in Russia.

Before the Bolshevik Revolution the Polish Left had established a temporary front of all Socialist groups. After October cooperation continued uneasily in some institutions and regions until the spring of 1918, but it could never take root. SDKPiL's rejection of Polish independence was unacceptable to the PPS, which, as one of its leaders put it, went along with the bourgeoisie on the national question and opposed it on social matters. Besides, this Socialist spokesman felt that "you cannot impose the government of Soviets" on others.[41]

The Polish Socialists took at first a favorable view of the Bolsheviks, but it soon became apparent that their views on national self-determination were miles apart. The activity of the PPS in Kiev, where it voted for the Third Ukrainian Universal (the term denoted a public manifesto) and supported the independence movement, clashed with Bolshevik policies.[42] The same was true in Belorussia and Lithuania, which the PPS hoped would ultimately link with Poland. But there was another issue on which the PPS could not see eye to eye with the Russian Communists. Leaders of the PPS in Russia insisted that theirs was a Polish party with its own aims and program. Although individuals and sections of the party, carried away by revolutionary enthusiasm, cooperated in the building of socialism in Russia, participating in soviets, local government, and the Bolshevik movement, the leadership felt that the PPS ought to help the revolution but avoid merging Polish socialism in the Bolshevik sea.[43] Under these conditions cooperation between the PPS and the Soviet regime was limited. If the Polish Socialists had qualms about the Bolsheviks there is little reason to suppose that the latter ever abandoned Lenin's view that the PPS was "no proletarian, no socialist, but a petty bourgeois party, something in the nature of Polish Social Revolutionaries. There never was and never could be question of any unity of purpose between the S[ocial] D[emocrats] and this party."[44] Besides, SDKPiL saw to it that no rapprochement between the Polish Socialists and the Bolsheviks ever took place.[45]

Polish Social Democrats in Russia clung tenaciously to their orthodox internationalism.[46] Bobiński, who represented the Polish cause at Brest-Litovsk, continued to assert that in the national question "we reject the outworn 'self-determining' democratic outlook." Stanisław Pestkowski, who acted as Stalin's deputy in the Commissariat for Nationality Affairs claimed credit for having fought against national self-determination, "unsuitable for revolution and contrary to the principles of Marxism."[47] Not content with maintaining their own views, SDKPiL wanted to force them on the Bolsheviks. In vain Lenin gave the SDKPiL leaders a lesson in political tactics reminiscent of his old tirades against Rosa Luxemburg. He reminded them that the Polish nation, long oppressed by the Russians, was "filled with one thought of revenge against to Moscovites." It was fine for the Social Democrats to declare that they would "never go to war for Poland's independence" but nonsensical to try to make the Russians take the same position. "We Russians," Lenin said, "must stress the freedom to separate and [you] in Poland, the freedom to unite."[48]

In spite of these divergences SDKPiL, having joined the Bolshevik party before the October Revolution, maintained its identity merely to "unite" and "use" the Polish workers in the struggle against nationalism, and identified itself completely with the Soviet cause. To quote one of the Social Democratic leaders: we "united ourselves organically with the Russian revolution."[49] This was no exaggeration. Dzierżyński (Dzerzhinskii), Radek, Pestkowski, Bobiński, Wesołowski, Unszlicht to mention only a few, assumed leading positions in the party and state apparatus. Three fourths of the members of SDKPiL devoted themselves to Soviet affairs, and their Central Committee found it necessary to apologize to the rank and file of the party that they had no time for Polish matters because "they were overburdened with Russian work."[50] The situation was favorable for SDKPiL in one important respect. The party could aspire to leadership of the Polish masses in Russia only through intimate association with the Soviet regime. SDKPiL's attitude toward national and peasant questions and its uncompromising stand vis-à-vis the PPS or even the PPS-Left—which it called "petty bourgeois parties"—marred the Social Democrats' chance of becoming a leading Polish political factor in their own right.[51]

The chief organ through which the Social Democrats sought to control Polish activities in Russia was the Commissariat for Polish Affairs. Early in December 1917 the Council of Peoples' Commissars nominated a prominent SDKPiL leader, Julian Leszczyński, as commissar for Polish affairs, and he promised to follow the Bolshevik line, rather than his own party's policies, with regard to nationalities.[52] A Soviet decree called the commissariat into existence on December 11, and a little later empowered it to take over the Liquidation Commission and all state and social institutions evacuated from the Kingdom of Poland. Soviet authorities received orders to consult the commissariat before issuing any new decrees on Polish matters.[53]

As defined in the first declaration of the commissariat, its tasks consisted of defending the national and cultural rights of the Poles, social and administrative protection of the refugees, assistance to "truly democratic" institutions, and general cultural, social, and organizational activities.[54] In contrast to the Liquidation Commission, the commissariat was not a mixed Russo-Polish body, and possessed more clearly the character of an all-embracing political organ. This corresponded to the nature of the new Soviet regime. As Leszczyński put it, the aim of the commissariat was "to accomplish a revolution in Polish social relations."[55] In practice this meant liquidation of non-Communist Polish organizations, control over the press, education, and propaganda, and a general policy of indoctrination of the refugee masses, constantly urged on to participate in the building of socialism in Russia.

Shortage of people, rather than good will, made SDKPiL accept delegates of the PPS and PPS-Left in the commissariat and in the Council of Polish Democratic and Revolutionary Organizations —its advisory body. Social Democrats were unhappy about it. With reason, they felt that the commissariat was "one of our institutions, and its activity in many respects coincides with the activity of our party organization."[56] The presence of outsiders raised problems. Socialists complained about the limitations on the competence of the advisory council, and stressed that the commissar ought to be democratically elected and not nominated. They opposed the project to dissolve the Exile Councils—a project inspired by the Bolshevik dissolution of the Constituent Assembly—in which the Left had obtained only a minority representation. Because SDKPiL clearly ruled the commissariat, the PPS feared to be drawn in an undesirable direction. Efforts to make the organ more Polish ran counter to the Social Democrats' idea that the commissariat was "a Soviet organ for Polish affairs and not some independent organization parallel to the Soviet government."[57] The commissariat had been called to life "by the will of the victorious revolution," and its character resulted from the near monopoly exercised over it by SDKPiL.

By the spring of 1918 the short-lived coalition of Social Democrats with the other Socialists came to an end; the activities of the Commissariat for Polish Affairs practically merged with that of SDKPiL. When the question of the dissolution of the commissariat came up in November 1918—largely because leading Social Democrats had no time for Polish affairs—discussion turned on the relations between it and SDKPiL. The commissariat was but one area of the revolutionary activity of SDKPiL, whose members occupied numerous positions in Stalin's Commissariat for Nationality Affairs, in the Cheka, and elsewhere.[58]

It is evident that Polish political life in Russia following the revolution was confused, and it could hardly have been otherwise. Except for the semi-independent Regency Council in the

Congress Kingdom, and Dmowski's National Committee in far-off Paris, there was no political center around which Poles could gather. The Social Democrats were the only group to cooperate with the Bolsheviks, but they did it not as Poles but as revolutionaries. The Council of Peoples' Commissars, beset by a host of other problems, devoted relatively little attention to Polish affairs. It lent support and sanction to SDKPiL and attempted to control the Poles through the Polish Commissariat, but apart from revolutionary slogans, which applied to Poland as well as to other countries, the Soviet regime had not yet, strictly speaking, developed a Polish policy. Nor did it show a consistent approach toward another matter which deeply affected Soviet-Polish relations at the time: the issue of Polish troops in Russia.

The idea of organizing separate units of Poles serving in the Russian army went back to the early stages of the war, but the opposition of the tsarist regime prevented its realization. The Provisional Government's proclamation on Poland brought the question of the six hundred thousand Poles, members of the fast disintegrating Russian army, into the open. The Minister of War favored the creation of a Polish army "imbued with Russian influence and Russian training," which could be opposed to Piłsudski's legions. Kerensky objected, believing that the separation of Polish units from the rest of the army would weaken the latter and become detrimental to the cause of freedom and revolution in both Russia and Poland. Differences on the Polish side were equally sharp. At the All-Russian Conference of Polish soldiers held in Petrograd in June 1917 several trends emerged. The Right advocated creation of a Polish army; Center groups opposed it partly not to antagonize Kerensky, partly to avoid a breach with the Provisional State Council in the kingdom which they viewed as the only existing Polish governmental institution. The Left shared this last view, and it also feared lest the Polish army in Russia become a weapon of the reactionaries. The extreme Left saw in a Polish army "a counter-revolutionary factor."[59]

The conference of Polish soldiers concluded with a series of compromises. It made a gesture toward the State Council in Warsaw, and elected the absent Piłsudski honorary chairman. Ignoring the Left, it decided to proceed toward the creation of an army and a governing committee (so-called Naczpol) to supervise it. The latter recommended to the Russian commander-in-chief a tsarist general, Józef Dowbór-Muśnicki, a Pole, to command the First Polish Army Corps.[60]

The passive or even negative attitude of the Center and Left parties placed rightist elements in control of the nascent army—a mistake which stemmed largely from inaccurate information from the kingdom. Piłsudski—on the eve of his arrest by the Germans —was planning to go to Russia and initiate talks with revolutionary leaders to form a democratically oriented Polish army.[61] He felt that the period of cooperation with the Central Powers was over, and he was willing to ignore the State Council in Warsaw. The PPS and the democratic parties in Russia failed to appreciate this development. Consequently the First Army Corps came into being under the influence of and following the model of the old tsarist army; its commander had no vision; and the Naczpol was a poor substitute for a political body.

The outbreak of the October Revolution raised the question of the attitude of Polish troops toward the Bolsheviks. Dowbór-Muśnicki and the commanders of the emerging Second and Third Corps, the Naczpol, and the vast mass of Polish soldiers favored a policy of neutrality toward internal Russian conflicts.[62] Neutrality proved almost impossible. The First Corps was stationed in Belorussia and the remaining two in the Ukraine; i.e., in the borderlands where the large Polish element was endangered by the revolution. Clashes were difficult to avoid, and in the Ukraine the Polish detachments sank to the role of guardians of landed estates and of landowners embattled with the peasantry and the Bolsheviks.

Some units became a refuge for russified or even Russian officers; Dowbór-Muśnicki could hardly be expected not to protect and sympathize with his former colleagues, generals in the tsarist army. Neutrality transformed itself into armed neutrality, imperceptibly merging into intervention. Belorussian peasant soviets protested against alleged attempts of the First Corps to "realize a national Polish idea to unite Belorussia with a monarchic Poland," and "tear away the Belorussian provinces from mother-Russia."[63] There were outcries about a Polish terror in the countryside.

All this played into the hands of the Polish Bolsheviks, who had opposed a Polish army and condemned statements on neutrality. Leszczyński proclaimed that the "Polish revolutionary soldier cannot be neutral in the struggle of the Russian proletariat."[64] SDKPiL announced it would "combat both the so-called neutrality of the Polish bourgeoisie and petty bourgeoisie in Russia . . . and the opportunist reserve of the PPS intelligentsia."[65] The Social Democrats sought to disband the Polish troops, do away with Naczpol, and use Polish soldiers for the revolution. They lacked the power to do it. Nor was there unity of action between SDKPiL and the Soviet High Command.

The number of institutions and organs involved in the affair of the Polish army was truly staggering. On the Polish side were the Naczpol and a rival committee representing first the entire Left, and later SDKPiL and its allies.[66] There was the Commissariat for Polish Affairs and its military section. There were branches of the commissariat on army levels. Finally on the Soviet side there was the commander-in-chief, Nikolai Krylenko, and the powerful commander of the Western Front and later master of Belorussia, the Armenian-born Aleksandr Miasnikov. The situation was chaotic, and the fact that Dowbór-Muśnicki's corps represented a serious military force complicated the situation.

In December the Bolsheviks began a political offensive against the First Corps. Recognizing the right of each nationality to form its regiments, as long as national will reflected the desires of the working masses, Krylenko emphasized that such units follow Russian revolutionary models. They could not adopt a policy of neutrality because the interests of the working masses of every nation were identical.[67] In practice this meant a "democratization" of the First Corps, and on December 10, 1917 the Soviet commander-in-chief ordered the creation of soldiers' soviets. Initiative for this move came from the Polish Commissariat; it also corresponded with the views of Trotsky.[68]

Long arguments and negotiations followed. Dowbór-Muśnicki's attitude, shared by practically all Polish military organizations, was that the First Corps was an army of independent Poland and its soldiers were Polish citizens. *Izvestia* rejected this position as ill-fitting an ex-tsarist and counterrevolutionary general. It contrasted the First Corps with other democratically oriented Polish troops, using a curious argument calculated to appeal to leftist Poles: "In Poland, already under the influence of the February Revolution, a democratization of part of the troops which were under the influence of comrade [*sic*] Piłsudski was taking place, and this was used by the German authorities as one of the reasons for arresting him."[69] It must have been a unique occasion for the Bolsheviks to have called Piłsudski a comrade.

The Poles protested Krylenko's interference, and objected to a Soviet division of Poles into bourgeois and proletarians.[70] To escape Bolshevik meddling, Naczpol ordered the nomination of fictitious political commissars in the corps. This did not improve matters, and toward the end of December Krylenko decreed the arrest of members of Naczpol. Some of them managed to escape, but the institution ceased to function a month later.* Conflict between the Soviet High Command and Dowbór-Muśnicki increased. Miasnikov ordered the corps to move to another area, and attempts to disarm it provoked a breach. Dowbór-Muśnicki behaved provocatively toward the Bolsheviks, addressing them an ultimatum on January 24, 1918; subsequently he began an armed struggle.[71] The move was politically unwise, and the Polish commander was driven to negotiation—coinciding with the Brest-Litovsk peace conference—with the German High Command. Neither these exchanges nor official subordination of the First Corps to the Regency Council in Warsaw saved Dowbór-Muśnicki's troops, and they capitulated to General Max Hoffmann. The First Corps had come to a somewhat inglorious end.

Was there no other way out? Officers belonging to the underground Polish Military Organization, POW (Polska Organizacja Wojskowa), which represented a continuation of Piłsudski's legions, had tried to prevent the capitulation. They were attempting to salvage the Polish troops in Russia, remove them from control of reactionary generals, and work out some *modus vivendi* with the Bolsheviks. In January 1918 a prominent Socialist and collaborator of Piłsudski, Tadeusz Hołówko, was dispatched to Russia with the double task of persuading the PPS to maintain its independent line and of organizing a Polish army controlled by Socialists and democrats. His hopes centered on the troops in the Ukraine which at this time had amalgamated with the second brigade of Polish legions under Józef Haller. This last unit had served under Austrian command and broke with the Central Powers after the treaty of Brest-Litovsk; it crossed the front and presented itself to the Bolsheviks, largely for tactical reasons, as a democratic or even revolutionary detachment.[72] It met at first with a friendly reception.

Though documentation is scarce, it is known that in the spring of 1918 Hołówko and other Polish Socialists conferred with Lenin and Trotsky about a democratic Polish army in Russia.† They apparently failed in their efforts. Nor were conditions in the

* It was replaced by the short-lived Supreme Council of Polish Armed Forces.
† Hołówko apparently acted on the authorization of Edward Rydz-Śmigly. A little earlier, Władysław Raczkiewicz of the Naczpol had sounded the Bolsheviks on the possibility of withdrawing the First Corps inside Russia and coordinating an anti-Germany policy. In June Tomasz Arciszewski (a PPS leader) proposed cooperation against the Germans. See Jerzy Holzer, *Polska Partia Socjalistyczna w latach 1917-1919* (Warsaw, 1962), pp. 115-116. Also Jerzy Osmołowski, "Wspomnienia z lat 1914-1921," III, 27, MS., Biblioteka Narodowa, Warsaw.

Ukraine favorable for organization of Polish troops there. After a hopeless battle against the Germans at Kaniov, Haller capitulated in May 1918.

The Third Polish Army Corps survived him by only two months. Subsequent attempts to organize military units in Russia were made in cooperation with the Entente. Stunned by Brest-Litovsk the Allies thought of reviving a second front in Russia, a policy which slowly gave rise to intervention. The rightist Polish Interparty Circle and POW tried to work out an agreement for shipping the remnants of Polish troops to France—through Allied-held Murmansk and Archangel—or to link their fate with Allied detachments in Russia. There were attempts to obtain a Soviet blessing for evacuation of Poles in exchange for promises of neutrality; but they produced no results.[73] Neutrality was as hard as ever to maintain. Operating with the Allies, the Poles at best could object to cooperation with the counterrevolutionary general Mikhail V. Alekseev, "given his uncertain attitude to the idea of [Polish] independence."[74] The Polish division formed under French auspices and commanded by Lucjan Żeligowski fought against the Ukrainians and the Bolsheviks. Another division under Walery Czuma struggled against the Red Army in Siberia. All this was a far cry from the original idea of an independent Polish army in Russia. As General Żeligowski wrote bitterly to Dowbór-Muśnicki: "History will judge if conditions existed for the creation of an army in the east; but even now it is self-evident that we did nothing to create such a force and to subordinate these difficult historical moments to our creative initiative."[75]

Naturally there were immense difficulties. A Polish army had to resist absorption by the revolution, maintain a genuine neutrality in Russian affairs, and avoid falling victim to the victorious Germans. It could not reject cooperation with the Entente, whose war aims included Poland's independence. In the chaotic situation of the day Polish troops, while professing neutrality, were engaged in a struggle against the Bolsheviks. Formed to fight the Germans, they eventually capitulated to them. Even when drawn into the schemes of intervention, the Poles failed to capitalize on their achievements.

To what extent did the policies of SDKPiL and of the Bolsheviks condition this development? Social Democrats opposed Polish national units and favored a Red army "built on the principle of internationalism, excluding all national divisions."[76] Conditions prevented a strict adherence to such a program. Polish revolutionary detachments emerged and were set in contrast to the "reactionary" Polish army. The experiences of these revolutionary troops were not always happy. The huge reserve regiment stationed at Belgorod for a while provided an example of a Polish Bolshevik unit, but in mid-December 1917 it was—"through misunderstandings and provocation"—disarmed by Red troops and its revolutionary commander Jackiewicz assassinated.[77] Its successors, named the Revolutionary Regiment of Red Warsaw, the Lublin regiment, the Siedlce regiment, the Mazovian regiment of Red Ulans, Warsaw Red Hussars, and others, later merged into the Western Division. This unit had only a Polish nucleus and served as a model of a truly international force.[78] In principle, regiments were formed on territorial and not a national basis, and only those national detachments were tolerated that would most likely not fall victim to "national bourgeois agitation."[79] Potential counterrevolutionaries were removed to areas from which they could not escape to Murmansk or Archangel. A delegate of the Cheka recommended that these "simple people be sent to Moscow where in a concentration camp, educational-propagandistic courses will make them return to the class to which they belong." Eventually they were to join the Red Army.[80]

While SDKPiL pursued a consistently negative policy toward Polish troops in Russia and attempted to make its forces as international as possible, the attitude of Soviet authorities lacked clarity. Polish Socialists criticized Krylenko for his "inconsistent and planless tactics, devoid of any program." They accused him of changing his position "by either supporting or even calling for the formation of national military formations, or combatting them by all available means."[81] There is no doubt that the Soviet commander-in-chief moved from one extreme to another. His order to the First Corps to advance into an area seething with national conflicts was bad enough, and it preceded orders to disarm the moving Poles. After the clash Krylenko called on the Belorussian peasantry to arrest all Polish officers and take the law in their own hands. All these measures, the PPS and PPS-Left asserted, were contrary to a democratic and Socialist sense of justice. It appears that Krylenko also was involved in the bloody events in the Belgorod regiment, and delegates of Polish soldiers called on Trotsky to have the commander-in-chief censured.[82]

SDKPiL criticized the Bolsheviks on different grounds. The Social Democrats considered them "poorly informed" and misguided with regard to the question of national troops. As in other instances, the differences of approach to the national question were at the bottom of the SDKPiL-Bolshevik controversy. The Social Democrats claimed that they attempted to correct the mistakes of Krylenko, and there is little doubt that they interfered in his conflict—possibly urging him on—with Dowbór-Muśnicki.[83]

Soviet policy toward the Polish troops indicated that circumstances prevented any clear program. Changing interpretations of self-determination, extreme military weakness of the Red Army, fear of German intervention—all contributed to contradictory tactics. Gaining time, consolidating the regime, waiting for an opportune moment: these were the characteristic Bolshevik policies during the spring and summer of 1918.

The establishment of German-Soviet diplomatic relations after the treaty of Brest-Litovsk brought out still another aspect of the Polish question: recognition of the Regency Council. The Council appointed Lednicki its representative in Russia, and the Germans applied pressure on the Narkomindel to recognize him. Ambassador Wilhelm von Mirbach wrote Chicherin on June 19, 1918 to enter into contact with Lednicki, and the commissar complied by addressing a brutal note to the Pole. Chicherin emphasized that although Russia had signed the peace treaty "which tore Poland away from Russia" she did not consider that this settlement gave the "Polish popular masses the right of self-determination." Hence the Council of Peoples' Commissars viewed the Regency Council as an organ of the German occupation, and would prefer to deal directly with Germany. Since Germany insisted on dealing with Lednicki—and the Germans had every right to appoint agents for talks concerning Polish refugees in Russia—the Peoples' Commissariat for Foreign Affairs would accede to Mirbach's request.[84]

Chicherin reiterated the Soviet attitude on Poland (as represented by the Regency Council) at the Fifth Congress of the Soviets. He explained that negotiations with Lednicki over concrete matters relating to the refugee problem in no way implied recognition of the state of affairs in the kingdom. Nor could one speak of establishment of Soviet-Polish diplomatic relations.[85] The Bolsheviks maintained their Brest-Litovsk line toward Poland, insisting that the Poles had not yet exercised the right of self-determination. Nor did the Soviet government renounce its freedom of action vis-à-vis Polish affairs.

Talks about re-evacuation of Poles from Russia did not proceed smoothly, and Mirbach's successor, Ambassador Karl Helfferich, had to remind Chicherin in early August 1918 to treat with Lednicki. It is obvious that the problem of refugees was difficult. The Commissariat for Polish Affairs made every effort to indoctrinate refugees so that they be "properly prepared to face the revolutionary tasks which awaited them in Poland."[86] The representative of the Regency Council, as well as German and Austrian authorities, were well aware of these attempts and displayed great caution in granting admission to Poles returning to the kingdom. As the commissariat admitted, the difficulty concerning repatriation consisted in each side wanting to have different people leave Russia and return to Poland.

German-Soviet relations underwent a significant change on August 27, with the signing of treaties supplementary to the main agreement of Brest-Litovsk. These documents reflect the decline of German power and bear the character of a give-and-take arrangement. While Soviet Russia renounced sovereignty over Estonia and Livonia and made other concessions, Germany agreed to withdraw from Belorussia and grant Russia access to the Baltic via Latvian ports. Two days after the signing of the supplementary treaties, the Council of Peoples' Commissars issued a decree which denounced a series of old agreements signed between the former Russian empire and the governments of Germany, Austro-Hungary, Prussia, Bavaria, Hessen, Oldenburg, Saxony-Meiningen, and the city of Lübeck. With one exception these agreements were of a technical nature and covered such issues as extradition of criminals, protection of shareholders of state loans, and deportation of vagrants and the unemployed. They were repudiated as contrary to the laws of the new Russian regime—their denunciation being "in conformity with the articles of the supplementary treaties."

The only clause which differed sharply from the rest of the decree was part three of the document, and it read: "All agreements and acts concluded by the Government of the former Russian Empire with the Governments of the Kingdom of Prussia and the Austro-Hungarian Empire which refer to the partitions of Poland, are irrevocably annulled by the present [decree] as contrary to the principle of national self-determination and to the sense of revolutionary legality of the Russian people which recognizes the inalienable right of the Polish people to independence and unity."[87]

This passage, often erroneously called *the* decree annulling Poland's partitions, represented the only official act by the Council of Peoples' Commissars referring to Poland, and as such it deserves examination. Why did the Bolsheviks unilaterally annul the partitions treaties, and why did they chose the autumn of 1918 to do so? If the object was propaganda it is strange that the denunciation of the partitions did not come simultaneously with Soviet rejection of all secret treaties concluded by the old regime, or even at the time of the Brest-Litovsk negotiations. It may well be that the Bolsheviks felt that such a move would be a challenge to the Central Powers, and they could afford to make it only in August 1918. This does not explain why this declaration—described by a prominent Polish Bolshevik as the "beginning of Poland's liberation"—was inserted in 'a document dealing with technical and non-controversial matters.[88] Surely this deprived it of the publicity which it otherwise could have achieved. The decree was made public in early September. One looks in vain for any evidence of Polish reaction. It would seem that the Bolsheviks, masters in revolutionary propaganda, did not direct the document at the Polish audience. It is also curious that the passage contained no reference to the Peace Decree or the Declaration of Rights of the Peoples of Russia but spoke in general terms about self-determination and revolutionary legality.[89]

A Polish historian wrote that "while in Brest, Russia had renounced its own part, she undermined by this act the legal foundations of the two remaining partitioners."[90] Such an interpretation could be greatly misleading if taken literally. The value of Soviet renunciation at Brest-Litovsk was at best problematic; later Russia simply repudiated the treaty.[91] An international agreement such as a partition pact could not become invalid with a unilateral denunciation. What one could say at most is that the decree of August 29 signified that Soviet Russia was no longer bound to uphold the rights of Germany and Austria to Polish territories acquired through the partition treaties. The Council of Peoples' Commissars merely announced that it had liquidated Russia's obligation arising out of the old treaties vis-à-vis the other two powers. In that sense it was logical to include the clause concerning Poland in a document which abrogated all Russian legal commitments to the Germanic states, even if the propaganda value of part three would greatly diminish.

Subsequent interpretations of the decree gave it a meaning it did not possess. Some Polish writers assumed that Soviet repudiation of the partitions meant not only that Russia no longer recognized German and Austrian rights to Poland but admittted the legal status quo ante 1772.[92] Such was not the Soviet intention. Nor did the Bolsheviks ever announce their lack of interest in the borderlands or Poland.

During the year between the outbreak of the October Revolution and the re-emergence of a Polish state in November 1918 the Polish issue did not require immediate Bolshevik attention. Following the complex moves with regard to Poles in Russia and the Polish army, studying Soviet declarations on Poland at Brest-Litovsk and elsewhere, one can see only broad lines of a

Soviet approach to the Polish question. By emphasizing the principle of national self-determination and denying the right of the Regency Council to represent Poland, the Bolsheviks maintained their freedom of maneuver. Except for the treaty of Brest-Litovsk, which they were ready to denounce at the first opportunity, they took no commitments to respect the status of the Kingdom of Poland. They repudiated the partitions and asserted that the Poles had a right to be free and united, but avoided making these assertions more precise. While using the Commissariat for Polish Affairs as a Soviet organ to deal with Polish matters, they made no attempts—and insofar as one can judge no preparations —to promote a Polish Communist government-in-exile. Was it because Lenin was wary to undertake anything that could remind the Poles of old tsarist policies of domination? Was it because his realism opposed any such premature ventures? We shall probably never know.

There were instances of Bolshevik preoccupation with Polish national sentiments; there were others in which Soviet leaders showed no interest in Poland.* One thing was incontestable. In the autumn of 1918, as the military power of Germany visibly declined and the war reached its final stage, Bolshevik hopes for a European revolution revived. Kamenev declared again that the victory of Communism in Russia could only come through an international upheaval.[93] Chicherin wrote Woodrow Wilson that the Soviet type of government would soon become the universally accepted political form.[94] No wonder that the Soviet government, realizing Poland's importance—if only for geographic reasons—was not going to commit itself to any solution of the Polish question that could have interfered with Bolshevik designs. Extension of the Communist revolution would naturally affect first the borderlands and contiguous countries in the west. At the Fifth Congress of the Soviets, Chicherin had denounced German interference with the "establishment of mutual economic relations between Russia and these states which had formerly created one economic unity—the Ukraine, Poland, the Baltic countries, the Caucasus."[95] The All-Russian Central Executive Committee (VTsIK) adopted a resolution on October 3, 1918

---

* The interest was evidenced by numerous decrees to protect Polish art treasures and cultural monuments in Russia and restore them eventually to the people of Poland. See *Materiały archiwalne do historii stosunków polsko-radzieckich,* ed. Natalia Gąsiorowska (Warsaw, 1957—), I, 541-542; *Dokumenty vneshnei politiki SSSR* (Moscow: Ministerstvo Inostrannykh Del SSSR, 1959—), I, 95-96, 370 (hereafter cited as *DVP. SSSR*). On the other hand it is strange that Lenin made no reference to Poland in his speech to the Warsaw Revolutionary regiment on August 2, 1918 (*Sochineniia* XXIII, 168).

which went further. After declaring that the "Soviet Government builds its entire policy on the prospect of a social revolution in both imperialist camps," the resolution stated: "binding the fate of the Ukraine, Poland, Lithuania, the Baltic, and Finland closely to the fate of the proletarian revolution, we reject any idea whatever of any rapprochement with Allied imperialism for the purpose of changing the provisions of the Brest-Litovsk treaty."[96]

The Bolsheviks were challenging all bourgeois governments. Lenin made this clear by announcing the need for a Red Army of three million men. The fate of Poland and its position and relation with Soviet Russia would depend not on agreements and declarations but the victorious march of the Communist revolution.

4

Nation or Class?

The collapse of Germany and Austro-Hungary in November 1918 opened wide prospects for the Bolsheviks. Never before, so Lenin asserted on November 8, "had we been so close to an international proletarian revolution as at present." But he warned that difficult times lay ahead.[1] This was true. The Soviet regime was menaced by counterrevolutionary armies and Allied intervention. It saw its salvation not in defense but in offensive action, for, as Lenin reiterated, "a complete victory of the Socialist revolution was unthinkable in one country," and it depended on spreading the proletarian fire to the large industrial states.

Aiming at European revolution, the Bolsheviks had to attempt a breakthrough in the West, and reconquer in the process the borderlands separated from Russia by Brest-Litovsk. Contemporary pronouncements by Communist leaders made it abundantly clear that this westward expansion was neither a defensive measure against new foes nor a spontaneous movement over which they had no control. Trotsky in his speech at Voronezh explained that the western front was no longer dangerous for Russia. It is we, he said, "who will complete our work there and establish Russia within frontiers that correspond to the will of popular masses inhabiting the old tsarist empire." Trotsky stated the Bolshevik objectives when he said: "Through Kiev goes the direct way of linking up with the Austro-Hungarian revolution, just as the way through Pskov and Vilna leads to a direct contact with the revolution in Germany." The *mot d'ordre* therefore was "offensive on all the fronts."[2] Stalin also spoke in fiery words about the "partition wall" between revolutionary Russia and the West, which had to be demolished.[3] Words were followed by deeds, and in mid-November the Western Defense Region changed its name to the Western Army. While the size of Red detachments was at first small, they received the order to advance. Their strength subsequently increased. As a Soviet historian put it, the immediate issue was who would capture the area first—the Bolsheviks, "Allied imperialism," or domestic "counterrevolution."[4]

Two days after Armistice was signed in the West—which included abrogation of Brest-Litovsk—Soviet Russia denounced the treaty. After stating that its terms were "null and void" the Soviet decree declared: "The working masses of Russia, Livonia, Poland, Lithuania, the Ukraine, Finland, the Crimea, and the Caucasus, freed by the German revolution from the yoke of an annexationist treaty, dictated by the German militarists, are now called upon to decide their own fate." The decree invited revolutionary soviets in Germany and in the former Austro-Hungarian Empire to begin negotiations with Russia, and recalled that Soviet principles of peace included evacuation of "all occupied provinces of Russia," and the granting of self-determination to "the working peoples of all nations." The decree proposed the creation of an alliance of workers of Russia, Germany, and Austro-Hungary, and hoped that in this "mighty alliance of the liberated nations of Russia"—here the countries of the former empire were enumerated—"Germany and Austro-Hungary will be joined by nations of all the other states that have not yet thrown off the yoke of capitalism." Until such a universal Communist league would be realized, the Soviet government, "supported by revolutionary forces throughout Central and Eastern Europe" promised to "resist every attempt to restore the power of capital, whether foreign or native."[5]

The meaning of the decree was clear. By repudiating Brest-Litovsk the Bolsheviks announced that they were no longer bound to recognize the sovereignty of the border states, and were defying all "bourgeois" governments of East Central Europe. While the decree called on the working masses of these countries to decide their own fate, it did not mean that this right was to be exercised without Soviet interference. *Ekonomicheskaia Zhizn* wrote that the separation of Lithuania, Belorussia, the Baltic countries, Poland, and the Caucasus was "contrary to common sense and economic laws."[6] Besides, the geographic position of these countries made them too important for the Bolsheviks to allow any real self-determination. To quote Trotsky again, the liberated border states would "no longer be a wedge but a connecting link between Soviet Russia and the future Soviet Germany and Austro-Hungary. Here is the beginning of a federation, of a European Communist federation."[7]

Thus, the future status of the border states was determined in advance. The principle of national self-determination, understood as a determination of the proletariat, provided the theoretical basis for the Soviet approach. Stalin wrote that it was evident that national liberation was unthinkable without "the overthrow of the bourgeoisie of the oppressed nationalities," and he castigated those who saw in national resistance "a struggle for national liberation against the 'soulless centralism' of the Soviet government."[8] Soviet propaganda took it for granted that the "masses"—a magic word—stood with the Bolsheviks, and Moscow took care not to test this assumption by plebiscites or referendums. When Chicherin refused to negotiate with an independent Georgia and Azerbaijan in the summer of 1918, he advanced as his reason that "national masses do not wish and do not recognize separation from Russia."[9] This approach would reappear again and again.

Undertaking their armed thrust in the direction of Belorussia, the Ukraine, and the Baltic countries, the Bolsheviks had to contend not only with their national resistance but also with the dogmatism of native Communist representatives. Most of these party members belonged to the "internationalist" trend and like the Polish Social Democrats saw no need for the formation of national states. At a conference of Communist delegates in Moscow in late October 1918 (the Poles were represented by Bobiński), these representatives of "occupied territories" had advocated an international republic with a Soviet regime imposed on the Ukraine, Poland, and the Baltic countries. The Central Committee of the Bolshevik party had to coerce them to subscribe to the principle of national self-determination.[10]

The story of the Soviet invasion of the borderlands at the turn of 1918 and the beginning of 1919 provides a supreme example of a travesty of national self-determination. The decision to advance and operate through largely fictitious governments was taken by Moscow alone. Toward the end of November Lenin informed Commander-in-Chief Ioakim I. Vatsetis (Jakums Vaciētis) about the creation of Soviet governments for the borderlands, and explained that this would "deprive the chauvinists of the Ukraine, Lithuania, Latvia, and Estland of the possibility of treating the offensive of our troops as an occupation." Without such governments the position of Red armies in the occupied countries would be extremely difficult, and the local "population would not treat them as liberators."[11] A month later Stalin, speaking at the All-Russian Central Executive Committee (VTsIK), explained—as if to allay fears that national self-determination might be taken seriously—that the right to independence had been given so as to permit these governments to eventually proclaim the unity of the Soviet republics.[12] Such assurances were hardly necessary; the problem was to convince the Latvian, Lithuanian, and Ukrainian Communists to play the game.

The leading Latvian Bolshevik, Petr Stuchka, candidly admitted that he had proclaimed an independent Soviet Latvia on the express orders of Moscow. Neither he nor his followers looked upon themselves as foreigners vis-à-vis the Russians, and they considered "independent" Latvia as a Russian province (*oblast*). The revolutionary Latvian Rifles, used to "liberate" Latvia, protested their separation from the Red Army, and passed a resolution in favor of integrating Latvia into Russia.[13] Even a decree of the Soviet Latvian government, which restored the laws passed by the Russian Socialist Federated Soviet Republic, justified it by repudiating Brest-Litovsk, through which Latvia "became again a part of Russia."[14] The Latvian Soviet government came from Russia to assume power over the country and Stuchka made no bones of the fact that only the argument that bourgeois nationalists would accuse Russia of imperialism made him agree to Lenin's scheme.

Lithuania offered parallels to Latvia. The two leading Bolsheviks, Vincas Mickiewicz (Mickievičius)-Kapsukas and Zigmas Aleksa-Angarietis, opposed Lithuanian independence. Again the Central Committee of the Russian Bolshevik party had to intervene and force them to issue a manifesto proclaiming a provisional revolutionary government of Lithuania. The manifesto, the date and place of issue of which were fictitious, was made more Lithuanian-sounding by the Bolsheviks, and Kapsukas explained his consent in similar terms to Stuchka, namely to prevent accusations that Soviet rule in Lithuania was "introduced by the bayonets of the Red Army."[15] Given the shortage of qualified Lithuanians in Russia, *Izvestia* carried announcements of the Commissariat for Lithuanian Affairs inviting specialists, irrespective of their nationality, to volunteer for new jobs in Soviet Lithuania. Because there were no Lithuanian troops in the Red Army, the Bolsheviks carried out the advance with the second Pskov division.[16]

The complex situation in the Ukraine required somewhat different methods. While the Council of Peoples' Commissars in early November ordered preparation of an army to invade the Ukraine, and a few days later created a Ukrainian Military Revolutionary Council (revvoensovet) with Stalin, Georgii L. Piatakov, Vladimir P. Zatonskii (Volodymyr Zatonskyi) and Vladimir A. Antonov-Ovseenko, the control of Kiev by the Directory made an easy conquest impossible. The manifesto of the Soviet Ukrainian Provisional Government of Workers and Peasants could not disguise the fact that the Ukraine under Volodymyr Vynnychenko and Simon Petliura was an existing reality. While Antonov-Ovseenko called for more Russian divisions, while Trotsky counseled an all-out offensive, Lenin preferred prudence.[17] Fighting alternated with negotiations, and at one point Moscow, officially remaining in the background, offered to mediate between the Directory and the Soviet Ukrainian government.[18] The Ukraine could not be included at once in the category of conquered borderlands, and the Red troops took Kiev only in February 1919.

Developments in Belorussia, which, except for Lithuania, had the most direct bearing on Soviet-Polish relations, followed a different course. The picture in that area was complicated by the mass expulsions of Belorussians during the World War and the flooding of the country by soldiers from other parts of the former empire. The soldiers, organized in soviets of workers' and soldiers' deputies, were represented by the ambitious Miasnikov who succeeded in gaining control over Belorussia. Efforts of the natives, originally grouped into peasant soviets, to assert themselves led to innumerable conflicts which necessitated intervention by Stalin and which delayed the proclamation of an independent Soviet Belorussia.[19] There were other reasons for this delay. Belorussia, was not originally included among the borderlands for which independent Soviet governments were prepared, and Moscow may not have thought it worthwhile. Indeed, in late December 1918 the revolutionary committee in Minsk spoke only of the rebirth of "a new great Russia."[20] The decision of the Central Committee to establish a Belorussian Soviet Republic stemmed largely from considerations connected with Poland.*

The general westward advance of Red troops was aimed at the Vistula, and its objective was first, occupation of Belorussia, and second, advance toward Warsaw up to the river Bug. As a Soviet historian put it, this offensive, developed at first successfully; "Poland, occupied elsewhere, weakly protected its eastern frontiers."[21] In January 1919, however, Soviet units began to meet resistance from Polish volunteer detachments, "legionaries," and POW, and the offensive slowed down. In Wilno Poles were the only element which, with slight assistance from Warsaw, attempted to stem the Russian tide. The Bolsheviks drew a lesson from this development and decided to establish a Belorussian state which "relying on the help of Soviet Russia would at the same time not involve her in open war with Poland."[22] The Central Committee of RKP(b) decided on January 16 that the Belorussian republic be limited in size and denied the gubernia of Smolensk, Vitebsk and Mohilev. Adolf A. Ioffe, dispatched to Minsk to organize the

* It is possible, however, that the fact of the declaration of an independent Belorussian Peoples' Republic, adopted during the night of March 24-25, 1918, may have also been taken into consideration. On the declaration see Jerzy Osmołowski, "Wspomnienia z lat 1914-1921," II, 184-185, Biblioteka Narodowa, Warsaw.

new state, explained that a small independent Soviet Belorussia would play the part of a buffer between Russia and Poland. "Polish claims," Ioffe declared, "may be settled by diplomacy," and it would be more convenient that Poland "be in conflict with buffers—Lithuania and Belorussia" than with the Russian Soviet Republic.[23]

The truncated Belorussian state was established under conditions which had nothing to do with national self-determination. Its brief existence ended when Moscow in mid-January decided that the policy of establishing buffer states required Belorussia's amalgamation with Lithuania. The local "governments" received word of this decision early in February, and Iakov M. Sverdlow came to see it through. The Bolshevik leader explained that the creation of a Lithuanian-Belorussian Soviet Republic—*Litbel*—was necessary because of the international situation, a tendency of nations to form larger units, more effective struggle against the enemy, and strife against nationalism and chauvinism. He emphasized that "whatever the divisions, we are at this time one party and the decision of the Central Committee is binding on all. This is axiomatic."[24] Sverdlov could not have been more explicit. It mattered little whether Moscow created independent republics, cut their territory, or amalgamated them with others. All these moves were of a purely tactical nature, determined by the interests of the Bolshevik revolution.

Leaders of the Soviet border republics, far from resenting rigid control by the Central Committee in Moscow and the fiction of independence, merely objected to the comedy of self-determination.[25] Vatsetis, who for a time combined the functions of commander-in-chief of the Red Army with that of commander of the Latvian army, in the spring of 1919 recommended ending the pretense of national Communist armies. He termed attempts to create such armies nonsensical. The Estonian army, he wrote, did not represent anything, and Lithuanian and Belorussian armies "are not even worth speaking of." Neither the Lithuanians nor the Belorussians could "justify their *raison d'être*," not having formed a single national unit. Besides, commanders of the Western Front wanted to get rid of Belorussian and Lithuanian soldiers because they were unreliable.[26] Stalin seemed to share Vatsetis's point of view, and already had assured the Estonian Communists that eventually they would all find themselves in a common Soviet federation.[27]

Such were the sentiments and moves behind the scene, but the Soviet government continued to pay lip service to the Leninist principle of national self-determination. In December Moscow solemnly recognized independent Soviet republics of Lithuania, Latvia, and Estonia. Recognition of Belorussia followed in February. Stalin publicly asserted that Russia "never looked upon the western regions as her possessions" but as the rightful property of the native proletariat. "It is self-understood," he added, "that this does not exclude but rather presupposes rendering them every assistance."[28] When, in February 1919, it was announced that Russia and Belorussia would be linked by federal ties and that a link with Lithuania would follow, Stalin commented: "Thus *from* the breakdown of the old imperialist unity *through* independent Soviet republics, the peoples of Russia are coming *to* a new, voluntary, fraternal unity."[29] Such was the practical realization of Lenin's theory of three stages—separation, revolution, unity—which made a mockery of this seemingly spontaneous process. Popular will nowhere had a chance to express itself, and even if one admits that revolutionary trends in the border countries facilitated Soviet advance, the conquest of the borderlands nonetheless remained the work of the Red Army.

All this had a direct bearing on Poland. That country, too, had been part of the old Russian empire; its geographical location disposed it to be either a link or a barrier between Russia and Western Europe; it had been enumerated alongside the other border countries in the statements and declarations quoted earlier.

How did Poland figure in the Soviet plans of a breakthrough to the west and was she to be treated similarly to Belorussia or Lithuania? It appears that the Bolshevik leaders realized their military weakness with regard to the nascent Polish state. Their offensive toward the Vistula was supposed to stop on the Bug River and not penetrate the Congress Kingdom. A Soviet historian called Poles "the most serious adversary,"[30] and it seems unlikely that the High Command assumed that the westward drive could bring Poland immediately under Russian control. The Germans still held, however ineffectively, a line in the east in accord with Article 12 of the Armistice, and this fact was bound to delay the Red Army. Besides, Lenin as a supreme realist must have known that the conquest of Poland would not be an easy matter. In his talks at Minsk Ioffe indicated that Russia wanted to avoid open war with the Poles. The Polish case had to be solved by internal revolution, which the Red Army would do its best to assist.

In late 1918 Poland faced the alternative of either becoming a "bourgeois" state, national and independent (barring westward Bolshevik expansion), or entering the Soviet orbit through a

Communist revolution. Polish Bolsheviks, belonging to a dogmatic "internationalist" wing of the party, doubtless would have to be coerced like their comrades in Latvia or Lithuania to promote the slogan of national self-determination, but one knows from the above-mentioned examples what self-determination meant in practice. So only a "bourgeois" state could become independent, and the dilemma narrowed to the question whether national or class feelings would predominate.[31] Because Poland was out of Russia's direct reach, she had the chance of resolving this dilemma herself.

On the eve of the Armistice in the West the Polish situation was extremely complex. The Regency Council in early October attempted to free itself from German tutelage; its cabinet in turn attempted a coup against the Regency Council, hoping to become an independent caretaker government. The Regents were still strong enough to dismiss the ministry, but their days were numbered. Galicia began to detach itself from the Austrian Monarchy, and a Polish Liquidation Committee appeared in Cracow. In an atmosphere of disintegrating institutions, the patriotic enthusiasm of the Poles mingled with radical social slogans. The chief political movements of the National Democrats and the PPS, together with their allies and the populist parties, stood for a constituent assembly which democratically would determine the character of the renascent state. But *faits accomplis* counted more than theories. The leaders of the Right were in Paris, and they based their calculations on Allied assistance and guidance. The Left, with strong links to Piłsudski, decided on immediate action to finish off the Regency Council and checkmate the extreme Left, which talked loudly about a Bolshevik revolution.

This last group was composed mainly of SDKPiL, and true to its former stand it rejected "the comedy of independence and of a democratic sejm."[32] Having drawn a lesson from the Bolshevik failure with the Constituent Assembly, the Polish extremists considered "an assembly of the representatives of the entire nation" as "absolutely unacceptable." They called instead for councils of workers', peasants', and soldiers' deputies. Their target was a Soviet Poland linked "with other liberated countries in one family of free and fraternal nations."[33]

Workers' councils began indeed to appear in some areas of the kingdom when the PPS and its allies on November 7, 1918 proclaimed a Polish Peoples' Republic headed by a government in which Socialists and radical populists (Wyzwolenie) had the principal part. The government, established in Lublin under the Galician Socialist leader Ignacy Daszyński, comprised Edward

Śmigły-Rydz, who acted as the substitute for the imprisoned Piłsudski and commanded the military force, POW. In its first proclamation—known as the Lublin Manifesto—the new regime demanded immediate dissolution of the Regency Council, and threatened to outlaw it in case of resistance. It promised to call a sejm, based on universal suffrage, and enumerated social reforms, some of which were to be put into effect immediately, others submitted to the sejm for approval.[34]

The guiding thought of the Socialists was to direct the state-building process into "democratic, or more precisely parliamentary-democratic channels." They considered that Poland's working class was too weak to rule by itself but too strong to be ignored.[35] The manifesto was based on a more realistic appraisal of the situation than the SDKPiL's demagogic demands for immediate dictatorship of the proletariat, and it took the wind out of Communist propaganda. No wonder the extreme Left savagely attacked the Lublin government.[36] The Right and the Center parties also objected, though on precisely opposite grounds.[37]

The result was deadlock. The Lublin government could not eliminate the Regency Council, nor vice versa. Polish political organizations in German Poland recognized only the National Committee in Paris. It seemed that a nationalist-populist government would emerge in Cracow. Piłsudski's return from Magdeburg to Warsaw on November 10 put an end to these divisions. Within four days the Regency Council, having passed its military and political powers to Piłsudski, withdrew from the scene. The Lublin government also resigned; the field was clear for a more representative ministry.

The cabinet appointed by Piłsudski—who in virtue of a decree of November 22, 1918 assumed dictatorial powers as the provisional chief of state—comprised mostly former members of the Lublin regime. It was no longer headed by Daszyński but by his fellow Socialist Jędrzej Moraczewski, who was more amenable to Piłsudski. Nor did it have the halo of a spontaneous, semirevolutionary creation, and it was hardly a "peoples' government" although the term continued for some time. The new ministry preserved some important items of the Lublin Manifesto, namely, the republican form of government and an impressive body of social legislation; it relegated other reforms to the future approval of the sejm. Piłsudski, who dominated the cabinet, explained its Socialist coloring by "taking into account the powerful trends which emerge victorious today in Western and Eastern Europe."[38] He favored reforms not so much because of his own radical leanings but out of belief that Poland had to shift from the eighteenth to the twentieth century. Above all Piłsudski wanted to discover a genuine majority in the country on which to base his government. He wrote Dmowski that only the National Democrats and the PPS were of consequence in Poland but even they represented leaders and staffs, and the allegiance of the masses was not yet certain. Hence, Piłsudski favored an early calling of the sejm to determine the strength of various political trends in the country, and he made clear his own determination not to lean on any party until general elections would reveal the true political picture.[39]

The Moraczewski government, which attempted "reforms of the West and not of the East, which engender chaos,"[40] struggled among untold difficulties. The extreme Left viewed it as a tool of the bourgeoisie; the Right saw in it pseudo-Bolshevik traits. The Entente suspiciously eyed a combination of an ex-Socialist chief of state who had fought on the side of the Central Powers and a Socialist-led cabinet. In vain the ministry tried to convince the West that "Peoples' Poland will be the best European bulwark against Bolshevism."[41] Unrecognized by the Allies, attacked by domestic foes, sabotaged by vested interests, Moraczewski's cabinet fought a lonely battle for moderate socialism and democracy.

Confident of French support, the National Democrats privately were not displeased with a cabinet they viewed as a stop-gap arrangement. They felt that only such a government could prevent the danger of a civil war.[42] A representative of Dmowski's National Committee suggested to Piłsudski that the appointment of Moraczewski's cabinet was dictated by the desire to "save the country from a Bolshevik revolution prepared by hundreds of agitators sent from Russia." Piłsudski replied that such a formula "did not correspond to the real state of affairs."[43]

Increasing domestic difficulties—there was even a theatrical coup d'état engineered by the Right on January 4-5, 1919—and pressure by the Entente, which had not yet recognized the existing regime, forced the resignation of the Moraczewski cabinet. A new ministry headed by the famous pianist and great patriot, Ignacy Paderewski, brought with it reconciliation with the National Committee and recognition by the Entente.[44] But it represented also a partial surrender to the Right and the end of Socialist hopes for a "democratic coalition." As a prominent Socialist put it, Moraczewski's cabinet fell because it found itself in a vacuum; it ceased to be a revolutionary government without becoming as yet a parliamentary ministry.[45] Its dismissal on the eve of elections to the sejm hurt the Socialists and their allies at the polls. On January 26 the block of the Right gained the largest number of seats, though no absolute majority. The Left fared worse than expected; the Communists—in mid-December SDKPiL and parts of the PPS-Left merged and set up a Polish Communist Workers' Party (KPRP)—boycotted the elections.

The nomination of Paderewski's cabinet, reconciliation between the National Committee in Paris and the regime in Warsaw, elections to the sejm which confirmed Piłsudski's position as chief of state, and Allied recognition of Poland—all these amounted to crystallization of the Polish state. An independent Western-oriented republic established itself; no Bolshevik revolution had taken place.

The Polish Communists during the winter of 1918-1919 enjoyed relative freedom. They had their own party headquarters, press organs, clubs, and in some cases, militia.[46] Rumors of a Bolshevik coup frightened some circles in Poland but Piłsudski and the PPS leaders did not take them too seriously.[47] While workers' councils appeared in most industrial centers of the former kingdom—and in a different form in other provinces—their revolutionary activity was not spectacular. The mining region of Dąbrowa constituted an exception, and Red Guard detachments came into existence there. The local council (rada) sent greetings to the Council of Peoples' Commissars in Russia, calling it "the leader of Socialist revolution,"[48] but even in this area the workers' councils were unable to maintain control against the government. In most places the councils comprised representatives of the PPS, the Jewish Bund, or even non-Socialist workers' organizations. Neither in Warsaw, nor in Łódź—the proletarian stronghold—were the Communists in a majority.

The situation was occasionally compared to that in Russia under the Provisional Government, but such an analogy was misleading. If one could argue that Bolshevism "agreed with the distinctive character of the Russian historical process,"[49] such argument was hardly valid for Poland. As a Bundist who stood at that time close to the Communists remarked, Polish Bolsheviks, while correctly evaluating external factors that helped Poland's rebirth, failed to appreciate the domestic elements, viz., the age-long struggle of the Polish people for independence.[50] Cultivating "illusions about the automatic solution of the national problem through an international revolution," they battled against the prevailing current in the country.[51]

Nor were the Communists fortunate in their approach to the peasant question. Their demands for nationalization of land could appeal to some groups of landless peasantry, but not to the politically organized masses who wanted agrarian reforms accomplished by the sejm. All populist parties favored complete independence of Poland and thought in terms of a parliamentary democratic state. Although there was a wave of agrarian strikes, sporadic outbreaks of peasant *jacquerie* were uncoordinated and dispersed, and their aims were often unclear.[52]

The Polish Communists had no Lenin. Their leaders, active in Russia and Germany, did not rush back to Poland to head the revolutionary movement. Those in Russia believed in 1918 that there was no need to go to Poland; Poland would come to them as part of a Russian Soviet republic.[53] Thus ideology, tactics, and lack of first-rate leadership made it impossible for Polish Communists to attempt a revolution. They naturally blamed their failures on betrayal by the PPS and on the perfidy of the bourgeoisie; and, indeed, the workers' councils became an arena of struggle between the Socialists and the Communists. The Socialists viewed the councils as subordinate bodies that fitted into the structure of the republic and bolstered the Daszyński and Moraczewski governments. The Communists, following blindly the Russian example, saw the councils as the sole legitimate organs of state control whose task it was to discredit and overthrow the respective governments. While the extreme Left castigated the PPS for disrupting proletarian unity, it tried hard to eliminate Socialists from the councils in which they had a majority. The Communists also refused to recognize the right of the councils in Galicia, which were purely Socialist, to participate in a planned national conference.*

Communist moves offended and antagonized national public opinion. While Poland was barely reviving, the Warsaw workers' council adopted a Communist motion to send delegates to Russia, Germany and Austria in order to coordinate the struggle against capitalism.[54] Such an appeal to the three former oppressors of Poland—be it even their proletariat—was hardly calculated to convince Poles of the patriotism of their native Communists. Nor were the accusations launched against the Moraczewski government by the Communists, of planning war against German and Russian proletarian states, an example of clever tactics.

The angered leaders of the PPS responded by accusing Russia of "Socialist Imperialism" and by calling the Polish Communists "allies of the bourgeoisie."[55] What they meant was that in the context of existing conditions in Poland, Communist tactics played into the hands of all the reactionary groups. The Right had its National Guard units, which were disarmed in January

* See Henryk Malinowski, "Walki polskiej klasy robotniczej w latach 1918-1919," in Tadeusz Cieślak and Ludwik Grosfeld, eds., *Rewolucja październikowa a Polska* (Warsaw, 1967), p. 86.

1919. A special organ for the struggle against the Bolsheviks had been created by the National Democrats in August 1918. The antinational and provocative attitude of the Communists provided ammunition for rightist attacks on Socialists, democrats, and radicals. Bolshevik slogans could only harm the cause of democracy and encourage persecutions of the Left on the pretext of combating Communism.

The Communist party (KPRP) was not impressed with such arguments. Its decision to boycott elections to the sejm and to ignore the Polish state showed the persistence of a dogmatic spirit which Soviet and Polish Marxist historians have subsequently condemned.[56] The Communists called the sejm a collection of "national democratic hooligans, dumb peasants, and socialist traitors"; the government, "agents of the French stock exchange," and "imperialist bandits"; the army "mercenaries"; the Polish state, an "incarnation of counterrevolution."[57]

These tactics made sense only if the Communists sought to create a revolutionary ferment which would excuse intervention by the Red Army. Without such assistance their chances were practically nil. The Polish general staff considered such a contingency. An anonymous officer carefully analyzed the problem of Communism in Poland, rejecting simple notions that Communism was merely a "Jewish plot" or a movement of brigands. Stressing that a Russian revolution was unthinkable in isolation, he wrote that the Bolshevik westward expansion was understandable because Poland could become an important element in Allied plans for counterrevolution. Under these circumstances Polish Communists had the choice either of starting a revolution in the country or of provoking an armed invasion. He called them "a fairly strong group inimical on principle to Polish statehood" and admitted that there was a serious danger for the country. He refused, however, to see a future struggle in ideological terms. "Poland," the officer wrote, "wants to escape revolution not because it wants to be a pillar of reaction or keep the prewar composition of social forces untouched, which is impossible," but because it wants to safeguard "its existence as a state."[58] This opinion, corresponding to Piłsudski's views, was not appreciated by the Communists, who could only think in terms of revolution and reaction. Did they plan a take-over of the country with assistance of the Red Army? This is an important question which will be attempted in the next chapter, in conjunction with Soviet-Polish relations in late January and early February 1919.

While the young Polish state struggled amid great domestic difficulties, its external situation was far from secure. From November 1918 to February 1919 the country existed within indeterminate frontiers, and it was hard to say what constituted state territory. Poles controlled the parts of the kingdom cleared of German troops, parts of Poznania, and western Galicia. The fate of other lands in the west and southwest depended on the decision of the Paris Peace Conference. In Eastern Galicia, Poles and Ukrainians were locked in struggle for mastery of the province. The whole area east of the former kingdom was in flux. The Lublin government had called for fraternal cooperation with Lithuanians, Belorussians, and Ukrainians on the basis of self-determination, voicing hopes for future association of all these nations in a free federation. Easier said than done. Poles who lived in the borderlands appealed to Warsaw, and it was felt that the government had an obligation to defend them.[59] The manifesto of the Moraczewski government—in which Piłsudski, Moraczewski, and Wasilewski constituted the inner working body—spoke vaguely about future cooperation with the borderlands.

With domestic and international conditions so unsettled, Warsaw found it hard to devise any clear-cut policy toward the eastern problems. The council of ministers agreed that the sejm ought to comprise ex-deputies of the Russian Duma to represent Lithuania and Belorussia, but the election decree of November 28, 1918 was a little less specific.[60] Piłsudski could give instructions only of a military nature to the commander of Polish forces in the southeastern area, because nobody as yet could determine the future borders between Poland and the Ukraine.[61] All the government could do was to explore the possibility of cooperation with Kiev, i.e., the Ukrainian Peoples' Republic, to solve the burning question of Eastern Galicia.[62]

The question of Polish borders in the east was connected with the advance of the Red Army, and even if many Poles were skeptical about the power of the Bolsheviks, it was the *fait accompli* which decided the issues.[63] Hence it seemed imperative to stop the Bolshevik offensive. Two obstacles had to be overcome: the military weakness of the Polish state, and presence of German troops who held a line in the east. The Polish army consisted of batallions, squadrons, and batteries—there were no larger units. While the occupying powers had left arms and munitions sufficient for some eighty thousand men, other supplies were badly lacking. The government decided to create an army based on volunteers, a decision variously interpreted by its political opponents.* The army could not move eastward and replace Ger-

---

* The National Democrat, Stanisław Głąbiński, viewed the volunteer army as Socialist-inspired. See *Wspomnienia polityczne* (Pelplin, 1939), p. 385. The Soviet historian Misko deemed it reactionary. In reality two factors explained the govern-

man troops until an agreement with Berlin. Negotiations proved difficult, and the Germans wanted Polish territorial concessions at the Paris Peace Conference in exchange for withdrawal of their troops. The local German command pursued its own objectives; Polish-German fighting in Poznania complicated the issue.[64] Only Allied pressure on the Germans was likely to prove effective, but until the formation of the Paderewski ministry it was unobtainable. The Polish chief of staff complained to Piłsudski that the Allies refused to help and treated the government in Warsaw as if it were a "Bolshevik representation."[65]

Warsaw could do little to prevent Bolshevik capture of Wilno. Local detachments called "self-defense" sprang into being, and Piłsudski sent an officer to take charge. The latter made the local commander, General Władysław Wejtko, discard the name "self-defense" and assume the title of chief of the Lithuanian and Belorussian military districts, so as to give impression that Warsaw was assuming defense of these border provinces. This did not prevent the fall of the city after a brief resistance by the Polish units.[66]

A Polish-German agreement was reached in early February 1919, and Polish troops passed through German lines. An eastern front came into being, and in mid-February Polish military units came into first contact with advancing detachments of the Red Army. Even at this stage Warsaw ordered no large-scale engagements but merely harassed the enemy to prevent an attack *en force*.

Soviet westward expansion into the borderlands, and the reemergence and consolidation of the Polish state form two aspects of the complex story in which both countries came to face each other. The third and principal aspect of events at this time concerns direct relations between Moscow and Warsaw.

It was paradoxical, though not from the Bolshevik point of view, that Soviet Russia spoke constantly of peaceful relations with the very states it aimed to overthrow by a Communist revolution.[67] Lenin subscribed fully to the old dictum that diplomacy was war by other means, and that one "should never be tied in war by formal considerations." Only those persons ignorant of military

---

ment decision: lack of administrative cadres for a large army based on conscription, and unwillingness to mobilize people worn-out by four years of war and military service. See Adam Przybylski, *Wojna polska 1918-1921* (Warsaw, 1930), p. 42, and Piłsudski's statement at the sejm's Committee on Military Affairs, February 26, 1919, Akta Adiutantury Generalnej Naczelnego Dowództwa/102, "Rokowania polsko-bolszewickie, materiały sejmowe i inne." Hereafter cited as AGND.

history, the Bolshevik leader asserted, did not know that a treaty was a "means of gathering strength," and he illustrated his point by references to Russian history.[68] It is curious indeed how often Lenin and especially his foreign commissar, Chicherin, thought in unmistakable Russian terms about matters of foreign policy. The heritage of the past was hard to forget.

The question of Soviet-Polish diplomatic relations came up after the treaty of Brest-Litovsk. Chicherin had agreed to deal with Lednicki as the representative of the Regency Council, but he made clear that this in no way implied recognition of the regime in Poland. Nevertheless in August 1918 the Narkomindel began to address official letters to the Polish representation and granted it the right to use its own couriers.[69] Finally on October 28 the foreign commissar informed the delegate of the Regency Council that Soviet Russia had named Julian Marchlewski as the diplomatic representative in Poland. In a peremptory note which appeared next day in *Pravda* and *Izvestia,* Chicherin told the Poles he would let them know when Marchlewski would leave for Poland. The note stressed that nomination of "one of the most outstanding and oldest leaders of the Polish workers' movement" ought to be understood by the working masses of Poland as proof "of absence of any inimical designs on the part of Soviet Russia with regard to Poland's national freedom," and of "full solidarity of the Soviet Government with the strivings of Polish popular masses toward social liberation."[70]

The reasons which prompted Moscow to appoint a representative to Warsaw—a seeming departure from the policy of non-recognition—were clear. The object, as explained at a SDKPiL conference, was to create in Poland a center "which could exist quite legally while conducting at the same time illegal activity." The Polish Commissariat, which originated the idea, had been pressing for such a move for months. SDKPiL dismissed the argument that establishing diplomatic relations would assist the Regency Council, "a cadaver which nothing will save anymore." As for any bad impression in Poland, even "the dumbest proletarian will have no illusions about the real meaning of the nomination" of Marchlewski. Representation in Warsaw would be another 'burning house' as "Comrade Lenin had called the mission of the [Soviet] Republic in Berlin."[71]

The Polish cabinet received Chicherin's note on November 4, and replied three days later that a decision on the Soviet proposal —though it was hardly a proposal—would be taken after the formation of a new ministry. Lednicki then would communicate it to Moscow.[72] There is no indication whether Warsaw saw through the Soviet game, although at least one political organization warned the government against Marchlewski's arrival.* Chicherin's note appeared in a Polish official journal and in some newspapers. No attempt was made to hide the Soviet overture.

Meanwhile, internal developments in Poland moved with rapidity. The Regency Council and the Lublin government disappeared from the scene, and Piłsudski on November 16 notified by radio the Allied governments, Germany, and all belligerent and neutral states of the establishment of the Polish Republic. Soviet Russia was not explicitly named in the radio message. Under the existing conditions this was quite natural; the Entente was suspicious of Piłsudski and his government. Ten days later the foreign minister, Leon Wasilewski, addressed a sharp note to Chicherin complaining about the treatment of representatives of the Regency Council in Russia. The mission's building, Wasilewski wrote, had been taken over by the Narkomindel and its members arrested. The minister threatened reprisals against "Russian citizens" in Poland—a naive threat. Wasilewski's radiogram of November 26 was repeated in a note sent by a special courier.[73]

Chicherin replied on November 28 describing the incident as caused by a Polish refugee committee in Russia which acted in belief that a Socialist revolution had occured in Poland and swept away the Regency Council. This seemed a clear allusion to the Lublin Manifesto. Neither the Soviet government, which always had looked on the Regency Council as an organ of German occupation, nor the Polish Commissariat felt obliged to intervene. Chicherin assured Wasilewski that the building was locked and protected, and that members of the delegation were free to leave provided the Germans would let them through. The commissar reminded Warsaw that he had not yet received an answer regarding Marchlewski—forgetting to mention that the note in question had been addressed to the unrecognized Regency Council —and expressed willingness to receive a Polish envoy in Russia. Diplomatic relations, the commissar wrote, were necessary to solve all conflicts which might arise between the two countries.[74]

Chicherin's message gave an impression of reasonableness which does not stand closer scrutiny. He cleverly contrasted the Regency Council with a popular government, trying to appeal to the Socialists. While the incident in Moscow may have been partly

* This was Związek Budowy Państwa Polskiego. See Materiały archiwalne, I, 397-398. The Socialist Bronisław Siwik wrote a little later in Robotnik about the desirability of having diplomatic relations with Russia, but he too had misgivings about Marchlewski. See Artur Leinwand, Polska Partia Socjalistyczna wobec wojny polsko-radzieckiej; 1919-1920 (Warsaw, 1964), p. 24n.

spontaneous, it is hard to believe that the Polish Commissariat had nothing to do with it. Indeed, Chicherin would speak later, enigmatically, about "a chosen Polish representation" which had replaced that of the Regency Council in Moscow.[75] Nor did he mention the archives, seized and not returned for nearly a month. The commissar may have underestimated the reaction which news about events in Moscow created in Poland. Newspapers wrote about "violation of the Polish legation [sic]" and expressed indignation about Soviet methods.[76] Chicherin's final point indicated that Russia was as intent as ever on establishing diplomatic relations with Warsaw. No wonder, since it meant having a "legal center" for "illegal activity" in the Polish capital.

It is obvious that Poland, still unrecognized and suspected by the Entente of radical leanings would have committed political suicide by responding to Soviet overtures. The ministry of foreign affairs instructed a representative going to Paris to tell the Entente that the country had no diplomatic relations with Russia nor was it planning them. Poland "will not recognize any Bolshevik representatives or allow them to enter the capital."[77] Wasilewski stated publicly that his attitude toward Soviet Russia was that of the PPS, which considered that not a minority dictatorship in Russia but a constituent assembly and a representative government were qualified to resolve fundamental political questions.[78]

Meanwhile, exchanges continued between Warsaw and Moscow. Wasilewski addressed a harsh note to Chicherin demanding the removal of seals on the doors of mission building and the return of Polish archives. The minister stressed that unless all Polish demands were satisfied it was pointless to talk about establishing diplomatic relations.[79] Wasilewski then asked the Danish minister in Moscow to represent Polish interests in the Soviet capital, to which the latter agreed.[80]

It is likely that Wasilewski's message had not yet been received when Chicherin addressed a brief radio message to Warsaw on December 2, written as if the whole incident were closed. The commissar asked the Poles when the mission was planning to return to Poland, and asked permission for Khristian Rakovskii—going to Vienna—to cross Polish territory.[81] Warsaw, seemingly ignoring the message, repeated once again on December 9 that unless Polish demands were satisfied there was no sense to talk about diplomatic relations. Wasilewski added that until his government would take new decisions the personnel of the mission of the Regency Council ought to be treated as members of Poland's legation.[82]

It would be interesting to speculate why Chicherin, obviously eager to close the incident, did not succeed in handing over at once the confiscated archives and funds. His original statement that nothing had been touched was obviously untrue. Were other Soviet agencies, possibly the Polish Commissariat, interested in exploring the archives, even at risk of letting the whole matter drag? The question cannot be answered, given the absence of sources.

The Chicherin-Wasilewski correspondence by radio continued. The commissar sent a long message on December 12, in which he repeated his points about the Regency Council. He disputed Wasilewski's accusation that the Bolsheviks had executed Polish citizens. As for the status of the mission in Russia, if the government in Warsaw were willing to consider it as Poland's legation, then Russia would return the archives and funds to the chargé d'affaires—Lednicki being in Warsaw throughout all this crisis. Other unspecified belongings would be handed back after the establishment of normal diplomatic relations. Thus Chicherin tried to use the incident to force Warsaw into relations with Moscow, and ended his note by asking whether and when such relations would be established.[83]

The commissar followed with another message three days later, submitting Warsaw to a veritable barrage of diplomatic missiles. He assured that the transfer of archives would soon finish, and since this would satisfy Polish demands, he inquired when Soviet representative might come to Poland. Chicherin cleverly used a new argument in favor of diplomatic relations. He pointed out that since the Soviet government had recognized a chargé d'affaires in Moscow, this surely required reciprocity on Poland's part.[84]

Wasilewski's new note to Moscow ignored Chicherin's message, and it is hard to tell whether he had not yet received it or preferred not to discuss the commissar's latest points. The new note was harsh—Chicherin had already objected to the phrasing of previous communications—and Wasilewski demanded the restitution of all goods of the mission, blaming the Soviets for the whole incident. He objected to what he termed Soviet attempts to meddle in internal Polish problems, and struck a new chord by strongly protesting the advance of Red Army toward the eastern frontiers of Poland.[85]

Was Wasilewski's protest against the Soviet offensive a tactical move designed to delay the embarrassing matter of opening diplomatic relations? The incident of the mission in Moscow was nearing its end, and Poland had no intent of receiving a Soviet envoy in Warsaw. While this may have been a reason for Wasilewski's stand, the penetration of Red Army into Lithuania and Belorussia presented a much bigger problem for Poland. It was at this time that a Soviet Lithuanian government was preparing to enter Wilno, and the Poles feverishly organized the defense of the city. Hence Wasilewski's statement that the Soviet offensive "forced" the Polish government to view this action as "an openly hostile act against our fatherland" was to strengthen weak military resistance by diplomatic pressure. Warsaw was warning Moscow to stop its offensive. This demarche, of course, produced no result.

Contemporary comments of the Soviet press emphasized the importance of Wilno for Russian-Polish relations. An article in *Izvestia* on December 25, significantly entitled "The Enemy," spoke about the counterrevolutionary center in Wilno. "The victorious march of Soviet armies assisted by the Germans, and the creation of the Soviet Lithuanian government put an end to the Lithuanian counterrevolution," Iurii Steklov wrote. "Now the Poles step forth to oppose us." *Pravda* commented on December 28 that the "Warsaw robbers seek a quarrel with Soviet Russia." Wasilewski's protest was seen as something more than a tactical maneuver to gain time.

While the affair of the mission in Russia was slowly liquidated, and chargé d'affaires Jan Żarnowski informed Warsaw that their headquarters were reopened and the personnel getting ready to leave, Chicherin replied at length to the last message of Wasilewski.[86] His radiogram of December 23 protested the sharp tone of the Polish communication. The commissar expressed amazement over constant repetition of demands concerning the mission, since the whole matter was in the process of liquidation. Chicherin countered Wasilewski's remark about the sinister reputation of the Red Army by accusing Polish troops of pogroms. Russia in no way endangered Poland since the two countries had no common border, being separated by Lithuania and Belorussia. Red troops were far "from the Polish borders." Finally, the commissar used a novel argument in favor of diplomatic relations. There were numerous Polish refugees in Russia, he said, who wanted to return home. Warsaw was complicating the solution of this task.

The Soviet note was revealing. It used the fiction of border republics as buffer states—Bolshevik reasoning was mentioned earlier in this chapter—to avoid direct conflict with Poland. By bringing in the question of refugees Chicherin was trying to open a new channel of communications with Warsaw, not necessarily on the official level. Not that he gave up the idea of sending a Soviet envoy to Warsaw—he demanded Polish agreement again on December 24—but he prepared the scene for informal talks about refugees.[87] The importance of this point was clear because on December 20, 1918 a mission calling itself a representation of the Soviet Russian Red Cross suddenly had descended on Warsaw.*

The status of the Soviet Red Cross was at this time tenuous and there is evidence that the organization was used for political purposes.[88] The representatives who arrived in Poland came apparently in three groups, although accounts are confused. Apart from the first group there was a second delegation headed by Pavel A. Hesse which encountered no difficulties, and a third led by a General Gubashev [?].[89] Their mutual relations are hard to determine and only the first group created an important crisis in Soviet-Polish relations.

The first group comprised five people, three of whom were prominent members of SDKPiL. Its leader was Bronisław Wesołowski, member of the Central Committee of SDKPiL in Petrograd, secretary of VTsIK, and chairman of the Highest Revolutionary Tribunal—a high dignitary indeed to preside over a Red Cross mission ostensibly concerned with Russian displaced persons in Poland. According to the later testimony of the one surviving member, Polish authorities had agreed to the coming of a mission in November, but no documentary evidence had ever appeared.[90] There is no indication that Moscow ever notified the Poles of the arrival of the delegation, and the above-mentioned delegate stated that "no one awaited us in Warsaw."[91]

The mission opened talks with Polish officials the day after its arrival, and toward the evening found itself interned in its quarters in the Brühl hotel. The Polish explanation was that the mission had no permission to enter the country, but it seems that there was more to it. There is strong probability that the mission had received credentials not from the Red Cross but from the Central College for Affairs of Prisoners and Refugees (Tsentroplenbezh) originally presided over by another leading SDKPiL man, Józef Unszlicht. This was a strictly Russian governmental institution.† It may well be that this fact, together with the unannounced arrival of the delegation made premier Moraczewski write retrospectively that Russia had "treated Poland as her own province."[92]

The Polish ministry of the interior explained later that it had grounds to believe that the objective of the mission was "agitation

---

* The date given by *Historia Polski* (Warsaw, 1966—). IV, part 2 (*makieta*), p. 142, is December 18.

† One of the documents refers to Wesołowski mission as being sent by the Tsentroplenbezh, while the Hesse group was constantly called a Red Cross mission. On the foundation of the former see *DVP SSSR*, I, 334.

in favor of the Soviet Republic," and if one bears in mind the composition of the delegation and Chicherin's constant attempts to have representation in Warsaw, this seems likely.[93] It is characteristic that when Leon Alter—one of the members of the mission—reached Russia, he presented his first report to the Central Committee of the Polish Communist party and not to any Red Cross authority.[94] Finally, the internment of the so-called Red Cross mission in Warsaw led to a huge Communist-led demonstration on December 29. In organizing the demonstration in front of the hotel in which the mission was interned, the party stressed that Wesołowski was a Communist.[95] Demonstrators clashed with military police. Six people were killed, including one policeman, and several were wounded.

The incident was highly embarrassing for the Socialist-led Moraczewski government, and the presence of the mission had already harmed it politically.[96] Consequently the Soviet delegates were transferred to the Warsaw citadel, and informed by the intermediary of Hesse that Poland did not want to have them on her territory. Wesołowski demanded that they be allowed to return to Russia. Wasilewski agreed. The group traveled under an escort of Polish gendarmes to Łapy, on the border, and were there assassinated under circumstances never fully elucidated. One of the members of the mission, Alter, was wounded and left for dead, and succeeded in crossing the border to Russia.*

The epilogue of the Wesołowski mission, which shocked responsible people in Poland and Russia, obscured its original character and purpose. Few Poles were aware of Hesse and his group, to which Wesołowski had been able to hand over the million rubles he had with him. Nor was Hesse over molested. The Communists received new ammunition for their anti-Polish campaign: the government in Warsaw would henceforth be accused not only of refusing peaceful relations with Russia but of harboring the assassins of innocent Red Cross representatives.

The tragedy had not yet occurred when Wasilewski answered Chicherin's note by a message of December 30. It is likely that the appearance of the mission in Warsaw and the bloody demonstration of the previous day made Wasilewski more suspicious than ever of Soviet motives. His radio message was not adroit. The Pole accused Moscow of bad faith and inconsistency. The Russians first created the incident of the Polish mission and backed down

---

* Alter's testimony indicated that the escort was changed near the border and that gendarmes of the second escort perpetrated the crime. Arrest and trial in Poland of people implicated in the Łapy murder did not convince anyone that justice was done. No capital sentences were passed.

under pressure. They spoke of good relations but simultaneously invaded Lithuania and Belorussia. Wasilewski emphasized that Poland had ethnic rights to some of the territories occupied by the Red Army, and therefore was directly concerned. The minister objected to the existence of Polish detachments within the Red Army bearing names of Polish towns. He saw them as troops prepared for invasion of Poland. He demanded the punishment of those guilty of the seizure of the mission, an investigation of executions of Poles in Russia, and payment of pensions to their families. Wasilewski concluded that in view of the hostile intentions of Moscow, Poland could not establish diplomatic relations with Soviet Russia. She might even have to oppose Russian westward expansion militarily.[97]

A day later came a telegram from Chicherin—not a reply to the above message—protesting the arrest of the Red Cross delegation and confiscation of their funds. The commissar declared that the Polish mission would be held in Russia until Soviet delegates would be released and money returned. A copy of the message was addressed to Hesse, called the president of the committee of the Red Cross.[98] Wasilewski replied four days later, explaining that the mission only had been interned and spent just one night in the citadel. He blamed the Soviet government for the whole incident, since the mission had not been authorized to enter Poland. As for funds, they had been returned to Hesse.[99]

Not yet aware of the tragic finale of the Wesołowski mission, Chicherin sent a long note on January 7, which constituted a reply to Wasilewski's note of December 30. It was a powerful blast with propagandistic overtones meant to embarrass the Polish government. Chicherin voiced indignation over the secrecy with which Warsaw surrounded his messages. He threatened that the day would come when revolutionary workers and peasants in Poland, kept in the dark and misled by their government, would learn the truth. There was no reason to punish Polish workers in Russia for having acted against the mission of the Regency Council, a German agency, which the Moraczewski cabinet, calling itself a peoples' government, saw fit to support. This mission, Chicherin asserted, had protected counterrevolutionaries whom Soviet Russia punished in accord with her laws. He challenged Wasilewski to produce a list of people who had been unjustly condemned. The commissar declared that there were numerous Poles fighting in the ranks of the Red Army, adding maliciously that some of them were members of the same party (PPS) as Poland's leading ministers. Polish military units did bear the names of Polish towns, to the satisfaction of the Polish proletariat. Chicherin denied that the Red Army anywhere had encroached on territories that could be considered part of Poland. Lithuania and Belorussia were independent states, and the Soviet government was not aware that their peasants and workers ever had expressed a wish to unite with Poland. The local Polish landowners who desired it constituted a tiny minority. The commissar warned that if Warsaw tried to impose its rule over Lithuania, Latvia, and Belorussia by force, she would find Polish revolutionary troops opposing her and fighting alongside the revolutionary units of these countries. The message concluded that there were numerous problems to be settled by direct Soviet-Polish negotiation, but Warsaw was constantly putting forward new reasons to delay talks and avoid opening relations with Soviet Russia. She thus victimized the Polish refugee masses in Russia. Chicherin remarked that he did not consider the matter of the Red Cross mission closed; he reserved judgment until detailed information would be forthcoming.[100]

The next day, on January 8, Warsaw received a strongly worded protest against the murder of the Red Cross delegates by "your agents." Chicherin asserted that it was the threat of "a revolutionary movement of Polish popular masses" which made the government imprison the delegates in the citadel. He called Moraczewski's cabinet "counterrevolutionary" and demanded investigation and punishment of those guilty of the assassination. The commissar announced that members of the Polish mission in Russia were arrested and held as hostages to guarantee proper treatment of Soviet citizens by the Poles.[101]

Moscow followed this protest by other messages addressed to Warsaw and to the International Red Cross. The Communist Party in Poland also made political capital out of the murders, presenting them as one of many outrages through which reactionary circles tried to make Poland "a fortress of counterrevolution" and prevent unification of Russian, German, and Polish revolutions.[102] Publicity given to the murder at Łapy was obscuring all other issues.

Moraczewski's government, harassed by the Right and Left, resigned about a week after Chicherin's last note. Paderewski became premier and minister of foreign affairs, and on January 29 he wired Chicherin, though the latter apparently never received the radiogram. Paderewski sent another message on February 7, 1919, in which he informed the Narkomindel that an energetic investigation was underway. He reproached Chicherin for his hasty and unfounded accusation of the Polish authorities, who were in no way responsible. The premier declared that to clarify the situation the government proposed to send Aleksander Więckowski as special envoy to Russia. He would be empowered to discuss with the Soviet government various questions—brought up by Russia—requiring solution in the interests of both countries.[103] The tone of Paderewski's note was firm but conciliatory. He followed it by another communication two days later which protested the continued imprisonment of the Polish mission in Russia. Paderewski called it "incomprehensible" in view of his government's prompt inquest into the Red Cross affair. The premier asked that members of the mission be freed and allowed to return to Poland.[104]

Chicherin's lengthy reply to Paderewski on February 10, which reviewed all fundamental questions between Soviet Russia and Poland—followed six days later by a message from the newly formed Soviet Lithuanian-Belorussian Republic—marked the opening of a new phase in Russo-Polish relations. Indeed, the end of January and beginning of February 1919 constitute a transition between the first turbulent months following the end of the World War and a somewhat more stable period in Poland. During the early period many things happened. Soviet westward expansion reached its maximum limits, to be exceeded only in the summer of 1920. The borderlands fell under Moscow's sway, cleverly camouflaged by slogans of national self-determination, and Red armies came suspiciously close to ethnic Poland. The Polish state which emerged, torn by rival political trends and unrecognized by the Allies, escaped the fate of Lithuania or the Ukraine. Native Communists showed activity but proved too weak to prevent a crystallization of the republic along national and parliamentary lines. Nation triumphed over class; a Communist revolution unsupported by the bayonets of the Red Army proved impossible.

The Russians, eager to neutralize Poland as a potential element of the "partition wall" between Communism and the West, tried to isolate the country from the Entente and entangle it in a net of diplomatic overtures. The Poles perceived the danger. Awareness of Soviet revolutionary designs mingled with apprehension of what seemed a new edition of Russian imperialism. Unable as yet to formulate a clear and consistent foreign policy, Warsaw pursued delaying tactics. This naturally made it vulnerable to accusations of an anti-Soviet stand. Two crises, centering around the Communist coup against the Polish mission in Russia, and the bloody affair of the "Red Cross" representation, added acrimony. These were merely symptoms of graver and deeper issues which set Soviet Russia and Poland in opposition.

The
Borderlands

In early February 1919 Polish troops moved eastward and clashed with units of the Red Army. A front opened and Belorussia and Lithuania slowly became a theater of operations. The question of the borderlands assumed a prominent place in Soviet-Polish relations; they received new emphasis in the continuing correspondence between Chicherin and Warsaw, and affected the plans of Polish Communists, whose activities in the area appeared as a preparation for a coup in Poland itself. The problem of the borderlands became a focal point in the formulation of Polish eastern policy, and caused heated discussion. It came up at the Paris Peace Conference in the context of Allied policy toward Russia. Finally, it influenced the Soviet interpretation of the principle of national self-determination at the Eighth Party Congress.

On February 10, 1919 Chicherin addressed a long telegram to Warsaw in reply to Paderewski's note, reviewing general political problems which Poland's premier barely had touched upon.[1] Soviet Russia, he said, wanted friendly relations with all countries including Poland. Chicherin recalled all the Soviet decrees to safeguard Polish art treasures in Russia which would eventually be returned to Poland's "brotherly popular masses," and he emphasized his desire to "liquidate the source of conflicts with the Polish government and establish normal relations with it." Guided by these feelings the commissar would receive Polish special emissary, Więckowski, and ask Lithuania and Belorussia to facilitate his journey through their territory. Moscow agreed with Warsaw on "the importance of questions to be discussed between the two Governments." Territorial issues concerned Lithuania and Belorussia, and Chicherin extended "good offices." Other issues related to Polish troops in Murmansk and Siberia and to Polish refugees in Russia. Moscow would raise all of them "in a completely peaceful spirit, filled with a desire to eliminate all cause of conflict."

Chicherin's note, as always, was adroit. He returned to his theme of formal relations with Poland, and implied that talks with Więckowski would range over general matters of foreign policy, not merely business on hand. He emphasized the independent status of Soviet Lithuania and Belorussia, and prepared the way for a communication from Minsk which reached Warsaw six days later. This last note signed by Miasnikov and Mickiewicz-Kapsukas on behalf of the Provisional Revolutionary Government of the Socialist Republic of Soviet Lithuania, and the Central Executive Committee of the Soviets of Deputies of the Socialist Republic of Soviet Belorussia, announced the creation of a joint Lithuanian-Belorussian republic. This new state, the radio message declared, strove after federation with Russia, the Ukraine, and Estonia—all in one Soviet republic. It believed in the proletarian solidarity of all countries and opposed solutions by force. Miasnikov and Mickiewicz-Kapsukas asserted that they could not believe that a neighborly state, even though not ruled by workers and peasants, would resort to violence to harm their republic, and they protested the Polish invasion of the Grodno-Białystok region. The working masses of Białystok "feel that their tie with Soviet Lithuanian and Belorussian republics is unbreakable." Besides, in this area the "Polish element constitutes a minority." The message concluded with the proposal of a mixed commission to settle the border controversies."[2]

The Lithuanian-Belorussian note was a clumsy maneuver. The attempt to gain recognition and prevent a Polish advance by means of a mixed commission was all too obvious. Assertion of the non-Polish character of Białystok was so palpably false that it could only act as an irritant.[3] The note could hardly diminish the Polish desire to eliminate Soviet rule from Lithuania and Belorussia, an occupation regime of areas in which Warsaw was interested, and an advance guard of Polish Communism menacing Poland. Wasilewski already had drawn Soviet attention to the first aspect of the question; Więckowski would raise the second after arrival in Moscow.

There is no doubt that Polish Communist leaders, to mention only Stanisław Berson, Unszlicht, Józef Kozłowski, Pestkowski, Kazimierz Cichowski, Bobiński and Jakub Zbiniewicz, who occupied crucial positions in the government of the Lithuanian-Belorussian republic, "treated their stay in Wilno as a revolutionary activity in the border region."[4] The SDKPiL party organ Młot announced as early as December 18, 1918: "We forge here [in Lithuania] a force which in the right moment will bring to it [Polish proletariat] the necessary aid."[5] The reference was to the Western Division which, as one of its declarations asserted, had been "created for the liberation of the proletariat of Poland from the bourgeois-capitalist yoke."[6] The Western Division had received the special attention of the Soviet government from

November 1918 onward.[7] On December 1, SDKPiL issued a special appeal to all Poles in Russia to join it. Addressing Polish railwaymen, the appeal promised that "an order will be issued shortly which will free you [and put you] at our disposal." The document went on to say that "we must be ready for any call of our brothers in Poland" and to "fight for the dictatorship of the proletariat" there.[8] While the division was supposedly composed of volunteers, Polish reports indicated that people were drafted in the Red Army "not excluding citizens of the former Kingdom of Poland."[9] Intense agitation among Poles to transfer from other Red Army units to the division went on through January 1919.[10] Efforts were made to polonize and expand this international formation,[11] which was concentrated on the western front.

In this connection the Central Committee of the Polish Communist Party in Russia submitted in January 1919 a plan to the Revolutionary War Council (revveoensovet) of the Soviet Republic which revealed the far-reaching ambitions of the Polish Communists. The Central Committee's memorandum proposed a transformation of the Western Division into a Polish Army group based in Lithuania and Belorussia.[12] The revolutionary council of the Western Division composed of such leading figures as Unszlicht and Bobiński would become a Polish revolutionary council (Polrevsovet) and assume exclusive control over the army. This proposal sounded much like a suggestion to create a nucleus of a Polish Soviet government with forces at its disposal. Sverdlov wrote Trotsky on January 22, 1919 about it and asked for an opinion about the possibility of a Red Polish army group crossing the borders of Poland. He felt this would greatly complicate "internal work," but whether he meant Communist work in Poland or work in Russia is not clear. Nor do we know whether the Soviet government, after formally approving the composition of the council of the Western Division, took any decision affecting the larger issue.[13] The whole thing is wrapped in mystery, and one can catch only glimpses of what was happening.

We know that Chicherin wrote early in February to his representative in Minsk to enjoin "the necessity of taking all measures to prevent Polish volunteers serving in the Red Army from crossing into the Polish provinces (gubernia of the former Kingdom of Poland)."[14] This might indicate that the Narkomindel knew of such preparations and had determined to stop them. At roughly the same time there appeared a curious notice in *Izvestia* concerning the Central College for Affairs of Prisoners and Refugees (Tsentroplenbezh). It stated that the Central College "decided in cooperation with the governments of *Poland,* Lithuania, and Belo-russia to assume the task of looking after prisoners and refugees on the territories of these republics."[15] What Polish government was meant here; surely not the one in Warsaw? Did a Soviet Polish government exist in Russia in February 1919? One looks in vain for other references.[16]

The revolutionary council of the Western Division un-doubtedly aimed at contact with the Communist movement in Poland. It launched an appeal which, after asserting that "We will not give Lithuanian-Belorussian lands to Polish imperialism," sounded the call: "Forward Red Polish soldiers under the flying banner of revolution toward the encounter of the native foe."[17] Did the Communist Party in Poland await and prepare a "libera-tion" by the Red Army? According to Communist historians, the Central Committee considered entry of Soviet troops into Poland, and worried lest it produce accusations of Soviet imperialism. The committee adopted a resolution that should military and political interests of Soviet Russia require such action, possibly in the Lublin region, Moscow ought to declare the absence of any designs on Poland's integrity. Polish Communists ought to be forewarned to create at once a "Lublin Commissariat of the Polish Soviet Republic."[18]

In mid-February 1919 the Party Council adopted a resolution which expressed things in a somewhat different way, namely that "armed assistance of the Russian proletariat, if needed by the ripening Polish revolution, would be neither an invasion nor an expression of imperialist tendencies," but the "realization of the watchword of international solidarity of the revolutionary pro-letariat."[19] Thus the possibility of Soviet intervention in Poland was calmly envisaged by local Communists. The resolution added that the party had to make some headway so that Bolsheviks would "be welcomed not only by the Communists, but by broad masses . . . as allies coming to help the Polish revolution."[20] This may have been no more than a pious wish, and a Bundist who stood close to the Polish Communists interpreted the resolution as an admission of weakness and of their hope for the help of the Red Army in seizing power.[21]

No wonder that in February 1919 the PPS deputies to the sejm issued a manifesto declaring that Poland stood in danger of inva-sion by Bolshevik troops. Poles realized that a successful advance into Lithuanian-Belorussian areas would eliminate an important outpost of militant Communism, and they were well informed about the Western Division and its activities.[22] The Polish High

Command ordered troops to move and in February the Poles took
Brześć, Wołkowysk, Białystok, and approached Grodno—the first
clash occurring on February 17, 1919. The aim of this advance
was, as Piłsudski put it, "to push back as far away as possible from
places where new life was being born, all attempts and aspirations
to impose on us, once again, a foreign way of life."[23] But there was
more to it. The Polish advance was not purely defensive. It connected with the broad question of a territorial settlement in the
east, and formed part of Poland's strategy and diplomacy. Hence
one must place it in the context of Polish foreign policy and relate
it to the Allied approach to Bolshevism and Russia at the Paris
Peace Conference.

The fundamental assumption of Poland's foreign policy in 1919
was that between Germany and Russia there was no place for a
small and weak state. Both Piłsudski and Dmowski expressed this
idea on several occasions. The simultaneous collapse of the
German, Austrian, and Russian empires created a unique chance
for Poland to regain the position it had occupied in East Central
Europe before the partitions. But if there were agreement on
this final objective, there was bitter controversy on how to achieve
it. Two main trends existed, corresponding roughly to the division between Left and Right, but with Polish Communists occupying a position apart.

The first orientation, called at various times nationalist, incorporationist, annexationist, or even imperialist, was best represented by the National Democrats. Dmowski, the greatest spokesman of modern Polish nationalism, stood for the creation of a
large and centralized state which would embrace all those eastern
areas where substantial Polish population, economic interests, and
historical traditions had left an imprint of "Polishness." Viewing
Belorussia and the Ukraine as largely artificial creations that could
maintain their existence only by relying on Germany, Dmowski
postulated disinterest in their national aspirations. Poland's
eastern borders ought to comprise the western parts of the borderlands, which would be assimilable, and leave the rest to Russia.
The National Democrats wanted to avoid permanently antagonizing the Russians, and Dmowski felt that his territorial program "did not harm the genuine interests of Russia."[24] The
Polish state as seen by Dmowski was to be a national state and
the percentage of native Poles must not fall below some sixty
percent of the total population.[25] Given the low national and
political level of the Belorussians, National Democrats believed
that polonization within twenty years would bring the Poles to

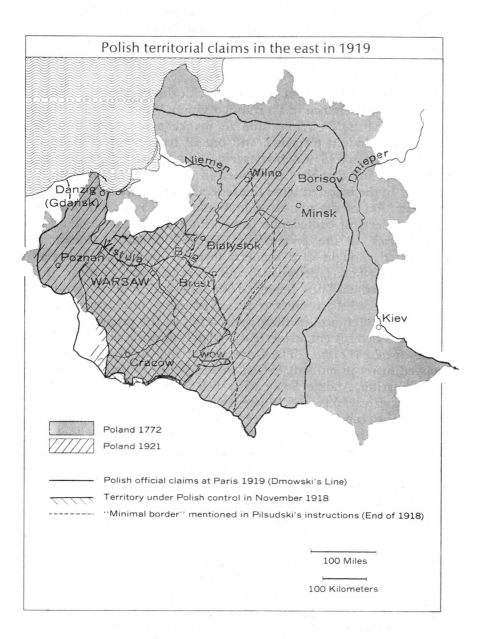

Polish territorial claims in the east in 1919

Danzig (Gdańsk)
Niemen
Wilno
Borisov
Dnieper
Minsk
Poznań
Vistula
Bug
Białystok
WARSAW
Brest
Kiev
Cracow
Lwow

Poland 1772
Poland 1921

———— Polish official claims at Paris 1919 (Dmowski's Line)
〰〰〰 Territory under Polish control in November 1918
- - - - - - - "Minimal border" mentioned in Pilsudski's instructions (End of 1918)

100 Miles
100 Kilometers

seventy-five or even eighty percent.* While Dmowski's program assumed that the prepartitions borders were the logical start of any territorial settlement, it did not claim the 1772 frontiers. The so-called Dmowski Line in the east conceded to Russia all territories annexed during the first partition and a large part of those taken in the second.

The nationalist program contrasted with the so-called federalist orientation. Federalism was a trend, a vision, "very audacious but slightly romantic."[26] While able to invoke a long tradition, it contained nebulous elements, and one of its supporters claimed that "in February 1919 nobody seriously supported the federalist principles," and that they developed in the course of subsequent events.[27] In the broadest sense the federalist orientation postulated the liberation of the non-Russian borderlands and their association by federal or confederate links with Poland. The federalists harked back to the prepartition Polish-Lithuanian Commonwealth and thought of a modern form of association between Poland, Lithuania, Belorussia, the Ukraine, and possibly the Baltic countries. They belonged to different political groups: Socialists, populists, conservatives, or nonparty intellectuals, and there were differences in their approaches to the program.†

The most consistent advocate of federalism was a weekly publication, *Rząd i Wojsko* ("The Government and the Army"), which grouped many prominent Leftist Piłsudskiites. Edited by a great Socialist writer, Andrzej Strug, with such contributors as Hołówko, Adam Skwarczyński and Wincenty Rzymowski, the periodical stressed the connection between democracy in Poland and a federalist approach.[28] Recognizing that Bolshevik Russia had an "imposing program," *Rząd i Wojsko* postulated that Poland oppose it with its own platform of democracy at home and union with free peoples in the east.[29] Rejecting the 1772 border as imperialistic, opposing Dmowski's demands as implying mutilation of historic Lithuania, *Rząd i Wojsko* insisted that nationalities of the old Lithuanian Grand Duchy receive the right of self-

* The German census of 1916, which showed the falsity of Russian figures of 1897, probably strengthened the conviction of Dmowski and his supporters of the justice of their claims.

† Federalists comprised Socialist leaders such as Ignacy Daszyński, Herman Lieberman, Mieczysław Niedziałkowski, Leon Wasilewski, and Bronisław Ziemięcki; populists like Stanisław Thugutt and Maciej Rataj; great conservative landowners such as Prince Eustachy Sapieha; intellectuals such as Professors Stanisław Kutrzeba, Marceli Handelsman, Ludwik Kolankowski, or Witold Kamieniecki. As Lewandowski remarks, their "concept of the union was not precise. The sixteenth-century conception needed greater precision and clarification in the twentieth century but this was not done." See Józef Lewandowski, *Federalizm: Litwa i Białoruś w polityce obozu belwederskiego, XI 1918—IV 1920* (Warsaw, 1962), p. 57n.

determination and then an invitation to join a federation with Poland.[30] The weekly stood for an independent Ukrainian state and advocated territorial concessions in Eastern Galicia to remove the friction between Warsaw and Kiev.[31]

Federalist writings appeared in different quarters. The Socialist *Robotnik* ran articles by Hołówko which criticized National Democratic plans for annexation and colonization in the east. Professor Stanisław Kutrzeba prepared a project for a Polish-Lithuanian union; another scholar, Witold Kamieniecki, favored the establishment of national cantons in historic Lithuania within a larger federal structure.[32] Ignacy Paderewski also showed federalist inclinations. During the war years he drew up a memorandum for Colonel Edward M. House suggesting a "United States of Poland" composed of Poland proper, Lithuania, Polesie (*sic*) and Galicia. He believed that with Allied, and particularly Wilson's support, such a project could work out after the war.[33] Addressing the sejm in February 1919, Paderewski denied any imperialist leanings, and asserted that while he recognized Polish historic rights in the east he recognized the right of the borderland nations to free and separate development.[34] Paderewski's deputy foreign minister, Władysław Skrzyński, shared a federalist viewpoint.

Was Piłsudski a federalist? His chief spokesman and collaborator on eastern questions, Leon Wasilewski—foreign minister in the Moraczewski cabinet and author of numerous studies of Ukrainian, Belorussian, and Baltic problems—had outlined a federal program by February 1918. In view of the national awakening of the border nations he rejected the historical and annexationist approach as obsolete, and favored union with Lithuania. Wasilewski considered that such a union would imply abandoning to Lithuania certain areas with a Polish majority. This would be no tragedy, for Poles within Lithuania might act as a force consolidating the union. But Wasilewski did not elaborate future solutions in detail, and intimated that while the federalist approach might be most desirable it could not be the sole way of solving Poland's eastern problems.

Neither Wasilewski's views, though they probably came close to Piłsudski's thinking, nor the federalist utterances of *Rząd i Wojsko* necessarily reflected the ideas of the chief of state.[35] Piłsudski's "federalism" becomes clearer when related to his general outlook, although his elusive personality makes this task difficult.

Piłsudski's personality was a curious combination of pragmatism and romanticism. He disliked abstract doctrines and quoted with approval Goethe's saying that *Die Theorie ist immer grau* (theory is always grey).[36] He was a man of action. As he put it, such a person "wants victory" and must reckon with "physical strength." He admired Napoleon, "the greatest man in the world." Though once a leading member of the Polish Socialist Party, he disliked Marxism and confessed lack of interest in doctrines.[37] It was not the class content of socialism which appealed to him but Marx's championship of Poland as a revolutionary force opposing Russia. "The historical role of socialism in Poland," Piłsudski wrote, "is the role of defender of the West against the aggressive, reactionary tsardom."[38]

Pragmatism and political flair blended with Piłsudski's romanticism.[39] This romanticism, for want of a better word, expressed itself in an appreciation of "imponderabilia": honor, courage, civic virtue. These he valued in the life of men and of nations. Born in the Lithuanian borderlands, Piłsudski was brought up in the tradition of the Polish-Lithuanian union and the Jagiellonian past. He was proud of this heritage. As one of his collaborators put it in 1919, Piłsudski's characteristic feature was pride, not conceit in the narrow sense but national pride; belief in the greatness of the Polish nation which he thought himself to symbolize. He wanted greatness for Poland, and showed contempt and impatience for those Poles who did not wish to follow his great designs.[40]

Piłsudski saw politics as an art and not a science.[41] Like a great artist, he despised mediocrity. Though raised in relative poverty he had the mentality of a *grand seigneur*. Educated in the rough conspiratorial school of revolutionary activity he retained a predilection for secrecy. He was followed blindly by some and hated by others; he had disciples but few genuine collaborators. His politics often resembled a military campaign in which one uses divergent tactics as elements of general strategy, and since he seldom explained them, many of his acts and pronouncements appeared obscure or contradictory. Such was the man who largely determined Poland's foreign policy and relations between Warsaw and Moscow.

Piłsudski viewed Russia as alien and inimical, and Bolshevism appeared to him "a purely Russian disease."[42] He claimed that "already in 1918 I adopted, irrespective of anyone else, a clear-cut objective of the struggle against the Soviets." He defined it as the elimination of all attempts to impose on Poland a foreign way of life, and he strove to achieve it by pushing Bolshevism as far from Polish frontiers as possible.[43]

But where were Poland's frontiers? In accord with his pragmatism Piłsudski distinguished between immediately practicable and long-range plans. Toward the end of 1918 when he sent his envoy Michał Sokolnicki to Paris to negotiate with the Entente, he gave characteristic instructions. The Allies had not recognized the government in Warsaw, and Polish possibilities of military action were restricted. Piłsudski stated that the question of Eastern Galicia could not be resolved at this stage; what mattered was military control of the area. Minimum claims comprised Lwów and Kałusz. Farther north the former boundary of the Kingdom of Poland was to be adjusted to secure the railroad from Wilno to Kowel. He recommended that this be achieved if possible through an understanding with Russia—probably meaning the White Russian representatives in Paris. Thus the eastern border of Poland was to run from Wilno through Baranowicze, Pińsk, Kowel, Lwów, and Drohobycz. In his second instructions, written some three weeks later, Piłsudski showed interest in a more general settlement in the east. Emphasizing the weakening of Russia as a condition of strengthening Poland, he wrote Sokolnicki that Polish support must go to an independent Lithuania and Ukraine.[44]

Even at this early stage he distinguished between the immediately practicable and the long range. The link between the two was to be secured by *faits accomplis* and not by a theoretical approach based on ideological premises. Confronted with Dmowski's proposed frontier in the east, Piłsudski characteristically replied that it would be acceptable "if no other possibilities should materialize."[45] This did not mean approval of the incorporationist approach, which Piłsudski openly termed "imperialistic." He felt that the "concept of a 'Great Poland' required a liberal treatment of the territories of the old Grand Duchy of Lithuania and of the Ukraine."[46] Moreover, simple annexation was a poor substitute for general reorganization of the political system in Eastern Europe. But such settlement depended on circumstances and not on theoretical blueprints. That was why Piłsudski did not want to get involved in a dispute between the federalists and the incorporationists, and he made caustic remarks about doctrinaire federalists.

"The principle of federation," he said, "cannot be applied to these lands. Surely we enter them with weapons in our hands which is contrary to the principles of federation. Besides I did not see people there who would want to join such a federation." And he added that his objective was to "create *faits accomplis* and later receive recognition *de jure*."[47] In a famous letter to Wasilewski, Piłsudski wrote that he did not want to be either a federalist or an imperialist as long as the eastern questions could not be approached in all seriousness and "with a revolver in the pocket." He spoke with derision about "American palavers" about the brotherhood of nations—a transparent allusion to Wilson in Paris—and added ironically that since these slogans had become fashionable he would "gladly lean toward the federalists." At the same time he instructed Wasilewski to keep an eye on Paderewski's activity at the Peace Conference, because the premier, despite being "a crazy federalist," might be led astray by the arguments of the imperialists.[48]

In early 1919, as through most of his life, Piłsudski stood alone. He opposed incorporations in the east, and viewed with some irony the doctrinaire federalism of his friends.[49] He believed in accomplished facts. Preparing to drive the Bolsheviks out of the borderlands, Piłsudski wanted to create conditions favorable for a separation of the area from Russia for future association with Poland. It was an arduous task in which the attitude of the Allies and of political parties in Poland were likely to take an important part.

The Russian problem at the Paris Peace Conference consisted of two interrelated aspects—Russia as a state, and Communism as a doctrine. The former concerned the European balance of power, because the loss of Russia as an ally greatly affected the policies of the Entente. The latter aspect was that of a fighting ideology which seemed to threaten the foundations of society, national as well as international. Should the Western powers try to re-establish Russia as a factor in international relations they would face the question of overthrowing the Bolshevik regime.

How could it be overthrown? There were several possible approaches: direct intervention, counterrevolution, or indirect action relying on border states and emancipated nationalities. Each was fraught with danger. After four years of war it seemed impossible to use Allied troops for a large-scale operation in Russia. Aid to counterrevolutionary armies was more likely, but it was hard to gauge the strength and support enjoyed by various White centers. Then there was the question of how to reconcile the slogan of Russia "one and indivisible" with the national aspirations of borderland countries. Reliance on the latter—Poland, the Baltic states, the Ukraine—who were engaged against the Bolsheviks required clarification of the Russian policy of the Entente. Did the Western powers seek reconstruction of great unified Russia to whom interests of the nationalities were subordinate? Or were they willing to take the disintegration of the tsarist empire as a starting point, and establish an Eastern block of states centering around a great Poland? And if they adopted this last policy, against White opposition, would not a greatly diminished Russia be forever hostile to such a bloc and to the Entente itself? There was another alternative; recognition of the new Bolshevik regime and a territorial settlement in Eastern Europe in cooperation with the new masters of Russia. Such a policy entailed ideological capitulation, and possibly the opening of gates to a revolutionary Bolshevik drive into the heart of Europe.

The Allies in Paris tried half-heartedly all of these courses of action, at times simultaneously pursuing contradictory approaches. They were divided among themselves, and there were divisions within each of the great powers, with a paralyzing effect on policies. The United States stood on the whole for a unified Russia. The British, apart from interest in the Caucasus and the Baltic region, also thought in terms of prewar Russian territory with exception of Poland and Finland.[50] France, in view of immediate interest in the area east of Germany, grappled with the question of who would be the French partner in Eastern Europe—a resurrected Russia, the ally of yesterday, or a strong Polish state—and the result was hesitation and inconsistency.[51] No one treated the complex borderland question on its own merit but only in conjunction with Russia or possibly Poland.[52]

The question of Russia's participation at the Peace Conference came up early at Paris. Lloyd George, with some support from Wilson, tried to bring Bolshevik representatives to the conference, or at least grant them a hearing. The prime minister argued that the Bolsheviks after all were a *de facto* government, and the Allies "had got themselves in a fix for the reason they had no definite policy in Russia."[53] The French objected. The Quai d'Orsay, especially, favored admission of anti-Bolshevik Russian leaders who had made Paris the center of their political activities.[54] The Americans and British would not agree, but an unofficial Conférence Politique Russe, comprising such personages as Prince Lvov, Sazonov, Nikolai Chaikovskii, Vasilii Maklakow, and others, received the right to communicate with the Peace Conference. They used this privilege to influence the Allies against the nationalities of the former empire, and in favor of an indivisible Russia.[55]

Under pressure of Lloyd George and Wilson the Supreme Council of the Peace Conference on January 22, 1919 issued an appeal to all goverments and centers in Russia to send representatives to the Princes' Islands (Prinkipo) to discuss the Russian question with Allied delegates. The appeal, transmitted by radio, demanded cessation of hostilities against nations not comprised within the Russian borders of 1914 and against peoples "whose autonomous action is in contemplation in the fourteen articles."[56] The French endorsed this proposal half-heartedly, and did their best to assist non-Bolshevik Russians to reject it. The hope in some Allied circles that Soviet refusal of the Prinkipo plan would strengthen Western propaganda and open possibilities for a more forceful anti-Bolshevik policy was frustrated by the stand taken by Moscow. Soviet Russia, after initial doubts whether the proposal was genuine and meant peace, embraced it eagerly.[57] To Lenin, Prinkipo was another Brest-Litovsk, and he was willing again to make far-reaching concessions to gain a respite and consolidate the Soviet position. As Chicherin put it, referring to possible territorial cessions: the "analysis of the results of Brest-Litovsk had shown that such annexations could be only of short duration."[58] Trotsky declared on February 24 that Russia was willing to make peace at the price of heavy sacrifices since "you and I know very well that all that we cede now will come back to us, because Soviet Russia gives in to the imperialists only temporarily."[59]

Soviet agreement to the Prinkipo proposal took a studiously insulting form. Moscow offered to make payments and submit to Allied annexations of Russian territory, implying that the Entente's only concern was for gold and land. For propaganda purposes, all the advantages were on the Bolshevik side.

Two days after the Allied appeal, the Moscow radio broadcast an invitation for the meeting of the Communist International. The gathering took place in Moscow, and the Comintern's manifesto adopted in early March emphasized peace, and appealed to workers in the West to force their governments to recognize the Soviet state. The emphasis on peace reappeared in Soviet dealings with Wilson's envoy, William C. Bullitt, sent to Russia behind the backs of the French but with knowledge of the British. But this sequel to the Prinkipo plan produced nothing. Wilson apparently felt that there was no future in exchanges with the Bolsheviks, given both the attitude of the other Allies and the international situation.

Failure of the Prinkipo approach brought to the fore plans for military intervention in Russia. Their chief advocates were Winston Churchill in Britain and Marshal Ferdinand Foch in France. In January Foch had urged that an international force invade Russia, and he returned to his projects in February and March.[60] Churchill spoke in favor of armed intervention in mid-February. These projects encountered the opposition of Lloyd George and Wilson and brought little encouragement from

Clemenceau. But the Quai d'Orsay and French army showed an interest in Foch's arguments in favor of strengthening Poland vis-à-vis Red Russia. The choice of Joseph Noulens, former ambassador to Russia and a well-known partisan of intervention, as head of an inter-Allied mission to Poland in early February 1919, indicated the desire of some French circles to make Poland a springboard for an invasion of Russia. General Barthélemy's proposals for an armistice in Eastern Galicia aimed at freeing Polish and Ukrainian forces for anti-Bolshevik action.[61]

When Noulens suggested that a French general be appointed commander of the Polish army so that the troops would not act contrary to Allied policy, the idea seemed in keeping with policy of intervention. The general in question, Paul Henrys, confided to Polish officers that "the plan of his action consists in making Poland a 'place d'armes' for operations against the Bolsheviks."[62] It is true that Henrys soon fell under Piłsudski's influence and undertook nothing contrary to the wishes of the chief of state, but the Bolsheviks may well have assumed that France was pushing Poland toward armed interference.[63]

Moscow skillfully exploited divergences among the statesmen in Paris. On February 18, 1919 Chicherin appealed to the governments of the Allied powers against the movement of Polish troops toward Lithuania and Belorussia. The Polish offensive, he said, was rendered possible by Allied pressure on Germany to let the Poles cross the German-held line, and it coincided with Noulens' stay in Warsaw. The Poles were operating against the Soviet republics "on the territory of the former Russian empire." How did the Allies reconcile such action with the principles of the Prinkipo offer?[64]

Some two weeks later the Soviet Lithuanian-Belorussian Republic (Litbel) sent a note to Paris agreeing to take part in the Prinkipo conference, and while this was only a propagandistic gesture it was likely to embarrass the Allies further.

Lloyd George was annoyed with the Poles for seemingly complicating the Russian question. On January 22 he was already worried lest the Poles "under this pretense [of fighting the Bolsheviks] . . . did not attempt to push their conquest eastwards and face the Congress with the capture of Kovno or Grodno."* After

* *Foreign Relations of the United States: The Paris Peace Conference 1919* (13 vols.; Washington, D.C., 1942-1947), III, 675. Hereafter cited as *F. R. Peace Conference*. It is likely that representations of the Conférence Politique Russe had something to do with this stand. The Conférence watched Polish moves eastward, and in April suggested to the Peace Conference that it issue a declaration in favor of purely ethnic Polish borders in the east. See Maklakov Archive, "Polsha 1919," Hoover Institution, Stanford, California.

receiving the Chicherin communication the prime minister told his secretary, Philip Kerr, that he saw "no evidence at the present moment that the Soviet Government have any intention or desire to invade these territories" [i.e. Poland and the Baltic countries].[65]

The statesmen in Paris moved in a vicious circle. They wanted to fight Bolshevism without injuring Russia; they played simultaneously with intervention and peaceful approaches; they desired that the states on Russia's western borders oppose the Bolsheviks but undertake nothing to further their own national interests. Italy's premier and chief delegate, Vittorio Orlando, expressed his view of these inconsistencies when speaking in the Supreme Council on March 27, 1919: "We had to choose in Russia between two policies equally logical and defendable. The first is that of intervention; go to Moscow if necessary and crush Bolshevism by force. The second consists in regarding Bolshevism as a government *de facto,* and to establish relations with it, if not cordial at least more or less normal. We did not know how to adopt either one or the other and we have suffered the worst consequences of pursuing both policies at the same time. Without going to war, we really are in a state of war with Russia."[66] This was certainly true, and consequences of this state of affairs were noticeable in the case of Poland, especially with regard to the eastern frontiers.

Dmowski wrote later that although the peacemakers asked the Polish delegation to submit territorial claims in the east, they "did not undertake any discussion with us about these demands." He remarked that there "existed first of all a serious doubt whether the Peace Conference could establish a boundary line between Poland and Russia in the absence of Russia,"[67] and he may have added, in the absence of any Russian policy of the Entente. Still, the Polish delegation submitted a note on eastern boundaries on March 3, 1919. Taking the frontiers of 1772 as a point of departure, they demanded inclusion in Poland of those territories which had retained a predominantly Polish character.[68] The proposed frontier was the Dmowski Line, and the whole note reflected the incorporationist approach of the National Democrats. The dominance of this approach was the result of their deal with Warsaw, leaving Dmowski with a virtual monopoly of representing Poland at the Paris Peace Conference.[69]

Piłsudski's representatives, who had joined the National Committee in Paris and then the peace delegation, made attempts to advocate the federalist solution but met with the stern veto of Dmowski and his collaborators. On the eve of the presentation of the note on eastern borders affairs came to a showdown at a joint meeting and Dmowski won over the opposition of the federalists. Dmowski was kept informed by the Allies, and he pointed out that a federalist approach would never be considered by the Peace Conference. The Allies, he declared, wanted a strong Poland and "federation means weakness not strength, especially as there is no one with whom one can federate."[70] This argument was not grounded in reality, nor were Dmowski's intimations that his eastern program could be accepted by non-Bolshevik Russians. The Allies were far from convinced of the need for a strong Poland; Miliukov used his British contacts to accuse Dmowski of imperialism.[71]

One of Piłsudski's envoys, Stanisław Patek, commented bitterly that Dmowski's program "is based on no criterion consistently applied (neither ethnic nor historical). It cuts and adjusts various borders depending on given needs." Belorussia is "cut into two halves," Lithuania restricted to "ethnic frontiers." The only issue was whether to annex more or less.[72] There was only one concession to the federalist viewpoint in the Polish note on eastern frontiers; Lithuania was to be a "separate land within the borders of the Polish state." Otherwise the voice of Polish federalists was not heard at the conference. Piłsudski's delegates in Paris continued to meet separately, and attempted direct conversations with Lithuanians, Latvians, and Ukrainians. The results were meager.[73]

Dmowski's note apparently failed to impress the Commission on Polish Affairs, which undertook a study of the eastern boundaries. The commission faced the difficulty "of ascertaining from what states Poland will be separated by these frontiers,"[74] and lacking precise instructions from the Supreme Council they decided on a line of least resistance—in accord with Russian views and based upon purely ethnic criteria corresponding to principles used in tracing Polish western frontiers. As the French member of the commission stated, there was one sure basis "namely the declaration [of March 30, 1917] of the last regular Russian government." And the Italian delegate added that the Allies "had always considered Russia an ally whose territorial integrity ought to be respected."[75] By integrity Marquis Della Toretta meant maintenance of the historic Russian state.

The commision took as its point of departure not the Polish—as Dmowski advocated—but the Russian historic borders. These borders were merely to be modified by concessions to ethnic Poland, placing the whole Polish case in jeopardy. If the ethnic criterion were to apply to Poland and not to Russia, then the borderlands would naturally be excluded from discussion. The federalists had insisted on the right to self-determination but

Dmowski had not. His denial of Lithuanian, Belorussian, or Ukrainian rights could easily be turned against Poland. If these lands had been part of Russia and were not ethnically Polish, Russia had better claims than Poland.

The Commission on Polish Affairs, after listening to Paderewski, who tried to interject federalist overtones, and after communicating with Russians in Paris, decided in early April to recommend a minimum border which roughly corresponded to the prewar boundary between the Kingdom of Poland and the tsarist state. This border excluded areas which even according to Russian statistics had Polish majorities; it represented a victory of protagonists of Russia "one and indivisible." The commission, probably aware of this state of affairs, qualified its recommendation by a proposal to set up an inquiry commission on the spot to determine what regions east of the line could be given to Poland. These changes were to be affected in argement with a future Russian government.

The commission's report, entitled "Eastern Frontier of Poland" and dated April 22, was submitted to the Peace Conference, but it was obvious that the Allies would not take any decisions for some time.[76] Still, the report indicated Allied thinking in Paris on Russo-Polish problems. It showed their insistence on respect for Russian territorial interests, a predilection for a minimum Polish border in the east, and neglect of Ukrainian, Belorussian, and Lithuanian claims and demands.*

Developments at the conference, culminating in Orlando's admission in late March that the Allies had no consistent Russian policy and in the April proposal of a minimum Polish frontier in the east, had direct bearing on Poland's diplomacy. Paris proved incapable of working out a solution of the Bolshevik problem, and by its fear of harming a non-Communist Russia tried to impose restrictions on Poland's aims in the east. Warsaw, dependent on the Entente for political and military support, faced the task of adopting a Russian policy which would not be in too blatant an opposition to that of the Allies. Such a policy also had to win approval at home, and Poles were far from united. Finally there was Moscow, which insisted on direct contacts with Warsaw and spoke in terms of peace, while maintaining a grip

* Britain favored consistently purely ethnic borders for Poland. See Foreign Office, *Peace Handbook*, no. 44 (London, 1920); and compare with Tytus Filipowicz report of April 13, 1919 in *Dokumenty i materiały do historii stosunków polsko-radzieckich* (Warsaw, 1962–), II, 229-231. The French were more hesitant but they kept Russian interests in mind. The Italian delegate on the Polish Commission was strongly pro-Russian.

on the borderlands. The early spring of 1919 was likely to be a period of difficulty and indecision.

From late February to mid-April 1919 the Russian question occupied a prominent place in the debates of the sejm, revealing a widening rift between the federalists and the adherents of incorporation. The issue of intervention against Bolshevism also came up, but created less excitement since most Poles felt that restoration of the old regime in Russia was neither Poland's business nor to her advantage. In most pronouncements at the sejm Bolshevism and Russia appeared as one and the same thing, and this attitude provided a sharp contrast to Allied thinking in Paris.

On February 20, Premier Paderewski spoke of the "bloody wave of Russian Bolshevism" threatening Poland. He stressed, however, that "The East had not changed. Bolshevism will collapse because it is bound to collapse, but, I wish I were a false prophet, out of its ruins there may arise not only a [new] republic, but some new tsardom."[77] Piłsudski expressed a similar sentiment in interviews with French journalists, by saying that "irrespective of what her government will be Russia is terribly imperialistic." The chief of state assured the French that Poles could beat the Bolsheviks without too much difficulty, provided they received enough equipment from the Allies.[78] This underestimate of the Communists,—Piłsudski was less positive when speaking to Poles—[79] linked with insistence on perennial Russian imperialism, was intentional. Polish leaders meant to show Paris that Russia rather than Bolshevism represented the danger. The French were annoyed, and believed that Piłsudski showed little energy in combating Communism, and even maintained contacts with the Bolsheviks.[80] A shrewd suggestion of Charles Richet in *Le Temps* that the Poles present an offer to destroy Bolshevism in exchange for the realization of their eastern program,[81] could not at that time have been adopted in Warsaw, nor would it have been favorably received in France.

The Polish Left made strong statements against associating Poland with intervention. "We want to be neither the advance guard nor the gendarmerie of the East" Daszyński said.[82] PPS deputies on March 27, 1919 issued a declaration favoring alliance with the Entente, but of an "exclusively defensive nature." The declaration also opposed "giving it any imperialist overtones," and rejected "any anti-Bolshevik intervention in Russia." A leader of the populists (Wyzwolenie) defined the views of his party by stating in the sejm that "fighting Bolshevism we fight against Russia, and fighting Russia we fight against Bolshevism, but a struggle against Bolshevism in particular is neither our aim nor our task."[83] Even a spokeman of the National Democrats (at that time chairman of the Foreign Affairs Committee) found it necessary to assure the sejm that "there were never any plans to use Poland as the gendarme of Europe," and irrespective of whether he believed it himself, the statement showed that intervention had few partisans in the country.[84]

As for a peaceful approach to Soviet Russia, the PPS and the Polish Communists for different reasons criticized the secrecy with which Warsaw surrounded Chicherin's overtures, and they accused the government of bellicose tendencies.[85] It was evident that the whole matter of Soviet-Polish exchanges had to be worked out, and after the Committee of Foreign Affairs met and discussed the question on March 5, 1919,[86] the sejm spent two days, April 3 and 4, on a major debate on Poland's foreign policy.

Grabski, in his capacity as chairman of the Foreign Affairs Committee presented a report which stated that the Soviet government had from the beginning tried to involve Poland into a discussion of Russo-Polish relations and especially of borders between the two countries. Moscow acted as "the legal government of the entire former Russian empire together with Lithuania, Belorussia, and Ruś [Ukraine]," and the Polish government "had done their best not to be drawn into such a discussion or recognize even indirectly Soviet authorities as a legal government."[87] Warsaw realized the danger of involvement in negotiations with the Bolsheviks—without prior understanding with the Entente—and Polish notes had dealt only with matters such as return of personnel of the diplomatic mission and of refugees. The government was justified in not publishing the individual notes of Chicherin—which Grabski described as "constructed in an extraordinarily perfidious manner"—but the committee had nothing against publication of the entire correspondence. Warsaw correctly ignored the communication from the Lithuanian-Belorussian Soviet authorities "imposed [on those peoples] by Bolshevik troops" which were no less imperialistic than those of the tsars.

The report contained an important statement on foreign policy objectives. The Polish eastern advance, it said, did not attempt to prejudice final decisions of the Peace Conference or bring forcible annexations, but only to defend the areas against foreign invaders. The Polish government ought to do everything to unify in one state all territories on which the Poles had left a permanent imprint. It should do its best to permit free expression of the local Polish, Belorussian and Ukrainian populations with regard to a union with Poland. Recognizing the right of the Lithuanians to statehood, the report called on the Polish government to strive for voluntary union.[88]

The report, which mainly represented the views of the rightist majority of the committee, was not free from ambiguities. It did not contain unconditional recognition of the right of self-determination, nor—except for Lithuania—did it advocate federalism. The assumption was that the peoples of the borderlands wanted to get rid of Russia and unite with Poland, and the report advocated that they receive the right to pronounce on the nature of such union, but not oppose it altogether. The government was to try to achieve maximum unity, and the report did not specify inducements or concessions to Ukrainians or Belorussians. The federalist Left did not fail to point all this out in the ensuing debate.

The debate brought the views of the Right and the Left into sharper relief. The federalists from the PPS and the populist Wyzwolenie had made statements about independent Lithuania and Belorussia in late February, and the Center and Right parties merely had countered by stressing the Polish character of Wilno and Lwów.[89] In mid-March Wyzwolenie had appealed for "an open and honest adoption of federalist aims" by other parties.[90] The PPS declared against annexations and imperialism and for union with Lithuania and Belorussia, although safeguarding their right to independence.[91] Socialist leaders in the sejm admitted, however, that one could not as yet determine eastern frontiers, and one of them warned that far from being a panacea federalism was a most difficult form of government.[92]

In the course of the debate which followed Grabski's report, the Left and the nonpartisan federalist Kamieniecki who advocated "disannexation" of the borderlands—a term meaning Russian withdrawal from the entire area west of 1772 borders—reiterated strong federalist sentiments. The most extreme position was that of a youthful PPS leader, Mieczysław Niedziałkowski, who favored strict observance of the principle of national self-determination, even if it meant concessions to Ukrainians in Galicia, and castigated the interests of the landowners in the borderlands.[93]

The Center replied with arguments in favor of a strong, hence a great Poland (some Socialists objected that the two were not necessarily identical); they said that Poland's eastward movement was in accord "with the natural tendency of expansion of nations"; and they forwarded ideas for the colonization of the sparsely inhabited eastern regions.[94] A spokesman of the nationalist block, the largest in the sejm, opposed the formation of the Ukraine or of any Lithuanian-Belorussian state. His formula was the Dmowski Line.[95]

When discussion ended, the sejm approved only the last point of a motion tabled by the PPS which provided (1) that the struggle in the east be of defensive character; (2) that the self-determination of Lithuania and Belorussia be explicitly recognized; and (3) that Soviet republics which were not based on free and popular will should be denied recognition. It passed a resolution which called on the government and Supreme Command to liberate from the Bolsheviks and unite with Poland "the northeastern provinces of Poland with their capital Wilno."[96] The Grabski report secured acceptance by a majority of the sejm on the same day; hence subsequent references to it as the April 4 resolution.

The federalists had suffered defeat—first at the hands of Dmowski in Paris and then in the Warsaw sejm. Only with regard to Lithuania was there a glimmer of hope, but chances of an attractive program of liberation of the borderlands were greatly restricted. Piłsudski's followers worried that without such a program the Polish eastern advance might just appear as an imperialist policy of aggrandizement.[97] Socialists continued to battle for recognition of Lithuanian and Belorussian rights. As for Piłsudski, he waited for an opportune moment to use his favorite method, that of creating *faits accomplis*. It came in late April when Piłsudski suddenly occupied Wilno. The issue of the borderlands appeared in a new light.

In contrast to the Polish federalist program which suffered from the political naïveté of some supporters and the distortions of opponents,[98] Soviet federalism labored under no such disadvantages. Deriving its strength from the highly centralized structure of the Bolshevik party, it presented the appearance of a democratic and progressive platform. Only the Leninist principle of national self-determination could raise questions; hence it mattered a great deal that the principle be both of universal validity and applicable to the complex situation in the borderlands.

As mentioned, Stalin's interpretation of the right of self-determination as self-determination "of the working masses," had been approved by the January 1918 Congress of the Soviets. The same congress adopted federalism as the basis of union of Soviet republics. These resolutions modified the original position of Lenin. The meaning of the right of self-determination needed clarification, and the Eighth Party Congress which met from March 18 to 23, 1919 turned to this question in connection with revision of the party program. Bolshevik leaders realized that the new program had to be general (though formally a Russian program it was to serve as a model for the international proletariat), concrete, and practical.[99] The same applied to national self-determination.

Bukharin was well aware of differences between the position of the "Left" which supported Stalin's formula, and that of Lenin, and he attempted a compromise. A nation, he said, was surely composed of all classes, and if one accepted the unqualified right of national self-determination it might mean that the will of the entire nation, as represented in a bourgeois parliament, would decide such issues as secession or unification. But acceptance of the formula of "proletarian self-determination" eliminated this danger, and Bukharin spoke in favor of it, giving, interestingly enough, Poland as an example. "If the Polish workers do not want to be together with us in one state we will not drag them in by force, we shall sanction and respect the will of the Polish proletariat. But we absolutely do not sanction and do not respect the will of the Polish bourgeoisie."*

So far Bukharin had followed Stalin's approach, but the formula of "proletarian self-determination," he said applied only to states that were socially advanced. In the case of colonial peoples where no class distinctions were visible, the unqualified right of national self-determination would be retained. This double standard, advantageous for the Communists, would be obscured by a general statement making the nature of self-determination dependent on the stage of development of a given nation.[100]

Lenin rejected this reasoning; Bukharin spoke of what ought to be and not of what was. A distinction between national and proletarian will could not be drawn even in an advanced state like Germany, and except for Soviet Russia there was no case where one could speak of proletarian will in a strict sense. "Each nation," Lenin went on, "should have the right of self-determination, and this will contribute to self-determination of the workers."[101] What he meant was that the desire for national self-determination was a fact to be recognized and used to Bolshevik advantage.

Vladimir Ilich also quoted the Polish example. In Poland, he

---

* *Vosmoi sezd RKP(b), Mart 1917 g: protokoly* (Moscow, 1959), p. 47. This view was shared by Polish Communists and fellow travelers. As Tadeusz Żarski expressed it, "the right to decide the fate of the nation is a right of the proletariat struggling for power" (August 1, 1919; *Dokumenty i materiały*, II, 304).

said, the process of proletarian self-determination was far advanced and the Communists had an impressive number of representatives on the Warsaw Council of Workers' Deputies. Judging from the Russian "revolutionary calendar," Poland was approaching its October.[102] This calendar could not be used uncritically. Polish workers, more cultured and advanced that the Russians, still mainly favored social-patriotism. There was no sharp contrast between their will and the national will, and "one could not speak of self-determination of the working masses." One had to wait, but at the same time it was impossible "not to grant the Polish nation the right of self-determination immediately." Lenin warned against rushing things, and stressed that Polish workers were still susceptible to the slogan that the Russians "who had always oppressed the Poles want to impose their Great Russian chauvinism on Poland under the cover of Communism." Proletarian unity could only be achieved "by propaganda, agitation, and voluntary union" and not by rejection of national aspirations. Lenin said that there were Communists who thought differently but "scratch such a Communist and you will find a Great Russian chauvinist." He repeated this twice, concluding that "he is in many of us and we have to fight him."

Lenin's approach was intensely practical. He wanted to retain the principle of national self-determination as a weapon of Socialism, and he could do it only if it were flexible enough. One of the Bolshevik delegates certainly understood it in this sense when expressing agreement "with our old opportunist, comrade Lenin."[103] A dogmatist such as Georgii L. Piatakov, who rejected the principle because it had united all the counterrevolutionary forces in the borderlands, was unable to grasp Lenin's subtleties. To Piatakov self-determination in a Soviet republic was only "a diplomatic game which in some cases it was necessary to play, but it was worse than a game if it were taken seriously."[104] Citing the Ukraine (he was a member of the executive committee of its Communist party), Piatakov asserted that one could not leave the decision concerning her fate even to the Ukrainian proletariat, because it affected Russia and indeed the Revolution. All this was true, but Piatakov's candor was astonishing. His comportment was that of a bull in a china shop.

The final formula of national self-determination adopted by the Congress was flexible enough for Lenin to use any way he wanted, and still had the merit of apparent consistency. It spoke of the need to overcome the suspicion of the proletariat of the oppressed countries toward the proletariat of the former oppressor countries, and it recognized the full equality of rights of nations, including political secession. "As for the question who is the carrier of the nation's will [with regard] to secession RKP represents the historical-class point of view, taking into consideration the level of historical development achieved by the given nation." Unity remained the goal of the Bolsheviks, and "federal unification of states organized on the Soviet pattern" was a transitional form. Establishment of "national Soviet republics around Soviet Russia" served as an example of "a genuinely close voluntary unification of various elements of the international proletariat."[105]

The Soviet federalist approach, based on the right of national self-determination, lent itself splendidly for propaganda purposes. If any doubt remains that practice differed greatly from theory, one can remove it by linking the above resolution on the national question with another resolution by the same congress which concerned party organization. This second resolution is revealing:

At the present time the Ukraine, Latvia, Lithuania, and Belorussia exist as separate Soviet republics. This is the solution of the given moment for the question of the form of political existence. This does not mean in any sense that RKP should in its turn be organized on the basis of a federation of independent Communist parties.

The Eighth Congress of RKP decides: it is necessary that a *single* centralized Communist party exist with a single TsK [Central Committee] directing all party work throughout all parts of RSFSR.

All decisions of RKP and its executive bodies are unconditionally binding on all parts of the party, irrespective of its national composition. Central Committees of the Ukrainian, Latvian, Lithuanian Communists enjoy the rights of provincial party committees and are totally subordinated to the TsK of RKP.[106]

Thus behind the façade of federalism there operated the most highly centralized and disciplined party of the world. The Soviet government could easily engage in talks with the Poles about the borderlands and use effectively its flexible principle of national self-determination while pulling party strings to undo any apparent concession.

The Polish extraordinary envoy, Aleksander Więckowski, reached Moscow two days before the opening of the Eight Party Congress.[107] The ostensible object of his mission was to settle the question of the Polish delegates arrested after the Red Cross incident. The Polish government assured both the sejm and the

Entente that Warsaw had no intention of establishing diplomatic relations with Moscow or starting political negotiations.[108] Paderewski instructed Więckowski to procure the release of members of the Polish mission, and to promise the Bolsheviks that Warsaw would do everything to find and punish the murderers of the Red Cross delegates. The envoy was to raise the question of Polish cultural treasures in Russia, but avoid "even touching on political questions." Should the Soviet government raise any, Więckowski was to refer back to Warsaw.[109]

The Polish envoy was also entrusted with a political note which did not emanate from the government but from the Central Committee of the PPS, addressed to the Central Committee of the Russian Communist Party. The document, dated March 4, contained the following statements and proposals.[110] Poland was independent and sovereign and any attempted invasion would mean encroaching on her integrity, which the Polish Socialists would actively oppose. Nor was any intervention by Soviet Russia in Polish internal affairs admissible, and since the "Polish Soviet government in Wilno" represented such an attempt, the PPS demanded its liquidation. Finally, the question of Polish eastern borders was to be decided on the basis of national self-determination, i.e., by a plebiscite held after a military evacuation of Lithuania and Belorussia. The alleged determination of the people of these countries to join Soviet Russia was pure fiction.

It is not known whether Paderewski approved of the PPS note to the Bolsheviks. Even if he did, he may have treated it as a *ballon d'essai* which in no way compromised the Polish government and could possibly clarify the Soviet stand on plebiscites in the borderlands. The reasons which prompted the PPS to put forward these proposals were largely domestic. The Socialists wanted to undermine Bolshevik propaganda in Poland and to demonstrate the desire of the Polish proletariat to find a peaceful solution of the borderlands.[111] Assuming that their overture produced some result, the PPS could use it as an argument for its eastern approach, as opposed to that of the incorporationists.

It is clear that the Bolsheviks were eager to start negotiations with Poland; they had so insisted for a long time. A respite on the Polish front was also desirable, although hostilities there were not yet a source of major concern for Russia.[112] Finally, the Soviet government seemingly desired not to show antagonism toward Paderewski, hoping to play him against the Socialists.* Only the

---

* Chicherin declared that the "purely bourgeois government of Paderewski took a less inimical attitude toward Soviet Russia" than the Polish Socialists. See Georgii V. Chicherin, *Stati i rechi po voprosam mezhdunarodnoi politiki* (Moscow, 1961), p. 121. According to Polish information, "the Bolsheviks do not intend to combat

Polish Communists adopted a negative attitude toward Więckowski's overtures. One of their leaders warned the Bolshevik Central Committee that "Więckowski has no wide powers. He was sent to pull wool over the eyes of broad working masses of toilers and peasants who do not want war."[113] Marchlewski later sneered at the PPS proposal, calling it "slightly comical" and "scandalous."[114] As for plebiscites in Lithuania and Belorussia preceded by troop evacuation, Polish Communists in Warsaw opposed them.[115]

Upon arrival in Moscow Więckowski gave Chicherin the judicial report on the murder of the Red Cross delegates, accompanied by a note from the Polish government expressing regret and promising punishment of the guilty.[116] He handed in the PPS note. The Bolsheviks were naturally most interested in the latter, and Lenin instructed that a reply should indicate that the Bolsheviks were in complete accord, and it was they who insisted on settlements by vote of the working masses. He added that "we agree to make concessions on details, etc."[117] Lenin spoke about a reply to Poland, and Chicherin, in answer to Więckowski on March 24, 1919, also asked that the envoy inform the Polish government about the Soviet stand. Thus both considered the PPS note as a government proposal sent through unofficial channels. The foreign commissar disclaimed any Soviet intention of invading Poland. There was no Polish government in Wilno, and PPS must have been misinformed. A "vote of the *working masses*" after the "evacuation by *foreign* troops" seemed a sensible way of settling the border question, and Chicherin felt sure the government of Litbel had nothing against it.[118] Chicherin's insistence on "proletarian self-determination," of course, perverted the sense of the Polish proposal. It is interesting that he used this formula after the Eighth Congress resolution, which had seemingly restored the original meaning of national self-determination.

Three days later Chicherin informed Więckowski that members of the Polish mission would be freed and sent back to Poland, and it seems that talks began concerning the refugees.[119] Were they the only subject of conversations? We must remember that Więckowski stayed in Moscow until late April, and surely political subjects were broached by the Bolsheviks.* What the latter

the Paderewski government because this could strengthen the influence of PPS." The Soviets allegedly believed that "the Paderewski government will compromise itself in the eyes of the masses." See Report No. 2, to Supreme Command, March 7, 1919, Akta Adiutantury Generalnej Naczelnego Dowództwa XV/478 (cited as AGND).

* It is also possible that the Bolsheviks raised the question of establishing economic relations with Poland, since Lenin had instructed L. B. Krasin "energetically and constantly" to conduct a policy of establishing such relations, and to notify Chicherin about it. See D. V. Oznobishin, *Ot Bresta do Iureva: Iz istorii vneshnei politiki Sovetskoi vlasti 1917-1920* (Moscow, 1966), p. 262.

said and what the Pole replied is still clouded in mystery. Chicherin later alleged that Więckowski "began unofficial negotiations for cessation of hostilities."[120] Marchlewski contradicted him, saying that Więckowski had avoided all concrete political negotiations.[121] According to one writer, the Pole assured the Bolsheviks that his country would not support the counterrevolutionary general, Anton Denikin. Another claims that Chicherin made offers of territorial concessions.[122] It is hard to imagine that no political exchanges took place during Więckowski's stay in Moscow, but given Polish instructions they could not have produced any tangible result.

On April 15, 1919 the foreign commissar addressed three notes to the Polish envoy.[123] In the first he stated that he had received a communication from the Soviet Ukrainian government which, worried by the likelihood of armed clash with the Poles, proposed to open negotiations about frontiers. The basis was to be "the expression of the will of the working masses."[124] The commissar asked that this information go to Warsaw. In the second note, after recalling that Russia had granted all facilities to a diplomatic courier sent to Warsaw, Chicherin asked whether there was still no reply and offered the use of Moscow radio. The third note developed the Soviet point of view on Russo-Polish negotiations. Chicherin explained that Moscow viewed a settlement concerning Polish mission and refugees as "partial understanding about secondary matters"; the real issue was the establishment of diplomatic relations. But Polish military preparations and statements in the sejm seemed to make such relations very difficult. Hence, the commissar suggested that Polish-Soviet exchanges, after the return of the members of the mission to Poland, be confined to the matter of refugees. Other problems—probably an allusion to the PPS proposal—must be put aside until Russia received "clarification of questions of basic interest" to her.

Five days later Chicherin protested the alleged atrocities perpetrated by Polish "legionaries" in the area of Białystok,[125] and on April 25, 1919 the bombshell exploded: Moscow learned about the sudden capture of Wilno by Piłsudski. Chicherin addressed a strong protest, accusing the Poles of aggression and of taking Wilno by subterfuge.[126] Więckowski was asked to leave, and he was taken under military escort to Finland. Prominent Poles were arrested in Russia as hostages for the Bolshevik leaders captured in Wilno.[127] A Polish newspaper reported that the Soviet government treated the seizure of Wilno as a declaration of war.[128] The theory arose that the object of Więckowski's mission had been "to raise the hopes of the Soviet government for a peaceful settlement so that Mr. Piłsudski could more effectively realize [his] military plans."[129]

All available evidence points to the Więckowski mission as a bona fide move. Paderewski was genuinely anxious to bring back Poles from Russia. The PPS wanted to have a chance to try its own approach to the Russian question and to fortify its position at home. Więckowski was no mere courier. He had played an important role in early 1917 when dealing with the Petrograd Soviet, and he would discuss delicate questions again with Bolshevik emissaries. He favored peace, though not at any price. It seems doubtful whether Piłsudski needed a smokescreen to execute his offensive on Wilno. The weakness of Soviet resistance and the difficulty of gathering reinforcements for the Western Front must have been fairly obvious, and Piłsudski's timing stemmed from domestic reasons and not the stage of Russo-Polish talks.

The capture of Wilno was not the beginning of war in an orthodox sense, but rather a move—a very important one—in the intricate game for the borderlands played by Moscow and Warsaw. In spite of all the uproar in Russia, Chicherin's note did not slam the doors and burn the bridges. It said that when hostilities would terminate the Soviet government would be willing to start new negotiations. Future events were to bear out this statement. Piłsudski's *fait accompli* cut the Gordian knot of the borderlands, creating genuine possibilities for a Polish federalist approach; it also opened another phase in Soviet-Polish relations.

Open Struggles and Secret Negotiations

After the capture of Wilno in April 1919 the Soviet-Polish story becomes increasingly involved. The Poles had challenged Russia, but neither side was strong enough to seek a solution by arms alone. Both were absorbed by a host of grave problems, domestic and international. While Polish troops fought the Red Army, diplomatic maneuvers and intricate political moves and countermoves acquired decisive importance.

The capture of Wilno opened a Pandora's box of Lithuanian and Belorussian issues, intensifying the federalist-incorporationist controversy in Poland. Ukrainian questions came also to the fore. The successes of the Russian Whites raised the specter of "one and indivisible" Russia, and affected not only the Bolshevik stand but Soviet-Polish relations. There began secret exchanges between the Soviet leaders and Piłsudski. Warsaw's repeated attempts to obtain a clarification of the Entente's attitude toward Russo-Polish issues largely failed, but some hope remained that Britain might be persuaded to cooperate with Poland. Piłsudski's Russian policy, although at times obscured by tactical considerations, remained unaltered: the chief of state continued his efforts to create accomplished facts. The Bolsheviks pursued a new version of the Brest-Litovsk policy of concessions in exchange for a respite. They assigned priority to a peaceful settlement with Poland—viewed as a "window to Europe"—over the question of the frontiers in the Belorussian-Lithuanian areas.

The first move had been made by Piłsudski. He took Wilno on his own initiative and the timing was due to domestic and international factors.* The swift Polish advance brought to light the bankruptcy of the Soviet regime in the Lithuanian-Belorussian Republic; peasant uprisings indicated hatred of the regime

* The sejm, which demanded an offensive in Eastern Galicia, had just gone into recess; Paderewski was in Paris; the first echelons of Haller's army which the Right wanted to use to enhance its own position began to arrive. See Józef Piłsudski, *Pisma zbiorowe* (10 vols.; Warsaw, 1937-38), VI, 109; Przybylski, *Wojna polska*, pp. 74-76. As for international aspects, the Commission on Polish Affairs in Paris indicated its preference for a strictly ethnic border for Poland, but reports reaching Warsaw suggested that the Peace Conference might change its attitude when confronted with a Polish *fait accompli*. See the report from attachés headquarters, March 19, 1919, Akta Adiutantury Generalnej Naczelnego Dowództwa, LV/519, Piłsudski Institute, New York (cited as AGND).

by the local population.[1] Wilno workers assisted the Polish troops; the people received them as liberators. While strategic reasons played a part in the move, the principal aim was political. Piłsudski viewed Wilno as the "key to Lithuanian-Belorussian affairs just as much as Warsaw is [the key] to Polish affairs."[2] Its seizure was not the end but the beginning of a campaign, and to quote Piłsudski again, "it placed the whole eastern question on the agenda."[3] But difficulties immediately arose. During the first three days Piłsudski tried to create another *fait accompli* by forming a government in Wilno which could become the center of attraction for Lithuania and Belorussia, and could prepare them for federation with Poland. He failed. The representatives of Poles, Lithuanians, and Belorussians were unwilling to commit themselves and looked for guidance to Warsaw, Kaunas, and Minsk. "I could not make them take any decision," Piłsudski wrote Paderewski.[4] He then decided on a second-best solution. On April 22 he issued a proclamation to the inhabitants of the former Grand Duchy of Lithuania—thus reviving the Jagiellonian tradition—promising a settlement of national, local, and religious issues according to the will of the population, and expressed without any violence or pressure on the part of the Polish side. Piłsudski proceeded to appoint a "Civilian Administration of the Eastern Lands" composed of natives and presided over by a local Pole, Jerzy Osmołowski.*

Piłsudski's proclamation did not determine the ultimate fate of Lithuania and Belorussia, and he made no legal engagements. He indicated his preference for a federalist solution, and morally committed himself to self-determination in the eastern borderlands.[5] His position occasioned an immediate showdown between the federalists and incorporationists. *Rząd i Wojsko,* after quoting with approval Piłsudski's proclamation and the orders issued by army commanders, wrote that since the Polish offensive meant war with Soviet Russia, the only worthy war aim was the liberation of Lithuania and application of the principle of self-determination.[6] The periodical asked the important question: "Will the sejm understand this great idea?"[7] Socialist and populist (Wyzwolenie) deputies certainly did, and emphasized in the sejm that war should not be for any other objective.[8] Paderewski telegraphed greetings to Piłsudski and his troops "in the old Lithuanian capital," asked for the text of the proclamation, and volun-

* Previously the Lithuanian and Belorussian areas were subject to military adminstration, and they were ruled by decrees jointly issued by the general staff and the Lithuanian-Belorussian department of the Ministry of Foreign Affairs in Warsaw.

teered to issue a manifesto to Lithuanians.[9] He shared Piłsudski's position, not only because of federalist leanings but also in general foreign policy.[10] Consequently, the premier clashed with Dmowski and his supporters.

The National Democrats and the Center parties attacked Piłsudski's Wilno proclamation, and asked if the government had approved it.[11] To them Wilno and its province with the large Polish population could not be treated as part of a separate entity—the former Grand Duchy—but as Polish territory. They strenuously opposed the Socialist idea that Polish troops should liberate eastern territories, proclaim them independent, and, only then, woo and persuade them to join a union with Poland. Areas with a predominantly Polish character were to be incorporated immediately.[12] Dmowski reasoned that Russia, a non-Bolshevik Russia of the future, might cede Lithuania and parts of Volhynia and Podolia to Poland, but she would never be reconciled to the grandiose plans of Polish federalists.[13]

The position of the National Democrats gained the approval of the majority of the sejm. A motion passed demanding the incorporation of Wilno and its surrounding region; and the sejm censured Piłsudski's proclamation as contrary to the resolution of April 4, 1919. A federalist motion of the Socialists was rejected.[14] Paderewski wired the marshal (speaker) of the sejm that such moves could produce "incalculable consequences" abroad, and asked that the whole matter be removed from the agenda until the premier's return from Paris. This, coupled with information that Poland was being accused of imperialist tendencies, had a sobering effect on the deputies. A new Socialist motion repudiating such accusations and calling for clarification of Polish eastern policy gained acceptance, although with some reservations of the Right. This shaky compromise "could not constitute a clear directive in the matter of foreign policy," commented one of Piłsudski's collaborators to Wasilewski.[15]

Upon his return to Poland Paderewski did his best to heal the breach. After discussions with leading politicians and members of the Foreign Affairs Committee,[16] he declared to the sejm on May 22 that Poland did "not oppose the self-determination and statehood of Lithuania and the Ukraine" and favored "the strivings of the Belorussian people for separate individual development." In the course of the ensuing debate the Left took the initiative, censuring chauvinism and imperialism in Poland, demanding not only self-determination for Lithuania and Belorussia, but also settlement with the Ukrainians in Eastern Galicia and recognition of a free Ukraine. The Right and Center showed restraint and

opposed only the last Socialist remarks. The sejm passed a resolution proposed by Grabski on behalf of the Foreign Affairs and
Military committees, stating that Poland would not annex unilaterally territories of the former Grand Duchy of Lithuania. The
sejm also reconciled its own resolution of April 4 with Piłsudski's
Wilno proclamation. It defeated a Socialist motion that favored
an independent Ukraine and proposed to leave borders of Eastern
Galicia undefined.[17]

The National Democrats, the most influential party of Poland,
thus agreed to a compromise solution, but they did not abandon
their own program. A month later, toward the end of June, a long
memorandum of Dmowski's National Committee in Paris in-
dicted the federalist position in unmistakable terms. It recalled
the Polish demands as presented to the Peace Conference, and
dealt with federalist criticism which it deemed unjustifiable and
confusing for the country. How could the National Democrats
simultaneously be imperialists and in favor of limited borders
in the east, the memorandum asked? The vague federalist program, it repeated, stood no chance of acceptance in Paris. Only
the argument that territories claimed in the east were Polish and
had to be incorporated could impress the Peace Conference and
the Russian Whites. All the talk about freeing "foreign" peoples
in the borderlands lessened the chances of a favorable territorial
settlement. The memorandum ended with a call for the unity of
Polish diplomacy, which in practice meant unreserved adoption
of Dmowski's theses.[18]

Piłsudski's program, as outlined on May 31, 1919 in a long
letter to Paderewski, indicated a completely different approach.
The chief of state noted that settlement of Poland's western
borders depended almost completely on the good will of the Allies.
Hence before a decision came "we must procrastinate in all other
matters in which we could come into conflict with the views of
the Entente." Once the conference made its decisions, Poland
"would become a first-rate force in the East with which everyone
not excluding the Entente would have to reckon." Piłsudski re-
gretted that domestic disagreements and political demagogy
already had caused some avenues to be closed; he would have
preferred more freedom of maneuver. Speaking of Polish policies
toward Eastern Galicia, the Ukraine, Lithuania, Belorussia, and
the Baltic countries, Piłsudski recalled the chief objectives of his
eastern policy: to prevent the acceptance of the idea that Great
Russia reach the Bug River (the old dividing line between the
Congress Kingdom and the Russian empire), and to propagate
the "union of all nations and peoples who live between us and

Russia proper with Poland and not with Russia, naturally on the basis of a federation."[19]

Here was the clearest formulation of Piłsudski's "great design," but how was it to be executed? The Right and Center opposed it, and their stand could only increase the border peoples' suspicion of Polish motives. Then there was Russia; and whether it was Red or White, Piłsudski's program endangered her position as a great power. Finally, the Allies had to agree. Those were formidable difficulties, and a closer examination makes them appear almost insurmountable.

To begin with the Lithuanians and Belorussians, Wilno was a key to their problems in the sense that it was both a historical center of the former Grand Duchy and a predominantly Polish city. Piłsudski meant to use it to attract ethnic Lithuania around Kaunas and Belorussian areas around Minsk into a combination with Poland—the local Poles becoming a consolidating factor. The incorporation of Wilno would defeat all chances of such a scheme. But would the new Lithuanian state, drunk with independence and nationalism, agree to a union with Poland? Would the politically immature Belorussians accept Polish guidance? Finally, would the Polish element in historic Lithuania appreciate the role it had to play and not antagonize the other two nationalities, ever suspicious and resentful of the privileged social position of the Poles? Finally the mainly Polish administration of the eastern territories would have to understand and execute its tasks.

The attitude of the ruling Lithuanian circles resembled that of Polish National Democrats. They opposed the re-creation of a historic Lithuania linked with Poland, and worked instead for a national state comprising Wilno and the western parts of Belorussia which could be assimilated and made Lithuanian.[20] Aware of their precarious position vis-à-vis Russia, Bolshevik or White, and suspicious of German machinations, the Lithuanians conducted protracted negotiations with Warsaw. But neither Piłsudski's threat that there were only two alternatives, union or Polish possession of Wilno, nor advantageous offers concerning the nature of federal ties made much headway. Even if the Poles committed some tactical errors the Lithuanians were intransigent.[21] Warsaw tried to force the issue by engineering a pro-Polish *Putsch* in Kaunas, but the scheme misfired.[22] The result was new acrimony and tension. Polish and Lithuanian troops stood separated by the Allied-approved Foch Line; but Piłsudski, who had been hesitant about the *Putsch*, opposed force not only because of the Entente but because he realized that aggression against Lithuania would kill the entire scheme of an eastern federation.[23]

While Lithuanian opposition to union with Poland undermined the federalist program, Belorussian issues created problems of a different kind. Here national aspirations were only awakening, and they mingled with the social demands of the peasantry. As a Polish intelligence report pointed out, "the Belorussian peasant can only be won over if it is shown in practice that Polish rule is not one of 'lords and magnates' but of a genuinely democratic and just authority."[24] Easier said than done. The administration of the eastern territories leaned heavily on local Poles, nationally conscious and reliable, many of whom shared the National Democratic program of incorporation and saw no reason to foster Belorussian nationalism. As a propertied class they were lukewarm toward social reform. Writing retrospectively, a prominent Pole from Lithuania asserted that "the chief mistake of the Polish groups in Lithuania and Belorussia was to treat these young, nascent nations as elements attached to the Polish nobleman's saddle, instead of adopting the stand of natives of these countries."[25] Many people realized it at the time and voiced severe criticism of the Polish administration in the northern borderlands.[26] Yet its position was difficult given the weakness of potential Belorussian partners and the competition of military authorities who often usurped prerogatives of a political character. An atmosphere of unreality surrounded the federalist program.

The Belorussians at first welcomed the entry of Polish troops and voiced approval of Piłsudski's proclamation. Such leaders as Vaclav Lastouski, Anton Lutskevich, Boleslaw Tarachkhevich took a pro-Polish line, and Piłsudski in a letter to Paderewski could claim that "the Belorussian government is on the Polish side."[27] But difficulties connected with the Lithuanian problem as well as local conditions made a genuine settlement impossible. Half-hearted attempts to organize self-government and encourage the formation of Belorussian detachments did not lead toward the creation of political organs. When the Poles captured Minsk on August 8, and Piłsudski addressed the inhabitants on September 19, he recalled his Wilno proclamation but indicated that things could not be rushed and that local administration represented the first step. "Later," he said, "the moment will come when you will be able to express yourselves freely on how your state will be organized." And he added that he would be proud when this country would "prove itself worthy of freedom."[28] Cautious words. And Belorussian leaders voiced complaints.[29] Piłsudski told Lutskevich that the time was not ready for raising the issue of independence and advised him to work for a "kind of Belorussian Piedmont." Only after clarification of Baltic and Ukrainian affairs would the Belorussian turn come. Piłsudski explained to the head of the civil administration that the new policy meant a retreat from supporting the council representing independent Belorussia and a move toward the encouragement of a local national council with restricted political authority.[30]

The application of a federalist program proved extremely difficult. No real partners had been found on the Lithuanian and Belorussian side; vested interests of local Poles hurt the scheme in practice; and military misrule raised opposition. By the autumn of 1919 the Poles had achieved "consolidation of borders and linking of the Lithuanian-Belorussian lands with Poland," but there was danger of bankruptcy of the entire federalist approach.[31]

Lithuanian-Belorussian issues formed the northern wing of Polish eastern policy; questions of Eastern Galicia and the Ukraine were its southern counterparts. As mentioned, Socialist deputies had made several references to Ukrainian problems during the Wilno debate in late April, and *Rząd i Wojsko* pointed out that Piłsudski's proclamation was also applicable to Kiev. National Democrats feared that federalist experiments in Wilno might be repeated in Eastern Galicia and would endanger the Polish possession of Lwów. Indeed there were some analogies but also striking differences between the situations in the north and south. With few exceptions, federalists and incorporationists were for the inclusion of Lwów and Eastern Galicia in the Polish state. Their ways parted with regard to a policy toward the Ukraine proper, i.e., the Ukrainian People's Republic. Piłsudski and the federalists favored recognition of and cooperation with the Ukraine, hoping to bring it within Polish sphere of influence. Dmowski and his supporters claimed the western fringes of the country and showed disinterest in the ultimate fate of the Ukrainian nation. The question of Eastern Galicia (Western Ukrainian Republic)—loosely linked with the Ukrainian People's Republic—did not constitute the same kind of impediment to Polish-Ukrainian cooperation as did Wilno between Kaunas and Warsaw. But it caused difficulties.

Then there were international complications. Because Galicia formerly had been part of Austrian and not Russian state territory the Paris Peace Conference had every right to settle its fate without the participation of Russia. But peacemakers in Paris were well aware of Russian interest in Eastern Galicia and took it into consideration. The fighting between Poles and Ukrainians in this area appeared prejudicial to a front against the Bolsheviks, and Paris attempted to impose a cease-fire. Poles rejected those attempts which favored Ukrainians, claiming that only Polish military control of the province could assure a continuous eastern front. Even if these assertions were sometimes exaggerated they were not without foundation.* Ukrainians countered with accusations that the Polish offensive against them prevented Eastern Galician aid to Petliura's People's Republic, then locked in struggle with the Bolsheviks. Petliura himself advised an armistice even on terms favorable to the Poles in order to remedy this situation.[32] To him Russia was the primary enemy, against whom all efforts had to be made; for Galician Ukrainians the Poles constituted the main danger.

An odd military and political situation developed. Petliura's forces, facing both the Bolsheviks and the Poles, concentrated in June on their eastern front. Their rear on the Polish side, after some clashes, remained undisturbed. Farther south the Eastern Galician troops proceeded to launch an important offensive westward, against the Poles. At one point a brief armistice with the Bolsheviks took place. Yet both Ukrainian armies were theoretically part of a common command. Relations between Eastern Galicia and Poland were those between two belligerents, but contacts existed between Warsaw and Petliura.

On May 24, 1919 a delegate from the Ukrainian foreign ministry of Petliura, Boris Kurdynovsky, signed a political agreement with Paderewski, stating that Ukrainian interests could best be assured by close union with Poland. Therefore the Ukrainian People's Republic, although not authorized to resolve the Eastern Galician question, renounced all rights to the province, as well as to parts of western Volhynia. In exchange Poland engaged to acknowledge the right of the Ukraine to independence, on condition of the establishment of a Ukrainian government recognized by Poland. The Poles further promised military assistance to such a Ukrainian government; duration of the stay of Polish troops in the Ukraine was to be fixed by common accord. Other articles provided for guarantees of rights and property of Ukrainians in Poland, and of Poles in the Ukraine, and for a military convention.[33] This far-reaching agreement was premature and the Ukrainians repudiated it. But it did indicate a line of development which would lead to close cooperation between Piłsudski and Petliura.

Late in June 1919 the Peace Conference authorized a Polish military advance to the river Zbrucz (the eastern border of Galicia) and the establishment of a civil administration there. The decision was based upon strategic considerations and did not prejudice

* On April 22, 1919 Lenin wrote Vatsetis that "An advance into a part of Galicia and Bukovina was essential for establishing contact with Soviet Hungary." See *The Trotsky Papers 1917-1922*, ed. Jan. M. Meijer (London, The Hague, Paris, 1964—), I, 374-375.

the future settlement of the province. The British felt strongly that Eastern Galicia ought eventually to be linked with Russia, a non-Bolshevik Russia of course.[34] The chances for a non-Bolshevik Russian state appeared bright in the spring and summer of 1919. Admiral Aleksandr V. Kolchak's drive, begun in early March, brought his armies to the upper Volga basin. Denikin's volunteer army started its rapid advance in May. The forces of Yudenich stood just outside Petrograd. Apart from the obvious threat to the Bolshevik rule, the successes of the Whites appeared ominous to the Ukraine and other nationalities of the former tsarist empire, and to Poland as well. As the American ambassador reported from Paris, the aim of the Whites was reconstitution of "one and indivisible" Russia "except possibly Poland and Finland, whose independence is accepted in principle but questioned in boundary."[35] The Poles were fully aware of this.[36]

The Entente had misgivings about the political tactics of the Whites, which were bound to antagonize the border states and preclude cooperation against the Bolsheviks. In late May the Peace Conference addressed a note to Kolchak laying down the conditions for Allied recognition and further support, including repayment of tsarist debts, summoning of a constituent assembly, recognition of Finnish and Polish independence, autonomy of the Baltic provinces and of Caucasian and Transcaspian territories. The Ukraine significantly enough was not mentioned. Kolchak's reply of June 4, 1919 was evasive. The Whites were not eager to make binding promises to nationalities, nor did they in practice respect the rights of nationalities. This lack of respect prompted a memorandum by representatives of the Baltic and Caucasian nationalities supported by Poland.[37] Warsaw sabotaged the formation of a common anti-Bolshevik front at Riga and, when a conflict developed between Latvia and the White forces of P. M. Bermondt-Avalov, offered help to the Latvians.[38]

While the signing of the Treaty of Versailles on June 28, 1919 relieved Poland of western worries and permitted transfer of troops to the east, Warsaw showed little interest in an anti-Bolshevik crusade. To assist the Whites would mean endangering the entire Polish eastern program, and the attitude of the Entente indicated that Russian interests would receive priority over Polish claims.* It is true that the Right still hoped for Russo-Polish reconciliation under the aegis of the Entente, but the Left and the Piłsudskiites were vociferous against cooperation with Kol-

---

* Article 87 of the Treaty of Versailles invoked Russian consent for the reestablishment of Poland, and subordinated any future settlement to Russian agreement.

chak. "Kolchak and Trotsky," wrote *Rząd i Wojsko,* on August 17, "are two enemies equally dangerous, and Poland has no right today to conclude an alliance with either of them." Piłsudski shared this point of view, and the continuing eastward advance of Polish troops was not meant to assist the Whites.[39] As Denikin commented, "the Polish invasion of Russia was never motivated either openly or secretly by a struggle against the Soviet government."[40]

Warsaw had to play a subtle game. It was interested in Petliura's overtures—the Ukrainian leader wrote Piłsudski on August 9, 1919 to propose cooperation—but could not openly defy the Entente, which demanded that the Poles press Petliura into collaboration with Denikin.[41] The Ministry of Foreign Affairs hastily explained to Paris that Poland had not officially recognized the Ukraine, that Petliura's renunciation of Eastern Galicia was a unilateral engagement, and that the purpose was to coordinate an anti-Bolshevik campaign in the south.[42] This was not the whole truth, and an important Polish memorandum advocated military infiltration in the Ukraine—under the pretext of combating the Bolsheviks—amnesty for Ukrainians in Galicia, and a "most active policy in the Ukraine."[43]

Meanwhile, events were driving Petliura more and more into the arms of Poland. Denikin took Kiev on August 30, and adopted an unfriendly attitude toward Ukrainian national aspirations. Only the Eastern Galician contingent agreed to cooperate with the Whites, which contributed to further estrangement between Petliura and the Galician leaders. Petliura on September 1 was able to sign an official armistice with the Poles, delayed so far by the Eastern Galician complications. The Polish Supreme Command noted with satisfaction the rapprochement with the Ukrainian People's Republic, although it was realistic enough to stress that "dire necessity and not a sincere desire for agreement has brought the Ukrainian mission to Warsaw."[44]

Allied pressure and the victories of the Whites in Russia forced Warsaw to make some overtures to Denikin. The Poles in July decided to send military and diplomatic missions to White Army headquarters, but they delayed matters until autumn. Warsaw was mainly intrested in learning Denikin's real attitude toward Poland and Ukrainian independence; genuine cooperation seemed possible only in the unlikely event of Denikin's recognition of Polish eastern aspirations.[45] Failing that, the Poles would have to consider the question raised by the Polish undersecretary of state in a letter to Paderewski: "whether we should continue fighting the Bolsheviks or sign peace with them."[46] This was a crucial question indeed, and the months to come indicated that it was difficult to resolve.

The initial Bolshevik reaction to Piłsudski's capture of Wilno was violent. Although not entirely unexpected, the swiftness of the Polish advance surprised the Soviet leadership.[47] Lenin urged the High Command and the Command of the Western Front to recapture the city, because with its fall "the Entente became even more impudent."[48] Bolshevik propaganda made efforts to ascribe the defeat to Polish treachery and to treasonable behavior of people in Wilno. Anger mingled with embarrassment about the collapse of the Soviet regime in Lithuania and Belorussia, later giving rise to recriminations between the Cheka and Mickiewicz-Kapsukas.[49] Because several ranking Communists fell into Polish hands, Moscow rearrested the luckless members of the former Regency mission and took several hundred hostages among prominent Poles in Russia. Mickiewicz-Kapsukas represented this move as retaliation against outrages allegedly perpetrated by Polish troops in Belorussian-Lithuanian territory. Warsaw issued a condemnation of the Soviet practice of taking hostages and proposed to exchange them for Communists arrested by Poland. Chicherin expressed agreement in a long note of June 3, which contained vehement denunciation of Polish aggressiveness and brutality.[50] But the bellicose tone of the Soviet note was not a prelude to a formal declaration of war on Poland. Quite the contrary. Moscow had no intention at this moment of waging a full-scale campaign on her western front.

The increasing internal danger stemming from the Whites dictated general Soviet strategy toward Poland. As the commander-in-chief put it, "A victory for us on the southern and eastern fronts will deliver into the hands of the Soviet regime the entire territory of the former Russian Empire, and hence a temporary reverse on the western front will not be reflected in the final result."[51] Thus the anti-Polish front—at this time of secondary importance—was to be barely covered, and the Polish danger allayed by peaceful overtures. The initiative for peace belonged to the Polish Communist, Julian Marchlewski.

The story of Marchlewski's first contacts in Warsaw is involved. In the spring of 1919, presumably around the middle of March, he came secretly to Warsaw and held talks with Undersecretary of State Józef Beck (then spelled Bek), and Stanisław Wojciechowski. He apparently influenced some of the PPS leaders.[52] Acting in agreement with a leading Polish Communist, Adolf Warski, Marchlewski offered his services to bring about an understanding between Poland and the Soviets, his main argument being that a White Russia constituted a mortal danger to both.[53] An important article in *Robotnik*, allegedly inspired by Marchlewski, showed that the Polish Left shared this point of view.[54]

This was not true of the Polish Communists in Russia. Marchlewski ran into stiff opposition from his comrades, who considered a suspension of hostilities and secret negotiations as prejudicial to the cause of the revolution in Poland. At best they could accept open talks which might have an "agitation advantage." Leszczyński insisted that revolutionary strategy may require the occupation of areas where Communism could hardly win by itself—"either the Red Army would support it or the Polish [army] would squash it" he said. Representing Lenin's point of view, Marchlewski countered with the argument that at this moment the entry of the Red Army would be "fatal for Communism in Poland." Besides, Bolshevik weakness precluded the possibility of a military advance.*

Backed by Lenin, Marchlewski's initiative prevailed, and on July 2, 1919 Chicherin wired Warsaw to suggest a resumption of talks concerning Polish refugees in Russia, interrupted by Więckowski's expulsion from Moscow. The note, calculated as always to achieve propagandistic effects—the commissar contrasted the Soviet humanitarian attitude with Polish indifference to human rights—was followed two days later by a radiogram that Kujawski (the pseudonym of Marchlewski) would be on the front line on July 10. The Poles acknowledged receipt of the message in a letter which stressed that the initiative had come from Soviet Russia.[55]

Talks betwen Marchlewski and Więckowski, joined later by Michał S. Kossakowski (Osmołowski's presence is uncertain), began about July 20 in a hunting lodge in the Białowieża forest. They lasted for about ten days. The Soviet representative submitted a proposal from his government to negotiate an agreement about hostages, refugees, exchange of prisoners, and related matters, on condition that it be through "official channels" and embodied in "formal conventions." It was obvious that Moscow once again was primarily interested in diplomatic relations and wanted to commit Warsaw to a recognition of the Soviet regime. On July 30 Marchlewski proposed a meeting of the delegates of the Polish and Russian Red Crosses on Polish-occupied territory to settle

* For the discussion among Polish Communists in Moscow and Minsk in June 1919 see Weronika Gostyńska. "Rola Juliana Marchlewskiego w tajnych rokowaniach polsko-radzieckich (czerwiec-lipiec 1919r.), *Z Pola Walki*, 9 (1966), 301-304. It may be significant that in July 1919 the Western Division became simply the 52nd Infantry Division, and its regiments dropped their Polish names.

the matter of hostages by abolishing the *usus* altogether. The meeting would also discuss the application of the Geneva Convention (ratified by Poland but not by Russia), protection of prisoners and refugees, and similar problems. Both interested governments were to give their approval by August 15.

These proposals were an overture to political discussion, and Marchlewski expressed disappointment when told by Więckowski that Poland could not treat with a government that was taking hostages.[56] The Bolshevik emissary said he had "expected something more." Surely hostages were "a trifle easy to settle," and he had been "empowered by Lenin to conduct far-reaching negotiations in the matter of peace." Polish delegates sensed that Moscow "would have gladly talked about a provisional demarcation line, even a final frontier with Poland."[57] Further remarks of Marchlewski confirmed this feeling. The Soviet envoy spoke openly, and assured the Poles that Lenin told him that "If the Poles have the intention of holding a plebiscite in Lithuania and Belorussia, we would not split over the way it would be conducted, nor would we split over the fate of Belorussia." Marchlewski made no bones about Soviet reasons for such concessions. First, the Bolsheviks needed a respite on the western front to concentrate against Denikin, and they feared lest the Poles give way to Allied pressure and cooperate with the Whites. Second, while Marchlewski admitted that a "bourgeois" plebiscite would yield anti-Soviet results, this would be merely a temporary defeat. All Europe would turn Communist in five years' time, and besides, "bourgeois Poland will never be able to maintain its rule over these Belorussian peasants." A Soviet republic would emerge in the contested territories sooner or later.

Marchlewski's political overtures stemmed from long-range expectations of a Communist victory, and reflected the temporary predicament of the Red Army. In early August Stalin painted a black picture of the western front. The Sixteenth Army was in retreat and demoralized, and there was a danger of its disintegration. While a month earlier he had believed that one Soviet division could have taken Baranowicze (Baranovichi) and Mołodeczno, now one division was not sufficient to hold the Borisov-Bobruisk-Mozyr line.[58] The Soviet position was critical.

The Białowieża talks ended without any Polish commitments, and Marchlewski wrote later that he had been given to understand that the time was not yet ready for diplomatic negotiation. Still, doors were open for further talks, because Piłsudski had consented to the proposed meeting of Red Cross delegations. Polish participants at Białowieża differed in their appraisals. Więckowski opined that peace with the Bolsheviks, or at least efforts in this direction that took the form of unofficial agreements, would not harm Poland's interests. Kossakowski disagreed. The vice-minister for foreign affairs thought that peace would be premature, given the attitude of the Entente, but he was vaguely pleased with the Białowieża exchanges. Piłsudski's attitude was of course decisive, and he stated his position in a long conversation with Kossakowski. Speaking about the possibility of peace he declared: "Let us imagine for a moment that I have concluded peace with them. I must demobilize the army . . . And then I will become powerless at the border. Lenin will be able to do what he wants because he will not hesitate to break even the most solemn word. I told Kujawski [Marchlewski] when he explained to me the possibility of reaching agreement with the Soviet government that I fully believe in the possibility of agreement about the borders but I doubt whether the Soviet government will agree to our conditions of a complete closing of the borders for export and propaganda. He grew silent and did not answer me."[59]

Piłsudski explained why he feared peace, but his mention of a conversation with Marchlewski was puzzling. When did such a conversation take place? Piłsudski did not elaborate, and he went on to speak about his war aims. He said that the Polish army could march on Moscow. But what then? One must have clear objectives, and Piłsudski defined them as "accomplishing great things in the East, taking the place of Russia but under different watchwords." He said that "we have such invaluable moments, such a splendid opportunity" and "we hesitate."

It is obvious that the chief of state alluded here again to his "great design," but realized that he had to move cautiously because of the Entente and the domestic situation. He was willing to probe deeper into Bolshevik thinking through the forthcoming conference of Red Cross delegates, and at the same time to try and obtain clarification of the stand of the Entente. An intricate diplomatic game began, and internal Polish divisions—the Left spoke of peace and federalism, the Right approved of a war coordinated with the great powers but devoid of federalist aims— obscured some of Warsaw's maneuvers.

On September 14, 1919 Paderewski had a long talk with Lloyd George, and the next day he addressed the Council of the Heads of Governments in Paris. The Polish premier stated that he was "anxious to learn the view of the Allies with respect to Russia." If they favored peace Warsaw wanted to be informed because "very advantageous terms of peace" had been made by the Bolsheviks. Polish territorial ambitions in the east "had been fulfilled" and the Poles could not fight on indefinitely without knowing what they were fighting for. If the Allies opposed peace then the Polish army could, with equipment and financial aid, march on Moscow with half a million men.[60]

The motive of Paderewski's startling proposal was not absolutely clear. He asserted later that he sought Allied permission to make peace, which he then wanted to impose on the Polish Right.[61] But what were the Bolshevik offers he mentioned? Did he have in mind the alleged feelers of Chicherin transmitted in the spring by Więckowski, Marchlewski's overtures, or some direct proposals which he was said to have received from Lenin?[62]

Insofar as Paderewski's demarche aimed to force the Allied hand it corresponded to Piłsudski's thinking, and it had been approved by him.[63] The premier's initial talk with Lloyd George was also in accord with Piłsudski's plan to concentrate efforts on Britain. The Polish minister there reported that while London had no definite Russian policy it wanted to devise one and was considering Polish federalist plans.[64] Piłsudski wished to impress on the Allies "the idea of combating Russian anarchy by stages, by detaching from Russia those non-Russian territories already fed up with Communism," and he sought to approach London.[65] Probably Paderewski's alternative of a march on Moscow embodied the idea of a complete reconstruction of Russia by Poland, with British blessing and cooperation. Be that as it may, the council refused to approve either course. Clemenceau opposed a march on Moscow on the grounds that it would mobilize all Russians against Poland; Lloyd George opposed it because of the immense cost. As for peace, the French premier offered the dubious advice that he "would not make peace nor would he make war," while Marshal Foch asserted that Poland's "true role" was "to provide a barrier on the one side against Bolshevism, and on the other against Germany."[66]

The German problem, mentioned by Foch, worried Entente statesmen. The activity of German troops in the Baltic countries raised suspicions, and a British Foreign Office expert said that "it would be better that Petrograd should not be captured at all than it should be captured by the Germans." The Poles agreed wholeheartedly, or may have even inspired this remark by constant warnings against German infiltration of Russia.[67] The council, rejecting Paderewski's proposals, toyed with the idea of using Polish troops to dislodge the Germans from the Baltic countries. The Polish premier expressed willingness and remarked that Warsaw must not be held responsible if people in eastern areas liberated by Poles should declare themselves for Poland. This may have been a reference to Lithuania, and the Allied statesmen passed the observation in silence. The whole scheme was dropped the next day, as creating too much danger of a German-Polish and a Lithuanian-Polish conflict.

Paderewski's initiative in Paris produced no results. If anything it revealed British hesitancies and French hopes for the success of Denikin. This was the time of Denikin's great advance on Moscow, and the French were not going to give the Poles a free hand in Russia to the detriment of the White leader. Polish military action and the problem of the eastern borders were subordinated to the interests of a future non-Bolshevik Russia. Should the latter prevail, a Polish diplomat wrote gloomily to Piłsudski, "Poland might be reduced in size to something resembling the Duchy of Warsaw."[68] Such fears were not groundless. The final report of the Commission on Polish Affairs, submitted on September 25, after recommending a provisional eastern boundary (coinciding once more with the division between Congress Kingdom and Russia) stressed the cooperation of a future regular Russian government which was "necessary to the definite determination" of such a boundary.[69] The Entente was unprepared to recognize in advance Poland's rights to any territory contested by Russians.

Under such circumstances the Poles had to establish some contact with Denikin, if only to demonstrate that their policy was not at complete variance with that of the Entente. General Karnicki's mission left for Denikin's headquarters at Taganrog; G. N. Kutepov received an *agrément* as the unofficial Russian representative in Warsaw. The Whites took pains to show cordiality to the Poles, but it was evident that their respective views were irreconcilable.[70] Denikin wrote to Piłsudski protesting the slowdown of the Polish offensive against the Bolsheviks and objecting to Polish rule in "Russian lands."[71] Even after Denikin sustained serious military defeats, the Whites still considered that the Poles could assist them by handing over to Denikin the gubernia of Vitebsk, Mohilev, Minsk, Wilno, Volhynia, Podolia, and part of Suwałki—most of the areas conquered from the Bolsheviks. Not only Belorussians but Lithuanians, Estonians, and Latvians were considered Russian subjects.[72] No wonder that Piłsudski treated exchanges with White Russians as purely formal talks and had no intention to proceed to negotiation.[73] Nor was he prepared to assist them militarily. Orders went out to the POW command in Kiev to support Petliura, oppose Denikin politically, and undertake no operation against the Bolsheviks to the advantage of the White general. Similar instructions allegedly were received by some commanders on the Bolshevik front.[74] General Tadeusz Rozwadowski recommended to the Supreme Command on September 24 that it would be best to wait until the Bolsheviks had defeated Denikin and then rout them in turn. He felt that during this second phase the Entente would have to reckon with Polish interests.[75]

Fighting had almost come to a standstill on the eastern front, and although the Poles explained it by technical difficulties it was clear they had no intention of fighting for the Whites. Talks in Taganrog—the *pourparlers fictifs* as Denikin later described them —were largely for the benefit of the Entente, particularly Britain, because Warsaw's concern was for cooperation with London on the Russian question.

The large-scale peace campaign waged by the Socialists in Poland played into the hands of the government, which used it as an argument to bring Britain closer to Poland. The government inspired an article in *Kurjer Poranny* on September 23, 1919, which discussed at length the pressure of public opinion in favor of peace. The newspaper stated that Bolshevism was imperialism in disguise and that Poland, by defending herself, also protected the West. If the West gave no help "we will be forced to end the war." Paderewski told the British envoy that the Socialists attacked his cabinet on the grounds that it did all the fighting for the Entente but received no support. What is more, Britain was systematically blocking Polish aspirations everywhere. Paderewski said that although he opposed Socialist reasoning his position was difficult. He repeated what he had already said in Paris—that he had advantageous peace offers from the Bolsheviks, and that Poland could realize all her aspirations in the east. The British diplomat replied that Britain "could not do everything for everybody," but simultaneously he advised against peace, mainly because of the Russian Whites.[76] It was hard to make the British see the Russian situation through Polish eyes.

The peace campaign in Poland was genuine enough, even if the Socialists used it to outbid the Communists in peace slogans.[77] Many groups in the country wondered what the Poles were fighting for. On September 24 Kossakowski noted in his diary: "Where are we going? This question intrigues not only the [Socialist] *Robotnik* but everybody ... To the Dnieper, to Dvina, and then? What then? Peace with the Bolsheviks? Perhaps." The Piłsudskiite *Kurjer Poranny* on August 10, 1919 had already repeated the Socialist phrase, "We shall not be a policeman of the West," but this was a negative formula. Did the Polish government have clear war aims which reflected the wishes of the people?

The rift between the federalist Left and incorporationist Right was still much in evidence. Paderewski's report to the cabinet and to the Foreign Affairs Committee of his experiences in Paris, revealed it clearly.[78] Impressed by the pro-Russian stand of the Entente, Paderewski showed himself critical of the armistice with Petliura. In addition, he criticized federalist ideas as lofty but impractical. Poles had to recognize that the Entente wanted a regenerated Russia and make the best of it. Paderewski told the cabinet that he expected advice from Lloyd George, and it was evident that he was worried by the turn of events and counted on Britain to help Warsaw. Sir Horace Rumbold reported that Poles "do not want to face a re-constitued Russia alone" and seek support "of a liberal power such as Great Britain."[79]

Piłsudski was skeptical of Denikin's chances, and reports from the mission at Taganrog fortified his belief that the Whites would never reach Moscow.[80] The chief of state did not approach the British from a position of weakness. He did not view them as protectors of Poland vis-à-vis a White Russia, but as partners in remaking Russia after the collapse of the counterrevolutionary armies. As the Polish minister in London put it, a defeat of Yudenich and Denikin was "a condition *sine qua non* of cooperation between Poland and England."[81] Such cooperation was to have economic advantages for Britain, and the Poles tried to offer their services as middlemen for future infiltration of Russian markets.[82] Though Rumbold may not have perceived all the nuances of Polish diplomacy he observed and reported to London that "Chief of the State and M. Paderewski do not see eye to eye."[83] This was certainly the case.

While the Poles watched the struggle between Denikin and the Bolsheviks and maneuvered to gain Britain over to the Polish point of view, Soviet diplomacy was far from idle. Moscow, like Warsaw, realized that Britain held the key position, and Russian diplomatic moves were aimed, although indirectly, at a future understanding with the British.

In a long memorandum to the Central Committee Trotsky speculated about the chances of revolution in Europe. He reached the conclusion that the situation had altered greatly from the early months of 1919. At that time, he wrote, the Bolsheviks controlled much of the Baltic region; "in Poland, as it appeared, the revolution was developing at a rapid pace"; Communists triumphed in Hungary and bid for power in Germany. Now things were different, and Moscow, after victory over the Whites, ought to turn to the East. The road to Paris and London led through Afghanistan, Punjab, and Bengal. Under such circumstances the "White Guard countries on our western periphery can establish a 'cover' for the time being" and add to Russia's safety.[84]

Irrespective of whether Trotsky's observations accorded with views of Lenin and other Bolshevik leaders, his remarks about the Baltic countries were realistic enough. It was perfectly obvious that Soviet Russia, waging a desperate struggle against Denikin and Kolchak, could not at the same time "prevent the Entente from establishing several bourgeois republics on our western frontier," as Chicherin expressed it.[85] Whether eventually useful as buffer states or not, the latter had to be neutralized. Peace offers to the Baltic countries would carry several other advantages. Moscow wanted to dispel the fears of their bourgeoisie, peasants, and workers that the Russians threatened the national independence of Finland, Estonia, Latvia, and Lithuania. The Bolsheviks counted also on the effect which peace treaties with these countries would have on Poland, the Ukraine of Petliura, and the Caucasus. Last but not least, talks with Estonia, which proved easiest, appeared as a prelude to future compromise with England. This was a "rehearsal," to borrow Chicherin's phrase, for negotiations with London, and the Bolsheviks hoped to appeal to British economic interests.[86]

The Soviet peace offensive toward the Baltic countries began in late July 1919 with assurances that the Red Army would not cross the border of the former gubernia of Estland. On August 31 Moscow addressed a note to Estonia recognizing her independence and frontiers; four days later the Tallinn government responded with a cautious agreement to negotiation. Soviet peace proposals to Finland, Latvia and Lithuania followed on September 22. Thus Allied reluctance to recognize officially the Baltic states—for fear of offending the Whites and prejudicing the cause of "one and indivisible" Russia—played into Bolshevik hands. Their peace offensive undermined chances of a future co-ordinated action of Poland and other border states against Soviet Russia. No wonder Chicherin termed the negotiations with Estonia "a turning point of our foreign policy in which the incomparable elasticity and political realism of Vladimir Ilich manifested itself."[87] Would renewed Soviet peace offers to Poland at the forthcoming conference of the Red Cross delegates crown the Bolshevik diplomatic edifice by neutralizing the largest and most important country on the western borders of Russia? Time was to provide an answer.

Nearly three and a half months separated the Białowieża exchanges from the meeting of Red Cross delegates in the forlorn railroad station at Mikaszewicze (Mikachevichi). These three months had been spent in fierce fighting between the Red Army and Denikin and in intricate diplomatic maneuvers by Poles and

Russians alike. Now the time had come for a confrontation of Soviet and Polish views and ideas.

In late August Moscow informed Warsaw that it agreed to a meeting, and because it was to be held on Polish territory Moscow demanded guarantees of safety for envoys, together with freedom of communication.. The Poles wired their agreement at the beginning of September, and it appears that technical difficulties and general political considerations were responsible for the subsequent delay.[88] In late September the Polish general staff proposed Mikaszewicze as the meeting place, and the command of the Lithuanian-Belorussian Front suggested October 10, 1919 as the opening date.

Warsaw was in no hurry to begin the talks. It was decided that the Red Cross mission be headed by Kossakowski, who had participated in the Białowieża meeting, and that he receive credentials from the ministries of war and the interior but not from the ministry of foreign affairs "because the Polish government should not enter into any official relations with the Soviet government."[89] On October 3 Piłsudski received Kossakowski and gave him instructions. The chief of state emphasized the need to settle first the matter of hostages, which he treated as a test of Soviet good will. In answer to Kossakowski's question on how to approach political matters, Piłsudski declared: "What we have taken we shall never give back. You can even mention the borders of 1772 and our determination to give the people [the right] of determining their own fate."

Piłsudski felt the general situation had altered greatly since the Białowieża exchanges, and that a more aggressive group in Russia led by Trotsky and Dzierżyński had gained the uper hand. One could talk meaningfully with Marchlewski, Leonid Krasin or Sverdlow, but not with diehard Polish Communists like Bobiński or Leszczyński. The chief of state intimated that, depending on the person heading the Soviet Red Cross delegation, he might choose a man "who could make contact with them and explain certain things in confidential talks." Piłsudski mentioned as a possible candidate the old Socialist Bronisław Ziemięcki, because Więckowski had died suddenly in September.[90]

Meanwhile the Bolsheviks were getting ready for the encounter. The Polish bureau of the Central Committee of the RKP(b) informed the president of the Russian Red Cross that a conference would be held with Poles which would "have officially a Red Cross character." The bureau had decided, together with the Narkomindel, that Marchlewski would lead the delegation, and asked for a Red Cross expert to deal with technical matters.

Credentials issued to Marchlewski consisted of papers from the
Soviet Red Cross empowering him to negotiate with the Poles,
and authorization from the Commissariat for Foreign Affairs.
There were also secret credentials signed by Chicherin. This
last document stated that Marchlewski, representing the Russian
Red Cross Society, was empowered "to conduct negotiations with
the representatives of the Polish government on all questions
that have arisen or may arise between the Polish Republic and
the Russian Socialist Federated Soviet Republic, and to ascertain
in general and in detail the basis of an agreement which could
guarantee peaceful relations" between the two countries.[91]

The Mikaszewicze conference began on October 11, 1919, and
it lasted until December 15.[92] Except for Marchlewski neither
delegation comprised important political figures. Kossakowski
reported to Warsaw that this might mean that Soviet Russia
"while desiring at all cost to conclude peace with Poland, absolutely disbelieves the possibility of beginning negotiations with
her at the present moment." The Polish delegate thought that
Chicherin treated the conference as a concession to Marchlewski,
who wanted to try peace negotiations, and that the commissar
was not hopeful of the result. "The *idée fixe* of the Bolsheviks,"
Kossakowski wrote Warsaw, "is the alleged alliance between
Poland and Denikin." Marchlewski showed his disappointment
in not finding Więckowski (of whose death he was unware) on the
Polish delegation, and he wondered why the Poles wanted to
talk about such trifles as hostages while there was a chance to
liquidate the source of it all—namely war itself. After some
hesitation the Bolshevik emissary handed to Kossakowski a copy
of his secret credentials and asked that they be sent to Warsaw.*

Formal negotiations started only on October 27, the sixteen-
day delay resulting from the Polish demand for credentials for
Marchlewski empowering him to sign binding agreements on
hostages. During this period both sides engaged in informal
conversation centering on political issues. The Poles gathered that
Moscow ascribed the sending of the Red Cross mission to Mikaszewicze to pressure of the workers' councils in Poland, practically
nonexistent at this time. Marchlewski also told them that Russia
had given up the idea of Communism conquering the world, or
Europe, or even Poland. He stated that he had made unequivocal
peace proposals during his Białowieża visit, but "the silence of
the Polish government was clearly a negative reply." He reiterated
Russian disinterest in Lithuania and Belorussia, and went so far

---

* Strangely enough, Kossakowski, who read the credentials, wrote that they were
signed by Lenin and not Chicherin.

as to state that in the Soviet-Polish conflict "territorial questions do not exist, and Poland will receive what she wants." Kossakowski felt—and this was a change from his attitude after Białowieża—that the moment was propitious for peace with the Bolsheviks, but he had no powers for political negotiation.

In mid-October two officers arrived from Warsaw and took some part in the informal talks. The first, Lieutenant Mieczysław Birnbaum from intelligence, was an ex-SDKPiL member, and he came to probe possibilities of political understanding with the Bolsheviks.[93] The second, Captain Ignacy Boerner, was a confidant of Piłsudski. He began a series of visits to Mikaszewicze on which he reported directly to the chief of state. In the course of conversations Marchlewski told Birnbaum that a Soviet-Polish cease-fire was possible without formal conventions. He also agreed that in future peace negotiations Russians (as for instance Sverdlov or Krasin) rather than Polish Communists ought to represent the Soviet side.

On October 26, 1919, when Marchlewski received his new credentials signed by Lenin and Lev Karakhan, the conference was able to begin officially.[94] The Soviet delegate on October 28,[95] submitted a declaration expressing the intention to abolish, on the basis of reciprocity, the practice of taking hostages—an important move designed to satisfy preliminary Polish demands, as stressed several times by Kossakowski in talks with Marchlewski. While great differences in interpretation remained, it was possible on November 2 to arrive at a formal agreement, followed a week later by a more detailed arrangement. These agreements on hostages, refugees, and other related issues fulfilled Piłsudski's condition that political talks could only begin after the Bolsheviks had demonstrated their good will. The chief of state, on November 3, summoned Captain Boerner and instructed him to communicate in Piłsudski's name the following seven points to Marchlewski as the representative of the Soviet government:

1. The chief of state will not order Polish troops to advance beyond the line they occupied at that moment.*

2. He advises the Soviet government, in order to avoid all misunderstanding, to establish a neutral zone 10 kilometers wide by withdrawing its troops along the front, except for a sector on the Dvina which could be neutralized if the Russians proposed to exchange prisoners through Polotsk.

3. If the Latvians demand that the Russians abandon Dünaburg (Daugavpils, Dvinsk), Piłsudski will support their demand,

* It was defined as running from Novogrod Volynskii (Zviahel), through Olevsk, along Ptich, Bobruisk, Beresina and its canal, to Dvina.

and he counsels the Soviet government to hand over that city to Latvia, by which act it will contribute to peace.

4. He demands categorically that the Soviet government stop all Communist agitation in the Polish army, warning that in places where it continues the Polish troops will advance.

5. He demands that the Bolsheviks do not attack Petliura.

6. He declares that he does not believe in the Soviet government's ability to maintain secrecy and warns that he will take appropriate measures in case of indiscretion on the Soviet's part.

7. He will await the effect of the preceding statement and, if the Soviet government fulfills points 2, 4, and 5, he will send a delegate to Moscow with credentials (to be shown to Marchlewski alone) to communicate all points in Piłsudski's mesage personally to Lenin. Finally, Piłsudski ordered Boerner to tell Marchlewski in his own (Boerner's) name that Poland "is not and does not want to be the gendarme of Europe." Poland "wants to, and will, look solely and exclusively after her own interests. The determinant of her policy can only be the exigencies of Poland's *raison d'état*. The support of Denikin in his struggle against the Bolsheviks cannot be Poland's *raison d'état*." Boerner was to add that a Polish offensive toward Soviet-held Mozyr could have assisted Denikin, perhaps decisively, yet the Poles had not undertaken it. Should this not open the eyes of the Bolsheviks?[96]

Captain Boerner conveyed Piłsudski's message to Marchlewski two days later, and the Soviet emissary promised to communicate it personally to Lenin. On November 14 the Politburo of the Central Committee heard Trotsky's report on the information brought by Marchlewski and decided to entrust Trotsky and Chicherin with working out the terms of the truce with the Poles. "The terms communicated by Comrade Marchlewski are to be considered generally acceptable, with the exception of the clause about the termination of military operations against Petliura." This was to be rejected on the grounds of separate negotiations with Petliura being conducted by the Bolsheviks. The Politburo agreed to respect the Polish demand for secrecy and consult only a few of the Soviet military leaders.[97]

The Russian reply, communicated through Marchlewski and Boerner to Piłsudski, was, as Marchlewski aptly described it, a counterproposal. The demarcation line was differently defined, and a neutral zone was to be created by mutual Soviet and Polish withdrawals (points 1 and 2). Moscow asked Poland to drop the question of Dünaburg (point 3) because it would be dealt with in negotiations with Latvia and would not be an insurmountable obstacle to peace. The Russians agreed that Communist agitation (point 4) would not be conducted by "state means." As for Petliura (point 5), the Bolsheviks felt that he could not be the object of negotiations between the Polish and Soviet governments, and they went on to explain the difficulties involved in Russo-Ukrainian talks. Moscow in turn made certain statements. It expressed concern over alleged collaboration between Poland and the Whites; reiterated preference for a formal armistice (without making it a condition for further talks); and made new proposals for a cease-fire at the three sectors at which hostages and prisoners would be exchanged.[98]

Marchlewski reported to Moscow that Boerner did not voice any basic objections to the Soviet note and disliked only the idea of mutual withdrawals.[99] But Boerner was obviously only a go-between, and it was clear that Piłsudski would not treat the Russian reply as satisfactory.

The chief of state's ideas at this time emerged clearly from talks he had with Kossakowski on November 13 and with the British minister a week earlier. Piłsudski corrected Kossakowski's use of the expression "negotiations," and told him he did not negotiate with the Bolsheviks but was telling them harsh things so as to force them "to be humble and begging in relations with us." Piłsudski said that Poland was a power while both White and Red Russia were "cadavers."[100] The chief of state also stressed his low opinion of Russians in conversations with Sir Horace Rumbold. He spoke of British-Polish cooperation in a future reconstruction of Russia, and mentioned his desire to hold elections (plebiscites) in areas east of the former Kingdom of Poland. He made no direct reference to the Mikaszewicze talks, although Rumbold knew already through Undersecretary Skrzynski that the chief Soviet delegate there had full powers to discuss peace. He merely alluded to a "possible agreement with the Bolsheviks," and said that Poland might declare "that she would disinterest herself in the affairs of Russia provided that the Bolsheviks left the Poles alone on their side."[101] As always in talks with the British, Piłsudski strove for collaboration on the Russian question. A coordination of views was especially important because the Mikaszewicze negotiations had a counterpart in talks between Maxim Litvinov and James O'Grady in Copenhagen. These also concerned prisoners, and Litvinov, like Marchlewski, had political credentials to conduct peace negotiations.

Piłsudski's remarks showed that he was in no mood to bargain with the Bolsheviks. Having learned their reply on November 23, he ordered Boerner to take a new message to Marchlewski. The message had a ring of annoyance. He repeated that his suggestion of a demarcation line was a voluntary statement on his part; the Soviet government had drawn unwarranted conclusions when they tried to bargain. They also misunderstood his intent with regard to the neutral zone; hence there would be no exchange of prisoners through Polotsk, and Polish troops would not withdraw anywhere. If the Russians had heeded Piłsudski's advice about Dünaburg they would have contributed greatly to peace. As things stood, Poland would assist Latvia if she asked for it. A mere declaration of the Bolsheviks about cessation of propaganda was insufficient. Piłsudski was not afraid to take severe measures against propagandists irrespective of who stood behind them. He merely preferred not to have to sign death warrants. As for Petliura, Piłsudski cared little whether the Bolsheviks negotiated with Petliura and what were the points at issue. Taking Polish interests into consideration he would not allow Petliura to be beaten, and if the Red Army attacked the Ukrainian leader the Poles would go to his defense. Piłsudski dismissed contemptuously Soviet accusations of Polish collusion with the Whites, and said the Russians were free to believe what they wanted.

The chief of state accompanied these statements with a declaration. He accused the Bolsheviks of wanting to draw him into far-reaching negotiations and agreements. They failed to realize that Piłsudski had taken it upon himself to conduct talks so far, and it was up to him to decide what form they should take and how they should be presented in Poland. His aim of preventing a triumph of reaction in Russia was seemingly misunderstood in Moscow but he would pursue it even if opposed by the Bolsheviks. "The Chief of State greatly regrets that there is no man in Soviet Russia who will take it upon himself to acknowledge this fact. If Lenin is such a man, the Chief of State will send a representative to him who will define more precisely the point of view of the Chief of State; but if Lenin is not or does not want to be such a man, he will not do it." Piłsudski stated emphatically that he did not want to fight the Soviets, but if they wanted to fight with Poland "he will take up the challenge." He stressed that he would not be impressed by words but by deeds: freeing of hostages and correct behavior of Soviet troops. As for a personal meeting with Marchlewski, Piłsudski did not reject the possibility but saw no chance at the present moment.[102]

Chicherin acknowledged Piłsudski's message to Marchlewski on December 6, 1919. Moscow accepted Piłsudski's statement that Polish troops would not advance, and the commissar urged Marchlewski to talk with the chief of state in order to elicit personal assurances which would "strengthen our military agreement" with the Poles. Soviet field commanders received orders to avoid encounters with Polish units. There was no indication, however, that Lenin wanted to respond to the overture implied in Piłsudski's last message.

The meeting between Piłsudski and Marchlewski never materialized, and Boerner did not return with any new communication to Mikaszewicze. Marchlewski waited until the word arrived on December 13 that "given the new circumstances Boerner would not come." He prepared to leave the conference; the work concerning hostages and refugees remained unfinished because of difficulties concerning a cease-fire and other technical arrangements. On December 15 the Polish delegation accompanied the Bolsheviks to the front, which they crossed the same day.

The Mikaszewicze conference showed plainly the impossibility of finding a common language between Warsaw and Moscow. Their interests coincided only insofar as concerned Denikin, and Piłsudski "consciously assisted the Soviet regime in its struggle against Denikin."[103] Marchlewski's assumption that Poland would be satisfied with territories already under her control seemed to be borne out by Paderewski's declarations in Paris, by Piłsudski's voluntary statement that the troops would not advance, and by other similar pronouncements.[104] Still, it was a mistaken view. The Bolshevik loss of the Ukraine to Denikin opened the possibility of occupation by Petliura, after defeat of the White general. Hence Piłsudski's emphatic insistence on a Soviet commitment not to touch the Ukrainian leader, and his threat of Polish intervention if they did.

Brest-Litovsk tactics had not been lost on the Poles. Piłsudski knew, and was telling the Bolsheviks that he knew, that they would use peace negotiations for revolutionary propaganda. This is why he insisted on the two other conditions he considered basic: withdrawal of the Red Army ten kilometers to the east; and cessation of all revolutionary propaganda among Polish soldiers.[105] Piłsudski never held out the prospect of a formal peace treaty. Given the attitude of the Entente and of the Right in Poland, this was hardly feasible.[106] What he probably envisaged was an arrangement by which Polish and Soviet armies would break contact, enabling the Poles to make a settlement in the borderlands and leaving the Bolsheviks free to establish their mastery at home.

Piłsudski overestimated the might of Poland and the extent of Russian fears of Polish intervention. The Ministry of Foreign Affairs, commenting on Marchlewski's overtures, concluded that the Bolsheviks "might accept all our conditions, especially in the sphere of territorial concessions."[107] Leading from strength, Piłsudski wanted Lenin to understand that he was a free agent who cared little about the collapse of the Communist regime, provided Moscow gave him a free hand in the border regions. In exchange he offered noninterference in domestic Russian affairs. His estimate of Soviet Russia erred in several respects. Lenin classed Poland together with the Baltic states in the category of "small nations," and assumed that the Polish offensive had slowed down because of domestic pressures on the government.[108] Trotsky wrote to the French Communists in September 1919 that the "weak Polish troops" had scored temporary gains at Russia's expense because of the Soviet struggle against Denikin, but once the Whites were defeated the situation on the western front would change.[109] Finally, the Bolshevik leaders suspected that Warsaw's eastern policy was influenced decisively by the West and they saw the Polish-Russian conflict only in terms of the general struggle between capitalism and Communism.

Under these conditions Moscow was not willing to pay any price for a peaceful settlement with Poland. Nor were the Bolsheviks prepared to renounce the Ukraine, which they considered of crucial importance. A peace settlement based on the status quo with all diplomatic advantages for Russia and political inconveniences for Poland was advisable; an acceptance of terms dictated by Piłsudski was not. Having satisfied themselves that the Poles would not assist Denikin, the Russians saw no reason to deal on terms other than their own.

If Piłsudski believed at first that his conditions might be accepted, he must have changed his mind after the Soviet reply.[110] His second message was an angry reiteration of old points with emphasis on statements that the Soviets chose to misunderstand his intent by assuming that he was open to bargaining. But Piłsudski did not break contacts immediately. He renewed his offer to send an envoy to Lenin if the Bolshevik leader was prepared to understand the chief of state. What was the purpose? Two well-informed writers from the opposite camps stated that Piłsudski's aim in the Mikaszewicze negotiations was to facilitate the Soviet struggle with Denikin.[111] Granted, but if this were the sole aim, why the renewed proposal of exchanges with Lenin? Surely the Bolsheviks knew by then that they need not fear any Polish intervention. Piłsudski's move made sense only if he wanted to gain absolute certainty that his terms were unacceptable to Red Russia.

At the time of the Mikaszewicze conference the Polish chief of state—striving after his eastern program—sought to find out if it could not be accomplished through peaceful means. Only after his second message did he come to the conclusion that this was impossible. A peace settlement based on his terms could come only after an armed struggle and a total defeat of the Bolsheviks. But if Piłsudski came to believe this, the Polish government, parliament, and public opinion did not see the Soviet-Polish issue in precisely those terms. Nor did the cabinets of Paris and London. During the crucial months which followed, the question of further war or peace between Poland and Soviet Russia hung in the balance, both sides trying to present their causes under the most favorable light.

War
or
Peace?

The breakdown of the Boerner-Marchlewski exchanges did not put an end to the search for peace. By December 1919 the Bolsheviks decisively defeated Denikin, Yudenich, and Kolchak. Having vanquished domestic foes, they needed time to consolidate their gains, and believed that they could better achieve their long-range objectives through peace than war. They strove to establish relations with the West and pursued a peace offensive in the Baltic region. The Poles were in a different situation. Piłsudski strengthened his hold over foreign policy after Paderewski's resignation and the appointment of the docile Skulski-Patek ministry, but he did not disarm his opponents. Nor was Warsaw successful in getting British support, and Polish diplomacy found itself operating under increasingly adverse conditions. The Allied attitude toward the eastern borders, the Russian Whites, and matters of war and peace failed to provide Poland with guidance. The Bolsheviks exploited this situation by addressing a direct and formal peace proposal to Warsaw. This left Poland with the difficult choice of either trying to win the war, or signing a treaty with Moscow. There was no unanimity of views either in the country or in the Allied camp.

By November and December 1919 the Bolshevik peace campaign was in full swing. The conclusion of agreements on exchanging hostages and prisoners between Russia and the Baltic countries led to the next step—a peace conference with Estonia. The Soviets wanted the Baltic states neutralized, and there were also unofficial contacts with the British about ceasing all hostilities in the area. The long-range aims were ideological. Lenin expressed them on December 28, 1919 by saying: "through the recognition of the independence" of the Baltic states "we gain the trust, slowly but surely . . . of the working masses of the neighboring tiny states . . . we detach them more and more from the influence of their native capitalists" and lead them "toward the future, single, international Soviet republic."[1]

The Bolshevik campaign received much publicity. The Seventh All-Russian Congress of Soviets passed a resolution which, after recalling efforts to establish peaceful relations with the Entente, instructed the government "to continue systematically the policy of peace by undertaking all measures necessary for its realization."[2] Chicherin assured the delegates that the Narkomindel was doing its best to bring peace "without such sacrifices as would harm the vital interests of the working masses," and he had asked Litvinov to inform the Allies of the resolution of the congress.

Litvinov was at this time in Copenhagen, ostensibly negotiating an exchange of prisoners with the British, but he also was empowered to conduct political talks. Although Lord Curzon refused to receive peace proposals from him, the Bolshevik emissary displayed great activity. He attempted to convince British diplomats of the need to raise the blockade of Russia, complained about London's alleged obstructions of a peace settlement in the Baltic area, and appealed to British industrial and commercial circles.[3] Still, London was not yet ready to devise a new Russian policy and merely considered alternatives. Churchill pressed for the creation of a common front of Denikin and the border states from Finland to Rumania. Denikin's short-sighted policy toward nationalities needed to be changed, however, and Savinkov, especially, criticized the White leader. Though pessimistic of Denikin's chances, Piłsudski told the British he wanted no conflict with the Whites, and promised to advance against the Bolsheviks in the spring.[4]

It was under these conditions that Curzon, in early December 1919, dispatched the scholar-politician Sir Halford Mackinder to Denikin with a mission to make the general more amenable to cooperation with the non-Russian nationalities and Poland.* Mackinder stopped en route in Warsaw, and on December 15 he had a long talk with Piłsudski. The chief of state developed his views on eastern questions, which he had already made known in conversations with Rumbold and Kossakowski. He stated that Poland could not afford to make peace with the Bolsheviks because it would be "a mere truce for the gaining of time by her enemies." One could not put any trust in Soviet assurances. Once again he declared he could march to Moscow, but what then? It seems he wanted to make Mackinder reply that the only solution was an alliance with non-Bolshevik Russia. Piłsudski did not reject such a possibility and, when asked about meeting Denikin, suggested the White general come to Warsaw. He thus intimated that Denikin ought to be treated as a junior partner. Piłsudski then introduced the question of the eastern borders, and Mackinder, visibly impressed, reported that the chief of state "made

* The fullest account of Mackinder's mission can be found in "Private Papers of Sir H. J. Mackinder relating to his Mission to South Russia, October 1919—February 1920," PRO, F.O. 800/251.

the important declaration that he was willing to allow the future position of the inhabitants of the country as far back as the [peace] conference line through Brest-Litovsk to be submitted to a plebiscite."[5]

The full implication of Piłsudski's statement becomes clear if one considers the two developments to which he referred: the declaration of the Allied Supreme Council on eastern frontiers, and the plebiscite which was then hotly debated in Poland. The Allied declaration of December 8 on a provisional, minimum frontier came ostensibly from a desire to introduce some order in Eastern Europe. It recognized Polish administration west of a provisional line—previously recommended by the Commission on Polish Affairs—and reserved Polish rights to territories east of it.[6] It did not establish any frontier but merely ackowledged Poland's rights to certain territories. It could have been and was understood to indicate Allied preference for this minimum boundary. The Russian Whites saw it as a triumph of their policy, and a question arose about the status of Polish-held eastern border-lands: were they to be administered by Poles on behalf of Denikin and the Whites? Some Russians thought so, and Piłsudski was approached to consider such a contingency. Naturally he refused.[7] But he held what seemed a trump card, namely, the idea of resolving the future of these territories by a plebiscite, and he showed his hand to Mackinder.

A solution by means of a plebiscite, though attractive, was fraught with great difficulties. The Socialists and their allies had consistently advocated it as part of the federalist program; the Right and Center parties spoke only of electing deputies from these regions, who would then express their views on the future fate of the borderlands. To rightist extremists the purpose of elections was to confirm that "this is a Polish land and wants to belong to Poland."[8] Even some nonparty federalists wavered after visiting the eastern territories, and felt that since the local population was not much interested in plebiscites the federalist-incor-porationist controversy might not be insoluble.[9] This was hardly the case, as shown by the heated debates in the sejm from August to November 1919. As on previous occasions the Right-Center majority defeated Socialist demands for a genuine plebiscite, and the sejm resolved on November 25 that general elections, organized by the civilian administration of the eastern territories, be held within ninety days. Deputies so elected would then express the will of their voters regarding legal and political relations with Poland.[10]

The government avoided carrying out this resolution, and the reason probably lay in Piłsudski's long-range plans and in the anticipated opposition of the Entente. Piłsudski treated the idea of a plebiscite seriously. He spoke of it to the Foreign Affairs Committee in November, and told Wasilewski that he wanted to solve the fate of "the entire former Grand Duchy of Lithuania" through a plebiscite. He recalled his Wilno declaration, and termed it a promise "on which one could not go back."[11] But the chief of state preferred to delay the plebiscite, or the elections, if the sejm's will were to prevail, until a showdown in the east. Eventually Allied opposition defeated such a scheme, and on March 6, 1920 the Supreme Council declared that eastern borders were to be determined in accord with Article 87 of the Treaty of Versailles and not by any elections held in former "Russian provinces." But in early December the chief of state believed that he could still use the plebiscite project to checkmate the Whites.[12]

Piłsudski's conciliatory stand on cooperation with Denikin, reported by Mackinder, did not represent a change of heart. The chief of state doubted the possibility of genuine collaboration with the White general, and he despised him for military failures. Although late in January 1920 Mackinder secured Denikin's grudging assent for a new policy toward Poland, this was a belated concession resulting from his hopeless position. As a non-Bolshevik Russian leader pointed out, had Denikin captured Moscow in late 1919 he undoubtedly would have clashed with Poland over the borderlands.[13]

The only reason which prompted Piłsudski's nonrejection of Mackinder's overtures was the continuing Polish desire to cooperate with Britain on the Russian question. It found new expression in the trip of Prince Stanisław Radziwiłł, an aide de camp of the chief of state, to England, and in also sending Stanisław Posner, a relative of Lewis Namier. Both received instructions to influence British circles.[14]

Meanwhile important changes were taking place in the West. The Supreme Council held a conference in London on December 11–13, 1919, and its outcome indicated an evolution in Allied policy toward Russia. Lloyd George and Clemenceau considered a meeting of anti-Bolshevik states leading toward a federation, and rejected it as a means of struggle against the Soviets. The British prime minister opposed such a plan because it would involve new commitments and expenses; the French premier opposed it for fear of antagonizing Russian nationalism. Both agreed on the uselessness of continuing active support of Denikin, and although the French still tried a few weeks later to press

Poland and Rumania to assist the White general, they eventually abandoned that position.[15] Instead the Allies proposed to "leave Bolshevik Russia, as it were, within a ring fence" or a "barbed wire entanglement," to prevent it from expanding. This was a negative formula which, while constituting a break with the past, placed the border states in an awkward situation.

The London conference made assistance to the Baltic countries dependent on circumstances—a policy which could evoke little enthusiasm in Riga or Tallinn. Lord Balfour wondered what the Entente planned to do since it did not consent to a peace settlement between these countries and the Bolsheviks. The French worried that, given the lack of Allied guidance and recognition, the Baltic countries would sign peace treaties after all. Polish efforts to consolidate their independence and to establish cooperation between these states and Warsaw received no backing.[16]

What place did the Allied statesmen assign to Poland? The conference singled her out for a special statement, and agreed to fortify the country "to keep Russia in check and to contain Germany" (Clemenceau), and equip her army but not "for an attack on Russia, but rather for future contingencies" (Lloyd George).[17] This ambiguous phrase alarmed the Poles. The rightist press wanted to know what the Entente expected of Poland; the Left voiced indignation at Allied plans to make Poland a guardian of Russia on behalf of the Anglo-French bourgeoisie. It seemed evident that Warsaw could not indefinitely maintain a state of neither war nor peace along her eastern borders, and the Polish minister in London complained to Clemenceau that the Allies seemingly wanted the Poles to do the impossible. The premier replied that the Pole was right, but that logic and politics did not always go together. Clemenceau added that for the time the only thing was to procrastinate. As for the British, the envoy suspected that Lloyd George secretly wished a Soviet-Polish peace, but without any encouragement on his part. Such a peace treaty, Sapieha speculated, would estrange Poland from France and leave London a free hand with regard to pending Polish problems, especially the German-Polish issues. The minister suggested to Warsaw a move reminiscent of Paderewski's initiative of September; Poland should propose either a joint action against the Bolsheviks, in exchange for recognition of borders in the east, or an official Allied approval of her own solution of the Russian question. This was not a realistic proposal, and Sapieha shortly withdrew it.[18] One thing was clear: Polish diplomacy was making no headway in London.

The Warsaw government had maintained great reserve in its

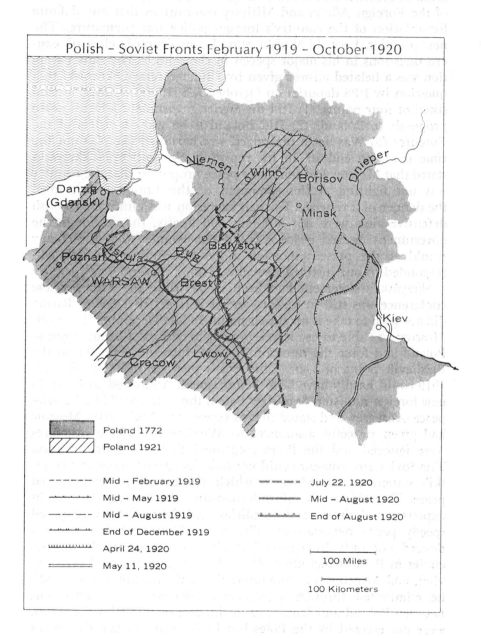

Polish – Soviet Fronts February 1919 – October 1920

Niemen
Wilno
Borisov
Dnieper
Danzig
(Gdańsk)
Minsk
Poznań
Wistula
Bug
Białystok
WARSAW
Brest
Kiev
Cracow
Lwow

Poland 1772
Poland 1921

- - - - - Mid – February 1919
—·—·— Mid – May 1919
— — — Mid – August 1919
—··—··— End of December 1919
ııııııııı April 24, 1920
═══════ May 11, 1920

═══ July 22, 1920
▬▬▬ Mid – August 1920
▬▬▬ End of August 1920

100 Miles

100 Kilometers

pronouncements on the Russian question. Piłsudski told members of the Foreign Affairs and Military committees that any definite formulation of the country's foreign policy was premature. The new premier, Leopold Skulski, stayed conspicuously clear off eastern questions in his major speech in the sejm.[19] The only exception was a belated answer given by Undersecretary Skrzyński to a question by PPS deputies on October 7, 1919. The question consisted of four points. (1) Did the Soviet government address peace proposals to Poland? (2) Did Poland wage war at orders of the Entente? (3) Was not a prolonged war harmful? (4) Was not the time ready to end it? In his reply on November 28 Skrzyński stated that Moscow had not made peace proposals; that the country was not fighting at the command of the Entente; that until the danger of a renewed Russian aggresion was eliminated Polish defensive aims were not fulfilled; and finally, that although the government desired peace it could not assume "that the enemy would at the present moment agree to conditions which corresponded to our justified demands."[20]

Skrzyński's statement had been made while the Mikaszewicze conference was still in session, and it is likely that Soviet Russia did not wish to take it up at that point. In late December, however, Moscow was able to use it as a pretext to address a formal note to Poland and force the question of peace into the open. From the Bolshevik point of view, Chicherin's message of December 22, 1919 could hardly have been better timed. Addressed to Poland's new foreign minister, Stanisław Patek, the note recalled all Soviet peace overtures, and stated that as recently as April 1919, Moscow had given peaceful assurances to Więckowski. These overtures were ignored and the Poles continued their eastward advance. The Soviet government could not hide its astonishment at Skrzyński's statement, according to which Rusia had never proposed peace. To remove all misunderstanding the Soviets once again expressed a desire to end hostilities, and they formally proposed speedy peace negotiations. The note affirmed that peace was desired not only by Russia but also by numerous democratic circles in Poland including all workers' organizations. Peace was vital, and Moscow was convinced that existing differences could be eliminated through agreements. Obstacles to a settlement between Poland and Russia, as in the case of other border states, were not erected by the Poles but by foreign powers. Chicherin ended his message by expressing hope that the peaceful efforts of the majority of the Polish people, coupled with the country's vital needs, would put an end to a war fought for alien interests.

Moscow asked Warsaw to indicate the place and time of peace negotiations.[21]

The Polish government made no reply to Chicherin's note. Unperturbed, the Bolsheviks went on with their peace offensive, which slowly transformed itself into a veritable barrage of offers and declarations. The Council of Peoples' Commissars issued on January 28, 1920 a statement addressed to Poland which announced that the country was now facing a decision likely to affect gravely both nations for many years to come. Extreme Allied imperialists, the note asserted, were trying to draw Poland into a senseless and criminal war against Russia. The Council of Peoples' Commissars, conscious of its responsibility for the fate of Russia's working masses, anxious to save both nations from disaster, declared as follows: the policy of Soviet Russia toward Poland was based on the principle of national self-determination and on unconditional recognition of Polish independence and sovereignty. Confirming the peace offer of December 22, 1919 the Council announced—in its own name and in that of the provisional Soviet Ukrainian government—that the Red Army would not cross the present front line running through Drissa, Disna, Polotsk, Borisov, Parichi, Ptich, Belokorovichi, Chudnov, Piliava, Derazhnia, and Bar. The council declared that Russia had no pacts with Germany or any other state directed against Poland. The nature of Soviet foreign policy precluded the possibility of agreements that would infringe Polish independence and territorial integrity. There was no question, territorial or economic, affecting the essential interests of both countries, that could not be settled by negotiations and agreement; Soviet-Estonian negotiations offered the best proof of it. The Council of Peoples' Commissars added that a declaration of Soviet intentions toward Poland would be submitted to the All-Russian Executive Committee of the Soviets (VTsIK) for ratification. It expressed hope that all questions in dispute would be resolved in a spirit of neighborliness.[22]

The declaration of the Council of Commissars appeared on the same day as an appeal against intervention which Chicherin addressed to workers of Allied countries. It was followed on February 2, 1920 by a statement of VTsIK which not only confirmed the council's message but elaborated on Soviet policy toward Poland.[23] This last document had a highly propagandistic content. Opening with an attack on Western capitalists—enemies of Polish and Russian workers—who had long tolerated tsarist oppression of Poland, it declared that Soviet Russia was offering peace. It knew that the age-long tsarist yoke had created a deep mistrust of the Russian nation among Poles; Russia's workers and peasants could not be responsible for the enslavement of the past. They had been the first to recognize Polish independence, which accorded with the true interests of both peoples. The Soviets wanted peace and opposed war; they were willing to make concessions to smaller countries to overcome old suspicions. After drawing a parallel between tsarist treatment of nationalities and of the Russian people, the address affirmed that "Freedom of Poland is the condition of a free development of Russia." The Soviets denied that they wanted "to introduce Communism into Poland on the bayonets of the Red Army. A Communist system is possible only where an important majority of the working people is imbued with the desire to build it by their own efforts." Hence, Russian Bolsheviks "do not think and could not even think of introducing Communism by force into foreign countries." The statement ended with an appeal to abandon mistrust, stop the war, and establish good relations.

Two days later, on February 4, Chicherin wired Patek to inform him of the VTsIK resolution, which, as he put it, constituted a solemn confirmation of Soviet peace proposals.[24]

A barrage of Soviet propaganda continued. There came a demagogic appeal of the union of agricultural workers to agrarian workers in Poland; Chicherin's address to the toiling masses of the Entente; Zinoviev's manifesto, on behalf of the executive committee of the Comintern, to workers of all countries; and two declarations of the Soviet Ukrainian government. All stressed peace between Russia and Poland and the end of intervention. Only the Comintern statement said that international revolution could bring genuine liberty to Poland.[25]

At first the Polish Communists were out of step with the Russian peace campaign. Tactics were never their strong point, and they argued with logic that the "war of capital with revolution cannot end by 'a peace' of understanding. To desire the end of war means to desire the victory of one of the belligerents." Consequently any campaign against war ought to be identical with action to overthrow the bourgeois regime in Poland.[26] Polish Bolsheviks in Russia were more sophisticated or amenable to Moscow's persuasion. In early February, Marchlewski submitted a declaration which spoke against revolution assisted by Red Army. "An invasion of Poland by any army," the document read, would "give the bourgeoisie the chance to strengthen nationalism . . . This is why the Communist Party has always rejected the thought of conquest of Poland by Soviet Russia." The only policy it favored was that of peace.* Thus admonished, the Polish Communist party fell into line, concentrating on antiwar propaganda. On the surface, at least, a unanimous front prevailed.

The unofficial representative of the Russian Whites in Warsaw reported on the dilemma posed by the Bolsheviks: continued fighting, he wrote, "will be bad," and peace "might be even worse."[27] The British envoy called Moscow's overture "rather embarrassing" because of the desire of the Left for peace, and indeed the Polish government could hardly ignore the campaign waged for several months by the PPS.[28] The Socialists opposed war partly for ideological reasons, fearing that it was being fought under pressure from the Entente, and partly for tactical motives, to prevent the hungry and war-weary masses from falling victim to Communist propaganda. *Robotnik* published leading articles entitled: "Will Poland be the Lackey of Reaction?" (Jan. 2, 1920), and "Peace, Quick Peace" (Jan. 21, 1920), and Socialist deputies protested the concealment of Chicherin's first note. They demanded a session of the Foreign Affairs Committee of the sejm and resented Premier Skulski's remark that "to desire peace in principle does not mean to desire it at the price of harming the state interests."[29]

PPS leaders could hardly be accused of advocating peace at any price. They insisted on the right of self-determination of the borderlands, and demanded only that the Bolsheviks be given a chance to prove the sincerity of their peace proposals.[30] But if self-determination in the east could not be achieved through peaceful negotiations, what then? This was the weakest point of the Socialist argument, and *Rząd i Wojsko* pointed it out in a polemic with *Robotnik*. The organ of leftist Piłsudskiites emphasized that the question of war and peace could not be treated independently of political aims, and now was the moment to say "firmly what peace should be like and what should war be fought for."[31] The Left was aware that its position posed a dilemma, and while it demanded a plebiscite in Belorussia and creation of a Belorussian government and army, it took a less clear stand on the Ukraine, for peace with the Bolsheviks could hardly be followed by liberation of Kiev. The PPS had no ready answer.

The Right differed from the Socialists both on the issue of war and peace and on the Polish program in the east. To the National Democrats and their allies the war was to achieve favorable borders

* The statement was signed by forty-two ranking Polish Communists in Russia including such diehards as Leszczyński, Unszlicht, and Pestkowski. See *Dokumenty i materiały do historii stosunków polsko-radzieckich* (Warsaw, 1962–), II, 575.

and to destroy Bolshevism. The former objective, they felt, had been realized, but not the latter. The National Democratic press voiced concern over rumors that Polish troops would advance on Kiev; the frontiers already won ought to be safeguarded by other means.[32] The military corollary of this approach was a defensive strategy permitting action only after a Soviet attack. But a formal peace treaty was not possible either. There was no partner on the Russian side with whom genuine peace could be made, and a settlement with the Bolsheviks seemed impossible were it only out of consideration for the Entente.[33] All this seemed much like a policy of neither war nor peace, and such a policy involved serious political and military risks. With the evolution of the views of the Entente, National Democrats began to favor some negotiation with the Bolsheviks, but their stand, like that of the PPS, was ambiguous.[34] Hence *Rząd i Wojsko* on January 25 could write with some justification that the sejm—as shown by the attitude of its leading parties—was incapable of formulating definite and consistent aims of either war or peace.

Polish public opinion was bewildered. An army memorandum prepared for Piłsudski stressed that "war aims originated and evolved during the war" and were still not clear to everybody.[35] Hołówko wrote that people as a whole did not really know "what we were fighting for."[36] There were divisions, misconceptions, and confusion. It was but imperfectly understood that the question of war or peace was badly put. The real question was whether peace or war would allow the realization of the country's eastern program. But there was no agreement on the program.

The government also failed to provide guidance, and both Right and Left joined forces in criticizing it. So did *Rząd i Wojsko*. It was tragic that at this crucial moment Poland was governed by the colorless Skulski cabinet. The ministers, as a conservative historian put it, were incapable of either supporting Piłsudski or resisting him.[37] Skulski gladly left foreign policy to the chief of state; Patek was Piłsudski's instrument but showed little talent even as the executor of his policy.[38] Piłsudski knew what he wanted but did not present his program to the people. Was it because he feared to see his views distorted and his plans sabotaged by predominantly rightist sejm? Or did he feel that his eastern program could only succeed by resorting to secretly prepared *faits accomplis?* Whatever the reason Piłsudski's policy was neither fully known nor understood by the nation.

Piłsudski's point of view found perhaps the most cogent expression in *Rząd i Wojsko*. The weekly stated that the Poles could defeat the Bolsheviks, hence they had the possibility of "dictating the conditions." International policies of intervention had ended in bankruptcy; pacifism was no alternative; therefore Poland could not sign peace without guarantees. Otherwise there would be grave dangers, not least of which was demoralization of people at home. "Peace must be the *embodiment of our program in eastern affairs,* and one can risk it only at that price."[39] Here one finds the key to Warsaw's attitude in months to come and an explanation of its diplomacy.

Piłsudski spent little time theorizing. He manipulated multiple strings and true to his nature preferred concrete arrangements to doctrinal solutions. Three areas were of utmost importance for his eastern policy: the Ukraine, Belorussia, and the Baltic countries, and in each field there was feverish activity.

Negotiations with representatives of the Ukrainian People's Republic led to an important declaration by the Ukraine—a prelude to the future full-fledged Polish-Ukrainian alliance. The document, signed in Warsaw on December 2, 1919, provided for recognition of a border between the Ukraine and Poland which left Eastern Galicia on the Polish side. Its status was to be decided by Warsaw in agreement with local Ukrainians. The Poles in the Ukraine were to receive national and cultural rights equal to those granted by Poland to Ukrainians. Pending solution of the agrarian question by a Ukrainian Constituent Parliament, a special Polish-Ukrainian agreement would deal with the legal rights of Polish landowners in the country. Closest economic relations between the two states, including reciprocal transit, were to be established. The document comprised four basic Ukrainian demands: first, Polish recognition of the Ukraine as an independent country, and conclusion of military, commercial, and consular agreements; second, liberation of Ukrainians arrested or imprisoned by Poles in former conflicts; third, military assistance; and fourth, free transit through Poland of Ukrainian prisoners, military supplies, and financial aid. Signed by Andrii Livytskyi, Petliura's foreign minister, the document expressed the conviction that Polish and Ukrainian nations "will create, through common cooperation, a powerful and invincible might which will become the basis of peace and order in Eastern Europe, and will contribute to a splendid cultural development of both nations."[40]

The Eastern Galician members of the mission resigned in protest over Livytskyi's declaration, but Petliura informed the Polish government that he considered it binding.[41] The Chief Ataman (Petliura) was already on Polish territory, and shortly thereafter went to Warsaw to confer with Piłsudski. Simultaneously Ukrainian detachments were transported across the front into Poland.[42]

All these moves, carried out in secrecy, gave rise to rumors in the Polish press and diplomatic circles.[43] The government said nothing; Piłsudski played his cards close to the chest.

The chief of state took as yet no commitments. Toward the end of December 1919 he told Wasilewski that one must secure "the possibility of raising the question of the Ukraine. Poland will help him [Petliura] at a moment which one must await."[44] In early January Piłsudski described the situation in the Ukraine as fluid and uncertain.[45] But he allowed his supporters to agitate in print for Polish-Ukrainian cooperation and present it as the only solution of the Eastern Galician problem. While critical of various Polish moves with regard to the Ukrainians, Petliura emphasized that the Poland of Piłsudski and his adherents understood the Ukrainian interests and would approach them in a chivalrous spirit.[46]

The Belorussian picture was less encouraging. Uncertainty over whether a federalist or incorporationist solution would eventually prevail led to a zigzagging Polish policy in the region. While a Belorussian national movement was encouraged around Minsk, it was discouraged in the Wilno-Grodno area.* Even Piłsudski, whom the Belorussians trusted more than any other political leader, spoke at times of the "Belorussian fiction," and forbade political concessions. A native military commission established in October 1919 received little scope for its activity; friction and difficulties multiplied.[47] A meeting of the Rada of the Belorussian Republic, authorized by one Polish official, was dissolved on the orders of another.[48] First Lastouski and then Lutskevich abandoned the pro-Polish orientation. The authorities had to treat with lesser figures, Vaclav Ivanouski and A. Smolich. The Belorussian Committee, later transformed into a political committee, created some trouble for the Poles who in January 1920 limited its activity. All these developments were discouraging and far-sighted Polish military and civilian circles saw it well enough. Kossakowski described the state of affairs in Belorussia as "chaos." Did Piłsudski realize it too? On the last day of December 1919 he told Wasilewski that the Belorussian question was not ready for solution, and for the time one must have a "Belorussian Piedmont in Poland."[49] In reality not even a Piedmont existed.

Piłsudski showed a profound interest in a common front with the Baltic countries. He felt that peace with Russia had to be

---

* "You must accept the fact," Piłsudski told Osmołowski, "that the Belorussians have Minsk and they lost Wilno which I gave to the *endeks* [National Democrats]. See Jerzy Osmołowski, "Wspomnienia z lat 1914-1921," III, 126, Biblioteka Narodowa, Warsaw.

signed simultaneously by those states and Poland. The key to the situation, Piłsudski said, "is in the north." It was in the north that during the first days of January 1920 the Polish army engaged in a new offensive in cooperation with the Latvians. The objective was Dünaburg, (Daugavpils, Dvinsk), which was captured. But neither the Polish gesture of handing over the city to the Latvians to prove the absence of imperialistic designs in the Baltic area, nor renewed efforts to make common front against the Bolsheviks, produced results, Deprived of Allied support, wary of throwing in their lot with the Poles, the Baltic countries preferred to negotiate with Moscow. No Eastern bloc under Polish leadership was coming into existence.

Neither domestic difficulties, nor problems connected with the borderlands deterred Piłsudski from his objectives. Nor did he shrink from the tremendous responsibility history had put on his shoulders.[50] He saw only two alternatives: either Poland would be "a state equal to the great powers of the world, or a small state that needed protection of the mighty."[51] He strove to obliterate the partitions and restore Poland to a position of power she had once occupied, or to put it differently, force Russia back into her pre-Petrine boundaries. Moscow was to disinterest itself in all areas west of the 1772 frontiers, but Piłsudski had no blueprint for final settlement of the borderlands. "I am a realist," he told a French journalist, "without prejudices or theories."[52] To his Polish advisers he spoke of plebiscites in the east and links with the whole former Grand Duchy of Lithuania.[53] In talks with anti-Soviet Russian leaders, Boris Savinkov and Chaikovskii, who came to Warsaw in mid-January, the chief of state proposed an anti-Bolshevik alliance of all nationalities of the former Russian empire. As for a Russo-Polish territorial settlement, both sides would renounce their historic borders of 1772 and 1914; a plebiscite would determine the fate of the Lithuanian and Belorussian lands.[54]

It is likely that Piłsudski's proposal stemmed from a genuine desire to reach a modicum of agreement with anti-Bolshevik Russians. Talking with them he did not abandon any of his aims, and cooperation with even a segment of the Russians was likely to weaken their united front. Denikin and the emigré leaders turned down Piłsudski's offer, although the latter repeated it again in late February. Only Savinkov continued to be interested.[55]

Piłsudski approached the question of war or peace purely in terms of power.* When asked by a British journalist if the Soviet

* He said in Wilno in April 1919 that he loved war "with all its horrors." A few months later in Suwałki he repeated "I love this war which either crushes a

peace offers were sincere, Piłsudski answered: "Is it possible to be sincere in politics? They [the Bolsheviks] must have an alternative ready in case their offer is rejected. They have good reason for wanting peace . . . They are at the end of their tether."[56] He told Hugh Gibson, the American envoy in Warsaw that from the Polish viewpoint peace would be a folly, because he would have to keep troops in the east for fear of sudden aggression, and it would be impossible to keep them alerted because of the strain on their morale. A day later Piłsudski indicated to Gibson that peace may be "a gambler's chance," because failing a settlement there was a danger of Soviet invasion and conquest of Poland.[57] Both remarks seemed calculated to obtain clarification of the American stand. Piłsudski and the government made efforts to persuade the West that a state of neither war nor peace could not continue. The chief of state felt that a lasting settlement embodying his eastern program could only be achieved after a victory over the Red Army; any other kind of peace would bring no permanent solution.[58] Piłsudski was not able to say this openly. Domestic opposition aside there were the powers of the Entente whose policies and opinions he had to take into consideration. That was why Warsaw left the Soviet peace overtures without an answer and why Foreign Minister Patek went to London and Paris to get a clear idea of views of the Entente.

At the beginning of January 1920, the foreign minister talked with Clemenceau and Foch, and they advised him not to enter any exchanges with the Bolsheviks and to pursue instead a defensive military strategy. This advice stemmed from their "barbed wire" policy.[59] But Allied ideas kept changing, and while on January 10 the Allies recognized the Transcaucasian states, on January 16 the Supreme Council lifted the blockade of Soviet territory. This latter decision, representing a victory of London over Paris, perplexed Polish diplomacy. Even the London *Times* commented on January 26 that England would "be equipping the Bolshevik forces for next spring, whether they attack in Poland" or elsewhere.

Patek's difficulties increased with a cabinet change in France. The Pole had to explain his country's position all over again, and ascertain the views of Alexandre Millerand and the new ministers. He reported "a greater than ever political disorientation."[60] In a memorandum dated January 20, 1920 Patek advocated the creation of a military conference to organize a single

man's character like glass or makes it strong like steel." In another public statement in January 1920, he called war "a mistress." See Józef Piłsudski, *Pisma zbiorowe* (10 vols.; Warsaw, 1937-1938), V, 76, 103, 135.

defensive front of all the border states, and he appealed for Allied political and military support.[61] Here was another version of the idea which Piłsudski had discussed with Savinkov and which was in general accord with Churchill's plans but not with those of the French government and the British prime minister.

Sensing that the center of Allied diplomacy had shifted to London, Patek went there to confer with Lloyd George. The chances of obtaining British commitments to Poland were slender, and the Polish legation's reports sounded pessimistic. What is more, the Poles suspected Lloyd George of having inspired a British press campaign against Polish "imperialist designs" in the east.[62]

Patek and Lloyd George held a long and important conversation on January 26, 1920, and the prime minister stated his position with clarity. He said that while it was for Poland to decide between peace and war, London did not advise the latter. Civil war and intervention in Russia were almost over; Poland would face the Bolsheviks singlehanded. The British government "did not wish to give Poland the slightest encouragement to pursue her policy of war, because if it were to give that advice it would incur responsibilities which it could not discharge." Lloyd George considered a Bolshevik offensive unlikely and by implication suggested the wisdom of a settlement. Regarding its nature, he said that if the Poles proposed reasonable peace terms (he meant ethnic borders) and the Russians either refused them, or having accepted them, violated the peace treaty, Poland could count on some support from Britain and France. None would be available if Warsaw claimed large areas from Russia. Lloyd George explained his "peace through trade" policy, adding that he did not want Poland to be an economic barrier between Russia and the West.

The Polish minister raised two questions. First, what guarantees would Poland have that a treaty with the Bolsheviks—whom the Allies did not recognize—would be internationally binding? The Bolsheviks might still be replaced by another regime. Second, did Lloyd George's views represent those of other powers of the Entente? The prime minister answered, regarding the first question, that admittedly there was a risk but it was a matter of "balance between the risk of making peace with an unstable Government and the risk of war." As for the second point, he believed that the other states would go along with the British government.[63]

Even if Lloyd George was less then honest in trying to obscure the Franco-British differences of opinion—and the Poles feared to antagonize Paris by following the advice of London—he made his own position clear. Britain was unwilling either to support a war to victory or guarantee a peace settlement. The British left the choice to Poland while indicating a preference for peace. Lloyd George spoke of aid in case of a Bolshevik offensive, following apparently the advice of the British minister in Warsaw who counseled such a promise "to have a hold over them [Poles]."[64]

Patek's conversations in Paris and London failed to bring the results Warsaw had hoped for. The foreign minister reported that the trend in Western Europe was for peace, and even France would not assume responsibility for advocating Polish military action in the east. "In one word," Patek concluded, "we can count only on our own forces and according to that conduct our policy toward Russia."[65] This was a realistic appraisal which brought little comfort to the Poles. Gibson reported that the British stand depressed Warsaw. People assumed that Lloyd George wished "to be free to claim the credit if the situation works out well, and disavow Polish action as treacherous and taken without Allied advice if it does not."[66] While executing instructions from his government—Washington declined responsibility for advising Poland on way or another—the American minister argued that the great powers could not "cut Poland adrift." He emphasized that Warsaw would sign peace if the Entente favored it, or continue war if the powers stated they supported such a policy. There was danger in leaving Poles entirely to their own counsels, he said. Yet this was happening.[67]

On his return to Warsaw on February 4 Patek addressed the Foreign Affairs Committee of the sejm. He reported that France advised against dealing with the Soviets or undertaking an offensive action, and instead counseled adherence to the "barbed wire" policy. Britain approached matters from a commercial position and refused to take responsibility. The minister, overconfidently, announced that "Polonia farà da se," paraphrasing the unfortunate old slogan of Charles Albert of Piedmont-Sardinia.[68] Next day he participated, together with the premier and the minister and deputy minister for war, in a joint meeting of the Foreign Affairs and Military committees. The question of hostilities arose, and General Sosnkowski argued that the Bolsheviks knew that they could not conquer Poland without a domestic upheaval, which was impossible. Hence they would strive for peace, hoping to bring about internal disintegration of the country. The general felt that the Poles had a good chance of defeating the Russians militarily. Then Patek spoke of peace, as if to stress that the government did not think it impossible. "We treat this question seriously," he said. He assured the committees that Warsaw would not present unacceptable peace terms to the Russians. Premier Skulski denied any agreements with the Ukraine and Belorussia. "In the matter of peace with the Bolsheviks it is necessary, given the divergences of opinions within the Entente, to adopt an independent stand without, however, offending the Entente." He added that during the transition period, i.e., from presentation of peace terms to their acceptance, the country had "to be ready for peace and for warlike action."[69]

Skulski's and Patek's statements indicated that the government had decided to prepare peace terms for the Bolsheviks. The exact date of this decision is not clear but seems to have been late January. As Kossakowski described the situation a few weeks afterward: "Patek and Piłsudski make peace. Piłsudski does not believe in it, Patek does. Piłsudski agrees to Patek's peacemaking but does not permit himself to be disarmed."[70] This was a fair summary of the state of affairs, and on February 4 Patek officially confirmed receipt of the message of the Council of Peoples' Commissars of January 28. He promised to send a reply after study of this note; Warsaw finally had responded to Moscow's overtures.

During February and March 1920 the Polish government prepared peace terms, discussed them with the sejm's Foreign Affairs Committee, and sounded the powers of the Entente. Toward the end of January, Patek informed Polish missions abroad that his ministry had begun to elaborate conditions based on the principle of Russian "disannexation" of territories west of the 1772 border, a free hand for Poland to reach agreement with borderland nations, and a *de jure* recognition of states which had emerged out of the old tsarist empire.[71] By February 11 a special committee comprising Wasilewski and Stanisław Gutowski drew up a list of preliminary conditions for negotiations: (1) recognition of states which arose out of tsarist empire and noninterference with their regimes; (2) Russian renunciation of rights acquired through the partitions; (3) solution of all territorial disputes on the basis of national self-determination; (4) abandonment of Soviet propaganda outside Russia; (5) withdrawal of Russian troops from territories within the 1772 Polish borders, which would then be occupied militarily by Poles and administered jointly by Poland and representatives of four countries (two invited by Poland and two by Russia) until final settlement by means of self-determination; (6) Soviet payment of reparations for war damages inflicted on Poland by tsarist Russia, and losses incurred as a result of the revolution, and return of art treasures and museum items; (7) facilities for Polish trade in Russia.[72]

The cabinet explored these conditions and made them into "peace theses," which it communicated on February 23 to the sejm's Foreign Affairs Committee.[73] Patek drew the attention of the deputies to practical difficulties. Who would ratify the treaty on Russia's side; how could one obtain guarantees of a lasting peace; how was one to apply the principle of national self-determination to the borderlands? The committee spent two days discussing the "peace theses" without achieving real unanimity. Members agreed that ratification by the highest Russian authority must not appear as a demand for ratification by a constituent assembly, for this would wreck all chance of negotiation. They showed less agreement on the principle of disannexation and the 1772 borders. National Democrats viewed them as fiction; Socialists preferred frank insistence on self-determination of the Ukraine and Belorussia. There was disagreement about the Ukrainian issue.

Premier Skulski presented his explanations. A recognition of the 1772 borders, he said, was a point of departure. What mattered were two lines, which he described as a strategic and a security line.* It appears, although the protocol is far from clear, that the former was to be drawn between the 1772 frontiers and the existing front, and the latter would be a border of Poland proper. A neutral zone was to be created between them for the purpose of popular consultation—referendum or elections—and Soviet Russia would be barred from all interference. Skulski tried to reconcile different views on the question of the Ukraine by asserting that no decisions had been taken. He also assured the Rightist deputies that Warsaw would keep in close touch with the Entente.

Discussion turned to methods of negotiating with the Bolsheviks, and the Socialist Herman Lieberman accused the government of delays. He proposed a note to Moscow, within a fortnight, setting the date and place of a peace conference. Warsaw would simultaneously notify the Entente. General Kazimierz Sosnkowski clashed with Lieberman. Military guarantees, he said, were necessary before one entered negotiations. If Poland proposed immediate peace talks and Moscow accepted "peace theses" as basis of discussion, there would come a *de facto* cease-fire, extremely dangerous for the morale of the army.[74] Sosnkowski's stand reflected

* A strictly confidential bulletin of the Command of the Volhynian Front indicated on March 1, 1920, that borders of 1772 were meant as point of departure for a line "which reflects the political thinking of the chief of state." See Akta Adiutantury Generalnej Naczelnego Dowództwa, VII/2797, Piłsudski Institute, New York (cited as AGND).

the thinking of Piłsudski, and betrayed a fear of what the Bolsheviks could do with the "peace theses." It is likely that they would have accepted them, arguing that Soviet Russia had fulfilled all the conditions. Had they not renounced rights derived from partitions? Had they not granted national self-determination and intervened only when called by the working masses?[75] There would be endless discussion reminiscent of Brest-Litovsk, with the Bolsheviks exploiting the demand for disannexation and the 1772 borders as proof of Polish imperialistic designs. There would be no chance of a speedy peace, and the military balance then favorable to the Poles would be upset to Russia's advantage.[76] It is not certain that the Foreign Affairs Committee realized all that, but it rejected Lieberman's proposal. Thus Warsaw was not committed to enter negotiations; war or peace remained an open question.

The Foreign Affairs Committee ended its session by adopting a vaguely phrased approval of the theses of the government. The shallowness of agreement appeared immediately when the chairman, Grabski, issued an official communiqué summarizing "peace theses." He toned down self-determination and emphasized ratification by a representative body of the Russian nation.[77] The Left was furious. It accused Grabski of falsification of the agreement reached in the committee. It spoke of a National Democratic intrigue against federalist principles and of sabotage of future peace negotiations.[78] Relations between the Right and the Skulski cabinet cooled.

The government was not very successful in gaining public support for its foreign policy. Nor was it able to succeed in dealing with the Entente, and a resolute stand of the powers was a condition of genuine peace negotiations with Soviet Russia. At least Patek thought so, and he made another effort "to get a final decision from French and British governments."[79]

London continued to adhere to the policy outlined by Lloyd George in January. Even Winston Churchill said that Britain would remain neutral in a Soviet-Polish war, although would not permit the crushing of Poland.[80] Sapieha reported that the British viewed Warsaw's peace terms as folly, and Rumbold did his best to intimate that Lloyd George opposed war.[81] The French were less consistent. Millerand told the Poles "not to trust the word of the Soviets" and to avoid official negotiations, but he was careful not to commit France to the Polish eastern program. In the Chamber of Deputies he spoke about Allied support in case of Soviet attack on Poland.[82] The French legation in Warsaw was apparently encouraging the Poles to fight, and Polish and French military leaders were engaged in far-reaching talks on military strategy.[83]

The Polish general staff sought Foch's advice on the armistice terms which would best guarantee Warsaw's peace conditions. They asked about the 1918 armistice with Germany, trying to find out if it was applicable to Russia. Foch and Maxime Weygand pointed out to Rozwadowski that a different situation existed then, and that "one could not obtain normal guarantees from the Soviets." The marshal advised the Poles either to demand that the Red Army withdraw behind the Dnieper pending an armistice, or improve their military position by capturing Mozyr and cutting Soviet communication between the northern and southern army groups.[84] Rozwadowski claimed later that Foch agreed that Polish troops advance on Kiev but there is no evidence to support this assertion.[85]

By mid-February 1920 Allied inconsistencies and hesitations increased. Warsaw kept receiving reports that France was coming closer to London's point of view, and that Polish-Soviet talks might be useful to "create a modus vivendi between Russia and the Entente."[86] This could have meant that the powers favored peace and were willing to guarantee it. The Poles wanted to know, and Patek complained to Gibson that he could not get a coherent statement from the Allies. Piłsudski said in an interview that "fear of Bolshevism should not become a pretext for doing nothing," and he added that the "moment for peace with Russia has come. This moment came not only for us but for all the states of the Entente."[87] This sounded much like a proposition that peace made sense only if signed by all the powers at once, but the Allied response was disappointing.

Meeting in London on February 24 the Supreme Council passed a resolution which attempted to reconcile the British and French positions. The Allies, it said, could not advise the border countries to continue war against Soviet Russia, not to speak of attacking. The Entente would assist them only in case of Soviet aggression "within their legitimate frontiers." The powers themselves could not enter into diplomatic relations with the Bolsheviks. Some ten days later the Supreme Council warned Poland not to attempt plebiscites in the eastern territories.

The Allied stand shattered the basis of the Polish peace policy as it had been conducted by Patek. The Entente simultaneously counseled against war and declined responsibility for peace. The phrase "legitimate frontiers" had an ominous ring. It could well mean the minimum line indicated in the December 8, 1919 Allied declaration. Piłsudski lashed out at the circuitous Franco-British policy.[88] He and his advisers concluded that Poland must not count on the Entente. The minister in London warned the government against submitting Polish peace terms for Allied approval. The Supreme Council, he wrote, would at best refuse any part in Soviet-Polish exchanges, at worst condemn the Poles for imperialist ambitions. He advised Patek not to visit London, where he would be subject to various pressures.[89] The foreign minister heeded this advice, at least for the time, and Gibson commented that Piłsudski apparently took a "firmer hold of the situation."[90]

Piłsudski was persuaded that Poland would face the Bolsheviks single-handed. Despite conferences held in Warsaw and Helsinki attempts to coordinate action with the Baltic countries failed. Estonia signed a peace treaty on February 2, 1920; Latvia concluded an armistice on January 30; and Lithuania negotiated with Moscow. Only Finland showed any interest in a common front with Poland. Speaking of the Warsaw conference, Piłsudski told a French journalist that "Poland recovers her historic role," and insofar as he meant independent Polish action to bring eastern plans into fruition, he was certainly correct.

Realizing that he lacked the support of the Entente, Piłsudski decided to negotiate only under conditions which guaranteed acceptance of Polish demands. Such guarantees were primarily military. Hence he strove to delay the opening of peace talks until early spring when climatic conditions would not interfere with large-scale operations. He was aware that the Bolsheviks might drag negotiations and improve both their military and political situation. Once peace negotiations started they would have to end quickly, otherwise Piłsudski would have to strike before Russia completed her concentration of troops and threw the vast resources of the country into the balance. The objective would be destruction of the bulk of Soviet armies followed by the conclusion of a victor's peace with Moscow.[91]

Piłsudski's insistence on military guarantees stemmed also from deep suspicion of Soviet motives. He told a French journalist that it was impossible to talk about a normal peace but only of peace "which the Bolsheviks want to snatch under threat," and he stressed that "we shall never be able or willing to agree to negotiations under any threat."[92] He seemed to exaggerate the military menace on purpose, for his whole plan was based on the idea that Polish forces were superior in the short-run. This confident estimate of the military situation was not Piłsudski's alone. General Rozwadowski and the officers of the French military mission seemed to share it.[93]

The British minister in Warsaw commented that Piłsudski "keeps his own counsel," and while having "a definite policy in his mind" he will reveal it only "at the moment it suits him, and, in the meantime, he is very skilful in the art of suggestion."[94] But as Jay P. Moffat, a junior American diplomat, observed, there were indications that the Polish desire for peace was "on the wane."

In early March the Polish general staff prepared a project for reorganizing the army. Their plan stated that if "peace negotiations will not produce positive results, our army will have to make a supreme effort to become victorious in this last war operation."[95] Army units began to move from the western parts of the country and deploy in the east. Piłsudski personally assumed command of the Russian front. Leading generals such as Józef Haller and Stanisław Szeptycki received no information. The former, asking about army moves, stated that "the aim of a larger offensive is so far unknown to me."[96] Meanwhile General Sosnkowski justified new budget credits for the army by the need of alertness vis-à-vis the Bolsheviks, "who want to talk with us with arms in hand."[97] Finally, on March 5, 1920, Polish troops mounted a local but important offensive and captured Mozyr and Kalinkovichi. Irrespective of whether this attack was inspired by the already mentioned advice of Foch to the Poles or resulted from obvious strategic considerations, it strengthened the Polish military position. The important north-south railroad linking the two Soviet armies was cut. Seen retrospectively the operation appeared as the prologue to the April offensive toward Kiev.

The Bolshevik riposte was military and diplomatic. The Red Army unsuccessfully counterattacked, and the Narkomindel addressed a new note to Warsaw. The Russian attack did not worry the Poles. There was no fear of a general offensive until after the breakdown of negotiations, and the attack seemingly sought to redress the situation and make the Russians appear as equals at the forthcoming peace talks.[98] As for Chicherin's message, the foreign commissar renewed assurances of peace and emphasized Soviet friendship for the smaller countries once oppressed by tsarist Russia. He complained that Warsaw, having promised on February 4 to reply to Soviet overtures, had given no answer thus far. Delay meant putting off discussions of peace. The Polish offensive forced the Red Army to defend itself, and if new acts of hostility would make the Bolsheviks cross the line they proposed on January 28, the Poles would be responsible. But if no agressive actions took place the line would be respected. Chicherin repeated that his government was awaiting the Polish answer to Moscow's peace offers.[99]

The same day a radio message come from Kiev, repeating the points made by Chicherin and recalling that Soviet Ukrainian messages of February 19 and 22 had remained unanswered by Warsaw.[100] A day later Chicherin and Rakovskii addressed a joint statement to the American, British, French, and Japanese governments, that responsibility for hostilities lay with the Poles, and that Soviet Russia wanted to begin peace talks with Warsaw. Russia and the Ukraine desired Poland to be "a strong and flourishing state."[101] The Polish general staff opined that this new diplomatic offensive sought to hasten the conclusion of peace "so much desired by the Bolshevik government."[102]

While Piłsudski directed military preparations the government continued to elaborate peace terms. A special committee set up on February 28, 1920 began work on a detailed draft of a Soviet-Polish treaty, and the Ministry of Foreign Affairs completed a note on principles of peace which it presented to Allied ministers in Warsaw on March 13.[103] The text of this note was later made public, and communicated to the Foreign Affairs Committee of the sejm.

Polish peace conditions in this document varied a little from those previously discussed by the sejm's committee. Russian renunciation of all rights to territories west of the 1772 borders received stronger emphasis. Their fate would be settled by Poland, though in conformity with wishes of the local population. The note demanded Russian restitution of state property comprised within the 1772 frontiers. It required ratification of the peace treaty by the highest representative body reflecting the will of the Russian people, although Patek privately explained that Warsaw did not ask the Bolsheviks to commit political suicide by calling a constituent assembly. The Poles wanted merely maximum assurance that the treaty would be binding.

Patek's note resulted from serious deliberations, and although the stress on the 1772 borders was his own, the cabinet discussed and approved it in a secret session on March 8.[104] On that occasion Premier Skulski explained the procedure to be followed in putting peace principles into practice. The Polish delegation would demand disannexation and the 1772 borders, and, if Russia agreed, Warsaw would determine how the local population would express its will. Assuming that Moscow would resist, the delegation was not to break off peace talks before proposing a line more to the west. Should this second line be accepted Poland would demand a popular referendum on both sides, the Poles supervising it on territory west of the line, Russia in the east up to the 1772 borders. Though the cabinet protocol is not distinguished by clarity, it appears that this kind of settlement would be applicable to the northern regions. In case of the Ukraine, Poles would promote her independence and draw a border between Poland and the Ukraine but take no engagements regarding the future Russo-Ukrainian boundary. Nor would they wage war to gain territory for the Ukrainian republic. Again, it is not clear how this was to be done in practice. Perhaps the ministers were not certain, though Piłsudski explained it a little later to Wasilewski. He said that "we shall oppose the Ukraine of Petliura to the Ukraine of Rakovskii" and "let the Ukrainians decide for themselves." He added that he would demand a neutralization of Kiev and a constituent assembly for all the Ukraine. Belorussia—and here the views of Piłsudski appeared identical with those of the cabinet —would be of purely Polish concern.[105]

The ministers agreed that Belorussia would only receive local autonomy in the area of Minsk and further east. Wilno would be part of Poland, and a frontier delimitation with Lithuania carried out after a Soviet-Polish peace treaty. As for technicalities of negotiations with the Bolsheviks, Warsaw would appoint a peace delegation composed of four representatives of the government and four sejm deputies. The conference was to assemble at a locality close to the front. Choice of a town in either Poland or Russia was considered inadmissible. The cabinet agreed to communicate peace conditions to the Entente but not subordinate them to Allied approval.

A certain vagueness of the note of March 13 and the insistence on the 1772 borders rather than on the more appealing principle of national self-determination resulted from numerous complications revealed at the cabinet meeting. Had self-determination prevailed, the Soviets could have claimed that the Ukraine had already determined her fate; the Belorussians would have demanded that the principle apply to them, and the Poles wanted to avoid any commitments to the Belorussian cause. It was only with great difficulty that the Belorussian Council gave in to Wasilewski's persuasion and voiced its approval of the idea of disannexation.[106]

If Patek assumed that phrasing of his note would appeal to the Entente and gain the ready approval of the sejm's Foreign Affairs Committee, he was mistaken. Neither the negative formula of disannexation nor insistence on Polish historic rights carried conviction. The principal objective of driving Russia to the east roused Allied dissatisfaction and criticism. The Russian Whites were indignant and their unofficial representative in Warsaw wrote that if Polish demands were not put forward "on purpose to wreck the possibility of negotiations" they were "simply monstrous."[107]

Only Savinkov and his followers, who saw in the note a prelude to an all-out war against the Bolsheviks, voiced satisfaction. They were ready to collaborate with Warsaw even on such terms, and Savinkov wrote to Piłsudski: "I am with you with all my soul."[108]

The American minister saw in Patek's note a change of heart, and ascribed the tough conditions to Allied desertion of Poland. The Poles left to their own devices had decided to get the best possible conditions.[109] Sir Horace Rumbold opined that Polish peace terms represented a gamble on the part of Warsaw, which thinks "it stands to gain either way," and he recommended that London give the Poles a free hand for a settlement with Russia. This did not mean approval of Polish demands, and the British diplomat reminded Patek, who was apparently much taken aback, that the Allies had the final say on fixing Poland's borders.[110] Meanwhile Sapieha reported from London about the difficulty, if not impossibility, of convincing the British government of "the justice of our demands."[111]

The French government was hardly enthusiastic, and considered that Poland as a state had not crystallized sufficiently to become a center of power in Eastern Europe. Paris feared the repercussions of a conflict which now seemed unavoidable; it felt that a plebiscite or referendum organized by Poles would never be recognized by a non-Communist Russia. "The attitude of France in the matter of our eastern borders is unfavorable to us," the Polish liaison officer with Foch's staff reported.[112] The Italian minister, Francesco Tommasini, wrote later that Warsaw's demand for the 1772 borders showed plainly that Poland was not approaching the negotiations in good faith. Thus the propagandistic effect of the note went against the Poles. Sapieha and Zamoyski further deplored the technique of handing the declaration to Allied ministers in Warsaw, and felt that it would have been far better if the two Polish envoys had presented it to the London and Paris governments.[113]

The premier and foreign minister faced the ordeal of informing the Foreign Affairs Committee of the sejm about the note, and the meeting on March 20 promised to be stormy. Rightist members accused the government of having departed from peace theses previously agreed upon. Skulski denied it and the Committee accepted his explanations, with National Democratic deputies abstaining from the vote. Then the content of the note came up for criticism. The Right declared that nobody would recognize the Polish claim to the 1772 borders; the passage in the note which spoke about Poland determining the fate of populations within these borders would simply discredit the Poles. The note had also attempted to smuggle in federalist ideas. "The drafting of the note is bad," declared Grabski, the chairman of the committee. The Socialist Feliks Perl felt that the principle of national self-determination had been played down, but otherwise considered the document acceptable. Once again it was clear that eastern programs of the Left and Right were irreconcilable, but this time the Right was being outvoted. The committee finally decided to accept the note by nineteen votes against seven. The government had secured freedom of action.[114]

The cabinet decided, and sejm's Foreign Affairs Committee agreed, that Warsaw would not present detailed peace conditions to Soviet Russia. Consequently Patek's note to Chicherin, sent on March 27, 1920, merely proposed to begin negotiations. It indicated the time—April 10; the place—the locality of Borisov near the northeastern front; and offered a local cease-fire to enable the Bolshevik delegates to reach the conference site.[115] These three proposals sounded innocuous but they were designed to ensure the realization of the Polish peace program.

Borisov
and
Kiev

The Polish proposal for a conference at Borisov began a verbal duel between Chicherin and Patek. Their exchanges lasted from late March into April 1920, with both of them playing to a large audience—domestic and international. On the whole, the Bolsheviks, masters in propaganda, got the better of the argument. A deadlock followed; only arms could resolve the issue.

Bolshevik overtures had stemmed from a realistic appraisal of the situation and not from humanitarian considerations. Lenin was no more a pacifist in early 1920 than in the past. He followed Clausewitz's dictum that war was a continuation of policy by other means, just as peaceful concessions were a continuation of war.[1] Nor did he condemn aggressive wars on moral grounds. "It is not the defensive or the offensive character of war," he said, "but the interests of the international proletariat which should determine our attitude toward the war."[2] If he advocated peace with Poland in early 1920 it was for good strategic, economic, and political reasons.

In the winter of 1919–1920 the Bolshevik leaders worried about the possibility of a large-scale Polish military operation. Marchlewski addressed a long report to the Central Committee warning about the danger of an offensive. If the Poles attacked soon, he wrote, they would reach Smolensk and Homel in "a parade march."[3] Trotsky wrote Lenin that the "Anglo-French interventionists are now constructing their policy on an alliance of the border States and attach vast importance to a link-up between Denikin's troops and the Poles."[4] In spite of some official statements which reflected Soviet optimism after victories over the Whites, there was anxiety about a showdown on the western front.[5]

Karl Radek, who in late January 1920 passed through Poland, by virtue of a secret Soviet-Polish arrangement, wrote about the Polish warlike tendencies to three PPS leaders—Daszyński, Herman Diamand, and Perl. He asserted that the Polish bourgeoisie was bellicose because it was afraid of popular discontent and the Entente; other groups were belligerent because they feared Russian aggression. Radek tried to dispel these fears and assured the Socialists that Russia needed peace. But she could not passively "observe Polish preparations for an offensive." He said that if he were to determine Russia's policy he would try to force Poland to make peace or fight a war. The state of neither war nor peace was impossible.[6] Radek's views were important. After reaching Moscow he spoke to Chicherin about the Polish situation, and the Poles suspected that he helped draft the note of January 28.

Soviet nervousness was evident in late January and through February. On January 13 *Pravda* warned the Poles to think twice about attacking Russia, and reminded them of the fate of the White generals. Trotsky wrote Zinoviev that all information pointed to "the possibility of an early Polish offensive along the entire front," and he suggested the mobilization of Polish Communists, increased propaganda, and military preparation.[7] Litvinov reported to the Narkomindel on the Savinkov-Chaikovskii visit to Warsaw, spoke of Polish army moves, and concluded that one had to watch developments in Poland.[8] Addressing a conference of the Presnev region Lenin mentioned the possibility of a Polish invasion of Russia and said that the Bolsheviks would resort to the same measures which in the past had ensured their victories.[9] Two weeks later he spoke again of attempts to make Poland invade Russia, and added in a more optimistic vein that these were breaking down "and the moment is near when we shall conclude peace with everyone."[10] In an interview with the *New York Evening Journal* he denied Moscow's intent to attack Poland, though the capitalists, he said, were pushing Warsaw against Soviet Russia.[11] Finally, in a letter to Trotsky, he spoke against entanglements in Siberia, because while the Soviets were engaged there Denikin might revive and the Poles attack.[12]

Bolshevik peace offers to Poland, dictated by military fears, were accompanied by preparations for war. Late in January the Soviet High Command issued instructions which read: "the general task remains the same—stubborn defense of the front line" accompanied by local counterattacks.[13] A month later the Council of Defense ordered the strengthening of the western front, but no large numbers of troops could be spared; a build-up proceeded fairly slowly.[14] At the same time the chief of operations of the Soviet field staff, Boris M. Shaposhnikov, began to elaborate the plan of an offensive against Poland to replace the old plan based on defensive strategy.[15] Military preparations proceeded together with political-military activity; commissars, Communist political workers, and activists began to arrive in larger numbers to bolster the revolutionary morale of the army.[16]

Did Soviet military moves imply that peace offers were a screen

behind which an all-out offensive was to gather momentum? Many
Poles thought so, and Polish historians have built a strong case
for such an interpretation. But this need not be the only explanation. As Radek told the Polish Socialists, Moscow would try to
impose peace; failing that, they would bring the war to its logical
conclusion—victory. Piłsudski spoke, as mentioned, of the two
Soviet alternatives. The American minister in Warsaw reported
that if there were no speedy peace the "only alternative left to
the Bolsheviks . . . is to attempt the military conquest of Poland."[17]
A change from defensive to offensive strategy reflected an improving military situation; it did not necessarily imply preference for
a warlike solution.[18]

The Bolsheviks had good reasons to avoid a large-scale campaign. The country was in a state of economic exhaustion. The
output of coal had fallen to a fraction of what Russia produced in
1914; there was a terrible shortage of grain. Steel production had
dropped catastrophically, and there was a crisis in transportation.
The precarious military situation led to a maximum effort in reconstruction of railroads, and while shortage in labor was partly
overcome by formation of the labor army (Trudarmiia) this was
a palliative since it did not mean demobilization and release of
men to peaceful work. The Ninth Congress of the RKP(b),
meeting in March 1920, devoted most of its attention to the
problems of economic reconstruction. Peace seemed indispensable
for raising the Russian economy from near ruin.[19]

Internationally, a peaceful settlement with Poland also offered
many advantages. If Lenin viewed the treaty with Estonia as "a
window cut out by the Russian workers to Western Europe," he
may have considered peace with Poland—to use Rumbold's
words—as the "first step towards admittance into family of
nations."[20] Moscow could present peace as proof of its friendly
disposition toward the small neighbors, detach these countries
from the Entente, and show the superiority of its methods over
those of the interventionists.[21] The Bolsheviks stood to gain from
peace because of the lifting of the Allied blockade and of Lloyd
George's policy of peace through trade. All this was unattainable
if war continued on the western borders. A treaty with Poland
offered chances of estranging Warsaw and Paris, London and
Paris, and Berlin and Warsaw, and Soviet peace messages showed
Moscow's intention of enhancing its diplomatic position and
isolating Poland.

A peaceful approach was also important for psychological
reasons. It served to destroy the picture of Soviet Russia—drawn
by Poles and their sympathizers abroad—as a continuator of the

old tsarist imperialism. The Bolsheviks had to consider "that special significance which the Polish question had always possessed,"[22] and Lenin stressed his awareness of the heritage of the past which had poisoned relations between Moscow and Warsaw. "We understand this hatred," he said, "which permeates the soul of the Pole." The partitions had been a crime and the Polish nation had long lived with a single thought of liberation. Soviet concessions aimed "to eradicate this accursed past when every Great Russian was seen as an oppressor."[23] Radek repeatedly urged new Russian and Comintern declarations affirming full recognition of Polish independence.[24] A military showdown was likely to destroy the patiently woven web of Soviet propaganda.

Pravda on February 6 explained why the Bolsheviks opposed war. In an article entitled "Why do we want peace?" the paper stated that it was "the most advantageous condition for introducing Communist ideas in the minds of workers of all the world, and for the victory of world revolution." Lenin angrily criticized those who saw in peace offers a Tolstoyan spirit of abnegation.[25] To "wage war for the overthrow of the international bourgeoisie" was "utterly ridiculous." The essence of Soviet policy since 1917 was compromise, retreat, zigzags, and exploitation of favorable moments.[26] In early 1920 peace with Poland was in accord with this policy, and peace offers were a means to further the internal decomposition of the Polish state.[27]

Peace with Poland was advantageous on all counts: military, economic, international, psychological. It never implied abandoning long-range goals. Zinoviev explained a little later that Soviet concessions to the Poles originated from a conviction that "the Polish workers, allies of the Russian proletariat" would "seize power and sooner or later put aside all injustices."[28] On February 12 *Pravda* asserted that the Polish masses, true to their revolutionary tradition, would side with Russia eventually and "help us to also gain peace with the West."*

To examine the kind of peace the Bolsheviks had in mind one must turn to the second point of the message of the Council of Peoples' Commissars of January 28, 1920, which stated that the Red Army would not cross the existing front line. It was not a formal proposal of a frontier, and some Polish historians feel that the Soviet leaders engaged in propaganda when they asserted

---

* Upon his return from Russia, Bertrand Russell said that the Bolsheviks were prepared to accept the existence and independence of the Baltic states and Poland, because they felt that these states "would necessarily be penetrated by Russian influence and if ever they became troublesome could easily be swallowed up." Memorandum of a conversation with Bertrand Russell by H. A. L. Fisher, July 26, 1920, PRO, Cab. 24/109.

that this is what they really suggested. In the absence of documentation for the council meetings at Moscow, one can only speculate whether the Russians were willing to give up territories occupied by the Poles. There is a good deal of circumstantial evidence to suggest that they were. Marchlewski had assured Polish envoys at Białowieża and Mikaszewicze that Lenin was ready to make territorial concessions. During the peace negotiations with the Baltic countries the Bolsheviks were less adamant on frontiers than on ideological provisions and political guarantees. Their thinking about territorial issues found expression in Lenin's statement on December 28, 1919, that determining the borders was a secondary question, since "we strive after a complete eradication of state frontiers."[29] Asserting that the front line was to serve as the basis for a territorial settlement with Poland— because the Soviets did not want to wage war for boundaries— Lenin added that this would be "a great gain for Poland."[30] Here he spoke with tongue in cheek, for neither he nor other Soviet leaders viewed this arrangement either as lasting or as advantageous for the Poles. Lenin, Zinoviev, and Radek made it clear that they thought Poland incapable of absorbing these "foreign lands"; Polish control over them would merely speed up the revolutionary processes.[31] While they spoke of sacrifices and of a disadvantageous treaty they believed that in the long run Soviet Russia would grow stronger than her enemies.

It is likely that the Bolsheviks "were ready to buy this peace"— to use Trotsky's words—at the price of a territorial settlement that coincided with the existing military situation.[32] This was the understanding of the Soviet proposal by the unofficial White Russian representative in Warsaw.[33] General Rozwadowski thought in similar terms. He wrote to the Supreme Command that the Bolsheviks "have no desire to risk a great military operation against Poland, intimating correctly that a probable defeat . . . would not only discredit their present successes but undermine generally the whole future of their leaders." He concluded that "they would rather pay for these advantages with serious concessions to Poland."[34] But Warsaw had to make certain of the Soviet intentions and find out whether the Bolsheviks were willing to consider other Polish peace conditions. Events of the next few weeks were to bring an answer to these questions.

Pravda acknowledged Patek's first message of February 4 two days later with a news item headlined, "Poland inclines toward negotiations." Then there was silence, as no new notes arrived, but the Bolsheviks began to glean an idea of the terms contemplated by the Poles. Lenin told VTsIK that the Polish demand for the separation of the Ukraine was "a crime."[35] He informed Trotsky that everything indicated that Warsaw would present "absolutely unacceptable and even impudent terms." It was necessary to strengthen the western front and "launch the slogan: get ready for war against Poland."[36] In an article entitled "We and They," *Pravda*, on February 27, contrasted Soviet moderation—though Russia was "at the summit of her victories"—with Polish demands for the 1772 borders. This was brigandage, the paper wrote, and if Poland was "an obedient lackey of the Entente," the Polish masses were on Russia's side. "Communism in Poland grows rapidly," the article concluded.

This appraisal of the domestic Polish situation may well explain why Lenin's war slogan was not launched. The Bolsheviks probably decided that a bellicose statement would play into the hands of the Warsaw government; it was better to stress peace. Besides, victories over Kolchak and Denikin had created a feeling of superiority: *Pravda* put Poland on the same level as Estonia; *Izvestia* called Poland a serious enemy only after the Polish victories in the spring of 1920. The press of the Western Front made no effort to prepare the troops for serious fighting.[37]

Lenin's speeches emphasized the political rather than the military aspects of the Polish situation. In an address on March 1 he pointed out that the Bolsheviks had won their victories not because of military superiority but because of the demoralization of foes. If the border states had combined against Soviet Russia "we would have suffered defeat." But they trusted the Entente less than Russia. Now the Allies wanted to push Poland against the Soviets, and Polish lords and capitalists put forward demands for 1772 borders although Moscow had denounced partitions and tried to wipe out the crimes of tsardom. Polish aggression would be madness. If Warsaw intended to pursue this course, the only Soviet reply was: "Try. You will be taught a lesson that you will never forget."[38] A week later Lenin repeated the threat and explained that although Poland was on the verge of internal collapse its government might want to save itself by a desperate military gamble.[39]

The Bolshevik leaders speculated in early March about the likelihood of a struggle. Lenin wrote Trotsky that "evidently the Poles will fight," and he said one must strengthen defenses and step up propaganda.[40] Trotsky inquired whether it was necessary to transfer units from the labor army (Trudarmiia).[41] Then came the Polish attack on Mozyr, and Trotsky tried to interpret it. He commented that this operation could mean two things. Either the Poles wanted to improve their position before negotiations and assumed that the Red Army would not offer much resistance, or they were trying to provoke the Soviets and use it as a justification for an all-out offensive. Trotsky suggested that Litvinov try to find out and respond to possible Polish propaganda.[42] Having received information from Chicherin and Litvinov, Lenin answered that hostilities seemed unavoidable; French officers were arriving in Poland, Russia had to get ready to fight.[43]

At this juncture there appeared among the Bolshevik leaders a serious difference of opinion over political tactics. Chicherin favored continuing the peaceful approach. Any threats were likely to strengthen the belligerent groups in Poland and weaken the peace party. Hence he avoided official comments on the Polish territorial program, and emphasized the need for peace. Trotsky and Litvinov disagreed. Litvinov asserted that "our peace proposals are taken for weakness," and Trotsky added that the last proposals to Poland "were unnecessary." He suggested a propaganda campaign in Russia to show Poles that the Bolsheviks were ready for a showdown. Among the measures he proposed were a manifesto to the Russian nation explaining the situation and calling on them to prepare for a war effort; public discussion by the party congress of the danger from Poland; mobilization of Polish Communists; sending of commissars and political workers to the western front. Trotsky insisted that the Politburo discuss the whole matter at the next meeting.[44]

It is not clear how other ranking Bolsheviks viewed the situation. In an enigmatic note, Lenin wrote Trotsky that in view of Polish military successes and in spite of Stalin's optimism he was ready to give effect to Trotsky's recommendations.[45] The war commissar elaborated his views in a lengthy memorandum. He argued that Chicherin's proposal to ignore the still uncommunicated Polish peace terms was mistaken, because it would make the Poles believe that "we shall accept their conditions." They would continue their policies "which undoubtedly will end by war." Trotsky termed Chicherin's approach "a provocation of war." He said that while the Entente could force the Poles to fight, the problem—at least formally—was still that of peace negotiations and not war. Warsaw had reacted to Soviet peace proposals and had prepared terms, which they had shown to the Entente. Russian silence could disarm the Polish workers politically. The latter heard no "determined protest of the Russian working masses against the impudent terms of the Polish government." Soviet failure to react could convey the impression that Polish conditions were acceptable. Trotsky concluded: "When we shall declare at the last moment that conditions are unacceptable, and the conflict becomes inevitable, this will come as a surprise to the broad masses of Polish workers, and it will be too late for them to take any measures to prevent the conflict."[46]

Judging by developments, Trotsky's theses did not prevail. He overestimated the effects of popular pressure on the government in Warsaw, and it is doubtful whether his approach would have helped to avoid the clash. Military preparations continued. The commander-in-chief, Sergei S. Kamenev, approved on March 10 the new offensive plan against Poland. Five days later the command and the revolutionary council (revvoensovet) of the Western Front ordered that the troops be ready. A rapid influx of party workers followed. Then on March 27 Moscow received Patek's note proposing peace negotiations at Borisov. Direct exchanges between Russia and Poland began.

The Polish proposal sought to bring about military and political provisions which would guarantee Soviet acceptance of Piłsudski's peace terms. Fearing that the Bolsheviks would drag out negotiations while completing the concentration of the Red Army, the Poles wanted to retain the means of preventing it. Two days after the receipt of Patek's note Lenin said that "each month gives us a gigantic increase of our forces,"[47] and Warsaw knew it too. Poland realized that a general armistice would immobilize Polish troops (in mid-March numbering 300,000, as opposed to 90,000 Russians) and allow Russia to swing the balance in her favor. Once an armistice would be signed and applied to a seven-hundred-mile front, it would be difficult to break. Poland would be obliged to negotiate even if circumstances changed to her disadvantage. Hence a local as opposed to a general cease-fire was a preliminary condition of the Polish peace program.

Nor was the choice of Borisov accidental. Protracted negotiations would permit Russia to use ideological weapons and try to revolutionize Poland. Lenin asked rhetorically "whether a Soviet republic of Poland will not come earlier than a peaceful or warlike move of the [Polish] government."[48] It was clear that the Bolsheviks planned to turn the peace conference into a propaganda debate. The little town of Borisov located in the front zone would lend itself less than any other place for such purposes. The Polish minister in Washington explained that Borisov was selected "because of the danger of possible propaganda and of direct contact of the delegates of Soviet Russia . . . with communists of other nationalities."[49] Sapieha said that the Bolsheviks sought to have negotiations "in a place well in the limelight" and that he was "determined not to allow this."[50] The Poles knew that the Entente was critical of Piłsudski's eastern program, and that the Allies still had the right—by virtue of Article 87 of the Treaty of Versailles—to determine Poland's eastern borders. Borisov, with no accommodations for foreign representatives and the press suited the Poles far better than any other locality.*

Chicherin answered Patek's note on March 28, expressing satisfaction that negotiations were to begin on April 10, and surprise that Poles proposed only a local and temporary cease-fire. Why should blood be spilled when a peace settlement was in sight?

The commissar opposed the choice of Borisov, because a conference could work much better in the peaceful conditions of a neutral country. He suggested a town in Estonia, adding that his government would seek the agreement of Estonian authorities. If Warsaw accepted his suggestions there would be no obstacles to negotiation.[51]

Official Soviet reactions were guardedly optimistic. At first *Pravda* and *Izvestia* reacted favorably to Patek's note but two and three days later expressed doubt about Polish sincerity, and stated that acceptance of Polish terms would be suicidal.[52] Lenin, addressing the Ninth Congress of the party, recommended caution because peace did not entirely depend on the will of a small country like Poland. He emphasized that the Soviet campaign for peace—or "war for peace" as he put it—would continue because it had brought Russia at least as many victories as had the Red Army. This was why, Lenin said, "we grasp at peace proposals with both hands, giving maximum concessions, in the conviction that peace with tiny states will advance the cause much more effectively than war," which only obscures the truth about Russia. Peace "opens the way to our influence."[53]

The Soviet leaders were not prepared to negotiate on the terms proposed by Patek. Their later comments revealed the full extent of their annoyance with the Poles. Marchlewski wrote of the "impudent tone" of the message which "unilaterally dictated" conditions; Radek said Warsaw wanted a "Polish peace"; Trotsky declared that the Polish government "demanded that our plenipotentiaries appear at Borisov to listen to lordly commands . . . as if we were defeated."[54] Moscow considered that the demand to negotiate at Borisov without a general armistice was a trick to

---

* Compare opinions expressed by Captain Miedziński on the Polish side (*Dokumenty i materiały do historii stosunków polsko-radzieckich* [Warsaw, 1962—], II, 470) and Radek on the Russian (Karl Radek and R. Stefanovich, *Perevorot v Polshe i Pilsudskii*, [Moscow, 1926], pp. 17-18) with the observation of the American minister in Warsaw that it would be "very difficult for the allied representatives here to find out what is going on at Borisov" (Rumbold to Curzon, March 29, PRO, F.O. 371/3913, no. 190050).

paralyze the Red Army in a most important sector, while permitting the Poles to continue military operations in the Ukraine. In their report to the Central Committee, the Polish Communists also emphasized this point.* Chicherin termed the Polish demand "absurd from a military point of view."[55] The Bolsheviks did not know that the Polish general staff, unaware of the concentration of Soviet armies along the northern front, assumed that the bulk of the Red Army was in the Ukraine.[56] It was politics rather than strategy that dictated Polish insistence on Borisov.†

Chicherin's reply indicated that Moscow's willingness to negotiate was conditional. Had the commissar agreed without reservation it would have meant that the Bolsheviks were prepared to accept a peace settlement along the lines envisaged by Piłsudski: preliminary conditions determining the nature of the final treaty. This was not the case, and the Poles knew what to expect. Patek told Gibson he thought the Bolsheviks would agree to his conditions. Piłsudski was primarily interested in his own goals and cared little if it were done through peace or a new military campaign. He told Gibson "he had no idea of what would be the outcome of the negotiations with the Bolsheviks." The Poles were capable of winning the war, and if they negotiated it was because Britain had forced their hand and because Piłsudski did not want to be accused of imperialism. He agreed that "conditions offered to the Soviet Government were severe" but "they were more moderate than the conditions imposed upon Germany by the victorious allies."[57]

Piłsudski thought of Russia as a defeated country to whom Poland could dictate conditions. He told Wasilewski after Chicherin's reply had reached Warsaw: "I do not believe in the possibility of concluding peace now." But since negotiations had to go on, he commented that either "we shall conclude a *serious* peace, or we shall strike, strike, strike."[58] He seemed to favor the "strike," in the belief that peace was only possible after a decisive defeat of the Red Army.

While Piłsudski began preparations for a spring campaign, the Ministry of Foreign Affairs went on with preliminary work for a

* See the report of the Polish bureau of propaganda and agitation of the Central Committee of RKP(b) of March 30, 1920 which spoke critically of Borisov and recalled the fate of Soviet envoys of the "Red Cross" who had negotiated on Polish territory. *Grazhdanskaia voina na Ukraine 1918-1920: sbornik dokumentov i materialov*, ed. S. M. Korolivskii, N. H. Kolechnik, and I. K. Rybalk (3 vols. in 4; Kiev, 1967), III, 24-25.

† It is interesting that a local cease-fire had been achieved at Borisov on January 1, 1920 in connection with the exchange of civilian prisoners and hostages. See *Dokumenty i materiały*, II, 523n.

conference in Borisov. The government appointed a peace delegation and made arrangements to house the peacemakers.* A special
commission worked out a draft peace treaty, and while only
fragments of it have been preserved, they give a good idea of the
Polish program. The document developed the theses previously
discussed by the ministers and the sejm's Foreign Relations Committee, and introduced new and far-reaching demands. Some
provided for demobilization of the Soviet army, others to secure
a privileged position for Polish trade in Russia. There were
articles which constituted interference with Russian sovereignty
and specified high reparations, almost a ransom. Wasilewski, who
seems to have been one of the authors of the draft, characterized
it as deliberately "kept on a maximum level for the purpose of
bargaining," and so formulated as if it were "addressed to a state
completely defeated by Poland."[59]

Patek answered Chicherin's message with a brief note on April
1. The Polish government adhered to its choice of the conference
site; it could not agree to an armistice along the entire front; a
local cease-fire around Borisov would not be temporary, as
Chicherin assumed, but would last during the whole negotiation.
This curt note ended with a statement that further delays would
postpone the opening of the conference. Warsaw asked for a
speedy Soviet reply.[60]

Chicherin consulted Lenin. He wrote that the Poles "are
evidently concerned how to break off [the negotiations] to their
greatest advantage in the eyes of public opinion." The commissar
said that Moscow "must absolutely reject Borisov" and propose
either Estonia or Russia. Negotiations in Poland "are unacceptable." He added that "We cannot insist on the question of an
armistice once we had conducted talks in Estonia without an
armistice. But in such a case there should be no armistice. Either
everywhere or nowhere."[61] Lenin commented that "in my opinion
Chicherin is right," but a subsequent Soviet radio to Warsaw
still made some reference to the armistice and to negotiation in
Poland for propaganda purposes.

Chicherin's message to Patek of April 2 was a long document. It

* According to Wasilewski the government delegates were Patek, Wasilewski,
Sapieha, and possibly Kossakowski. See *Józef Piłsudski jakim go znałem* (Warsaw,
1935), p. 219. Gibson reported that the following were members of the delegation:
Patek, Wasilewski, General Sosnkowski, Kazimierz Olszowski, Moraczewski, Anusz,
and Stanisław Grabski. See Gibson to Secretary of State, March 30, 1920, Record
Group 59, "Political Relations between Poland and the Soviet Union," 760c.61/38,
National Archives. Preparation of the lodgings at Borisov was in the hands of
Boerner. See MS Diariusz Kossakowskiego, March 30, 1920, Archiwum Polskiej
Akademii Nauk, Warsaw.

said that the working masses of Russia had extended a fraternal hand to the Polish people and proposed peace. A conference could proceed normally if hostilities came to a halt, and the Polish government by rejecting an armistice assumed responsibility for continued bloodshed. Poland's reasons were obscure if the country desired peace. Warsaw's insistence on Borisov was incomprehensible, for it was not a convenient location, and led to a suspicion of concealed strategic motives. Patek's proposal was unacceptable, and Russia could find no convincing arguments for the Polish case. If the Poles preferred negotiations in Petrograd or in Moscow, even in Warsaw—assuming that they provided guarantees—this was agreeable. Chicherin said he awaited a Polish reply.[62]

Five days passed before Patek dispatched his answer, the last communication addressed to Moscow, and it is likely that the Poles took pains to phrase it carefully. The note repeated that the Polish government had chosen Borisov because of its convenient location—good railroad communications with Warsaw and Moscow, and easy radio and telegraph contacts with both capitals. The Poles had rejected a general armistice, because given the length of the front armistice arrangements would require as much time as preliminary peace talks. The Polish army had no intent of hindering negotiations through aggressive action, and it imposed no restrictions on Soviet military freedom. As for guarantees—a veiled Russian allusion to the murder of the "Red Cross" delegates in January 1919—Poland took them for granted. A peace conference, given the delays resulting from Soviet counterproposals and long exchanges, could not start before April 17, and Warsaw expected a final answer. Further discussion of Borisov and the armistice was fruitless. Patek terminated his message by objecting to some expressions used by Chicherin which could make negotiation difficult.[63]

The foreign commissar replied briefly. Polish insistence on Borisov sounded like an ultimatum. A deadlock on account of the choice of a meeting place was unprecedented in the history of international relations. The Soviets had rejected a town in the front zone because the Poles would not agree to an armistice, but were willing to negotiate elsewhere, even in London or Paris. The only way out was to ask for the mediation of the Entente, and Chicherin informed Patek that he was dispatching a note to Britain, France, Italy, and the United States.[64] He thus implied that final decision rested with the Allies, and simultaneously emphasized the conciliatory spirit of Soviet diplomacy.

Chicherin's note to the Entente cleverly appealed to the economic interests of the powers: Polish warlike actions against the

Soviet republics interfered not only with peaceful policies but "hampered the development of their resources and the possibility of delivering to other countries products which were needed by them." The commissar sought to gain sympathy for Russia, stating that Warsaw had blindly imitated German policies at Brest-Litovsk. He repeated that it was a unique case in the history of diplomacy when peace negotiation broke down on the choice of place for a conference. Chicherin reiterated Soviet willingness to talk in Estonia, Petrograd, Moscow, Warsaw, or even in London or Paris. He asked the Allies to use their influence with the Poles, since Poland was largely their responsibility.[65]

Chicherin complemented his communication with an interview to the *Manchester Guardian*. His remarks were intended to convey the impression of moderation. Repeating some of the points of his note, he added that he could not believe that the Poles, despite their last message, wished to make peace impossible. The Polish masses were peaceful and there were only a handful of warmongers. Perhaps Warsaw opposed a meeting in Estonia because that country had been the first to make peace with the Bolsheviks. The Poles disliked talks in a Russian city, because they feared to look as if they had been defeated. As for a conference in Warsaw, the government seemingly feared the Polish workers. Perhaps the Poles might agree to negotiate in Paris or London.[66]

All this was brilliant propaganda, for Chicherin must have known that neither France nor Britain would favor Soviet-Polish peace talks in their capitals.[67] In a note to Litvinov he wrote that the Soviets would be willing to negotiate in Białystok, Grodno, or any other place in Poland provided it would not lie closer than 300 versts behind the front.[68] This was an important qualification, tied to Bolshevik military preparations. The same day Chicherin replied to Patek, the Soviet commander-in-chief telegraphed the commander of the Western Front, Vladimir M. Gittis, that the last Polish note indicated the possibility of an impending Polish offensive. Kamenev ordered preparations for a counterattack. If the Poles failed to strike, the commander-in-chief went on, Gittis was to continue to concentrate his troops and get ready for the planned operation.[69] This referred to the Soviet offensive in the north, approved on March 10, 1920. Chicherin's insistence that the negotiation site be far from the front line was to ensure noninterference with the contemplated action of the Red Army.

The Allies gave no answer to the Soviet note, but the Polish government was disappointed that they did not take a stand favoring Warsaw. Foch and Weygand wanted to help the Poles get conditions from the Bolsheviks "which would guarantee

Poland a stable peace in the east," but the French government prefered noninvolvement.[70] Millerand said he had no intent of intervening over the place for peace talks. Nor was he willing to strengthen Poland by recognizing the pro-Polish Petliura.[71] The British, while appreciating that Chicherin's telegrams were "to represent Poland in a bad light," tried to soften the Polish stand with regard to Borisov.[72] Warsaw disliked these subtle pressures, and assured London that Polish willingness to desist from aggressive action, provided the Bolsheviks would do the same, "showed best the desire to conclude a rapid peace."[73] As for the United States, the Polish minister in Washington wrote that the State Department shared Warsaw's point of view on Borisov.[74]

Patek then went on another tour of Western capitals, and reported that "all the governments leave us a free hand and will either not reply to Chicherin's note or wash their hands of it." He concluded, optimistically, that "they all consider that we have been managing the affair of peace with the Bolsheviks very well." The French gave him to understand "that the Bolsheviks wanted to deceive us [the Poles] but we have been cautious." Paris would exercise no pressure to hasten a Soviet-Polish settlement.[75]

In the absence of Allied mediation the deadlock continued, and both Warsaw and Moscow attempted to justify their positions. The Polish Ministry of Foreign Affairs issued on April 20 a communiqué which contained its version of the breakdown of exchanges. According to this release, Poland had indicated Borisov as the most convenient place for negotiations. In reply the Soviet government demanded an armistice which in view of technical difficulties and in absence of guarantees was likely to cause friction. Its result would have been a state of "neither war nor peace," allowing negotiations "to drag on endlessly." Warsaw favored immediate discussion of peace conditions, and showed good will by declaring that the army did not intend to hinder negotiation by aggressive action. The Soviets, so the communiqué said, responded by increasing their concentration of troops and by attacks along the front. Moscow sent a note to the Entente asking for intervention, although the Bolsheviks originally had left the choice of a place for the peace conference to the Polish government. Thus "the controversy about the place is only a pretext to delay the opening of negotiations." If the Soviet government would show a "sincere will" to conclude peace, it would find the Poles ready.[76]

The Polish communiqué illustrated Warsaw's suspicion of Soviet motives, and indeed many people feared the Bolsheviks would exploit the negotiations to strengthen their position and

then try to impose a "Soviet peace."[77] Instructions to Polish
missions abroad emphasized that "the Polish government considers
that the attitude of the Council [of Peoples' Commissars], coinciding with a concentration of Soviet armies along the front,
betrays the desire of the Council—masked by misleading ap-
pearances—to prolong preliminary negotiations for strategic and
tactical reasons, in the hope that fortune of arms would cease to
favor the Polish troops or that the Council would succeed in gaining the good will and support of the Entente."[78]

All this made good sense to many Poles, even if the Socialists
had doubts whether the government had handled negotiations in
good faith, and the National Democrats were unhappy about
the course of events. The Piłsudskiites were belligerent. In an
article entitled "Peace," *Rząd i Wojsko* wrote that "in the existing
conditions there can be no question of a peace of understanding."
War against Russia was an "unavoidable consequence of the resurrection of the Polish state." Chicherin knew it well, and his notes
were propaganda to gain more time for the Bolsheviks.[79]

The Narkomindel fired its broadside on April 23. The Soviet
communiqué said that in view of the deadlock about the meeting
place and the Polish interpretation of events, it was necessary to
state the following facts: Russia had never agreed in advance to a
Polish choice of a conference site; she "is not a defeated country
to which the victor may dictate his will." Poland had rejected
talks about the meeting place, and did it on purely formal grounds.
The Poles aimed at "the capitulation of the Soviet government."
They had not published the text of Soviet proposals and allowed
the press to attack the Bolsheviks. The Soviets had rejected Borisov because of a Polish refusal of an armistice, and the connection
ought to be obvious. Warsaw's insinuation that Russia had secret
plans connected with an armistice were groundless; even some
Polish papers viewed the armistice as a natural arrangement. The
Warsaw government had declared over the radio that it gave
orders to its troops not to hinder peace negotiations by aggressive
action, but this assurance, as phrased in Patek's note, was vague.*
The Soviets were still ready to conclude a peace treaty. Current
hostilities were not caused by Soviet attacks but by the Polish
troops acting against an alleged concentration of the Red Army.
The Narkomindel stated that the last Polish note indicated that

* It is not clear what Chicherin had in mind because the phrasing of this
point in Patek's note and in the communiqué of April 20 was virtually identical.
He may have referred to an alleged broadcast by Warsaw radio supposedly repeated by Radio Lyons. See Chicherin to Tsentrosoiuz delegate, April 9, 1920,
Dokumenty vneshnei politiki SSSR (Moscow, 1959—), II, 452. (Cited as *DVP SSSR*.

Warsaw did not treat the question of the conference site as an ultimatum.* The Soviet government also noted the informal declaration that the Polish army would not undertake aggressive action. Moscow desired a solution to the problem of a place for the conference, and assumed the Poles would not object to a town in their own territory. Hence the Soviet government proposed Grodno or Białystok.[80] Two days later Chicherin issued a statement to the Soviet press covering the same ground as the communiqué.[81] It was clearly for people at home, but its effectiveness must remain in the realm of conjecture.

The communiqués of both governments sought to present their respective cases to domestic and international public opinion. In this verbal duel the Bolsheviks got the better of the argument. Not only was Chicherin more adroit than Patek, but his position was easier. The Bolsheviks spoke consistently of peace, favored an armistice, and showed themselves reasonable regarding the site of a conference. They implied willingness to make territorial concessions beyond those contemplated at the Paris Peace Conference. All this was bound to create sympathy abroad. In contrast to Moscow, Warsaw appeared unreasonable. The Poles had rejected an armistice, wanted to negotiate at the front, and their peace program seemed excessive if not imperialist. They showed a tenacity and self-confidence annoying to the public at large.

Closer scrutiny reveals that the Soviet approach was not all white and the Polish not all black.† The Soviet idea of peace was a "revolutionary peace," a temporary arrangement dictated by expediency and based on the hope of the ultimate victory of Communism. No documents have appeared to indicate what kind of a settlement the Russians had in mind. There are no drafts of a peace treaty, no listings of demands which the Bolshevik delegates were to present at a conference table. Nor is there any indication that a Soviet delegation had been appointed. All this lends support to Polish suspicions that the Bolsheviks viewed negotiations as marking time until a reassertion of Russian might.

The Soviet "revolutionary peace" contrasted with Piłsudski's "strategic peace." Warsaw felt that even a compromise settlement would favor Russia in the long run. Poland seemed to have a unique opportunity to recover the position she once occupied in East Central Europe. She did not want to be disarmed by Bol-

---

* There is nothing to indicate that the Polish note or communiqué softened on the issue of Borisov.

† As E. Malcolm Carroll has observed, Chinese-North Korean negotiations with the United Nations at Panmunjon in 1953-1954 were on exactly the same conditions as proposed by the Poles in 1920. See his *Soviet Communism and Western Opinion, 1919-1921* (Chapel Hill, N.C., 1965), p. 256n.

shevik propaganda and made to abandon a temporarily advantageous situation. Failing concerted diplomatic action with the West, Piłsudski sought military guarantees for a peace which would stabilize the young Polish republic, and he thought of obtaining them through a victorious campaign.

The Ukrainian question occupied a central place in Piłsudski's designs. Polish insistence on renunciation by Russia of the 1772 borders implied Soviet withdrawal up to the Dnieper, and Warsaw had to adopt a definite policy vis-à-vis the Ukraine. Political and military reasons favored alliance with the exiled leader Petliura, and the Poles thought of opposing him to the Soviet masters of the Ukraine.

Having driven out Denikin, the Bolsheviks seized Kiev in mid-December 1919, and began to re-establish their rule over the country. Their position was precarious, and Lenin tried hard to obliterate mistakes which had so signally contributed to the collapse of Communism in the Ukraine. The old Central Committee of the KP(b) of the Ukraine was dissolved, and the majority of former officials of the republic suspended. The Eighth Conference of the Russian Communist Party, held in early December 1919, issued a resolution "On the Soviet rule in the Ukraine," which foresaw concessions to the separatists.[82] A new All-Ukrainian Revolutionary Committee emerged. Lenin explained the lines of policy in a message to workers and peasants of the Ukraine. He admitted that the Bolsheviks were divided into supporters of full Ukrainian independence, federalists, and those who advocated a merger with Russia. The last group could well be suspected of Great Russian chauvinism, but those who favored independence might become victims of local nationalism. He saw the solution in subordination of these diverse tendencies to long-range revolutionary goals. He said that the Bolsheviks strove "after close unity and full merger of workers and peasants of all nations of the world into a single universal Soviet republic," but they wanted "a voluntary union of nations." Hence one had to move cautiously to overcome national suspiciousness. He warned the orthodox Communists against neglecting the "national" weapon, which was important if one realized its limitations.[83]

Caution was the *mot d'ordre*, for the Ukraine was far from pacified. Remnants of Petliura's troops were active, and units led by General Mykhailo Omelianovych-Pavlenko fought during their famous "winter march." The government, presided over by Isaak Mazepa, held out in Khmelnik. Anti-Soviet partisans abounded. Although Denikin had helped the Bolsheviks by having partly

suppressed peasant revolts, "the wave of kulak uprisings." as a
Soviet historian put it, "organized by Petliura's agents swept
large parts of the provinces of Kiev, Kharkov, Kherson, and
Volhynia."[84] Several months after effective occupation by the Red
Army and establishment of a Soviet Ukrainian government,
Trotsky alarmed Moscow with news of trouble. He asked for
political workers and party agitators, and spoke of need for "heroic
efforts."[85] In the spring of 1920 he said that Petliura's military
organization in the rear of the front was "much stronger than the
Soviet government.[86] The Southwestern Front had to hold back
four divisions against the partisans.[87] While dismissing Petliura
as a negligible quantity, Zinoviev conceded that his movement
(Petliurovshchina) was the most serious adversary in the
Ukraine.[88] By the spring of 1920 the fate of the Ukraine was far
from settled to the advantage of the Bolsheviks. As Trotsky remarked a few months later: "The Soviet rule of the Ukraine has
been largely maintained so far (and badly maintained) through
the authority of Moscow, Great Russian Communists, and the
Russian Red Army." Economically there was chaos under the
"bureaucratic centralism of Moscow."[89] Petliura and Piłsudski
had reason to believe that the Ukraine could be torn away from
Russia and get a chance to decide her own future.

Polish-Ukrainian cooperation against the Bolsheviks was likely
to arouse the opposition of several groups of Poles and Ukrainians.
The National Democrats and the Center parties felt that a pro-
Ukrainian policy would permanently antagonize Russia, any
Russia. Mistrusting the Ukrainians and worried about Eastern
Galicia, the Polish rightists and moderates saw no reason why
Poland should commit herself to Ukrainian independence. The
Socialists, while favoring an independent Ukraine and willing to
defend her in peace talks with the Bolsheviks, were not keen on
military action.[90] Ukrainians from Eastern Galicia feared that
any arrangement with the Poles would leave them under Polish
control. Others felt that a Ukraine allied with Poland would become Warsaw's satellite. There was fear of economic exploitation
in view of the existence of vested interests of Polish landowning
and industrial circles in the Ukraine. Need rather than free choice
was driving the Ukrainians toward collaboration with the Poles.

In the long run Piłsudski saw a Ukraine detached from the
Bolsheviks as a barrier between Poland and Russia, weakening
the latter.[91] In the forthcoming campaign the Ukraine would
become the main battlefield, for Piłsudski planned an offensive
toward Kiev. He hoped to destroy the bulk of Soviet armies—
which the Polish general staff erroneously assumed to be con-

centrated there—and then leave the defense of the Ukraine to Petliura and his troops. This operation would shorten the Polish-held front by some 160 miles, and permit a second blow to the Red Army in the north. The military advantages of cooperation with the Ukrainians seemed perfectly clear. As for political benefits, a paper prepared by the Ministry of Foreign Affairs in Warsaw stated: "In case Petliura should maintain himself in the Ukraine, Poland would secure economic advantages and undoubted general influence on the shaping of relations in the right bank [of the Dnieper] Ukraine."[92] Piłsudski later summed up the factors in favor of his Ukrainian policy by saying that it would free Poland from "the whims of the Entente," eliminate the menace of Russian Bolshevism and imperialism, and secure economic profits through the use of the riches of the Ukraine.[93]

The Polish-Ukrainian *pourparler* began in earnest in March 1920 and ran parallel to the Patek-Chicherin exchanges. The negotiating power of the Ukrainians was obviously weak, and Petliura was aware of it.[94] Writing to his minister of war, the Chief Ataman asserted that a realistic politician could not be influenced by memories of past misunderstandings and had to strive for cooperation with Poland, a necessary stage in political evolution. He criticized those Ukrainians who favored federation with Russia, and condemned the Galicians for shortsightedness. He wrote that Piłsudski and his supporters who favored Ukrainian independence also had to overcome domestic opposition. What mattered most was Polish recognition of the Ukrainian state and its government and military help.[95] Petliura believed in Piłsudski's sincerity, but was ready to ally with the devil to save Ukrainian independence. Petliura's faith in Piłsudski was justified, and when Livytskyi, the Ukrainian foreign minister who conducted the negotiations, objected to the first Polish draft, the chief of state ordered concessions to the Ukrainians.[96]

There were many points of friction. Livytskyi suggested on April 14 that the question of borders be transferred from the political pact to the military convention; the Polish general staff protested. A day later the Polish draft treaty was completed and new exchanges took place. The draft contained ten points: it recognized Petliura's regime as a *de facto* government; defined the Ukraine as comprised within the Dnieper and the prewar Austrian frontier; provided for Polish evacuation of the Ukraine by mutual agreement; engaged the Ukrainian government to call a constituent assembly to which it would hand over power within six months after liberation of the country; precluded the possibility of Ukrainian agreements directed against Poland or a separate peace treaty with the Bolsheviks; stipulated reciprocal national and cultural rights for Poles in the Ukraine and Ukrainians in Poland; provided for an economic agreement and military convention; and stated that the pact would be secret.[97]

More discussion followed, in the course of which the Polish side agreed to some territorial concessions. The obligation not to conclude a separate peace treaty or sign other pacts became binding on both partners. In the final text, signed on April 21, 1920 by Andrii Livytskyi and Jan Dąbski, there were some changes. Clauses dealing with Polish evacuation of the Ukraine and with the constituent assembly disappeared. Instead of *de facto* recognition there was full recognition of the Ukrainian government as presided over by Petliura.[98]

A military convention followed three days later. The document, meant to be later replaced by a permanent treaty, dealt with technical cooperation during hostilities. Its salient points were the supreme Polish command over allied troops while operating west of the Dnieper, Polish control of the railroad system, Ukrainian engagement to supply the Polish army with food, and promise of payment for equipment provided by the Poles. Except for conquered armored trains and movable equipment, all war booty was to become property of the Ukrainian Republic. Final evacuation of the Ukraine by Polish armies would begin after a proposal emanating from either side, and would be carried out following agreement between Polish and Ukrainian supreme military authorities. The text of the military convention was top secret.[99]

An economic convention, foreseen by the political pact, was not concluded. There was merely agreement that the rights of Polish landowners in the Ukraine—pending a final solution of the agrarian question by the constituent assembly—would be regulated by a special accord. The Poles prepared a draft of an economic treaty on May 1, and subsequently had other demands: concessions to exploit some iron ore and manganese mines in the Ukraine, free zones in Black Sea ports, and trade and communication privileges. The Ukrainians resisted. Piłsudski showed apprehension lest the Poles try to exploit the Ukraine economically, and Sosnkowski had to assure him that this was not the case. It was, he reported, merely a question of keeping open the possibility of eastward economic expansion. Later military developments prevented any binding agreements.[100]

The Polish-Ukrainian pacts of April 21 and 24, 1920 were neither an example of Poland's altruism nor a plot to enslave the Ukraine. They represented a political bargain in which the weaker side made greater concessions, although Piłsudski did his best to show magnanimity. Existing evidence shows that Warsaw paid more attention to Polish industrial and commercial interests than to those of the Polish landowners in the Ukraine. The Poles sought to obtain some measures of control over political and economic life of the country but no more than that.[101] Even when their bargaining power was at its highest, they made concessions, agreeing among other points that only one cabinet minister (instead of three) and one undersecretary of state should represent the Polish minority in the Ukraine.[102] Both men, incidentally, were staunch supporters of Ukrainian independence.

Piłsudski called his Ukrainian policy "an experiment."[103] The word was well chosen, for the pact went against the mental habits of most Poles and Ukrainians. Eastern Galician leaders denounced it; the senior statesman of the Ukrainian national movement, Professor Mykhailo Hrushevsky, opposed it; so did Volodymyr Vynnychenko, the former leader of the Directoriat gone over to the Bolsheviks. Even Mazepa, Petliura's premier, was critical, and resigned. Many Ukrainians questioned Petliura's right to conclude such an alliance. Instead of closing Ukrainian ranks the treaty contributed to new splits. As Premier Mazepa wrote retrospectively, "the Warsaw pact did not create a basis for the unification of Ukrainian national forces."[104]

Although the Polish cabinet had approved negotiations for an alliance on April 13, the matter came up for discussion in the Foreign Affairs Committee only nine days later, i.e., after signing of the pact. The National Democrats, who had introduced a motion in the sejm protesting a policy of buffer states in the east and demanding that the government explain its "real war aims," attacked the cabinet.[105] Grabski ostentatiously resigned his chairmanship of the committee and withdrew from the peace delegation. He accused the government of having broken the compromise with the sejm. The government, he said, not only approved the Ukrainian venture but also inserted new points in the draft treaty with Soviet Russia which had never been approved by the Right. Skulski accused the National Democrats of not having kept their part of the bargain, and the Ministry of Foreign Affairs censured Grabski for abusing his position in the peace delegation by betraying secret documents to the sejm. The discussion ended with the committee outvoting the National Democrats and approving the policy of the government, but a scar remained.[106]

Three days after debate in the Foreign Affairs Committee the Polish army, accompanied by two divisions of Petliura, started an all-out offensive in the Ukraine. On May 7, 1920 the troops entered Kiev. The final struggle had begun. Piłsudski launched his armies at the earliest moment, given the climatic conditions in the Ukraine, and struck, as a Russian historian wrote, "so as to forestall by his offensive an attack by the Soviet troops."[107] In this sense the operation was a "preventive offensive," as General Weygand later called it, designed to destroy the Red Army before it would complete its concentration. This made good sense militarily, especially since the raw Polish troops were likely to be more effective in offensive action, and the vast theater of war precluded the possibility of trench warfare. There is no evidence that the French had "masterminded" the Polish attack, or that it was part of a "third Allied offensive" against the Bolsheviks, as Stalin and several Soviet historians have asserted ever since.[108] Nor was it a new war. Mikhail Kalinin pointed out in a speech in mid-May 1920, that "Poland had been all the time in a state of war with Russia."[109] True, the French general staff was in close contact with the Polish command, and the military mission in Poland was involved in preparation of the campaign.[110] The government in Paris was not involved, although it knew of the approaching showdown. Nor can one accuse Washington or London of having encouraged or helped to prepare the offensive.

Polish and Ukrainian troops advanced rapidly. Their successes could be attributed to a certain element of surprise, a good plan, and assistance from the Ukrainian population. Trotsky fumed against the "bandits" who "facilitated and accelerated the advance of the Polish units."[111] The Eastern Galician brigades serving with the Red Army went over to the Poles, weakening the Soviet front by some eleven thousand men and forty-four artillery guns.[112]

Piłsudski announced his political objectives in an appeal on April 26 to the inhabitants of the Ukraine.[113] Polish armies had marched into the country to clear it of "foreign invaders," and would remain only long enough to enable the legitimate Ukrainian government to establish control. When the national government created proper state institutions and when Ukrainian forces, capable of defending the country, took a position at the frontiers, Polish armies would go home. The "hosts of her [the Ukraine's] valiant sons under the leadership of the Chief Ataman Simon Petliura," were now returning together with the Poles.

Petliura's proclamation "To the Ukrainian Nation" followed on April 27. The Ataman spoke in it of the three-year struggle of the Ukrainians against "the Red invaders, the Moscovite Bolsheviks." He recalled how the other Great Russian enemy, Denikin, had taken Kiev and tricked the Galician troops into surrender. But the struggle had gone on: Omelianovych-Pavlenko fought during his winter march, Aleksandr Udovychenko struggled in Podolia. Then came "a great change" when the Polish nation, respecting the right of the Ukrainians to independence, recognized the republic. Poland was now giving support, and her troops had come "as allies against a common foe." This joint struggle, Petliura said, would obliterate past mistakes. The "blood spilled together in battles against the perennial historical enemy, Moscow, which had once destroyed Poland and the Ukraine" would cement "mutual friendship between the Ukrainian and Polish nations." He ended his proclamation by promising to fight until all the Ukraine was free of the enemy.[114]

The two appeals stressed national liberation from foreign, Moscovite, oppression. Piłsudski and Petliura countered Communist slogans of the international solidarity of the proletariat with national appeals. But these watchwords had certain inherent weaknesses. Given the old Ukrainian-Polish antagonism, and the thorny issue of Eastern Galicia, they could prove a double-edged sword. Moreover, traditional class differences between the Ukrainian peasantry and the Polish landowners were bound to create difficulties. As the Polish Socialist Adam Pragier wrote retrospectively, the Ukrainians were to lose Eastern Galicia and possibly the land which they got during the revolution in exchange for democracy and some ties with Poland. This was not an overwhelmingly attractive program.

The initial reaction of the Ukrainians nonetheless was favorable to the Poles.[115] Piłsudski assured their leaders at Vynnitsia that they must not see in the Polish troops "a new imposition of a foreign will."[116] The general staff ordered all units to remember that it was not their business to vindicate the claims of Polish landowners or disarm the Ukrainian population.[117] Piłsudski made efforts to secure international recognition of Ukrainian independence and succeeded in gaining recognition by Finland. Vynnychenko paid an involuntary tribute to the Poles when he commented that they had learned from the mistakes of Kolchak and Denikin, as evidenced by Polish policies of discouraging Polish landlords, sending goods into the Ukraine, and helping to organize a national army.[118]

Still, the general picture was not without shadows. Piłsudski wrote Premier Skulski that once the Bolsheviks lost the Ukraine west of the Dnieper and north of the Black Sea, which seemed imminent, the Polish army could withdraw. In actual practice the troops would have to stay to watch over the settlement in the country and would leave only after the signing of all Ukrainian-Polish conventions. Piłsudski was aware that such a prolonged occupation would irritate the inhabitants and complicate matters, and he sought a way out.[119] Some friction was already apparent. The Ukrainians complained about the internment of Eastern Galician units by the Poles; they protested the behavior of the temporary Polish administration; and grumbled about the seizure of war booty which belonged to the Ukrainian republic. Most of these accusations against lower echelons of the Polish army and administration were justified, and Piłsudski wrote bitterly about "our looting army," which he dared not lead into areas where pro-Polish uprisings were taking place.[120]

The formation of Ukrainian units proceeded slowly. The Poles blamed the apathetic population—the Ukraine had changed masters so many times since 1917—but there were delays on the Polish side. Premier Mazepa suspected that Poland did not wish to see the promised six Ukrainian divisions organized too quickly.[121] All these were problems inherent in a difficult situation and did not seriously affect the Polish-Ukrainian brotherhood in arms. Ukrainian units fought bravely and loyally during the advance—and during the subsequent retreat, even when fighting took place on Eastern Galician soil. None deserted to the Bolsheviks.[122] Politically, however, the prospects of Ukrainian-Polish cooperation were uncertain, and there was some truth in the gloomy assertions of Savinkov that the whole venture was doomed because the Poles were hated in the Ukraine, because they did not enter with a clear-cut program of agrarian reform, and because the Ukrainians did not fully realize what was at stake.[123] Nor were the Polish people united behind Piłsudski's Ukrainian program. Many had paid little attention to the eastern war. The man in the street assumed that Polish territorial claims had been fulfilled and wondered about the need to fight for the Ukraine. The National Democrats censured Piłsudski's proclamation and questioned his right to issue statments unapproved by the sejm. Grabski predicted that the offensive on Kiev was likely to share the fate of Napoleon's invasion of Russia of 1812.[124] Even the premier had doubts and needed to be persuaded to go along with Piłsudski.[125] The Socialists, while approving liberation of the Ukraine, favored a speedy peace. They demanded on April 27 that negotiations with Soviet Russia be reopened, and they criticized the former Polish insistence on Borisov. Some PPS leaders felt that a constituent assembly ought to be called in the Ukraine in June, and Polish troops withdrawn within three months. The Seventeenth Congress of the party, held in late May, demanded peace based "on understanding and a genuine defense of the right of self-determination of nations."[126] Criticism came from other quarters as well, and a liberal such as Lednicki warned about policies built on the "quicksand of Polish-Ukrainian community." He asserted that the military offensive made sense only if its outcome were a new federated Russia based on Moscow and Kiev.[127]

Still, military victories and the entry of Polish troops into Kiev overshadowed domestic disputes. These were the first major victories won since the eighteenth-century partitions, and Poles basked in national pride. Piłsudski received a hero's welcome in Warsaw after his return from the front on May 18; there was genuine enthusiasm over the army's accomplishments.

Piłsudski strove for a victorious peace. Four days after launching his offensive he wrote Sosnkowski about peace but felt that the time was not yet ready for talks. "I do not have as yet a clear idea what effect our victories have on them," he said, "and I do not know what political impression they [the victories] created in Europe."[128] When the first reports about a favorable Western reaction began to come in, Piłsudski informed the premier he would complete military operations within ten days and then "the moment will come to propose new negotiations to the Bolsheviks."[129] The marshal—Piłsudski received a marshal's baton in late March—felt that once Moscow lost hope of applying military pressure on Poland, it would agree "to end the useless war and bloodshed." As for conditions, he would propose the same terms as before the offensive, bearing in mind "engagements undertaken by us toward other nations"—a clear reference to the pact with Petliura. There would be no armistice, negotiation would take place at the front, and should the Bolsheviks agree to immediate talks there would be a halt of "our military action in the sense of moves of strategic character."[130]

Premier Skulski informed the sejm's Foreign Affairs Committee on May 12 that resumption of peace negotiations was near, and he intimated that Warsaw was willing to give up certain preliminary requirements, such as Borisov.[131] Skulski refused to divulge the text of the treaty with Petliura, and he avoided any discussion of peace terms. It was obvious that the eastern program of the National Democrats was still irreconcilable with that of the government. The Supreme Command struck a little later at the rightists by means of an inspired article entitled "Communists and Defeatists," which criticized the idea of a border cutting across the Ukraine and Belorussia, and attacked plans of aid to counterrevolution in Russia. "Even if we could reconcile the oppression of other nationalities and the negation of their right to free existence with the Polish *raison d'état*," the article said, "the assumption that we could find in a future Russia an ally and a friend against Germany . . . is obviously the product of a febrile mind." It concluded that a "reduction of Russia to her historical frontiers is a condition of existence just as much as the prevention of Germany's militarization."[132]

As in the past, Piłsudski's goal was the defeat of Russia, not Communism. The Bolsheviks doubted it. Trotsky wrote in May that after capturing Kiev the Poles aimed at Kharkov and Moscow. Stalin commented later on an alleged Polish plan involving the advance of White Guard armies into the heart of Russia and the installation of Mikhail V. Rodzianko or some other counterrevolutionary leader in Moscow. But there is no evidence that such plans existed.[133]

Polish cooperation with Savinkov's group was limited; there was none with Wrangel. In May 1920, a representative of Savinkov and Chaikovskii asked General Sosnkowski if Poland was ready to support an anti-Bolshevik Russian government and allow the formation of an army; whether she required that Russians recognize an independent Ukraine; and if the demand for 1772 borders implied Polish annexation of territories west of them. Sosnkowski commented on the last question, and explained the idea of disannexation. He refused to answer the first two.[134] In early June 1920 Savinkov wrote in French newspapers that the Russians wanted to know if the Soviet-Polish war was "a war of liberation." He suggested that territorial disputes between Poland and a non-Bolshevik Russia be resolved by means of plebiscites.[135] Received by Piłsudski on June 10, Savinkov reported that the marshal saw a future Russia as a grouping of free states, and added that the Piłsudski-Petliura agreement was hard to swallow. Still, Savinkov hoped that a constituent assembly in Kiev might voluntarily agree to federation with Russia.[136]

Cooperation between Savinkov's committee, set up in Warsaw in July 1920, and the Polish Supreme Command gained momentum when Poland's military situation became bleak. Even then, contacts between the Poles and Wrangel did not go beyond overtures by the latter. Piłsudski told the unofficial Russian envoy in Warsaw that given Polish experiences with the tsarist regime he would prefer the Bolsheviks to the Whites. Poland, Piłsudski said, could only contemplate rapprochement with a democratic Russia, and he voiced skepticism whether Wrangel was her representative.[137] The Ministry of Foreign Affairs clearly stated that "the aim of Polish eastern policy is in no way interference with Russian domestic affairs, and in that sense Poland does not fight against Bolshevism . . . future developments of the Russian revolution and its consequences ought to be left to the will and the force of the Russian people."[138]

The April offensive in the Ukraine was thus unrelated to anti-Bolshevik intervention, and strove to force Russia to sign a peace treaty that would undo Poland's partitions and re-establish the country as a great power in Eastern Europe.[139] Lenin grasped that purpose when he said in November 1920 that the war was a continuation of a struggle by Poland "which at one time had been a great power and which now opposes another great power—Russia. Poland cannot abandon this old, perennial struggle even now."[140] Piłsudski's political objectives, imperfectly understood at home and criticized abroad, precluded the possibility of genuine cooperation with anti-Bolshevik Russians. Except for Petliura, the Poles had begun their grandiose military operation without allies. Its outcome was to be decided on the battlefield.

"Give Us Warsaw!"

The military campaign of 1920 brought the Soviet-Polish war to its dramatic height. Piłsudski's thrust in April had led to the capture of Kiev; the Bolshevik July offensive reached deep into Poland, menacing her capital. The battle cry of *"Daesh Varshavu!"* ("Give us Warsaw!") resounded through the ranks of the Red Army, marking a new stage in the old conflict. Both sides played for large stakes, and it was only when these great goals became unattainable that the chances of a compromise peace would appear.

The Polish offensive in the Ukraine did not take the Bolsheviks unaware but their military preparations had not been completed, and the "peace offensive" had prevented elaboration of political directives and war aims. All the Soviet propaganda apparatus turned now to explain the character of the struggle with Poland, and there were signs of improvization.[1] A conference of the Ukrainian KP(b) declared on April 26, 1920 that the task of the Ukraine was not only to chase away the Polish aggressors but to help the proletariat in Poland overthrow its own bourgeoisie.[2] This was merely a slogan, and Soviet propagandists attempted a reply to Piłsudski's proclamation only on April 28. The riposte was a series of clichés about Polish lords and the traitor Petliura who had come to impose slavery on Ukrainian peasants.[3] Only one idea, namely that there could be no national liberation without social liberation, showed a more serious effort to offset the impact of Piłsudski's and Petliura's appeals. A more sophisticated explanation of the war was necessary, and Bolshevik leaders took pains to provide it. The Polish offensive, Lenin now declared, was a new version of the Allied policy of intervention, and the Poles— acting as tools of French imperialists—sought to extend the barrier which separated Soviet Russia from the German proletariat. Fearing that Russia might recover economically and become one of the most powerful states of the world, the Entente had chosen the rich Ukraine as a target for the Polish attack.[4] Why did Poland lend herself to this scheme? Trotsky advanced two reasons: the greediness of Polish landlords and capitalists who wanted land and power in the Ukraine; and Piłsudski's desire to disarm the revolutionary forces at home through an expansionist war. All this, Trotsky claimed, was a kind of third-rate Bonapartism.[5]

If the Bolsheviks presented the conflict as a war imposed on them by the Entente and Warsaw, was it primarily a class struggle or should the war be viewed also as a national conflict? Extremists such as Karl Danishevskii and Miasnikov argued that national wars belonged to the past, for all wars now were essentially civil wars between the capitalists and the exploited masses. Others saw the war as a national conflict. There was a wave of Russian chauvinism and hatred of the Poles. *Krasnaia Zvezda* called on the Fifteenth Army to fight for a "one and indivisible Red Russia." Another army newspaper, *Voennoe Delo,* referred to the Poles as "Lakhs"—a derogatory term—and spoke of their "inborn Jesuitism." Even *Izvestia* printed nationalist articles.[6]

This trend toward open statements of Russian-Polish national antagonism, likely to harm Bolshevik slogans of international proletarian unity, alarmed Soviet leaders. Lenin instructed the secretariat to avoid chauvinistic overtones, and insisted on a distinction between the Polish lords, and the peasants and workers.[7] Trotsky later took disciplinary action against the army newspapers.[8] *Pravda,* commenting on May 7 on the decision of the Polish Communists to serve in the Red Army, said that this constituted the best proof that the war against Poland was not national.

But the question was not that simple. *Pravda* ran a series of articles in May under such titles as "On the National Pride of the Great Russians," "National and International Aspects of the Russo-Polish War," and "National War." The articles attempted to reconcile the notions of a class war and a national struggle.[9] Radek, with his usual perspicacity, observed that although one had to avoid exciting Russian chauvinism, it was necessary to encourage the "healthy patriotic instincts" of the Russian masses.[10]

In their effort to mobilize all resources against the Poles the Bolsheviks could not easily discard the national element. While the fall of Kiev came as a blow to Soviet rule in the Ukraine it awakened the country.[11] Patriotic feelings ran high, and the former tsarist commander-in-chief, General Aleksei A. Brusilov, issued an appeal to Russian ex-officers: "irrespective of the flag and promises with which the Poles would be coming to us in the Ukraine," he said, "we must firmly remember" that "the present chief objective of their offensive lies exclusively in the fulfillment of Polish annexationist designs." Stating that the Poles sought to seize Lithuania and Belorussia and detach the Ukraine, Brusilov warned his countrymen that future Russian generations would curse them if for ideological and class reasons "we would forget our Russian nation and destroy our Mother Russia."[12]

Brusilov's manifesto—the general soon became chairman of a special advisory board to the Soviet High Command which comprised other high ranking ex-tsarist officers—produced considerable effect. Other appeals followed; the Bolsheviks multiplied their efforts to gain support of non-Communist or even anti-Communist Russians. Even nationalist articles from the emigré press were reprinted in Soviet newspapers.[13]

The government did its best to whip up warlike enthusiasm, which had been weak at the onset.* Trotsky stressed that Kiev fell not only to the lords but to foreign lords, and he told his troops that the fate of "the Russian nation" would be decided on the western front.[14] Maxim Gorky, addressing the departing soldiers, said that past Russian-Polish struggles weighed heavily on the present strife. This, he said, "may give this war a national character which could unite all classes, irrespective of their divergent interests."[15] With a keen sense of the paradox, Karl Radek pointed out that it was a curious sign of the times when a Soviet war commissar publicly lauded the ex-tsarist commander-in-chief, (Brusilov) to the applause of a Bolshevik gathering.[16]

To consolidate the country and strengthen its hold over the people, the Defense Council and the VTsIK issued a decree on May 11, "On Measures Against the Polish Advance," which announced that the enemy wanted to conquer Russia from within. Consequently twenty-four gubernia came under martial law: revolutionary order had to prevail. Bolshevik fears of Polish-inspired sabotage were exaggerated. The Poles were aware of the Russian nationalist upsurge and could do little to hinder it. Piłsudski's eastern program imposed severe limits on cooperation with anti-Soviet Russians. Wasilewski suggested sending the partly Russian, partly Belorussian partisan unit commanded by Stanisław Bułak-Bałachowicz to the region of Pskov to organize a diversion.[17] Later the Poles tried to support Savinkov and his committee in Warsaw—which assumed control over various White

---

* Some Red Army regiments refused to attack because they favored only a defensive war. See P. V. Suslov, *Politicheskoe obespechenie sovetsko-polskoi kampanii 1920 g.* (Moscow and Leningrad, 1930), pp. 53, 63, and J. Paluch's report, June 26, 1920, Akta Adiutantury Generalnej Naczelnego Dowództwa, VIII/3965, Piłsudski Institute, New York. Desertion assumed serious proportions, and even before the campaign in March there were thirty thousand deserters in the gubernia of Smolensk, Vitebsk, Homel, and Chernikhov. See the protocol of July 23, 1920 of Smolenk gubernial committee, The Smolensk Archive, Kommunisticheskaia partiia Sovetskogo Soiuza, Smolenskii oblastnoi Komitet, Partiinyi arkhiv, WKP 6, Widner Library, Harvard University, Cambridge, Mass. Compare with Trotsky's order of May 10, Trotsky, *Kak vooruzhalas revoliutsiia* (3 vols. in 4; Moscow, 1924), II/2, 133; and information about the desertion problem in the Soviet press.

units—to show that they fought Bolshevism and not the Russian nation. All these efforts produced little result.

The Bolsheviks formulated their war aims in the last days of April and during May and June, 1920. Three documents were particularly important: the "theses" called "The Polish Front and Our Tasks," prepared by Trotsky on April 30; and two appeals to the Polish workers, peasants, and soldiers issued by VTsIK, and dated May 7 and June 16.[18] All three asserted the inviolability of Poland's independence, predicting at the same time the ultimate triumph of Communism in the country. They stressed the defensive nature of the war, while simultaneously hinting at the forthcoming European revolution. The emphasis on any particular idea—as developed in numerous addresses, especially in Radek's speech on May 5, 1920—varied according to the speaker and the type of pronouncement. There was also a noticeable evolution from Trotsky's theses to the June appeal, determined by the changing military situation.

The statement that the Polish offensive "did not change for one iota our attitude toward Poland's independence" (April 30 theses) came out most forcibly in the May 7 appeal, coinciding with the fall of Kiev. This document contained a phrase never again repeated in the same form, that "after defeating your lords, the Soviet government will leave to the Polish nation the right to build your own life in accord with your own views. You, yourselves, Polish workers and peasants, will resolve whether you will want to maintain the existing order, or take the land and the factories in your own hands." The appeal said the Poles need not fear that the Red Army wanted "to impose Communism on you by force." Other statements emphasized respect for Polish national independence.*

Yet most of the appeals also mentioned a Soviet Poland. Even the above quoted May 7 appeal ended with the words: "down with the government of landlords and capitalists." Trotsky told the workers, peasants, and Red Army soldiers that "over its [the bourgeoisie's] cadaver we shall conclude a brotherly alliance with a Workers' and Peasants' Poland"; other Soviet declarations ended with the slogan, "long live Poland of peasants and workers," or "long live Soviet Poland."[19] *Pravda* wrote on May 1 that the

---

* Lenin said on April 29, that "we have not the slightest designs on Poland's independence, just as we have none on the independence of Lithuania and Belorussia" (*Sochineniia*, XXV, 252.) Another statement on the same day described Polish independence as "inviolable," and Chicherin asserted a little later that "We do not carry either our system or our government on bayonets." See *Dokumenty vneshnei politiki SSSR* (Moscow, 1959—) II, 495, 638.

moment was near when the insurgent Polish workers would chase away Piłsudski and take the power into their own hands. The war, most Bolshevik leaders declared, was bound to end with emergence of a Soviet Poland.[20]

If one were to ask how the Bolsheviks reconciled their slogan of an independent Poland, free to choose her own regime, with the ultimate goal of a Soviet Polish republic, the answer would be complicated. In the first place, insistence on Polish independence was largely propagandistic, to calm the fears of the Poles. Trotsky's theses make this fairly clear.[21] Also, the Bolsheviks did not look upon national independence as a final form of government. Lenin stressed that the Soviets planned to solve national questions by means of a federation which was "a transitional form toward full unity."[22] Stalin agreed, but advocated adding another transitional form, namely, confederation. Such states as Poland, Hungary, or Finland, he wrote, may find it difficult to accept the status of a federal unit, and Lenin's scheme would give them no more rights than, say, to the Bashkirs.[23] As for the independence of the border states, it was an illusion. "It suffices to glance at Georgia, Armenia, Poland, Finland, etc.," Stalin wrote, "which have seceded from Russia but have retained only the appearance of independence," to see that these countries either must stay with Russia or fall to Allied imperialism. The right of secession was a valid principle, suited to the colonial situation, but was "profoundly counterrevolutionary" when applied to the border states.[24] It is evident that when the Bolsheviks spoke of Polish independence they did it mainly for tactical reasons.

But there was more to the explanation. The Soviet leaders said that bourgeois Poland was to blame for hastening her own eventual disintegration. The Poles, aided by Western capitalists, had attempted to smash Communist Russia and thus gambled away their own existence. The Polish government offered the best proof that a bourgeois Poland could not coexist with Soviet Russia; Warsaw itself provided an opportunity for the Polish proletariat to seize power in the country.[25] Ultimately a true Poland would emerge, and as Lenin told the Red Army conscripts, "we have recognized the independence of Poland and of the *Polish people's republic*."[26] Thus Trotsky's theses strove to explain to every Russian that the war with Poland was "his war for the alliance with the Polish proletariat and the proletariat of all Europe and all the world."

Radek provided the clearest and most logical interpretation of the Soviet point of view in his speech on May 5, 1920. He said that the Bolsheviks were not presenting any definite war aims, nor were they saying that they could conclude peace only with a Soviet Poland. They were ready for peace even with the existing Polish government. But, he warned, if the war went on, its final outcome would be a Soviet Poland. "If the White Guard Poland does not want to be a peaceful neighbor of Soviet Russia, then there is no place for a White Guard Poland." Should things continue the way they were, the slogan of a peasants' and workers' Poland would not be a slogan brought on the bayonets of the Red Army, but a watchword of the Polish laboring masses.[27] Hence, according to Radek the war would bring a spontaneous revolution in Poland.

This latter was an important point. Trotsky's theses had contributed to the idea that the Red Army would not invade ethnic Polish territories or try to introduce Communism from outside. Not everyone in Russia adhered to this idea. As early as May 25 one of the army commanders had declared that "our Red eagles will hoist the Red star on the Warsaw citadel to the accompaniment of the joyful acclamations of the liberated Polish proletariat."[28] Three days later *Krasnaia Armiia* launched the battle cry, "On to Minsk, Brest, Warsaw." Soviet leaders were more prudent. Trotsky spoke of a revolution in Poland *after* Soviet victories, and Stalin in late June criticized "the boastfulness and self-conceit" of some of the comrades who, "not content with defending our Republic," would only be satisfied with a "red Soviet Warsaw."[29]

In the early stages of the military campaign the Bolsheviks used the idea of a revolution in Poland largely for domestic consumption. The Russians were told that they had allies in the Polish people; they fought a defensive war but they also struggled for the proletariat in Poland.[30] The old Polish watchword, "For your freedom and for ours," was revived and received wide currency. The first victories of the Red Army brought a change of emphasis, and the June 16 appeal to Polish workers, peasants, and soldiers reflected it. This document repeated the slogan that the war was against Polish lords and did not menace Poland's independence, but the earlier phrase about the Poles being free to choose their regime disappeared. "A workers' and peasants' Poland stands in no danger from the Red Army," the document proclaimed. "On the contrary we are ready to bring you fraternal aid against your domestic and foreign enemies." There was a new optimism in the appeal, stressing the might of the Soviet army and warning against prolonged resistance. Opposing the Red troops, the appeal went on, "you are committing treason toward a future Socialist Poland." The document urged desertion to the Soviet ranks, and ended with the slogan: "Long live the independent peasants' and workers' Poland in a fraternal union with a peasants' and workers' Russia and the Ukraine."[31] Former phrases about a defensive war, self-determination, and peace were receding. Radek's prediction that peace after this war would be "more complex than before," and Lenin's sneering remarks about rumored Polish peace overtures showed an evolution in Soviet thinking.[32] On June 12 Lenin declared that the Bolsheviks would talk peace only with the Polish workers and peasants in whom they placed their entire trust.[33]

At this point the Bolshevik leaders still played down the connection between Communism in Poland and a European revolution. Trotsky's theses had mentioned the alliance with the European proletariat as a war aim; Marchlewski linked the Polish question with revolution in Europe; Lenin and Zinoviev spoke of Poland as a barrier between the proletariat in the West and Soviet Russia.[34] But the existing situation precluded a meaningful elaboration of this theme. In May and June, Moscow merely protested Allied support of Poland, and warned that it would draw appropriate conclusions from the behavior of the Entente. Simultaneously, Zinoviev, acting as head of the Communist International, launched appeals to the proletariat of the world.[35]

Events on the front had affected the tone and content of Bolshevik propaganda. The Polish offensive in the Ukraine had halted on the Dnieper without accomplishing its task, the destruction of the Soviet Twelfth Army. In the north the Red troops forestalled a Polish attack and launched their offensive, based on a new plan, on May 14. A Polish counterattack of June 1 restored the situation but five days later the First Cavalry Army of Semen Budenny broke through the front in the Ukraine. General Edward Rydz-Śmigły, commanding the troops in Kiev, escaped encirclement but failed to engage Budenny. So far neither side had won decisive victories. The Bolsheviks were disappointed with the meager results of their action in the north. Army morale sank. Fearing the political effect of harsh treatment of prisoners of war, Soviet authorities issued repeated orders that Polish soldiers, mere tools of the capitalists, must not be ill-treated.[36]

Military events revealed the peculiar character of the war. As compared with the World War, campaigns were fought under primitive conditions. Troops were underfed and badly clothed. Both sides lacked effective communication and signals system. The size of armies in relation to the vast areas of operation was small. The Polish forces on the eastern front, at the time of its greatest effort, were below half a million men; the Russian Western and Southwestern Fronts numbered eight hundred thousand.

This was a war of movement with rapid advances and retreats, accompanied by demoralization of troops, and frequent confusion in the higher echelons of command. At first the Poles were stronger in the Ukraine, but they lacked sufficient cavalry to oppose the mounted cohorts of Budenny. In the north the Red Army had superiority, and Polish reserves were rapidly exhausted. While later Soviet historians and propagandists attempted to picture a great technical preponderance of the Polish army, contemporary sources do not bear it out.*

A turning point in the military situation came on July 4. Troops of the Western Front, commanded since April 29 by the youthful ex-tsarist lieutenant, Mikhail Tukhachevskii, began a major offensive and drove deep into Belorussia. Strategically and politically this operation was more important than the continuing advance of the Russian Southwestern Front under the command of another ex-tsarist officer, A. I. Egorov, for it aimed directly at Warsaw. What is more, the Poles could now see the practical realization of a Soviet war aim: the liberation of Belorussia.

The Bolsheviks had no definite idea on how to solve the Belorussian question. The Central Committee of the Communist party of Lithuania and Belorussia in January 1920 had split on whether the country, after conquest by the Red Army, ought to be rebuilt as a Soviet republic or be annexed. Mickiewicz-Kapsukas favored re-creation of the former Litbel; his opponents argued that international conditions which had favored such an arrangement in 1919 no longer existed. The discussion lasted until May 1920. Expediency rather than concern for Belorussian national rights governed Soviet policy.[87] Although the organ of the Lithuanian and Belorussian Communist party, *Zvezda*, announced on May 10 that the war must become a war "for the liberation of Belorussia from Polish occupation" and "for the re-creation of the brotherly union between Russia and Belo-

---

* Exact figures at any given time are hard to determine. Poles and Russians calculated front troops and rear units differently. There are discrepancies between sources. General Stachiewicz mentions 370,000 Poles on the entire eastern front; General Kukiel 300,000 on the Ukrainian front; Kuzmin, citing another Polish source, speaks of 65,000, but these were presumably only "sabres" and "bayonets," i.e., front troops directly participating in the offensive. The most fantastic figures appear in Fedor G. Zuev, *Mezhdunarodnyi imperializm organizator napadenia panskoi Polshi na sovetskuiu Rossiiu 1919-1920* (Moscow, 1954), and are faithfully reproduced by some Polish Marxist historians. As for the technical superiority of the Poles, even if we assume that some contemporary Soviet speeches were deliberately optimistic—for instance Kalinin's address on May 16, 1920 (*Dokumenty i materiały do historii stosunków polsko-radzieckich* [Warsaw, 1962—], III, 52) or Sokolnikov's remarks on May 5 (in *Sowjetrussland und Polen* [Moscow, 1920], pp. 30-31)—the testimony of an army commander such as I. N. Sergeev (*Od Dźwiny ku Wiśle* [Warsaw, 1925], p. 51) still sounds convincing.

russia," there was no immediate application of the slogan.[38] Political organs of the army began to establish revolutionary committees (*revkoms*) in territories evacuated by the Polish troops, but even the revkom of Minsk did not receive the name "Belorussian." Programs of nationalist leaders such as Lastouski, who appealed to the Entente for help, were, of course, ignored. The declaration of the Central Committee of the Lithuanian and Belorussian party, issued about July 16, included no slogan about national independence, and instead spoke of Polish terror and called the Belorussians to arms against their oppressors.[39]

Although a sizeable part of the Belorussian peasantry, which had suffered from abuses of the Polish army and administration, welcomed the Bolsheviks,[40] their hopes were largely disappointed. The advancing Red Army and its political units eyed Belorussian volunteers suspiciously; the revkoms' agrarian policy disregarded the wishes of the peasantry; mass confiscations—the Sixteenth Army alone appropriated fifteen thousand horse carts—contributed to widespread discontent. Sovietization of Belorussia, a Russian historian admitted, was carried out "to a large extent by the hands of Russian and Jewish workers and followed the tried-out Russian patterns."[41]

An important tactical change occurred on July 30, 1920 when the Minsk revkom changed its name to the Belorussian revkom and a day later proclaimed the creation of an independent Belorussian Soviet Socialist Republic. The declaration defined only the western borders of the new state, which were to follow ethnic lines. Borders with Russia were to be determined later "by common agreement."[42] Though the declaration stated that it was issued in accord with the revvoensovet of the Western Front, the latter did not bother to announce Belorussian independence until August 12. The independence of the new republic was purely fictional. The new state had no military units or cadres of command, and no separate legislation; all orders and decrees of the Russian Socialist Federated Soviet Republic applied without any limitations to this territory.

The Poles did hardly anything to expose this comedy and failed to show concern for the Belorussians. It is true that their own position was difficult, and their record in Belorussia was weak.[43] New talks between Polish and Belorussian representatives took place in July, but proved inconclusive. Warsaw did not take up suggestions to establish a Belorussian government.[44] Wasilewski communicated with Lastouski, who showed interest in cooperating with Poles, and he tried to induce the Belorussian leader to join the pro-Polish council of Ivanouski. Lastouski demanded an independent Belorussia, allied or even federated with Poland, and national military units. All these talks produced no result, and the Poles approved the creation of a new Belorussian military commission and recruitment only in September 1920.[45] Even this was meant as a diversion—tied up with the short-lived adventure of Bulak-Balakhovich—and ended with the peace treaty of Riga. Used by both sides, though more effectively by the Bolsheviks, Belorussia could never become an independent factor in the course of the Soviet-Polish war.

The continuing advance of Tukhachevskii brought the Red Army into the vicinity of Wilno. On July 12 the Soviets signed a peace treaty with Lithuania, and two days later captured Wilno, which they handed over to the Lithuanian government. Red troops remained in control; Lithuanian neutrality was constantly violated. In some areas revkoms came into existence. Soviet designs on Lithuania can be surmised from Lenin's instruction to exploit fraternization with Lithuanians, and to "leave the most trustworthy troops in Lithuania," using less reliable units for the offensive against the Poles.[46] The increasing self-confidence of the Bolsheviks showed in their new tone toward Latvia and Finland. While the Russians previously had merely complained about the Latvians, and Lenin spoke of the boldness of the Baltic countries, they began to think now about pressure against recalcitrant Riga and Helsinki.[47] Angered by Latvian obstinacy in negotiation, Lenin played with the idea of overawing them by terrorism. He suggested penetrating the country "for ten or twenty versts, under the guise of the green brigades (on whom we shall put the blame later) and hang kulaks, priests and landowners. Premium: 100,000 rubles for a hanged man."* No price was too high for accomplishment of revolutionary goals.

The retreat from Kiev provoked a political crisis in Poland. Skulski's cabinet fell on June 9, 1920, and after prolonged strife there emerged a nonparty government headed by Władysław Grabski. The Ministry of Foreign Affairs went to Eustachy Sapieha. The Right and Center parties tolerated the new cabinet; the Left adopted a negative attitude. Grabski's ministry began by considering peace overtures. Piłsudski opposed them on the ground that Poland would negotiate from weakness.[48] He was right. The Soviet High Command had an inkling of Polish peace

* Lenin's note for Sklianskii, August 1920, Trotsky Archive, T. 555, Houghton Library, Harvard University, Cambridge, Mass. The scheme apparently appealed to Lenin, for he scribbled still another note which suggested passing "the frontier somewhere behind Balakhovich, be it only for one verst, and hang there 100–1,000 of their officials and rich people" (ibid., T. 554).

tendencies, and surmising that the Poles would try to improve their military situation first, considered that peace overtures should in no way influence the Red Army offensive.[49]

The tense political situation led to the creation of a State Defense Council, approved by the sejm on July 1, 1920. Presided over by Piłsudski, this new body consisted of the marshal of the sejm, the premier and three principal ministers, three delegates of the Supreme Command, and ten deputies representing leading political parties. Its main function was to control matters of war and peace. Because the cabinet was unrepresentative of major political trends, and the sejm too large and unwieldy, the State Defense Council appeared as a step toward internal consolidation. Its rightist sponsors saw in it also an institution which would limit the power of Piłsudski. Four days after its inauguration the council issued appeals to the soldiers and the nation which stressed that Poland fought the Bolsheviks and not the Russian people.[50] Kossakowski commented that the pronouncement marked "a new political stage of our struggles."[51] Its emphasis on the ideological character of the war sought to satisfy a large segment of Polish public opinion, influenced by the Church and the Right; to please the Entente; and to facilitate colaboration with non-Bolshevik Russians. General Sosnkowski confidentially commented that the determined stand of the Soviet government, the vagueness of anti-Russian slogans, and the Savinkov issue had forced the Poles to this declaration. He added that it did not imply abandoning the Ukrainian plans.[52]

The PPS continued to assert that the war was being fought against Russia and not the Bolsheviks, which annoyed the Entente.[53] They also continued their agitation against the government, demanding a ministry based on parties of workers and peasants. Other groups welcomed the council's declaration. Savinkov and his Russian Political Committee issued a manifesto to the Russian nation proclaiming that the war was against the Bolsheviks. Their newspaper, *Svoboda*, espoused the Polish cause and spoke of plebiscites in the borderlands. A Polish-White Russian agreement resulted in the organization of a Russian force in Poland, subordinated politically to the committee and tactically to the Polish Supreme Command. While not numerous—Russian troops comprised the regular infantry units of General B. S. Permykin, Cossack cavalry of *essaul* Iakovlev, and partisans of Bulak-Balakhovich—this force fought loyally on the Polish side.[54] Even Wrangel informed Warsaw that he regarded the Poles as allies. A final settlement of territorial and political questions, he said, would take place after the war.[55] The Poles also received notification of the coming to Warsaw of an allegedly liberal and pro-Polish envoy of Wrangel, General Petr Makhrov.[56]

All these developments could not change the fact that the Polish army was in full retreat. Tukhachevskii had launched his great offensive on July 4, and next day the State Defense Council met in an atmosphere of gloom. Peace was almost on everyone's lips. The Socialist Norbert Barlicki suggested direct approaches to the Bolsheviks; the majority favored turning to the Entente. Piłsudski alone was for all-out war. He spoke of ringing "the great bell of war," and said that if the army was "ill" it was because the Polish people as a whole were sick and needed shock treatment. The marshal did not believe that effective aid could come from the Entente. Asking for it was like administering morphine to the Polish nation; what it needed was to build its own resistance.[57] But Piłsudski had been confident of victory, and there had been defeats. He personified the army, and the army was retreating. His prestige had suffered. The decision to ask for assistance from the Allied conference at Spa was taken against Piłsudski's wishes. Sapieha was also lukewarm.[58]

The Polish delegation at Spa, led by Patek, soon discovered that talks with the Allies were going to be difficult. Lloyd George criticized the Poles for imperialism; the French showed dissatisfaction with the Polish army.[59] Only the French minister of war seemed to favor a barrier against the Russians consisting of Poland, Czechoslovakia, Hungary, Rumania, and the Baltic states.[60] Acting in conformity with the resolution of the State Council, Sapieha on July 6 addressed an appeal to the conference, announcing that Warsaw was ready to sign a reasonable peace with the Soviets and asking for Allied support.[61] Shortly after dispatch of this note, Premier Grabski went largely on his own initiative to Spa to present the Polish case.[62] His hopes to receive French backing did not materialize. Millerand was caught in the ambiguities of France's eastern policy, and Lloyd George forced the French premier to admit that he could send no troops. Nor could Paris compromise its position by interceding with the Bolsheviks.

Lloyd George had full initiative to deal with the Russo-Polish question, and he made the most of it. In a meeting on July 9, Grabski assured the Allied statesmen that Poland had abandoned her eastern ambitions and was willing to sign peace. He confessed that the critical situation had resulted from Polish mistakes, and he criticized Piłsudski. The premier threw himself on the mercy of the Entente, asking it to "help Poland to make peace" and lend "moral support." Long exchanges ensued which took a good part of July 10. Lloyd George again accused the Poles of imperialism, and said Britain would only consider helping Poland if Warsaw agreed to purely ethnic frontiers in the east and submitted all other controversial questions—Wilno, Teschen, Danzig—to an Allied decision. Grabski consented and signed—despite the opposition of other Polish delegates—an agreement containing the following points: Poland would withdraw to the minimum frontier line proposed in Paris on December 8, 1919; she would participate in a peace conference in London together with Russia, the Baltic countries, and delegates of Eastern Galicia; she would abide by the Allied verdict on all other unsettled borders.[63] In exchange for these concessions the Allies promised to mediate between Soviet Russia and Poland, and should Moscow reject an armistice proposal, provide assistance. Military support being excluded, it was not clear either to the Poles or the Allies what kind of assistance would be available.

Allied mediation took the form of a note signed by Lord Curzon—the French did not want to have any dealings with the Soviet government—and dispatched on July 11. It proposed a Polish-Russian armistice along the December 8 line, but created some confusion in the case of Eastern Galicia by mentioning both the line of actual hostilities in Eastern Galicia (to which Grabski had agreed) and the so-called line A which placed all of Eastern Galicia outside of Poland. The British previously had favored line A, and it is still not clear whether at this time they meant to reopen the whole Eastern Galician question or mistakenly had inserted line A in the note.[64]

Grabski's capitulation at Spa, coinciding with Polish loss of plebiscites in East Prussia, was a great blow. Soviet acceptance of the Curzon Line would have forced Warsaw to give up large areas in the north and in Eastern Galicia. Any attempts at evasion would have mobilized the British against Russia. Seeking to justify his stand by concessions which he allegedly obtained, Grabski claimed to have salvaged part of Eastern Galicia and to have received the assurance that Wilno would go to Lithuania and not to Russia.[65] He realized that he had a heavy responsibility, but since the State Defense Council had failed to give precise instructions, what else was he to do?

Only too glad to put the blame on the premier, several members of the State Defense Council criticized Grabski and the Spa settlement. Piłsudski, obviously unhappy with the result, censured all those who refused to face reality. "Those who agitated for peace," he said, "now [agitate] for war, and those who [wanted] war, now speak of peace." The decision oscillated "like a candle flame" in windy weather. The marshal reiterated that he had foreseen what the views of the Entente were going to be, and stressed again that "war can be won if the country wants war."[66]

The State Defense Council accepted Grabski's agreement at Spa by a majority vote but no one was satisfied with this arrangement. Piłsudski, Sapieha, and many others wished that the Bolsheviks would reject Curzon's note and release Poland from her onerous obligations vis-à-vis the Allies.[67] The government did not think of a peace treaty amounting to a surrender. Sapieha instructed Polish missions abroad that Warsaw would still strive to achieve union with Lithuania, even at heavy territorial sacrifice, and retain Eastern Galicia by granting it a wide autonomy. Nor would the Poles drop immediately their request for a constituent assembly in Kiev, though they would not insist.[68]

The Curzon note which created such dissatisfaction in Warsaw confronted the Bolsheviks with a dilemma. Should they accept Allied mediation and seek peace on presumably favorable conditions; or exploit their military victories, march on Warsaw, and create a Communist Polish republic? The Red Army, drunk with success, favored the offensive. War appeared as a "direct means of rapid progress and spreading of the revolution," and Tukhachevskii, the would-be Bonaparte of the Red Army, appeared as a chief exponent of this doctrine.[69] His order of July 2 was more fiery than the typical Soviet pronouncement. "Avenge the burnt Borisov, humiliated Kiev, destroyed Polotsk," Tukhachevskii addressed his troops. "In the blood of the smashed Polish army you will drown the criminal government of Piłsudski." Saying that "over the corpse of White Poland lies the path toward world conflagration," the commander of the Western Front ordered his soldiers to advance "On Vilna, Minsk, Warsaw."[70]

On the day when Minsk fell to the Red Army, Piatakov launched the slogan which shortly thereafter became the battle cry of the Red Army: *"Daesh Varshavu!"*[71] As the commander of the Soviet Twelfth Army recalled, "nobody except for some divisional commanders thought about stopping." Trotsky wrote later that the view that the struggle "which started as one of defense should be turned into an offensive and revolutionary war began to grow and acquire strength."[72]

In the days following receipt of Curzon's note, the Bolshevik leaders tried to evaluate the chances of a revolutionary war. Trotsky favored caution. In his note of July 13 to the Politburo he suggested a reply to Curzon that Poland was a sovereign state whose integrity the Soviets had always respected. Still, they would be willing to accept British mediation if London guaranteed the proposed frontiers, without prejudicing the final settlement which must conform to the principle of national self-determination. The Entente should also guarantee the armistice. He favored a rejection of that part of Curzon's note which proposed an armistice with Wrangel.[73]

Trotsky favored stopping the offensive, not because he objected in principle to a revolutionary war but because he doubted the possibility of an outbreak of revolution in Poland. In the absence of one the advance on Warsaw would be "only a partisan affair." He wondered whether the Red Army might be strong enough to march on, let alone storm, Warsaw, and his skepticism about the chances of a Polish revolution apparently derived from the realistic thinking of Marchlewski.[74]

Lenin held an opposite view. He considered that the Treaty of Versailles had made Poland "a buffer which is to fence off Germany from a contact with Soviet Communism." Poland was a "battering ram" against Bolshevik Russia, and the destruction of Poland would not only bring security but open the road to Germany. "If Poland had become Soviet," Lenin ruminated a little later, "if the Warsaw workers had received from Russia the help they expected and welcomed, the Versailles Treaty would have been shattered, and the entire international system built by the victors would have been destroyed." Seen in this light the struggle against the Polish army meant "destroying the Versailles Peace on which the entire present system of international relations is based."[75]

In Lenin's mind the choice between further war or peace became subordinated to the great objective of a junction with Germany and carrying the revolution westward. Trotsky commented later upon the "boldness of Lenin's thought," and remarked that the failure of this plan "involved no danger for the existence of the Soviet Republic itself."[76] No wonder Lenin reacted unfavorably to Curzon's note. The British proposal, he wrote Sklianskii, "necessitates furious acceleration of the advance in Poland." And he asked: "Are you doing it? All of you? Energetically?"[77] Writing to Stalin, he advocated an all-out offensive, and described the Curzon note as an Allied attempt to snatch victory from the Bolsheviks.[78]

Although there is only circumstantial evidence, it appears that Stalin, who not so long ago criticized those who called for the seizure of Warsaw, gave in to Lenin's persuasive powers. So apparently did the other members of the Politburo.*

---

* Trotsky recalled that only Rykov shared his point of view, but according to other testimony he did not. At any rate Rykov was not then a member of the Politburo. See Leon Trotsky, *Moia zhizn*, (2 vols.; Riga, 1930), II, 192; Isaac

To probe Bolshevik thinking at the time one must look at their estimates of military possibilities, revolutionary chances in Poland, and general international trends. The Soviet High Command submitted its report to Trotsky on July 16, announcing that the Western Front could continue operations for two more months, given existing supplies, and if Poland were left on her own, then two months would suffice to win the war. The report mentioned the possibility of the armed intervention of Rumania, Finland, or Latvia—at the orders of the Entente—and asked for the Central Committee's opinion on what was to be done in such a case. The Glavkom recommended stopping on the Curzon line.[79] Lenin did not see any danger of an Allied intervention.[80] The Curzon note masked Western fears, and was merely a clumsy maneuver to deceive the broad masses, give Poland a breathing spell, and permit preparation for a new attack. There were no military reasons for stopping the offensive.

On July 17 the Central Committee and the revvoensovet of the Soviet Republic took the momentous decision to continue the offensive and issued orders to speed up operations. Trotsky instructed the High Command to pay no attention to the Curzon Line, "in case circumstances would force us to cross temporarily this border." The action was to be carried out "quickly and energetically."[81]

The army responded with enthusiasm. Tukhachevskii wrote Grigorii Zinoviev that a revolutionary war could be "concluded only with the coming to power of the universal dictatorship of the proletariat."[82] A member of the revvoensovet of the Western Front, Ivan Smilga, reported that the Polish left wing was smashed, and that events moved with increasing rapidity. Kamenev, the commander-in-chief ordered on July 22 that Red troops take Warsaw not later than August 12, and telegraphed Efraim M. Sklianskii that since the Poles no longer had a line on which they could stop the advance, "the possibility of executing the task within three weeks must not be ruled out."[83]

Military possibilities were linked with an estimate of revolution in Poland. Many Polish Communists were doubtful of the possibility of revolution and advocated caution. They had not encouraged Lenin to take the risk, but once he made up his mind few were willing to oppose him. Nor were they in a position to do it. The Polish Communist party in Russia and Poland was in a state of disintegration. After the Bolshevik Seventh Congress of March 1919 the party had transformed itself into sections of

Deutscher, *Stalin: A Political Biography* (London, 1949), p. 215; Ruth Fischer, *Stalin and German Communists* (Cambridge, Mass., 1948), p. 136.

RKP(b); its Central Committee in Smolensk ceased to function in the summer of 1920. At first the highest organ was the Polish bureau of agitation and propaganda in the Central Committee of the Russian party. It lost much importance with creation on July 4 of a Polish bureau to act in territories occupied by the Red Army (Polburo). Its initiators were Marchlewski and Dzierżyński, and the date on which it appeared coincided with the beginning of the great Soviet offensive.* The structural integration of the Polish Communist party within the RKP(b) deprived it of the small amount of national character it had possessed. In the words of a Soviet historian, Polish Communists simply became "an organ of the Russian Communist Party (bolsheviks) for work among the Polish population."[84] Similarly, Polish Red Army units had long ago ceased to exist as independent detachments.

Polish Communist leaders naturally expressed their views on the chances of revolution in Poland and an invasion by the Red Army. Radek and Marchlewski privately warned against an invasion, and expressed skepticism about the possibilities of a spontaneous revolution.[85] In public utterances they maintained a façade of unity, as evidenced by Marchlewski's speech on July 19 at the Second Congress of the Comintern. This enabled Zinoviev to claim later that the Polish representative declared that "the party adopts entirely the Russian point of view."[86] Lenin found Radek's pessimism annoying, and he said afterward that "I was very angry with him."[87] What Vladimir Ilich wanted to hear was a confirmation of his own views, and failing to receive support from Radek he turned to Unszlicht. In a telegram Lenin demanded: "Indicate your opinion and that of your Polish comrades on the following tactics. (1) We shall declare very solemnly that we guarantee to the Polish workers and peasants a frontier more to the east than that given by Curzon and the Entente. (2) We shall make every effort to finish off Piłsudski. (3) We are entering Poland proper only for a short time to arm the workers, and we shall leave it immediately. (4) Do you consider a Soviet revolution likely and how soon?"

Unszlicht replied that he agreed with the idea of a declaration

---

* The first bureau comprised Marchlewski, Kon, Stefan Brodowski, Bobiński, Brodzki, Jakub Dolecki and Samuel Łazowert, and after May 1920 Marchlewski, Próchniak, Dolecki, Brodowski, Budziński, Kazimierz Cichowski, and Adam Sławiński. The Polburo headed by Dzierżyński included Marchlewski, Kon, Próchniak, and Unszlicht. See *Dokumenty i materiały,* III, 541, and R. Ermolaev, "K istorii polskikh kommunisticheskikh organizatsii i organov RKP(b) dlia raboty sredi polskogo naseleniia na territorii Sovetskoi respubliki v 1917-1921 gg," in A. Ia. Manusevich, ed., *Oktiabrskaia revoliutsiia i zarubezhnye slavianskie narody* (Moscow, 1957), p. 57, 60-61.

and a border further east "if it would correspond to the wishes of the workers." Military means permitting, "we shall continue the war to a complete defeat of the Polish White army and the fall of the bourgeois government." Ethnic borders should be crossed if there were no genuine agreement with the Entente—guaranteeing a long period of respite—and if no revolution occurred in Poland. "We shall make our stay in Poland dependent on the will of the Polish workers and peasants." Finally, Unszlicht said that "I consider a Soviet revolution in Poland, with the advance of our troops toward her borders, most likely within a short time." The revolution would meet with fierce resistance in the Poznań area, which could be overcome by the German revolution. He did not commit himself to any particular date, but pointed out that the revolution would depend largely on "coordination of our activities on Poland's territory with those of the Polish Communist Party."[88]

Thus Unszlicht's reply contained no objection to the Red Army's invasion of Poland, although he and other ranking Polish Communists in Russia had signed the February 4, 1920 declaration which opposed the idea. His stand reflected the internationalist outlook of Polish Communists in Russia, which subordinated national considerations to broad revolutionary interests. No less a person than Dzierżyński admitted this mistake a few years later when he remarked: "By rejecting independence in general we failed to understand it and we lost our struggle for an independent Soviet Poland."[89]

The thinking of Communists within Poland ran along parallel lines. There were individuals who were unwilling to forget slogans about a revolution accomplished by native forces; they constituted a minority.* The Central Committee—according to one of its leaders, Adolf Warski—did not pass any resolutions on whether the Red Army ought to cross the ethnic border, advance on Warsaw, and assist in sovietization of Poland. Members of the

---

* Henryk Stein (Domski, Kamieński) wrote in the German Communist *Rote Fahne* on July 22, 1920 that the Bolsheviks who had respected Lithuanian rights to Wilno would sign an armistice with Poland without trying to impose Communism by force. Zinoviev subsequently denounced the article as heresy, but according to Roman Jabłonowski, *Wspomnienia* (Warsaw, 1962), p. 260, there were "many other important comrades who saw the matter in this fashion." Compare Jan A. Reguła, *Historia Komunistycznej Partii Polski* (Warsaw, 1934), pp. 43-44; also references in Suslov, *Politicheskoe obespechenie*, p. 18, and *Grazhdanskaia voina 1918-1921*, ed. A. S. Bubnov, S. S. Kamenev, and R. P. Eideman (3 vols.; Moscow, 1928-1930), III, 399. Warski speaks with contempt of the group. See *Dokumenty i materiały*, III, 496. For the Zinoviev-Stein (Domski) clash see *Protokoll des vierten Kongresses der Kommunistischen Internationale* (Hamburg, 1923), pp. 208-209, 218. Also "Protokoły II Zjazdu KPRP," *Z Pola Walki*, I (1958), 1170-1171. I am indebted to Professor Wiktor Sukiennicki for drawing my attention to this incident.

committee were cut off from the world, and they felt that this decision must be taken by Russia "not from the point of view of our partisan and political interests in Poland but from the viewpoint of the interests of the Russian revolution and the world situation." Crossing of the ethnic border "did not interest us at all." Nor was anyone "frightened by the thought that Poland may become Soviet with the aid of Bolshevik bayonets." It was only when the Red Army began to menace Warsaw that Polish Communists worried about an outburst "of petty bourgeois chauvinism" which could "sweep away our organization."[90] This fear was justified. Viewed as enemies of the Polish state, many of the leaders had to escape or found themselves in prison.[91] The party went to pieces.

Lenin ignored all this. He felt that the Red Army could take Warsaw and kindle a revolution. The Polish proletariat would become an auxiliary force of Russia and Soviet Poland a bridge to the West. He said that taking Warsaw was important only because it meant the destruction of the Treaty of Versailles.[92] Piatakov wrote that it was for the cause of a general revolution that "White Poland must be destroyed, a proletarian Poland established, and the Red flag unfurled over Warsaw."[93] In spite of propagandistic statements that Russia was "accomplishing the great mission of handing back crucified and violated Poland to the Polish workers and peasants," little sentimentality surrounded Poland's liberation.[94] The country was to be a means to a higher end.

Soviet optimism reached its peak when on July 19 the Second Congress of the Comintern convened in Moscow. It was a large and impressive gathering. In the main hall hung a huge map of Europe on which the advance of the Red Army into Poland was marked daily. Tukhachevskii called on the Comintern to prepare for a general war ending with proletarian victory.[95] Lenin's theses on the fundamental tasks of the Comintern, which originally stipulated that the parties' work lay in preparing the proletariat and "not in accelerating the revolution," appeared in final form with the emphasis on acceleration.[96] The Comintern's appeal to proletarians of the world for solidarity against Poland expressed belief in the imminent collapse of the Polish state. There was little discussion at the congress, and the Mensheviks, profoundly opposed to the attempt to spread Communism by force of arms, later accused the Bolshevik leaders of having dictated their own will. As Martov said, neither the congress nor the Russian people were ever asked whether they favored peace or wanted war for the purpose of artificial revolutions in Poland and the West.[97]

Internationally, the Soviet government was playing an astute game. Encouraging pro-Bolshevik activity of the Western proletariat, which helped maintain a virtual blockade of Poland, it did not neglect official contacts with governments. Hopes of a revolution in Germany, which appeared grossly exaggerated to such German Communists as Paul Levy—Lenin saw the Kapp Putsch of March 1920 as a Kornilov-like affair—did not preclude exchanges with leading circles in Berlin.[98]

While the Bolsheviks worried about the possibility of German-Polish cooperation, they encouraged the widespread belief that the Soviet-Polish war had created a chance for the Germans to undo the provisions of Versailles.[99] Here were possibilities of cooperation. Did not Lenin say later that "one of the reasons why this monstrous peace holds together is the fact that Poland divides Germany into two parts"?[100] Victor Kopp was active in Berlin; there were military contacts; and Moscow intimated it had no intention of crossing the borders of Germany.[101] Could this mean the prewar frontiers of Reich? There were indications that it did.

Enver Pasha reported to General Hans von Seeckt that Trotsky and an important group of Bolshevik leaders favored the borders of 1914.[102] Perhaps Lenin thought the same.[103] The Polish legation in Bern alarmed Warsaw with news of an alleged pact between Kopp, Radek, and Ago von Maltzan which concerned "the corridor." [104] When the Red Army reached the little town of Działdowo (Soldau), commissars and officers assured its German population that Russia would return "West Prussia" to Germany.* No less a person that the German Undersecretary of State for Foreign Affairs, Edgar von Haniel, assumed that the "corridor" and Poznania might, through a process of self-determination, return to Germany without raising any Russian objections.[105] Sir Maurice Hankey, in his report for the British government, wrote that one of the results of a Soviet victory might be German recovery of the "corridor," and retention of Upper Silesia.[106]

Berlin tried to explore all avenues of revisionism. The Germans approached the British, attempted to press the Poles, finally declared Germany's neutrality and forbade all export and transit

---

* Martov publicly referred to this incident (see Unabhängige Sozialdemokratische Partei Deutschlands (USPD), *Protokoll uber die Verhandlungen des ausserordentlichen Parteitages in Halle: vom 12 bis 17 Oktober 1920* (Berlin, n.d.), pp. 212-213). A German correspondent with the Red Army quoted the remarks of a Soviet major who said: "I do not think that the Polish Soviet Republic will lay claim to this German territory." See Rolf Brandt, "With the Soviet Army," *Living Age*, 307 (1920), 28. Compare Christian Höltje, *Die Weimarer Republik und das Ostlocarno-Problem 1919-1934* (Würzburg, 1958), pp. 24-30; Josef Korbel, *Poland between East and West* (Princeton, 1963), pp. 28-30, 72-75.

of war material to Poland.[107] Meanwhile Danzig assisted the German game by proposing ingenious schemes of rectifying its borders in a manner which would have included most of the "corridor" within the Free City.[108]

The German situation offered possibilities of a revolutionary and territorial upheaval. Lenin said that "with the advance of our troops on Warsaw all Germany began to boil," and he felt that current developments warranted the risk of a continued offensive.[109]

As for the Entente, the prevalent trends also operated to Russia's advantage. The Bolsheviks knew of the profound Franco-British differences on Poland, and they could observe the vacillating policies of the Allies.[110] The Soviet trade mission to London had a good knowledge of Lloyd George's ideas, which were far from friendly to the Poles. Moscow could be reasonably certain that the prime minister had no intention of intervening actively in the Soviet-Polish war, and the trade mission tempted him with prospects of economic concessions.[111]

Chicherin replied to the Curzon note on July 17, that is, the same day on which the Central Committee had decided to continue the military advance on Warsaw. The message was phrased with its propaganda value in mind. The foreign commissar viewed the British note with satisfaction, especially because Britain had not done anything so far toward restraining the Poles or contributing to peace. Soviet Russia always stood for peace, but in view of past policies Britain could hardly aspire to the part of an impartial arbiter. It was up to Warsaw to approach the Soviets directly. A settlement without a third party whose interests might interfere would surely be much easier. Moscow had signed peace treaties with Estonia and Lithuania, hence a conference in London with the participation of the Baltic countries would be superfluous. As for the League of Nations, mentioned in Curzon's note, the Soviets had never been informed officially of its existence. The border which Curzon indicated in his "ultimatum" had been drawn by the Supreme Council "under the influence of counter-revolutionary elements," and in the Chełm (Kholm) district it followed a line of the "anti-Polish policy of Tsarism and the imperialist White Russian bourgeoisie." Russia was "the more ready to meet the interests and the wishes of the Polish people with regard to peace terms" the more the Poles advanced "in their internal life along a road which will create a firm foundation for truly fraternal relations between the working masses of Poland, Russia, and the Ukraine." Chicherin's message ended by expressing a desire to eliminate all the obstacles to Russo-British peace and good relations.[112]

Chicherin had administered a neat snub to the Allies. Millerand termed his reply "impudent." Lloyd George used the expression "incoherent," which hardly corresponded to reality. The Polish military attaché in London shrewdly appraised the document when he wrote that the Bolsheviks sought to overthrow the Polish government, paralyze London's intervention, and promote anti-British feelings in Poland.[113]

Soviet leaders did not seriously envisage an armistice or even a peace with the existing Polish regime. New political directives of July 21 stated these points, adding that it was inadvisable "to say openly that we shall conclude peace only with a Soviet Poland."[114] Smilga, speaking of the government in Warsaw, said that "with these people there can be no peace," and added that the "historical strife between Russia and Poland must end by friendship and unification of the Russian and Polish Soviet Republics."[115] Official pronouncements were more circumspect. An appeal to the workers, peasants, and honorable citizens of Russia, issued on July 20, left out several passages of the original draft containing a direct call for an overthrow of the Polish government and a promise of Soviet assistance.[116] It said merely that together with "genuine representatives of the Polish nation we shall without difficulty settle a border with Poland, more just and corresponding more accurately to the interests of the Polish nation" than did the Curzon Line. The proclamation ended with "Forward, against the bourgeois-noble oppressors of Poland!"[117]

In answering Chicherin's note on July 20 Curzon deplored the controversial statements in the Soviet message, but welcomed the mention of a more favorable frontier and the offer of direct talks with Warsaw. The British, he said, advised Poland to address herself to Moscow. The foreign secretary was surprised that the Bolsheviks rejected an international conference but he did not insist on the proposal. He warned that British-Soviet trade negotiations could not continue if the Red Army crossed into ethnic Poland.[118]

Lenin instructed Chicherin to wait for two days before answering: "What is the point of spoiling them," he remarked. He told the commissar to say that a conference with the great powers would be acceptable, but as far as Wrangel was concerned the Allies must curb him. As for Poland, if she "wants peace, we are *for it,* and we said it clearly and repeat it now: let her propose it."[119] Chicherin's note of July 23 developed these points and expressed surprise—in accord with instructions—about the British threat to interrupt the trade talks. Surely these talks had been a result of British initiative.[120]

Curzon agreed to continue trade negotiations. He stressed that the proposed London conference ought to comprise, in addition to the great powers and Russia, Poland and the other border states. Its aim would be a general peace settlement guaranteeing the independence of Poland and safeguarding the interests of both sides.[121]

The Soviet-British exchange formed the setting for direct Polish approaches to Moscow. Piłsudski was unhappy about them, and told Osmołowski that he only needed ten days to reorganize the army and redress the situation. If there were no armistice "so much the better for us," but if Poland had to sign one she ought at least to delay peace until her military chances improved.[122] The State Defense Council once again engaged in debates, and Piłsudski, who on previous occasions had demanded either full trust or leave to resign, asked a vote of confidence. The council passed it during its July 19 session, and then turned to discuss a coalition government. Debate proved inconclusive and continued the next day. Sapieha informed the council that the British minister in Warsaw insisted on a speedy Polish acceptance of an armistice, and there were doubts whether this should be at once or left to the new coalition government. Seconded by Generals Rozwadowski and Stanisław Haller, Sapieha stressed that an armistice might help the nation to "catch its breath." Finally, it was agreed that the new government would send a radio message to Moscow within the next twenty-four hours.[123]

The coalition cabinet formed at this point was presided over by the peasant leader, Wincenty Witos. The Socialist Daszyński became deputy premier; General Józef Leśniewski took the Ministry of War (to be replaced by General Sosnkowski on August 9); and Sapieha retained his post at foreign affairs. The ministry was a symbol of national consolidation, and received the endorsement of all sejm deputies with exception of a lonely Communist fellow traveler, Tomasz Dąbal. In joining the cabinet the PPS announced that it was sacrificing its principle of a workers' and peasants' government on the altar of national defense. The sejm had already passed a law on agrarian reform, and the Ministry of War issued stern orders to restore discipline in the army; the Poles were taking all measures to make a final stand.

Witos defined the aims of his government as the defense of the country, the end of war, and the conclusion of a just and lasting peace. He declared that "we will not give in to any threat to

violate the rights of the Polish nation to freedom and unity."
Though he indicated no peace conditions, Sapieha thought in
terms of a compromise which would involve Polish disinterest in
the Ukraine and Russian in Lithuania and Belorussia. Both states
would pledge noninterference in each other's affairs.[124] Witos confirmed that Warsaw had made overtures for a cease-fire with the
Bolsheviks, and he added that an armistice "does not yet prejudge
the fate of peace."[125]

Polish armistice proposals took the form of two radiograms sent
on July 22 by Sapieha to Chicherin, and by General Rozwadowski
to the High Command of the Red Army. The first invoked the
Soviet reply to Curzon and proposed an immediate armistice and
opening of peace talks. The second proposed armistice negotiations, and said that Warsaw would await a Soviet answer until
3:00 A.M. on July 25. Chicherin replied on July 23 that his government had ordered the High Command to enter into negotiations with the Poles to conclude an armistice and prepare a
future peace. At the same time the Glavkom answered Rozwadowski that it was sending representatives to a meeting place. The
command of the Western Front would inform the Poles where
this place would be and when Polish delegates should present
themselves.[126] Then came Tukhachevskii's radio message, sent on
July 24, which dealt with these points in detail: In view of technical difficulties and because of Belorussian hatred for the Poles
it was difficult to fix a place to begin talks at once. Hence, the
commander of the Western Front suggested that the Polish delegates cross the front on the Baranowicze-Brest road, and conform
to the rules of the Red Army "for the reception and passage of
parliamentaries." The earliest date for the meeting would be
July 30—the date "mentioned in the radiogram" of the Polish
chief of staff. The delegates would then be taken to Baranowicze.[127]

It appears that Warsaw received the first two Soviet notes on
July 25, and the third on July 26.[128] The Polish government
agreed to accept the Soviet proposal, but pointed out that it had
never indicated the date of July 30, which Tukhachevskii ascribed
to Rozwadowski. The latter called this to Tukhachevskii's attention on July 27. He agreed to the meeting and demanded clarification about Red Army rules, with which the Polish army was not
familiar.[129] Two days later Tukhachevskii wired back that these
rules did not differ from internationally accepted procedures.[130]
All this was rather puzzling. Radio Moscow had received the
original Rozwadowski message without any mistakes except for
the date, which mysteriously had changed from July 25 to July

30.* Tukhachevskii found it necessary to speak of special regulations which turned out to be no different from any others. Finally, Baranowicze, where the talks were to be held, was quite far from the front and bound to cause further delays. It seemed clear that the Bolsheviks viewed Polish overtures as a sign of weakness, and were intent on procrastinating while the Red Army moved forward.[131] Rumbold, who had originally pressed the Poles to start negotiating, reported to London that Warsaw was doing its best; the Bolshevik moves showed that they "hoped to improve their military and strategic situation during the week." He assured Curzon that there was "no foundation for the allegations that the Polish Supreme Command had delayed the armistice negotiations until July 30."[132] Martov expressed the same opinion some six weeks later when he publicly accused Soviet diplomacy of having begun "openly, for all the world to see, to drag the negotiations."[133]

The Polish cabinet and the State Defense Council discussed the armistice on July 28 and 29. The military and international situation was bad, but not hopeless. The army was still retreating, but it had not been destroyed. There were great difficulties with the transit of war material through Czechoslovakia and Danzig. None of the East Central European countries pursued a friendly policy toward Poland—except for Hungary, which had made offers of military help. These offers were not realistic, given the lack of a common frontier, and could only lead to complications.[134] The French military mission was doing its best to assist the Polish army, and an inter-Allied mission comprising Ambassadors Jules Jusserand and Lord D'Abernon, Sir Maurice Hankey, and Generals Weygand and Sir Percy Radcliffe arrived in Warsaw around July 25. Two days later Weygand became counselor to the Polish chief of staff, and although this raised some personal difficulties it showed French interest in the survival of Poland.[135]

The Boulogne conference between Lloyd George and Millerand on July 27 had stiffened the attitude of the prime minister, and Lord Curzon on July 29 addressed a new message to Chicherin urging that an armistice be followed by an international peace conference in London.[136] Still, French and British policies toward Russia continued to differ appreciably, with London intent on a Soviet-Polish armistice even if unfavorable to Poland, and Paris doubtful of its practicability. From the far-off Crimea came a message from General Wrangel that he was ready for another offensive—his operation in early June had brought some

* This is the explanation in *Dokumenty i materiały*, III, 208, which prints the message as sent and as received.

success—to relieve the Poles and draw off Bolshevik forces. The general expressed belief in a common victory and spoke against even a temporary cease-fire.[137]

The Poles had to take all these complex military and international factors into consideration, but in the final analysis the decision and risk was theirs alone. Daszyński presented three principles for negotiating with the Bolsheviks. The armistice line could not be farther west than the Curzon Line; no disarmament demands would be acceptable; no interference in Polish domestic affairs would be tolerated. Daszyński made it clear that armistice negotiations must not "prejudice questions which belong to peace negotiations."[138] The cabinet approved, and Daszyński explained the instructions for the Polish delegation to the State Defense Council. He stated that the "government will not allow armistice negotiations to drag"; nor would it seek an armistice at any price. The council agreed, and the government appointed a delegation headed by Deputy Foreign Minister Władysław Wróblewski.[139]

The cabinet approved final instructions for the delegates at a secret session on July 29 when it decided that a minimum armistice line should be that indicated by Curzon. If that line proved unacceptable there could be some changes—up to fifteen kilometers—to Russian advantage. The line of hostilities would represent the final concession. The delegates were authorized to break off negotiations if the Bolsheviks demanded a more advantageous line, insisted on Polish disarmament, or wanted to interfere in Poland's domestic affairs. The latest date for signing the armistice was August 2, and its minimum duration was to be eight days. Matters pertaining to peace were not to be treated in armistice negotiations—especially in view of the decisions of the Boulogne Conference and the advice of Allied ambassadors in Warsaw —so as not to prejudice the final settlement. A peace treaty with Soviet Russia, ignoring the Allies, could only be considered if the Bolsheviks offered advantageous conditions. Should the Russian delegates demand immediate peace the Polish representatives were to return to Warsaw to inform the government.[140]

The Polish delegation crossed the front on July 30 and went east to its meeting with the Bolsheviks. The same day, in the little town of Białystok, occupied by the Red Army, there emerged a Provisional Polish Revolutionary Committee presided over by Marchlewski—a would-be government of Soviet Poland. The conflict was entering its crucial phase.

The Decisive Battle

From the end of July until late August 1920 the Bolsheviks sought a decisive victory over the Poles. In their all-out effort they relied on ideological, diplomatic, and, above all, military means. The Provisional Polish Revolutionary Committee (Polrevkom) was the ideological weapon; peace negotiations seeking Poland's capitulation represented the diplomatic arm; and finally there was the Red Army coming ever closer to Warsaw. In the last analysis Soviet success or failure hinged on its achievements.

On July 28 Russian troops occupied Białystok, the first sizable Polish town west of the Curzon line. A Soviet army order reminded troops that they were fighting the Polish oppressors and not the people who strove "to make Poland a full-blooded sister of the workers' and peasants' Russia." The High Command threatened penalties for soldiers who disregarded this order.[1] The Polish bureau of the Central Committee of RKP(b), which had gone to the front on July 25, arrived in Białystok five days later and proclaimed the creation of a Provisional Polish Revolutionary Committee. Marchlewski presided over the body; Dzierżyński, Kon, Próchniak, and Unszlicht were its leading members.[2] All available evidence suggests that Marchlewski, Dzierżyński, and the other members of the Polish bureau took the decision to create this committee on the spur of the moment. On August 2, when Lenin informed Stalin of the event, he did not sound as though this were a long-planned development.[3] The Polish Communist, Jakub Fürstenberg-Hanecki, described the Polrevkom a result of Marchlewski's initiative.[4]

Polish Communists in Russia, at their conference in May 1920, had advocated mobilizing the Poles en masse and sending them to the western front. The Central Committee of the RKP(b) showed little haste. Dzierżyński, with several thousand members of the Cheka, was in the Ukraine establishing "order," and Lenin took some time before recalling him for work in Poland.[5] Marchlewski had been busy at the Second Congress of the Comintern; in early July he signed the peace treaty between Soviet Russia and Lithuania. Feliks Kon headed a section in the Ukraine dealing with behind-the-front diversion. Presumably other leading Polish Communists in Russia could not be spared. Hence while the Bolsheviks were making a gigantic propaganda effort to undermine the morale of Polish soldiers and the populace, they were slow in preparing an organization to work on Polish territories.[6]

Then came the Soviet decision of July 17 to continue the offensive toward Warsaw. This immediately affected the Polish Communists, and the next day Dzierżyński informed his colleagues of a directive from the Central Committee of RKP(b) to proceed with the general mobilization of Polish party members in Russia, "given the likelihood of the entry of the Red Army into Poland's territory." He proposed the creation of an organ to carry out the mobilization and to prepare a plan of action. Those present at the meeting agreed, and voted to set up a board composed of Marchlewski, Kon, Unszlicht, Dolecki, Dzierżyński and Próchniak. The Central Committee of RKP(b) officially approved this initiative on July 22, and a day later the Polish bureau resolved to set up revkoms in localities occupied by the Red Army. Theses revkoms were to rebuild the old councils of workers' deputies, organize trade unions and cooperatives, and create a basis for Communist operations.[7]

All this activity was belated. Marchlewski and most Polish Communists voiced complaints. The mobilization proved inefficient and there were other mistakes. These errors, as the Polish bureau later charged, "were one of the elements of the defeat."[8]

When the Red Army entered purely Polish territories it soon discovered that the attitude of the population differed from that encountered before.[9] Revkoms set up by political organs of the army had an oddly assorted membership. In some cases members of the PPS joined for diversionary purposes. In Łomża local National Democrats entered a revkom to advance their own political designs. In the absence of genuine Polish Communists, "non-party anarchists," Jewish leftists, and other individuals whom a Soviet historian called "in their majority completely useless or even harmful" came to the fore.[10] With Russian nationalism rampant, anti-Polish measures seemed permissible. After the occupation of Białystok the commissars recognized Russian and Yidish—the town had a large Jewish proletariat—as the official languages, and gave positions only to those persons who knew them. Jews took over schools, and Polish students received the status of a minority.[11]

On his arrival in Białystok Marchlewski saw it all and decided not to delay the formation of a Polish Communist authority. A leading Polish Bolshevik explained privately that "If Marchlewski had decided to take the known step, it was because the Polish Communists wanted to save Poland from further bloodshed."[12] This makes sense only insofar as the activity of the Red Army was likely to stiffen Polish resistance and prolong the conflict. The Polrevkom was to ensure that Soviet methods and policies would assist and not hinder a Communist revolution in the country. At the same time the committee strove to change the anti-Russian feelings of the population and mobilize, at all cost, the workers and peasants of Poland.

Marchlewski's task was not easy, and he began by issuing a manifesto to the Poles and informing Lenin of the creation of his committee. In a telegram on July 30 he thanked Lenin for the friendly assistance of the Red Army and declared that the Polrevkom had been set up "to administer the territory liberated from the lords." He hoped that within a short time the Red flag would wave over "the bastion of imperialism and reaction" next to Russia.[13] Four days later Lenin instructed the command of the Western Front to give publicity by all available means to the Polrevkom manifesto. Its text appeared in *Pravda*.[14] Four days were wasted, and one cannot tell if the delay resulted from technical reasons or some doubt in Moscow.

Tukhachevskii's order, presumably influenced by the Polrevkom, appeared on August 5, and forbade the replacement of Polish names with Russian; ordered the use of the Polish language in appeals and ordinances; and decreed the playing of Polish revolutionary songs together with the Internationale at public meetings. Government announcements were to carry the heading, "Polish Socialist Soviet Republic," and the motto, "For your freedom and for ours."[15] A day later Marchlewski and Smilga issued joint instructions to Communists and political workers in the Red Army on proper behavior in Poland. Soldiers were told to act so that the Polish people could regard them as liberators. They must refrain from any action that could recall the tsarist occupation. Soldiers ought "to facilitate and not hinder our Polish comrades in their task of building Socialism"; they should help make Poland "a strong ally of Soviet Russia." The commissars were to explain all this to the Red Army, and wage a relentless struggle against looting, rape, ill-treatment of prisoners, and wanton destruction.[16]

Time was pressing, yet army commissars received detailed instructions on political work in Poland only by September 1. Nor was the Polrevkom well assisted. It had no apparatus of its own until August 10 and relied on political units of the Red Army. Theoretically a quasi-government in the occupied territories, the Polrevkom exercised no direct control over the numerous revolutionary committees set up by the commissars; it could establish and confirm only the large revkoms on the level of a province.

Soviet propaganda was slow to give publicity to the committee and did so on a small scale. The army paid little attention.[17]

Soviet propaganda had failed to explain the place of a Polrevkom in Bolshevik policy and strategy. Lenin may have believed that revolution in Poland was around the corner and would develop spontaneously. Perhaps the grandiose vision of a triumphant westward march obscured the need for practical measures in Poland. The real goal of the march on Warsaw was Germany, and there may have been opposition to commit Soviet Russia to definite arrangements in Poland. Once the committee appeared, however, Lenin showed great interest in it. He offered advice to Dzierżyński, granted a credit of one billion rubles, and manifested displeasure when a Soviet official criticized the Polrevkom on the grounds that it created an unfavorable impression in Britain.[18]

Marchlewski admitted that his committee had no mandate from the Polish masses. It was impossible to establish contact with the disintegrating Communist Party in Poland. The Polrevkom had called itself provisional because it planned—after the capture of Warsaw—to hand over power to the Polish Communist Party. It was up to the KPRP to organize the elections of councils of workers and peasants.[19] The Polbureau which was the supreme party organ—the Polrevkom was the highest legislative and executive body—discussed these elections on August 6 and 10, but no details are available.

The committee's program appeared in its manifesto of July 30, calling on workers to take over factories, which would become the property of the nation, and on peasants to establish laborers' committees to administer the estates of the landowners. All land would become national property. Taking political power in their hands, peasants' and workers' councils would create a Polish Socialist Soviet Republic.[20] The manifesto did not elaborate on how its principles would apply in practice. In accord with long-held theories about agrarian solutions in Poland, the Polrevkom did not distribute land among the peasantry, but planned to transform the estates into state farms. There was disagreement within the committee, and Lenin intervened, urging that land be given at once to the landless peasants.[21] As for industry, the committee issued several decrees nationalizing the factories in Białystok, but it made no definite statements with regard to future policies.[22]

The Polrevkom showed feverish political and military activity. It launched appeals to the proletariat of Warsaw, demanding that workers seize the city before it should fall to the Red Army. "You must not wait passively," an appeal said, and it sounded the call to arms.[23] A few days later the committee "ordered" the Polish army to arrest officers and establish soldiers' councils.[24] The order, just like the previous appeals, produced no effect. Nor did Dzierżyński's attempts to form a Polish Red army.[25]

The committee defined its stand on the Soviet-Polish war by declaring in its manifesto that "a lasting peace is possible only between Socialist Russia and a Socialist Poland of workers' councils." It appealed on August 5 to the proletarians of the world, stressing solidarity with Russia and the Red Army. "The Polish revolutionary proletariat," it said, "finds in it [the Red Army] assistance in the struggle of liberation from the yoke of Polish capitalists and the yoke of the capitalists of France and England."[26]

The balance sheet of the attempted sovietization of Poland during the first two weeks of August was not impressive, but it affected Bolshevik thinking about revolution in that country. Although conditions in the countryside were not satisfactory and there was much resentment, the largest class, the peasantry, adopted a negative attitude.[27] The poorest stratum of agricultural laborers was more receptive to revolutionary propaganda, but the group was in no position to assume leadership.[28]

The greatest disappointment to the Bolsheviks was the working class. Lenin tried later to explain the collapse of Soviet expectations by saying that the Red Army had failed to capture any of the large industrial cities.[29] Dzierżyński, who knew Poland better, wrote to his wife that although the workers in Białystok were friendly, "one felt no power, there were no active revolutionary developments." Writing about the expected entry into Warsaw, he expressed fear that Warsaw would "not greet us as we would wish it." He blamed the leadership of the Polish Communist Party. They "did not know how to master the masses or the political situation," he complained. "They miss a leader—a Lenin."[30] Others also noted the weakness of the Polish Communists.[31] Leaders were in exile, prison, or hiding. Moscow worried about their fate and threatened reprisals against captured Polish officers. Lenin scribbled on a note for Trotsky: "Threaten. For shooting Communists in Poland—100 Poles [to be shot] here *or* no peace."[32] But Communist activity was almost nonexistent. There were no mass strikes in the factories. In the summer of 1920 the PPS with its patriotic slogans represented the Polish working class. Agitation among prisoners of war produced feeble results. Out of 24,000 prisoners subjected to Communist indoctrination, only 123 agreed to join the Bolshevik party.[33] When the very existence of Poland seemed at stake, the war was popular among almost all classes. The advancing Red troops met with an increasingly hostile reception.[34]

The brutality of certain units of the Red Army provoked reaction.* The ruthlessness and anti-Semitism of Budenny's cavalry, including the commissars, was notorious, and required such orders as: "Our main and basic shortcomings are our attitude toward the population, toward the prisoners, and anti-Semitism."[35] In the province of Siedlce—which, judging by the number of revkoms, had proved susceptible to Soviet propaganda—the Red Army had to fight partisans even more than the regular troops. During the Soviet retreat the same was true for Białystok.[36] No wonder that an army commander wrote that "expectations of an outbreak of the Polish revolution could only have been seriously entertained in political offices, and only in those which were very far from the front." The army hardly believed in it.[37]

The Soviet advance shook the foundations of the Polish state and brought many of its social problems into the open,[38] but a Communist Poland could have been established only by Soviet bayonets. A realization of this fact considerably influenced the final peace settlement between Russia and Poland.

The Polish Revolutionary Committee had its counterpart in the revkom of Eastern Galicia. Two days before the Poles had begun their offensive toward Kiev, the Central Committee of the Communist party of the Ukraine established an organizational committee for Eastern Galicia and Bukovina. After the all-out advance of the Red Army there emerged on July 8 an Eastern Galician revkom presided over by Zatonskii, which issued its first manifesto from Tarnopol on August 1. In subsequent declarations and decrees, the committee spoke of an independent Galician Republic and its unification with Soviet Ukraine. The revkom denied all Polish rights to Eastern Galicia, and in that sense constituted a reply to the Piłsudski-Petliura alliance.[39]

The Galician committee received recognition from the Polrevkom which welcomed it as an ally against the "common enemy."[40] Lenin's interest in the work of Zatonskii's committee took the form of telegrams urging stern measures against the "kulaks," and asking what Zatonskii was doing to provoke a revolution of the Galician peasants.[41] While none apparently occurred, there were instances of collaboration of the people with the revkom and the Red Army. At the same time, as Zatonskii complained later, the

---

* Piłsudski stated, however, on August 18, 1920, that in some areas the Red Army behaved quite well. See "Protokoły Rady Obrony Państwa," ed. Artur Leinwand and Jan Molenda, in Z Dziejów Stosunków Polsko-Radzieckich: Studia i Materiały, I, (1965), 259.

highly nationalist character of Russian propaganda produced bad results in Eastern Galicia and harmed the revolutionary cause.[42]

The Polish committee turned its eyes on Warsaw, the Galician aimed at Lwów, and the command of the Southwestern Front ordered the army to take the city by July 29.[43] This it failed to accomplish, and one can only speculate if the ambitions of the Galician revkom had anything to do with Stalin's famous insistence—he was a member of the army's revvoensovet—to concentrate all efforts in the south to the detriment of the more important operations then taking place near Warsaw.

The *Polrevkom* was formed on July 30 and the Eastern Galician Committee on August 1; between these two dates there emerged the Belorussian Soviet Republic. This closeness of events may have been coincidental, but it could have had a connection with the opening of Soviet-Polish armistice talks. The Bolsheviks may have wanted to show the Poles that Belorussia had already determined her fate and that Warsaw was not the sole spokesman for the people of Eastern Galicia and even of Poland.

Be that as it may, the Polish armistice delegation on the evening of July 30 went to its meeting with the Bolshevik representatives. It presumably reached Baranowicze the next day. The Poles presented their credentials on August 1, but it was only a day later that delegates of the Soviet Western Front came up with a note on Russian conditions.* The document contained the following points: to speed up the negotiations the Poles must have a written mandate signed by Piłsudski, empowering them to sign not only an armistice but the preliminaries of peace. To obtain it the Polish delegates either could return to Poland; ask that the mandate be sent by a courier; or bring in new representatives with full powers. It was desirable to have the mandate by August 4, because peace negotiations would then begin in Minsk. If there was not enough time, the Bolsheviks would accept Warsaw's confirmation by radio that the mandate was on the way. Finally, the note said that the Soviet authorities had been obliged to alter the text of the telegram sent by the Polish delegation to Warsaw.[44]

The Poles responded with a written statement: messages exchanged thus far between Moscow and Warsaw did not speak of peace negotiations but of an armistice. This was the reason for limited Polish credentials. Given the Soviet stand the delega-

---

* There is some confusion regarding chronology. If the Poles crossed the front around 8:00 P.M. on July 30, they could not have reached Baranowicze the same day, as some historians indicate. Even so its seems that the Russians were in no hurry to start negotiations since nothing happened on July 31 and August 1.

tion had no choice but to go back to the Polish capital, and at the same time protest Bolshevik interference with freedom of communications. Simultaneously the chief delegate Wróblewski wired Sapieha Russian demands, and said that the Poles would return at once to Warsaw.[45]

The abortive encounter at Baranowicze resulted in a loss of four days during which the Red Army continued its advance. Bolshevik tactics showed a lack of good will, and Chicherin attempted to alter the bad impression. He radioed Sapieha that interference with the Polish telegram in no way implied Russian disregard of the right of the delegation to communicate with its government.[46] The Narkomindel issued a statement interpreting the exchange of telegrams between Sapieha, Chicherin, Rozwadowski and Tukhachevskii in the sense that they implied simultaneous armistice and peace negotiations.[47] The Poles contested these assertions, saying that the telegrams merely indicated that after the conclusion of an armistice, peace talks would follow.

One thing was evident. The Bolsheviks were not interested in stopping their offensive, and they objected to a cease-fire. As for the wisdom of signing peace, views differed once again. Lenin telegraphed Stalin that "Within the C[entral] C[ommittee] there grows a tendency immediately to conclude peace with bourgeois Poland."[48] Those who advocated such a course felt the need to concentrate against Wrangel, and were discouraged by the absence of revolutionary developments in Poland.* Indeed the White general again expressed a readiness to launch an offensive to take the pressure off the Poles, and he asked for French assistance.[49] This increased the possibility of a serious struggle on two fronts and worried the Bolshevik leaders. But not Lenin.[50] A plenary session of the Central Committee discussed the military situation and on August 5 decided to continue the offensive until victory. The Soviet government emphasized that this was a purely military operation which in on way endangered the independence of a Polish state within its ethnic borders. It said that peace negotiations would begin as soon as the Polish delegates returned.[51] On the same day the revvoensovet of the republic expressed a conviction that Warsaw would be captured on August 16. In order to overcome the duality between the Western and Southwestern commands, Tukhachevskii became the supreme commander of the entire Polish front on August 6. He was now as optimistic as the

* One can appreciate the extent of Soviet preoccupation with Wrangel, if the geographically remote gubernia of Smolensk was ordered in July 1920 to send Communists to the Southern Front. See protocol of July 31, 1920, Smolensk Archive, WKP 6, Widener Library, Harvard University, Cambridge, Mass.

revvoensovet.[52] It was only a week later that he began to worry about his left wing and unsuccessfully ordered Budenny's cavalry to transfer to the north. In early August the Bolsheviks, sanguine about the campaign, were determined not to allow anything to interfere with their victory.

The outcome of the Baranowicze encounter discouraged the Poles. The State Defense Council met on July 4 to consider further action. The government was not unanimous. Sapieha favored a note to the Bolsheviks requesting their peace proposals. Should this note remain without answer, Warsaw ought to wait. Daszyński, supported by the majority of the cabinet, advocated sending a peace delegation to Minsk on the grounds that a new exchange of notes would mean delay, and this could only benefit the Russians. The State Defense Council debated the pros and cons of both tactics. General Sosnkowski remarked that irrespective of what one did it was impossible to obtain peace. The council then decided by a unanimous vote to send a note to Chicherin announcing the departure of Polish delegates to Minsk, and saying that Poland awaited the Soviet peace terms. The note was to make clear that Warsaw could never admit Soviet interference in Polish domestic affairs.[53]

Sapieha sent the note on August 5. He accused the Soviet government of deliberate delays and stated Polish willingness to start negotiations at Minsk. He recalled the right of the delegates to communicate freely with Warsaw, and suggested, in view of the Soviet rejection of an armistice, a halt in offensive operations. After saying that negotiations would not be possible if they aimed at interference with Poland's sovereign rights, Sapieha concluded that his government awaited a Soviet statement on the principles of the future peace.[54]

Polish fears that the Bolsheviks would continue to drag matters out were not groundless. Sapieha's message, radioed August 5 and repeated the next day, was not received by Moscow's station. On August 7 the message came through in garbled form, and radio Moscow allegedly called Warsaw thirteen times for clarification. Finally, the next day, the full message came in.

If atmospheric conditions made it impossible for radio Moscow to receive the Polish message—as Chicherin claimed in his later notes—one can only say that the weather singularly favored the Bolsheviks. The foreign commissar radioed Warsaw on August 6 to complain about the lack of news, and on August 7 to confirm Polish consent to dispatch a delegation to Minsk. He demanded that Polish delegates appear on August 9 at the Siedlce-Międzyrzec-Brest road and it is odd that he should have given such a short notice in view of the difficulties in radio communications.[55] The Poles never received this message and belatedly learned via London about the proposed encounter. The cabinet then dispatched two delegates, Zdzisław Okęcki and Major Stamirowski, to the front. During the night of August 11-12, they signed an agreement—with the representative of the revvoensovet of the Sixteenth Army, V. Mulin—on a meeting of delegates on August 14.[56] This game of hide and seek, if really coincidental, was strange indeed. The Poles did not think that weather was the main cause of all the difficulties. Nor did the British minister in Warsaw, who spoke of "strong evidence" of Soviet "bad faith and calculated delay."[57]

The Bolsheviks blamed the Poles. Trotsky, in an interview for *Pravda*, and Kamenev, in a note to Lloyd George, explained that Poland was procrastinating to force the Red Army to take Warsaw and provide the Entente with an excuse for military intervention.[58] Given the decision of the Central Committee to take the Polish capital by August 16, this sounded like a preposterous accusation, made to cover up Soviet tactics. Strangely enough Trotsky believed there was something to it; perhaps he could find no other explanation for the absence of an unconditional Polish surrender.[59] Dzierżyński saw things more clearly and wrote Lenin that the Poles wanted to maintain themselves in Warsaw at the beginning of the negotiations.[60] Delays seemed to the Bolshevik advantage, and commenting on the failure of Polish delegates to appear at the front on August 9, Lenin wrote: this was "arch-convenient for us."[61] Other Soviet leaders must have shared this opinion privately.

Russian-Polish moves and countermoves coincided with Lloyd George's talks with the Soviet representatives in London. Leonid Krasin, who had come to England to discuss Russo-British trade, left on June 31, to return with Lev Kamenev on August 4. At this point the Poles had already returned from Baranowicze as a result of Soviet insistence to have an armistice and peace terms discussed at the same time. This ran counter to British ideas, and on August 4 the prime minister spoke sternly to the two Bolshevik representatives. He accused Russia of delaying tactics, and threatened to order the fleet out, reimpose the blockade, and strengthen Poland by forcing deliveries through Danzig, paralyzed by dockers' strikes. Lloyd George softened his "ultimatum" by promising not to divulge it to the parliament or to Warsaw. He made it conditional upon Russian willingness to present acceptable terms to the Poles.

The prime minister wanted a peaceful way out, and Kamenev

tried to reassure him with a palpably untrue statement that Moscow did not want "to mix the question of armistice with that of peace with Poland."[62] The Soviet delegate reported Lloyd George's position to Moscow, but the Soviet government claimed that it received the message only five days later and did not respond.[63] This silence permitted Kamenev to indulge in vague assurances that the Bolsheviks did not intend to tie an armistice with the final treaty but merely sought guarantees that the armistice would not be exploited against them. These guarantees, Kamenev thought, should include partial disarmament and demobilization, turning over of some war supplies to Russia, a withdrawal of foreign instructors, the end of Allied assistance to Wrangel, and an effective supervision of all such measures. Kamenev stressed that the advance of the Red Army "did not prejudice in the slightest degree the question of the nature of the peace treaty, and constituted no attempt against the independence and integrity of the Polish state in its ethnic borders." As for the London conference which Curzon had proposed, only Russia and the Entente ought to participate.[64]

The Soviet objective was clear: as Chicherin later explained, Russia absolutely opposed any form of Allied control over her relations with the border states.[65] Kamenev sought to confuse Lloyd George regarding the Polish situation, and to keep the London conference separate from any arrangements which the Bolsheviks would devise vis-à-vis Poland.

Taking Kamenev's statements at face value, the prime minister tried to outline armistice terms which might be acceptable to the Bolsheviks. He prepared a memorandum on August 6, proposing a ten-day armistice to begin at midnight on August 9, and providing guarantees that the Poles would not use the cease-fire to strengthen their military position.[66] The whole thing seemed pointless because the Bolsheviks had already forced the Poles to link the matters of armistice and peace, and Moscow was in no hurry about a peace conference.

The prime minister was annoyed, because two new notes from Kamenev and Chicherin, sent on August 8, gave no formal reply to his armistice proposal.[67] Four days had passed since he had presented his "ultimatum," and nothing had happened. Just as in the case of the Soviet crossing of the Curzon line, London threatened and the Bolsheviks called the bluff.

Meanwhile the French were growing suspicious of British dealings with Kamenev and Krasin. Paris worried about increasing differences among the Allies, and to restore some Anglo-French unity Millerand, accompanied by Marshal Foch, went to Britain.

There, at the Lympne residence at Hythe, the statesmen and their military advisers spent August 8 and 9. The meeting began in a chilly atmosphere. The French were alarmed about the possible breakdown of the Polish barrier—meant to keep the Bolsheviks and Germans apart—and Lloyd George's inability to see how the Soviet advance would affect the Treaty of Versailles. But Millerand had little chance to coordinate French and British policies; he was too much handicapped by his unwillingness to have any dealings with the Bolsheviks. Nor could the French free themselves of illusions concerning the re-emergence of a non-Soviet Russia. Millerand and Lloyd George were unanimous in heaping abuse on Piłsudski and Poland for getting them into a difficult position. Otherwise their views were miles apart, and the final agreement at Lympne merely obscured Anglo-French differences. It said that the Allies would advise Poland to do her best to sign an armistice that would not harm Polish independence within ethnic borders. Should Soviet terms violate such independence, Britain and France would take collective measures in Poland's defense. These were to consist of a blockade of Russia, maintenance of the freedom of communication with Poland, and the shipment of military equipment and advisers. No Allied troops would be available.[68]

The Lympne accord hinged on a Franco-British agreement about exactly what constituted a threat to Polish independence. Its flimsiness was exposed two days after the conference ended. On August 10 Kamenev presented a note to Lloyd George (dated August 9) which contained Soviet terms for an armistice and peace with Poland. Apparently the prime minister had an earlier inkling of these terms from an intercepted Russian radiogram, but said nothing about it to the French.[69]

The Russian conditions were a far cry from what Kamenev had intimated and Lloyd George proposed. They comprised the following demands: demobilization of the Polish army to fifty thousand men (administrative and command staff not to exceed ten thousand); handing over to Russia all weapons beyond the needs of the small army and a civic militia; dismantling of Polish war industries and no importation of war matériel; exclusive Soviet management of the Wołkowysk-Białystok-Grajewo railroad to ensure transit to Baltic ports and Prussia; grants of land to Polish war victims and their families by the Polish government. With fulfillment of these conditions—and Kamenev added that minor alterations and additions could still be made—the Red Army would withdraw. In the meantime its size would gradually diminish. The armistice line would coincide with the front, but under no circumstances would it be farther east than the Curzon line. The Polish troops would withdraw fifty versts (over thirty miles) from the armistice line, creating a neutral zone between the two armies. The final Russo-Polish border would follow the Curzon Line with some rectifications to Poland's advantage.[70]

British reaction to these terms, clearly endangering Poland's independence, was hardly in keeping with the spirit of the Lympne agreement. Lloyd George thought the Soviet conditions acceptable, and Curzon telegraphed the British envoy in Warsaw to tell the Poles that His Majesty's Government could not undertake hostile acts against Russia to force her to grant any better.[71] Millerand indignantly protested. He said that if Poland accepted the Bolshevik conditions she "would have no means of guaranteeing her independence."[72] A day later France recognized General Wrangel, and London took it as a retaliation against the unilateral British move with regard to Poland. The English were annoyed by what appeared to be a deliberate French attempt to prevent a settlement in Eastern Europe; both governments indulged in recriminations.

Lenin gloated and wrote Stalin that Lloyd George had agreed to all the Soviet terms, including disarmament and the handing over of weapons to the Bolsheviks and to the workers in Poland (the civic militia). He termed it "a great victory."[73] The neutral zone which the Polish troops were to evacuate would comprise Warsaw—though it is not clear that the British ever thought of it—and that was another achievement. Lenin wired Karl Danishev-skii, the chairman of the peace delegation in Minsk: "You have learned from Chicherin about our great diplomatic success in England on account of Poland. I hope that you will fully appreciate it, and will also insert Warsaw in the terms as we discussed them with you, and [get] fullest guarantees of everything else."[74]

The gloom in Warsaw contrasted with Soviet jubilation. Rumbold reported to London on his "painful" interview with Sapieha and the awkward position of the British as compared with the French.[75] Two weeks later he commented that Polish acceptance of the Soviet terms, especially as amplified at the Minsk conference, would have placed the country at the mercy of the Soviets. "It is certain," he wrote, "that if the Soviet troops had captured Warsaw a Soviet regime would have been set up in that town," and if the Polish government had moved elsewhere there would have been ideal conditions for a civil war in Poland under the aegis of the Bolsheviks.[76]

The fortunes of Poland never seemed so bleak as during the second week of August 1920. The Councils of Action in Britain and similar pro-Soviet movements in other Western countries kept a steady pressure on their governments to prevent deliveries of arms to the Poles. The Franco-British mission in Warsaw vainly appealed for help. In his report for Lloyd George, Sir Maurice Hankey virtually wrote off Poland. French officers led by Weygand and Henrys performed valuable service; the French general staff was for continuation of the war, but it was annoyed with Weygand's difficulties in Warsaw, and continued to distrust Piłsudski.[77] Diplomatically the Poles derived some comfort from the note of Brainbridge Colby, the American Secretary of State, to the Italian Ambassador, Romano Avezzana. The note said the United States could not recognize the Bolshevik regime, based as it was on a negation of honor and good faith. Nor was it possible to sign treaties with it. As for Poland all means ought to be used to preserve her independence and integrity.[78] But the effects of this statement were offset by Lloyd George's willingness to recognize Soviet demands.

In Poland the coalition government continued its attempts to mobilize public opinion and to impress the nation and the army with the gravity of the situation.[79] It was largely successful, even though party politics kept interfering with full realization of national unity.[80] Holding Piłsudski responsible for the military and political catastrophe, the Right intrigued against him. The marshal, on August 9, "exhausted by the absence of moral strength among us"—as he put it—offered General Weygand a share in the Supreme Command. The latter consulted Paris and refused.[81] On August 12, Piłsudski handed Witos a letter expressing his willingness to resign as chief of state and commander-in-chief if circumstances demanded it. He based his decision on several considerations. He knew that in spite of the vote of confidence the Defense Council mistrusted him. Dmowski had withdrawn from this body. The marshal wrote: "I was and am a partisan of a war à outrance against the Bolsheviks, because I see absolutely no guarantee that they would keep such and such agreement or treaty." Despite this conviction he had been forced to make concessions to the peace party in Poland. Finally, assuming that the peace talks in Minsk would fail, the Entente would remain the last card Poland had, and the country would have to follow blindly Allied demands. This, Piłsudski said, he would be incapable of doing.[82]

One can understand his feelings.* The Entente was suspicious

---

* Did Piłsudski have other reasons he did not reveal? Henryk Jabłoński suggested that the marshal planned, in case the Bolsheviks overran Poland, to make some of his supporters collaborate with the new regime while secretly remaining under his orders. See "Wojna polsko-radziecka 1919-1920," *Przegląd Socjalistyczny*, 7-8 (1948), 29.

of him to an extent which seemed almost unbelievable. Millerand said at the conference of Lympne that Piłsudski "had probably only one aim, to keep himself in power, and to do this he might negotiate tomorrow with the Bolsheviks." Lloyd George considered it probable that Piłsudski was playing a double game and was a traitor.[83] In their telegram to Warsaw the two Allied statesmen demanded the nomination of a commander-in-chief of the Polish army with no other functions—clearly a cut at Piłsudski.

The marshal's letter remained secret,[84] and the situation he envisaged never arose. Having delivered his letter to Witos, Piłsudski concentrated on preparing a military plan which was ultimately to result in a Polish victory.

The military situation was dramatic. Soviet guns could be heard in the Polish capital, and the little town of Radzymin, which protected the approaches to Warsaw, was contested in hand-to-hand combat. Trotsky on August 14 issued an order to the Red Army. After accusing Poland of playing a game with Russia, he promised the Poles a lesson. He ended with the words: "Red armies forward! Heroes, on to Warsaw!"[85] The next day Chicherin disclaimed any intention of imposing a Soviet form of government on Poland, and he declared that "Maintenance of peace will rest with armed Polish workers instead of with Russian Army of Occupation."[86] On August 16 the Polrevkom moved with the advance Red units and installed itself in Wyszków, less than forty miles (fifty versts) from the capital. It prepared for entry into Warsaw on August 17.

Polish armies regrouped, and Piłsudski on August 16 launched a counterattack which outflanked the Red Armies. To borrow Lord D'Abernon's expression, the battle appeared to contemporaries as "the eighteenth decisive battle of the world." While not ending the campaign it inflicted a telling blow on the Red Army, exhausted by its rapid advance and strategically outmaneuvered.[87] At first the Bolsheviks failed to recognize the importance of their defeat. They viewed it as a temporary reversal, and both civilian and army leaders clamored for a counterattack. At a meeting of the Central Committee, Lenin scribbled several notes for Sklianskii: "Happen what may," he wrote, "it is necessary to take Warsaw within three to five days." If the High Command does not refuse to seize Warsaw, it must be captured, and "what extreme measures are needed for it? Tell me?" He added, presumably contesting somebody's opinion: "to talk about *speeding up* the armistice now that the enemy is advancing is an idiocy."[88]

On August 18 Lenin instructed Smilga, a member of the revvoensovet of the Western Front, to issue "an order to the troops to the effect that by multiplying their efforts now, they are securing favorable peace terms for Russia for many years to come."[89] Two days later an order declared that "peace can be concluded only on the ruins of White Poland." It struck at defeatists: "Shame on him who thinks about peace near Warsaw," and ended with "Victory or death."[90] The idea that peace with bourgeois Poland was unthinkable prevailed on all levels of party and administration.[91]

Reality proved stronger than theory. Military casualties were heavy, and the losses of Communist "activists" amounted to 70 percent in the Sixteenth Army and almost 90 percent in the Third Army.[92] After analyzing the situation on the western front Trotsky reached pessimistic conclusions. Reinforcements had to be untrained recruits; the policy of filling the gaps with party members had proved costly. It would be impossible to take Warsaw. The Polish army, he now believed "was on a higher level than that of Kolchak or Denikin."[93]

Bolshevik leadership wavered. The Politburo decided on August 19 "to recognize the Wrangel front as the main front," a decision which logically entailed restricted activity against the Poles.[94] Lenin began to feel less optimistic, and wrote the commander-in-chief that "we can hardly take Warsaw soon."[95] The Bolsheviks wondered whether to prepare for a winter campaign against Poland. Stalin persuaded the Central Committee that they should. Trotsky was against it, and Lenin was coming round to the opinion that it would be better to "get a smaller part of Belorussia" than to risk a winter campaign.[96] Lenin's view prevailed at the meeting of the Politburo on August 25.[97] Russia was ready to talk peace.

As for the Poles, the anti-Piłsudski Right termed the victory at Warsaw "the miracle on the Vistula," and did its best to prevent the chief of state from deriving political advantages from the success. As a Polish writer put it, the people "rendered thanks to God for the August battle and poured maledictions on Piłsudski for the Kievan campaign."[98] A month later, the marshal of the sejm expressed what many Poles thought at the time. "The guns near Warsaw," he said, "became a tocsin which warns and awakens. We cannot allow that such humiliation and such danger could ever be repeated in the future."[99]

As the supreme commander Piłsudski had to make certain that the Warsaw victory would be properly exploited. It was not immediately clear whether the Red Army had lost its offensive power, and reports indicated that Soviet resistance was stiffening.

One could not rule out a counteroffensive. But how far should the Poles pursue the retreating Red troops? This was not only a military but also a political question.

Piłsudski told the State Defense Council on August 27 that he saw two alternatives: either his troops stopped on the Curzon Line and Poland signed peace, or they would cross the line and then the "logical consequence [was] an alliance with Wrangel and agreement on spheres of influence." He stressed Wrangel's disinterest in Lithuania, and though he spoke cautiously it was evident that he favored continuation of war until the fulfillment of his plans. He concluded that "We must work out things with some kind of Russia." In an interview which appeared two days later, Piłsudski reiterated his belief that the Curzon Line was an "illusory eastern border," strategically untenable and politically unsound. He warned that even after a peace treaty Poland would continue to be a potential object of Russian aggression, and complained that the Polish people were already cooling off.[100]

The National Democratic member of the Defense Council demanded that, in view of "rumors that the aim of the present offensive was also Kiev," the Supreme Command should submit strategic and political aims of the offensive.[101] The Right favored a peace settlement acceptable to the Entente, and everyone knew that the Allies would object to Polish occupation of territories much to the east of the Curzon Line. The minister in Paris strongly recommended that Polish eastern borders be determined "in close cooperation with the interested parties and with the Allies."[102]

The military experts of the Entente shared Piłsudski's view that the Curzon Line was not a sound military boundary. Weygand advocated Polish advance to the so-called German line (the line of German trenches during the First World War), which could eventually become a border acceptable to political parties. At the above-mentioned session of the State Defense Council, members agreed to authorize the crossing of the Curzon Line, and accepted the line of the German trenches as a basis for negotiations with the Bolsheviks.[103]

To calm domestic public opinion and the Entente Witos issued a declaration stating that "the victory of the Polish troops in no way changed the stand of the Polish government on the matter of concluding peace." The Poles wanted a just and lasting settlement, and delegates at Minsk had received instructions to that effect. He concluded that "we have not waged war against the Russian nation, nor do we desire to annex foreign lands."[104] Privately, Sapieha assured the American chargé d'affaires in

Warsaw, and presumably other diplomats as well, that there would be no repetition of a march on Kiev or of demands for the frontiers of 1772. Either peace would be concluded on Polish terms (i.e., the German line), or the war would go on and the army "would have to cooperate with Wrangel."[105]

The continuing eastward advance of Piłsudski's armies, deliberations in Warsaw and Moscow, and the changing international scene all affected the course of Soviet-Polish peace negotiations at Minsk.

On the eve of the battle of Warsaw a Polish peace delegation, led by Deputy Foreign Minister Jan Dąbski, had left Warsaw and crossed into Soviet-occupied territory.* The delegation had received general instructions. It was to reject any Bolshevik demand of disarmament and be flexible on an armistice line. As for peace preliminaries, which the delegates were empowered to sign, the cabinet gave several stipulations: an exchange of prisoners and mutual engagement to stop propaganda could be inserted in the treaty. The question of transit could be mentioned but finally resolved in a commercial agreement. With regard to frontiers, no definite settlement, and if doubts arose as to principles the delegates ought to consult Warsaw. The Poles were to protest the Bolshevik cession of Wilno to Lithuania, and demand the right to arrange Polish-Lithuanian affairs by direct talks. If the Soviet delegates were to raise the Belorussian issue, the Polish side should recognize the country's independence but avoid discussing borders. In regard to the Ukrainan question they ought to stress self-determination but guard against wrecking the peace conference because of it. If the question of Petliura's or Balakhovich's troops came up, the delegates could promise withdrawal from the front at the time of the armistice, and disbanding after the peace.[106]

Many of these points were vague and reflected differences within Poland. Piłsudski and the government were unhappy about the possible abandonment of Petliura; the Right, which had long disapproved of the alliance with the Ukraine, feared that negotiations might founder on the Ukrainian rock.† Recognition of

* It comprised General Antoni Listowski; two government officials, Władysław Wróblewski and Kazimierz Olszowski; and six deputies representing major parties of the sejm—Norbert Barlicki, Stanisław Grabski, Władysław Kiernik, Adam Mieczkowski, Ludwik Waszkiewicz, and Michał Wichliński.

† In mid-July Sapieha wrote the minister in Washington that one could not think of "tearing up our agreement with Petliura," because this would discredit the Polish government and nation. Besides, the Ukrainians were a loyal and useful ally. See "Pertraktacje pokojowe polsko-rosyjskie 1920-21," July 12, 1920, Ciechanowski Deposit, Hoover Institution, Stanford, California. For the debate in the State Defense Council see *Dokumenty i materiały do historii stosunków polsko-*

Belorussian independence may well have taken into account the constitution of the Soviet Republic of Belorussia on July 31, assuming the Poles were aware of it. As for borders, it appears that the cabinet thought in terms of the line of the German trenches as a minimum frontier.[107]

The Polish delegation traveled by cars to Brest and then by train to Minsk—a long and painful journey. Amid the jeers of Communists, who at one point attempted to persuade Polish drivers to desert the capitalists and join the proletarian liberators, the representatives passed through little towns bedecked with Red flags. Finally they reached Minsk, and the first plenary session took place on August 17.

Neither side appeared in a great hurry to arrive at a settlement; the Poles even less than the Russians. The Bolsheviks were engaged in the decisive battle at Warsaw, and still thought in terms of a total victory. The Poles could achieve little through a peace conference and hoped for a favorable outcome of hostilities. The first days were spent in shadow boxing, with each side presenting its point of view largely for the benefit of a domestic and international audience.*

The chief Soviet delegate, Karl Danishevskii, appeared nervous, and Lenin had to admonish him by telegram.[108] His instructions were to make the most of Soviet willingness to recognize Polish independence; offer better borders than the Curzon Line; and renounce all reparations.[109] All of these were calculated to impress Lloyd George and show how reasonable the Bolsheviks were.

At the first session Danishevskii read a declaration reviewing Soviet-Polish relations over the last two years, with an emphasis on Poland's imperialism supported by the Entente. The paper recognized Poland's independence in wider borders than those proposed in the Curzon note, and stated that the Red Army would evacuate Poland if Russia received genuine guarantees that Warsaw had abandoned its aggressive policies. The declaration said that Soviet conditions were meant neither as an ultimatum nor a dictation.[110] The Bolsheviks evidently sought to retain some freedom of maneuver.

The conference then turned to technical matters. Credentials were exchanged and verified, and Danishevskii raised the problem that the Poles had no definite powers to deal with the Soviet Ukraine. He required additional credentials and entered into a

radzieckich (Warsaw, 1962—), III, 310-314, and "Protokoły Rady Obrony Państwa," ed. Artur Leinwand and Jan Molenda, in *Z Dziejów Stosunków Polsko-Radzieckich: Studia i Materiały*, I (1965), 249-254.
    * Plenary sessions were open to the press.

debate with Wróblewski on the nature of constitutional links between the RSFSR and the Ukrainian SR. The Poles eventually received vague additional credentials and the whole incident revealed a Soviet desire to force Poland to recognize the Soviet Ukraine, and Polish reluctance to do so.[111]

Dąbski presented the Polish declaration at the next session on August 19. The one-day interval resulted from a Polish desire to study more fully the Soviet statement, which they had only heard and not read. The chief delegate accused the Russians of having imposed the war on Poland by the invasion and occupation of Lithuania and Belorussia in 1918 and the threat of introducing a Bolshevik revolution into Poland. Dąbski denied imperialistic designs. He recalled Piłsudski's Wilno proclamation and resolutions of the sejm, and pointed out that Polish troops had never set foot on ethnic Russian soil. But the Red Army now stood at the gates of Warsaw, and the Soviets sought to impose a Communist regime on Poland.[112]

Both declarations were a prelude to real business. There was more fencing, in the course of which the Ukrainian question reappeared together with Danishevskii's accusation that the Poles were delaying the work of the conference. Dąbski countered by accusing the Bolsheviks of interfering with Polish radio communications with Warsaw. Then the head of the Soviet delegation presented fifteen "theses" concerning a peace settlement. He said that the Poles were probably familiar with them, insofar as their outlines had been sent to London. He thus implied that the conditions were identical with those which Lloyd George had received favorably some ten days earlier.[113] The truth was that the conditions now appeared in an amplified form which made them look like a new document.

The first three points referred to recognition of Poland's independence, her right to establish a regime without outside interference, and Soviet renunciation of reparations together with acceptance of the Curzon Line modified by minor concessions to the Poles. Point four provided for reduction of the Polish army to fifty thousand, and its completion by a workers' civil militia. According to point five Poland was to complete demobilization within one month after the armistice and the preliminary peace. Point six said that armaments beyond those needed by the small Polish army would be turned over to Soviet Russia and the Ukraine, which would use some of the equipment to arm the workers' militia. Point seven provided for demobilization of war industries. In accord with point eight Poland would prohibit transit inimical to Russia and tolerate no organizations pretending to the role of foreign governments. Point nine said that military operations would cease seventy-two hours after the signing of the armistice. The armistice line would correspond to the front, except where it ran east of the Curzon Line. Polish troops were then to withdraw fifty versts westward and a neutral zone would be set up, administered by Polish civilian officials under the control of a mixed commission and a committee of the trade unions. Point ten stipulated that during the period of demobilization the Red Army would withdraw, leaving no more than two hundred thousand troops along the line of the neutral zone. According to point eleven Poland promised to return all inventory, rolling stock, and other goods originating in the territories occupied by the Polish army. She would also rebuild destroyed bridges and buildings. Point twelve said that as part of a general agrarian reform the Polish government would provide free land to the families of soldiers who had lost their lives during the war. According to point thirteen Poland would guarantee free transit to Russia and place under exclusive Soviet control the Wołkowysk-Białystok-Grajewo railroad. Points fourteen and fifteen provided an amnesty for political prisoners in Poland and publication of peace preliminaries and all diplomatic documents relating to the Soviet-Polish war.[114]

The Bolshevik peace conditions were equivalent to a demand for complete surrender. The first three points were propaganda, and were meaningless when taken in conjunction with those that followed. Deprived of the army, with war industries dismantled, Poland would have been at Soviet mercy. The Russian-armed workers' militia was to ensure Communist mastery of the country. Soviet members of the mixed commission would have ruled the neutral zone including Warsaw. Learning from the agrarian mistakes of the Polrevkom, the Bolsheviks sought to win over the peasantry by a free distribution of land. Political amnesty would free the imprisoned Communists; the 200,000-strong Red Army would be standing by to interfere if and when necessary.

Did Moscow assume that the Poles would accept such peace "theses"? Kamenev told Lloyd George a little later that "I do not wish to conceal that inside the Russian Government a certain struggle went on regarding the exact formulation of the terms of peace or armistice to be offered to Poland."[115] Assuming this to be true the partisans of stiff terms must have prevailed. Why was that? Dąbski wired Warsaw on August 20 that the Bolsheviks were "surely not naive enough to suppose that we would accept" such conditions.[116] Martov later accused the Soviet government of deliberately presenting demands which the Poles would have to reject.[117] One day after Danishveskii's fifteen theses Lenin ordered Smilga to have leaflets dropped accusing the Poles of breaking off peace talks and forcing the people to shed more blood.[118] Since at that point the Polish delegation had not yet replied to the theses, Lenin anticipated their rejection.

Dąbski assumed that the Bolsheviks merely wanted to prolong the talks. This is not a convincing explanation. The conditions must have been prepared at the time when entry of the Red Army into Warsaw seemed a matter of days. Perhaps Moscow anticipated that it would sign peace with the Polrevkom, already transformed into a Soviet Polish government.[119] An adamant stand of the delegation in Minsk could be used as proof—for the benefit of Lloyd George and the Polish masses—that bourgeois Poland had refused peace to the last moment. Even if the Soviet position deteriorated militarily a new effort was still possible, and a diplomatic game at Minsk could assist the Bolsheviks. Finally, it cannot be ruled out that the Soviets hoped that the Polish delegation would lose its nerve and sign on the dotted line.

The radio transmitters of the delegation were constantly and mysteriously breaking down. The Poles in Minsk were isolated and deprived of news from Warsaw.[120] The Tukhachevskii-Smilga order of August 20 contained a vitriolic passage about the spies and saboteurs who made up the Polish delegation. The local commander of the Cheka told the Poles about the popular furor against them, and expressed doubts whether he would be able to protect them. On August 21 the Polish delegates heard for the first time of the Warsaw victory.* Their mood changed, and they could now make countermoves. Dąbski had already capitalized on Soviet interference with radio communications; now he could protest the unheard of afront offered to his delegation.[121]

The conference met in its third plenary session on August 23, and the chief Polish delegate demanded apologies and the revocation of Tukhachevskii's order. Moscow was embarrassed and messages circulated between Lenin, Smilga, and Danishevskii.[122] Dąbski eventually received full satisfaction; the whole incident enhanced the Polish position. As for the main business, the Poles now presented their analysis of the fifteen Soviet theses. In a long declaration Dąbski rejected a dictated peace and demanded one "in which the interests of both nations would receive equal recognition." He stated that unilateral acknowledgment of Polish independence was uncalled for; both sides ought to renounce

---

* Grabski said they heard about it on the radio five days after their arrival in Minsk. This would make it August 21, 1920. See Stanisław Grabski, *The Polish-Soviet Frontier* (London, 1943), p. 24.

reparations; the Curzon Line corresponded to the boundary of the third partition and was unacceptable; demands for reduction of the Polish army were reminiscent of the policies of Peter the Great and Catherine II. Demobilization ought to be reciprocal. As for dismantling Polish war industries and Russian arming of a workers' militia, these were demands which could create a real threat to peace. Dąbski described points referring to the transit and dissolution of foreign organizations on Polish soil as interference in domestic affairs. Nor could one accept the presence of 200,000 Soviet troops along a neutral zone. Reparations of war damages were contradictory to the avowed Bolshevik principle of no reparations. Exclusive Soviet control over a Polish railroad, and a demand for land reform were contrary to Poland's sovereignty. Political amnesty had to be reciprocal. Finally, Dąbski deemed the Soviet request for publication of diplomatic correspondence incomprehensible.[123]

Almost endless arguments and recriminations ensued, occupying the rest of the third session and most of the fourth held on August 25. Dąbski was answering earlier statements of Danishevskii. The Soviet delegate complained that the Poles had rejected eleven out of fifteen points of his theses. He asserted that a lost battle was not yet a lost campaign, and even a lost campaign did not necessarily mean a lost war.[124] Despite the sharpness of argument, the Poles noted a weakening of the Soviet stand. Dąbski reported that the Bolshevik delegation "was inclined to make concessions."[125] Moscow had plenty of reasons to revise its policy toward Poland. Ideologically the Russians had failed in promoting a revolution in Poland. Militarily they were defeated, and the Wrangel front required immediate attention. In the international field a change in Poland's favor became noticeable.

At the time of the Minsk negotiations and the Battle of Warsaw Lloyd George was on a brief holiday. On his return he affected a *volte face* which amazed the Bolsheviks. He took strong exception to the Minsk theses, and accused the Russians of having mislead him by adding conditions to those communicated by Kamenev. It is true that the latter had successfully obscured the meaning of "civic militia," and the British only gradually discovered that there was more to it than they thought. Lloyd George was annoyed and he attacked the clause about the workers' militia, terming it a gross infringement of Poland's independence.[126] Angry British-Soviet exchanges followed. Lloyd George accused Kamenov of deception, saying he could not deal with a government which could not "conform to the ordinary obligations of honor." In vain Chicherin protested that Britain had recognized the Soviet right as victor to deal with Poland, and there were no grounds for a change of policy. Only one operation had failed, but neither the campaign nor the war. London disagreed and somewhat belatedly ordered the fleet into the Baltic to keep free the lines of communication with Poland. Whether the Bolsheviks liked it or not the situation had changed to their disadvantage.

By late August both Moscow and Warsaw were willing to contemplate a compromise peace. Neither side was sure of the other and Radek came to Minsk to talk confidentially with the Poles. In a meeting in which Barlicki, Perl, Kiernik and Lucjan Altberg participated, together with Radek and Smidovich of the Soviet delegation, the situation became clearer. Radek found that the Poles were not planning to continue the war to please France and Wrangel. He also realized that they would abandon Petliura in exchange for Soviet noninterference in Polish-Lithuanian affairs and for a reasonably good border. Radek intimated that the Russians would withdraw their demand for Polish disarmament and make territorial concessions. He attached little importance to frontiers and stressed only the need to recognize the Soviet Ukraine.[127]

The contours of a Soviet-Polish peace settlement began slowly to take shape. Both sides were now willing to negotiate seriously and to arrive at a treaty that could be voluntarily signed. But it was necessary to change the place of the conference, for Minsk stood as a symbol of Polish humiliation and defeat.

The Peace Settlement

Proposals for the transfer of the peace conference to a neutral country came up during the last days of August 1920. The Polish State Defense Council instructed the delegates at Minsk to raise the matter, and Sapieha on August 28 wired Chicherin to suggest the Latvian capital of Riga. His radio message presumably crossed that of Chicherin, who a day earlier proposed that the conference move to a town in Estonia.[1] Russian preference for Estonia, just as the Polish preference for Latvia, was bound up with considerations of prestige. Estonia had been the first country to sign a peace with the Bolsheviks, and Moscow wanted to stress that fact. Latvia had cooperated with Poland, especially in the conquest of Dünaburg (Daugavpils), and the Poles favored negotiations in that country.

In the ensuing exchanges both sides were reluctant to give up their proposed conference sites. The foreign commissar pointed out on August 29 that the demand for Riga would delay the opening of negotiations, and he criticized the Poles for stressing past misunderstandings. He protested Polish attacks on the Tukhachevskii-Smilga order and on Soviet interference with radio communications. By contrasting Sapieha's demand for Riga with Witos' speech in which the latter had merely objected to working conditions in Minsk, Chicherin tried to insinuate that the Poles disagreed among themselves. He urged haste and added that he had already approached the Estonian government.[2] Sapieha checkmated him in a message sent the next day, which said that Latvia had agreed to a peace conference in Riga. The Polish minister remarked that responsibility for further delays would now fall on the Russians.[3] Chicherin reluctantly agreed, on the condition that Latvia guarantee full freedom of communication and immunity of the Soviet delegates. The episode was characteristic of Soviet-Polish negotiations. Both sides had determined to drive a hard bargain, using every opportunity to gain diplomatic advantages, be they only of symbolic value.

The Bolsheviks informed Poland that Adolf A. Ioffe would head the delegation and would have powers to negotiate preliminaries and the final treaty.[4] Danishevskii, a Latvian Communist, would hardly be at ease in Riga. Sapieha responded that the Polish delegates who would leave Danzig for Riga on September 12 would receive similar credentials.[5] Meanwhile the Latvians provided the guarantees Moscow demanded.[6] The scene was set for the conference.

The last session in Minsk took place on September 2, but by that time the principal delegates had departed. The meeting was devoid of importance. The Bolshevik Smidovich tried to have the last word, and remarked that while the Poles knew the Russian peace terms, Polish conditions were still unannounced. He represented the transfer to Riga as caused by technical difficulties in Minsk. There had been no break in negotiations. The Pole Wróblewski agreed with this last formula, and the rest of the session was spent on a discussion of technical arrangements.[7]

If peace appeared a foregone conclusion, everything nevertheless was not smooth sailing. From late August into September the Polish troops continued their march eastward. They drove Budenny from Eastern Galicia and prepared for the important Niemen campaign in the north. Was all this merely a completion of the Warsaw victory, putting more pressure on the Bolsheviks, or revival of the eastern program?

Piłsudski did not suddenly become a partisan of a compromise settlement. He still believed in total victory, and as he later put it, was forced to stop the eastern advance because of the "lack of moral strength of the nation."[8] Petliura also believed that the Warsaw victory had opened possibilities for a reversal of the Ukrainian situation, but Polish domestic factors prevented their realization.[9] The marshal's acquiescence in peace resulted from the fiasco of the federalist program. This was probably his greatest political drama, and after the war he apologized to the former Ukrainian soldiers for letting them down.[10]

Not only domestic opposition but the international situation made a resumption of the grand design impossible. Here the attitude of the Entente and the problem of the White Russians influenced the course of events. Sapieha told the American chargé in Warsaw that if war was to continue, the Poles would need definite Allied commitments. They wanted to have the assurance that a non-Bolshevik Russian government would make the same territorial concessions as the Soviets.[11] Here was the crux of the matter. Reports from Paris indicated that the French might assist Poland in a campaign coordinated with Wrangel.[12] Szymon Askenazy wrote Piłsudski that Russian emigré circles in Paris pressed for a continuation of the war "for their benefit."[13] The Whites worked for the creation of an army in Poland, eighty thousand strong, consisting of the Permykin and Balakhovich units. Called the Third Army, this group was to operate on the right wing of the Ukrainian front. In early September, Wrangel's chief of staff, General Petr Makhrov, came to Warsaw. He was received by Sapieha who allegedly told the general that circumstances might force Poland to sign a quick peace with the Bolsheviks. Sapieha asked what delays Wrangel would need to consolidate. He tried then to find out what the Whites thought of a territorial settlement, and the Russian unofficial envoy in Warsaw, Gorlov, commented that the minister wanted to obtain Wrangel's agreement to borders east of the Curzon Line. Hence the friendly attitude to the Whites. But the talk was apparently inconclusive.[14] Cooperation with Wrangel and the continuation of the war without Allied backing of the Polish territorial program made little sense.

French and, later, British approval of the Polish eastward advance did not imply their political support. The Allies warned against any designs on Wilno, recalled Grabski's engagements at Spa, and worried about Piłsudski, whom Rumbold called an "unknown factor." Sapieha made it clear that Grabski's engagement at Spa was void because the Allies had not prevented an invasion of ethnic Poland. The British were annoyed but failed to press Warsaw to adhere to the Spa decision. Nor did the Entente make a serious effort to make use of Article 87 of the Treaty of Versailles and impose an eastern frontier. Hugh Gibson wrote that it was "impossible to coerce Poland into being reasonable through conflicting advice and in the absence of material support."[15] As in the past, the West tried to restrain Poland without proposing a working scheme; it advised and pressed, but took no responsibility.[16]

Under the circumstances the Poles were left largely to their own devices. Piłsudski took half-measures: a Ukrainian offensive—for which Poland would decline responsibility—aiming at a junction with Wrangel. The Polish political parties would not stand for anything more. The State Defense Council authorized Sapieha to transmit a note of Ukrainian Foreign Minister Livytskyi to the Bolsheviks asking when his delegation could meet with Soviet Ukrainian representatives. This was no more than a gesture, and Chicherin replied that he never had heard of Mr. Livytskyi. There was only one legitimate Ukrainian government, namely the Soviet regime in Kiev.[17]

Poland could do nothing to support the Ukrainian cause at a peace conference; talks in Minsk, especially with Radek, made clear that the Bolsheviks would have none of it. This was confirmed later through an intercepted Bolshevik message of September 15, 1920, which spoke of insurmountable difficulties if Poland were to raise demands concerning a "bourgeois" Ukraine.[18] When the Polish minister in Riga assured the Ukrainians that Piłsudski would not allow a treaty disregarding their rights, he expressed only wishful thinking.[19]

Everything combined to hasten peace. Poland was exhausted, threatened with bankruptcy, and on the threshold of economic chaos. In the absence of Allied commitments to Polish territorial claims in the east, a direct settlement with Soviet Russia seemed the only course.

The State Defense Council on August 27 had approved the German line as a basis of territorial settlement. In early September the government and army favored going beyond it. Sapieha wrote Polish missions abroad that there was a good chance of obtaining a frontier running a little farther east, namely through Barano-wicze-Łuniniec-Sarny-Równo.[20] General Rozwadowski counseled that the armistice line be drawn along the Dvina and Dnieper rivers, and that the final frontier approximate the front held by Poles in December 1919.[21]

On September 11 the State Defense Council debated the instructions for the Polish peace delegation. The document consisted of eighteen points and occasioned a lively discussion, revealing differences regarding aims and tactics. The first point stated that the delegates ought to present principles governing a border settlement rather than propose a concrete frontier and an armistice line. The latter ought to be drawn only after both delegations reached an agreement on the preliminaries of peace. As for territorial delimitation between Poland, Russia, and the Ukraine, it should put an end to secular conflicts by reconciling vital interests of the participants; recognize the will of the local population and strive after joining compact national groups to their respective nations; and promote reciprocal security. According to point two, after the above principles gained acceptance negotiations ought to proceed in a mixed commission. Points three to six dealt with the means of achieving a final border settlement. The council instructed the delegates to seek an armistice line and a frontier approximating those indicated on the enclosed map. While the map unfortunately has disappeared from the available documents, the debate permits its general reconstruction. The delegation was to negotiate so as to prevent a breakdown on the grounds of excessive Polish demands. It first was to reach agreement on an armistice line—corresponding to the military situation—and then convert it into a final frontier. This frontier was to be described as one between Russia and the lands taken away from Poland during the partitions. The

Poles would renounce their historic rights east of the frontier, and the Russians should declare their disinterest in territories to the west.

The State Defense Council favored moderation. As a member recalled, Sapieha had said that Danzig, Upper Silesia, and Eastern Galicia were the important questions to be settled by the Entente and there was no need to antagonize the Allies by exaggerated claims in the east. Rozwadowski's proposal for an armistice line on the Dvina and Dnieper rivers and for a final border approximating the Dmowski Line was rejected—only four members voting for it. The delegates in Riga were to strive after the German line, revised in several points to Poland's advantage.* If the Bolsheviks rejected it, the Poles were to refer to Warsaw.

Point seven of the instructions allowed delegates to recognize the RSFSR (Russian Socialist Federated Soviet Republic) and the Ukrainian Soviet Republic, but not before obtaining a favorable frontier settlement. To offset the effect of recognizing the Soviet Ukraine, point eight stipulated that the peace treaty should declare that Poland acknowledged the right of the Ukrainian nation to independence and a free choice of its regime. Point nine forbade delegates to recognize in any way the Soviet-Lithuanian treaty of July 1920. According to point ten each side engaged itself not to interfere with the domestic affairs of the other, nor to tolerate emigré organizations. Point eleven dealt with determining the size of armies along the borders. In accord with point twelve, Poland would guarantee the rights of Russians and Ukrainians in Poland, on the basis of reciprocity.

Point thirteen of the instructions spoke of the future signing of commercial and technical conventions, and the fourteenth indicated the lines of a financial settlement. Both sides were to renounce reparations and claims to state property on the territory of the other state. Both would return movables and property of individuals, whose claims would be reciprocally settled. Russia had to agree that Poland incurred no charges and obligations from her former inclusion in the tsarist empire. Russia had to restore archives and art and cultural treasures taken from Poland since the partitions. She would grant the Poles the most-favored-nation clause with regard to possible restitution and damages resulting

* It was to run east of the Stołpce-Baranowicze-Łuniniec-Sarny railroad. See Andrzej Ajnenkiel, *Od "rządów ludowych" do przewrotu majowego* (Warsaw, 1964), p. 121. Władysław Pobóg-Malinowski called it a modified Dmowski Line (*Najnowsza historia polityczna Polski 1864-1945* [3 vols.; Paris, 1953, London, 1956-1960], II, 369), while Stanisław Grabski not quite accurately wrote that it did not go beyond the old German trenches *Z codziennych walk i rozważań* [Poznań, 1923], p. 104).

Frontier proposals 1919 – 1920

Niemen

Danzig (Gdańsk)

Wilno

Borisov

Dnieper

Minsk

Poznań

Vistula

Bug

Białystok

WARSAW

Brest

Kiev

Cracow

Lwów

Poland 1772

Poland 1921

——————— Treaty of Riga

– – – – – Line of German trenches north of Galicia September 28, 1916

- - - - - - Line of December 8, 1919 (extended into Galicia as Curzon Line)

–·–·–·– Soviet proposal of January 28, 1920

═══════ Ioffe's line I of September 28, 1920

═══════ Ioffe's line II of October 2, 1920

+++++++ Line A eastern Galicia

100 Miles

100 Kilometers

from revolution and civil war. Point fifteen referred to the right of option by citizens of both states; the sixteenth provided for mixed commissions to deal with prisoners and hostages. Mutual amnesty to Poles and Russians constituted point seventeen. The last point said that immediately after signing of preliminaries, negotiations would begin for a final peace treaty.[22]

As the secretary of the peace delegation observed, the instructions were a "skeleton" and provided for a good deal of lattitude.[23] They reflected not only a desire for flexibility in negotiation but also differences about the final settlement. Moderation and a wish to conclude peace appeared in clauses which spoke of a mutually acceptable treaty and warned against a breach. Differing views of the army and government, and of the federalists and the incorporationists found expression in ambiguous statements about the frontier and the armistice line. While Belorussia was not mentioned, and Lithuanian affairs were considered of no concern of the Bolsheviks, the Ukraine was to be finally abandoned. Still, the phrase about the border being a western frontier of Russia rather than an eastern boundary of Poland indicated hope that the fate of the borderlands was not yet sealed.[24] It was up to the delegation, representing people of divergent views and parties, to give reality to the instructions.

Public opinion in Poland was cautious and uncertain about the negotiations. People realized that the Bolsheviks would drive a hard bargain; some papers had doubts about their sincerity.[25] The same was largely true for the Russians. They doubted Poland's peaceful intentions, and speculated whether Russia should approach the conference seriously. After Sapieha's dispatch of the Livytskyi note and some belligerent speeches in Poland, the Bolsheviks wondered if Piłsudski's views on war until victory would not prevail. When the State Defense Council deliberated in Warsaw, Trotsky wrote articles entitled "A Second Lesson Is Necessary," "We Are Stronger Then Ever," and "The Lords Do Not Want Peace."[26]

These bellicose writings did not show a desire to resume a new march on Warsaw. The troops were in poor condition and could not even stem the Polish advance.[27] Soviet leaders realized fully "the Warsaw mistake." As Lenin told Klara Zetkin a little later: "in the Red Army the Poles saw enemies, not brothers and liberators." He admitted that "the revolution in Poland on which we counted did not take place."[28] A few years later Trotsky asked Chiang Kai-shek, then visiting Russia, to inform Dr. Sun Yat-sen that "after the war with Poland in 1920 Lenin had issued a new directive regarding the policy of World Revolution," stating that while Russia must give "utmost moral and material assistance" to revolution, she should "never again employ Soviet troops in direct participation."[29]

Public utterances were more circumspect. Lenin admitted in December 1920 that the Battle of Warsaw was an "extremely heavy defeat," and added, three months later, that during the war with Poland "we committed an evident mistake." Other ranking Bolsheviks shared this point of view.[30]

Soviet propaganda returned to the old theme of peace. Chicherin instructed Kamenev to point out to Arthur Balfour that Russia had always sought peaceful solutions and that the "war between Russia and Poland" was "only an episode in this struggle for peace."[31] Trotsky claimed that "Our invasion of Poland aimed at finally forcing the lords to conclude peace."[32] Marchlewski made a more plausible point later when he wrote that from the beginning it was obvious that only a decisive defeat would sober up the Polish bourgeoisie and make it peaceful. He advanced the theory that the march on Warsaw had achieved this object.[33]

Whatever the rationalizations, Moscow realized that peace was badly needed. A conquest of Poland was out of the question; the Bolsheviks had failed on both counts—ideological and military. The Crimean front and an uprising in the Kuban worried Lenin.[34] The attitude of the West was disquieting—especially French interest in Wrangel. In mid-September, Lenin asked Ioffe for a report on the Polish attitude toward peace, chances of a settlement, and probable peace conditions. He also demanded detailed information concerning Lithuania, Belorussia, and Eastern Galicia.[35] The Central Committee probably discussed the report, and produced a draft declaration on principles of peace with Poland, which Lenin eventually revised.[36] The document was then submitted to the Ninth All-Russian Conference of RKP(b) on September 22, i.e., one day after the opening of sessions at Riga. Approved by the conference, it came before the VTsIK. There Bukharin opposed the declaration on the grounds that concessions would only weaken the Russian war effort by creating ephemeral hopes of peace. Apparently Radek succeeded in persuading other members to vote for the document, and "after stormy debates" the VTsIK approved the declaration by a two-thirds majority on September 23. The document, which amounted to an abandoning of the Minsk peace theses, was sent to the Soviet delegation at Riga the same day, to be presented at a plenary session.[37]

Preparations for the conference were under way. The Polish delegates on September 14 went to Danzig where they embarked on British destroyers for Liepaja (Libau, Libava). From there they traveled by train to Riga. The head of the delegation was the Deputy Foreign Minister, Jan Dąbski, who had handled the Minsk talks. The group comprised two other government representatives: the chargé in Riga, Witold Kamieniecki, and the minister to Estonia, Leon Wasilewski; a representative of the Supreme Command, General Mieczysław Kuliński; and the same six sejm deputies who had been to Minsk. Several experts and a secretariat presided over by Aleksander Ladoś accompanied the delegates.

Dąbski, an adherent of the peasant party *Piast* and hardly an experienced diplomat, was mildly sympathetic to the federalist trend in Poland. Its main exponents were Wasilewski and Kamieniecki. Its principal opponent was the most influential political figure in the delegation, Stanisław Grabski. The latter succeeded in creating an almost unanimous front of the "sejm delegation," as opposed to the "government delegation." Even the Socialist Norbert Barlicki followed his lead, fearing that the PPS might be accused of dragging out the negotiations. General Kuliński, whom the Supreme Command instructed to be stiff with regard to an armistice and sympathetic to the cause of Petliura, was not a forceful personality; his influence over the delegation was limited. Military experts resented their exclusion from sessions of the delegation and blamed Kuliński for not asserting his position and theirs.

The contact with Warsaw was frequent but not intimate. Sapieha does not seem to have guided the delegates through the various phases of negotiations. As for Piłsudski, his influence was felt only indirectly. The marshal allegedly had said that because people were dissatisfied with his Ukrainian policy he would leave all the responsibility to the government and concentrate on military matters.[38]

The Soviet delegation consisted of its chairman, Adolf A. Ioffe, at that time a member of the Collegium of the Commissariat for Control and an experienced negotiator; the commissar of agriculture of the Ukraine, Dmitri Z. Manuilskii; a member of the Collegium of the Finance Commissariat, Leonid L. Obolenskii; and the Soviet representative in Georgia, Sergei M. Kirov. The Soviet secretary was J. Lorenz. As compared with its Polish counterpart the group was smaller and more closely knit. Lenin maintained strict control. He exchanged telegrams almost daily, and supervised activity throughout the conference.[39]

The delegations installed themselves in Riga: the Poles in Hotel Rome, the Russians in Hotel St. Petersburg, an amusing coincidence. Dąbski and Ioffe met on September 18, three days before the official opening of the sessions. The Pole found the Bolshevik delegate impressive, and discovered that the Soviets would demand a definitive peace settlement, recognition of the status quo in the Ukraine, and political amnesty in Poland. Ioffe apparently was sanguine about the conference, and expected it to complete its work within a month.[40] Both sides were eager to negotiate and bring peace between their respective countries.

On the afternoon of September 21, 1920 the two delegations, members of the diplomatic corps in Riga, representatives of the Latvian government, and foreign correspondents assembled in the State Hall of the Schwarzhäupterhaus (Melngaluju Nams), an old, stately building. The atmosphere was solemn and formal. Foreign Minister Zigfrids Meierovics opened the session with a welcoming speech in French; then Dąbski and Ioffe took the floor. They spoke of need for a just and lasting peace, and thanked Latvia for hospitality. Ioffe used the expression "democratic peace," though the word had not appeared in the printed version given to the press. The correspondents felt that the Russians were "reticent" and that the Poles had barricaded themselves "behind excessive politeness."

The press soon discovered that the techniques of the delegations differed considerably. "Ah, these Russians understand propaganda," a reporter commented. While the Poles promised official texts "early the next morning," by that time "the Russian side of the case and Ioffe's speech" was already "in print across the Atlantic."[41] The smart Polish uniforms and good manners of the civilian delegates contrasted with the drab appearance of the Russians, including the Havana-smoking Ioffe. But the skill of the latter was evident.

The conference faced problems of magnitude. Delegates representing two different *Weltanschauungen* sought not only to liquidate the war but the intricate state of affairs arising out of the past. A separation of Poland from Russia, after a century and a half of enforced dependence, raised many issues, particularly economic ones. The Soviet delegates were unprepared to deal with them and favored a clean sweep of the past. The Poles could not accept it, and when the more immediate political and territorial questions were out of the way, economic and financial matters came to the fore.

The Bolsheviks won the first round at the opening of the conference by making the Poles recognize Soviet Ukrainian credentials. Though Polish instructions had permitted it after some bargaining, the quick recognition came as a surprise to correspondents and a blow to the Ukrainians of Petliura. To many of them it was the betrayal of the Polish-Ukrainian alliance.[42]

The Soviet delegation took the initiative during the second session (seventh, counting those in Minsk) on September 24. Ioffe insisted on presenting, before a Polish statement, the above-mentioned VTsIK declaration. The reasons which prompted him to place it on the agenda derive from a message he received from the Central Committee. "For us," the message ran, "the crux of the matter lies first, in having within a short time an armistice, and second . . . in having within ten days real guarantees of an effective peace." The Central Committee ordered the delegation to achieve this object and estimate the effectiveness of the guarantees. In exchange Ioffe could offer territorial concessions, namely a frontier running along the Shara (Szczara) river, the Ogiński canal, the Iaselda (Jasiołda) and Styr rivers, and then following the prewar Russo-Austrian frontier. Except in the southern sector this border did not coincide with Polish claims. It fell short even of the German line. The Central Committee instructed Ioffe that should agreement on this basis prove impossible, he was to denounce the Poles before the world and declare a winter campaign unavoidable.[43]

Soviet insistence on a speedy armistice was understandable. The Polish troops took Grodno, seeking to drive a wedge between the Russian and the Lithuanian armies. Hostilities against Wrangel caused the creation on September 21 of a special Southern Front; the Red Army was preparing an all-out offensive in the Crimea. Time mattered a great deal, as well as the assurance that peace would prevail in the west.

The Russians gave great publicity to the VTsIK declaration. Lenin prepared the scene by announcing that Poland would receive an advantageous peace.[44] Trotsky issued an order to the Red Army and Navy that the Soviets were offering maximum concessions to end bloodshed. In an interview he threatened the Poles with a new offensive if they rejected this offer.[45] The Comintern appealed to all Communists, workers, and peasants to press Poland to accept it.

The VTsIK declaration clothed the Bolshevik proposal in propagandistic garb. After painting a gloomy picture of a winter war, it proposed to end the struggle and sign a peace on the basis of self-determination. The document recalled Soviet recognition of the independence of Poland, the Ukraine, and Belorussia in 1917 and 1918. It mentioned the peace treaty with Lithuania. The VTsIK declaration proposed that both Poland and Russia solemnly recognize the principle of the independence of these countries and of Eastern Galicia. As for their future fate it ought to be determined by the existing institutions: parliaments, soviets, or whatever they might be. In the case of Eastern Galicia, the Russian government agreed to a "bourgeois" plebiscite.

After this long preamble the declaration admitted that the Poles differed from the Bolsheviks in their notion of national self-determination, and consequently there might be no agreement. Should this prove to be the case, the VTsIK proposed a direct Soviet-Polish settlement along the following lines: first, Soviet withdrawal of the demands for a demobilization of the Polish army and control of the Wołkowysk-Grajewo line; second, a more favorable boundary than the Curzon Line. The offer was valid for ten days, and should preliminaries of peace still be unsigned by October 5, Russia reserved the right to change her conditions. An outright rejection of the offer would prove that the Poles wanted to fight a winter campaign.

Ioffe's unexpected presentation of the VTsIK declaration produced a sensation at the conference. Commotion increased when after a half-hour interval Dąbski declared that he would still read the previously prepared Polish statement on peace conditions. He acknowledged Ioffe's proposal by merely welcoming Soviet withdrawal of the Minsk theses, and asserting that Polish attitude toward national self-determination would come out clearly from his statement. The latter followed closely the instructions which the delegation had received in Warsaw. Dąbski began with a general preamble stressing Poland's desire for a just peace, understanding, and reconciliation of vital interests of both sides. He enumerated the principles of a settlement, and said that the Poles proposed no definite boundary because they wanted to work it out jointly with the Russians. In accord with instructions he stated that an armistice would be concluded as soon as both sides had agreed on the basic conditions of a preliminary peace. He elaborated on economic provisions, declaring that Poland demanded part of the gold reserve of Russia, because the country had contributed to the treasury of the former Russian Empire.[46]

Two days elapsed before the next conference session, and both sides prepared replies to statements made on September 24. But the main question was the VTsIK proposal, which sounded like an ultimatum, although Ioffe denied that it was.[47] If the Poles accepted it they would deprive themselves of their chief means of pressure, namely the eastward military advance. Would the Russians grant Poland a favorable peace once this sword over their heads was withdrawn? But if the Poles rejected the VTsIK offer and trusted only to force of arms, a winter campaign would become unavoidable, opening prospects of new victories, but also carrying dangers of defeats.

There was no agreement. The American minister in Warsaw reported that military circles around Piłsudski opposed a speedy conclusion of peace, talked about cooperation with Wrangel, and dispatched officers to Riga to press for a tough line.[48] The French supposedly approached Piłsudski to send a representative to Paris to discuss the possibility of an alliance with Wrangel. The Italians urged the Poles to continue fighting. Even the British in Warsaw pointed out the danger of allowing the Red Army to regroup. Sapieha, the American minister wrote, opposed those overtures and favored peace with the Bolsheviks. Only a clear-cut Allied statement supporting further hostilities could change his views, but he did "not propose to angle for such a statement."[49] Nor did Premier Witos appear bellicose, and he assured the sejm on September 24 that Warsaw put forward no conditions that could occasion a breach, provided the Bolsheviks approached the negotiations in good faith.

The government was inclined to assume that one could talk at Riga without the additional military pressure to which the Soviets strongly objected.[50] Dąbski felt that the Russians would make no difficulties in ceding Volhynia, Eastern Galicia, and possibly parts of Belorussia. But the delegation was not unanimous on what constituted Polish maximum aims.[51] Grabski now favored a more extensive border than the modified German line; other delegates were undecided. Some advocated a speedy peace, others believed in borders gained by the continuing Polish offensive. As for the nature of peace only Dąbski and a few other members believed it possible to achieve a lasting settlement. Several delegates viewed the forthcoming treaty as an episode, because counterrevolution would triumph in Russia and a new settlement would have to be negotiated. They cared less for actual acquisitions, and more for creating legal titles and precedents of use in the future. Divergences must have been pronounced, because on Grabski's initiative the delegation decided to exclude experts and secretaries from its meetings, and have no protocols of the sessions. The secretary of the delegation may have only exaggerated slightly when he wrote later that nearly as much energy was spent on internal squabbles as on actual bargaining with the Bolsheviks.[52]

The Poles reached no decision as the conference went into another session on September 27. Dąbski answered the VTsIK declaration evasively. He said he wanted to avoid polemics, and would welcome concrete proposals to be discussed in commissions unattended by journalists and foreign observers. He made critical remarks about the quasi-ultimatum character of the Soviet declaration. In turn, Ioffe analyzed point by point the Polish statement on the principles of peace. He noted Polish peaceful dispositions with satisfaction, and assured the audience that Russia had always respected the sovereignty of others and favored noninterference. The Soviets had never claimed Polish territory; they already expressed themselves for an option and guarantees for minorities; they agreed with nonreparations and exchange of prisoners. As for amnesty, Ioffe felt it ought to apply not only to foreigners but to one's own citizens. The Soviet delegation was all for a speedy negotiation of a final treaty and special conventions. Economic and financial matters could best be settled in such a treaty. Ioffe ended by saying that the Poles as yet had given no reply to the offer in the VTsIK declaration. This was no ultimatum, but he was not in position to sustain the offer after the ten days had elapsed.[53] The session ended with an agreement to set up mixed commissions—a General Commission comprising all delegates, and commissions on territorial, legal, and economic-financial questions. Meetings would not be open to the public.

The General Commission met next day, and Ioffe presented a seventeen-point proposal. The first point recognized self-determination and the sovereignty of the Belorussian, Lithuanian, and Ukrainian republics. According to the second, the independence of Eastern Galicia, while recognized in principle, would—given the absence of any state forms—be determined through a universal, secret, direct, and equal referendum. Point three proposed the recognition of existing forms of government in all of above-mentioned countries. In accord with point four, Russia would confirm her renunciation of sovereign rights over Polish territory. The fifth point proposed a boundary between Poland, Belorussia, and the Ukraine running from the point where the Swisłocz entered the Niemen, then along the Swisłocz to Białowieża, Kamieniec Litewski, to Brest, then through Piszcza, Lubomla, Włodzimierz and Hrybowice to the former Austro-Russian border. Forty-eight hours after signing a preliminary agreement, hostilities would cease, with Polish troops withdrawing twenty-five versts to the west of the above border, and with the Red army staying twenty-five versts east of it. A neutral zone thus established would come under joint administration. The Poles were to retreat twenty versts daily from the positions they occupied on the front and take nothing from the evacuated territories.

Point six said that neither side would tolerate organizations which promoted war against the other, nor grant transit privileges to powers in war with one of the parties. Points seven to eleven were similar to Polish proposals regarding option, minorities, reparations, and exchange of prisoners. The twelfth point said than an amnesty ought to cover one's own citizens together with foreigners. Point thirteen provided for the immediate negotiation of a final treaty. Financial matters figured in point fourteen and contained the following provisions: no obligations for either side from former inclusion of Poland in the empire; restitutions would be mutual; Russia would return archives and objects of art to Poland "provided these objects have genuine significance for Poland and their transfer would not constitute a real hardship for Russian archives, galleries, museums, and libraries in which they are preserved." Point fifteen spoke of the future negotiations of consular, commercial, transit, and other technical conventions. The sixteenth provided that the treaty be drawn in Russian, Polish, and Ukrainian; while the seventeenth point foresaw mutual ratification of the peace preliminaries.[54]

Dąbski termed the statement a new proposal, to which Ioffe objected, and the Polish delegate asked for an interval to study it in detail. This amounted to suspension of the conference, and the beginning of a brief war of nerves between the delegations. Ioffe's statement was indeed much more extreme than the Poles could have assumed after his original declaration and the VTsIK message. It contained several unacceptable points. Eastern Galicia, which had never been legally part of Russia, found its place in the document. The border—which the Poles wanted to treat as the western border of Russia—was defined as the eastern frontier between Poland and Belorussia and the Ukraine. The Bolsheviks evidently sought to maintain exclusive control over the borderlands. The proposed frontier was more disadvantageous to Poland than that which the Central Committee had described in its note to Ioffe. The latter wanted to have more scope for bargaining. The armistice line was to be identical with the proposed border, which implied immediate Polish withdrawal to the west. What is more, Polish troops were to stay away from the frontier, and a neutral zone fifty versts wide would be established. All this would constitute a reversal of the military situation to Russian advantage, and would allow the Red Army to finish off Wrangel. Amnesty for one's own nationals was designed to protect Polish Communists; Ioffe hardly could have meant it to apply to counterrevolutionaries in Russia. Economic and financial matters were relegated to a future peace treaty. As for art treasures, which the Bolshevik propaganda as early as 1917 had promised to return to the Poles, the statement showed no sign that a full restitution would ever take place.

The press bureau of the Polish delegation issued a communiqué saying that if fruitful negotiations were to continue the Russians would have to drop their demands concerning Eastern Galicia, give Poland frontiers guaranteeing her security, hand over part of the gold reserve, and return works of art and culture.

Ioffe realized he had pushed the Poles too far, and showed himself most conciliatory in an interview to the local press. This did not help. Dąbski forbade any Polish-Russian meetings, and Sapieha told the journalists in Warsaw that Soviet proposals of September 28 were contrary to the original stand. The question of Eastern Galicia, he said, under no circumstances could be an object of peace negotiations. Soviet nervousness increased. Polish troops were just engaging the Red Army in an important encounter at Lida; Petliura's units advanced into the Ukraine; Wrangel registered success along his front.[55]

Two days after the September 28 session Ioffe wrote Dąbski to ask how long negotiations would be suspended, and when he could expect another meeting of the General Commission. "I agree to any proposal," he said. The chief Polish delegate replied vaguely that the secretaries of both delegations would soon arrange this matter.[56] Ioffe again took the initiative on October 1, and proposed a confidential meeting of heads of delegations accompanied only by the two secretaries. Dąbski agreed, and both diplomats met late in the evening and talked until midnight in German.

Dąbski accused Ioffe of being less conciliatory than the VTsIK. Surely the latter had said that if a settlement on the basis of national self-determination proved impossible, discussions could proceed along different lines. Ioffe countered that both Poland and Russia wanted to create buffer states in the borderlands; but the Soviets had succeeded and one had to recognize the state of affairs. He admitted that he had raised the Eastern Galician issue to prevent the Poles from bringing up the Ukrainian question, and he was willing to drop it as a quid pro quo. Poland, he said, needed Galician oil, and Russia needed Ukrainian grain. This was a clever tactic, for Grabski and many other Polish delegates were sensitive to the Eastern Galician question and cool toward the Ukraine.[57]

Ioffe warned that negotiations had to be speeded up, because otherwise a war party which existed in Moscow might gain the upper hand. Was this true or merely tactical move? Lack of documentation prevents a definite opinion, but Ioffe used this argument again in the continuing negotiations. He explained that Moscow was bound by a treaty to Lithuania and had moral obligations toward Belorussia. The latter, in any event, would have to figure in a peace settlement. Regarding boundaries, Ioffe's attempts to get an answer from Dąbski were only partly successful.

The Soviet diplomat mentioned that Russia must at least control the Lida-Baranowicze-Łuniniec-Równo-Brody railroad, at which Dąbski said that the Poles could never abandon it. The Pole recalled that in January 1920 the Soviets had proposed a vastly better frontier. Ioffe replied that they had offered a demarcation line and not a final border. The meeting ended with an engagement to continue private and secret exchanges.[58]

It is likely that Ioffe's new method of direct talks was well chosen. Dąbski enjoyed these frank discussions, and the Bolshevik diplomat knew how to handle him. Besides, Dąbski genuinely wanted to conclude a peace treaty, and he wanted to be the peacemaker. Should no progress be made in Riga Sapieha was likely to intervene, because Warsaw worried about the slow pace. The cabinet decided that peace should be concluded rapidly, and considered sending new delegates to the Latvian capital. Socialists and National Democrats for once joined in opposing any additional military advance. At the session of the State Defense Council, Daszyński severely criticized the eastward march and said that the government could not tolerate a breakdown of negotiations. Sapieha remarked that the Soviet offer of September 28 was not acceptable, but he also favored speeding up talks. He mentioned that he and possibly Daszyński would have to go to Riga. Even General Sosnkowski felt that peace was necessary. The French encouraged further war and alliance with Wrangel, but gave no real assurances or commitments.[59]

Given this atmosphere in Warsaw and the possibility of negotiations falling into the hands of Sapieha and Daszyński, Dąbski had all the more reason to show progress. After the first session with Ioffe he informed his colleagues about the talks, and obtained their agreement concerning frontiers. The agreement was half-hearted. Wasilewski and Kamieniecki pressed for a federalist solution in the north—creation of a free Belorussia linked with Poland. The majority opposed this suggestion, which was quite realistic since the Polish armies were approaching Belorussian lands. Nor were the delegates willing to formulate demands on Minsk.[60] Still, the consensus enabled Dąbski to inform Ioffe of Polish territorial claims when they met again on October 2.

The Pole told the Bolshevik diplomat that Poland proposed a line running along the eastern administrative borders of the former Wilno gubernia, then along the river Łań, south to Równo, and then along the old Russo-Austrian frontier. Ioffe said that the Soviet government could only consider a line much more to the west, and he went on to describe it. This was the line which the Central Committee had authorized Ioffe to propose. He told

Dąbski that such a line represented a considerable concession, and when the Pole replied that they needed a territorial junction with Latvia—a kind of corridor—he remarked with a smile that the Poles had a special predilection for corridors. Dąbski and Ladoś denied it and said it was merely a necessity.

The Soviet diplomat did not reject the Polish demand. He wanted to make sure that this was a proposal of the government and not merely of one party—an allusion to differences between the Poles. When Dąbski assured him that it was, Ioffe suggested that for a time frontiers be left aside, and that the delegates reach agreement before October 5 on other matters. He warned that many Russians believed the Poles wanted to drag out the negotiations and were not genuinely interested in peace. He promised to ask Moscow about Dąbski's territorial claims, and suggested another secret encounter soon.[61]

Dąbski's position was not easy, for Sapieha telegraphed him on October 2 that the government was interested in a free Belorussia cleared of Soviet troops and administration.[62] Simultaneously the Supreme Command urged General Kuliński to persuade the delegation to demand better frontiers in the east.[63] It is likely that Ioffe was aware of these conflicting trends on the Polish side and proceeded with caution.

On October 3 the Soviet diplomat met with Dąbski, accompanied this time by Grabski, Barlicki, and Kiernik. The head of the Polish delegation wanted to show that he spoke with approval of his principal colleagues. Grabski justified the need for the Brody-Równo-Sarny-Łuniniec-Baranowicze railroad on strategic grounds. He also assured Ioffe that once Poland would sign an advantageous peace with the Bolshevik government, she would be foolish to try to overthrow the Soviet regime.[64]

Next day the two chief delegates went into another secret session. In reply to Dąbski's question about Moscow's reaction to Polish territorial claims, Ioffe said he had no news. Keeping Dąbski in suspense, he expressed fear that a preliminary treaty might be greatly delayed if the Poles insisted on such matters as division of gold and return of cultural treasures in the preliminaries. He proposed that they be discussed in commissions, which implied shelving them at least temporarily. Dąbski reluctantly agreed. This meant that commissions would meet and the conference return to normal. Ioffe then intimated that Moscow might consent to territorial concessions, except in the northern part. It was here that the Poles sought contiguity with Latvia and strove to separate Russia from Lithuania. But Ioffe was not categorical. He tried to find out if Poland would agree to far-reaching transit privileges for Russia, in case there would be no Russo-Lithuanian border. Dąbski gave an evasive answer.[65]

The meeting of the General Commission which followed was important for two reasons. It put an end to the alarmist rumors that the conference was about to break down, and made Dąbski see that secret talks with Ioffe were more fruitful than general sessions. In the General Commission, Dąbski discussed Ioffe's seventeen points and contrasted them unfavorably with the VTsIK statement and Ioffe's original reply to the Polish peace principles. He also criticized the Soviet interpretation of national self-determination. The Russian delegate retorted with a brilliant speech. He characterized the difference between the VTsIK declaration and the seventeen points as implicit: one was a general message, the other a concrete proposal. He attacked the Poles for failing to submit counterproposals—Dąbski's statement on borders had been only in a private talk. Ioffe declared that since the Polish delegation questioned national self-determination as a suitable basis of peace, negotiations should be along different lines, as foreseen in the VTsIK message.[66] In this verbal duel Ioffe proved the better fencer, and made Dąbski glad to return to the privacy of direct talks.

The two diplomats met the following day in the early hours of the afternoon. Ioffe played his hand well. He said that the General Commission meeting had made him pessimistic. One could go on endlessly discussing such things as noninterference and economic and financial matters. He confronted Dąbski with a choice. Either both delegations would make a joint statement that they were in general agreement and would sign the armistice and peace preliminaries within the next few days, or Ioffe would request a plenary session to make a public declaration which would not facilitate understanding. This was blackmail, though in a discreet form. One could trust Ioffe to make the most out of a plenary session attended by foreign press and observers.

Faced with this choice Dąbski asked about the territorial settlement, and Ioffe like a magician produced a winning card from his diplomatic bag. He said that if the Poles agreed to replace the clause about gold with a general formula for settling accounts; consented to a wording of the treaty which would not make it appear like a *Diktat*; accepted the Soviet demand for free transit to Lithuania and Germany; and engaged to sign the treaty on October 8, Russia would agree to Polish territorial demands. This sounded like a quid pro quo. The Poles would gain their frontier in the east, and the Soviets would obtain an armistice and assurances of peace; the basic demands of both sides would be satisfied.

Dąbski asked for a break to consult his colleagues. He shortly returned to resume the conversation, and then both men signed— at 7:00 P.M., according to Dąbski, at 5:00 P.M., according to a contemporary report—a protocol proposed by Ioffe.[67] This brief document said that given general agreement, the heads of both delegations decided to sign an armistice and peace preliminaries between Poland, Russia, and the Ukraine not later than Friday, October 8. Well aware of possible Polish opposition Dąbski acted in a hurry. Ioffe was more relaxed; this was his finest hour at the conference.

The signing of the protocol came as an unpleasant surprise to several Polish groups. Some delegates apparently had not been consulted, and military experts fumed about Dąbski's "quiet coup d'état" against Sapieha and the Supreme Command.[68] The officers made General Kuliński submit a *votum separatum* on October 6. His note said that the following points ought to appear in the peace preliminaries: border rectifications in the Polesie region; withdrawal of the Red Army beyond the Dvina and Dnieper while the Polish troops would occupy the existing front line; guarantees of the return of war matériel to Poland; an armistice line coinciding with the front as it existed before the Kievan campaign of April 1920; a provision allowing the Supreme Command to determine the date of the armistice.[69]

Kuliński's *démarche* could have little practical effect. As Dąbski put it later, the protocol "made Polish-Soviet understanding a political fact; it could neither be withdrawn nor erased."[70] Still, the general's statement was revealing of the aims of the Supreme Command. The latter still hoped to salvage as much as possible of Piłsudski's grand design. Officers in Riga kept assuring the Ukrainians that Piłsudski would not consent to a destruction of their alliance.[71] The protocol dealt a heavy blow to these hopes. A rapid armistice was bound to endanger Petliura's troops in the Ukraine. The officers in Riga favored an immediate advance to the Zhitomir-Berdichev line or even farther east to protect the Ukrainian army.[72] Leading Ukrainians in Riga, S. P. Shelukhin and Volodymyr Kedrovskyi, solemnly protested against the term "Ukraine" in the protocol and said that only Petliura's government, whose delegates had not been admitted to the conference, could speak for the Ukraine.[73]

Sapieha sent a critical note on September 10. He complained that he had not received a report on the signing of the protocol. He considered Dąbski's haste ill-advised and mentioned adverse French reactions, because the protocol said nothing about the

Red Army's transfer to Wrangel's front. "We are the victors," Sapieha went on; Dąbski's policy was bound to cost Poland some fruits of victory, notably in the matter of gold. The State Defense Council had not authorized any secret talks with Ioffe, and these produced a bad impression on the Right. The minister intimated that Dąbski's tactics could cause the fall of the coalition cabinet, and expressed doubt whether the peasant party—to which Dąbski belonged—would profit thereby.[74]

The protocol looked like a Soviet victory. The Bolsheviks had given the ten-day ultimatum and the Poles had submitted to it. Moscow's diplomatic and military situation greatly improved, for its army could turn against Wrangel. Did the Bolsheviks pay the highest price in terms of territorial concessions? Grabski, writing many years later, did not think so. He contended that it was possible to gain a boundary coinciding with that offered by the Soviets in January 1920.* Dąbski and other members of the delegation did not press for further concessions because of domestic reasons. Fearing a possible revival of Piłsudski's eastern plans they decided to prevent it by making further was impossible.[75] In this respect they enjoyed the backing of the majority of Polish public opinion.

On October 7, when Premier Witos informed the sejm of the signing of the protocol, the deputies responded with prolonged applause. Even a Socialist leader such as Moraczewski, although critical of a settlement that would bring neither liberation nor federation to the borderlands, concluded that after the experience of war both Poland and Russia opposed the beginning of a new one.[76] The Poles clearly wanted peace.

There is no direct evidence of what Piłsudski thought or said at the time Dąbski and Ioffe signed the protocol in Riga. One can imagine that he felt a certain contempt for the bargaining there, and sought to influence events by his favorite method of creating *faits accomplis.* Three days after the signing of the protocol, the so-called Lithuanian-Belorussian Division commanded by General Lucjan Żeligowski "rebelled" and began a march on Wilno, which it captured on October 8.

Żeligowski's coup, executed at Piłsudski's secret orders, had been in preparation for some time.[77] Ever since the advance after the Battle of Warsaw, the Poles were making vain efforts to con-

---

* "I must admit that if we had, by drawing out the peace negotiations, given our army the necessary time to push for a further hundred kilometres to the east, the Soviet Union would indeed, according to all available data, have agreed to a frontier with Poland along the armistice line, through Dryssa and Bar . . . which it had proposed in January" (Stanisław Grabski, The *Polish Soviet Frontier* [London, 1943], p. 28).

vince the Entente that an occupation of Wilno was necessary on strategic grounds. They had to proceed cautiously. Polish-Lithuanian talks began concerning a demarcation line between the two armies, and a vaguely phrased agreement reached on October 7. The next day Żeligowski began his march, proclaimed the creation of a new state, Central Lithuania, and proceeded to organize its administration.

Piłsudski's move—no one was taken in by his stratagem, though Sapieha's participation was so well concealed that he escaped all blame—created a great stir.[78] The Wilno affair transcended the limits of a local Polish-Lithuanian conflict. As two officials of the Ministry of Foreign Affairs wrote in mid-October, this question, "like the Belorussian or the Ukrainian issue [is] connected with the whole question of Polish-Russian relations, i.e., with the still open problem of the continuing course of the Russian revolution."[79] The British quickly came to realize that the Poles sought to bring about "the creation of a greater Lithuania, perhaps organized on a cantonal basis, with its Lithuanian, Polish and White Russian component elements, in federation with the Polish State."[80]

The Wilno coup brought Piłsudski's design to light. The new "Central Lithuania" could revive the federalist idea in the north. But Piłsudski could not bring himself to follow up the march on Wilno by an advance on Kaunas, although General Rozwadowski thought that this was the only course, and that swift occupation of Lithuania would forestall Soviet demands for Polish recognition of Lithuanian sovereignty.[81] As for Belorussia, the troops were entering its territory, but its fate could only be resolved by the conference at Riga.

No wonder that the Żeligowski coup revived controversies within the Polish delegation. "We have gone through a hot campaign on Belorussia," reported one of the Polish experts to Warsaw.[82] Dąbski asked for instruction whether he was to demand a Russian "disannexation" of Belorussia, and he sounded out Ioffe. The Bolshevik diplomat cunningly answered that there were only two possibilities: Poland could obtain the already agreed to borders, or remain restricted to the Curzon line, with a bourgeois Belorussian buffer state coming into existence. Ioffe well knew that the latter solution would be unacceptable to the Polish Right and Center. While Secretary Ładoś and some of the experts wondered if Ioffe might be amenable to more pressure, other delegates reacted violently to the exchanges. A storm broke. The question of Minsk, which Wasilewski saw as a symbol of Belorussian nationality, came up for discussion; federalist sentiments revived. News circulated again that Sapieha would come to Riga either to force the Bolsheviks to make new concessions or to break off the conference.

The delegation was split unequally. Nobody knew for certain who stood behind the federalist policy in Warsaw. Piłsudski made no pronouncements, and the federalists in Riga lacked support and guidance. Dąbski did not want Sapieha to come and rob him of his diplomatic laurels. Grabski, who at one point was willing to press for a cession of Minsk, swung the scales in favor of a speedy peace in accord with the protocol of October 5. His forceful personality and the logic of his arguments contrasted with the nebulous plans for opening the Belorussian question.[83]

While the Poles debated the preliminary peace treaty, there was no unanimity on the Bolshevik side. Lenin said later that peace with Poland "at first encountered strong resistance in the Party," and he had been attacked for favoring it. He recalled that most of the Russian experts had advocated holding out longer because of Poland's economic plight, but he did not disclose their names. The Bolshevik leader said that while he was not for peace at any price, he thought it wiser from a political and military point of view—Wrangel was still active—to come to terms with the enemy.[84] Chicherin, in a retrospective report of the Riga negotiations, pointed out that acceptance of Dąbski's borders was a price the Soviets had to pay for Polish renunciation of a system of buffer states under Warsaw's leadership.[85]

Lenin explained his reasons for peace with Poland in a speech on October 9: Soviet concessions were an indication of Moscow's peaceful intentions, but the Poles would derive little benefit from territorial acquisitions and reparations. "In those localities which we give them according to the peace agreement," he said, "Poland will maintain herself only by force." As for reparations, they will pay for the debts which Poland owed France. Warsaw was not getting as much as could be imagined. The Bolsheviks, Lenin concluded "will gain time and we shall use it for strengthening our army."[86] The Soviet leader did not believe that the Polish delegation in Riga might break off the talks. He received assurances from Ioffe that the "Poles fear a breach even more than we do," and he suggested to Trotsky that some divisions be moved from the Polish front to the Crimea. Trotsky objected. This was a dangerous proposal and it could act as "a provocation to Piłsudski to seize Kiev."[87]

One can appreciate Trotsky's nervousness, because the date foreseen for signing an armistice and preliminaries for peace had passed. Lenin was unruffled. An armistice and peace was already a foregone conclusion; a few more days mattered little. It was humanly impossible for the delegates to work out a peace treaty within three days, from October 5 to 8. Even if the Polish Supreme Command asked their delegation at Riga to delay so the troops could capture Minsk, liberate some individuals, and recover some secret documents, this could not change the picture.

All the commissions at Riga worked at full speed to dispose of last-minute disagreements. Since the Polish side was interested in inserting detailed economic provisions in the treaty, haste naturally operated against it. At last the document was ready, and on the evening of October 12 the two delegations met in a plenary session and signed the preliminaries of peace and the armistice convention between Poland on the one side and Soviet Russia and the Soviet Ukraine on the other.

Ioffe spoke first, and expressed satisfaction. Dąbski followed, emphasizing that the peace that had been signed was one without victors and defeated. It was a peace of understanding, and this was why "it gives a guarantee of stability." The heads of delegations thanked each other. The next day at a Polish banquet the new frontier was called a "compromise boundary."[88]

The preliminary peace treaty consisted of a preamble and seventeen articles. In the preamble the signatories expressed their desire to end the war and prepare conditions "which could form the basis of a lasting and honorable peace based on mutual understanding." In accord with the principle of national self-determination, the first article recognized the independence of Belorussia and the Ukraine, and drew a border between them and Poland. Russia and the Ukraine renounced all claim to territories west of it, Poland to those in the east. Contested Polish-Lithuanian areas were to be settled by the two interested parties. Thus Eastern Galicia was not mentioned, and a compromise formula adopted with regard to Wilno. Belorussia did not figure as a party to the treaty; only her independence was recognized, as a gesture toward the Belorussian people. The Bolsheviks did not want to bring a Belorussian delegate to Riga, and while the Poles wished to show their concern for that country, they apparently did not insist.[89]

The second article dealt with respect for each other's sovereign rights and noninterference in domestic affairs. It said that more precise engagements would be worked out in the final treaty. The signatories agreed after ratification of the peace preliminaries to withdraw all support from foreign military operations. The former formula was at least partly a Soviet success; the latter enabled the Poles to give assistance to Petliura, Balakhovich, and Savinkov until the ratification date.

The third article concerned the right of option to be exercised by Poles, Russians, and Ukrainians. Practical details which promised to be controversial were relegated to the final treaty. Article four contained an agreement to include in the final treaty guarantees of the rights of Poles in Russia and the Ukraine, and of Ukrainians and Russians in Poland. In accord with article five, both sides renounced war reparations—defined as state expenses for war—and compensations for losses suffered by the countries and their citizens. Article six removed to the final treaty stipulations concerning exchange of prisoners of war and reimbursement of costs of their maintenance. Article seven provided for mixed commissions to deal with hostages, civilian prisoners, internees, and, if possible, prisoners of war. A special agreement was to be signed immediately. According to article eight, both sides would take measures to suspend proceedings against civilian prisoners, internees, hostages, refugees, emigrants, and prisoners of war. No penalties would apply, and those accused or condemned would be handed over to authorities of their respective countries. Article nine said that the final treaty would contain provisions governing amnesty for Russian and Ukrainian citizens in Poland, and Polish citizens in Russia and the Ukraine. The above articles (three to nine) by-passed a number of controversial issues by relegating them to the final peace treaty. While the Poles had resisted Soviet demands that amnesty in Poland apply to Polish citizens, the question was not yet resolved. By opting for Russia the Polish Communists retained the chance of escaping articles eight and nine.

Article ten provided for insertion in the final treaty of stipulations governing the settlement of mutual accounts. The following principles were to apply: Poland incurred no charges or obligations resulting from former inclusion in the empire; each side renounced claims to state property on the territory of the other; active participation of Polish lands in the economic life of the empire would be considered in the final liquidation of accounts; both sides agreed to return movables belonging to state and local institutions, organizations, or individuals—taken away after August 1, 1914—except for war booty; Russia promised to honor her engagement to return Polish archives, libraries and objects of art and culture removed from Poland since the partitions; there would be a settlement of mutual claims of individuals and organizations; the final treaty would determine the obligation of Russia and the Ukraine to grant Poland and her citizens the most-favored-nation clause with regard to restitution of property and compensation for losses during the revolution and civil war.

This long article, together with the territorial settlement, represented the most important part of the preliminary peace. Except for the Polish demand for gold, which was put into a separate secret protocol, all other claims were enumerated, and Russia took cognizance of them. But she made no commitment that they would be settled to Poland's advantage. This was the price Dąbski paid for Polish territorial acquisitions.[90]

Article eleven declared that both parties agreed to negotiate economic and technical conventions after signing the peace treaty. The twelfth article stated that transit arrangements would be worked out in the final treaty. Article thirteen provided an armistice convention signed simultaneously with the preliminaries and equally binding. According to article fourteen, Russian and Ukrainian obligations and rights vis-à-vis Poland applied to all territories east of the established border. An engagement to begin immediate negotiation of the final treaty appeared in article fifteen. The sixteenth article established equal validity of the Polish, Russian, and Ukrainian texts of the preliminaries. The last article said that the preliminary treaty was to be ratified within fifteen days, and the instruments of ratification exchanged six days later in Liepaja. In the absence of ratification the armistice provisions would no longer bind, but hostilities could not recommence earlier than forty-eight hours from the date foreseen for exchange of ratifications.[91]

A secret protocol dealt with the question of gold. Composed of four clauses, the document referred to article ten of the preliminary treaty and recognized Poland's right to part of the gold reserve of the former Russian State Bank. Leaving to the final peace treaty the method of settling Poland's favorable balance, Russia and the Ukraine engaged to make advance payments to Poland in gold, raw materials, and concessions in state forests. They promised to return to Poland the property of the state and of natural and legal persons. The question of transit also figured in the protocol. Signatories agreed that while the document would not be published it had the same force as the preliminaries and armistice convention.[92]

The third and last document signed at Riga was the armistice convention, consisting of fourteen articles. All hostilities would end by midnight, October 18, i.e., more than six days after signature. This concession was important for the Poles, and their army raced east to occupy as much territory as possible before the deadline. Troops eventually reached a line approximating that prior to the Kievan campaign in the south and a somewhat less advanced front in the north. The convention established an armistice line which would coincide with the new state borders in the north and the front in the south. This necessitated a Polish evacuation of Minsk. The Red Army had to stay fifteen kilometers east of the armistice line. With ratification of the peace preliminaries both armies would withdraw to the frontiers and remain fifteen kilometers east and west of them. The two neutral zones would be administered by civil authorities.

The armistice agreement was of twenty-one days' duration and each side could denounce it at a forty-eight-hour notice. After the first twenty-one days the armistice would be prolonged automatically until ratification of the final peace treaty; each side could denounce it on fourteen-days' notice.[93]

The wording of the armistice reflected Polish military and political preoccupations. By having the demarcation line in the south correspond to the front, the Poles meant to protect Petliura's army. They were obliged to withdraw to the state frontier only by November 2—the date of the exchange of ratifications—and this gave them time to assist the Ukrainians. Ioffe objected but was obliged to give in.[94] The short notice on which the armistice could be denounced was also a Polish gain. In the absence of military operations, which served as means of pressure on the Bolsheviks, the Poles meant to keep them in a state of uncertainty. Piłsudski emphasized it in his order of the day, issued on October 18, the day of the armistice. "You have finished the war through a magnificent victory," the marshal told his troops, and although peace in final form was not yet realized, the Polish soldier must await it patiently in an "order arms" position. He must be ready to defend "the fruits of his victory, should the enemy want to abandon [the preliminaries] before the final consolidation."[95]

The Polish Supreme Command and Sapieha viewed the preliminary treaty of Riga with marked lack of enthusiasm. In a circular to missions abroad the minister commented that he did not trust Soviet good will. Poland had to continue support of anti-Bolshevik forces; Russian, Ukrainian, Belorussian, Caucasian. The permanence of the Soviet regime was questionable, hence it was imperative to keep in contact with those groups which might seize power in Russia. Nor could Poland remain indifferent to the fate of the lands which had once been linked with her. She favored the Ukrainian and Belorussian strivings for independence.[96]

In a letter to Dąbski, Sapieha considered that the signing of preliminaries without consultation with the friendly powers was inopportune. A settlement with Russia without some participation of the Entente could only be temporary. The minister remarked caustically that the instructions of the State Defense Council did not order Dąbski to worsen relations between Poland and the Allies. He assured him that the Supreme Command did not seek further war, but did not want an estrangement from France.[97] Some National Democrats in their party meeting harped on the same theme. Dąbski, they said, was pursuing an anti-French policy. What did they mean, for surely neither the Ministry of Foreign Affairs nor the Right could share French objection to extended Polish frontiers in the east? Sapieha dealt adequately with a Franco-British protest on October 12 against the treaty of Riga and the occupation of Wilno, which said that Polish frontiers in the east would antagonize a non-Bolshevik Russia.[98] One can only conclude that the minister and some of the Polish rightists objected to the lack of provisions protecting Wrangel, and to the *de jure* recognition of Soviet Russia. In this respect their views corresponded to those of the French.

Whatever other misgivings they had, the sejm and Polish public opinion greeted the preliminary peace with relief and satisfaction. Witos called the treaty "a testimony of good will to [reach] understanding and eliminate the causes of all conflicts."[99] Deputies of the Center and Right lauded the settlement, and even though some Socialists criticized the territorial provisions, the sejm ratified the treaty unanimously. Those who felt that the Riga compromise meant a breakdown of the eastern program, destroying its last manifestation—the Balduri conference of August 1920 which prepared a confederated block of Poland, Latvia, Estonia, the Ukraine and Belorussia—were in a minority. Hołówko wrote bitterly that "We have betrayed Petliura at Riga," and commented that this had happened not so much because of fear of Soviet Russia but because such people as Grąbski did not want to antagonize a future non-Bolshevik Russia which would never accept an independent Ukraine.[100] Little was said about Belorussia, which, as an officer commented, constituted "the weakest point of the treaty." It was paradoxical that the preliminary peace "recognized the sovereignty of the Belorussian Republic while partitioning at the same time its territory."[101]

To the Right the treaty justly appeared as a victory over Piłsudski and the federalists. Grabski wrote later that in his modest capacity as a member of the delegation he had "carried out the whole program devised by the National Committee, way back in Paris."[102] Six months later Dmowski allegedly said that his party took entire responsibility for the Riga peace treaty because it had "dictated the preliminaries.[103]

The reaction of the Ukrainians of Petliura was bitter, and Belorussian leaders of stature, such as Lastouski and others, protested the decisions of the Riga Conference.[104] White Russian circles generally condemned the peace settlement and its territorial provisions.[105]

The Bolshevik reaction was complex. While censuring the Poles for territorial gains, they asserted that Poland would derive little benefit. Comparing Soviet offers at the beginning of 1920, they concluded that the Poles could have received much more had they not gone to war.[106] Thus Lenin could assert that eventually "we turned out to be the winners."[107] Emphasizing peace, the principal Soviet objective, Radek commented that although the settlement involved the annexation of border areas by Poland, "not a single vital interest of Russia had been harmed by its terms."[108] Looking for additional reasons to explain the concessions, the Bolsheviks blamed Wrangel, whose struggle against the Soviets had cost Russia important territory.

One of the peace delegates, Manuilskii, struck a different tone. He attacked the imperialist character of the treaty, which allowed the Poles to annex numerous foreign groups. Calling Poland a new Austro-Hungary he ominously remarked that Brest-Litovsk had shown that no frontiers were impervious to change.[109] The Polish Communists in Russia shared this sentiment. Marchlewski called the frontier a "senseless boundary" because it cut Belorussia in half and separated parts of Podolia and Volhynia from the Ukraine. But he approved of peace because it "gives Soviet Russia a possibility to achieve stability while simultaneously it revolutionizes Poland." He foresaw nothing but trouble for the Poles as a result of the territorial settlement. He admitted, however, that the preliminaries were a compromise. The Polish bourgeoisie had to agree to peace; Soviet Russia had to withdraw the Minsk conditions "which were designed to render aggressive attacks by bourgeois Poland impossible." Like other Bolsheviks, Marchlewski insisted that Warsaw could have attained more advantageous terms before the showdown of 1920.[110]

Communists in Poland took an even sharper view of the preliminary peace. A manifesto issued by the Central Committee of KPRP termed Riga a "peace with open annexations and masked contributions," and asserted that a real peace would come to Poland only after the overthrow of the capitalist regime.[111]

The preliminaries of Riga obtained the ratification of the sejm on October 22, and of the All-Russian Central Executive Committee of the Soviets (VTsIK) on October 23. The Soviet Ukraine ratified the document in Kharkov on October 20. Formal instruments of ratification were duly exchanged in the Latvian town of Liepaja on November 2, 1920. Since hostilities had officially ended on October 18, peace between Soviet Russia and Poland was an accomplished fact.

Epilogue

The preliminaries of Riga did not bring an immediate *détente* to Soviet-Polish relations. Although the two countries were no longer at war, armed clashes continued for which the Poles were largely responsible.

Piłsudski had favored continued Ukrainian action, and felt bound to end honorably the comradeship in arms with former Polish allies. Immediately after the armistice the marshal gave Savinkov the choice either of evacuating his troops to the Crimea or beginning an independent offensive against the Bolsheviks.[1] Savinkov preferred the second alternative. He had made agreements with Petliura and had achieved control over the Bulak-Balachovich forces; he also had the assurance of some Polish support.[2]

Warsaw officially dissociated itself from Petliura, Savinkov, and Balakhovich. The Ministry of War declared on November 2 that all Russian, Ukrainian, and Cossack troops would have to leave Polish territory. But it was easy to guess where Piłsudski's sympathies lay.

In late October Balakhovich began his offensive and captured Mozyr. He telegraphed Piłsudski and Wrangel that this was a struggle for a free Belorussia; members of the Belorussian Political Committee who accompanied him proclaimed themselves the government of the country. The expedition was hardly more than an adventure. Surrounded and defeated by the Red Army, Balakhovich partisans streamed back into Poland where they were disarmed and interned.

Petliura's offensive around November 11 was a more serious affair, and his appeal to the Ukrainians carried more weight than the manifestos of Balakhovich. The Poles were also privy to this operation.[3] Although Petliura had signed an agreement with Savinkov's Russian Committee, which recognized Ukrainian independence, cooperation was limited. General Permykin's forces operating on the northern wing failed to coordinate action, and the chances of an uprising in the Ukraine were slender. By late November the Ukrainians were driven across the Zbrucz into Poland. Polish authorities had no choice but to disarm and intern the soldiers.

Such activities of Poland's eastern allies, coupled with delays in the withdrawal of Polish troops, evoked Soviet protests. There were recriminations on the level of armistice commissions and through diplomatic channels. Leading Bolsheviks denounced Warsaw. An article in *Izvestia* asked whether the Riga preliminaries were a "scrap of paper," and suggested that Piłsudski sought to revive "the famous conception of the buffer states."[4] There was widespread suspicion that Poland was behind the anti-Soviet uprisings. But if Moscow was annoyed and suspicious, there was nonetheless no cause for alarm. Polish troops had not intervened to save the Ukrainian and Belorussian detachments. The Red Army had proved adequate to deal with them, and the Soviet military situation greatly improved on November 7 with the final assault on the Crimea. Still, there was tension as Ioffe and Dąbski returned to Riga to begin negotiations for the final peace treaty, and Ioffe met the Polish delegate with accusations and complaints. Dąbski recognized the justice of some of them, and on November 14 both diplomats signed a protocol for the withdrawal of Polish troops to the state borders.[5] Their failure to do so earlier was explained on the ground of technical difficulties and epidemics in the south.

The Peace Conference resumed its labors on November 17, and four months of hard bargaining lay ahead. Both delegations had been reconstituted. There were no longer any sejm deputies on the Polish side, and Dąbski was accompanied by four government officials—Stanisław Kauzik, Henryk Strasburger, Edward Lechowicz, and Leon Wasilewski. The Soviet delegation consisted of Ioffe, Jakub S. Fürstenberg-Hanecki, Leonid Obolenskii and Emanuel J. Kviring. A Ukrainian, Jur Kotsubinskyi joined before the signing of the treaty. The Polish Communist Leszczyński, though only an adviser, appeared to many the gray eminence of the Bolshevik representation. Colonel Ignacy Matuszewski replaced Kuliński as the representative of the Supreme Command. As before, Polish military instructions were more far-reaching than those of the government, but unlike the earlier period Matuszewski had a greater say than General Kuliński.

During the first stages the question of fulfilling the protocol of November 14 occupied the two delegations. While Dąbski wanted strict adherence to the protocol and Matuszewski wondered about the feeling in Warsaw, Ioffe threatened to suspend the conference unless Polish troops withdrew immediately. Dąbski angrily retorted that the affair was of secondary importance and he was doing his best to resolve it. A crisis developed. Matuszewski rightly pointed out that the Soviets could now afford to be less tractable than in October. Then they had wanted a speedy armistice and assurances of peace. Now they had both. Most of the advantages from the final treaty were likely to go to Poland.[6]

Warsaw became alarmed and sought to speed up negotiation by the direct intervention of Sapieha. But his telegram to Chicherin and Rakovskii accusing the Bolsheviks of delays misfired. The foreign commissar exploited the Polish desire to fix a date for the final treaty and obtain military guarantees, and he made a number of propagandistic statements. He expressed astonishment at direct communication while there were plenipotentiaries at Riga to conduct the negotiations.[7] Exchanges once again centered in Riga and took the form of direct and secret talks between Dąbski and Ioffe. Their first meeting occurred on November 29, and while special commissions spent long hours in bargaining, the two diplomats deliberated.

The principal issues became clearer. The Bolsheviks strove to lengthen the period at which the armistice could be denounced in order to obtain greater assurance that peace would not be broken. They were also interested in transit privileges. In return they were willing to consider minor frontier rectifications favoring Poland, to send back the prisoners of war, and to make economic concessions. They were adamant regarding gold, one of the main Polish demands. An agreement along these lines was hard to reach, and the Poles differed among themselves regarding tactics. Warsaw instructed Dąbski to keep the armistice question open as a means of pressure on the Russians. The chief delegate favored dispelling Russian fears of Polish military designs. Matuszewski and the Supreme Command believed that occasional war scares might make the Bolsheviks more tractable.

In early December Ioffe complained that "Central Lithuania" was becoming a new area of activity for Savinkov and Balakho-vich. This was dangerous because although Żeligowski was theo-retically independent of Poland, Russia would hold Warsaw responsible if anything happened. It is doubtful that the Bolshe-viks were genuinely worried. They probably tried to reopen the Polish-Lithuanian question which the preliminaries had declared to be of exclusive concern to Warsaw and Kaunas. Arguments were exchanged until mid-December; the conference was hardly making progress.

Meanwhile the question of gold became the center of nego-tiations. Both sides mentioned figures which were miles apart, and tried to press each other. Aware that the Poles were using the armistice extension for tactical purposes, Ioffe began now to discount its importance for the Russians. He dwelt instead on the matter of speeding up the negotiations, which he knew the Poles desired. He recalled that the date of the plebiscite in Upper Silesia had been fixed for March 1921. Surely Warsaw would want to sign a final peace treaty before the plebiscite. This last question was a sore point. Dąbski worried about the possibility of a Soviet-German agreement. "The date of the Upper Silesian plebiscite hangs over me like a nightmare," he wrote Witos. If the plebiscite was lost, everyone would blame the delegates in Riga.[8]

Agreement was nowhere in sight. There was progress on minor matters such as repatriation of civilian prisoners, hostages and refugees, but economic issues were no nearer solution. Finally, about February 19 Dąbski resolved to have a secret talk with Ioffe which even the secretaries did not attend. The Pole agreed to accept the Russian offer of thirty million gold rubles, though Ioffe said that even this sum would not be paid exclusively in gold. Economic matters were then discussed between the Polish minister of finance, Jan Steczkowski, who came to Riga, and Krasin. This helped clarify matters.

On February 24, more than three months after the opening of the conference, an unusual and almost forgotten spectacle took place in Riga. The two delegations assembled in a plenary session to sign the first series of agreements: on repatriation; a supplementary protocol to the agreement; a protocol on the armistice; and a protocol establishing a mixed border commission.[9] The first two were a concession to the Poles, the latter—especially extension of the armistice notice to forty-two days—to the Russians.

Four days after the signing of the protocols, Lenin made a speech in which he explained the need for concessions toward border countries, once oppressed by tsarist Russia. In the case of Poland, he said, these concessions sought to obliterate national hatred, tear away Polish workers and peasants from the Entente, and demonstrate Soviet peacefulness and toleration. He said that while a few weeks earlier the Riga Conference had gone through a crisis, "we decided to make some more concessions, not because we thought them just but because we considered it important to smash the intrigues" of White Guardists and the Entente. He felt that peace would be signed "in the nearest future."[10]

On March 1, 1921 the Kronstadt sailors and workers rebelled against Soviet rule. The regime was shaken, and the Poles felt that the revolt, together with persistent rumors of a new Soviet-Polish clash, hastened the signing of the final treaty. By March 9 Dąbski reported three fourths of the document drafted; problems of gold, restitution of property, art treasures and archives, and commercial matters still delayed the negotiators. Finally these issues were settled, at least on paper.

The day of the signing of the treaty had arrived. On Friday, March 18, 1921, both delegations, the Latvian government, the diplomatic corps, and the press assembled again in the State Hall of the Schwarzhäupterhaus. The treaty was read in Polish, Russian, and Ukrainian, and duly signed. Speeches followed. Dąbski said this was a "peace of understanding." Poland did not want to be "a barrier between East and West" but a "bridge facilitating their contacts." Ioffe stressed that the treaty satisfied "all the essential, vital and just demands of the Polish people." It completed, he said, "the circle of peaceful relations between all the states which had previously formed part of the old Russian Empire." The main merit of all these treaties was that "not one question in any of these treaties has been decided on the basis of a simple relationship of power," and hence none contained "seeds of a new war." The foreign minister of Latvia commented that the treaty was "the essential condition for a rapprochement and union of the nations of Eastern Europe."[11]

The Treaty of Riga consisted of the articles agreed upon in the preliminaries, which now appeared in a more detailed form, and of those which had been reserved for solution in the final document.[12] There were minor changes regarding territorial settlement—to Poland's advantage—and the border defined as separating Poland, the Ukraine, Belorussia *and* Russia. Belorussia, whose legal status had altered between October 1920 and March 1921, figured in the treaty. The highly complex economic settlement represented on the whole a compromise between Polish claims and Soviet reluctance to allow a weakening of the Russian economy. Even so, a good deal depended not on the phrasing of articles but on the Soviet intent to fulfill them. In some cases, as in the matter of gold, Soviet pledges remained empty.

The Treaty of Riga was ratified and the documents exchanged in the Sutin Hotel in Minsk on April 30. With the creation of the Union of Soviet Socialist Republics on July 6, 1923, Moscow solemnly affirmed the validity of the treaty; the same year the Conference of Ambassadors granted it international recognition.

Was the Treaty of Riga a genuine compromise, that is to say, following the definition of Webster's Dictionary, "a reciprocal abatement of extreme demands or rights resulting in an agreement"? To give an answer, one must consider the treaty in connection with demands at the Riga Peace Conference, in the light of historic Polish-Russian relations, and in regard to the fundamental objectives of Soviet Russia and Poland.

If one compares the respective programs of the peace delegations he finds that the final settlement corresponded to a mutual agreement to withdraw more extreme demands and meet the opponent halfway. As viewed by the negotiators this was a give-and-take arrangement. The positions of the peacemakers had not been irreconcilable. There was room for compromise, and various provisions represented a judicious balancing of claims.

Looking at the Riga settlement from the perspective of old Polish-Russian territorial controversies, one notices also a mutual abandoning of historic advantages. Once the borders of the Polish-Lithuanian Commonwealth had been close to Moscow; then through the partitions of Poland and the inclusion of the Congress Kingdom, Russian frontiers had moved far into the center of Europe. A glance at a map reveals that the Riga borders were somewhere halfway between extremes. When compared with the territorial losses of the prepartition Commonwealth, Russian sacrifices were relatively minor. The area ceded at Riga constituted only two and one half percent of the entire European Russia (Congress Kingdom excluded), and four and one half percent of the population. Russia lost a little over four percent of her arable land and over twenty eight percent of forests. Only the last figure was of importance.

As for the borderlands, the historic bone of contention, a Ukrainian politician compared Riga to the seventeenth-century treaty of Andrusovo, which had split the Ukrainian lands. The frontiers of Riga and Andrusovo were of course different, but the compromise they embodied was not dissimilar. The western portions of the borderlands closer to Poland, culturally and religiously, went to that country. Those subject to stronger Russian influence came under Moscow. While several million Ukrainians and Belorussians, and a handful of Russians, found themselves under Polish rule, nearly three million Poles remained within the Soviet republics.[13] Advantages or disadvantages were not one-sided.

Did the Treaty of Riga represent a reasonable reconciliation of extreme Polish and Soviet political objectives? In contrast to the two aspects examined above, the answer must be "no." Far from being a compromise, the settlement represented a negation of both Piłsudski's eastern program and the Bolshevik plan of making Soviet Poland a bridge to the West.

Piłsudski's federalist designs—for want of a better word—sought a radical transformation of Eastern Europe. The marshal wanted to undo the partitions, and restore Poland, though in a new form, to her former might. Warsaw was to become the rallying point of smaller states in the East, with Russia driven back to the borders of Peter the Great's reign. Such a plan could either win or fall. It could not become the object of any compromise. At Riga, Piłsudski's program crumbled. The Polish conception of incorporating and digesting the western parts of the borderlands prevailed. The Polish state in 1921 found itself in the position of a second-rate power between two giants—Germany and Russia—who, although temporarily weakened, were bound to revive. From the point of view of Piłsudski's great design this was not a compromise but a catastrophe.

The extreme plans of the Bolsheviks, as revealed in the days of their military victory in the summer of 1920, had been equally grandiose. They assigned to Poland the part of a small ethnic Communist republic—at best a satellite, at worst a member of the future Union of Soviet Socialist Republics. Poland would open the way to the West. The dependence of Polish Communists on Bolshevik leadership and their dogmatic internationalist outlook indicated the path of future developments. Even if Lenin, with his keen sense of national susceptibilities, had preserved the appearance of Polish independence, it is by no means certain how long his approach would have prevailed. Nor must one forget that Lenin gambled against Polish nationalism in 1920 to achieve higher stakes, namely, a revolution in the West. There was a possibility of Poland in one form or another joining the Soviet Federation, and one may recall the statement of the Second Congress of the Comintern in the summer of 1920 that: "Federation is a transition form toward full unification of working masses of different nations."

It is likely that Poland might have been required to make further sacrifices on the altar of international Communism. The conquest of Poland was only a means of bringing revolution to Germany—the most advanced industrial state of continental Europe. Would the provisions of Versailles regarding German-Polish borders remain intact in case of Bolshevik victory? The mysterious goings on between Germany and Russia in 1920, Lenin's castigation of Versailles, casual remarks about German rights to the lost provinces, the pro-German attitude of Polish Communists toward the Upper Silesian plebiscite, all this indicated possible territorial cessions by a Soviet Poland to Germany. Foreign observers thought it probable, and it was not mere demagogy that prompted the PPS to say in its party order of August 9, 1920 that the existence of Poland was at stake, for in the case of defeat the country would be partitioned between Russia and Germany.[14]

Seen in this light the Treaty of Riga could hardly be considered a compromise. Commenting later on the peace settlement "that cut us off from Germany," Trotsky wrote: "The counterrevolutionary significance of the Riga treaty for the fate of Europe can be best understood if you picture the situation in 1923 [Ruhr occupation and the crisis in Germany] under the supposition that we had had a common frontier with Germany."[15] Nothing could be more clear. The settlement of 1921 stopped the Soviet westward advance, stabilized the situation in Eastern Europe—and indeed in Europe—and excluded Russia from international politics for at least sixteen years. This was a breakdown of the Bolshevik revolutionary program. It opened the new period of "Socialism in one country" and the New Economic Policy.

In the long run the negative effects of Riga were more pronounced in the case of Poland than of Russia. The former lost the chance of becoming a great power; the plans of the latter were merely delayed. Even the existence of "bourgeois" states on Russia's western borders, from Finland to Rumania, brought some advantages to Moscow. These weak countries acted as a shield or a buffer behind which Russia quietly could gather strength. Strangely enough, few Poles appreciated the real implications of the war and of the peace which followed. The Treaty of Riga seemed a compromise reflecting Polish reasonableness after a victorious war. Contrary to reality many Poles came to believe that their country was a power in European politics. Together with the Upper Silesian plebiscite and the adoption of a constitution, the Treaty of Riga stood as a symbol of a new period in Poland's history. There was a feeling of satisfaction for having overcome the first turbulent years of independence.

The Bolsheviks had no illusions. Their long-range goals remained unchanged, and their re-entry into European politics in 1939 began with the tearing up of the Treaty of Riga. A reconquest of the Baltic states followed. With the Red flag over the ruins of Berlin by the end of the Second World War, the dream of 1920 had come true.

The sequence of historical events may not be inevitable. It is the historian rather than participant who perceives and constructs logical patterns and causal relations. And yet it is difficult to escape the feeling that given the situation from 1917 to 1921 things could not have happened any other way. That is not to say that the Soviet-Polish conflict was determined by laws of Marxist dialectics. To present it as a mere fragment of the general struggle between revolution and reaction is to oversimplify its complex nature. For the Poles it was much more than strife between Red Russia and White Poland, although there were circles primarily interested in fighting the Bolsheviks. The government and the Supreme Command had more sophisticated notions, and they realized that the struggle had roots in the past. Seen from the Soviet side the struggle came because the Bolsheviks did not believe in a victorious revolution in one country. But even in their case ideological motives blended with the requirements of Russian *raison d'état*.

Both countries did not start with a clean slate in 1917. Even the new and universal doctrine of the Bolsheviks should not make one forget that "Both the Tsarist and Soviet government—the former rarely; the latter invariably—claimed to be acting in the name of an ideal identified with an international cause."[16] The new Russia contained many of the characteristics of the old: contempt for the West, which she simultaneously sought to emulate; censorship; self-criticism and breaking of individual will; a belief in the basic peacefulness of the Russians. For all the internationalism of the Bolsheviks, Russian chauvinism, as Lenin admitted, was in all Bolsheviks, and had to be overcome.

The Poles did not fail to point out that their strife against the Soviets was a new version of the struggle between the civilized West and barbarian East. The Poles acted—or thought they did—as defenders of Christendom, assuming a part which the West had not assigned them, and which the Russians resented. The two countries fought anew the old battle for leadership in Eastern Europe, which had been decided in Russia's favor at the time of the partitions. The stakes were the borderlands. To both Lenin and Piłsudski it was evident that Belorussia and the Ukraine would have to come under the wings of either Warsaw or Moscow. In the age of nationalism and awakening of the masses they sought to accomplish it by promoting the principle of national self-determination and a federalist solution. Federalism became the means and the end; the Soviet version of federalism confronted the revived Jagiellonian federalism of the Poles.

If Polish federalism as a detailed program was hard to define, its application proved more difficult. The powerful Right opposed it, the Entente viewed it as screen for Polish imperialism. Western parts of the borderlands with their sizable Polish population had either to be sacrificed to an ill-defined federalism, or incorporated into Poland, raising the opposition of Lithuanians, Ukrainians, and Belorussians. The national and economic interests of the local Poles, a privileged class, complicated the picture. Poland's potential partners in the borderlands were the nationalist leaders whose programs were in opposition both to the Poles and Russians. Federalism as a doctrine transcending nationalism could never be successfully formulated. Domestic Polish opposition and the complex situation in the borderlands made it virtually impossible. Had Piłsudski gained the support of the leading Polish political

groups, captivated the imagination of the Belorussian and Lithuanian politicians, and obtained the backing of the Entente, he
might have succeeded. He failed on all three counts. The federalist conception "dug a chasm of misunderstanding between
Piłsudski and the majority of the nation."[17] He had to fight his
battles alone.

The Bolsheviks labored under no such disadvantages. The two
factors which harmed Polish federalism, social contradictions and
Polish stakes in the western parts of the borderlands (Wilno and
Eastern Galicia), assisted the Soviets. The Russians could theoretically favor indivisibility of the borderlands, and base their federalist slogans on appeals against social inequality. Russian partners
in Lithuania, Belorussia, or the Ukraine were Communists whose
only allegiance was to the common cause of the revolution. Their
program went beyond national antagonisms. It could be clear
and logical, even if only on paper. A centralized and highly disciplined party could carry it out. No corresponding body existed
on the Polish side.[18] Soviet federalism carried with it complete
subjection of the borderlands to Russia, but it was clothed in
lofty internationalist slogans. Polish federalism at best could
encroach on the sovereign rights of Lithuania, Belorussia, and
the Ukraine, but it also evoked historic associations which the
masses in the borderlands wanted to repudiate. Soviet slogans
appeared to bring a new future; the Polish sounded anachronistic.

Control of the borderlands determined the power position of
Russia and Poland. This was imperfectly understood by most
Poles and misunderstood in the West. Hopes that the Soviet
regime was a passing phenomenon, to be replaced by a vigorous
non-Communist Russia, blinded people to realities. The existence
of Russia as a great power was taken for granted; a new and
friendly Russia was needed as an element of the balance of power.
The re-emergence of Poland as a dominant factor in Eastern
Europe appeared to be turning back the wheel of history. Hardly
any one in the West believed it possible or desirable.

At times the Soviet-Polish strife looked like a duel between
Lenin and Piłsudski. Lenin, as Pokrovskii put it, and many others
confirmed, "personally directed the foreign policy" of Russia.[19]
Piłsudski as the chief of state and supreme commander united in
his hands political and military powers. Lenin's authority, despite
occasional disagreements, was never seriously challenged. Piłsudski was constantly at odds with the "sovereign" sejm, which
questioned and distorted his policy. The old strife between the
Left and Right continued, and the National Democrats could at
times set the country against the chief of state, and as an impartial

observer remarked, "have been doing their utmost to goad him into exasperation."[20] It was a paradoxical situation, and as a Polish writer put it, "Dmowski had realized his principles and achieved his conception of an independent Poland, though he did not rule the country. Piłsudski did govern Poland but he failed to fulfill his ideas."[21]

Poland's policy toward Russia was a result of this dualism. Piłsudski pursued one plan, the Dmowski-led delegation in Paris another. After his Wilno proclamation the chief of state inclined toward federalist solutions; dominated by the Right, the sejm applied brakes. The idea of a plebiscite in the borderlands had a different meaning for the federalists and incorporationists. While the Borisov episode, the alliance with Petliura, and the march on Kiev resulted from Piłsudski's initiative, the peace settlement was a victory of his opponents. The government's position was weakened by this dualism. Nothing comparable existed on the Soviet side. There were internal differences which reached their height in the summer of 1920, and there were changes and tactical retreats. But at every important turn, Lenin prevailed over his colleagues.

Could the Soviet-Polish conflict have been avoided? Though one can only speculate and conjecture, it is hard to conceive of an alternative. The Poles were united in their opposition to being confined to the borders of the Congress Kingdom and revolutionized from outside. When at the turn of 1918–1919 the Red Army began its advance, Warsaw had to react. It was not only fear of a spreading revolution but territorial considerations which prompted the Polish move on Wilno in the spring of 1919. In the summer of that year the secret Soviet-Polish talks revealed a minimum of agreement with regard to counterrevolutionary Russia. They showed at the same time that Piłsudski's aims were irreconcilable with those of Moscow. Nor were the Polish rightists, whose views followed those of the Entente, any more conciliatory.

Serious chances of peace appeared at the turn of 1919 and 1920. Even then, neither side trusted the other. While peace messages circulated, both countries prepared for a showdown.[22] Piłsudski and the Right differed on the Ukraine and on military tactics, but neither took Soviet offers at face value. Even if the Bolsheviks were sincere in their peaceful protestations, they viewed peace as a temporary expedient. The goal was the revolutionization of Poland and expansion further west. They may have preferred to accomplish it through peaceful means and time was on their side, but the Poles could have no assurance that armed intervention would not come sooner or later. The subsequent fate of Georgia showed that their fears were not groundless. Peace became possible only after both sides had tried to accomplish their aims and failed. At that point there was no alternative.

The Soviet-Polish war of 1919–1920 profoundly affected the two countries and their relations. It produced hardship for Poland, resulting in nearly a quarter of a million people killed, wounded, or taken prisoner. Estimated war damages amounted to some ten billion gold francs. Corresponding losses and damages for Russia, the Ukraine, and Belorussia, were also heavy. Traditional Russian-Polish hostility received new impetus; throughout the interwar period the formative years weighed on the relations between the two countries.

From the European point of view the stalemate of Riga brought no lasting solution to continental security and the balance of power. Although hostile to Soviet Russia, the West, seeking counterrevolutionary mirages, had not assisted Piłsudski in a permanent weakening of the Russian colossus. The Entente had antagonized the Bolsheviks, discouraged the Poles, and failed to preside over a settlement in the East. Its share of responsibility for events which later arose from the 1917–1921 period was heavy indeed. In this larger failure, unfortunately, the Poles could take little comfort.

Bibliography
Notes
Index

Bibliography

This list of references includes only those works cited in the text. A few titles which concern historical background and are only indirectly relevant for Soviet-Polish relations are not listed. Unless otherwise stated the third edition of Lenin's works is cited, and although there are English translations of the works of Lenin and Stalin I relied on the original Russian texts. I chose the Polish language publication, *Dokumenty i materiały do historii stosunków polsko-radzieckich,* in preference to the Russian *Dokumenty i materialy po istorii sovetsko-polskikh otnoshenii* because the former prints all the documents in the original language while the latter translates them into Russian.

1   Manuscript Collections and Government Documents

Polish

New York
  Józef Piłsudski Institute of America
    Akta Adiutantury Generalnej Naczelnego Dowództwa 1918-1922
    Akta Generała Tadeusza Rozwadowskiego
    Akta Ukraińskiej Misji Wojskowej
    Archiwum Michała Mościckiego
  Polish Institute of Arts and Sciences
    MS Karol Wędziagolski Memoirs (in Polish)
  Archive of Russian and East European History and Culture, Columbia University
    Alexander Minc, "Der Kommunismus in Polen: Erinnerungen"

Montreal
  Archive of the Polish Government-in-Exile, documents from the Polish Embassy in London

Warsaw
  Archiwum Polskiej Akademii Nauk
    MS Diariusz Michała S. Kossakowskiego
  Biblioteka Narodowa
    Jerzy Osmołowski, "Wspomnienia z lat 1914-1921"
  Zakład Historii Stosunków Polsko-Radzieckich
    Archiwum Paderewskiego. Copies from Archiwum Akt Nowych

Stanford, Calif.
  Hoover Institution
    Ciechanowski Deposit. Archives of the Polish Embassy in

Washington, D.C.
Wislowski Collection. Miscellanea

Russian

New York
Archive of Russian and East European History and Culture, Columbia University
Denikin Papers, Rukopisi proizvedenii Gen. A. I. Denikina
MS Dnevnik P.N. Miliukova
MS Zapiski P.N. Shatilova
Anatolii P. Velmin, "Russkaia emigratsiia v Polshe v 1919-1921 gg"
————, "K istorii russkoi pressy v Polshe v 1919–1939 gg"

Stanford, Calif.
Hoover Institution
M.N. Giers Archives
V.A. Maklakov Archives
MS Borisa Savinkova

Cambridge, Mass.
Widener Library, Harvard University
Smolensk Archive: Kommunisticheskaia Partia Sovetskogo Soiuza, Partiinyi Archiv
Houghton Library, Harvard University
Trotsky Archive

American, British, and German

Washington, D.C.
National Archives
Department of State Records, Record Group 59
St. Antony's Collection, Akten betreffend das Verhältniss Deutschlands zu Russland

London
Public Record Office
Cabinet Records
Foreign Office Records

Cambridge, Mass.
Houghton Library, Harvard University
Jay Pierrepont Moffat, Diplomatic Papers and Correspondence

New Haven, Conn.
Sterling Library, Yale University
Edward M. House Collection
Louis S. Fischer Collection: Chicherin Correspondence 1929–1932

2 Published Documents, Diaries and Memoirs, Eyewitness Accounts, and Speeches

Akty i dokumenty dotyczące sprawy granic Polski, 1918-1919. 4 vols. Paris: Sekretariat Generalny Delegacji Polskiej, 1920-1926.

Angaretis, Zigmas. "Litva i Oktiabrskaia revoliutsiia," *Zhizn Nat-sionalnostei*, 1 (January 1923), 217-220.

Anrufe des Executivkomitees der kommunistichen Internationale zur polnischen Frage. Berlin, 1920.

Antonov-Ovseenko, Vladimir A. *Zapiski o grazhdanskoi voine*. 4 vols. Leningrad and Moscow, 1932-1933.

Baranowski, Władysław. *Rozmowy z Piłsudskim, 1916-1931*. Warsaw, 1938.

Bonch-Bruevich, Mikhail D. *Vsia vlast Sovetam*. Moscow, 1957.

Brandt, Rolf. "With the Soviet Army," *Living Age*, 307 (October 2, 1920), 28-30.

British Foreign Office. *Peace Handbook: No. 44*. London, 1920.

Browder, Robert P., and Kerensky, Alexander F., eds. *The Russian Provisional Government, 1917: Documents*. 3 vols. Stanford, 1961.

Carton de Wiart, General Sir Adrian. *Happy Odyssey*. London, 1950.

Chambre des deputés. *Débats*. Paris.

Chernov, Victor M. *Pered burei*. New York, 1953.

Chicherin, Georgii V. *Stati i rechi po voprosam mezhdunarodnoi politiki*. Moscow, 1961.

Conférence Politique Russe. *Considérations sur les frontières orientales de la Pologne et la paix en Europe*. Paris, 1919.

D'Abernon, Edgar V., Lord. *The Eighteenth Decisive Battle of the World*. London, 1931.

Dąbski, Jan. *Pokój ryski, wspomnienia, pertraktacje, tajne układy z Joffem, listy*. Warsaw, 1931.

Daszyński, Ignacy. *Pamiętniki*. 2 vols. Cracow, 1925-1926.

Degras, Jane, ed. *The Communist International 1919-1943: Documents*. 2 vols. New York, 1956-1960.

——— *Soviet Documents on Foreign Policy, 1917-1941*. 3 vols. New York, 1951-1953.

Degtiarev, L. "Politotdel v otstuplenii: vospominaniia iz voiny s Poliakami 1920 g.," *Proletarskaia Revoliutsiia*, 12/34 (December 1924), 212-247.

Denikin, Anton I. *Ocherki russkoi smuty*. 5 vols. Berlin 1921-1926.

——— *Kto spas sovetskuiu vlast od gibeli?* Paris, 1937.

Deviatyi sezd RKP(b). Moscow, 1960.

Desiatyi sezd RKP(b), Mart 1921 g. Moscow, 1962.

Dmowski, Roman. *Polityka polska i odbudowanie państwa*. Warsaw, 1925.

Documents diplomatiques concernant les relations polono-lithuaniennes: déc. 1918—sept. 1920. Warsaw: République Polonaise, Ministère des Affaires Étrangères, 1920.

Documents on British Foreign Policy, 1918-1945. Ed. E. L. Woodward and R. Butler. First series, London, 1947—.

Dokumenty i materiały do historii stosunków polsko-radzieckich. Warsaw: Polska Akademia Nauk i Akademia Nauk ZSRR, 1962—.

Dokumenty vneshnei politiki SSSR. Moscow: Ministerstvo Inostrannykh Del SSSR, 1959—.

Dowbór-Muśnicki, Józef. *Moje wspomnienia.* Poznań, 1936.

Dzierżyńska Zofia (Dzerzhinskaia Sofiia). *V gody velikikh boev.* Moscow, 1964.

Dzierżyński, Feliks E. (Dzerzhinskii). *Dnevnik: Pisma k rodnym.* Moscow, 1958.

———— *Izbrannye proizvedeniia.* 2 vols. Moscow, 1957.

Eudin, Xenia J., and Fischer, Harold H., eds. *Soviet Russia and the West, 1920-1927: A Documentary Survey.* Stanford, 1957.

Ezovitov, K. *Belorussy i Poliaki: dokumenty i fakty iz istorii okkupatsii Belorussii Poliakami v 1918-1919 gg.* Kovno, 1919.

Foreign Relations of the United States: The Paris Peace Conference, 1919. 13 vols. Washington, D. C., 1942-1947.

Foreign Relations of the United States: 1919, Russia. Washington, D.C., 1937.

Foreign Relations of the United States: 1920. 3 vols. Washington, D.C., 1935-1936.

Girinis, S. "Kanun i sumerki Sovetskoi vlasti na Litve," *Proletarskaia Revoliutsiia,* 8, (1922), 71-92.

Głąbiński, Stanisław. *Wspomnienia polityczne.* Pelplin, 1939.

Gorky, Maxim. *Sobranie sochinenii.* 30 vols. Moscow, 1948-1953.

Grabski, Stanisław. *The Polish-Soviet Frontier.* London, 1943.

———— *Z codziennych walk i rozważań.* Poznań, 1923.

Grazhdanskaia voina na Ukraine, 1918-1920: sbornik dokumentov i materialov. Ed. S. M. Korolivskii, N. H. Kolechnik, and I. K. Rybalk. 3 vols. in 4. Kiev, 1967.

Haller, Józef. *Pamiętniki.* London, 1964.

Hołówko, Tadeusz. *Przez dwa fronty.* 2 vols. in 1. Warsaw, 1931.

———— "Skutki pokoju w Rydze," *Przymierze,* Nov. 28, 1920.

Horst, Leonhard. "At the Riga Peace Conference," *Living Age,* 307 (November 20, 1920), 458-460.

Howard, Sir Esme. *Theatre of Life.* 2 vols. Boston, 1935-1936.

Istoriia Sovetskoi konstitutsii v dokumentakh, 1917-1956. Moscow, 1957.

Jabłonowski, Roman. *Wspomnienia.* Warsaw, 1962.

Jastrzębski, Wincenty. "Między Piotrogrodem a Warszawą," *Najnowsze Dzieje Polski: materiały i studia z okresu 1914-1939,* 12 (1967) 155-189.

Kalendarz Robotniczy PPS. Warsaw, 1919.

Kamenev, Sergei S., "Vospominaniia," in *Vospominaniia o Vladimire Iliche Lenine,* vol. II. 3 vols. Moscow, 1956-1960.

Kedrovskyi, Volodymyr. *Ryzhske Andrusovo: spomyny pro rosiisko-polski myrovi perehovory v 1920 r.* Winnipeg, Canada, 1936.

Kennedy, A. L. *Old Diplomacy and New: 1876-1922.* London, 1922.

Kirimer, Cafer Seydahmet. "Moje wspomnienia z rozmowy z marszałkiem Józefem Piłsudskim," *Niepodległość,* n.s., 2 (1950), 41-50.

Kliuchnikov, Iu. V., and Sabanin, A. V., eds. *Mezhdunarodnaia politika noveishego vremenii v dogovorakh, notakh i deklaratsiakh.* 3 parts. Moscow, 1925-1928.

Kozicki, Stanisław. *Sprawa granic Polski na konferencji pokojowej w Paryżu*. Warsaw, 1921.

KPP w obronie niepodległości Polski: materiały i dokumenty. Warsaw: Zakład Historii PZPR, 1953.

Kridl, Manfred, Malinowski, Władysław, Wittlin, Józef, eds., *For Your Freedom and Ours: Polish Progressive Spirit through the Centuries*. New York, 1943.

———— *'Za Waszą i naszą wolność': Polska myśl demokratyczna w ciągu wieków*. London, 1945.

Krzewski (Lilienfeld, J.). *Zasady federacji w polskiej polityce kresowej*. Cracow, 1920.

Kumaniecki, Kazimierz W., ed. *Odbudowa państwowości polskiej: najważniejsze dokumenty*. Warsaw and Cracow, 1924.

Ładoś, Aleksander. "Wasilewski w rokowaniach ryskich," *Niepodległość*, 16 (1937), 230-250.

League of Nations Treaty Series. Vols. IV and VI. 1921.

Lednicki, Aleksander. *Nasza polityka wschodnia*. Warsaw, 1922.

———— "P. N. Miliukov i polskii vopros," in *P. N. Miliukov: sbornik materialov po chestvovaniiu ego semidesiatiletiia 1859-1929*, ed. S. A. Smirnov *et al*. Paris, 1929.

Lenin, Vladimir Ilich. *Sochineniia*. 3rd ed. 30 vols. Moscow, 1935-1937.

———— *Sochineniia*. 4th ed. 38 vols. Moscow, 1942-1950.

———— *Polnoe sobranie sochinenii*. 5th ed. Moscow, 1958—.

Leninskii Sbornik. Moscow, 1924—.

Liberman, Simon. *Building Lenin's Russia*. Chicago, 1945.

Lipiński, Wacław. "Wywiad u marszałka Piłsudskiego w Sulejówku z 10 XI 1924," *Niepodległość*, 7 (1933), 63-80.

Livre rouge: recueil des documents diplomatiques relatifs aux relations entre la Russie et la Pologne 1918-1920. Moscow: RSFSR, Commissariat du Peuple pour Affaires Étrangères, 1920.

Lloyd George, David. *The Truth about the Peace Treaties*. 2 vols. London, 1938.

Lockhart, Bruce. *Memoirs of a British Agent*. London, 1932.

Lunacharskii, Anatolii V. *Stati i rechi po voprosam mezhdunarodnoi politiki*. Moscow, 1959.

Luxemburg, Rosa. *Die industrielle Entwicklung Polens*. Leipzig, 1896.

———— *The Russian Revolution and Leninism or Marxism*, trans. Bertram D. Wolfe. Ann Arbor, Mich. 1961.

Mandelstam, André. *Mémoire sur l'application du principe des nationalités à la question polonaise*. Paris, 1919.

Mannerheim, Carl. *The Memoirs of Marshal Mannerheim*. New York, 1954.

Mantoux, Paul. *Les délibérations du Conseil des Quatre: 24 mars—28 juin 1919*. 2 vols. Paris, 1955.

Manuilskii, Dmitrii Z. "O Rizhskikh peregovorakh," *Kommunisticheskii Internatsional*, no. 15 (1920), 3077-3082.

Marchlewski, Julian (Markhlevskii). "Mir s Polshei," *Kommunisticheskii Internatsional*, no. 14 (1920), 2751-2754.

———— *Pisma wybrane.* 2 vols. Warsaw, 1952-1956.

———— *Polsha i mirovaia revoliutsiia.* Moscow, 1920.

———— "Polski vopros i oktiabrskaia revoliutsiia," *Zhizn Natsional-nostei,* 1 (January 1923), 227-231.

Marx, Karl. *Manuskripte über die polnische Frage: 1863-1864.* Ed. Werner Conze and Dieter Hertz-Eichenrode. The Hague, 1961.

Marx, Karl, and Engels, Friedrich. *The Russian Menace to Europe.* Ed. Paul W. Blackstock and Bert F. Hoselitz. Glencoe, Ill., 1952.

———— *Marks i Engels o Polsce.* Ed. Helena Michnik. 2 vols. Warsaw, 1960.

Materiały archiwalne do historii stosunków polsko-radzieckich. Ed. Natalia Gąsiorowska. Warsaw, 1957—.

Mazepa, Isaak. *Ukraina v ohni i buri revoliutsii 1917-1921.* 3 vols. Prague, 1942-1943.

Melgunov, Sergei P. *N. V. Chaikovskii v gody grazhdanskoi voiny: materialy dlia istorii russkoi obshchestvennosti 1917-1925 gg.* Paris, 1929.

Mickiewicz-Kapsukas, Wincas (Vincas Mitskevich-Kapsukas). "Walka o władzę radziecką na Litwie i Białorusi Zachodniej," *Z Pola Walki,* nos. 9-10 (1930), 5-35.

Miliukov, Pavel N. "Aleksander Lednicki jako rzecznik polsko-rosyjskiego porozumienia," *Przegląd Współczesny,* no. 3/303 (March 1939), 25-71.

Miller, David Hunter. *My Diary at the Conference of Paris.* 21 vols. New York, 1926.

Mirnye peregovory v Brest-Litovske s 22/9 dekabria do 3 marta/18 febralia 1918 g. Moscow: Narodnyi Kommissariat Inostrannykh Del, 1920.

Moraczewski, Jędrzej. "Wspomnienia o współpracy z Leonem Wasilewskim," *Niepodległość,* 16 (1937), 210-220.

Mordacq, General Henri. *Le Ministère Clemenceau: journal d'un témoin.* 4 vols. Paris, 1931.

Nagórski, Zygmunt, Sr. "Aleksander Lednicki, 1866-1934," *Zeszyty Historyczne,* 1 (1962), 27-66.

"Nieznane listy Petlury do Piłsudskiego," ed. Piotr S. Wandycz, *Zeszyty Historyczne,* 8 (1965), 181-186.

Pestkowski, Stanisław (Pestkovskii). "Ob Oktiabrskikh dniakh v Pitere," *Proletarskaia Revoliutsiia,* 10 (October 1922), 94-104.

Petliura, Simon. *Statti, lysty, dokumenty.* New York, 1956.

Piłsudska, Aleksandra. *Piłsudski: A Biography by his Wife Alexandra.* New York, 1941.

———— *Wspomnienia.* London, 1960.

Piłsudski, Józef. *Pisma zbiorowe.* 10 vols. Warsaw, 1937-1938.

Poznański, Karol. "Jak to naprawdę było w Rydze z Mińskiem?" *Tydzień Polski,* Nov. 28, 1964.

"PPS, XVII Kongres: 21-25 V 1920," ed. Władysław Mroczkowski and Jan Tomicki, *Najnowsze Dzieje Polski: materiały i studia z okresu 1914-1939,* 6 (1963), 239-288.

Proceedings of the Brest-Litovsk Peace Conference: 21 November 1917—3 March 1918. Washington, 1918.

Protokoll des zweiten Weltkongresses der Kommunistichen Internationale. Hamburg, 1921.

Protokoll des vierten Kongresses der Kommunistischen Internationale. Hamburg, 1923.

"Protokoły II zjazdu KPRP," *Z Pola Walki*, 1 (1958), 819-891, 1141-1213.

"Protokoły Rady Obrony Państwa," ed. Artur Leinwand and Jan Molenda, *Z Dziejów Stosunków Polsko-Radzieckich: Studia i Materiały*, 1 (1965), 136-317.

"Protokoły posiedzeń Komitetu Narodowego Polskiego w Paryżu z okresu 2 października 1918 do 23 stycznia 1919 r. (wybór)," ed. Tadeusz Kuźmiński, *Najnowsze Dzieje Polski: materiały i studia z okresu 1914-1939*, 2 (1959), 111-182.

Putna, Vitovt K. *K Visle i obratno.* Moscow, 1927.

Radek, Karl. *Die Auswärtige Politik Sowjetrusslands.* Hamburg, 1921.

——— *Die innere und äussere Lage Sowjetrusslands und die Aufgaben der KPR.* Leipzig, 1921.

——— "Polskii vopros i internatsional," *Kommunisticheskii Internatsional*, no. 12 (1920), 2173-2188.

——— "Das Selbstbestimmungsrecht der Völker," *Lichtstrahlen*, October 13, 1915.

——— *Voina polskikh belogvardeitsev protiv Sovetskoi Rossii.* Moscow, 1920.

Rady delegatów robotniczych w Polsce 1918-1919: materiały i dokumenty. 2 vols. Warsaw, 1962-1965.

Ransome, Arthur. *Russia in 1919.* New York, 1919.

Rataj, Maciej. *Pamiętniki, 1918-1927.* Warsaw, 1965.

Recueil des actes de la conférence, Conférence de la Paix: 1919-1920. 36 vols. Paris, 1923-1934.

Revoliutsionnye komitety BSSR XI 1918—VI 1920: sbornik dokumentov i materialov. Minsk: Tsentralnyi gosudarstvennyi arkhiv, 1961.

Riddell, Lord. *Intimate Diary of the Peace Conference and After: 1918-1922.* New York, 1934.

Roja, Bolesław. *Legendy i fakty.* Warsaw, 1931.

Savinkov, Boris. *Boris Savinkov pered voennoi kollegiei verkhovnogo suda SSSR.* Ed. I. Shubin. Moscow, 1924.

Sedmoi ekstrennyi sezd RKP(b): stenograficheskii otchet. Moscow, 1962.

Seeckt, Hans von. *Aus seinem Leben, 1918-1936,* Ed. Friedrich von Rabenau. Leipzig, 1941.

Sergeev, I. N. (Siergiejew, J. N.). *Od Dźwiny ku Wiśle.* Warsaw, 1925.

Seyda, Marian. *Polska na przełomie dziejów: fakty i dokumenty.* 2 vols. Poznań, 1927-1931.

Shaposhnikov, Boris M. *Na Visle: K istorii kampanii 1920 g.* Moscow, 1924.

Śliwiński, Artur. "Marszałek Piłsudski o sobie," *Niepodległość,* 16 (1937), 367-373.

Snowden, Mrs. Philip [Ethel]. *Through Bolshevik Russia.* London, 1920.

Sovetskaia Ukraina i Polsha: sbornik diplomaticheskikh dokumentov i istoricheskikh materialov. Kharkov, 1921.

Sowjetrussland und Polen: Reden von Kamenev, Lenin, Trotski, Marchlewski, Radek und Martov . . . 5 Mai 1920. Moscow, 1920.

Sprawozdanie stenograficzne 1919-1921. Sejm Ustawodawczy R.P.

Sprawy polskie na konferencji pokojowej w Paryżu 1919 r.: dokumenty i materiały. 2 vols. Warsaw, 1965-1967.

Stalin, J. V. *Sochineniia.* 13 vols. Moscow, 1946-1951.

Stepanov, Ivan [Skvortsov]. *S krasnoi armiei na panskuiu Polshu.* Moscow, 1920.

"Stosunki polsko-węgierskie w 1919 r.: materiały archiwalne," ed. Jarosław Jurkiewicz. Mimeographed. Warsaw: Polski Instytut Spraw Międzynarodowych, zeszyt 5, 1957.

Stuchka, Petr I. *Piat mesiatsev sotsialisticheskoi sovetskoi Latvii.* 2 parts. Moscow, 1919-1921.

———— *Za Sovetskuiu vlast v Latvii, 1919-1920: sbornik statei.* Riga, 1964.

Sverdlov, Iakov M. *Izbrannye proizvedeniia.* 3 vols. Moscow, 1957-1960.

Szeptycki, Stanisław. *Front litewsko-białoruski 10 III 1919—30 VII 1920.* Cracow, 1925.

Szmidt, O. B., ed. *Socjaldemokracja Królestwa Polskiego i Litwy; materiały i dokumenty 1914-1918.* Moscow, 1936.

Tommasini, Francesco. *La Risurrezione della Polonia.* Milan, 1925.

Tretii vserossiiskii sezd sovetov rabochikh, soldatskikh i krestianskikh deputatov. St. Petersburg, 1918.

Trotsky, Leon. *Kak vooruzhalas revoliutsiia.* 3 vols. in 4, Moscow, 1923-1924.

———— *Lenin.* New York, 1962.

———— *Moia zhizn.* 2 vols. Riga, 1930.

———— *My Life.* New York, 1931.

———— *Na frontakh.* Moscow, 1919.

———— *Sochineniia.* Moscow, various dates, incomplete.

———— *Sovetskaia Rossiia i burzhuaznaia Polsha.* Speech at Homel, May 10, 1920, n.p., n.d.

———— *The Trotsky Papers, 1917-1922.* Vol. I: *1917-1919.* Ed. Jan M. Meijer. London, 1964.

Tukhachevskii, Mikhail N. *Voina klassov: stati 1919-1920.* Moscow, 1921.

Tymczasowy Komitet Rewolucyjny Polski. Warsaw: Wydział Historii Partii KC PZPR, 1955.

Unabhängige Sozialdemokratische Partei Deutschlands. *Protokoll über die Verhandlungen des ausserordentlichen Parteitages in Halle: vom 12 bis 17 Oktober 1920.* Berlin, n.d.

Velikaia oktiabrskaia sotsialisticheskaia revoliutsiia v Belorussii, Okt. 1917—Mart 1918: dokumenty i materialy. 2 vols. Minsk: Institut Istorii Partii TsK KPB, 1957.

Vosmoi sezd RKP(b), Mart 1919 g.: protokoly. Moscow, 1959.

Vosmoi vserossiiskii sezd sovetov: stenograficheskii otchet. Moscow, 1921.

Vsesoiuznaia Kommunisticheskaia Partiia (bolshevikov) v rezoliutsiakh i resheniiakh sezdov, konferentsii i plenumov TsK: 1898-1932. Moscow, 1933.

Wasilewski, Leon. *Józef Piłsudski jakim go znałem.* Warsaw, 1935.

Wasilewski, Zygmunt, ed. *Proces Lednickiego.* Warsaw, 1924.

Wędziagolski, Karol (K. Vendziagolskii). "Savinkov," *Novyi Zhurnal,* no. 71 (1963), 135-155; no. 72, 169-197.

Weygand, Maxime. *Mémoires.* Vol. II: *Mirages et réalité.* Paris, 1957.

Wierzbicki, Andrzej. *Wspomnienia i dokumenty, 1877-1920.* Warsaw, 1957.

Witos, Wincenty. *Moje wspomnienia.* 3 vols. Paris, 1964-1965.

Żegota-Januszajtis, Marian. *Strategiczne granice Polski na wschodzie.* Warsaw, 1919.

Zetkin, Klara. *Reminiscences of Lenin.* London, 1929.

Zhurnal zasedanii vremennago pravitelstva. 2 vols. Petrograd, 1917.

Zinoviev, Grigorii. *Le prolétariat européen devant la revolution: discours . . . à Halle le 14 octobre 1920.* Petrograd, 1921.

3   **Secondary Works: Books and Articles**

Ajnenkiel, Andrzej. *Od "rządów ludowych" do przewrotu majowego: zarys dziejów politycznych Polski 1918-1926.* Warsaw, 1964.

Angress, Werner T. *Stillborn Revolution: The Communist Bid for Power in Germany, 1921-1923.* Princeton, 1963.

Arenz, Wilhelm. *Polen und Russland, 1918-1920.* Leipzig, 1939.

Arski, Stefan. *My Pierwsza Brygada.* Warsaw, 1962.

Askenazy, Szymon. *Uwagi.* Warsaw, 1924.

Bagiński, Henryk. *Wojsko polskie na wschodzie 1914-1920.* Warsaw, 1921.

Bardoux, Jacques. *De Paris à Spa.* Paris, 1929.

Berdyaev, Nicolas. *The Origin of Russian Communism,* trans. R. M. French. Ann Arbor, Mich., 1962.

Bobińska, Celina. *Marks i Engels a sprawy polskie do osiemdziesiątych lat XIX wieku.* Warsaw, 1955.

Bobrzyński, Michał (anon.) *Wskrzeszenie państwa polskiego.* 2 vols. Cracow, 1920-1925.

———. *Dzieje Polski w zarysie.* 3 vols. Warsaw, 1927-1931.

Bolotin, Aleksei I. *Deviataia konferentsiia RKP(b).* Moscow, 1956.

Borkenau, Franz. *The Communist International.* London, 1938.

Borys, Jurij. *The Russian Communist Party and the Sovietization of the Ukraine: A Study of the Communist Doctrine of the Self-determination of Nations.* Stockholm, 1960.

Brand, Edward, and Walecki, Henryk. *Der Kommunismus in Polen* Hamburg, 1921.

Bril, I. "Politicheskaia podgotovka letnei operatsii v 1920 g.," *Voina i Revoliutsiia*, 11 (1926), 86-105.

Brinkley, George A. *The Volunteer Army and the Allied Intervention in South Russia 1917-1921*. Notre Dame, 1966.

Bułat, Wojciech. "Zjazd polsko-rosyjski w Moskwie 21-22 kwietnia 1905 r.," *Studia z Najnowszych Dziejów Powszechnych*, 2 (1962), 187-206.

Carr, E. H. *The Bolshevik Revolution, 1917-1923.* 3 vols. London, 1950–1953.

Carroll, E. Malcolm. *Soviet Communism and Western Opinion, 1919-1921*, ed. Frederick B. M. Hollyday. Chapel Hill, N. C., 1965.

Charaszkiewicz, Edmund. "Przebudowa wschodu Europy: materiały do polityki wschodniej Józefa Piłsudskiego w latach 1893-1921," *Niepodległość* n.s., 5 (1955), 125-167.

Chiang kai-shek. *Soviet Russia in China.* New York, 1957.

Chocianowicz, Wacław. "Historia dywizji litewsko-białoruskiej w świetle listów Józefa Piłsudskiego," *Niepodległość*, n.s., 7 (1962), 200-218.

Churchill, Winston S. *The Aftermath.* London, 1929.

Ciołkosz, Adam. *Róża Luksemburg a rewolucja rosyjska.* Paris, 1961.

Dallin, Alexander. "The Future of Poland," in Alexander Dallin et al., *Russian Diplomacy and Eastern Europe 1914-1917.* New York, 1963.

———— "The Use of International Movements," in *Russian Foreign Policy*, ed. Ivo Lederer. New Haven, 1962.

Daniszewski, Tadeusz. "Lenin a polski ruch komunistyczny," *Z Pola Walki*, 3 (1960), 247-276.

Deutscher, Isaac. *The Prophet Armed: Trotsky, 1879-1921.* Oxford, 1954.

———— *Stalin: A Political Biography.* London, 1949.

Dziewanowski, Marian Kamil. *The Communist Party of Poland.* Cambridge, Mass., 1959.

Epstein, Fritz T. "Studien zur Geschichte der 'Russischen Frage' auf der Pariser Friedenskonferenz von 1919," *Jahrbücher für Geschichte Osteuropas*, 7 (1959), 431-478.

Ermolaev, R. "K istorii polskikh kommunisticheskikh organizatsii i organov RKP(b) dlia raboty sredi polskogo naseleniia na territorii sovetskoi respubliki v 1917-1921 gg," in *Oktiabrskaia revoliutsiia i zarubezhnye slavianskie narody*, ed. A. Ia. Manusevich. Moscow, 1957.

Erickson, John. *The Soviet High Command: A Military Political History, 1918-1941.* New York, 1962.

Feldman, Wilhelm. *Dzieje polskiej myśli politycznej w okresie porozbiorowym.* 3 vols. Cracow and Warsaw, 1913-1920.

Fischer, Louis. *The Soviets in World Affairs.* 2 vols. London, 1930.

Fischer, Ruth. *Stalin and German Communists.* Cambridge, Mass., 1948.

Florinsky, Michael. *Russia: A History and an Interpretation.* 2 vols. New York, 1946.

Gałęzowska, Irena. "Myśl Józefa Piłsudskiego w świetle filozofii współczesnej," *Niepodległość,* n.s., 7 (1962), 127-146.

Gatzke, Hans W. "Russo-German Military Collaboration during the Weimar Republic," *American Historical Review,* 63 (April 1958), 565-597.

Giertych, Jędrzej. *Pół wieku polskiej polityki.* London, 1947.

Gostyńska, Weronika. "Rola Juliana Marchlewskiego w tajnych rokowaniach polsko-radzieckich (czerwiec-lipiec 1919 r.)," *Z Pola Walki,* 9 (1966), 291-308.

———— "Tajne rokowania polsko-radzieckie w Mikaszewiczach (sierpień-grudzień 1919r.)," *Z Pola Walki,* 10 (1967), 961-986.

Graham, Malbone W. *The Recognition of the Border States.* Vol. III: *Latvia.* Berkeley and Los Angeles, 1941.

Grazhdanskaia voina 1918-1921, ed. A. S. Bubnov, S. S. Kamenev, and R. P. Eideman. 3 vols. Moscow, 1928-1930.

Grinberg, Maria, "Z zagadnień wojny polsko-radzieckiej," in *Ruch robotniczy i ludowy w Polsce w latach 1914-1923.* Warsaw, 1961.

Grosfeld, Leon. *Polskie reakcyjne formacje wojskowe w Rosji 1917-1919.* Warsaw, 1956.

———— "Wpływ rewolucji lutowej na Królestwo w świetle świadectw austriackich," *Kwartalnik Historyczny,* 63, nos. 4-5 (1956), 381-394.

———— "Piłsudski et Savinkov," *Acta Poloniae Historica,* 14 (1966), 49-73.

Grünberg, Karol, "Socjaldemokracja polska a ruch liberalny w państwie rosyjskim w 1904r.," *Materiały i Studia,* 1 (1960), 33-45.

Gumplowicz, Władysław, *Kwestya polska a socjalizm.* Warsaw, 1908.

Haller, General Stanisław. "Nasz stosunek do Denikina," *Kurjer Warszawski,* June 13, 1937.

Haluskko, I. M. *Narysy istorii ideologichnoi ta orhanizatsiinoi diialnosti KPZU v 1919-1928 rr.* Lvov, 1965.

Historia Polski. Warsaw: Polska Akademia Nauk, 1958—.

Höltje, Christian. *Die Weimarer Republik und das Ostlocarno-Problem 1919-1934.* Würzburg, 1958.

Holzer, Jerzy. *Polska Partia Socjalistyczna w latach 1917-1919.* Warsaw, 1962.

———— and Molenda, Jan. *Polska w pierwszej wojnie światowej.* Warsaw, 1963.

Hulse, James W. *The Forming of the Communist International.* Stanford, 1964.

Iarosh, Kiprian N. *Russko-polskiia otnosheniia.* Kharkov, 1898.

Istoriia grazhdanskoi voiny v SSSR. 5 vols. Moscow, 1935-1960.

Iwański, Gereon. "Z dziejów Komunistycznej Partii Galicji wschodniej," *Z Pola Walki,* 10 (1967), 933-960.

Jabłoński, Henryk. "Międzynarodowe warunki odbudowy niepodległości Polski w 1918 r.," in *Ruch robotniczy i ludowy w Polsce w latach 1914-1923*. Warsaw, 1961.

—— *Narodziny drugiej Rzeczpospolitej 1918-1919*. Warsaw, 1962.

—— *Polityka Polskiej Partii Socjalistycznej w czasie wojny 1914-1918r*. Warsaw, 1958.

—— "Wojna polsko-radziecka 1919-1920," *Przegląd Socjalistyczny*, nos. 7-8 (1948).

—— "Z dziejów genezy sojuszu Piłsudski-Petlura," *Zeszyty Naukowe Wojskowej Akademii Politycznej*, seria historyczna, no. 5/21 (1961), 40-58.

Jędruszczak, Tadeusz. "Stanowisko Polski i mocarstw Ententy w sprawie polskiej granicy wschodniej," *Sprawy Międzynarodowe*, no. 6/87 (1959).

Jędrzejewicz, Wacław. "Rokowania borysowskie w 1920 roku," *Niepodległość*, n.s., 3 (1951), 47-59.

Jundziłł, Zygmunt. "Niefortunna wyprawa kowieńska," *Niepodległość*, n.s., 5 (1955), 206-212.

—— "Z dziejów polskiej myśli politycznej na Litwie historycznej," *Niepodległość*, n.s., 6 (1958), 61-77.

Kakurin, N. E. *Kak srazhalas revoliutsiia*. 3 vols. Moscow, 1925-1926.

—— *Russko-polskaia kampania 1918-1920*. Moscow, 1922.

—— and Melikov, V. A. *Voina s belopoliakami*. Moscow, 1925.

Kalinichenko, P. "O deiatelnosti polskogo vremennogo revoliutsionnogo komiteta," in *Oktiabrskaia revoliutsiia i zarubezhnye slavianskie narody*, ed. A. Ia. Manusevich. Moscow, 1957.

Kamenskaia N. V. *Belorusskii narod v borbe za Sovetskuiu vlast*. Minsk, 1963.

Kancewicz, Jan. "SDKPiL wobec zagadnień wojny, rewolucji i niepodległości Polski w latach 1914-1918," in *Ruch robotniczy i ludowy w Polsce w latach 1914-1923*. Warsaw, 1961.

Katelbach, Tadeusz. "Rola Piłsudskiego w sprawie polsko-litewskiej," *Niepodległość*, n.s., 1 (1948), 101-116.

Komarnicki, Titus. "Piłsudski a polityka wielkich mocarstw zachodnich," *Niepodległość*, n.s., 4 (1952), 17-106.

—— *Rebirth of the Polish Republic*. London, 1957.

Komarnicki, Wacław. "Odbudowa państwowości polskiej na ziemiach wschodnich," *Rocznik Prawniczy Wileński*, III (1929), v-l.

Kon, Feliks. *Natsionalnyi vopros v Polshe*. Moscow, 1927.

Kondrashev, I. F., and Kirillov N. V. *Ocherki istorii SSSR 1917-1962*. Moscow, 1963.

Korbel, Josef. *Poland between East and West: Soviet and German Diplomacy toward Poland, 1919-1933*. Princeton, 1963.

Kowalski, Józef. "Z zagadnień rozwoju ideologicznego KPRP w latach 1918-1923," in *Ruch robotniczy i ludowy w Polsce w latach 1914-1923*. Warsaw, 1961.

Kozłowski, Leon (L. Kozlovskii). *Russkaia revoliutsiia i nezavisimost Polshi*. Paris, 1922.

Krasuski, Jerzy. *Stosunki polsko-niemieckie 1919-1925*. Poznań, 1962.

Kucharzewski Jan. *Od białego caratu do czerwonego*. 7 vols. Warsaw, 1923-1935.

Kukiel, Marian. *Dzieje Polski porozbiorowe, 1795-1921*. London, 1961.

Kulichenko, Mikhail I. *Borba kommunisticheskoi partii za reshenie natsionalnogo voprosa v 1918-1920 godakh*. Kharkov, 1963.

Kutrzeba, Stanisław. *Przeciwieństwa i źródła polskiej i rosyjskiej kultury*. Lwow, 1916.

Kutrzeba, Tadeusz. "Odpowiedź Gen. Denikinowi," *Gazeta Polska*, December 9-12, 1937.

―――― *Wyprawa kijowska 1920 roku*. Warsaw, 1937.

Kutschabsky, W. *Die Westukraine im Kampfe mit Polen und dem Bolschewismus in den Jahren 1918-1923*. Berlin, 1934.

Kuzmin, N. F. *Krushenie poslednego pokhoda Antanty*. Moscow, 1958.

Lapinskii, M. N., ed. *Russko-polskie otnosheniia v period mirovoi voiny*. Moscow, 1926.

Lappo, I. I. *Zapadnaia Rossiia i eia soedinenie s Polsheiu*. Prague, 1929.

Lapter, Karol. "Rewolucja październikowa i niepodległość Polski," *Sprawy Międzynarodowe*, 10, no. 11 (1957), 13-25.

―――― "Zarys stosunków polsko-radzieckich w latach 1917-1960." Mimeographed. Warsaw, 1961.

Leder, V. "Natsionalnyi vopros v polskoi i russkoi Sotsial-demokratii," *Proletarskia Revoliutsiia*, nos. 2-3 (Feb.–March 1927), 148-208.

Leder, Z. "Lenin i niepodległość Polski," *Z Pola Walki*, nos. 9-10 (1930) 88-107.

Lednicki, Wacław. "Rosyjsko-polska Entente Cordiale: jej początki i fundamenty 1903-1905," *Zeszyty Historyczne*, 10 (1966), 9-138.

―――― *Russia, Poland and the West: Essays in Literary and Cultural History*. New York, 1954.

Leinwand, Artur. *Polska Partia Socjalistyczna wobec wojny polsko-radzieckiej, 1919-1920*. Warsaw, 1964.

Lewandowski, Józef. *Federalizm, Litwa i Białoruś w polityce obozu belwederskiego:listopad 1918—kwiecień 1920*. Warsaw, 1962.

Libert, Feliks, "Nowy cel wojny," *Niepodległość*, n.s., 3 (1951), 30-45.

Likholat, A. V. *Razgrom natsionalisticheskoi kontrrevoliutsii na Ukraine 1917-1922*. Moscow, 1954.

Lipiński, Wacław. "Sprawy wojskowych formacyj polskich na wschodzie według relacji ks. Kazimierza Lutosławskiego," *Niepodległość*, 16 (1937), 633-645.

――――. *Walka zbrojna o niepodległość Polski 1905-1918*. Warsaw, 1931.

―――― *Z dziejów dawnych i najnowszych* Warsaw, 1934.

Łossowski, Piotr. *Stosunki polsko-litewskie w latach 1918-1920*. Warsaw, 1966.

―――― "Próba przewrotu polskiego w Kownie w sierpniu 1919 r.,"

Najnowsze Dzieje Polski: materiały i studia z okresu 1914-1939, 8 (1964), 51-74.

Łukasiewicz, Juliusz, *Polska w Europie w polityce Józefa Piłsudskiego*. London, 1944.

———— "Uwagi o polityce ukraińskiej marszałka Piłsudskiego," *Wiadomości Polskie*, 50/92 (1941).

Łukawski, Zygmunt. "Polityka polskich organizacji w Rosji w sprawie powrotu uchodźców do kraju 1917-1918," *Kwartalnik Historyczny*, 74 (1967).

Mackiewicz, Stanisław. *Historia Polski od 11 listopada 1918 r. do 17 września 1939 r.* London, 1941.

Maiskii, I. *Vneshniaia politika RSFSR 1917-1922*. Moscow, 1923.

Malinowski, Henryk. "Walki polskiej klasy robotniczej w latach 1918-1919," in *Rewolucja październikowa a Polska*, ed. Tadeusz Cieślak and Leon Grosfeld. Warsaw, 1967.

Manusevich, A. Ia. "Deiatelnost polskikh sotsial-demokraticheskikh organizatsii v Rossii v period podgotovki oktiabrskoi revoliutsii: mart-oktiabr 1917 g.," in *Oktiabrskaia revoliutsiia i zarubezhnye slavianskie narody*, ed. A. Ia. Manusevich. Moscow, 1957.

Meissner, Boris. *Sowjetunion und Selbstbestimmungsrecht*. Cologne, 1962.

Meyer, A. G. *Leninism*. Cambridge, Mass., 1957.

Mezheninov, S. A. *Nachalo borby s Poliakami na Ukraine v 1920 g.* Moscow, 1926.

Miedziński, Bogusław. "Wojna i pokój," *Kultura*, nos. 5/223, 6/224, 9/227, 11/229 May, June, September, November, 1966.

Mienski, J. "The Establishment of the Belorussian SSR," *Belorussian Review*, 1 (1955), 5-33.

Misko, M. V. *Oktiabrskaia revoliutsiia i vosstanovlenie nezavisimosti Polshi*. Moscow, 1957.

Molenda, Jan. "Masy chłopskie i ruch ludowy w czasie wojny 1914-1918," in *Ruch robotniczy i ludowy w Polsce w latach 1914-1923*. Warsaw. 1961.

Mościcki, Henryk. *Pod berłem carów*. Warsaw, 1924.

Najdus, Walentyna. "Polacy we władzach republiki litewsko-białoruskiej 1919," *Kwartalnik Historyczny*, 74 (1967).

Nettl, J. P. *Rosa Luxemburg*. 2 vols. London, 1966.

Nicolson, Harold. *Curzon: The Last Phase, 1919-1925*. London, 1934.

Nikulin, Lev. *Tukhachevskii*. Moscow, 1964.

Ochota, Jan. "Unieważnienie aktów rozbiorowych przez Rosję," *Sprawy Obce*, 1 (1930), 283-314.

Oznobishin, D. V. "Vneshnepoliticheskie pobedy sovetskogo naroda i mezhdunarodnaia solidarnost trudiashchikhsia v 1919 g." in *Reshaiushchie pobedy sovetskogo naroda nad interventami i belogvardeitsami v 1919 g.*, ed. C. F. Naida. Moscow, 1960.

———— *Ot Bresta do Iureva: Iz istorii vneshnei politiki sovetskoi vlasti 1917-1920 gg.* Moscow, 1966.

Page, Stanley W. "Lenin and Self-Determination," *Slavonic and East European Review*, 28 (April 1950), 342-355.

—— *Lenin and World Revolution.* New York, 1959.

Perl, Feliks (Res.) *Dzieje ruchu socjalistycznego w zaborze rosyjskim do powstania PPS.* Warsaw, 1958.

Pipes, Richard, E. "Domestic Politics and Foreign Affairs," in *Russian Foreign Policy,* ed. Ivo J. Lederer. New Haven, 1962.

—— *The Formation of the Soviet Union: Communism and Nationalism, 1917-1923.* Cambridge, Mass., 1964.

Pobóg-Malinowski, Władysław. *Najnowsza historia polityczna Polski, 1864-1945.* 3 vols. Paris, London, 1956-1960.

Pogodin, A. L. *Glavnyia techeniia polskoi politicheskoi mysli 1863-1907.* St. Petersburg, 1908.

Pokrovskii, Mikhail N. *Vneshniaia politika Rossii v XX veke.* Moscow, 1926.

Pragier, Adam. "Polityka ukraińska Piłsudskiego," *Wiadomości Polskie,* 42/84 (1941).

Próchnik, Adam (Henryk Swoboda). *Pierwsze piętnastolecie Polski niepodległej 1918-1933.* Warsaw, 1957.

Przybylski, Adam. *Wojna polska 1918-1921.* Warsaw, 1930.

Rabinovich, Samuil E. *Istoriia grazhdanskoi voiny.* Moscow, 1933.

Radek, Karl, and Stefanovich, R. *Perevorot v Polshe i Pilsudskii.* Moscow, 1926.

Rauch, Georg von. *Russland, staatliche Einheit und nationale Vielfalt.* Munich, 1953.

Reguła, Jan A., *Historia komunistycznej partii Polski.* Warsaw, 1934.

Reshetar, John S. *The Ukrainian Revolution 1917-1920.* Princeton, 1952.

Rosenfeld, Günther. *Sowjetrussland und Deutschland, 1917-1922.* Berlin, 1960.

Rozwadowski, Adam. *Generał Rozwadowski.* Cracow, 1929.

Ryazanov, David (Rjazanoff, N.). "Karl Marx und Friedrich Engels über die Polen Frage," *Archiv für die Geschichte des Sozialismus und der Arbeiterbewegung,* 6 (1916), 175-221.

Schapiro, Leonard. *The Communist Party of the Soviet Union.* New York, 1959.

Shelukhin, S. P. *Varshavskyi dohovir mizh Poliakamy i S. Petliuroiu 21 kvitnia 1920 roku.* Prague, 1926.

Shub, David. *Lenin: A Biography.* Garden City, N.Y., 1948.

Sieradzki, Józef. *Białowieża i Mikaszewicze.* Warsaw, 1959.

Skrzyński, Count Aleksander. *Poland and Peace.* London, 1923.

Slisz, Andrzej. "Odbicie rewolucji październikowej w czasopismach polskich w Piotrogradzie i Moskwie," in *Rewolucja październikowa a Polska,* ed. Tadeusz Cieślak and Leon Grosfeld. Warsaw, 1967.

Sokolnicki, Michał. "Józef Piłsudski a zagadnienie Rosji," *Niepodległość,* n.s., 2 (1950), 51-70.

Speidel, Hans von. "Reichswehr und Rote Armee," *Vierteljahrshefte für Zeitgeschichte,* 1 (1953), 9-45.

Spustek, Irena. "Sprawa Polski w polityce Rosji w roku 1916," *Najnowsze Dzieje Polski: materiały i studia z okresu 1914-1939,* 2 (1959), 5-33.

Stachiewicz, Julian. *Działania zaczepne 3 armii na Ukrainie.* Warsaw, 1925.

Stankiewicz, Witold. "Ruch ludowy w Polsce w latach 1918-1923," in *Ruch robotniczy i ludowy w Polsce w latach 1914-1923.* Warsaw, 1961.

Starzewski, Jan. "Zarys dziejów polskiej polityki zagranicznej." Mimeographed. London, 1944.

Stein, B. E. *Die "Russische Frage" auf der Pariser Friedenskonferenz 1919-1920.* Leipzig, 1953.

Sukiennicki, Wiktor, "Przyczyny i początek wojny polsko-sowieckiej 1919-1921," *Bellona,* 45 (1963), 11-42, 145-201.

―――― "Stalin and Belorussia's 'Independence,' " *Polish Review,* 10 (Autumn 1965), 84-107.

Suslov, P. V. *Politicheskoe obespechenie sovetsko-polskoi kampanii 1920 goda.* Moscow and Leningrad, 1930.

Szandruk, Paweł. "Organizacja wojska ukraińskiego na Podolu z początkiem r. 1920 i wyprawa na Mohylów," *Bellona,* 29 (1928), 202-218.

Taracouzio, T. A. *The Soviet Union and International Law.* New York, 1935.

Teslar, Tadeusz. *Polityka Rosji sowieckiej podczas wojny z Polską.* Warsaw, 1937.

―――― *Propaganda bolszewicka podczas wojny polsko-rosyjskiej 1920 roku.* Warsaw, 1938.

Thompson, John M. *Russia, Bolshevism, and the Versailles Peace.* Princeton, 1966.

Trukhanovskii, V. G., ed. *Istoriia mezhdunarodnykh otnoshenii i vneshnei politiki SSSR, 1917-1960 gg.* Moscow, 1961.

Trzciński, Wit. "Uznanie niepodległości Polski przez Rosję," *Niepodległość,* 8 (1933), 301-304.

Tych, Feliks. "Stosunek SDKPiL, PPS-Lewicy i KPRP do rewolucji październikowej," in *Rewolucja październikowa a Polska,* ed. Tadeusz Cieślak and Leon Grosfeld. Warsaw, 1967.

―――― "Z dziejów PPS-Lewicy w latach wojny 1914–1918," in *Ruch robotniczy i ludowy w Polsce w latach, 1914-1923.* Warsaw, 1961.

―――― and Schumacher, Horst. *Julian Marchlewski: szkic biograficzny.* Warsaw, 1966.

Ulam, Adam B. *The Bolsheviks.* New York, 1965.

―――― "Nationalism, Panslavism, Communism," in *Russian Foreign Policy,* ed. Ivo J. Lederer. New Haven, 1962.

Umiastowski, Roman. *Russia and the Polish Republic 1918-1941.* London, 1945.

Valenta, Jaroslaw. "Polská otázka a říjnová revoluce," *Slovanské Historické Studie,* 5 (1963) 125-204.

Vygodskii, S. Iu. *V. I. Lenin: rukovoditel vneshnei politiki Sovetskogo gosudarstva, 1917-1923.* Leningrad, 1960.

Wandycz, Piotr S. *France and her Eastern Allies, 1919-1925.* Minneapolis, 1962.

———— "General Weygand and the Battle of Warsaw of 1920," *Journal of Central European Affairs,* 19 (January 1960), 357-365.

———— "Secret Soviet-Polish Peace Talks in 1919," *Slavic Review,* 24 (September 1965), 425-449.

Warski, Adolf. "SDKPiL wobec II zjazdu SDPRR: 20 letni spór z Leninem," *Z Pola Walki,* nos. 5-6 (1929), 8-50.

Wasilewski, Leon (L. Płochocki). *Rosyjskie partye polityczne i ich stosunek do sprawy polskiej.* Cracow, 1905 (?).

Wehler, Hans-Ulrich. *Sozialdemokratie und Nationalstaat.* Würzburg, 1962.

Wereszycki, Henryk, *Historia polityczna Polski w dobie popowstaniowej 1864-1918.* Warsaw, 1948.

Wolfe, Bertram D. *Three Who Made a Revolution.* Boston, 1948.

Zdziechowski, Marian. *U epoki mesjanizmu.* Lwow, 1912.

———— "Z historii stosunków polsko-rosyjskich nazajutrz po wojnie światowej 1919-1920," *Przegląd Współczesny,* 58 (August 1936), 33-55.

Żółtowski, Adam. *A Border of Europe: A Study of the Polish Eastern Provinces.* London, 1950.

Zubov, Nikolai I. *F. E. Dzerzhinskii: biografiia.* Moscow, 1965.

Zuev, Fedor G., *Mezhdunarodnyi imperializm organizator napadenia panskoi Polshi na sovetskuiu Rossiiu, 1919-1920.* Moscow, 1954.

4   Additional Journals and Newspapers

The following includes only those journals and newspapers for which specific articles have not been listed in the bibliography.

Gazeta Warszawska
Izvestia
Kurjer Polski
Kurjer Poranny
Monitor Polski
Pravda
Rząd i Wojsko
Z Dokumentów Chwili

Abbreviations Used in the Notes

AGND   Akta Adiutantury Generalnej Naczelnego Dowództwa, Józef Piłsudski Institute of America, New York.

AMM   Archiwum Michała Mościckiego, Józef Piłsudski Institute of America, New York.

APGE   Archive of the Polish Government-in-Exile (Documents from the Polish Embassy in London), Montreal.

AR   Akta Generała Rozwadowskiego, Józef Piłsudski Institute of America, New York.

AREEH   Archive of Russian and East European History and Culture, Columbia University, New York.

DBFP   *Documents on British Foreign Policy, 1918-1945*, 1st series, ed. E. L. Woodward and R. Butler. London: 1947—.

DVP SSRR   *Dokumenty vneshnei politiki SSSR*. Moscow: Ministerstvo Inostrannykh Del SSSR, 1959—.

PRO, Cab.   Public Record Office, Cabinet Records, London.

PRO, F.O.   Public Record Office, Foreign Office Records, London.

Notes

Chapter 1.   The Heritage of the Past

1. V. I. Lenin, *Sochineniia* (3rd ed.; 30 vols.; Moscow, 1935-1937), XXV, 482. Unless otherwise noted, all quotations are from the 3rd edition.

2. "Lettres sur la philosophie de l'histoire 1829-1831," in Mikhail O. Gershenzon, ed., *Sochineniia i pisma P.Ya. Chaadaeva* (2 vols.; Moscow, 1913-1914), I, 138.

3. K. N. Iarosh, *Russko-polskiia otnosheniia* (Kharkov,1898), *passim.* Compare with Stanisław Kutrzeba, *Przeciwieństwa i źródła polskiej i rosyjskiej kultury* (Lwow, 1916), pp. 25-40.

4. *Russia: A History and an Interpretation* (2 vols.; New York, 1946), II, 1475.

5. See Manfred Kridl, Władysław Malinowski, and Józef Wittlin, eds., *For Your Freedom and Ours: Polish Progressive Spirit through the Centuries* (New York, 1943), pp. 32, 67.

6. The phrase is Dostoevsky's, cited in Wacław Lednicki, *Russia, Poland and the West: Essays in Literary and Cultural History* (New York, 1954), p. 32.

7. See an interesting discussion of this point in Michał Bobrzyński, *Dzieje Polski w zarysie* (3 vols.; Warsaw, 1927-1931), II, 290-292.

8. See Wilhelm Feldman, *Dzieje polskiej myśli politycznej w okresie porozbiorowym* (3 vols.; Cracow and Warsaw, 1913-1920), I, 230; Iarosh, *Russko-polskiia otnosheniia*, p. 27.

9. See *Slavs in European History and Civilization* (New Brunswick, 1962), pp. 221-222.

10. *Istoriia gosudarstva rossiiskago* (12 vols.; St. Petersburg, 1892), XII, 153. Compare Bobrzyński, *Dzieje*, II, 192.

11. Wacław Sobieski, *Żółkiewski na Kremlu* (Warsaw, 1920), pp. 211-213.

12. Chancellor Nikolai Panin viewed the acquired lands as "resembling Poland in habits and customs of the people." Cited by Adam Żółtowski, *A Border of Europe: A Study of the Polish Eastern Provinces* (London, 1950), p. 69. Nicholas I felt that the "former Polish provinces" were inhabited by the compatriots of the Poles, and a nineteenth-century Russian geography textbook described the Poles as a "nation comprising the largest part of the population of the Kingdom of Poland and of the gubernia detached from Poland." Cited by I. I. Lappo, *Zapadnaia Rossiia i eia soedinenie s Polsheiu* (Prague, 1929), pp. 28-29, 69.

13. See Robert H. Lord, *The Second Partition of Poland* (Cambridge, Mass., 1915), pp. 41-43.

14. Sir Robert Wilson, cited in Żółtowski, *A Border of Europe*, p. 89.

15. Cited in Feldman, *Dzieje polskiej myśli politycznej*, I, 82. Kościuszko imagined the relationship between Russia and Poland similar to that between Austria and Hungary. See his letter to Czartoryski, June 13, 1815, in Leonard Chodźko, *Recueil des traités, conventions et actes diplomatiques concernant la Pologne* (Paris, 1862), pp. 700-701.

16. Chodźko, *Recueil*, p. 735.

17. This is well brought out by Hedwig Fleischhacker, *Russische Antworten auf die polnische Frage, 1795-1917* (Munich, Berlin, 1941), pp. 29-31.

18. Richard Pipes, ed., *Karamzin's Memoir on Ancient and Modern Russia* (Cambridge, Mass., 1959), p. 145.

19. Statement ascribed to Pozzo di Borgo in 1814, cited in Karl Marx, *Manuskripte über die polnische Frage: 1863-1864,* ed. Werner Conze and Dieter Hertz-Eichenrode (The Hague, 1961), pp. 145-146.

20. See the map in Pestel, "Russkaia pravda," in *Vosstanie dekabristov: dokumenty* (11 vols.; Moscow, 1925-1954), VII, 130.

21. Cited by Jan Kucharzewski, *Od białego caratu do czerwonego* (7 vols.; Warsaw, 1923-1935), II, 306.

22. Cited in Kridl, Malinowski, and Wittlin, *For Your Freedom and Ours*, p. 81.

23. Karol Libelt, cited by Feldman, *Dzieje polskiej myśli politycznej*, I, 205.

24. A. I. Herzen, "Byloye i dumy," *Sobranie sochinenii* (Moscow, 1954—), XI, 367.

25. Cited by Marceli Handelsman, *Adam Czartoryski* (3 vols.; Warsaw, 1948-1950), II, 184.

26. Cited in Chodźko, *Recueil*, pp. 1117-1118.

27. Quoted by R. F. Leslie, *Reform and Insurrection in Russian Poland, 1856-1865* (London, 1963), pp. 138-139.

28. So wrote Prince Bariatynskii to Alexander II, cited by Kucharzewski, *Od białego caratu*, IV, 80.

29. For a recent discussion see Henryk Wereszycki, "Spór o powstanie styczniowe," *Odra*, no. 5 (27), May, 1963, 33-40.

Chapter 2.   The Background

1. Quoted in Hans Kohn, ed., *The Mind of Modern Russia* (New York, 1962), p. 216.

2. Quoted in Henryk Wereszycki, *Historia polityczna Polski w dobie popowstaniowej 1864-1918* (Warsaw, 1948), p. 69.

3. For a Russian description see A. L. Pogodin, *Glavnyia techeniia polskoi politicheskoi mysli 1863-1907* (St. Petersburg, 1908), pp. 10-11, 47-49.

4. See details in Henryk Mościcki, *Pod berłem carów* (Warsaw, 1924), p. 193.

5. This point is well developed in R. F. Leslie, *Reform and Insurrection in Russian Poland, 1856-1865* (London, 1963), p. 249.

6. See the program of *Kraj* in Wilhelm Feldman, *Dzieje polskiej myśli politycznej w okresie porozbiorowym* (3 vols.; Warsaw and Cracow, 1913-1920), II, 258-259.

7. As evidenced by Imeretinskii's report to the tsar, copied and circulated by Polish socialist organizations.

8. Stanisław Kozicki, *Historia Ligi Narodowej: okres 1867-1907* (London, 1964), pp. 473-474.

9. Ignacy Daszyński cited in Kridl, Malinowski, and Wittlin, eds., *For Your Freedom and Ours* (New York, 1943), p. 176.

10. See especially D. Ryazanoff, "Karl Marx und Friedrich Engels über die Polenfrage," *Archiv für die Geschichte des Sozialismus und der Arbeiterbewegung,* 6 (1916); *Marks i Engels o Polsce,* ed. Helena Michnik, (2 vols.; Warsaw, 1960); Karl Marx and Friedrich Engels, *The Russian Menace to Europe,* ed. Paul W. Blackstock and Bert F. Hoselitz (Glencoe, Ill., 1952); Marx, *Manuskripte über die polnische Frage: 1863-1864,* ed., Werner Conze and Dieter Hertz-Eichenrode (The Hague, 1961); Hans-Ulrich Wehler, *Sozialdemokratie und Nationalstaat* (Würzburg, 1962); Władysław Gumplowicz, *Kwestya polska a socjalizm* (Warsaw, 1908); Celina Bobińska, *Marks i Engels a sprawy polskie do osiemdziesiątych lat XIX wieku* (Warsaw, 1955).

11. See *Neue Rheinische Zeitung,* August 20, 1848.

12. *Commonwealth,* March 31, 1866.

13. See Marx's statement in 1875, Engels' letter to Kautsky of 1882, and the preface to the Polish edition of the *Communist Manifesto.* See *Marks i Engels o Polsce,* II, 103-104, 205; and Marx and Engels, *The Russian Menace,* pp. 116-120.

14. Program of 1894 cited in Wereszycki, *Historia polityczna,* p. 143.

15. *Die industrielle Entwicklung Polens* (Leipzig, 1896). For a refutation of Rosa Luxemburg's position see Gumplowicz, *Kwestya,* pp. 65-115, and the famous article by Karl Kautsky, "Finis Poloniae," *Die Neue Zeit,* 2, nos. 42-43 (1895-1896), 484-491, 513-535. Compare J. P. Nettl, *Rosa Luxemburg* (2 vols.; London, 1966), II, 842-862.

16. Quoted by Jan Kucharzewski, *Od białego caratu do czerwonego* (7 vols.; Warsaw, 1923–1935), III, 229.

17. Quoted in *Marks i Engels o Polsce,* II, 73.

18. See Feliks Perl (Res), *Dzieje ruchu socjalistycznego w zaborze rosyjskim do powstania PPS* (Warsaw, 1958), pp. 208-225.

19. Marx wrote Engels on March 24, 1870 that "the main task of the Russian section [of the International] is to work for the cause of Poland," and he added in parentheses, *"viz.,* to free Europe from their own [Russian] neighborhood" (*Marks i Engels o Polsce,* II, 74).

20. Thus Engels wrote Marx on May 23, 1851 that Poland could be useful as long as Russia herself "would not be drawn into the

whirlpool of agrarian revolution." He added: "what is Warsaw and Cracow, compared to Petersburg, to Moscow?" (*ibid.*, I, 251, 253).

21. Engels in 1874. See Marx and Engels, *Russian Menace*, p. 115.

22. Among the numerous works that discuss Lenin's theory of national self-determination the following are particularly useful: Richard Pipes, *The Formation of the Soviet Union: Communism and Nationalism, 1917-1923* (Cambridge, Mass., 1964), pp. 29-49; E. H. Carr, *The Bolshevik Revolution, 1917-1923* (London, 1950-1953), I; Stanley W. Page, "Lenin and Self-Determination," *Slavonic and East European Review*, 28 (April, 1950), 342-358; Boris Meissner, *Sowjetunion und Selbstbestimmungsrecht* (Cologne, 1962); Bertram D. Wolfe, *Three Who Made a Revolution* (Boston, 1948), pp. 578-590.

23. "Zadachi russkikh sotsial demokratov," 1898, in Lenin, *Sochineniia* (3rd ed., 30 vols., Moscow, 1935-1937), II, 175-178.

24. Lenin, *Sochineniia*, V, 338.

25. "Natsionalnyi vopros," 1903, *ibid.*, V, 337.

26. As the Soviet historian M. N. Pokrovskii observed, "You will not find in Lenin a single purely theoretical work; each has a propaganda aspect"; cited by Adam B. Ulam, *The Bolsheviks* (New York and London, 1965), p. 146.

27. See for instance "O manifeste armianskikh sotsial-demokratov," 1903, *Sochineniia*, V, 243.

28. "Tezisy po natsionalnomu voprosu," 1913, *ibid.*, XVI, 513.

29. *Ibid.*, XVI, 508.

30. "Kadety i pravo narodov na samoopredelenie," 1913, *ibid.*, XVII, 108-109; Letter to Shaumian, December 6, 1913, *ibid.*, XVII, 90.

31. "O natsionalnoi programe," 1913, *ibid.*, XVII, 120. Compare "K voprosu o natsionalnoi politike," 1914, *ibid.*, XVII, 327.

32. Letter to Shaumian, *ibid.*, XVII, 90.

33. See "Natsionalnyi vopros," 1903, *ibid.*, V, 338-341, and "Tezisy po natsionalnomu voprosu," 1913, *ibid.*, XVI, 508-509.

34. "O karikature na Marksizm i o imperialisticheskom ekonomizme," 1916, *ibid.*, XIX, 228.

35. See Władysław Pobóg-Malinowski, *Najnowsza historia polityczna Polski 1864-1945* (3 vols.; Paris, 1953; London, 1956-1960), I, 74; and Wereszycki, *Historia polityczna*, p. 146.

36. See Adam Ciołkosz, *Róża Luksemburg a rewolucja rosyjska* (Paris, 1961), p. 108. PPS-Frakcja will be later referred to simply as PPS while the other splinter group will be known as PPS-Left.

37. "Natsionalnyi vopros v nashci programe," 1903, *Sochineniia*, V, 338-341.

38. See *ibid.*, XVII, 713; and "O natsionalnoi programme," *ibid.*, XVII, 120.

39. "O prave natsii na samoopredelenie," 1913, *ibid.*, XVII, 427-474. Compare with the excellent analysis of Ciołkosz in *Róża Luksemburg*, p. 108-113. For a detailed discussion of Lenin's views on Polish independence as compared with those of SDKPiL, see Adolf Warski, "SDKPiL wobec II zjazdu SDPRR: 20 letni spór z Leninem," *Z Pola*

Walki, nos. 5-6 (1929), 8-50; Z. Leder, "Lenin i niepodległość Polski," *ibid.,* nos. 9-10 (1930), 88-107, and V. Leder, "Natsionalnyi vopros v polskoi i russkoi Sotsial-demokratii," *Proletarskaia Revoliutsiia,* nos. 2-3 (February–March 1930), 148-208.

40. See M. K. Dziewanowski, *The Communist Party of Poland* (Cambridge, Mass., 1959), pp. 33-34; and Leonard Schapiro, *The Communist Party of the Soviet Union* (New York, 1960), p. 107.

41. Leon Wasilewski (L. Płochocki), *Rosyjskie partye polityczne i ich stosunek do sprawy polskiej* (Cracow, 1905 [?], p. 130. Also V. M. Chernov, *Pered burei* (New York, 1953), pp. 295-296.

42. Stanisław Witkiewicz cited by Kridl, Malinowski, and Wittlin, *'Za Waszą i naszą wolność': Polska myśl demokratyczna w ciągu wieków* (London, 1945), p. 181.

43. A declaration of the Central Committee of the PPS in 1903, quoted in Pobóg-Malinowski, *Najnowsza historia,* I, 116. Compare Pipes, *Formation of the Soviet Union,* pp. 11-12.

44. See Wasilewski, *Rosyjskie partye,* pp. 130-135; Karol Grünberg, "Socjaldemokracja polska a ruch liberalny w państwie rosyjskim w 1904 r.," *Materiały i Studia,* 1, (1960), pp. 40-44.

45. See Pogodin, *Glavnyia techeniia,* introduction; Marian Zdziechowski, *U epoki mesjanizmu* (Lwów, 1912), pp. 42, 113; Wasilewski, *Rosyjskie partye,* pp. 123–135. A wealth of information is contained in Wacław Lednicki, "Rosyjsko-polska Entente Cordiale," *Zeszyty Historyczne,* 10 (1966), 9-138.

46. See Wojciech Bułat, "Zjazd polsko-rosyjski w Moskwie 21-22 kwietnia 1905 r." *Studia z Najnowszych Dziejów Powszechnych,* 2 (1962), 202-204.

47. See Pipes, *Formation of the Soviet Union,* p. 29.

48. Compare Marian Kukiel, *Dzieje Polski porozbiorowe, 1795-1921* (London, 1961), p. 472; Wereszycki, *Historia polityczna,* p. 263; Kozicki, *Historia Ligi,* pp. 290-296; Pobóg-Malinowski, *Najnowsza historia,* I, 174.

49. Polish activities in the second Duma allegedly provoked Russian fears that the Poles were preparing to struggle for cultural supremacy in Lithuania and the Ukraine. See Pogodin, *Glavnyia techeniia,* p. 615.

50. Still, as a historian rightly pointed out, the PPS-Left was never "ideologically uniform." See Feliks Tych, "Z dziejów PPS-Lewicy w latach wojny 1914-1918," in *Ruch robotniczy i ludowy w latach 1914-1923* (Warsaw, 1961), p. 192.

51. A brilliant and convincing analysis of Piłsudski's evolution is in Wereszycki, *Historia polityczna,* pp. 281-282. Compare with comments by the Socialist leader from Galicia, Daszyński, who at this time called Piłsudski a "Polish saint"; Ignacy Daszyński, *Pamiętniki* (2 vols.; Cracow, 1925-1926), I, 215.

52. As a member of the Polish Supreme National Committee (NKN) shrewdly observed in 1915, "Socialist slogans played [in the case of PPS] the same part as the watchword of peasant emancipation in the old Polish insurrectionary movements; a means of uniting broad

masses of workers behind the Polish cause." Cited by Tych, "Z dziejów PPS-Lewicy," p. 205.

53. For Piłsudski's speculations at a lecture in Paris in January 1914, see Chernov, *Pered burei,* pp. 296-297. For his subsequent denials that he had calculated the chances of victory of one side or the other see Wacław Lipiński, "Wywiad u marszałka Piłsudskiego w Sulejówku z 10 II 1924," *Niepodległość,* 7 (1933), 71. Compare Józef Piłsudski, *Pisma zbiorowe* (10 vols.; Warsaw, 1937-1938), V, 265-268; VI, 202-203.

54. See Pobóg-Malinowski, *Najnowsza historia,* I, 300.

55. See Chernov's account of his dramatic talk with Jodko-Narkiewicz in *Pered burei,* pp. 297-304.

56. See O. B. Szmidt, ed., *Socjaldemokracja Królestwa Polskiego i Litwy: materiały i dokumenty 1914-1918* (Moscow, 1936), p. xxv. Compare Jan Kancewicz, "SDKPiL wobec zagadnień wojny, rewolucji i niepodległości Polski w latach 1914-1918," *Ruch robotniczy i ludowy w latach 1914-1923* (Warsaw, 1961), pp. 136-137; also Lenin's ironic remark about Rosa Luxemburg in *Sochineniia,* XVII, 451.

57. See Kancewicz, "SDKPiL wobec zagadnień wojny," p. 130. Also Karl Radek "Das Selbstbestimmungsrecht der Völker," *Lichtstrahlen,* Oct. 13, 1915.

58. Tych, "Z dziejów PPS-Lewicy," p. 194.

59. In 1915 Dmowski stated that when the Poles spoke of Poland they meant "ethnographic Poland." See the minutes of a Russo-Polish meeting presided over by Premier I. L. Goremykin and cited in Szymon Askenazy, *Uwagi* (Warsaw, 1924), p. 400.

60. The Russian diplomat, Rosen, cited by Alexander Dallin, "The Future of Poland," in A. Dallin *et al., Russian Diplomacy and Eastern Europe, 1914-1917* (New York, 1963), p. 4.

61. M. N. Lapinskii, ed., *Russko-polskie otnosheniia v period mirovoi voiny* (Moscow, 1926), p. 15. Also Dallin, "The Future of Poland," pp. 14-15.

62. Cited in Dallin, "The Future of Poland," p. 58.

63. See Irena Spustek, "Sprawa Polski w polityce Rosji w roku 1916," *Najnowsze Dzieje Polski: materiały i studia z okresu 1914-39,* 2 (1959), 28-32.

64. "The Future of Poland," pp. 74-75.

65. For an excellent discussion of the effect this had on the problem of nationalities, see Pipes, *The Formation of the Soviet Union,* pp. 50-53. Compare Titus Komarnicki, *Rebirth of the Polish Republic* (London, 1957), pp. 152-153.

66. *Materiały archiwalne do historii stosunków polsko-radzieckich,* ed. Natalia Gąsiorowska, (Warsaw, 1957), I, 41; cited hereafter as *Materiały archiwalne.* Compare Zygmunt Nagórski, Sr., "Aleksander Lednicki: 1866-1934," *Zeszyty Historyczne,* 1 (1962), 28.

67. The most detailed account of the events discussed here can be found in Nagórski, "Aleksander Lednicki"; Leon Kozłowski, *Russkaia revoliutsiia i nezavisimost Polshi* (Paris, 1922); Askenazy, *Uwagi;* and

Komarnicki, *Rebirth of the Polish Republic*. All the dates are given here according to the Western calendar.

68. See Robert P. Browder and Alexander F. Kerensky, eds., *The Russian Provisional Government 1917: Documents* (3 vols.; Stanford, Calif., 1961), I, 320.

69. For a stenogram of this important meeting see *Zhurnal zasedanii vremennago pravitelstva* (2 vols.; Petrograd, 1917), session of March 15/28, pp. 1-2.

70. Browder and Kerensky, *Provisional Government*, I, 328.

71. The text of the clause is cited in *Z Dokumentów Chwili*, no. 37, May 17, 1917, pp. 61-62.

72. English text in Browder and Kerensky, *Provisional Government*, I, 321. Russian text, accompanied by speeches of representatives of PPS-Left and SDKPiL in the Soviet, in *Materiały archiwalne*, I, 1-3 and in *Dokumenty i materiały do historii stosunków polsko-radzieckich* (Warsaw: Polska Akademia Nauk and Akademia Nauk ZSRR, 1962–), I, 8-10 (hereafter cited as *Dokumenty i materiały*).

73. See *Kalendarz Robotniczy PPS* (Warsaw, 1919), p. 25; Askenazy, *Uwagi*, p. 458; Wit Trzciński, "Uznanie niepodległości Polski przez Rosję,"*Niepodległość*, 8 (1933), 302; Tadeusz Teslar, *Polityka Rosji sowieckiej podczas wojny z Polską* (Warsaw, 1937), p. 22.

74. See M. V. Misko, *Oktiabrskaia revoliutsiia i vosstanovlenie nezavisimosti Polshi* (Moscow, 1957), pp. 56-57.

75. See P. Miliukov, "Aleksander Lednicki," *Przegląd Współczesny*, 18, no. 3 (203) (March, 1939), 207. Compare A. Lednicki, "P. N. Miliukov i polskii vopros," *P. N. Miliukov: sbornik materialov . . . 1859-1929,* ed. S. A. Smirnov *et al.* (Paris, 1929), pp. 216-217.

76. For instance Komarnicki, *Rebirth of the Polish Republic*, pp. 155-156.

77. *Zhurnal zasedanii*, March 10/23, 1917, I. 6.

78. For a fairly convincing analysis see Kozłowski, *Russkaia revoliutsiia*, pp. 40-41.

79. See protocol of the meeting in *Zhurnal zasedanii*, March 29/16, 1917, pp. 11-13. The English translation of the declaration is in Browder and Kerensky, *Provisional Government*, I, 322-323.

80. It is interesting that while the declaration was widely discussed in *Z Dokumentów Chwili* on April 21, the first mention of the Soviet's manifesto appeared only on April 30, 1917. See nos. 33-35. For the impact on the kingdom see Leon Grosfeld, "Wpływ rewolucji lutowej na Królestwo," *Kwartalnik Historyczny*, 63, nos. 4-5 (1956), 381-394.

81. Declaration of April 6, 1917, *Materiały archiwalne*, I, 418-419.

82. See for instance the declaration adopted between May 19 and 22, 1917 and signed by National Democrats, PPS, Polish Peasant Party (PSL) and ten other parties, in the Wislowski *Collection*, box 3, Hoover Institution, Stanford, Calif. Also see the resolutions of the 13th congress of PPS in box 1.

83. For the message of April 5, 1917 see *Materiały archiwalne*, I, 417-418.

84. Askenazy, *Uwagi,* p. 179.
85. Cited in Browder and Kerensky, *Provisional Government,* I, 323–347.
86. Askenazy, *Uwagi,* p. 461.
87. Quoted in Pobóg-Malinowski, *Najnowsza historia,* I, 319n.
88. MS Dnevnik P. N. Miliukova, pp. 21-22. Archive of Russian and East European History and Culture, Columbia University, (hereafter cited as AREEH). For a somewhat optimistic appraisal of the Russian attitude toward Poland see Lednicki to Paderewski, August 1917, Archiwum Paderewskiego, t. 1384, Archiwum Akt Nowych, select documents in Polska Akademia Nauk, Zakład Historii Stosunków Polsko-Radzieckich, Warsaw.
89. "O prave natsii," 1914, *Sochineniia,* XVII, 448.
90. *Ibid.,* XX, 278.
91. Lenin won by a narrow margin of 42 votes against 21 and 15 abstentions. See Georg von Rauch, *Russland, staatliche Einheit und nationale Vielfalt* (Munich, 1953), p. 202.
92. "Rech v zashchitu rezoliutsii o voine," *Sochineniia,* 4th ed., XXIV, 231.

Chapter 3. The Bolshevik Revolution

1. See "O levom rebiachestve i o melkoburzhuaznosti," in *Sochineniia* (3rd ed., 30 vols., Moscow, 1935-1937), XXII, 510. Compare Lenin's remarks about pacifism in "O mire bez anneksii i o nezavisimosti Polshi kak lozungakh dnia v Rossii," and "O programme mira" in 1916, *ibid.,* XIX, 30-32, 49-54. Also see the statements at the Seventh Party Conference in May 1917 in *ibid.,* XX, 278.
2. Numerous statements of Lenin that revolution in one country was unthinkable are conveniently listed in A. G. Meyer, *Leninism* (Cambridge, Mass., 1957), p. 220.
3. See the English text in Jane Degras, ed., *Soviet Documents on Foreign Policy, 1917-1941* (3 vols.; London, and New York, 1951-1953), I, 1; Russian text in *Dokumenty vneshnei politiki* SSSR (Moscow: Ministerstvo Inostrannykh Del SSSR, 1959), I, 11-14. Hereafter cited as *DVP SSSR.*
4. Russian text in *DVP SSSR,* I, 14-15.
5. *Mirnye peregovory v Brest-Litovske s 22/9 dekabria 1917 do 3 marta 18 febralia 1918 g.,* Tom I: *plenarnye zasedaniia, zasedaniia politicheskoi komissii* (Moscow: Narodnyi Kommissariat Inostrannykh Del, 1920), pp. 92-93. *Proceedings of the Brest-Litovsk Peace Conference: 21 November 1917-3 March 1918* (Washington, 1918), pp. 80-81. Hereafter cited respectively as *Mirnye peregovory* and *Proceedings of Brest-Litovsk.*
6. *Mirnye pregovory,* pp. 7-8, 29; *Proceedings of Brest-Litovsk,* p. 39, 44. Italics added.
7. See the declaration of the PPS, Polish Peasant Party, and others,

January 1, 1918, in Henryk Jabłoński, "Międzynarodowe warunki odbudowy niepodległości Polski w 1918 r.," *Ruch robotniczy i ludowy w latach 1914-1923* (Warsaw, 1961), pp. 38-39; and in *Materiały archiwalne do historii stosunków polsko-radzieckich,* ed. Natalia Gąsiorowska (Warsaw, 1957—), I, 515-517.

8. See text of resolution in *Materiały archiwalne,* I, 429; also *Dokumenty i materiały do historii stosunków polsko-radzieckich* (Warsaw, 1962) I, 47.

9. "Sudby Polshi," *Izvestia,* Dec. 10/23, 1917; reprinted in *Dokumenty i materiały,* I, 555-557; and also see "Eshche o sudbakh Polshi," *Izvestia,* Dec. 17/30, 1917.

10. "Beseda s tov. Trotskiim," *Izvestia,* Dec. 20, 1917/Jan. 2, 1918; English translation in Degras, *Soviet Documents,* I, 27.

11. On Feb. 3, 1918, *Proceedings of Brest-Litovsk,* p. 149; *Mirnye peregovory,* p. 158.

12. Henryk Wereszycki, *Historia polityczna Polski w dobie popowstaniowej 1864-1918* (Warsaw, 1948), p. 329; Leon Grosfeld, *Polskie reakcyjne formacje wojskowe w Rosji 1917-1919* (Warsaw, 1956), p. 83; Henryk Jabłoński, *Polityka Polskiej Partii Socjalistycznej w czasie wojny 1914-1918 r.* (Warsaw, 1958), p. 622. Only the last author mentions a source by referring to the "Scandinavian press." My search for more information yielded no result.

13. Kamenev wrote that the German program opposed the extension of the principles of the Russian revolution "to territories exploited by Polish capitalists and the Baltic barons"; *Izvestia,* Jan. 12/25, 1918.

14. Pipes's view that "It is not far-fetched to assert that at the beginning of 1918 Russia, as a political concept, had ceased to exist" (*The Formation of The Soviet Union* [Cambridge, Mass., 1964], p. 108) corresponds to a contemporary opinion of a Polish Socialist, Bronisław Siwik, who wrote on December 2, 1917 that "In actual fact Russia is no more; there are individual gubernia, towns, districts, which live a life of their own" (*Materiały archiwalne,* I, 124).

15. See "Kontrrevoliutsiia i narody Rossii," Aug. 13, 1917, in J. V. Stalin, *Sochineniia,* (13 vols.; Moscow, 1946-1951), III, 208.

16. "Otvet tovarishcham Ukraintsam," Dec. 12, 1917, *ibid.,* IV, 8. Italics added.

17. *Ibid.,* IV, 31-32.

18. See *Tretii vserossiskii sezd sovetov rabochikh, soldatskikh i krestianskikh deputatov* (St. Petersburg, 1918), pp. 74-94.

19. *Ibid.,* p. 94; *DVP. SSSR,* I, 93-94.

20. See especially articles 6, 7, and 49B in *Istoriia Sovetskoi konstitutsii v dokumentakh, 1917-1956* (Moscow, 1957), pp. 142-157. The constitution was purposely vague about the territorial limits of the federation.

21. Interviews in *Pravda,* April 3, 4, 1918. See Stalin, *Sochineniia,* IV, 69, 73.

22. "Ocherednye zadachi sovetskoi vlasti" [project] March 28, 1918, Lenin, *Sochineniia*, 4th ed.; XXVII, 181.

23. At the Third All-Russian Conference of the PPS; see *Materiały archiwalne*, I, 575.

24. See Rosa Luxemburg, *Russian Revolution and Leninism or Marxism*, trans. Bertram D. Wolfe (Ann Arbor, 1961), p. 51.

25. Quoted in Degras, *Soviet Documents*, I, 39. Lenin, "Tezisy po voprosu o zakliuchenii separatnogo mira," *Sochineniia*, 4th ed.; XXVI, 408. Compare "O revoliutsionnoi fraze," *ibid.*, XXVII, 9.

26. See *Materiały archiwalne*, I, 155-156, 575-576.

27. Memorandum in *Mirnye peregovory*, 171-175; also *Materiały archiwalne*, I, 549-553. There is only a brief summary in the *Proceedings of Brest-Litovsk*, pp. 156-157.

28. For the stand of SDKPiL see the resolution of January 28, 1918, *Materiały archiwalne*, I, 531-533.

29. See Bobiński's article in *Trybuna*, April 12, 1918; *Dokumenty i materiały*, I, 557-559. Compare Karol Lapter, "Rewolucja październikowa a niepodległość Polski," *Sprawy Międzynarodowe*, 10, no. 11 (1957), 19-21.

30. Radek in his criticism of the treaty at the Seventh Party Congress did not even mention Poland. See *Sedmoi ekstrennyi sezd RKP(b): Stenograficheskii otchet* (Moscow, 1962), pp. 57-61. SDKPiL stated on February 28, 1918 that it opposed the peace not from the "point of view of narrow interests of our country" but on revolutionary grounds. See *Materiały archiwalne*, I, 568-571. Compare p. 601.

31. "The Central Executive Committee is given all powers to abrogate at any moment all the peace agreements with the imperialist and bourgeois states and also declare war on them" (*Sedmoi ekstrennyi sezd*, p. 176). Compare V. G. Trukhanovskii, ed., *Istoriia mezhdunarodnykh otnoshenii i vneshnei politiki SSSR, 1917-1960 gg.* (Moscow, 1961), p. 55.

32. Lenin at the Seventh Congress, *Sochineniia*, XXII, 331.

33. This is conceded even by Karl Radek and R. Stefanovich in *Perevorot v Polshe i Pilsudskii* (Moscow, 1926), p. 11.

34. See the report of the meeting of Polish National Committee, May 27, 1918, *Materiały archiwalne*, I, 297-298.

35. See the resolutions in *Materiały archiwalne*, I, 38, 172, 417, 515; also Henryk Jabłoński, *Polityka Polskiej Partii Socjalistycznej*, pp. 400, 421-422, 456.

36. *Naprzód*, Nov. 14, 1917; *Materiały archiwalne*, I, 462.

37. *Materiały archiwalne*, I, 45, 62, 435. Compare Jerzy Holzer, *Polska Partia Socjalistyczna w latach 1917-1919* (Warsaw, 1962), pp. 45-47, 83-87.

38. See Jerzy Holzer and Jan Molenda, *Polska w pierwszej wojnie światowej* (Warsaw, 1963), pp. 273-274; *Materiały archiwalne*, I, 209.

39. See O. B. Szmidt, ed., *Socjaldemokracja Królestwa Polskiego i Litwy: Materiały i dokumenty, 1914-1918* (Moscow, 1936), p. 249.

40. For Lednicki's refusal see Zygmunt Wasilewski, ed., *Proces*

Lednickiego (Warsaw, 1924), pp. 147-148, 164. For the dissolution see *Materiały archiwalne*, I, 488. The Polish Economic Council presided over by Lednicki carried on some work of the commission; see *ibid.*, I, 278-280.

41. This was Kazimierz Pużak. See *Materiały archiwalne*, I, 574-575.

42. For Polish support of Ukrainian independence see, among others, Jurij Borys, *The Russian Communist Party and the Sovietization of Ukraine: A Study of the Communist Doctrine of the Self-determination of Nations* (Stockholm, 1960), pp. 98-99.

43. See Tadeusz Hołówko, *Przez dwa fronty* (2 vols. in one; Warsaw, 1931), pp. 73-74, 252-253. Also see *Materiały archiwalne*, I, 124-126, 479-480, 573, 576, 648-655.

44. Lenin, "O prave natsii," 1914, *Sochineniia*, XVII, 454.

45. "We absolutely opposed all attempts at establishment of relations between *fraki* [PPS-Frakcja] and the Soviet government"; Third Conference of SDKPiL, Nov. 14-17, 1918, *Materiały archiwalne*, I, 673. Italics added.

46. This is evident from all documents, and even the Soviet historian M. V. Misko had to admit that: "In Russia also the Polish Social Democrats rejected the watchword of Polish independence"; *Oktiabrskaia revoliutsiia i vosstanovlenie nezavisimosti Polshi* (Moscow, 1957), pp. 75-76.

47. See *Materiały archiwalne*, I, 594, 599.

48. Lenin at the Seventh Conference, *Sochineniia*, XX, 275-276.

49. The phrase is Julian Leszczyński's. See *Materiały archiwalne*, I, 639.

50. See the May 1918 conference of SDKPiL, *ibid.*, I, 596.

51. As Misko put it, SDKPiL in Russia faced genuine difficulties because the "influence of Polish bourgeois and petty bourgeois organizations and of the Catholic clergy on Polish working masses was quite significant"; *Oktiabrskaia revoliutsiia*, p. 93. An Austrian report estimated that while the Poles wanted far-reaching reforms they stood aloof of the Russian Revolution. See *Materiały archiwalne*, I, 208. Compare Witold Stankiewicz, "Ruch ludowy w Polsce w latach 1918-1923," *Ruch robotniczy i ludowy w Polsce w latach 1914-1923* (Warsaw, 1961), p. 416, and Zygmunt Łukawski, "Polityka polskich organizacji w Rosji w sprawie powrotu uchodźców do kraju 1917-1918," *Kwartalnik Historyczny*, 74 (1967), 632. These important facts are overlooked by Jaroslav Valenta, "Polská otázka a říjnová revoluce," *Slovanské Historické Studie*, 5 (1963), 158-159.

52. On December 7, 1917. See *Leninskii Sbornik*, XXI (1933), 95.

53. See *Materiały archiwalne*, I, 488, 490, 512-513.

54. *Ibid.*, I, 473-474.

55. Speech of December 23, 1917, *ibid.*, I, 489.

56. *Ibid.*, I, 668. Compare I, 472-473, 546.

57. See *Dokumenty i materiały*, I, 428.

58. See Stanislav Pestkovskii, "Ob oktiabrskikh dniakh v Pitere," *Proletarskaia Revoliutsiia*, 10 (1922), 94-104. For SDKPiL member-

ship in the Commissariat for Nationality Affairs see Wiktor Sukiennicki, "Przyczyny i początek wojny polsko-sowieckiej 1919-1921," *Bellona*, 45 (1963), 34.

59. See declaration of SDKPiL and PPS-Left, June 17 (misdated 23), 1917, *Materiały archiwalne*, I, 441, also I, 28-29.

60. On the conference see Henryk Bagiński, *Wojsko polskie na wschodzie 1914-1920* (Warsaw, 1921), pp. 111-120; Tadeusz Hołówko, *Przez dwa fronty*, pp. 250-252; Nagórski, "Aleksander Lednicki, 1866-1934," *Zeszyty Historyczne*, 1 (1962), 48; Grosfeld, *Polskie reakcyjne formacje*, pp. 30-39.

61. See Michał Sokolnicki, "Józef Piłsudski a zagadnienie Rosji," *Niepodległość*, n.s., 2 (1950), 61-62; Józef Piłsudski, *Pisma zbiorowe* (10 vols.; Warsaw, 1937-1938), V, 272; Leon Wasilewski, *Józef Piłsudski jakim go znałem* (Warsaw, 1935), pp. 148-150; Lipiński, "Wywiad u marszałka Piłsudskiego," p. 77. Stefan Arski misinterprets the episode in *My pierwsza brygada* (Warsaw, 1962), p. 142.

62. See among others, *Materiały archiwalne*, I, 469-470, 484-485.

63. *Ibid.*, I, 467-468. A Polish historian of a pro-Piłsudski orientation wrote that the activities of Dowbór-Muśnicki in Belorussia would "remain a black page in Polish history." See Wacław Lipiński, *Walka zbrojna o niepodległość Polski, 1905-1918* (Warsaw, 1931), p. 300.

64. On December 23, 1917, *Materiały archiwalne*, I, 489.

65. *Ibid.*, I, 546.

66. A story of Leszczyński's offer of cooperation with the committee (Komitet Główny Igo Zjazdu Polaków Wojskowych-Lewica) appears in *Z Dokumentów Chwili*, no. 84 (Dec. 15, 1917), 32-36.

67. See Krylenko's order to Miasnikov in *Velikaia Oktiabrskaia sotsialisticheskaia revoliutsiia v Belorussi: Okt. 1917—Mart 1918* (2 vols.; Minsk: Institut Istorii Partii Tsk KPB, 1957), II, 394.

68. *Materiały archiwalne*, I, 538-539. See also "Razgovor tov. Trotskogo so Stavkoi," *Izvestia*, Dec. 8, 1917.

69. *Izvestia*, Nov. 27/Dec. 10, 1917, cited in *Materiały archiwalne*, I, 471.

70. See the telegram to Krylenko in *Z Dokumentów Chwili*, no. 95 (February 1, 1918), 56-58.

71. See the highly critical appraisal of Dowbór-Muśnicki by Wacław Lipiński, *Z dziejów dawnych i najnowszych* (Warsaw, 1934), p. 317.

72. See the letter to Soviet authorities in *Materiały archiwalne*, I, 284-286; Hołówko, *Przez dwa fronty*, pp. 10-11, 211-241.

73. See the report of Colonel Michał Żymierski, Jan. 7, 1919, in Akta Adiutantury Generalnej Naczelnego Dowództwa, II/182, Józef Piłsudski Institute of America, New York. Hereafter cited as AGND. For Polish exchanges with the Entente, see *Materiały archiwalne*, I, 322-323, 345-346, 347. As for the Soviet attitude, V. D. Bonch-Bruevich was allegedly willing to agree to Polish representations. Trotsky was not. See Wacław Lipiński, "Sprawy wojskowych formacji polskich na wschodzie według relacji ks. Kazimierza Lutosławskiego," *Niepodległość*, 16 (1937), 637.

74. General Haller's report, *Materiały archiwalne*, I, 327.

75. June 3, 1918, AGND, III/460.

76. Declaration of January 28, 1918, *Materiały archiwalne*, I, 534.

77. See *ibid.*, I, 563. For Polish protests see *Z Dokumentów Chwili*, no. 98 (February 10, 1918), pp. 52-56. On Jackiewicz's assassination: Sukiennicki, "Przyczyny i początek wojny," p. 22 and 38n; letter of F. Piotrowski in *Wojskowy Przegląd Historyczny*, 9, no. 1/30 (1964), 416-417. Also Józef Dowbór-Muśnicki, *Moje wspomnienia* (Poznan, 1936), annex no. 13, pp. 14-17; and Bagiński, *Wojsko polskie na wschodzie*, p. 191.

78. See *Materiały archiwalne*, I, 267-269, 306-307, 309, 595, 596, 627, 628. Compare Misko, *Oktiabrskaia revoliutsiia*, pp. 94-95.

79. SDKPiL resolution of May 1918, *Materiały archiwalne*, I, 604, 606-607.

80. Report of S. Szymański, *ibid.*, I, 361-364.

81. *Ibid.*, I, 565.

82. *Z Dokumentów Chwili*, no. 98 (February 10, 1918), 55-56.

83. See *Materiały archiwalne*, I, 604, also 474-478. It appears that Trotsky allowed the formation of national units on the condition that SDKPiL approve such a policy. See Andrzej Slisz, "Odbicie rewolucji październikowej w czasopismach polskich wydawanych w Piotrogrodzie i w Moskwie," in Tadeusz Cieślak and Leon Grosfeld, eds., *Rewolucja październikowa a Polska* (Warsaw, 1967), p. 413.

84. See *DVP SSSR*, I, 371-372; *Materiały archiwalne*, I, 620-621.

85. G. V. Chicherin, *Stati i rechi po voprosam mezhdunarodnoi politiki* (Moscow, 1961), p. 43.

86. See resolution of SDKPiL of May 1918 in *Materiały archiwalne*, I, 603. The military section of the Commissariat stated its aim was to "organize and unite these masses, to make them conscious workers of the revolution, and to send them home as such" (August, 1918, *ibid.*, I, 331).

87. *DVP SSSR*, I, 460; *Materiały archiwalne*, I, 647. An English translation slightly different from the above is in Degras, *Soviet Documents*, I, 98.

88. Feliks Kon, *Natsionalnyi vopros v Polshe* (Moscow, 1927), p. 4.

89. See Sukiennicki's comments in "Przyczyny i początek wojny," pp. 37-38.

90. Jabłoński, "Międzynarodowe warunki odbudowy niepodległości Polski," p. 43.

91. In virtue of a decree of December 24, 1918 the Ukrainians were considered citizens of the Russian Socialist Federated Soviet Republic, though at Brest Russia had renounced all her rights to the Ukraine. See T. A. Taracouzio, *The Soviet Union and International Law* (New York, 1935), p. 31. In the Soviet-Latvian peace treaty of August 11, 1920, Moscow renounced "voluntarily and for ever all sovereign rights which belonged to Russia." There were similar clauses in peace treaties with Lithuania and Estonia. This may mean that until 1920 Soviet Russia considered herself sovereign over these countries.

92. That view was represented by Roman Umiastowski in *Russia and the Polish Republic, 1918-1941* (London, 1945), p. 79. For criticism of this position see Wacław Komarnicki, "Odbudowa państwowości polskiej na ziemiach wschodnich," *Rocznik Prawniczy Wileński, 3* (1929), 3; Jan Ochota, "Unieważnienie aktów rozbiorowych przez Rosję," *Sprawy Obce*, 1, (1930), 296-299.

93. At the Twenty-fifth Congress of SDKPiL, August 27, 1918; *Materiały archiwalne*, I, 637.

94. August 24, 1918, Degras, *Soviet Documents*, I, 115; *DVP SSSR*, I, 535.

95. Chicherin, *Stati i rechi*, p. 49.

96. Degras, *Soviet Documents*, I, 111.

Chapter 4. Nation or Class?

1. See V. I. Lenin, "Rech o mezhdunarodnom polozhenii," *Sochineniia* (3rd ed.; 30 vols.; Moscow, 1935-1937), XXIII, 269, 261.

2. November 18, 1918. Leon Trotsky, *Kak vooruzhalas revoliutsiia* (3 vols. in 4; Moscow, 1923-1924), I, 394, 398.

3. November 17, 1918. J. V. Stalin, *Sochineniia* (13 vols.; Moscow, 1946-1951), IV, 168-170.

4. *Grazhdanskaia voina 1918-1921*, ed. A. S. Bubnov, S.S. Kamenev, and R. P. Eideman (3 vols.; Moscow, 1928-1930), III, 120.

5. Russian text in *DVP SSSR*, I, 565-567. English translation in Jane Degras, ed., *Soviet Documents on Foreign Policy, 1917-1941* (3 vols., New York, 1951-1953), I, 124-125.

6. On November 16. Cited in Sukiennicki, "Przyczyny i początek wojny polsko-sowieckiej 1919-1921," part II, *Bellona*, 45 (1963), 187n. Based on the contemporary Soviet press, this article brings a wealth of information.

7. Speech of November 18, 1918; Trotsky, *Kak vooruzhalas revoliutsiia*, I, 394.

8. See Stalin's articles in *Pravda*, November 6 and 9, 1918; *Sochineniia*, IV, 161, 163. A few years later Stalin pictured the strife as one between the industrialized center and the peasant borderlands. See "Zakliuchitelnoe slovo," April 25, 1923, *Zhizn Natsionalnostei*, 3-4 (1923), 25.

9. See Georgii V. Chicherin, *Stati i rechi po voprosam mezhdunarodnoi politiki* (Moscow, 1961), p. 46.

10. See Sukiennicki, "Przyczyny i początek," part II, 26-28; Zigmas Angaretis, "Litva i Oktiabrskaia revoliutsiia," *Zhizn Natsionalnostei*, 1 (January 1923), 219; Mikhail I. Kulichenko, *Borba kommunisticheskoi partii za reshenie natsionalnogo voprosa v 1918-1920 g.* (Kharkov, 1963), pp. 38-40; Petr Stuchka, *Piat mesiatsev sotsialisticheskoi Sovietskoi Latvii* (2 parts; Moscow, 1919-1921), I, 23ff, and his "Nashi zadachi v otnoshenii Latvii," November 24, 1918 in *Za Sovetskuiu vlast v Latvii, 1918-1920: sbornik statei* (Riga, 1964), pp. 44-49.

11. Lenin to Glavkom, November 29, 1918, in *Leninskii Sbornik,* XXXIV (1942), 53-54.

12. *Izvestia,* December 24, 1918.

13. See Stuchka, *Piat mesiatsev,* I, 16, 21ff, 58. Also many details in Sukiennicki, "Przyczyny i początek," part II, 161-163.

14. Stuchka, *Piat mesiatsev,* II, 9.

15. See Wincas Mickiewicz-Kapsukas, "Walka o władzę radziecką na Litwie i Białorusi Zachodniej," *Z Pola Walki,* nos. 9-10, (1930), 14.

16. See Sukiennicki, "Przyczyny i początek," part II, 164-167.

17. See Trotsky to Lenin, January 2, 1919, in *The Trotsky Papers, 1917-1922* ed. Jan M. Meijer (The Hague, London, Paris, 1964—), I, 230-233. Later, Trotsky's dispatches became less sanguine as he recognized the strength of Ukrainian separatism and the unreliability of pro-Communist units. A wealth of material is contained in V. A. Antonov-Ovseenko, *Zapiski o grazhdanskoi voine* (4 vols.; Moscow and Leningrad, 1932-1933), III, 1-141.

18. See Chicherin, *Stati i rechi,* pp. 120-121.

19. For an analysis of this highly involved story see Sukiennicki "Przyczyny i początek," part II, 168-183, and his "Stalin and Belorussian 'Independence,'" *Polish Review,* 10 (Autumn 1965), 84-107. Also J. Mienski, "The Establishment of the Belorussian SSR," *Belorussian Review,* 1 (1955), 5-33.

20. *Revoliutionnye komitety: XI, 1918—VI, 1920 BSSR: sbornik dokumentov i materialov* (Minsk: Tsentralnyi Gosudarstvennyi Arkhiv, 1961), p. 71.

21. *Grazhdanskaia voina,* III, 153-154.

22. Kulichenko, *Borba,* p. 54.

23. *Ibid.,* p. 249. Compare Tadeusz Teslar, *Polityka Rosji Sowieckiej podczas wojny z Polską* (Warsaw, 1937), p. 78.

24. Kulichenko, *Borba,* p. 254. Compare Iakov M. Sverdlow, *Izbrannye proizvedeniia* (3 vols.; Moscow, 1957-1960), III, 141-143, 145-146, 159.

25. The reader will find much revealing material in Kulichenko, *Borba,* pp. 230-231, 249-250, Stuchka's memoirs, and Sukiennicki's article.

26. Vatsetis to Lenin, April 23, 1919 cited in N. E. Kakurin, *Kak srazalas revoliutsiia* (3 vols., Moscow, 1925-1926), II, 406; also in *The Trotsky Papers,* I, 352-353.

27. Stalin on December 26, 1918. See Kulichenko, *Borba,* pp. 439-440.

28. On December 15, 1918, *Sochineniia,* IV, 178.

29. February 9, 1919, *ibid.,* IV, 229.

30. Kakurin, *Kak srazhalas revoliutsiia,* II, 97.

31. For somewhat different phrasing of this dilemma compare Feliks Kon, *Natsionalnyi vopros v Polshe* (Moscow, 1927), p. 5 and Henryk Jabłoński, *Narodziny drugiej Rzeczpospolitej, 1918-1919* (Warsaw, 1962), p. 126.

32. *Materiały archiwalne do historii stosunków polsko-radzieckich,* ed. Natalia Gąsiorowska (Warsaw, 1957—), I, 384.

33. *Ibid.,* I, 672, 675.

34. See text in Kazimierz W. Kumaniecki, ed., *Odbudowa państwowości polskiej: najważniejsze dokumenty* (Warsaw and Cracow, 1924), pp. 130-132. English translation in Kridl, Malinowski, and Wittlin, *For Your Freedom and Ours* (New York, 1943), pp. 219-221.

35. Views of Mieczysław Niedziałkowski cited by Jabłoński, *Narodziny drugiej Rzeczpospolitej,* pp. 146-147.

36. See their statement on November 8, 1918 in *Materiały archiwalne,* I, 398-399.

37. A prominent historian and an enlightened conservative considered that this government "was preparing Poland to enter alongside with the Ukraine and Lithuania into Soviet Russia." See Michał Bobrzyński (Anon.), *Wskrzeszenie państwa polskiego* (2 vols.; Cracow, 1920-1925), II, 18.

38. Józef Piłsudski, *Pisma zbiorowe* (10 vols.; Warsaw, 1937-1938), V, 19.

39. Piłsudski's letter, published in *Niepodległość,* n.s., 7 (1962), 14, may never have been mailed but it reflected his mode of thinking at the time. Compare Piłsudski, *Pisma zbiorowe,* V, 35, 37, 44-45.

40. Moraczewski's statement at cabinet meeting of November 25, 1918, Protocol, Akta Adiutantury Generalnej Naczelnego Dowództwa, Piłsudski Institute, I/66 (cited as AGND).

41. Tytus Filipowicz's interview in *Kurjer Polski,* December 7, 1918.

42. See Dmowski's instructions to Grabski. "Protokoły posiedzeń Komitetu Narodowego Polskiego w Paryżu" (wybór), ed. Tadeusz Kuźmiński, in *Najnowsze Dzieje Polski: materiały i studia z okresu 1914-1939,* II (1959), 148.

43. See letters exchanged between Piłsudski and Grabski, December 11, 1918, AGND, LIV/246.

44. For Paderewski's appraisal and hopes of Allied support see two messages to Colonel House of January 1 and 12, 1919; Edward M. House Collection, Sterling Library, Yale University.

45. See comments of Adam Próchnik (Henryk Swoboda), *Pierwsze piętnastolecie Polski niepodległej 1918-1933* (Warsaw, 1957), p. 44.

46. See the work by two Polish Communists, Edward Brand and Henryk Walecki, *Der Kommunismus in Polen* (Hamburg, 1921), p. 21.

47. See *Materiały archiwalne,* I, 364-368, 376, 382; *Dokumenty i materiały do historii stosunków polsko-radziekich* (Warsaw, 1962—), II, 70-71; AGND, I/3, I/20, I/119, II/118; also Leon Wasilewski, *Józef Piłsudski jakim go znałem* (Warsaw, 1935), pp. 158-159.

48. *Dokumenty i materiały,* II, 3.

49. Nicolas Berdayev, *The Origin of Russian Communism,* trans. R. M. French (Ann Arbor, Mich., 1962), p. 107.

50. Alexander Minc, "Der Kommunismus in Polen: Erinnerungen,"

Archive of Russian and East European History and Culture, Columbia University (cited as AREEH).

51. See Jabłoński, *Narodziny drugiej Rzeczpospolitej*, pp. 196-197; M. V. Misko, *Oktiabrskaia revoliutsiia i vosstanovlenie nezavisimosti Polshi* (Moscow, 1957), p. 221.

52. See M. V. Misko, *Oktiabrskaia revoliutsiia*, p. 220; compare Jan Molenda, "Masy chłopskie i ruch ludowy w czasie wojny 1914-1918," *Ruch robotniczy i ludowy w Polsce w latach 1914-1923* (Warsaw, 1961), *passim*.

53. See reminiscences of Minc, "Der Kommunismus," p. 9. As a Polish Communist later recalled, "The notion that the Red Army of the USSR or possibly of a Soviet Germany will make a revolution in our country is still alive among our comrades" (Roman Jabłonowski, *Wspomnienia* [Warsaw,1962], p. 337).

54. *Dokumenty i materiały*, II, 11.

55. See *Rady delegatów robotniczych w Polsce 1918-1919: materiały i dokumenty* (2 vols.; Warsaw, 1962-1965), I, 133, 145.

56. See Józef Kowalski, "Z zagadnień rozwoju ideologicznego KPRP w latach 1918-1923," *Ruch robotniczy i ludowy w Polsce w latach 1914-1923* (Warsaw, 1961), pp. 261-291. The author admits that the PPS slogans reflected the thinking of the masses. For a detailed discussion of Polish Communist tactics see numerous articles in *Z Pola Walki* (1959-1960); also Jaroslav Valenta, "Polska otázka a říjnová revoluce," *Slovanské Historické Studie*, 5 (1963), 194-204.

57. *Dokumenty i materiały*, II, 209, 117, 165-171.

58. See "Bolszewicy a sprawa polska," referat VI oddziału Sztabu, AGND, XV/325.

59. See *ibid.*, I/40; *Dokumenty i materiały*, II, 77-78.

60. See protocol of the meeting of November 23, 1918, AGND, I/66; and Kumaniecki, *Odbudowa państwowości polskiej*, p. 147.

61. See Piłsudski, *Pisma zbiorowe*, V, 23. Compare Bolesław Roja, *Legendy i fakty* (Warsaw, 1931), p. 138.

62. See J. Wołoszynowski to Piłsudski, January 23, 1919, AGND, XV/255; a confidential statement from the Ukraine, January 10, 1919, *ibid.*, 253; report of B. Kutyłowski, January 27, 1919, *ibid.*, 299.

63. For Polish underestimation of the Bolsheviks see Zygmunt Jundziłł, "Niefortunna wyprawa kowieńska," *Niepodległość*, n.s., 5 (1965), 207. Also the statement of Undersecretary Tytus Filipowicz, that since the days of Batory Polish chances were never so great (*Kurjer Polski*, December 7, 1918).

64. See *Dokumenty i materiały*, II, 50-51, 83, 85-89; AGND, I/8, II/102; Günther Rosenfeld, *Sowjetrussland und Deutschland, 1917-1922* (Berlin, 1960), pp. 196-200. The topic is treated extensively in Titus Komarnicki's *Rebirth of the Polish Republic* (London, 1957), see especially pp. 443-450.

65. See the memorandum of General Stanisław Szeptycki of January 10, 1919 in *Dokumenty i materiały*, II, 64-66. Also Wacław Chociano-

wicz, "Historia dywizji litewsko-białoruskiej w świetle listów Józefa Piłsudskiego," *Niepodległość*, n.s., 7 (1962), *passim*; and Piłsudski to Clemenceau,, December 29, 1918, *Documents diplomatiques concernant les relations polono-lithuaniennes* (Warsaw, 1920), p. 5.

66. See Piłsudski to Wejtko, December 19, 1918, AGND, I/55; Captain Zygmunt Klinger to Piłsudski, December 30, 1919, *ibid.*, II/127. The defense of Wilno was badly organized but one must remember that Klinger had at his disposal only four machine guns and 750 rifles. See S. Mickiewicz's report on the fall of Wilno, January 17, 1919 in Archiwum Michała Mościckiego, no. 351, Piłsudski Institute, New York (cited as AMM).

67. For this topic see observations by Adam B. Ulam, "Nationalism, Panslavism, Communism," and Richard E. Pipes, "Domestic Politics and Foreign Affairs," in Ivo J. Lederer, ed., *Russian Foreign Policy* (New Haven, 1962).

68. See Lenin, *Sochineniia*, XXII, 334.

69. See Zygmunt Wasilewski, ed., *Proces Lednickiego* (Warsaw,1924), p. 214.

70. *Materiały archiwalne*, I, 657.

71. *Ibid.*, I, 671-672. Valenta's interpretation of Soviet motives in "Polská otázka," pp. 172-173 is not convincing.

72. *Materiały archiwalne*, I, 397.

73. Original French text in *Dokumenty i materiały*, II, 16-17, based on *Livre rouge: recueil des documents diplomatiques relatifs aux relations entre la Russie et la Pologne* (Moscow, 1920), pp. 22-23. Hereafter cited as *Livre rouge*. Russian translation in *Dokumenty vneshnei politiki SSSR* (Moscow, 1959—), I, 581 (cited as *DVP SSSR*). The note sent by courier has never been published.

74. *Dokumenty i materiały*, II, 17-18; *DVP SSSR*, I, 579-581.

75. Chicherin, *Stati i rechi*, p. 121.

76. See *Kurjer Warszawski*, Nov. 26, 1918; *Kurjer Polski*, Nov. 26, 1918. For a description of the seizure of the Polish mission's building see among others Zygmunt Wasilewski, *Proces Lednickiego*, p. 243.

77. Note by Ministry of Foreign Affairs for Michał Sokolnicki [?] December 5, 1918, AMM, no. 235.

78. Article in *Naprzód*, December 19, 1918, cited in Artur Leinwand, *Polska Partia Socjalistyczna wobec wojny polsko-radzieckiej 1919-1920* (Warsaw, 1964), pp. 21-22.

79. The date of this note is not clear. *Livre rouge*, pp. 25-26, dates the message December 6, 1918. *Dokumenty i materiały*, II, 22-23, corrects it to December 4. A copy in AGND, II/179 is dated December 1.

80. See Wasilewski's note to Minister Scavenius and the latter's note to Chicherin protesting the occupation of the Polish mission by strangers who "take away documents"; *Livre rouge*, pp. 25-26.

81. *Ibid.*, pp. 24-25.

82. *Dokumenty i materiały*, II, 24-25.

83. *Ibid.*, II, 28-30; *DVP SSSR*, I, 607-609; *Livre rouge*, pp. 27-29. The last publication gives the date of December 10.

84. *Dokumenty i materiały,* II, 30-31; *DVP SSSR,* I, 610; *Livre rouge,* pp. 29-30.

85. *Dokumenty i materiały,* II, 33-34; *DVP SSSR,* I, 626; *Lire rouge,* pp. 30-31. According to the above the note was dated December 22, 1918. A copy in AGND, II/79 gives the date of December 19, 1918, and includes a phrase about "acts of cruelty and vandalism committed" by Soviet troops. Compare a promemoria to this note probably drawn up by Sokolnicki, AMM, Misc.

86. *Dokumenty i materiały,* II, 33, 34-35; *DVP SSSR,* I, 625-626; *Livre rouge,* pp. 31-32.

87. *Dokumenty i materiały,* II, 36; *Livre rouge,* pp. 32-33.

88. For incidents connected with the Soviet Red Cross in Hungary and Germany, and for French refusal to admit Red Cross missions see numerous dispatches in *DVP SSSR,* I and II.

89. *Kurjer Poranny* referred to it as the third mission in succession of the Russian Red Cross. See issue of January 3, 1919.

90. Such a permission with the signature of Wasilewski was allegedly given to Leon Alter by minister Bronisław Ziemięcki.

91. The story of the mission is based here mainly on documents printed in *Dokumenty i materiały,* II, 41 42, 46-50, 52-53, 57-60, 71-72, 176-178, 812-814; and *Livre rouge,* pp. 38-39

92. See Jędrzej Moraczewski "Wspomnienia o współpracy z Leonem Wasilewskim," *Niepodległość* 16, (1937) 218-219.

93. See the reply of Stanisław Wojciechowski to interpellation by Polish Socialists tabled on February 26, 1919. Also see the discussion in the Foreign Affairs Committee, AGND/101, "Wyciągi z protokółów Komisji Spraw Zagranicznych."

94. See telegrams of Jakub Fürstenberg-Hanecki, January 8, 1919, and of the Central Committee to Chicherin, *Livre rouge,* pp. 38-39.

95. See Maria Grinberg, "Z zagadnień wojny polsko-radzieckiej," *Ruch robotniczy i ludowy,* p. 475. Compare Fedor G. Zuev, *Mezhdunarodnyi imperializm organizator napadenia panskoi Polshi na sovietskuiu Rossiiu 1919-1920* (Moscow, 1954), p. 21. For details of the manifestation see Tadeusz Teslar, *Propaganda bolszewicka podczas wojny polsko-rosyjskiej 1920 roku* (Warsaw, 1938), p. 68.

96. See the protocol of cabinet meeting in *Dokumenty i materiały,* II, 41.

97. *Dokumenty i materiały,* II, 42-44; *Livre rouge,* pp. 33-34; a summary in *DVP SSSR,* II, 17.

98. *Dokumenty i materiały,* II, 46-47; *DVP SSSR,* I, 636; *Livre rouge,* p. 34. Only the last publication mentions the copy to Hesse. For another reference to him see Fürstenberg-Hanecki to Chicherin, January 8, 1919, *Livre rouge,* p. 39.

99 *Dokumenty i materiały,* II, 52-53; *Livre rouge,* p. 35.

100. *Dokumenty i materiały,* II, 54-56; *DVP SSSR,* II, 15-17; *Livre rouge,* pp. 35-37.

101. *Dokumenty i materiały,* II, 62; *DVP SSSR,* II, 17-18; *Livre*

rouge, pp. 39-40. For names of those arrested see the telegram of January 18, 1919 in AGND, XV/234.

102 *Dokumenty i materiały*, II, 61.

103. *Ibid.*, II, 99-100; *DVP. SSSR*, II, 70; *Livre rouge*, p. 41.

104. *Livre rouge*, p. 42.

Chapter 5. The Borderlands

1. *Livre rouge: recueil des documents diplomatiques relatifs aux relations entre la Russie et la Pologne 1918-1920* (Moscow, 1920), pp. 43-44; *Dokumenty vneshnei politiki SSSR* (Moscow, 1959—), II, 68-70 (cited as *DVP SSSR*); *Dokumenty i materiały do historii stosunków polsko-radziekich* (Warsaw, 1962—), II, 102-103.

2. February 16, 1919. *DVP SSSR*, II, 74-76; *Dokumenty i materiały*, II, 109-111; *Livre rouge*, which gives the date of February 17, pp. 44-46.

3. Marchlewski certainly knew better. See "Rosja proletariacka a Polska burżuazyjna," *Pisma wybrane*, (2 vols.; Warsaw, 1950-56), II, 773-774.

4. Józef Lewandowski, *Federalizm, Litwa i Białoruś w polityce obozu belwederskiego listopad 1918–kwiecień 1920* (Warsaw, 1962), p. 73. Also see Walentyna Najdus, "Polacy we władzach republiki litewsko-białoruskiej 1919," *Kwartalnik Historyczny*, 74 (1967), 611-624.

5. Lewandowski, *Federalizm*, p. 74. *Młot's* publication increased from 3,000 to 15,000 copies between December 1918 and April 1919. See Tadeusz Teslar, *Propaganda bolszewicka podczas wojny polsko-rosyjskiej 1920 roku* (Warsaw, 1938), p. 290.

6. *Dokumenty i materiały*, II, 250.

7. See Lenin's directives of November 16, 1918, *Leninskii Sbornik*, XXXIV (1942), pp. 50-51.

8. *Dokumenty i materiały*, II, 21.

9. See Colonel A. Sikorski's report on a journey from Moscow to Warsaw, December 18, 1918, Akta Adiutantury Generalnej Naczelnego Dowództwa, I/57, Piłsudski Institute (cited as AGND). His evidence was partly borne out by Chicherin who complained several months later to Trotsky about the forcible conscription of foreigners and the shooting of those who refused to join. See Chicherin to Trotsky, October 22, 1919, *Trotsky Papers, 1917-1922* (London, 1964), I, 722-723.

10. See communiqués of the Central Committee of the Polish Communist Party in Russia, *Dokumenty i materiały*, II, 68.

11. See report of Dr. B. Nakoniecznikow, November 9, 1918, AGND, I/4, and compare with analysis of the composition of the Western Division, in *ibid.*, III/545.

12. *Dokumenty i materiały*, II, 79-81.

13. Iakov M. Sverdlov, *Izbrannye proizvedeniia* (3 vols.; Moscow, 1957-1960), III, 137-138.

14. *DVP SSSR*, II, 732.

15. *Izvestia*, February 6, 1919. Italics added. My attention to this notice was drawn by Professor Wiktor Sukiennicki.

16. In early February 1919 there were rumors in Berlin of a Communist revolution in Germany coordinated with the Red Army's march through Poland. See David Shub, *Lenin: A Biography* (Garden City, N.Y., 1948), p. 342. Teslar mentions that members of the Polish Commissariat in Belorussia, notably Stefan Heltman, had ideas about creating a government-in-exile. See Tadeusz Teslar, *Polityka Rosji sowieckiej podczas wojny z Polską.* (Warsaw, 1937), p. 89.

17. On February 19, 1919; *Dokumenty i materiały*, II, 115-116.

18. See Józef Kowalski, "Z zagadnień rozwoju ideologicznego KPRP w latach 1918-1923," in *Ruch robotniczy i ludowy w Polsce w latach 1914-1923* (Warsaw, 1961), p. 289. Compare Artur Leinwand, *Polska Partia Socjalistyczna wobec wojny polsko-radzieckiej 1919-1920* (Warsaw, 1964), citing the text of the resolution as reconstructed by Edward Próchniak.

19. Edward Brand and Henryk Walecki, *Der Kommunismus in Polen* (Hamburg, 1921), p. 17. Also Jan A. Reguła, *Historia komunistycznej partii Polski* (Warsaw, 1934), p. 40, citing a contemporary Communist pamphlet *W sprawach partyjnych*, p. 25. Interestingly enough this resolution is left out in *KPP w obronie niepodległości Polski: materiały i dokumenty* (Warsaw, 1953), and included without the above-quoted phrase in *Dokumenty i materiały*, II, 107-109.

20. *Dokumenty i materiały*, II, 108.

21. Alexander Minc, "Der Kommunismus in Polen: Erinnerungen," Archive of Russian and East European History and Culture, Columbia University (cited as AREEH). Compare the views of Henryk Walecki as cited by Tych, "Stosunek SDKPiL, PPS-Lewicy i KPRP do Rewolucji październikowej," in Cieślak and Grosfeld, *Rewolucja październikowa a Polska*, pp. 179-180.

22. See report on the Western Division and its recruiting practices in Wilno by Kuszel (A. Sługocki) of February 19, 1919 forwarded by Pużak to Piłsudski, and a report of April 15, 1919; AGND, XV/592, XVI/665.

23. Józef Piłsudski, *Pisma zbiorowe* (10 vols.; Warsaw, 1937-1938), VII, 147. The quotation is somewhat shortened for reasons of adequate translation.

24. Roman Dmowski, *Polityka polska i odbudowanie państwa* (Warsaw, 1925), p. 36.

25. See Stanisław Kozicki, *Sprawa granic Polski na konferencji pokojowej w Paryżu 1919* (Warsaw, 1921), pp. 118-119; Lewandowski, *Federalizm*, pp. 30-41; minutes of the 193rd meeting of the Polish National Committee in Paris in "Protokoły posiedzeń Komitetu Narodowego Polskiego w Paryżu z okresu 2 października 1918 do 23 stycznia 1919r. (wybór)," ed. Tadeusz Kuźmiński, in *Najnowsze Dzieje Polski: materiały i studia z okresu 1914-1939*, II (1959) 128-129. For a discussion of strategic considerations see Marian Żegota-Januszajtis, *Strategiczne granice Polski na wschodzie* (Warsaw, 1919). See also Dmowski's memoranda for Balfour and Wilson in Sekretariat Jeneralny Delegacji Polskiej, *Akty i dokumenty dotyczące sprawy granic Polski 1918-1919* (4 vols.; Paris, 1920-1926), I, 12, 58-69.

26. Alexander Skrzyński, *Poland and Peace* (London, 1923), p. 36.

27. Krzewski (J. Lilienfeld, *Zasady federacji w polskiej polityce kresowej* (Cracow, 1920), p. 12.

28. See especially no. 2 (33), January 12.; no. 4 (34), January 19.; no. 7 (38), February 16, 1919.

29. See "Wojna z Rosją," no. 8 (39), February 23, 1919.

30. "W sprawie Litwy i Białorusi," no. 9, March 2, 1919.

31. See especially "Niepodległa Ukraina," no. 7 (38), February 16, 1919; "Linie wytyczne polityki narodowej," no. 6 (37), February 9, 1919; "Wojna z Rosją czy wojna z Ukrainą?" no. 16 (47), April 20, 1919; also issues of July 27, November 9, and November 23, 1919.

32. See Lewandowski, *Federalizm*, pp. 91-95. Also "Państwa bałtyckie," Ciechanowski Deposit, Hoover Institution, Stanford, Calif.

33. The memorandum, preceded by a lengthy historical introduction is in the Paderewski file in the Edward M. House Collection, drawer 15, Sterling Library, Yale University. Compare Kozicki, *Sprawa granic*, pp. 119-120; Piłsudski, *Pisma zbiorowe*, VI, 122; Marian Seyda, *Polska na przełomie dziejów: fakty i dokumenty* (2 vol.; Poznań, 1927-1931), II, 474; *Akty i dokumenty*, I, 99.

34. February 20, 1919; *Sprawozdanie stenograficzne 1919-1921*, Sejm Ustawodawczy R.P., III/67-68.

35. Many historians tend to confuse the views of Piłsudski and of his followers. A clear distinction between the two is inherent in the work of Lewandowski.

36. See Irena Gałęzowska, "Myśl Józefa Piłsudskiego w świetle filozofii współczesnej," *Niepodległość*, n.s., 7 (1962), 128.

37. Piłsudski, *Pisma zbiorowe*, II, 299; IV, 104; VII, 15.

38. *Ibid.*, I, 95. And he added years later that "A Socialist in Poland must strive after the independence of his country" (*ibid.*, II, 45).

39. "Perhaps I am a romantic," Piłsudski declared in 1914; *ibid.*, IV, 21. To the end of his life, the Polish Romantic poets, especially Juliusz Słowacki, were especially dear to him.

40. Characterization by Władysław Skrzyński. See MS Diariusz Michała Stanisława Kossakowskiego, October 5, 1920, Archiwum Polskiej Akademii Nauk, Warsaw.

41. For Piłsudski's dislike of all systems and systematic theories see Artur Śliwiński, "Marszałek Piłsudski o sobie," *Niepodległość*, 16 (1937), 369.

42. See Piłsudski, *Pisma zbiorowe*, V, 110. Compare Michał Sokolnicki, "Józef Piłsudski a zagadnienie Rosji," *Niepodległość*, n.s. 2 (1950), 51-70. On Piłsudski's attitude to Russia there are interesting observations in the unpublished memoirs of Karol Wędziagolski, who acted as Piłsudski's representative in dealings with Boris Savinkov. See MS Wędziagolski, Polish Institute of Arts and Sciences, New York.

43. Piłsudski, *Pisma zbiorowe*, VII, 147.

44. Instructions of November 27, and December 18-19, 1918; AMM, nos. 211-212, 529.

45. Władysław Baranowski, *Rozmowy z Piłsudskim, 1916-1931* (War-

saw, 1938), p. 124. Piłsudski told Dmowski's representative, Grabski, that he favored a border running along Ula-Beresina-Słucz-Horyń. See "Protokoły posiedzeń Komitetu Narodowego," p. 171.

46. Leon Wasilewski, *Józef Piłsudski jakim go znałem* (Warsaw, 1935), p. 172. Piłsudski emphasized the distinctive "physiognomy" of Lithuania and Belorussia in instructions for General Gołogórski on March 16, 1919. See *Niepodległość*, new series 7 (1962), 21.

47. Piłsudski *Pisma zbiorowe*, VI, 122.

48. Wasilewski, *Piłsudski jakim go znałem*, pp. 175-176. The letter is reprinted in Piłsudski, *Pisma zbiorowe*, V, 73-74. A copy is in AGND, XV/612.

49. Compare Stanisław Mackiewicz, *Historia Polski od 11 listopada 1918 r. do 17 września 1939 r.* (London, 1941), pp. 101-107; T. Komarnicki "Piłsudski a polityka wielkich mocarstw zachodnich," *Niepodległość*, n.s., 4 (1952), 64.

50. See F. T. Epstein, "Studien zur Geschichte der 'Russischen Frage' auf der Pariser Friedenskonferenz von 1919," *Jahrbücher für Geschichte Osteuropas*, 7 (1959), 450-460.

51. The secretary of the Polish delegation in Paris reported that "There were elements which were inclined to take disintegration of Russia as a starting point and strive to replace it with Poland; others, however, did not cease to count on the resurrection of the old United Russia and did not want to injure [Franco-Russian] relations by supporting Poland to Russian disadvantage" (Kozicki, *Sprawa granic*, p. 115). Compare Piotr S. Wandycz, *France and her Eastern Allies* (Minneapolis, 1962), pp. 124-125.

52. For an elaboration of this point see Wacław Komarnicki, "Odbudowa państwowości polskiej na ziemiach wschodnich, "*Rocznik Prawniczy Wileński*, 2 (1929), 15ff.

53. *Foreign Relations of the United States: The Paris Peace Conference 1919* (13 vols.; Washington, D.C., 1942-1947), III, 490. Hereafter cited as *F.R. Peace Conference*.

54. See especially V. A. Maklakov Archive, I, no. 40, Hoover Institution, Stanford.

55. See *ibid.*, packet II, file 2, "Rossiia, zapad, 1919: Litva, Estoniia, Latviia"; III, 5, "Polsha 1919." Also Giers Archive, file 73, Hoover Institution, Stanford. See also André Mandelstam, *Mémoire sur l'application du principe des nationalités à la question polonaise* (Paris, 1919), and Conférence Politique Russe, *Considérations sur les frontières orientales de la Pologne et la paix en Europe* (Paris, 1919). An unpublished memorandum of May 24, 1919 is in Archiwum Michała Mościckiego, Piłsudski Institute (cited as AMM). Compare Epstein, "Studien zur Geschichte der 'Russischen Frage'," pp. 433-445. John M. Thompson, *Russia, Bolshevism, and the Versailles Peace* (Princeton, 1966), pp. 77-78.

56. *F.R. Peace Conference*, III, 677.

57. See Chicherin to V. V. Vorovskii, January 24, 1919; Chicherin to Wilson, January 28, 1919; and note of February 4, 1919; *DVP SSSR,*

II, 42-44, 52, 57-60. In its reply Moscow failed to mention the question of an armistice in Russia. See the discussion in Thompson, *Russia*, pp. 114-118.

58. D. V. Oznobishin, "Vneshnepoliticheskie pobedy sovetskogo naroda i mezhdunarodnaia solidarnost trudiashchikhsia v 1919 g.," in C. F. Naida, ed., *Reshaiushchie pobedy sovetskogo naroda nad interventami i belogvardeitsami v 1919 g.* (Moscov, 1960), p. 629. Compare Lenin's speech at the Eighth Congress of RKP(b), *Sochineniia*, XXIV, 116-130. Also M. N. Pokrovskii, *Vneshniaia politika Rossii v XX veke* (Moscow, 1926), p. 90.

59. Leon Trotsky, *Na frontakh* (Moscow, 1919), p. 26.

60. See *F.R. Peace Conference*, III, 477, 674; IV, 120-125, 379; David Lloyd George, *The Truth About the Peace Treaties* (2 vols.; London, 1938) I, 291; Paul Mantoux, *Les délibérations du Conseil des Quatre: 24 mars—28 juin, 1919* (2 vols.; Paris, 1955), I, 22-23; Titus Komarnicki, *Rebirth of the Polish Republic* (London, 1957), pp. 399-406.

61. The Eastern Galician aspect is discussed in some detail by W. Kutschabsky, *Die Westukraine im Kampfe mit Polen und dem Bolschewismus in den Jahren 1918-1923* (Berlin, 1934), pp. 207-212.

62. Report from the attachés headquarters, April 4, 1919, AGND, LV/641.

63. Still, it is incorrect to write that "Piłsudski obtained the support of the Entente for his aspirations to Belorussian, Lithuanian, and Ukrainian lands," and to call Noulens head of the "military mission" and Henrys "chief of Polish general staff." See Oznobishin, "Vneshnepoliticheskie pobedy" in Naida, ed., *Reschaiushchie pobedy*, p. 631. M. V. Misko's assertion that government circles of the Entente "encouraged with all means at their disposal the annexationist strivings of the Polish exploiting classes" is equally misleading (*Oktiabrskaia revoliutsiia i vosstanovlenie nezavisimosti Polshi* [Moscow, 1957], p. 194).

64. *Dokumenty i materiały*, II, 112-114; *Livre rouge*, pp. 46-48; Iu. V. Kliuchnikov and A. V. Sabanin, eds., *Mezhdunarodnaia politika noveishego vremenii v dogovorakh, notakh i deklaratsiiakh* (3 parts; Moscow, 1925-1928), II, 229-230.

65. Lloyd George, *The Truth About the Peace Treaties*, I, 377.

66. Mantoux, *Délibérations du Conseil*, I, 56.

67. Roman Dmowski, *Polityka polska i odbudowanie państwa*, (Warsaw, 1925), p. 477.

68. *Ibid.*, annex XII, pp. 623-625; *Akty i dokumenty dotyczące sprawy granic*, I, 130-131.

69. As Dmowski put it, "only this will be said on our side at the Conference with which I shall agree" (*Polityka polska*, p. 432).

70. *Dokumenty i materiały*, II, 145; compare Lewandowski, *Federalizm*, pp. 106-116.

71. See MS Dnevnik P.N. Miliukova, February 2, 8, March 2, 5, 1919, Archive of Russian and East European History and Culture, Columbia University. (cited as AREEH).

72. Patek to Piłsudski, presumably around March 3, 1919, AGND, LV/501.

73. Piłsudski's delegates continued their separate sessions until July 1919. See "Protokóły posiedzeń delegacji Naczelnika Państwa w Paryżu" (January 12-July 9, 1919), AMM, no. 132. For contacts with representatives of the borderlands see Leon Wasilewski, *Józef Piłsudski jakim go znałem,* (Warsaw, 1935), pp. 175-178; Sokolnicki to Piłsudski, February 3, 1919, AGND, LIV/402; also note on Socialist Committee of Cooperation among Nationalities, AMM, no. 259.

74. David Hunter Miller, *My Diary at the Conference of Paris* (21 vols.; New York, 1926), XVII, 180-181.

75. *Recueil des actes de la conférence* (Conférence de la Paix, 1919-1920; Paris, 1923-1934), IV, C (2), 95. Hereafter cited as *Recueil.*

76. Text in Miller, *My Diary,* IX, 14-28; *Recueil,* IV, C (2), 129-139.

77. *Sprawozdanie stenograficzne,* III/66.

78. *Le Petit Parisien,* March 16, 1919; *Le Matin,* March 31, 1919; cited in Piłsudski, *Pisma zbiorowe,* V, 67, 70.

79. Addressing the Military Committee of the sejm on February 26, 1919, Piłsudski said that "the Bolsheviks have not shown their strength as yet"; AGND/102, "Rokowania . . . materiały sejmowe."

80. Report of Lieutenant Olszamowski of a talk with General Henry Niessel, March 11, 1919; AMM, no. 108.

81. Report from attachés headquarters, March 12, 1919, AGND, LV/506.

82. March 26, *Sprawozdanie stenograficzne,* XVIII/1094. For similar statements of Perl see March 27 session, *ibid.,* XIX/1146.

83. Maciej Rataj on March 26, 1919, *ibid.,* XVIII/1079.

84. Stanisław Grabski on March 27, 1919, *ibid.,* XIX/1155.

85. See the PPS interpellation of February 26, 1919, *Sprawozdanie stenograficzne* VII/245; AGND/102 "Rokowania . . . materiały sejmowe." For KPRP stand see *Dokumenty i materiały,* II, 165-167, 192-193; compare Misko, *Oktiabrskaia revoliutsiia,* p. 187.

86. In the committee the Socialist Perl criticized the lack of coordination between the committee and the Ministry of Foreign Affairs, and pressed for publication of the entire correspondence with Chicherin. See excerpts from protocol in AGND/102, "Rokowania . . . materiały sejmowe."

87. It was obvious, as Marchlewski put it, that "to send an envoy to Russia meant recognizing the Soviet government." See Marchlewski, "Rosja proletariacka a Polska burżuazyjna," *Pisma wybrane,* II, 749.

88. Grabski's presentation in sejm in *Sprawozdanie stenograficzne,* April 3, XXIV/6-10. Text of report as adopted on April 4, in the form of *sejm's* resolution, *ibid.,* XXV/26. Report in *Dokumenty i materiały,* II, 219-220.

89. See the statements of Błażej Stolarski, Daszyński, Witos, Bolesław Fichna and others in sejm: *Sprawozdanie stenograficzne,* IV/110, 129, 134, V/167, VII/280-293.

90. *Ibid.*, XIX/1124. See also Lewandowski, *Federalizm*, pp. 87-88.

91. Manifesto of the PPS deputies, March 9, 1919. See Jerzy Holzer, *Polska Partia Socjalistyczna w latach 1917-1919* (Warsaw, 1962), pp. 360-361.

92. This was Feliks Perl. See *Sprawozdanie stenograficzne*, XIX/1146. Compare XVIII/1094.

93. See Kamieniecki's statement, *ibid.*, XXV/4; Niedziałkowski's, XXIV/37-43.

94. Dąbski's speech, *ibid.*, XXIV/26-33.

95. W. Jabłonowski's speech, *ibid.*, XXIV/12-17.

96. *Ibid.*, XXIV/44-45; XXV/27-28.

97. Władysław Baranowski wrote Piłsudski that "It is necessary that Polish eastward expansion be accompanied by a more idealistic program, a program of federalism without which all our potential conquests become unmanageable and will put us in a disadvantageous light," April 4, 1919, AGND, LV/619. Dłuski, writing from Paris on April 14, developed a compromise federalist formula which he thought acceptable to Dmowski. See AGND, LVI/716.

98. See Maciej Rataj, *Pamiętniki 1918-1927* (Warsaw, 1965), p. 48.

99. See Nikolai Bukharin's remarks in *Vosmoi sezd RKP(b), Mart 1919 g: protokoly* (Moscow, 1959), p. 37.

100. Compare Bukharin's note in *Leninskii Sbornik*, III (1925), 483.

101. *Vosmoi sezd*, p. 138.

102. Some two months earlier the Soviet press announced that "according to all data there is no doubt that Poland is on the eve of its October." See *Izvestia*, January 10, 1919.

103. *Vosmoi sezd*, p. 69. For the quotations of Lenin, see *ibid.*, pp. 139 and 155.

104. *Ibid.*, pp. 80-81. Piatakov's candor can only be compared with that of a Latvian Communist who on March 11, 1919 published an article entitled "Proletarian Imperialism." See Petr I. Stuchka, *Za Sovetskuiu vlast v Latvii, 1919-1920: sbornik statei* (Riga, 1964), pp. 176-180.

105. *Vosmoi sezd*, p. 398; also *Vsesoiuznaia Kommunisticheskaia Partia (b) v resoliutsiakh i resheniiakh sezdov, konferentsii i plenumov Ts. K.: 1898-1932* (Moscow, 1933), I, 331-332. See English text in Richard Pipes, *The Formation of the Soviet Union: Communism and Nationalism, 1917-1923* (Cambridge, Mass. 1962), p. 110, in which the word "no" should be added before "full rights" in the last line of point 2.

106. *Vosmoi sezd*, p. 425; italics in text. Compare Sverdlov's remarks about the Ukraine in *Izbrannye proizvedeniia*, III, 189.

107. He left Warsaw on March 7, and there is some controversy about the date he crossed the demarcation line. He arrived in Moscow on March 16, 1919 unaccompanied by any other delegate. Compare accounts in *Izvestia*, March 9, 1919; *Livre rouge*, pp. 49-50; Chicherin's letter to Fischer, September 30, 1929 in Louis S. Fischer Collection: Chicherin Correspondence 1929-32, I, Sterling Library, Yale University;

and intercepted radio message of Chicherin to Paderewski, March 11, 1919, F.O. 371/3912, no. 40430 and 46675, Public Record Office, Foreign Office, London (hereafter cited as PRO F.O.).

108. See communiqué in *Monitor Polski*, March 3, 1919. There exists a draft of a memorandum of March 1, 1919, ostensibly prepared for the Allies, which develops this point. See AMM, no. 5.

109. Paderewski to Więckowski, February 24, 1919, AGND, XV/441.

110. Text in *Dokumenty i materiały*, II, 172-173; *Livre rouge*, pp. 48-49.

111. Compare Teslar, *Propaganda bolszewicka*, p. 82.

112. While Stalin complained to the Eighth Party Congress that elements "composing the majority of our army do not want to fight voluntarily for Communism," and called for stern discipline to combat revolts and strengthen the Red Army (*Sochineniia*, IV, 249-250), Trotsky, discussing the united efforts of the enemies of the Revolution, did not even mention Poland. See telegram to Lenin, March 17, 1919, *Trotsky Papers*, I, 302-305.

113. Konstanty Brodzki to Central Committee, March or April 1919, *Dokumenty i materiały*, II, 234n.

114. *Pisma wybrane*, II, 753. Compare Misko, *Oktiabrshaia revoliutsiia*, p. 196.

115. For instance on March 4, 1919 in the Council of Workers' Deputies.

116. Text in *Dokumenty i materiały*, II, 202-203.

117. Lenin to Central Committee, date uncertain, 1919. See *Polnoe sobranie sochinenii* (5th ed.; Moscow, 1958—), L, 266.

118. *Dokumenty i materiały*, II, 201-202; *Livre rouge*, pp. 54-55. Italics added.

119. Note of March 27, 1919, *Dokumenty i materiały*, II, 206-207; *Livre rouge*, pp. 55-56.

120. Chicherin's message of June 3, 1919 to the Entente: *Livre rouge*, p. 63. The statement may have been made to embarrass the Poles. Only one Polish writer seems to consider it true, namely, Jan Starzewski, "Zarys dziejów polskiej polityki zagranicznej" (mimeographed), (London, 1944), part II, p. 57.

121. "Rosja proletariacka," *Pisma wybrane*, II, 753. Compare Fedor G. Zuev, *Mezhdunarodnyi imperializm organizator napadenia panskoi Polshi na sovetskuiu Rossiiu 1919-1920* (Moscow, 1954), pp. 35-36.

122. Louis Fischer, *The Soviets in World Affairs* (2 vols.; London, 1930), I, 239 and Stanisław Głąbiński, *Wspomnienia polityczne* (Pelplin, 1939), pp. 456-457.

123. *Dokumenty i materiały*, II, 231-234; *Livre rouge*, pp. 56-58.

124. See text of Rakovskii's telegram to Chicherin, April 13, 1919, in *Sovetskaia Ukraina i Polsha: sbornik diplomaticheskikh dokumentov i istoricheskikh materialov* (Kharkov: Narodnyi Komissariat po inostrannym delam USSR, 1921), p. 21.

125. *Dokumenty i materiały*, II, 237-238; *Livre rouge*, pp. 58-59.

126. *Dokumenty i materiały*, II, 243-244; *DVP SSSR*, II, 142-143; *Livre rouge*, pp. 59-60.

127. See Więckowski's telegram from Finland, AGND, XVI/764.

128. *Kurjer Poranny*, May 7, 1919. Note inspired by Polish Ministry of Foreign Affairs.

129. Marchlewski, "Rosja proletariacka," *Pisma wybrane*, II, 745.

Chapter 6. Open Struggles and Secret Negotiations

1. See S. Girinis, "Kanun i sumerki Sovetskoi vlasti na Litve," *Proletarskaia Revoliutsiia*, no. 8 (1922), 83-87; articles of Mickiewicz-Kapsukas in *Izvestia*, May 5, 1919, and of S. Dimianshtein in *Pravda*, May 6, 1919; remarks on the "kulak uprisings" in N. V. Kamenskaia, *Belorusskii narod v borbe za sovetskuiu vlast* (Minsk, 1963), pp. 43-49; Józef Lewandowski, *Federalizm, Litwa i Białoruś w polityce obozu belwederskiego* (Warsaw, 1962), pp. 123-124; *Dokumenty i materiały do historii stosunków polsko-radzieckich* (Warsaw, 1962—), II. 771-773. For contemporary Polish reports from Wilno and Minsk of February, March, and April, 1919, see Akta Adiutantury Generalnej Naczelnego Dowództwa, XV, LVI, Piłsudski Institute, New York (cited as AGND).

2. Piłsudski to Szeptycki, April 7, 1919, AGND, III/610. Compare Piłsudski's letter to Wasilewski, in Leon Wasilewski, *Józef Piłsudski jakim go znałem* (Warsaw, 1935), pp. 175-177.

3. See Piłsudski to Paderewski cited in Wasilewski, *Piłsudski jakim go znałem*, p. 185. Compare Józef Piłsudski, *Pisma zbiorowe*, (10 vols.; Warsaw, 1937-1938) V, 80.

4. See Wasilewski, *Piłsudski jakim go znałem*, p. 183; compare Piłsudski, *Pisma zbiorowe*, VI, 122.

5. Lewandowski termed this a "pseudo-accomplished fact," *Federalizm*, p. 128.

6. "Z powodu zajęcia Wilna," no. 17 (48), April 27, 1919. Orders of General Edward Rydz-Śmigły and Colonel Władysław Belina-Prażmowski emphasized the liberation of the *capital of Lithuania* and repudiated any intention of imposing a solution by force.

7. T.H[ołówko], "Równi z równymi, wolni z wolnymi," *Rząd i Wojsko*, no. 18 (49), May 4, 1919.

8. See speeches on May 22 and 23, 1919, *Sprawozdanie stenograficzne 1919-1921*, Sejm ustawodawczy R.P., XXXX/35-34, XL/3-14, XLI/36-45. Also proceedings of the PPS Council in *Dokumenty i materiały*, II, 288-289. The Communists viewed the march on Wilno as a counterrevolutionary crusade. See *ibid.*, II, 247-248, 252-253, 297-303.

9. Piłsudski to Paderewski, April 27, May 2, 1919, AGND, LVI/701, 702. Compare Czesław Świrski's statement to Piłsudski that Paderewski wanted to coordinate his action with that of the chief of state and was "genuinely loyal." *Ibid.*, LVI/730.

10. Notes of Patek, May 6, 1919; Wasilewski to Piłsudski, April 28, 1919; Sokolnicki to Piłsudski, May 6, 1919, AGND, LVI/790, LVI/305, LVI/770. Compare Paderewski's interview for *Le Matin* May 30, 1919 in *Sprawy polskie na konferencji pokojowej w Paryżu w 1919 r.: dokumenty i materiały* (2 vols., Warsaw, 1965-1967), I, 194.

11. See, for example, *Gazeta Warszawska*, April 28, 1919.

12. See report of Sosnkowski to Piłsudski, April 20, 1919, AGND, LVI/762.

13. Wasilewski to Piłsudski, June 12, 1919, *ibid.*, LVI/998.

14. See *Sprawozdanie stenograficzne*, XXXI/55-56. April 29, 1919. Piłsudski wrote the Minister of the Interior, Stanisław Wojciechowski, on April 22 to assume the responsibility before the sejm for Piłsudski's declaration. See Archiwum Michała Mościckiego, no. 358, Piłsudski Institute, New York (cited as AMM).

15. Kazimierz Świtalski to Wasilewski, May 17, 1919, AGND, XVI/822.

16. See AGND/101, "Wyciągi z protokołów Komisji Spraw Zagranicznych."

17. See *Sprawozdanie stenograficzne*, XXXX/24-25, 32-33, 35-45.

18. Text in *Dokumenty i materiały*, II, 292-295.

19. See text, first printed by Karol Lapter in *Sprawy Międzynarodowe*, 10, no. 11 (1957), in *Dokumenty i materiały*, II, 262-267. Compare with more guarded statements in Piłsudski, *Pisma zbiorowe*, V, 79.

20. For Lithuanian statements and territorial claims in Paris see Miller, *My Diary*, XVII, 398-402; Record Group 59, General Records of the Department of State, "Government of Lithuania," 860M.01/77, National Archives. Compare Skrzyński to Ministry of Foreign Affairs, May-June 1919, *Dokumenty i materiały*, II, 273-274; Polish memorandum by J. Ziabicki, August 19, 1919, AGND, XIX/146.

21. For details of these complex negotiations see among others: *Documents diplomatiques concernant les relations polono-lithuaniennes, passim*, Wasilewski, *Piłsudski jakim go znałem*, p. 203ff; AGND, XVI/711, 909, XVII/1070, XVIII/1268; *Dokumenty i materiały*, II, 239-243, 281-283.

22. On the *Putsch* see *Dokumenty i materiały*, II, 452-455; AGND, XVIII/1335, XIX/1402, 1407, XX/1627, 1628, 1632, 1633; MS Diariusz Kossakowskiego July 18, August 20, 31, September 4, 1919, Archiwum Polskiej Akademii Nauk, Warsaw. The most recent treatment of the plot, emphasizing its negative aspects, is Piotr Łossowski, "Próba przewrotu polskiego w Kownie w sierpniu 1919 r.," *Najnowsze Dzieje Polski: materiały i studia z okresu 1914-1939*, 8 (1964), 51-74, and in his, *Stosunki polsko-litewskie w latach 1918-1920* (Warsaw, 1966), pp. 117-149.

23. On Piłsudski's ideas about Lithuania see AGND, XIX/1484, XX/1631; *Dokumenty i materiały*, II, 332-334, 439-441. Piłsudski's reluctance to use force comes out in a letter to Szeptycki, September 5,

1919, AGND, XIX/1423, and is emphasized by MS Diariusz Kossakowskiego, September 24, 1919.

24. Report of Lieutenant Bobrowski forwarded by Captain Walery Sławek to Piłsudski, n.d., AGND/111, "Odpisy różnych akt Oddziału II, r. 1919."

25. Zygmunt Jundziłł, "Z dziejów polskiej myśli politycznej na Litwie historycznej," Niepodległość, n.s., 6 (1958), 76.

26. For instance Rząd i Wojsko, July 6, November 9, 1919. For criticism of the Polish gendarmerie see Dokumenty i materiały, II, 365, 465-472.

27. May 4, 1919. Cited in Lewandowski, Federalizm, p. 210.

28. Piłsudski, Pisma zbiorowe, V, 107.

29. See the memoranda of the Council of the Belorussian People's Republic for Piłsudski, September 19, 1919, AGND, XIX/1591, 1596.

30. Piłsudski to Osmołowski, September 21, 1919, Niepodległość, n.s., 7 (1962), 67-71.

31. General Szeptycki to Piłsudski, July 19, 1919, AGND, IV/1147. For a criticism of the military see the unpublished memoirs of the General Commissioner of Eastern Territories (Jerzy Osmołowski, "Wspomnienia z lat 1914-1921," III, 92-93 Biblioteka Narodowa, Warsaw); for a general appraisal, see memoranda of his political adviser (Dokumenty i materiały, II, 314-320, AGND, XX/1685). Also Stanisław Gutowski's report in AGND, XIX/1529. For achievements, "Rola i praca administracji polskiej na kresach wschodnich w latach 1919-ym i 1920-ym," "Referaty i raporty informacyjne MSZ, 1920-21," Ciechanowski Deposit, Hoover Institution, Stanford. For extreme Belorussian criticism see K. Ezovitov, Belorussy i Poliaki: dokumenty i fakty iz istorii okkupatsii Belorussii Poliakami v 1918, 1919 g. (Kovno, 1919).

32. See Henryk Jabłoński, "Z dziejów genezy sojuszu Piłsudski-Petlura," Zeszyty Naukowe Wojskowej Akademii Politycznej, seria historyczna, no. 5/21 (1961), p. 54. Compare Dokumenty i materiały, II, 129-133.

33. English text in Dokumenty i materiały, II, 259-260; French in AGND, XVI/899-900.

34. Numerous statements to that effect were made at the Peace Conference and in British diplomatic correspondence. For instance on September 19, 1919 the British emphasized that "No obstacle should be placed in the way of an ultimate union of Eastern Galicia with Russia." Foreign Relations of the United States: The Paris Peace Conference, VIII, 272-273.

35. Wallace to Secretary of State, June 28, 1919, Foreign Relations of the United States: 1919, Russia (Washington, D.C.: Department of State, 1937), pp. 764-765; hereafter cited as Foreign Relations: 1919 Russia.

36. See Skrzyński to Ministry of Foreign Affairs, May-June 1919, Dokumenty i materiały, II, 274; Bolesław Wieniawa-Długoszowski to Piłsudski, May 27, 1919, AGND, LVI/881.

37. *Foreign Relations: Peace Conference*, VI, 73-75; and *Foreign Relations: 1919 Russia*, pp. 766-768.

38. See Feliks Libert, "Nowy cel wojny," *Niepodległość*, n.s., 3 (1951), 35.

39. See Juliusz Łukasiewicz, *Polska w Europie w polityce Józefa Piłsudskiego* (London, 1944), p. 11; Marian Zdziechowski, "Z historii stosunków polsko-rosyjskich nazajutrz po wojnie światowej 1919-1920," *Przegląd Współczesny*, nr. 176 (1936), pp. 184-185; Piłsudski's own statements in *Pisma zbiorowe*, VI, 123-124.

40. Anton Denikin, *Ocherki Russkoi smuty* (5 vols.; Berlin, 1921-1926) IV, 31.

41. For the text of Petliura's letter see my translation in "Nieznane listy Petlury do Piłsudskiego," *Zeszyty Historyczne*, 8 (1965), 182-183; Ukrainian original in AGND, XIX/1144.

42. See *Dokumenty i materiały*, II, 330-332.

43. Memorandum of Roman Knoll, September 25, 1919, AGND, XX/1601.

44. Internal communiqué of the eastern section of Supreme Command, October 9, 1919, AGND/111, "Odpisy różnych akt Oddziału II."

45. See General Stanisław Haller to Ministry of War, July 8, 1919, *Dokumenty i materiały*, II, 307-308, and drafts of instruction for the mission, August 1919, AGND, XVIII/1286, 1289. For mutual recriminations concerning Polish relations with Denikin see Denikin, *Ocherki*, V, 175-181; and his *Kto spas sovetskuiu vlast od gibeli* (Paris, 1937), and *Sprostowanie historii, odpowiedź Polakom* (Paris, 1937); also "Russko-polskaia rana," Rukopisi proizvedenii Generala A. I. Denikina, Denikin Papers, Archive of Russian and East European History and Culture, Columbia University, New York (cited as AREEH). Stanisław Haller, "Nasz stosunek do Denikina," *Kurjer Warszawski*, June 13, 1937; Tadeusz Kutrzeba, "Odpowiedź gen. Denikinowi," *Gazeta Polska*, December 9, 10, 11, and 12, 1937.

46. Skrzyński to Paderewski, July 10, 1919, cited in Lewandowski, *Federalizm*, p. 152.

47. There was talk at the VTsIK about Polish preparations against Wilno already in late February 1919. See Arthur Ransome, *Russia in 1919* (New York, 1919), p. 168.

48. Lenin to *Glavkom* and *Zapfront*, April 24, 1919, *Sochineniia*, 4th ed., XXXV, 319, *Leninskii Sbornik*, XXXIV (1942), p. 122. Compare *Trotsky Papers*, I, 378-379, and AGND, LXIV/1933.

49. See the latter's "Walka o władzę radziecką" and article in *Izvestia*, cited in *Dokumenty i materiały*, II, 771-773.

50. See notes in *Dokumenty i materiały*, II, 257-258; *Livre rouge: recueil des documents diplomatiques relatifs aux relations entre la Russie et la Pologne 1918-1920* (Moscow, 1920), pp. 61-67; *Dokumenty vneshnei politiki SSSR* (Moscow, 1959—), II, 180-185 (cited as DVP SSSR). Polish Communists opposed the exchange (except of those condemned to death) for fear of depleting their ranks in Poland.

51. Vatsetis to Lenin, April 23, 1919, *Trotsky Papers*, I, 354-355. For a criticism of the *Glavkom* for underestimating the western front see Mikhail D. Bonch-Bruevich, *Vsia vlast sovetam* (Moscow, 1957), pp. 345-346.

52. For a detailed discussion of Marchlewski's negotiations with the Poles see Piotr S. Wandycz, "Secret Soviet-Polish Peace Talks in 1919," *Slavic Review*, 24 (September 1965), 425-449; and the two articles by Weronika Gostyńska: "Rola Juliana Marchlewskiego w rokowaniach polsko-radzieckich (czerwiec-lipiec 1919 r.)," and "Tajne rokowania polsko-radzieckie w Mikaszewiczach (sierpień-grudzień 1919 r.)," in *Z Pola Walki*, 9 (1966) and 10 (1967). Also the most recent biography by Feliks Tych and Horst Schumacher, *Julian Marchlewski* (Warsaw, 1966), pp. 306-313; Józef Sieradzki, *Białowieża i Mikaszewicze* (Warsaw, 1959), pp. 13-14; Lewandowski, *Federalizm*, p. 135; Louis Fischer, *The Soviets in World Affairs*, (2 vols.; London, 1930), I, 239; Marchlewski's own remarks in *Pisma wybrane*, (2 vols.; Warsaw, 1952-1956), II, 755-756 and an entry in MS Diariusz Kossakowskiego for July 31, 1919, which mentions a talk with Piłsudski. In early 1919 there was another Soviet emissary in Warsaw, a former PPS member, Wincenty Jastrzębski. See Tadeusz Daniszewski, "Lenin a polski ruch komunistyczny," *Z Pola Walki*, 3 (1960) p. 254n; and the revealing reminiscences of Jastrzębski himself, "Między Piotrogrodem a Warszawą," *Najnowsze Dzieje Polski: materiały i studia z okresu 1914-1939*, 12 (1967), 155-171.

53. Marchlewski, *Pisma wybrane*, II, 755. See also his "Polsha i mirovaia revoliutsiia," written in September 1919 and published in *Kommunisticheskii Internatsional*, no. 6, 7/8, September, October, November, December 1919, and then in an enlarged form as a book in 1920.

54. J. M. Borski "Kołczak," June 11, 1919, reprinted in *Dokumenty i materiały*, II, 775-778.

55. Text of first message in *DVP SSSR*, II, 200-201; second cited in Wandycz, "Soviet-Polish Peace Talks," p. 428n.

56. Given the nature of statements about hostages made by Ukrainian Communists, the Poles questioned Marchlewski's powers to speak in their behalf. See Rakovskii to Paderewski, n.d., and Chicherin to Rakovskii, August 9, 1919, in *Sovetskaia Ukraina i Polsha: sbornik diplomaticheskikh dokumentov i istoricheskikh materialov* (Kharkov, 1921), pp. 25-26.

57. MS Diariusz Kossakowskiego, July 24, 1919.

58. Letter to Lenin, August 11, 1919, in J. V. Stalin, *Sochineniia*, IV, 272-274.

59. MS Diariusz Kossakowskiego, July 31, 1919. This is the only reference to a talk between Piłsudski and Marchlewski, and it is not confirmed by any other source.

60. *Foreign Relations: Peace Conference*, VIII, 204, 218-219.

61. Paderewski stated on February 21, 1921: "I went to the Supreme

Council with a demand that I be allowed to conclude peace. I met with a refusal." Cited by Lewandowski, *Federalizm*, p. 139n.

62. The story of direct Lenin-Paderewski communications, based partly on Paderewski's recollections and on testimony of Edward Ligocki is told by Sieradzki, *Białowieża i Mikaszewicze*, pp. 23-26.

63. See Bogusław Miedziński, "Wojna i pokój," *Kultura*, 9/227 (1966), 92-93.

64. Sapicha to Ministry of Foreign Affairs, September 2, and to Paderewski, September 11, 1919, *Dokumenty i materiały*, II, 336-338. Other reports of September 15, 1919 in AGND, LXIV/1701.

65. Wasilewski, *Piłsudski jakim go znałem*, p. 202.

66. *Foreign Relations: Peace Conference*, VIII, 212, 221. Even Winston Churchill opposed the two alternatives of Paderewski. See Churchill's *The Aftermath* (London, 1929), pp. 262-263.

67. *Documents on British Foreign Policy, 1918-1945*, ed. E. L. Woodward and R. Butler, 1st ser. (London, 1947—), III, 142 (hereafter cited as *DBFP*). The Polish envoy in London tried to convince the British that "cooperation of Germany in any anti-bolshevik action can be considered at present as being solely a masked means employed by Germany to regain contact and influence Russia." Memorandum cited in *ibid.*, III, 78-80. Paderewski, writing Churchill about British help to Poland, added "provided that no association with Germans of any kind . . . be imposed upon us" (*Dokumenty i materiały*, II, 398). Piłsudski stated in an interview for the London *Times* on October 8, 1919 that "If we were compelled to associate either with the Germans or the Bolshevists . . . Poland's civilizing mission would remain unfulfilled" (London *Times*, Oct. 16, 1920, *Pisma zbiorowe*, V, 111).

68. Gutowski to Piłsudski, September 15, 1919, AGND, LVII/1531.

69. *Foreign Relations: Peace Conference*, VIII, 372. Denikin commented retrospectively that any "further [Polish] expansion was left for the 'Russian Executive Committee' to decide upon." See "The Russian Problem," January 1940, Denikin Papers, AREEH.

70. For contemporary Russian and Polish reports see Maklakov Archive, "Polsha 1919," III, 5 and Giers Archive, files 81, 123, Hoover Institution, Stanford. Also Karnicki to Supreme Command, October 15, November 12, 1919, AGND, XX/1827, 1864, Ministry of Foreign Affairs to Zamoyski, November 15, 1919, *Dokumenty i materiały* II, 439.

71. Denikin to Piłsudski, September 29, 1919, AGND, XXXI/5847.

72. General Palitsyn to General D. G. Shcherbachev, November 28, 1919, Giers Archive, file no. 80.

73. Confidential note of Major Świtalski, November 2, 1919, AGND, XX/1808.

74. See *Dokumenty i materiały*, II, 346-347; MS Diariusz Kossakowskiego, November 3, 1919.

75. Note in AGND, LVII/1636.

76. Rumbold to Curzon, October 30, 1919, *DBFP*, III, 621-622.

77. For Socialist insistence on peace see protocols of secret meetings of Committees on Foreign Affairs and Military matters, October 15, 16, 17, 1919 in AGND/102, "Rokowania . . . materiały sejmowe."

78. Excerpt of protocol of cabinet's meeting on October 20, 1919 in *Dokumenty i materiały*, II, 406-408; summary of committee's discussion on October 29 in *Kurjer Poranny*, October 30, 1919.

79. Rumbold to Curzon, October 24, 1919, *DBFP*, III, 611. Compare Francesco Tommasini, *La risurrezione della Polonia* (Milan, 1925), p. 112.

80. See Rumbold to Curzon, October 24, 1919, *DBFP*, III, 612. Compare Sir Adrian Carton de Wiart, *Happy Odyssey* (London, 1950), pp. 118-119.

81. Sapieha to Ministry of Foreign Affairs, October 28, 1919, *Dokumenty i materiały*, II, 417.

82. See Skrzyński to Sapieha, October 18, 1919, *ibid.*, II, 339-401; Rumbold to Curzon, October 20, 1919, *DBFP*, III, 605; Gutowski's memorandum, November 1, 1919, AGND, LXIV/1805.

83. Rumbold to Curzon, October 24, 1919, *DBFP*, III, 612.

84. August 5, 1919, *Trotsky Papers*, I, 620-627.

85. Report to plenary session of the VTsIK, February 4, 1920, Georgii V. Chicherin, *Stati i rechi po voprosam mezhdunarodnoi politiki* (Moscow, 1961), p. 135.

86. For Bolshevik thinking see numerous exchanges in *Trotsky Papers*, I, 718-745, *Leninskii Sbornik*, XXXIV (1942), pp. 233-234. Also Chicherin, *Stati i rechi*, pp. 138-140, 282.

87. Chicherin, *Stati i rechi*, p. 282.

88. See both messages in *DVP SSSR*, II, 235, *Dokumenty i materiały*, II, 341, *Livre rouge*, pp. 75-76.

89. Cited in Wandycz, "Soviet-Polish Peace Talks," p. 434. Most of the narrative which follows is based on this article, which relies extensively on Kossakowski's diary and the other documentation available so far.

90. MS Diariusz Kossakowskiego, October 3, 1919.

91. Copies of the Red Cross documents and the Narkomindel authorization with the date October 7, 1919 are in AGND, XX/1733; for the secret credentials dated October 4, see photograph in Louis Fischer, *The Soviets in World Affairs*, I, 238. A handwritten copy in Russian is in AGND, XX/1733.

92. Dates based on Kossakowski's diary. Both Komarnicki and Fischer give wrong dates for the negotiations.

93. See Stanisław Haller, "Nasz stosunek do Denikina," *Kurjer Warszawski*, June 13, 1937.

94. Protocols of meetings are in AGND, LXXXIV/2158.

95. The date of October 23, 1919 given by *Dokumenty i materiały* and *DVP SSSR* and based on Livre rouge is clearly a mistake.

96. Boerner's diary, as reproduced in General Tadeusz Kutrzeba, *Wyprawa kijowska 1920 roku* (Warsaw, 1937), pp. 26-27.

97. Text of protocol in *Trotsky Papers,* I, 758-761.

98. Boerner's diary quoted by Kutrzeba, *Wyprawa kijowska,* pp. 27-29.

99. Text of message to Trotsky, *Trotsky Papers,* I, 764-765.

100. MS Diariusz Kossakowskiego, November 13, 1919.

101. See Rumbold's dispatches to Curzon, *DBFP,* III, 630n, 633-636.

102. Boerner's diary, cited by Kutrzeba, *Wyprawa kijowska,* pp. 29-31.

103. Kutrzeba, *Wyprawa kijowska,* p. 25.

104. See *Rząd i Wojsko,* November 23, 1919.

105. Although the Polish army did not greatly fear Communist propaganda (see report of Miedziński to General Leśniewski and the latter's order in AGND, V/1681), the intense activity of Polish Communists and the elaborate system of fraternization promoted by Lenin and Trotsky could not be ignored. On this last aspect see *Trotsky Papers,* I, 709, and *Leninskii Sbornik,* XXXIV (1942), 232.

106. For Paderewski's statement in the sejm on November 12, 1919, see *Sprawozdanie stenograficzne,* XCVII/16; for the press conference, see *Kurjer Poranny,* November 30, 1919.

107. Note for Sapieha, November 13, 1919, "Rosja, I," Archive of the Polish Government-in-Exile, Montreal; hereafter cited as APGE.

108. Lenin, *Sochineniia,* XXIV, 496, 546.

109. *Die Kommunistische Internationale,* no. 5, September 1919, p. 651.

110. As Kutrzeba put it, "Piłsudski came to the conclusion that a peace settlement based on his terms would not come about," *Wyprawa kijowska,* p. 32.

111. *Ibid.,* p. 24; and Karl Radek and R. Stefanovich, *Perevorot v Polshe i Pilsudskii* (Moscow, 1926), p. 16. Lewandowski seems to share their views in his *Federalizm,* pp. 145-146.

Chapter 7. War or Peace?

1. V. I. Lenin, *Sochineniia* (3rd ed.; 30 vols.; Moscow, 1935-1937), XXIV, 657.

2. December 5, 1919, *Dokumenty vneshnei politiki SSSR* (Moscow, 1959—), II, 298-299.

3. See correspondence in *Documents on British Foreign Policy, 1918-1945,* ed. E. L. Woodward and R. Butler, first series (London, 1947—), III, 670-672, 682-683, 688-690; cited as *DBFP.* Compare with D. V. Oznobishin, "Vneshnepoliticheskie pobedy sovetskogo naroda i mezhdunarodnaia solidarnost trudiashchikhsia v 1919 g.," in *Reshaiushchie pobedy sovetskogo naroda nad interventami i belogvardeitsami v 1919 g.,* ed. C. F. Naida (Moscow, 1960), pp. 670-671.

4. For Churchill's plans see his memoranda of November 12 and December 1, 1919 in PRO. Cab. 24/94 and 93. Piłsudski's views emerge from an interview with Major General W. H. Greenly of

November 19, 1919 (*ibid.*, 24/97), and talks with Mannerheim in early December. Compare Mannerheim's account in *The Memoirs of Marshal Mannerheim* (New York, 1954), pp. 236-237, with a contemporary account which also shows his willingness to coordinate Finnish action with the Poles (Rumbold to Curzon, Dec. 13, 1919, PRO, F.O. 371/3731, no. 162298).

5. See Rumbold to Foreign Office, December 16, 1919, *DBFP*, III, 787-788; compare Mackinder's report in *ibid.*, III, 768-798. In his later talks with Denikin, the British envoy emphasized that Poland could not be expected to throw her whole weight on his side until the principle of determining the boundaries was accepted.

6. Text in *Foreign Relations of the United States: The Paris Peace Conference, 1919* (13 vols.; Washington, D. C., 1942-1947), IX, 447. For Zamoyski's underestimation of its importance see report of December 4, 1919, Akta Adiutantury Generalnej Naczelnego Dowództwa, LVII/1984, Piłsudski Institute, New York (cited as AGND). For the odd view that the declaration was a secret encouragement of further Polish expansion see Fedor G. Zuev, *Mezhdunarodnyi imperializm organizator napadenia panskoi Polshi na sovetskuiu Rossiiu 1919-1920* (Moscow, 1954), pp. 69-70.

7. Józef Piłsudski, *Pisma zbiorowe* (10 vols.; Warsaw, 1937-1938), VI, 123-124.

8. See Lutosławski's speech on November 21, 1919 in *Sprawozdanie stenograficzne, 1919-1921*, Sejm ustawodawczy R. P. CII/53.

9. See Kamieniecki's remarks on November 7, 1919, *ibid.*, XCVI/24-28.

10. See the ambiguously phrased resolution (*Druk sejmowy*, nos. 531 and 1176) in "Państwa bałtyckie 1919-1920-1921," Ciechanowski Deposit, Hoover Institution, Stanford. Also *Sprawozdanie stenograficzne*, especially CII/55-60, CIII/3-7, 9, 13-15, 39. For a rather pessimistic comment see MS Diariusz Kossakowskiego, January 7, 1920, Archiwum Polskiej Akademii Nauk, Warsaw.

11. Leon Wasilewski, *Józef Piłsudski jakim go znałem* (Warsaw, 1935), p. 215. Compare Titus Komarnicki, *Rebirth of the Polish Republic* (London, 1957), p. 455; Francesco Tommasini, *La Risurrezione della Polonia* (Milan, 1925), pp. 113-114, 115, and Piłsudski's remarks in Równo and Łuck, *Pisma zbiorowe*, V, 132-133.

12. See Zamoyski to Ministry of Foreign Affairs, March 8, 1920, AGND, LVIII/2806.

13. S. P. Melgunov quoting Chaikovskii in *N. V. Chaikovskii v gody grazhdanskoi voiny: materialy dlia istorii russkoi obshchestvennosti 1917-1925 gg.* (Paris, 1929), p. 189. The incompatibility of Piłsudski's and Denikin's political objectives emerges clearly from *Dokumenty i materiały do historii stosunków polsko-radzieckich* (Warsaw, 1962—), II, 486, 527; AGND, XXII/3072, 3217, 3222, LVII/2032; Giers Archive, file 81, 123, Maklakov Archive, packet III, 1, Hoover Institution, Stanford.

14. See Radziwiłł's report of January 13, 1920, AGND, LXV/2266, and Patek to Piłsudski, November 24, 1919, *ibid.*, LXIV/1967.

15. See *Foreign Relations: Peace Conference*, IX, 784-785; and Wallace to Department of State, January 8, 1920, Record Group 59, "Termination of the European War," 763.72119/8609, National Archives.

16. Under Polish influence the Ukraine of Petliura officially recognized Latvian independence on December 10, 1919. See Malcolm W. Graham, *The Recognition of the Border States*, vol. III: *Latvia* (Berkeley and Los Angeles, 1941), 435-436. For the efforts of Polish diplomacy see a retrospective report entitled "Polska a państwa bałtyckie," January 20, 1921 in Ciechanowski Deposit, "Referaty i raporty informacyjne MSZ 1920-21." Mackinder told Paderewski openly that the independence of Baltic countries "was regarded as subject to limitation in respect of superior interests" (Rumbold to Foreign Office, December 16, 1919, *DBFP*, III, 789).

17. *Foreign Relations: Peace Conference*, IX, 849-850.

18. Sapieha's report, December 12, 1919, AGND, LXV/2169. Compare Zwierkowski's report of December 28, 1919, *ibid.*, 2304; and Gutowski to Patek, December 22, 1919, *ibid.*, LVIII/2251.

19. See *Gazeta Polska*, November 6, 1919, and *Sprawozdanie stenograficzne* CV/6-17, Session of December 18, 1919.

20. *Dokumenty i materiały*, II, 451.

21. *DVP SSSR*, II, 312-313; English translation in Jane Degras, ed., *Soviet Documents on Foreign Policy, 1917-1941* (3 vols.; New York, 1951-1953), I, 177-178.

22. *DVP SSSR*, II, 331-333. English translation in Degras, *Soviet Documents*, I, 179-180.

23. *DVP SSSR*, II, 355-357.

24. *Ibid.*, II, 359.

25. These appeals were launched between February 10 and 22, 1920. See *DVP SSSR*, II, 363-364, 375-377, 386-387; *Dokumenty i materiały*, II, 619-620; *Anrufe des Executivkomitees der kommunistischen Internationale zur polnischen Frage* (Berlin, 1920), pp. 3-10; and English translation in Jane Degras, ed., *The Communist International, 1919-1943: Documents* (2 vols.; New York, London, Toronto, 1956-1960), I, 80-82.

26. *Czerwony Sztandar* cited by Artur Leinwand, *Polska Partia Socjalistyczna wobec wojny polsko-radzieckiej 1919-1920* (Warsaw, 1964), p. 106. The Warsaw committee of KPRP stated on February 3, 1920, that "the only way to genuine peace is a proletarian revolution" (*Dokumenty i materiały*, II, 577).

27. Kutepov on January 31, 1920, Giers Archive, file 81.

28. Rumbold to Curzon, December 31, 1919, *DBFP*, III, 745. Skrzyński told General Carton de Wiart that by November "The Left will have such arguments [in favor of peace] that it will force any government, wishing to continue the struggle against the Bolsheviks, to give in"; Skrzyński to Sapieha, November 3, 1919, AGND,

LXIV/1902. While this was a standard argument used to convince Britain of the need for more Allied help to Poland, it contained some truth.

29. On January 23, 1920. See *Sprawozdanie stenograficzne*, CXIII/72. The chairman of the Foreign Affairs Committee, while favoring an early session, made the surprising statement that it was naive to assume "that great developments are taking place at the moment"; *ibid.*, CXIII/70.

30. See Lieberman's speech on February 27, 1920, *ibid.*, CXXIV/70-76; also CXLI/58. Compare Leinwand, *Polska Partia Socjalistyczna*, pp. 120-121; *Dokumenty i materiały*, II, 610-611; Maciej Rataj, *Pamiętniki 1918-1927* (Warsaw, 1965), p. 78.

31. J. O., "Pokój czy wojna?" *Rząd i Wojsko*, no. 7, February 15, 1920.

32. Compare Stanisław Szeptycki, *Front litewsko-białoruski* (Cracow, 1925) p. 117, and MS Diariusz Kossakowskiego, February 1, 1920.

33. See speeches of Seyda and Father Maciejewicz on November 21 and December 19, 1919; *Sprawozdanie stenograficzne*, CII/24-32, CVI/44-53.

34. Grabski wrote retrospectively that at one point, possibly in February or March, he, together with Premier Skulski and Daszyński, told Piłsudski that Soviet offers provided a chance for understanding. Consequently negotiations ought to start. See Stanisław Grabski, *The Polish-Soviet Frontier* (London, 1943), p. 22.

35. Memorandum of the Command of the Volhynian Front, January 27, 1920, AGND, XVI/2345.

36. T. H.[ołówko], "O uzgodnienie naszej polityki zagranicznej," *Rząd i Wojsko*, no. 5, February 1, 1920. Compare the note "Stronnictwa polityczne a kwestia pokoju," sent to the London legation in April 1920, APGE, "Rosja," 5.

37. Michał Bobrzyński, *Wskrzeszenie państwa polskiego* (2 vols., Cracow, 1920-1925), II, 146.

38. See Rataj, *Pamiętniki*, pp. 68-69, 75-76.

39. J. O., "Pokój czy wojna?" *Rząd i Wojsko*, no. 7, February 15, 1920. Italics in text.

40. *Dokumenty i materiały*, II, 461-463.

41. Note of December 11, 1919. Polish translation in Ciechanowski Deposit, "Wydział Wschodni MSZ, Referaty i Raporty 1920-21."

42. See Paweł Szandruk, "Organizacja wojska ukraińskiego na Podolu z początkiem r. 1920 i wyprawa na Mohylów," *Bellona*, 39 (1928), *passim*.

43. Jay P. Moffat, the American diplomat in Warsaw, noted on January 10 that Petliura negotiated secretly with Piłsudski. See Jay Pierrepont Moffat Diplomatic Papers and Correspondence, v. 26, Houghton Library, Harvard University. Hereafter cited as Moffat Papers.

44 Wasilewski, *Piłsudski jakim go znałem*, p. 216.

45. Interview in *Journal de Pologne,* January 5-6, 1920, cited in Piłsudski, *Pisma zbiorowe,* V, 130.

46. See memorandum of January 22, 1920 in Simon Petliura, *Statti, lysty, dokumenty* (New York, 1956), pp. 244-254.

47. See Kazimierz Stamirowski's report, April 17, 1920, and memoranda of the Military Commission, March 19, 25, 1920, AGND, XX/1889, 3516, 3975.

48. See details in Józef Lewandowski, *Federalizm* (Warsaw, 1962), pp. 237-238; Edmund Charaszkiewicz, "Przebudowa wschodu Europy: materiały do polityki wschodniej Józefa Piłsudskiego w latach 1893-1921," *Niepodległość,* n.s., 5 (1955), 154-155.

49. Wasilewski, *Piłsudski jakim go znałem,* p. 216.

50. Piłsudski wrote that "During the two years of our war with the Bolsheviks I, as Chief of State, was in this rare position that I concentrated in my hands political and military powers and exercised therefore decisive influence on the course of events" (*Pisma zbiorowe,* VI, 208).

51. Speech in Lublin, February 11, 1920, *ibid.,* V, 137-138.

52. Interview for *L'Echo de Paris,* February 12, 1920, cited in *ibid.,* V, 147.

53. Piłsudski's remarks to Osmołowski. See MS Diariusz Kossakowskiego, February 22, 1920.

54. Compare the somewhat different accounts in Sergei P. Melgunov, *N. V. Chaikovskii,* pp. 194-196; Savinkov to Wrangel, July 1920, PRO, F.O. 371/3915, file 208987/40430/55; Rumbold to Curzon, January 23, 1920, *DBFP,* III, 800-801. Also *Boris Savinkov pered voennoi kollegiei verkhovnogo suda SSSR,* ed. I. Shubin (Moscow, 1924).

55. Even Savinkov found it difficult to accept the self-determination of the Ukraine and the other nationalities. For details of the January, February, and March negotiations see the above cited letter of Savinkov to Wrangel; a note in French containing a summary of points discussed in Paris by Piłsudski's envoy Karol Wędziagolski, Giers Archive, file 81; and two articles by Wędziagolski, (K. Vendziagolskii), "Savinkov," *Novyi Zhurnal,* no. 71 (1963), pp. 133-155, no. 72 (1963), pp. 168-197. Also Leon Grosfeld, "Piłsudski et Savinkov" *Acta Poloniae Historica,* 14 (1966), 56-66.

56. Interview of February 9 in the London *Times* of February 14, 1920; also see *Pisma zbiorowe,* V, 144.

57. Gibson to Secretary of State, January 17, 18, 1920, in *Foreign Relations of the United States: 1920* (3 vols.; Washington, D.C. 1935-1936), III, 371, 375.

58. For Piłsudski's disbelief in peace see Tadeusz Kutrzeba, *Wyprawa kijowska 1920 roku* (Warsaw, 1937), p. 39; Melgunov, *N. V. Chaikovskii,* p. 197; note on Wędziagolski's mission, Giers Archive, file 81.

59. See Patek's reports to Okęcki, January 1, and to Piłsudski, January 5, 7, 12, and 14, 1920; AGND, LVIII/2262, 2250, 2255, 2318, 2319. Compare General Henri Mordacq, *Le Ministère Clemenceau: journal d'un temoin* (4 vols.; Paris, 1931), IV, 232-233.

60. See Patek to Piłsudski, January 19, 22, 24, 1920, AGND, LVIII/-2303, 2321, 2385; compare Zamoyski's report of January 26, 1920, *ibid.*, LVIII/2450.

61. A copy of the memorandum is enclosed in Derby to Curzon, January 26, 1920, PRO, F.O. 371/3912, no. 173960.

62. See Sapieha to Ministry of Foreign Affairs, January 28, 1920, *Dokumenty i materiały*, II, 567-568; Ciechanowski's report of January 16, 1920, *ibid.*, II, 534-536; Rozwadowski to Supreme Command, January 20, 22, 1920, AGND, LVIII/2397, 2451.

63. See British account in Curzon to Rumbold, January 27, 1920 also Curzon to General Keys, February 9, 1920, *DBFP*, III, 803-805, 814. Polish account in Patek to Piłsudski, January 27, 1920, and minutes, AGND, LXVa/2438 and LXX/5844. The British version of the conversation does not contain Patek's statement that "we owe too much to France to disregard her opposition."

64 Rumbold to Curzon, January 19, 1920, *DBFP*, III, 764-766.

65. Lieutenant Michał Mościcki on behalf of Patek to General Staff, January 28, 1920; compare General Rozwadowski to Supreme Command, January 29, 1920, AGND, LVIII/2477, 2493.

66. Gibson to Secretary of State, February 2, 1920, Record Group 59, "Political Relations between Poland and the Soviet Union," 760c.61/9, National Archives.

67. See Lansing to Gibson, February 5, 1920, and Gibson to Secretary of State, February 8, 1920. *Foreign Relations: 1920* III, 378, 379-380.

68. Incomplete protocol in AGND/102, "Rokowania . . . materiały sejmowe."

69. Protocol of meeting of February 5, 1920, *ibid.*

70. MS Diariusz Kossakowskiego, March 9, 1920. Compare Patek's statement to the British envoy that he believed the sincerity of the first Soviet approaches. Rumbold to Curzon, May 22, 1920, *DBFP*, XI, 345.

71. Patek to legation in Washington, January 24, 1920, "Pertraktacje pokojowe polsko-rosyjskie 1920-21," Ciechanowski Deposit.

72. *Dokumenty i materiały*, II, 583-584.

73. Protocol of sessions of February 23 and 24, 1920, AGND/102 "Rokowania . . . materiały sejmowe."

74. See details in Rataj, *Pamiętniki*, pp. 79-80.

75. All these assertions are made interestingly enough in comments on the peace conditions in *Dokumenty i materiały*, II, 585n.

76. Polish intelligence warned the Supreme Command that protracted negotiations would alter the military ratio to Moscow's advantage. See Kutrzeba, *Wyprawa kijowska*, pp. 69-72.

77. See text in Jan Dąbski, *Pokój ryski: wspomnienia, pertraktacje, tajne układy z Joffem, listy* (Warsaw, 1931), pp. 16-17.

78. See Lieberman's speech on February 27, 1920, *Sprawozdanie stenograficzne* CXXIV/70-75; A. Skwarczyński, "N. Demokracja wobec

warunków pokoju," *Rząd i Wojsko,* no. 10, March 7, 1920; Leinwand, *Polska Partia Socjalistyczna,* p. 129.

79. This is what he told the American envoy. See Gibson to Secretary of State, February 16, 1920, RG 59, 760c.61/17, National Archives.

80. Savinkov to Piłsudski, February 13, 1920, AGND, XXI/2639.

81. See *Dokumenty i materiały,* II, 630-632; and *Foreign Relations: 1920,* III, 380-381. Zwierkowski reported from London that Britain wanted to see a peace settlement but not on Polish conditions. February 13, 1920, AGND, LXV/2865.

82. Zamoyski to Ministry of Foreign Affairs, February 6 and 12, 1920, AGND, XXI/2574, LX/5369; Patek to Millerand, February 10, 1920, PRO, F.O. 371/3913, no. 183097. Compare Savinkov to Piłsudski, February 8, 1920, AGND, XXI/2593. Millerand's speech in Chambre des deputés, *Débats,* Session ordinaire, 1920, 106.

83. See Gibson to Secretary of State, February 19, 1920, *Foreign Relations: 1920,* III, 380-381.

84. Rozwadowski to Supreme Command, February 10 and 11, 1920, AGND, LVIII/2529, 2656. Compare report of Major H. S. Howland, February 19, 1920, RG 59 760c.61/29, National Archives.

85. Adam Rozwadowski, *Generał Rozwadowski,* (Cracow, 1929), pp. 76-77.

86. Zamoyski to Ministry of Foreign Affairs, February 18, 1920, AGND, LVIII/2636.

87. Piłsudski, *Pisma zbiorowe,* V, 148-149.

88. February 28, 1920, *ibid.,* V, 150-152.

89. Sapieha to Ministry of Forcign Affairs, February 27, 1920, *Dokumenty i materiały,* II, 614-616. The envoy pointed out that several groups in England were likely to oppose the Polish eastern program: industrialists interested in Russian markets, pro-Russian political circles, Leftists who sympathized with the Bolsheviks, and pacifists who took Moscow's peace overtures at face value.

90. Gibson to Secretary of State, March 3, 1920, RG 59, 760c.61/28, National Archives.

91. See Kutrzeba, *Wyprawa kijowska,* pp. 20, 39-40, 74; Adam Przybylski, *Wojna polska, 1918-1920* (Warsaw, 1930), p. 132; Wacław Jędrzejewicz, "Rokowania borysowskie w 1920 roku," *Niepodległość,* n.s., 3 (1951), 151; Tommasini, *La Risurrezione della Polonia,* p. 115; Rumbold to Curzon, May 22, 1920, *DBFP,* XI, 325-328.

92. Piłsudski, *Pisma zbiorowe,* V, 150. Compare Juliusz Łukasiewicz, "Uwagi o polityce ukraińskiej marszałka Piłsudskiego," *Wiadomości Polskie,* no. 50 (92) (1941).

93. See Rozwadowski to Supreme Command, February 9, 1920, AGND, LVIII/2541, 2684; Rumbold to Curzon, March 13, 1920, *DBFP,* XI, 242.

94. Rumbold to Curzon, March 21, 1920, *DBFP,* XI, 261.

95. Draft amended by Piłsudski, March 5, 1920, AGND, VII/2744.

96. J. Haller to Piłsudski, March 11, 1920, *ibid.*, VII/2790. Compare the somewhat inaccurate account in Józef Haller, *Pamiętniki* (London, 1964), pp. 218-219.

97. Protocol of meeting of Military and Budget Committees, March 4, 1920, AGND/102, "Rokowania . . . materiały sejmowe."

98. See a paper prepared by the General Staff, April 1, 1920 in Archiwum Michała Mościckiego, no. 170, Piłsudski Institute, New York (cited as AMM). Compare *Rząd i Wojsko*, which wrote on March 14 that the Soviet counterattack was perfectly natural because he who wants peace must show his strength.

99. Chicherin to Patek, March 6, 1920, *DVP SSSR*, II, 397-399.

100. See *ibid.*, II, 399-400.

101. *Ibid.*, II, 400-402.

102. A paper prepared by General Staff, March 15, 1920, AMM, no. 158.

103. English text in *DBFP*, XI, 243-245; French in *Dokumenty i materiały*, II, 677-678 (erroneously dated March 15, 1920).

104. *Dokumenty i materiały*, II, 638-640. Patek's authorship is stressed by Tommasini, *Risurrezione della Polonia*, p. 116; Rumbold in *DBFP*, XI, 326; and Gibson, RG. 59, 760c.61/34, National Archives.

105. Wasilewski, *Piłsudski jakim go znałem*, pp. 219-220.

106. The Belorussian Council demanded self-determination, participation at the peace conference, equality of Belorussian and Polish languages, and the creation of a government. After negotiating with them Wasilewski could satisfy only some moderate cultural demands. See *Dokumenty i materiały*, II, 687-691; Wasilewski, *Piłsudski jakim go znałem*, p. 218; Lewandowski, *Federalizm*, p. 247ff; see also note of Belorussian Central Council of Wilno and Grodno, March 28, 1920, AGND, XXII/3068, and "Report on Belorussia" (in Polish), January 24, 1921, CD.

107. Kutepov to Sazonov, March 21, 1920, Giers Archive, file 81.

108. On March 14, 1920, AGND, XXII/3196. Compare Porębski to Piłsudski, March 2, 1920, *ibid.*, XXI/2666.

109. Gibson to Secretary of State, March 22, 1920. *Foreign Relations: 1920*, III, 381-382.

110. Rumbold to Curzon, March 14 and 26, 1920, *DBFP*, XI, 246, 264-265.

111. Sapieha to Ministry of Foreign Affairs, March 16, 1920, AGND, LXVI/3134. Compare British comments by Rumbold and Lewis Namier in PRO, F.O. 371/3913, no. 185750, 371/3914, no. 192377, and Cab. 24/101.

112. Captain Morstin to Rozwadowski, March 17, 1920, Akta Generała Rozwadowskiego, II, Piłsudski Institute, New York. Also Zamoyski to Patek, March 18, 1920, *Dokumenty i materiały*, II, 679-681. Compare Jan Starzewski, "Zarys dziejów polskiej polityki zagranicznej" (London, 1944), mimeographed, p. 68.

113. See Sapieha to Zamoyski, March 23, 1930, *Dokumenty i materiały*, II, 685-686.

114. See protocol of March 20, 1920 meeting AGND/102, "Roko-wania . . . materiały sejmowe."

115. *Dokumenty i materiały,* II, 693; *DVP SSSR,* II, 428.

Chapter 8. Borisov and Kiev

1. See Lenin's remarks on December 21, 1920, *Sochineniia* (3rd ed., 30 vols.; Moscow, 1935-1937), XVI, 6. Compare M. N. Pokrovskii's observation that Lenin had never been a pacifist (*Vneshniaia politika Rossii v XX veke* (Moscow, 1926), p. 80). A copy of Clausewitz's book on war with Lenin's annotations was found in Lenin's library in Poronin. See Bogusław Miedziński, "Wojna i pokój," *Kultura,* no. 5/233 (1966), 109-110.

2. Lenin, *Sochineniia,* XII, 318.

3. Marchlewski to the Central Committe of RKP(b), December 24, 1919, *Dokumenty i materiały do historii stosunków polsko-radzieckich* (Warsaw, 1962—), II, 502-505.

4. December 22, 1919, *The Trotsky Papers, 1917-1922* (London, 1964), I, 800-801.

5. For an optimistic speech on November 21, 1919 see Anatolii V. Lunacharskii, *Stati i rechi po voprosam mezhdunarodnoi politiki* (Moscow, 1959), pp. 163-165.

6. See Radek's letter in Artur Leinwand, *Polska Partia Socjali-styczna wobec wojny polsko-radziechiej 1919-1920* (Warsaw, 1964), pp. 251-256. Compare Radek's speech of January 27, 1920 in *Die innere und äussere Lage Sowjetrusslands und die Aufgaben de K.P.R.* (Leipzig, 1921), p. 10; and his "Noiabr: stranichka iz vozpominanii," *Krasnaia Nov,* October 1926, pp. 172-175.

7. Trotsky to Zinoviev, copy to Lenin and Krestinskii, January 22, 1920, Trotsky Archive, T. 422, Houghton Library, Harvard University.

8. On January 26, 1920, *Dokumenty vneshnei politiki SSSR,* (Moscow, 1959—), II, 331. Litvinov erroneously asserted that Sazonov also came to Warsaw.

9. January 24, 1920, *Sochineniia,* 4th ed., XXX, 278-279. The third edition only summarizes the speech and gives the date of January 26.

10. February 9, 1920, *Sochineniia,* XXV, 27.

11. *Sochineniia,* 4th ed., XXX, 340.

12. Lenin to Trotsky, February 19, 1920, Trotsky Archive, T. 446.

13. N. E. Kakurin and V. A. Melikov, *Voina s belopoliakami* (Moscow, 1925), p. 14.

14. Exact figures are hard to establish. Compare Tadeusz Kutrzeba, *Wyprawa kijowska 1920 roku* (Warsaw, 1937), p. 68; Polish intelli-gence report of February 13, 1920, Akta Adiutantury Generalnej Nac-zelnego Dowództwa, XXI/2538, Piłsudski Institute, New York (cited as AGND); I. N. Sergeev (J. N. Siergiejew), *Od Dźwiny ku Wiśle* (Warsaw, 1925), p. 15.

15. See Kakurin and Melikov, *Voina s belopoliakami,* p. 67; Wilhelm

Arenz, *Polen und Russland* (Leipzig, 1939), p. 77; Boris M. Shaposhnikov, *Na Visle: K istorii kampanii 1920 g* (Moscow, 1924), p. 9; Kutrzeba, *Wyprawa kijowska,* pp. 131-133.

16. See I. Bril, "Politicheskaia podgotovka letnei operatsii v 1920 g," *Voina i Revoliutsiia,* 11 (1926), *passim.*

17. Gibson to Secretary of State, January 17, 1920, *Foreign Relations: 1920,* III, 372.

18. Kutrzeba commented that from a military point of view the Russian chief of operations could do nothing else but to prepare for a campaign. See *Wyprawa kijowska,* p. 131. Rumors about an impending Soviet attack against Poland were especially strong in Germany, but they had slender foundation. See two reports of Dr. Victor Naumann, February 9 and 11, St. Antony's Collection, roll 33, National Archives, Washington, D.C. Compare Chicherin to Litvinov, February 14, 1920, *DVP SSSR,* II, 370-371.

19. For an economic analysis and statistical data see N. F. Kuzmin, *Krushenie poslednego pokhoda Antanty* (Moscow, 1958), pp. 10-12, 19; S. E. Rabinovich, *Istoriia grazhdanskoi voiny* (Moscow, 1933), p. 92; P. V. Suslov, *Politicheskoe obespechenie sovetsko-polskoi kampanii 1920 goda* (Moscow and Leningrad, 1930), pp. 7-9; compare Titus Komarnicki, *Rebirth of the Polish Republic* (London, 1957), p. 512; Fedor G. Zuev, *Mezhdunarodnyi imperializm . . .* (Moscow, 1954), p. 124.

20. Lenin on February 5, 1920, *Sochineniia,* XXV, 23. Rumbold to Curzon, January 30, 1920, *Documents on British Foreign Policy* (first series, London, 1947—), XI, 203-204 (cited as *DBFP*).

21. Lenin made all these points on February 2, 1920; *Sochineniia,* 4th ed., XXX, 291-303.

22. Zinoviev in *Pravda,* June 4, 1920.

23. Lenin on March 1, 1920, *Sochineniia,* XXV, 58-59.

24. Radek, "Polskii vopros i internatsional," *Kommunisticheskii Internatsional,* no. 12, (1920), pp. 2186-2188.

25. On June 12, 1920, *Sochineniia,* XXV, 295.

26. Lenin, "Detskaia bolezn," *Sochineniia,* XXV, 210-230.

27. February 2, 1920, *ibid.,* 4th ed., XXX, 300.

28. Appeal of May 16, 1920, in *Anrufe des Executivkomitees der kommunistischen Internationale zur polnischen Frage* (Berlin, 1920), p. 11.

29. *Sochineniia,* XXIV, 657.

30. March 1, 1920, *ibid.,* XXV, 58-59.

31. See, among others, Lenin on June 12, 1920, *ibid.,* XXV, 294; *Anrufe,* p. 11; Karl Radek, *Voina polskikh belogvardeitsev protiv Sovetskoi Rossii* (Moscow, 1920), p. 17.

32. See Trotsky's speech at Homel on May 10, 1920, published as *Sovetskaia Rossiia i burzhuaznaia Polsha* (1920). This view is shared by the following Polish writers: Stanisław Szeptycki, *Front litewsko-białoruski* (Cracow, 1925), p. 13; Stanisław Grabski, *The Polish-Soviet Frontier* (London, 1943), p. 21; Wincenty Witos, *Moje wspomnienia*

(3 vols.; Paris, 1964-1965), II, 363; Feliks Libert, "Nowy cel wojny," *Niepodległość*, n.s., 3 (1951), 36. While Ioffe told the Poles later that the Soviets had proposed "only a demarcation line and not a boundary which would have had to run quite differently," he was then bargaining at the Riga peace conference. See Jan Dąbski, *Pokój ryski, wspomnienia, pertraktacje, tajne układy z Joffem, listy* (Warsaw, 1931), p. 108.

33. See Kutepov to Sazonov, February 1, 1920, Giers Archive, file 124, no. 244, Hoover Institution, Stanford, Calif.

34. February 9, 1920, AGND, LVIII/2541.

35. February 2, 1920, *Sochineniia*, 4th ed., XXX, 302.

36. February 27, 1920, *ibid.*, XXX, 373.

37. See Suslov, *Politicheskoe obespechenie*, pp. 25-30.

38. *Sochineniia*, XXV, 59.

39. March 6, 1920, *ibid.*, XXV, 65-66.

40. Lenin to Trotsky, March 1, 1920, Trotsky Archive, T. 465.

41. Trotsky to Krestinskii, March 2, *ibid.*, T. 467.

42. Trotsky to Lenin, March 9, 1920, *ibid.*, T. 478.

43. Lenin to Trotsky, March 11, 1920, *Leninskii Sbornik*, XXXIV (1942), 275. Trotsky Archive, T. 482. Compare Lenin to Unszlicht, March 11, 1920, in Rabinovich, *Istoriia grazhdanskoi voiny*, p. 96.

44. See Lenin to Trotsky, March 11, 1920, *Leninskii Sbornik*, XXXIV (1942), 275; Trotsky to Lenin, March 12, 1920, Trotsky Archive, T. 484; Trotsky's criticism of the Narkomindel in Leon Trotsky, *Kak vooruzhalas revoliutsiia* (3 vols.; in 4, Moscow, 1923-1924), II/2, 103. Compare Isaac Deutscher, *The Prophet Armed* (Oxford, 1954), p. 459.

45. Lenin to Trotsky, undated (editors suggest that the note was written between March 8 and 20, 1920, and it would seem that the latter date is more likely), Lenin, *Polnoe sobranie sochinenii* (5th ed.; Moscow, 1958—), LI, 154.

46. Trotsky to Lenin, Kamenev, Krestinskii, Bukharin, copy to Chicherin, March 24, Trotsky Archive, T. 490.

47. On March 29, 1920, in *Sochineniia*, XXV, 101.

48. *Ibid.*

49. Lubomirski to Secretary of State, April 19, 1920, *Foreign Relations: 1920*, III, 383. Compare a similar statement by Ciechanowski to Gregory, PRO, F.O. 371/3913, no. 191556.

50. Rumbold to Curzon, April 6, 1920, PRO, FO 371/3913, no. 190665.

51. *DVP SSSR*, II, 427-428; English translation in Jane Degras, ed., *Soviet Documents on Foreign Policy, 1917-1941* (3 vols., New York, 1951-1953), I, 183-184.

52. See especially *Pravda*, March 28 and 31, 1920.

53. On March 29, 1920, in *Sochineniia*, XXV, 101-102.

54. Julian Marchlewski, *Pisma wybrane*, (2 vols., Warsaw, 1952-1956), II, 759; Radek, *Voina polskikh belogvardeitsev*, pp. 3-4; Leon Trotsky, *Sochineniia*, XVII/2, 453.

55. Chicherin, in introduction to *Livre rouge: recueil des documents diplomatiques relatifs aux relations entre la Russie et la Pologne 1918-1920* (Moscow, 1920); compare Lenin on April 29 and October 2, 1920, *Sochineniia*, XXV, 252, 399; Karl Radek, *Die auswärtige Politik Sowjetrusslands* (Hamburg, 1921), p. 59; Trotsky, *Sovetskaia Rossiia*, p. 8; Marchlewski in *Dokumenty i materiały*, II, 719n; Narkomindel to president of Tsentrosoiuz in Reval, April 9, 1920, *DVP SSSR*, II, 451. For the opinions of Soviet historians see *Grazhdanskaia voina 1919-1921*, ed. A. S. Bubnov, S. S. Kamenev, and R. P. Eideman (3 vols.; Moscow, 1928-1930), III, 307-308; Suslov, *Politicheskoe obespechenie*, p. 59; N. Kakurin, *Russko-polskaia kampania 1918-1920* (Moscow, 1922), p. 33; I. Maiskii, *Vneshniaia politika RSFSR 1917-1922* (Moscow, 1923), p. 87.

56. See Julian Stachiewicz, *Działania zaczepne 3 armii na Ukrainie* (Warsaw, 1925), p. 5; Adam Przybylski, *Wojna polska 1918-1921* (Warsaw, 1930), p. 133; Kutrzeba, *Wyprawa kijowska*, p. 46; staff reports, AGND, VII/2345, VIII/3377.

57. Gibson to Secretary of State, April 6, 1920, Record Group 59, "Political Relations betwen Poland and the Soviet Union," 760c.61/44, National Archives.

58. Wasilewski, *Piłsudski jakim go znałem*, pp. 220-221.

59. See text in *Dokumenty i materiały*, II, 699-716; Wasilewski's comments on p. 716.

60. *Ibid.*, II, 718-719; *DVP SSSR*, II, 437-438.

61. Chicherin to Lenin, April 2, 1920, Trotsky Archive, T. 494. In the negotiations with Estonia the "Russian delegation declared from the start that hostilities would not cease and an armistice would not be signed until so-called 'war guarantees' were given by the other party." Ioffe's statement quoted in Xenia J. Eudin and Harold H. Fisher, eds., *Soviet Russia and the West, 1920-1927: A Documentary Survey* (Stanford, 1957), p. 50.

62. *DVP SSSR*, II, 436-437; *Livre rouge* (Moscow, 1920), pp. 103-105.

63. *Dokumenty i materiały*, II, 722-723; *DVP SSSR*, II, 448.

64. April 8, 1920, *DVP SSSR*, II, 447-448; *Livre rouge*, pp. 106-108, which gives the date of April 9, 1920.

65. April 8, 1920, *DVP SSSR*, II, 445-447; English text in *DBFP*, XI, 280-282.

66. April 9, 1920, published on April 15, 1920, reprinted in Degras, *Soviet Documents*, I, 185-186.

67. Curzon, for one, wanted to have nothing to do with it. See *DBFP*, XI, 281n. Also PRO, FO 371/3913, no. 191556.

68. April 9, 1920, *DVP SSSR*, II, 452-453. Compare Narkomindel to delegate of Tsentrosoiuz in Reval, *ibid.*, 451-452.

69. Kamenev to Gittis, April 8, 1920 cited in Kakurin and Melikov, *Voina s belopoliakami*, pp. 422-423.

70. Morstin to Supreme Command, April 14, 1920, AGND, LVIII/-3253.

71. Piltz to Ministry of Foreign Affairs, April 15, 1920, *ibid.*, LVIII/3358.

72. Rumbold to Curzon, April 13, 1920, and Lord Hardinge to Rumbold, April 19, 1920, *DBFP,* XI, 282, 287.

73. Ciechanowski to Ministry of Foreign Affairs, April 14, 1920, AGND, LXVI/3477.

74. Lubomirski to Ministry of Foreign Affairs, April 20, 1920, *ibid.,* LXVI/3350.

75. Excerpts of Patek's note to Skulski, April 28 [?], 1920, *ibid.,* XXIV/3708.

76. Communiqué of April 20, 1920, *Dokumenty i materiały,* II, 743-744; Kazimierz W. Kumaniecki, ed., *Odbudowa państwowości polskiej* (Warsaw, 1924), pp. 262; Kutrzeba, *Wyprawa kijowska,* pp. 75-76.

77. Kossakowski later told a Soviet diplomat that peace had not materialized in the spring because of "lack of faith in the sincerity of your intentions." Kossakowski to Ministry of Foreign Affairs, August 3, 1920, AGND, XXVII/4520, printed with omissions in Józef Sieradzki, *Białowieża i Mikaszewicze* (Warsaw, 1959), pp. 101-116. The same opinion is expressed by Kutrzeba, *Wyprawa kijowska,* p. 62; Przybylski, *Wojna polska,* p. 130; and Grabski, *Polish-Soviet Frontier,* p. 22.

78. Note in French, April 23, 1920, marked "for the envoy." Not clear when dispatched and to which legations. See Archiwum Michała Mościckiego, no. 613, Piłsudski Institute, New York (cited as AMM).

79. On April 11, 1920. A few days later Captain Bogusław Miedziński, addressing intelligence officers, said that "history does not know a peace of understanding." Peace comes only after a victory, and since both the Poles and the Bolsheviks had so far been successful in their campaigns, the Red Army had to be defeated before peace negotiations could begin. See *Dokumenty i materiały,* II, 739-740.

80. Text of declaration of April 23, 1920 in *DVP SSSR,* II, 481-482.

81. See *Pravda,* April 25, 1920.

82. *Vsesoiuznaia Kommunisticheskaia Partiia (bolshevikov) v rezoliutsiakh i resheniiakh sezdov, konferentsii i plenumov TsK: 1898-1932* (Moscow, 1933), pp. 368-370. The order of the revvoensovet of the Republic to the Southern Front, dated November 30, 1919 and sent on December 2, contained the phrase "long live free and independent Soviet Ukraine." See *Grazhdanskaia voina na Ukraine 1918-1920: sbornik dokumentov i materialov,* ed. S. M. Korolivskii, N. H. Kolechnik, and I. K. Rybalk (3 vols. in 4, Kiev, 1967), II, 517.

83. On December 28, 1919, *Sochineniia,* XXIV, 656-659.

84. A. V. Likholat, *Razgrom nationalisticheskoi kontrrevoliutsii na Ukraine* (Moscow, 1954), p. 459.

85. Trotsky to Lenin, Serebriakov, Stalin, Dzierżyński, Kamenev, April 26, 1920, Trotsky Archive, T. 500.

86. Trotsky to Central Committee, May 11, 1920, *ibid.,* T. 516.

87. See Suslov, *Politicheskoe obespechenie,* p. 42. See a map showing centers of partisan activity in S. A. Mezheninov, *Nachalo borby s Poliakami na Ukraine v 1920 g.* (Moscow, 1926), p. 42.

88. Zinoviev, "Kto nash glavnyi vrag na Ukraine?" *Pravda,* June 10, 1920; compare Komarnicki, *Rebirth of the Polish Republic,* p. 578.

89. Trotsky to Lenin, Bukharin, Krestinskii, Kamenev, copy to Rakovskii, November, 2, 1920, Trotsky Archive, T. 616.

90. Petliura wrote War Minister Salskyi on March 31, 1920 that the PPS had promised to demand, in the course of peace negotiations, that the Bolsheviks evacuate the Ukraine, so that Petliura's forces could move in and organize a constituent assembly. See Simon Petliura, *Statti, lysty, dokumenty* (New York, 1956), p. 266.

91. See confidential bulletin of the Command of the Volhynian Front, March 1, 1920, AGND, VII/2797.

92. "Referat o Ukrainie," January 18, 1921, Ciechanowski Deposit, Hoover Institution, Stanford, Calif.

93. Piłsudski to Sosnkowski, April 29, 1920, *Niepodległość*, n.s., 7 (1962), 98.

94. He wrote Mazepa it was necessary to pay a heavy price for the alliance. See Isaak Mazepa, *Ukraina v ohni i buri revoliutsii 1917-1921* (3 vols.; Prague, 1942-1943), III, 11.

95. Petliura to Salskyi, March 31, 1920 in Petliura, *Statti,* pp. 263-264.

96. See Mazepa, *Ukraina,* III, 13-14.

97. See draft of Polish-Ukrainian agreement, April 15, 1920, AGND, XXII/3148, compare 3124.

98. See Polish text in *Dokumenty i materiały,* II, 745-747; English translation from the Ukrainian text in John S. Reshetar, *The Ukrainian Revolution 1917-1920* (Princeton, 1952), pp. 301-302.

99. Signed on April 24, 1920 by Major Walery Sławek and Captain Wacław Jędrzejewicz on the Polish side and General Volodymyr Sinkler and Lieutenant Colonel Maksym Didkovskyi on the Ukrainian side. Polish text (binding in case of disagreement) in *Dokumenty i materiały,* II, 749-753 and in Kutrzeba, *Wyprawa kijowska,* pp. 83-86 (with some stylistic differences).

100. See the draft in *Dokumenty i materiały,* III, 26-29. Compare Piłsudski's talk with Skulski, May 9, 1920, *Niepodległość,* n.s., 7 (1962), 113; Sosnkowski to Piłsudski May 12 and 14, 1920, AGND, VIII/3698 and IX/4329, also report of May 27, *ibid.,* XXVI/4331, and Leinwand, *Polska Partia Socjalistyczna,* pp. 146-148.

101. Extreme interpretations of the Piłsudski-Petliura pact abound. S. P. Shelukhin, *Varshavskyi dohovir mizh Poliakamy i S. Petliuroiu 21 Kvitnia 1920 roku* (Prague, 1926) views it as a conspiracy to enslave the Ukrainian nation. Reshetar in *The Ukrainian Revolution* sees only shadows of the agreement. On the opposite side Komarnicki argues that Poland could never have dominated the Ukraine because of the latter's size. He overlooks the point that Petliura's Ukraine could hardly have extended beyond the Dnieper and thus would have been weaker and smaller than Poland. See Komarnicki's *Rebirth of the Polish Republic,* p. 575.

102. See Mazepa, *Ukraina,* III, 8, 29, 32; Leinwand, *Polska Partia Socjalistyczna,* p. 144. The two cabinet members were Stanisław Stempowski, minister of agriculture and then of health, and Henryk Józewski.

103. Interview for the *Daily News,* May 21, 1920, cited in *Pisma zbiorowe,* V, 158.

104. Mazepa, *Ukraina,* III, 32.

105. See text in Andrzej Wierzbicki, *Wspomnienia i dokumenty, 1877-1920* (Warsaw, 1957), pp. 589-590; compare Grabski, *Polish-Soviet Frontier,* p. 23.

106. For the debate see the protocol of April 22, 1920 in AGND/102 "Rokowania . . . Materiały sejmowe." Compare Kumaniecki, *Odbudowa państwowości polskiej,* pp. 262, 264; Kutrzeba, *Wyprawa kijowska,* pp. 87-88; Maciej Rataj, *Pamiętniki: 1918-1927* (Warsaw, 1965), pp. 81-82; Stanisław Głąbiński, *Wspomnienia polityczne* (Pelplin, 1937), pp. 467-468.

107. *Grazhdanskaia voina,* III, 318.

108. For a Soviet presentation of the alleged evidence, with an emphasis on the sinister role played by the United States, see *Istoriia grazhdanskoi voiny v SSSR* (5 vols.; Moscow, 1935-1960). V, 39ff.

109. On May 16, 1920, see *Dokumenty i materiały,* III, 51.

110. See telegram to Foch of April 25, 1920 in *ibid.,* III, 3. Compare with Piotr S. Wandycz, *France and her Eastern Allies, 1919-1925* (Minneapolis, 1962), pp. 145-148.

111. See "V chadu i khmelu," May 13, 1920, *Kak vooruzhalas revoliutsiia,* II/2, 138. Compare accounts of the first stages of the Polish offensive in Kakurin and Melikov, *Voina s belopoliakami,* pp. 82, 90; L. Degtiarev, "Politotdel v otstuplenii," *Proletarskaia Revoliutsiia,* no. 12/35 (December 1924), pp. 212-247; Kuzmin, *Krushenie poslednego pokhoda,* p. 69.

112. For details see Piłsudski to Sosnkowski, April 29, 1920, *Niepodległość,* n.s., 7 (1962), 95, 98-99; Suslov, *Politicheskoe obespechenie,* p. 34; Kakurin and Melikov, *Voina s belopoliakami,* p. 93; Kutrzeba, *Wyprawa kijowska,* p. 99; Stachiewicz, *Działania zaczepne,* p. 67.

113. Piłsudski, *Pisma zbiorowe,* V, 155-156.

114. See text in Kumaniecki, *Odbudowa państwowości,* pp. 267-269.

115. See Piłsudski to Skulski on April 26, May 1, 6, 1920, *Niepodległość,* n.s., 7 (1962), 87-88, 101-105, 111. The American diplomat Moffat praised Polish "tact and cleverness" and reported on the delight of the inhabitants of Kiev "to be ridden of the Bolsheviks" (Moffat Papers, v. 26). Rumbold informed Curzon that the British were impressed with Polish behavior in Kiev; *DBFP,* XI, 360-361. The London *Times* on May 13 wrote that Polish and Ukrainian troops entering Kiev were "received with the greatest enthusiasm by the population."

116. Piłsudski, *Pisma zbiorowe,* V, 159.

117. See the commentary to the Polish-Ukrainian pact, AGND, XXIII/3699.

118. See Suslov, *Politicheskoe obespechenie,* p. 37.

119. Piłsudski to Skulski, May 6, 1920, *Niepodległość,* n.s., 7 (1962), 110-111.

120. See Piłsudski to Sosnkowski, May 6, 1920, *ibid.,* 114-115. Compare with another letter of April 29, 1920, *ibid.,* 95-99; also draft of a note from the Ukrainian Chief of Staff to the Polish General Staff,

July 24, 1920, Akta Ukraińskiej Misji Wojskowej, I/5, Piłsudski Institute, New York.

121. Mazepa, *Ukraina,* III, 42n. Compare Grabski's criticism of the Ukrainians, *Polish-Soviet Frontier,* pp. 23-24.

122. See the testimony of Polish generals, Kutrzeba, *Wyprawa kijowska,* pp. 182, 304, and Marian Kukiel, *Dzieje Polski porozbiorowe, 1795-1921* (London, 1961), p. 587. For problems connected with Eastern Galicia see Petliura's letters to Piłsudski in Petliura, *Statti,* pp. 266-269, and in "Nieznane listy Piłsudskiego do Petlury," ed., Piotr Wandycz, *Zeszyty Historyczne,* 8 (1965), 184-186; also material in AGND, VIII/4135, IX/4208, XXIII/3514, XXVI/4381, XXVII/4529 and 4557.

123. See Moffat to Foster, June 20, 1920, Moffat Papers, v. 26.

124. Grabski's interview in *Gazeta Warszawska,* April 27, 1920, cited in Kutrzeba, *Wyprawa kijowska,* pp. 88-89.

125. See Sosnkowski to Piłsudski, April 29 and May 3, 1920, AGND, VIII/3697 and 3657; also Piłsudski to Skulski, May 1, 1920, *Niepodległość,* n.s., 7 (1962), 101-105.

126. See Leinwand, *Polska Partia Socjalistyczna,* p. 161; compare "XVII Kongres PPS (21-25 V 1920)," ed. Władysław Mroczkowski and Jan Tomicki, in *Najnowsze Dzieje Polski: materiały i studia z okresu 1914-1939,* 6 (1963), 239-288. Also *Dokumenty i materiały,* III, 23, and Lieberman's motion of April 27, in AGND/102, "Rokowania . . . materiały sejmowe."

127. In articles written on May 9 and June 27, 1920, which appeared later in a booklet, *Nasza polityka wschodnia* (Warsaw, 1922), pp. 5-12, 23.

128. Piłsudski to Sosnkowski, April 29, 1920, *Niepodległość,* n.s., 7 (1962), 99.

129. Piłsudski to Skulski, May 6, 1920, *ibid.,* 106-107. For reports from abroad see extracts from Patek's report of April 28, 1920, AGND, XXIV/3708; Sosnkowski to Piłsudski, May 3, 1920, *ibid.,* VIII/3697; paper by Ministry of Foreign Affairs, May 5, 1920, *ibid.,* XXIV/3708; Rozwadowski's report, May 16, 1920, *ibid.,* XXII/3453; Zamoyski to Ministry of Foreign Affairs, May 8, 1920, *ibid.,* LVIII/3534.

130. Piłsudski's letter to Skulski of May 6 radiated optimism. Compare his letter to Mrs. Piłsudska, May 1, 1920. Aleksandra Piłsudska, *Piłsudski: A Biography by his Wife Alexandra* (New York, 1941), pp. 296-297, and original text in Aleksandra Piłsudska, *Wspomnienia* (London, 1960), pp. 246-247. In a letter to Sosnkowski, Piłsudski wrote on May 6 that the capture of Kiev was a political symbol. A seizure of Odessa by the Ukrainians with Polish aid would follow. Then negotiations could start. See *Niepodległość,* n.s., 7 (1962), 114.

131. See Kumaniecki, *Odbudowa państwowości,* p. 273; Ministry of Foreign Affairs to legation in London, May 19, 1920, "Rosja 4, A.B." Archive of Polish Government-in-Exile, Montreal (cited as APGE); Rumbold to Curzon, May 22, *DBFP,* XI, 326-327.

132. "Defetyści i komuniści," *Kurjer Poranny,* no. 163, June 17, 1920.

Although the article appeared a month after the events discussed it represented ideas current in late April and May. For the stress on disannexation see a confidential circular of the Polish Ministry of Foreign Affairs of April 26, 1920, Ciechanowski Deposit; also Sapieha to legation in Washington, May 10, 1920, "Pertraktacje pokojowe," *ibid.* One may mention in this connection Polish interest in the nations of the Caucasus, where Tytus Filipowicz acted as Poland's envoy. See Marian Uzdowski, "Niepodległość narodów Kaukazu," *Rząd i Wojsko,* no. 10, March 7, 1920; and Cafer Seydahmet Kirimer, "Moje wspomnienie z rozmowy z Marszałkiem Józefem Piłsudskim," *Niepodległość,* n.s., 2 (1950), 41-50.

133. See Trotsky, "V chadu i khmelu," *Kak vooruzhalas revoliutsiia,* II/2, 139; Stalin to Lenin, July 18, 1920, *Leninskii Sbornik,* XXXVI (1959), 110-111. Many Soviet historians have later repeated a story, according to which Wrangel was to help the Poles conquer Belorussia and the Ukraine in exchange for assistance against the Bolsheviks. France, Britain, and the United States allegedly promoted this plan. See I. F. Kondrashev and N. V. Kirillov, *Ocherki istorii SSSR 1917-1962* (Moscow, 1963), p. 129.

134. Sosnkowski to Piłsudski, May 12, 1920, AGND, VIII/3698.

135. Article in *L'Éclair,* June 2, 1920; interview in *La Victoire,* June 3, 1920.

136. Translation of a deciphered Russian message, June 16, 1920, and other reports in AGND, XXVIII/4817, 4768. In a telegram to Wrangel, sent the same day, Savinkov added he had Piłsudski's assurance that the war was against the Bolsheviks and not Russia. Wrangel thus ought to view the Poles as liberators. See *Dokumenty i materiały,* III, 91-92. Compare Savinkov to Wrangel, July 1920, PRO, F.O. 371/3915, no. 208987.

137. Gorlov to Giers, July 5, 1920, Giers Archive, file 81. The Poles seemingly left without answer an earlier proposal of cooperation made by Petr Struve. See AGND, XXII/3271. For a negative stand of Wrangel toward Savinkov's action in Warsaw see *Boris Savinkov pered voennoi kollegiei verkhovnego suda SSSR,* ed. I. Shubin (Moscow, 1924), p. 101.

138. Ministry of Foreign Affairs to legation in Paris, June 8, 1920, *Dokumenty i materiały,* III, 93n.

139. Compare General Rozwadowski's memorandum for Marshal Foch and Sir Henry Wilson, July 6, 1920, AGND, XXV/4119.

140. Lenin, *Sochineniia,* XXV, 482.

Chapter 9. "Give Us Warsaw!"

1. It appears that the orders for mobilization of Communists for the western front came out later than originally anticipated. For instance the Smolensk gubernial committee discussed them only on April 28, 1920. See protocol no. 17 in Smolensk Archive: Kommunisticheskaia

Partia Sovetskogo Soiuza. Smolenskii oblastnoi komitet, Partiinyi Arkhiv, Widner Library, Harvard University, Cambridge, Mass.

2. See *Dokumenty i materiały*, III, 4-5.

3. See the critical comments of P. V. Suslov in *Politicheskoe obespechenie sovetsko-polskoi kampanii 1920 goda* (Moscow, and Leningrad, 1930), p. 47. Also *Dokumenty i materiały do historii stosunków polsko-radzieckich* (Warsaw, 1962—), III, 6-7, 8-9.

4. See Lenin on April 29, and May 5, 1920. Compare his statements on October 2, 1920 in *Sochineniia* (3rd ed.; 30 vols.; Moscow, 1935-1937), XXV, 251-252, 257-261, 399. See Chicherin's remarks on June 17, 1920 in *Dokumenty vneshnei politiki SSSR* (Moscow, 1959—), II, 641; Stalin's retrospective remarks, on November 6, 1920, in Stalin, *Sochineniia* (13 vols.; Moscow, 1946-1951), IV, 388. An interesting explanation of the war on the grounds of Allied interests—which minimizes Polish vested interest—was made in a publication (no. 23) of the politburo of the Sixteenth Army revvoensovet. See Tadeusz Teslar, *Propaganda bolszewicka podczas wojny polsko-rosyjskiej 1920 roku* (Warsaw, 1938), p. 199.

5. Trotsky on May 2, 9, 10 and 11 in *Kak vooruzhalas revoliutsiia* (3 vols. in 4; Moscow, 1923-1924), II/2, 102-104, 130-131, 133, 135.

6. See Suslov, *Politicheskoe obespechenie*, p. 21, 31, 64-65; Steklov's article in *Izvestia*, May 18, 1920.

7. See *Leninskii Sbornik*, XXXIV (1942), 293.

8. Trotsky's order of June 30, 1920, in *Kak vooruzhalas revoliutsiia*, II/2, 153. Compare William H. Chamberlin, *The Russian Revolution, 1917-1921* (2 vols.; New York, 1935), II, 303; Isaac Deutscher, *The Prophet Armed: Trotsky, 1879-1921* (Oxford, 1954), p. 460.

9. On May 7, 12, and 23, 1920.

10. Speech on May 5, 1920. Karl Radek, *Voina polskikh belogvardeitsev protiv Sovetskoi Rossii* (Moscow, 1920), pp. 22-23.

11. See Leon Trotsky, *My Life* (New York, 1931), p. 456. Compare telegram of Rakovskii and Berzin to Trotsky in N. E. Kakurin and V. A. Melikov, *Voina s belopoliakami* (Moscow, 1925), p. 82.

12. *Pravda* and *Izvestia*, May 30, 1920.

13. See the appeal of Lenin, Trotsky, and Kurskii to White officers in *Pravda* on June 3, 1920; Trotsky's declaration on May 7 in *Kak vooruzhalas revoliutsiia*, II/2, 119-120; account of an anti-Polish meeting of former officers of Kolchak in *Pravda*, April 30, 1920. Many anti-Communist Russians may have agreed with A. Pogodin's words printed in *Russkaia Gazeta* in Belgrade on June 11, 1920 that "in the place of Poland there emerged from the tomb the frightening ghost of *Rzeczpospolita*."

14. On May 8 and 9, 1920, *Kak vooruzhalas revoliutsiia*, II/2, 121, 124, 125.

15. Maxim Gorky, *Sobranie sochinenii* (30 vols.; Moscow, 1948-1953), XXIV, 215. Also account in *Pravda*, May 5, 1920.

16. On May 5 at the meeting in the Bolshoi Theater.

17. Wasilewski to Piłsudski, May 15, 1920. Akta Adiutantury Gene-

ralnej Naczelnego Dowództwa, XXIII/3532, Piłsudski Institute, New York (Cited as AGND). On Balakhovich and his troops, who resembled seventeenth-century cossack bands rather than a modern army see reports in *ibid.*, XXVIII/4304; and the description by Karol Wędziagolski in "Savinkov," *Novyi Zhurnal* (1963), 135-155, and 169-197.

18. The drawing up of directives was decided by the Central Committee on April 28. Their text of April 30 appears in Trotsky, *Kak vooruzhalas revoliutsiia*, II/2, 93-96. They seem to have been published on May 23, 1920; see N. F. Kuzmin, *Krushenie poslednego pokhoda Antanty* (Moscow, 1958), p. 80; and *Istoriia grazhdanskoi voiny v SSSR* (5 vols.; Moscow, 1935-1960), V, 69. Suslov speaks of early May (*Politicheskoe obespechenie*, p. 32). The texts of appeals are in *DVP SSSR*, II, 507-509, and 576-578.

19. See Trotsky, *Kak vooruzhalas revoliutsiia*, II/2, 91; VTsIK's declaration, April 29, 1920 in *DVP SSSR*, II, 495; Zinoviev on May 4, 1920, in *Pravda*, May 5, 1920.

20. See resolution of May 5, 1920 in *Sowjetrussland und Polen: Reden von Kamenev, Lenin, Trotski, Marchlewski, Radek und Martow . . . 5 Mai 1920* (Moscow, 1920).

21. See Point 9, Trotsky, *Kak vooruzhalas revoliutsiia*, II/2, 94. Compare Radek, "Polskii vopros," *Kommunisticheskii International*, no. 12, pp. 2186-2188.

22. Lenin, *Sochineniia*, XXV, 287.

23. Stalin's letter of June 12, 1920 in *ibid.*, XXV, 624. For a lengthy excerpt in English see Titus Komarnicki, *Rebirth of the Polish Republic* (London, 1957), pp. 585-586. Compare comments in Mikhail I. Kulichenko, *Borba kommunisticheskoi partii za reshenie natsionalnogo voprosa v 1918-1920 godakh* (Kharkov, 1963), pp. 440-441.

24. Stalin, *Sochineniia*, IV, 352-354.

25. See point 8 of the theses, Trotsky, *Kak vooruzhalas revoliutsiia*, II/2, 94. Compare Kalinin's speech on May 18, 1920, *Dokumenty i materiały*, III, 53.

26. Lenin, *Sochineniia*, 4th ed., XXXI, 106. Italics added.

27. Radek, *Voina polskikh belogvardeitsev*, p. 17.

28. See Suslov, *Politicheskoe obespechenie*, p. 51. The army order of the day appeared in *Pravda* on May 25, 1920.

29. Trotsky on May 3, 1920, *Kak vooruzhalas revoliutsiia*, II/2, 114-115; Stalin, *Sochineniia*, IV, 333.

30. See assurances of Kon to the All-Ukrainian Soviets in late May, 1920, *Dokumenty i materiały*, III, 55n.

31. Incomplete English translation of the document is in Jane Degras, ed., *Soviet Documents on Foreign Policy, 1917-1941* (3 vols.; New York, 1951-1953), I, 189-190.

32. Radek on May 5, 1920, in *Sowjetrussland und Polen*, p. 32. Only the Menshevik leader Martov spoke in favor of a peace settlement acceptable to both sides; *ibid.*, pp. 34-36.

33. Lenin, *Sochineniia*, XXV, 298. For Lev Kamenev's views, expressed in a pamphlet on "Lloyd George, Wrangel and Piłsudski,"

see Teslar, *Polityka Rosji sowieckiej podczas wojny z Polską* (Warsaw, 1937), p. 173.

34. Lenin on April 29, Zinoviev on May 3, Marchlewski on May 5, 1920.

35. See Chicherin's notes of May 19 and June 11, 1920, *DVP SSSR*, II, 530-532, 565-566. Also notes to Czechoslovakia, and Austria, *ibid.*, II, 551, 568. Zinoviev's are in *Anrufe des Executivkomitees der kommunistischen Internationale zur polnischen Frage* (Berlin, 1920), pp. 11-15, and extracts in Jane Degras, ed., *The Communist International 1919-1943: Documents* (2 vols.; New York, 1956-1960), I, 90-92.

36. See orders of Trotsky and Tukhachevskii *Kak vooruzhalas revoliutsiia*, II/2, 134, 155-156; *Dokumenty i materiały*, III, 97.

37. See Kulichenko, *Borba*, pp. 292-298.

38. Cited in *Istoriia grazhdanskoi voiny*, V, 73. Compare Suslov, *Politicheskoe obespechenie*, p. 68; and Kuzmin, *Krushenie poslednego pokhoda*, pp. 86-87.

39. Text in *Dokumenty i materiały*, III, 168-170.

40. Stalin spoke at length about anti-Polish revolts in Belorussia (*Sochineniia*, IV, 343). Guerilla activity around Minsk was confirmed in Warsaw. See Moffat to Gibson, June 2, 1920, Moffat Papers, v. 26, Houghton Library, Harvard University. The Lithuanian and Belorussian party had created in November 1919 a special bureau for underground action. See Kuzmin, *Krushenie poslednego pokhoda*, pp. 178-179.

41. Suslov, *Politicheskoe obespechenie*, p. 126.

42. Text in *DVP SSSR*, III, 73-75.

43. See the highly critical report of Captain Kazimierz Stamirowski, April 28, 1920, *Dokumenty i materiały*, III, 9-11.

44. Suggested by Stamirowski to Colonel Tadeusz Piskor, July 23, 1920, AGND, IX/4209.

45. Wasilewski to Świtalski, July 30, 1920, *ibid.*, XXVI/4481, also XXVIII/5852.

46. Lenin to Smilga, July 20, 1920, Trotsky Archive, T. 547, Widener Library, Harvard University.

47. See report of Soviet peace delegation, May 27, 1920, *ibid.*, T. 521. Also Lenin's remarks on June 12, 1920. *Sochineniia*, XXV, 297.

48. See Rumbold to Curzon, June 25, 1920, *Documents on British Foreign Policy* (first series, London, 1947—), XI, 362 (cited *DBFP*). Compare Józef Piłsudski, *Pisma zbiorowe* (10 vols.; Warsaw, 1937-1938), VII, 93. Moffat informed the American Commission in Berlin that the Polish Undersecretary for Foreign Affairs sent a circular to missions, which said that "the Ukrainian adventure is now definitely liquidated." This apparently produced conflicts within the ministry. See Moffat to N. G. Foster, June 28, 1920, Moffat Papers, v. 26.

49. See Kakurin and Melikov, *Voina s belopoliakami*, p. 495.

50. Text in Kazimierz W. Kumaniecki, ed., *Odbudowa państwowości polskiej: najważniejsze dokumenty* (Warsaw and Cracow, 1924), pp. 281-283.

51. MS Diariusz Kossakowskiego July 5, 1920, Archiwum Polskiej Akademii Nauk, Warsaw. Compare Aleksander Lednicki's statement that this was "the only government act determining the character and aims of the war" (*Nasza polityka wschodnia* [Warsaw, 1922], p. 45).

52. Sosnkowski to General Pomiankowski, July 16, 1920, *Dokumenty i materiały*, III, 166-167.

53. See Adam Próchnik, *Pierwsze piętnastolecie Polski niepodległej 1918-1933* (Warsaw, 1957), p. 89. Moffat wrote Gibson on July 6, 1920 that the stand of the *Robotnik* played into the hands of the Russians. See Jay Pierrepont Moffat Papers, v. 26, Houghton Library, Harvard University.

54. There are many letters and memoranda of Savinkov to Piłsudski, as well as agreements between Savinkov, Balakhovich, General Petr Glasenapp, and Wrede in AGND. The proclamatión to the Russians, signed by Savinkov, Dimitrii Merezhkovskii, Glasenapp, F. I. Rodichev, Dimitrii Filosofov, and Z. Hippius is in Giers Archive, file 81, Hoover Institution, Stanford. See also *Dokumenty i materiały*, III, 146, and A. P. Velmin, "Russkaiia emigratsiia v Polshe v 1919-1921 gg.," and "K istorii russkoi pressy v Polshe v gg. 1919-39," Archive of Russian and East European History and Culture, Columbia University (cited as AREEH).

55. Gorlov to Giers, July 11, 1920, Giers Archive, file 81.

56. See Polish reports from Sevastopol, June 27, July 15, 1920, AGND, XXV/4155 and XXVI/4447.

57. See protocol and notes of July 5 meeting of the Council in "Protokoły Rady Obrony Państwa," ed. Artur Leinwand and Jan Molenda, *Z Dziejów Stosunków Polsko-Radzieckich: Studia i Materiały*, I (1965), 151-176.

58. Sapieha telegraphed Patek on July 3, 1920 to warn him against asking for Allied mediation in the Soviet-Polish peace; *Dokumenty i materiały*, III, 133.

59. On the Lloyd-George and Patek conversation of July 6, 1920 see *DBFP*, VIII, 441-442; and Patek's report to Ministry of Foreign Affairs in *Dokumenty i materiały*, III, 137-140. Also General Rozwadowski's report in *Dokumenty i materiały*, III, 142-144.

60. Report of Military Mission from Paris, July 9, 1920, *Dokumenty i materiały*, III, 153-154.

61. English text in *DBFP*, VIII, 505-506; Polish in Kumaniecki, *Odbudowa państwowości*, p. 291.

62. Patek did suggest on July 3 that Grabski and Sapieha come to Spa. See AGND, LIX/4059. Compare Rataj's statement (*Pamiętniki, 1918-1927* [Warsaw, 1965], p. 95) that everyone was simultaneously for and against Grabski's journey.

63. See minutes of the meetings in *DBFP*, VIII, 502-506, 524-530; contemporary Polish translation in *Dokumenty i materiały*, III, 155-162. Maxime Weygand, *Mémoires*, II: *Mirages et réalité* (Paris, 1957), pp. 89-91; Rozwadowski's telegram stating that Grabski "signed in spite of our protests," July 14, 1920, AGND, LIX/4159. Compare Adam

Rozwadowski, *Generał Rozwadowski* (Cracow, 1929), p. 79. Also Piotr S. Wandycz, *France and her Eastern Allies* (Minneapolis, 1962), pp. 153-155.

64. For a detailed discussion of this point see Witold Sworakowski, "An Error Regarding Eastern Galicia in Curzon's Note to the Soviet Government," *Journal of Central European Affairs*, 4 (April 1944), 1-26.

65. See Stanisław Stroński's interview in *Kurjer Warszawski*, July 18, 1920.

66. Grabski's report and discussion in the State Council in *Dokumenty i materiały*, III, 163-165, and "Protokoły Rady Obrony Państwa," pp. 177-195.

67. See White to Secretary of State, July 18, 1920, Record Group 59, "Political Relations between Poland and the Soviet Union," 760c.61/161, National Archives. Compare Moffat's views, July 20, 1920, Moffat Papers, v. 26.

68. Sapieha's instructions of July 15, 1920, AGND, IX/4223.

69. See Mikhail Tukhachevskii, "Revoliutsiia izvne," *Voina klassov: stati 1919-1920 g.* (Moscow, 1921), pp. 50-59. Compare Deutscher, *Prophet Armed*, p. 472. Samuil E. Rabinovich, *Istoriia grazhdanskoi voiny* (Moscow, 1933), p. 101 ascribes the theory of a revolution from outside to Trotsky.

70. See text in Ivan Stepanov, *S krasnoi armiei na panskuiu Polshu* (Moscow, 1920), p. 78. See also Kakurin and Melikov, *Voina s belopoliakami*, p. 470; Suslov, *Politicheskoe obespechenie*, p. 72. Compare comments in Teslar, *Propaganda bolszewicka*, p. 213; and Franz Borkenau, *The Communist International* (London, 1938), p. 194.

71. Suslov, *Politicheskoe obespechenie*, p. 77. According to Teslar, *Propaganda bolszewicka*, p. 165, that slogan had already been in use by June 1920.

72. I. N. Sergeev, *Od Dźwiny ku Wiśle* (Warsaw, 1925), p. 109; Trotsky, *My Life*, p. 456.

73. Trotsky to Politburo, July 13, 1920 (2 notes), Trotsky Archive, T. 544, T. 541. The Politburo consisted at this time of Lenin, Kamenev, Krestinskii, Trotsky, and Stalin (members), and Zinoviev and Bukharin (candidates).

74. See Leon Trotsky, *Lenin* (New York, 1962), p. 116; *My Life*, p. 457; *Moia zhizn* (2 vols.; Riga, 1930), II, 190-192; *Kak vooruzhalas revoliutsiia*, III/1, 97. Compare Ruth Fischer, *Stalin and German Communists* (Cambridge, Mass., 1948), p. 136; Boris M. Shaposhnikov, *Na Visle: k istorii kampanii 1920 g.* (Moscow, 1924), p. 22.

75. Lenin on October 2, 1920, *Sochineniia*, XXV, 402. Translation of excerpts, mistakenly dated October 8, in Degras, ed., *Soviet Documents on Foreign Policy*, I, 217-219.

76. Trotsky, *Lenin*, p. 116.

77. Lenin to Sklianskii (presumably not later than July 13, 1920), *Polnoe sobranie sochinenii* (5th ed., Moscow, 1958—), LI, 238. The note is also in Trotsky Archive, T. 540.

78. Lenin, *Sochineniia*, 4th ed., XXXI, 179.

79. *Grazhdanskaia voina na Ukraine, 1918-1920*, ed. S. M. Korolivskii, N. H. Kolechnik, and I. K. Rybalk (3 vols. in 4; Kiev, 1967), III, 395; Kuzmin, *Krushenie poslednego pokhoda*, p. 219.

80. See Georgii V. Chicherin, "Lenin," *Stati i rechi po voprosam mezhdunarodnoi politiki* (Moscow, 1961), p. 283.

81. Trotsky to Glavkom, July 17, 1920, Kakurin and Melikov, *Voina s belopoliakami*, pp. 475-476; also *Grazhdanskaia voina*, III, 396.

82. On July 18, 1920; Tukhachevskii, *Voina klassov*, pp. 138-140.

83. See Kuzmin, *Krushenie poslednego pokhoda*, p. 251. Compare Kakurin and Melikov, *Voina s belopoliakami*, p. 212; *Grazhdanskaia voina*, III, 399; Shaposhnikov, *Na Visle*, p. 23. These works mention different dates of Kamenev's order.

84. R. Ermolaev, "K istorii polskikh kommunisticheskikh organizatsii i organov RKP(b) dlia raboty sredi polskogo naselenia na territorii sovetskoi respubliki v 1917-1921 gg," in A. Ia. Manusevich, ed., *Oktiabrskaia revoliutsiia i zarubezhnye slavianskie narody* (Moscow, 1957), p. 36.

85. See especially Trotsky, *My Life*, p. 457; Borkenau, *Communist International*, p. 94; *Grazhdanskaia voina*, III, 391; Martov's speech on October 15, 1920, Unabhängige Sozialdemokratische Partei Deutschlands, *Protokoll über die Verhandlungen des ausserordentlichen Parteitages in Halle, vom 12 bis 17 Oktober 1920* (Berlin, n.d.), p. 212 (hereafter cited as USPD, *Protokoll*). A report of the Polish bureau recalled its ineffective warnings of the Russian comrades; see *Dokumenty i materiały*, III, 543.

86. Grigorii Zinoviev, *Le prolétariat européen devant la revolution: discours . . . à Halle le 14 octobre 1920* (Petrograd, 1921), p. 65.

87. Klara Zetkin, *Reminiscences of Lenin* (London, 1929), p. 20.

88. Both texts in Russian in Artur Leinwand, *Polska Partia Socjalistyczna wobec wojny polsko-radzieckiej, 1919-1920* (Warsaw, 1964), p. 184, quoting from Unszlicht Papers.

89. Cited in Suslov, *Politicheskoe obespechenie*, p. 18.

90. Warski to Zofia Dzierżyńska, October 16, 1920; excerpts in Maria Grinberg, "Z zagadnień wojny polsko-radzieckiej," in *Ruch robotniczy i ludowy* (Warsaw, 1961), pp. 503-504; text in *Dokumenty i materiały*, III, 495-499.

91. Clandestine appeals of the Polish Communist Party against the government, the State Defense Council, and recruiting, and for collaboration with the Red Army gave ample grounds for arrests. See *Dokumenty i materiały*, III, 71-73, 88-90, 108-110, 120-122, 259-263.

92. Lenin on October 2, 1920, *Sochineniia*, XXV, 402.

93. Cited in Suslov, *Politicheskoe obespechenie*, p. 76.

94. Trotsky on August 7, 1920, *Protokoll des zweiten Weltkongresses der Kommunistischen Internationale* (Hamburg, 1921), p. 681.

95. "Pismo k tovarishchu Zinovevu," Tukhachevskii, *Voina klassov*, pp. 138-140.

96. See James W. Hulse, *The Forming of the Communist Interna-*

tional (Stanford, Calif., 1964), p. 189. On the atmosphere of the Congress see the often-quoted remarks of Zinoviev of May 16, 1921. *Desiatyi sezd RKP(b), mart 1921 g.* (Moscow, 1962), pp. 500-501.

97. See speech in Halle, October 15, 1920 in USPD, *Protokoll*, p. 212.

98. Lenin astounded Levy by asking him about the chances of a Communist revolution in East Prussia, the stronghold of conservatism. To Levy this seemed like a poor joke. See the episode in Werner T. Angress, *Stillborn Revolution: The Communist Bid for Power in Germany 1921-1923* (Princeton, 1963), p. 67.

99. On the fear of German-Polish cooperation see the resolution of the Politburo, June 4, 1920, Trotsky Archive, T. 534.

100. Lenin on October 2, *Sochineniia*, XXV, 401.

101. See Hans W. Gatzke, "Russo-German Military Collaboration during the Weimar Republic," *American Historical Review*, 63 (April, 1958), 567; Kakurin and Melikov, *Voina s belopoliakami*, p. 212; Kopp to Maltzan, June 22, 1920, *DVP SSSR*, II, 583; compare Josef Korbel, *Poland between East and West* (Princeton, 1963) pp. 79-93; Christian Höltje, *Die Weimarer Republik und das Ostlocarno-Problem 1919-1934* (Würzburg, 1958), pp. 24-26; E. H. Carr, *Bolshevik Revolution, 1917-1923* (3 vols.; London, 1950-1953), III, 323-328.

102. Enver's letter in Hans von Seeckt, *Aus seinem Leben 1918-1936*, ed. Friedrich von Rabenau (Leipzig, 1941), p. 307.

103. See Hans von Speidel, "Reichswehr und Rote Armee," *Vierteljahrshefte für Zeitgeschichte*, 1 (1953), 13; *Berliner Zeitung*, August 13, 1920. While Lenin ordered Kopp on July 22 to talk only about trade relations with the Germans. (Lenin, *Sochineniia*, 4th ed., XXXV, 387), Trotsky insisted that Ioffe conduct some unspecified talks with Germany (August 4, 1920 note for the Politburo, Trotsky Archive, T. 560). For Kopp's alleged activities see also Teslar, *Polityka Rosji*, p. 246.

104. The note is in "Rosja," I, Archive of the Polish Government-in-Exile, Montreal (cited as APGE).

105. Haniel at a secret session of the Foreign Affairs Committee of the Reichstag, on August 17, 1920; cited in Höltje, *Die Weimarer Republik*, pp. 29-30. Compare a Polish report from Berlin in Jerzy Krasuski, *Stosunki polsko-niemieckie 1919-1925* (Poznan, 1962), pp. 84-85.

106. See *DBFP*, XI, 429-434

107. On these maneuvers see especially, Günther Rosenfeld, *Sowjetrussland und Deutschland 1917-1922* (Berlin, 1960), pp. 274, 292-293; E. Malcolm Carroll, *Soviet Communism and Western Public Opinion*, (Chapel Hill, N.C., 1965) pp. 148-152; *Dokumenty i materiały*, III, 272-273.

108. See Tower to Curzon, August 8, 10, 1920, *DBFP*, XI, 447, 457-459.

109. Lenin on September 22, 1920, *Sochineniia*, XXV, 378.

110. See Lenin's remarks on December 21, 1920, *ibid.*, XXVI, 13.

111. On British policies see Sir Esme Howard, *Theatre of Life* (2 vols.; Boston, 1935-1936), II, 297; Harold Nicolson, *Curzon: The Last*

Phase, 1919-1925 (London, 1934), pp. 205-210, 333; Lord Riddell, *Intimate Diary of the Peace Conference and After, 1918-1923* (New York, 1934), pp. 229-235; Komarnicki, *Rebirth of the Polish Republic,* Chap. 7; and the revealing, still unpublished third volume of Richard H. Ullman, *Anglo-Soviet Relations, 1917-1921.*

112. Text in *DVP SSSR,* III, 47-53. Incomplete translation in Degras, *Soviet Documents,* I, 194-197.

113. Telegram of July 20, 1920, AGND, XXV/4212.

114. Cited in Suslov, *Politicheskoe obespechenie,* p. 80. Karol Lapter remarks cautiously that when the Soviets spoke of peace with the Polish government they meant "in this case perhaps already a revolutionary government." See "Zarys stosunków polsko-radzieckich w latach 1917-1960" (mimeographed; Warsaw, 1961), p. 19.

115. On July 21, 1920, cited in Stepanov, *S krasnoi armiei,* pp. 89-90.

116. For discrepancies compare Trotsky, *Sochineniia,* XVII/2, 428-429; *Kak vooruzhalas revoliutsiia,* II/2, 161; *DVP SSSR,* III, 59; and *Izvestia,* July 21, 1920. This point is brought out in the yet unpublished third volume of Ullman, *Anglo-Soviet Relations.*

117. *DVP SSSR,* III, 60. Trotsky's original text concluded with "Long live a free, fraternal Poland of workers and peasants within large and just frontiers" (*Kak vooruzhalas revoliutsiia,* II/2, 161).

118. *DBFP,* VIII, 649-650.

119. Lenin to Chicherin, July 22, 1920, *Sochineniia,* 4th ed., XXXV, 387.

120. *DVP SSSR,* III, 61-62.

121. Note of July 26, 1920, *DBFP,* VIII, 662.

122. MS Diariusz Kossakowskiego, July 17, 1920. Piłsudski expressed similar views to the chief of the French military mission. See White to Secretary of State, July 19, 1920, RG 59, 760c.61/96, National Archives.

123. See minutes in *Dokumenty i materiały,* III, 193-194; "Protokoły Rady Obrony Państwa," pp. 214-219. Compare Rumbold to Curzon, July 19, 21, 23, 1920, *DBFP,* XI, 386, 393-394, 397.

124. Sapieha was eager to negotiate and sought contact with Litvinov in Copenhagen and Ioffe in Riga. See MS Diariusz Kossakowskiego, July 24, 1920. Compare Hanecki to Chicherin, August 2, 1920, *Dokumenty i materiały,* III, 275-276.

125. Witos on July 24, 1920, *Sprawozdanie stenograficzne 1919-1921,* Sejm ustawodawczy R.P. CLXVI/7-9.

126. See text in *Dokumenty i materiały,* III, 207-208 and *DVP SSSR,* III, 60-61, 64.

127. *DVP SSSR,* III, 65; *Dokumenty i materiały,* III, 211-212.

128. See Rozwadowski's request of July 25 for the indication of time and place of meeting; *Dokumenty i materiały,* III, 215.

129. *Ibid.,* III, 221; Kumaniecki, *Odbudowa państwowości,* p. 311.

130. *Dokumenty i materiały,* III, 221n.

131. Glavkom radioed the revvoensovet on July 21, that if the Poles started negotiations it would mean that they could not count on outside support. Only if they did not make overtures the Soviet

advance was to be more cautious. See Kakurin and Melikov, *Voina s belopoliakami*, p. 210.

132. Rumbold to Curzon, July 31, 1920, *DBFP*, XI, 422. Compare Edgar V., Lord D'Abernon, *The Eighteenth Decisive Battle of the World* (London, 1931), pp. 60, 74-75, 100-105. For a discussion of Soviet tactics see Komarnicki, *Rebirth of the Polish Republic*, pp. 644-651.

133. USPD, *Protokoll*, p. 212.

134. Hungarian proposals date back to June 1919 when the idea originated of creating a Hungarian unit in Poland to fight the Bolsheviks and then be used to pacify Hungary. See Władysław Skrzyński to Paderewski, June 18, 1919, Polski Instytut Spraw Międzynarodowych, zeszyt historyczny, no. 5, "Stosunki polsko-węgierskie w 1919 r.: materiały archiwalne," ed. Jarosław Jurkiewicz (mimeographed; Warsaw, 1957), p. 63. For contacts in 1920 see my *France and her Eastern Allies*, p. 152.

135. See Weygand, *Mirages et réalité*, p. 96-97; Piotr S. Wandycz, "General Weygand and the Battle of Warsaw of 1920," *Journal of Central European Affairs*, 19 (January 1960), 357-365; D'Abernon, *The Eighteenth Decisive Battle, passim*. Also see the revealing report by Major General Sir Percy Radcliffe of September 1, 1920, PRO, Cab. 21/180.

136. *DBFP*, VIII, 663-664; compare American chargé to State Department, July 30, 1920, RG 59,861.00/7195, National Archives.

137. See the telegram of the Polish liaison officer, July 27, 1920, *Dokumenty i materiały*, III, 221-222.

138. Protocol of the cabinet meeting, July 28, 1920, *ibid.*, III, 225-226.

139. Protocol of State Defense Council, July 28, 1920, *ibid.*, III, 222-225; also "Protokoły Rady Obrony Państwa," pp. 226-232.

140. Protocol of July 29, 1920, *Dokumenty i materiały*, III, 232-234.

Chapter 10.   The Decisive Battle

1. Order of July 31, 1920. See Ivan Stepanov, *S krasnoi armiei na panskuiu Polshu* (Moscow, 1920), p. 86.

2. Próchniak had recently come to Russia, thanks largely to Kossakowski, as a result of an exchange of prisoners. See MS Diariusz Kossakowskiego, March 30, 1920, Archiwum Polskiej Akademii Nauk, Warsaw. Unszlicht was not in Białystok and consequently could not participate actively. See Zofia Dzierżyńska (Sofiia Dzerzhinskaia), *V gody velikikh boev* (Moscow, 1964), p. 327.

3. Lenin to Stalin, August 2, 1920, in Lenin, *Sochineniia* (4th ed.; 38 vols.; Moscow, 1942-1950), XXXI, 239. The telegram said that Dzierżyński and his friends had formed a Polish revkom and issued a manifesto.

4. In a conversation with Kossakowski on August 9, 1920; MS Diariusz Kossakowskiego, August 9, 1920.

5. See *Dokumenty i materiały do historii stosunków polsko-radzieckich* (Warsaw, 1962—), III, 542-543. Also see *Istoriia grazhdanskoi voiny v SSSR* (5 vols.; Moscow, 1935-1960), V, 103; compare Mikhail I. Kulichenko, *Borba kommunisticheskoi partii za reshenie natsionalnogo voprosa v 1918-1920 godakh* (Kharkov, 1963), p. 134; N. I. Zubov, *F. E. Dzerzhinskii: biografia* (Moscow, 1965), pp. 226-230.

6. The Bolsheviks published some 10 million pamphlets and propaganda tracts addressed to the Poles, and attempted to indoctrinate Polish prisoners of war. See P. V. Suslov, *Politicheskoe obespechenie sovetsko-polskoi kampanii 1920 goda* (Moscow and Leningrad, 1930); I. Brill, "Politicheskaia podgotovka letnei operatsii v 1920 g.," *Voina i Revoliutsiia*, 2 (1926), 100. Tadeusz Teslar, *Propaganda bolszewicka podczas wojny polsko-rosyjskiej 1920 roku* (Warsaw, 1938).

7. *Dokumenty i materiały*, III, 177, 243.

8. *Ibid.*, III, 543; compare 544; also Julian Marchlewski, *Pisma wybrane* (2 vols.; Warsaw, 1952-1956), II, 765.

9. This is admitted even by Samuil E. Rabinovich in *Istoriia grazhdanskoi voiny* (Moscow, 1933), p. 108.

10. Suslov, *Politicheskoe obespechenie*, p. 144. On the revkoms compare Wincenty Witos, *Moje wspomnienia* (3 vols.; Paris, 1964-1965), II, 342, Roman Jabłonowski, *Wspomnienia* (Warsaw, 1962), p. 263; Artur Leinwand, *Polska Partia Socjalistyczna wobec wojny polsko-radzieckiej 1919-1920* (Warsaw, 1964), pp. 213-214; P. Kalinichenko, "O deiatelnosti polskogo vremennogo revoliutsionnogo komiteta," in A. Ia. Manusevich, ed., *Oktiabrshaia revoliutsiia i zarubezhnye slavianskie narody* (Moscow, 1957), pp. 182-188; *Tymczasowy Komitet Rewolucyjny Polski* (Warsaw, 1955), p. 100ff. Compare the discussion in the sejm on October 15, 1920, *Sprawozdanie stenograficzne*, Sejm ustawodawczy R.P., CLXXIII/22-34.

11. See Marchlewski, *Pisma wybrane*, II, 768, 773-775. For subsequent criticism of Russian nationalist propaganda see the remarks of Zatonskii on March 10, 1921, *Desiatyi sezd RKP(b), Mart 1921 g.* (Moscow, 1962), p. 204.

12. Summary of a talk between Fürstenberg-Hanecki and Kossakowski on August 9, 1920, Akta Adiutantury Generalnej Naczelnego Dowództwa, XXVII/5420. Piłsudski Institute, New York (cited AGND). Compare MS Diariusz Kossakowskiego, August 9, 1920.

13. *Dokumenty i materiały*, III, 243.

14. Lenin to Smilga and Tukhachevskii, August 3, Trotsky Archive, T. 559, Houghton Library, Harvard University. Also *Leninskii Sbornik* (Moscow, 1924—), XXXIV (1942), 342, which omits the names. Compare Kalinichenko in Manusevich, *Oktiabrskaia revoliutsiia*, pp. 151-152.

15. See Suslov, *Politicheskoe obespechenie*, p. 138. For text, signed by Tukhachevskii, Smilga, Schwarz, and Shutko, see *Dokumenty i materiały*, III, 294-295.

16. Text in Stepanov, *S krasnoi armiei*, pp. 86-87; Suslov, *Politicheskoe obespechenie*, pp. 170-171. The Polish translation in *Tymczasowy Komitet Rewolucyiny*, pp. 69-70, is incomplete.

17. See Suslov, *Politicheskoe obespechenie*, pp. 109, 137, 143; and compare Teslar, *Propaganda bolszewicka*, p. 274.

18. For Lenin's interest, see among others *Leninskii Sbornik*, XXXIV (1942), 342; Kalinichenko in Manusevich, *Oktiabrskaia revoliutsiia*, pp. 152-169; Zubov, *Dzerzhinskii*, p. 232. Also Simon Liberman, *Building Lenin's Russia* (Chicago, 1945), p. 121.

19. Marchlewski, *Pisma wybrane*, II, 765. Lenin said the same thing on October 2, 1920, *Sochineniia*, XXV, 405. See also Kalinichenko in Manusevich, *Oktiabrskaia revoliutsiia*, pp. 181, 188; compare Jabłonowski's remarks that among Polish Communists in Warsaw "there was already talk about the composition of the future government of people's commissars" (*Wspomnienia*, p. 259).

20. Polish text in *Dokumenty i materiały*, III, 244-247; and in *Tymczasowy Komitet Rewolucyjny*, pp. 81-82 (photograph); Russian text in Stepanov, *S krasnoi armiei*, pp. 92-95; English translation of excerpts in Xenia J. Eudin and Harold H. Fisher, ed., *Soviet Russia and the West, 1920-1927* (Stanford, 1957), p. 16.

21. See Lenin to Radek, August 19, 1920, in Lenin, *Polnoe sobranie sochinenii*, LI, 264; note of August 20, 1920, Trotsky Archive, T. 572. See Dzierżyńska, *V gody*, pp. 327-328, who mentions differences between Dzierżyński and Kon. Compare N. F. Kuzmin, *Krushenie poslednego pokhoda Antanty* (Moscow, 1958), pp. 228-230, and Zubov, *Dzerzhinskii*, p. 232.

22. See *Tymczasowy Komitet Rewolucyjny*, p. 98; Suslov, *Politicheskoe obespechenie*, p. 137.

23. August 5, 1920, *Dokumenty i materiały*, III, 292-294.

24. On August 11, 1920. See text in Teslar, *Propaganda bolszewicka*, pp. 261-262.

25. Text of appeal to join the First Białystok Workers' regiment in *ibid.*, p. 272, and in *Dokumenty i materiały*, III, 305-306. See Dzierżyński to Lenin, August 6, 15, 1920, in F. E. Dzierżyński, *Izbrannye proizvedeniia* (2 vols.; Moscow, 1957), I, 294-297. Compare Kalinichenko in Manusevich, *Oktiabrskaia revoliutsiia*, pp. 176-179; Suslov, *Politicheskoe obespechenie*, p. 144; I. N. Sergeev, *Od Dźwiny ku Wiśle* (Warsaw, 1925), p. 108.

26. *Dokumenty i materiały*, III, 290-291.

27. See Marchlewski, *Pisma wybrane*, II, 780; Kalinichenko in Manusevich, *Oktiabrskaia revoliutsiia*, p. 163; Vitovt K. Putna, *K Visle i obratno* (Moscow, 1927), p. 238-239; Stepanov, *S krasnoi armiei*, p. 56.

28. Witos, *Moje wspomnienia*, II, 374; Stepanov, *S krasnoi armiei*, p. 56.

29. On September 22, 1920, Lenin, *Sochineniia*, XXV, 378.

30. See F. E. Dzierżyński, *Dnevnik: Pisma k rodnym* (Moscow, 1958), pp. 258-260. Letters of August 17 and 25, 1920.

31. Putna, *K Visle*, p. 238. Jabłonowski recalled that Communist influence in the Białystok area was nil (*Wspomnienia*, p. 259).

32. Trotsky Archive, T. 546. See also Hanecki to Meierovics, July 24, and Chicherin to Curzon, July 26, 1920, about treatment of officers as hostages for Communists in Poland, *Dokumenty vneshnei politiki SSSR* (Moscow, 1959—), III, 66, 67 (cited as *DVP SSSR*).

33. Suslov, *Politicheskoe obespechenie*, p. 115.

34. *Ibid.*, pp. 140 141, which quotes letters of Red soldiers; Putna, *K Visle*, p. 73; compare a captured report of the Fourth Army, no. 331, August 8, 1920, AGND, XXVII/4558.

35. Order of August 11, 1920, text in Suslov, *Politicheskoe obespechenie*, pp. 160-161. Compare Suslov's remarks on pp. 52, 82-85. For justifications of the Red Army behavior see Marchlewski, *Pisma wybrane*, II, 765-777.

36. Piatakov's telegram to Central Committee, August 28, 1920, cited in Suslov, *Politicheskoe obespechenie*, pp. 140-141.

37. Sergeev, *Od Dźwiny*, p. 108.

38. See Trąmpczyński's remarks on September 24, 1920, *Sprawozdanie stenograficzne*, CLXVII/5; compare with Witos, *Moje wspomnienia*, II, 374.

39. See origins in Kuzmin, *Krushenie poslednego pokhoda*, p. 178. Text in *Dokumenty i materiały*, III, 263-266. The deputy chairman was Mykhailo Baran; other members were Mykhailo Levytskyi, K. Lytvynovych, and A. Baral (Savka). See I. M. Haluskko, *Narysy istorii ideologichnoi ta orhanizatsiinoi diialnosti KPZU v 1919-1928 rr.* (Lviv, 1965), p. 262; and Gereon Iwański, "Z dziejów komunistycznej partii Galicji wschodniej," *Z Pola Walki*, 10 (1967), 933-960. Compare Tadeusz Teslar, *Polityka Rosji sowieckiej podczas wojny z Polską* (Warsaw, 1937), pp. 182-211 where the author quotes from the collected decrees and documents of the Galrevkom.

40. Telegram of August 9, 1920, *Dokumenty i materiały*, III, 304-305.

41. Lenin to Zatonskii, August 19, 1920, in Lenin, *Polnoe sobranie*, LI, 264-265. Also see Trotsky Archive, T. 569. Compare Suslov, *Politicheskoe obespechenie*, pp. 145, 147.

42. Zatonskii on March 10, 1921, *Desiatyi sezd RKP(b)*, p. 204.

43. See Kuzmin, *Krushenie poslednego pokhoda*, p. 252.

44. *Dokumenty i materiały*, III, 269-270.

45. *Ibid.*, III, 270-271. According to Kazimierz W. Kumaniecki, ed.. *Odbudowa państwowości polskiej: najważniejsze dokumenty* (Warsaw and Cracow, 1924), p. 315. Wróblewski's message was of August 3 and not August 2, 1920.

46. Chicherin to Sapieha, August 2, 1920, *DVP SSSR*, III, 78.

47. Declaration of August 3, 1920, *ibid.*, III, 79-80.

48. Lenin, *Sochineniia*, 4th ed., XXXI, 239, also *Leninskii Sbornik*, XXXV (1945), 141. The existence of different trends must have been well known, because even Mrs. Snowden heard in Moscow that there was a peace party and one which stood for war until complete victory.

See Ethel (Mrs. Philip) Snowden, *Through Bolshevik Russia* (London, 1920), p. 84.

49. See Foch to Millerand, August 4, 1920, *Dokumenty i materiały*, III, 284-285.

50. For Lenin's interest in the campaign see reminiscences of S. S. Kamenev in *Vospominaniia o Vladimire Iliche Lenine* (3 vols.; Moscow, 1956-1960), II, 263.

51. See Kuzmin, *Krushenie poslednego pokhoda*, pp. 256-257.

52. See Lev Nikulin, *Tukhachevskii* (Moscow, 1964), pp. 126-127; compare John Erickson, *The Soviet High Command: A Military-Political History, 1918-1941* (New York, 1962), p. 95. The order to begin an attack on Warsaw, by an outflanking maneuver, was issued on August 10. See Kuzmin, *Krushenie poslednego pokhoda*, p. 260.

53. *Dokumenty i materiały*, III, 278-283; "Protokoły Rady Obrony Państwa," pp. 233-239.

54. *Dokumenty i materiały*, III, 289-290.

55. Chicherin's notes of August 6 and 7, in *DVP SSSR*, III, 90-91. See White to Secretary of State, August 8, 1920, *Foreign Relations: 1920*, III, 387.

56. *Dokumenty i materiały*, III, 310n.

57. Rumbold to Curzon, August 6 and 8, 1920, *Documents on British Foreign Policy* (first series; London, 1947—), XI, 441, 449-451 (cited DBFP).

58. On August 12, 1920. See Leon Trotsky, *Sochineniia*, XVII/2, 423-425, and Kamenev's note in *DVP SSSR*, III, 122.

59. See Trotsky's thesis presented to Lenin, Krestinskii, Chicherin, Zinoviev, Bukharin, and Steklov, on August 11, 1920, in *Kak vooruzhalas revoliutsiia* (3 vols. in 4, Moscow, 1923-1924), II/2, 164-165.

60. On August 17, 1920, Dzierżyński, *Izbrannye proizvedeniia*, I, 298-299.

61. Lenin to Stalin, August 11, 1920, in Lenin, *Sochineniia*, 4th ed., XXXI, 241. Chicherin proposed this meeting in his note of August 7, which the Poles received via London four days later. Lenin apparently assumed that it would take place, for he wrote Stalin that a proposal to include a representative of the Eastern Galician revkom in the Soviet delegation had come too late. Lenin to Stalin, August 10, 1920, *Leninskii Sbornik*, XXXIV (1942), 343.

62. An account of the conversation is in *DBFP*, VIII, 670-680.

63. See Kamenev's report to Lenin, August 4, 1920, *DVP SSSR*, III, 81. Compare the Narkomindel declaration, August 12, 1920, *ibid.*, III, 119-120.

64. Kamenev to Lloyd George, August 5, 1920, *ibid.*, III, 83-86. Notes on the August 6 meeting are in *DBFP*, VIII, 681-708.

65. See Georgii V. Chicherin, *Stati i rechi po voprosam mezhdunarodnoi politiki* (Moscow, 1961), p. 325.

66. See *DBFP*, VIII, 707-708.

67. See *DVP SSSR*, III, 95-96; also *DBFP*, VIII, 722-723.

68. For the Lympne negotiations and agreements see *DBFP*, VIII,

709-755; Alexandre Millerand, "Au secours de la Pologne," *Revue de France*, 4 (1932), 580; Harrison to Secretary of State, August 10, 11, 1920, Record Group 59, "Political Relations between Poland and the Soviet Union," 760c.61/162 and 163, National Archives; Lord Riddell, *Intimate Diary of the Peace Conference and After: 1918-1922* (New York, 1934), p. 229, 247; Jacques Bardoux, *De Paris à Spa* (Paris, 1929), p. 363; Titus Komarnicki, *Rebirth of the Polish Republic* (London, 1957), pp. 657-660, 661, 664; and Ullman's still unpublished third volume of *Anglo-Soviet Relations*.

69. According to Lloyd George, the intercepted message was tantamount to a refusal of truce. See Conclusions of Cabinet Meetings, August 9, 1920, PRO, Cab. 23/22.

70. Kamenev's note of August 9, 1920, *DVP SSSR*, III, 100-101; English text in *DBFP*, XI, 456. Before August 5 Lenin had already wired Kamenev that the Bolsheviks would give Poland a border east of the Curzon Line but not "much more" east (Lenin, *Polnoe sobranie sochinenii*, LI, 249).

71. Curzon to Rumbold, August 10, 1920, *DBFP*, XI, 546n; compare Lord D'Abernon, *The Eighteenth Decisive Battle of the World* (London, 1931), pp. 70-72.

72. Millerand, "Au secours de la Pologne," p. 587.

73. Lenin to Stalin, August 11, 1920, *Leninskii Sbornik*, XXXIV (1942), 345; *Sochineniia*, 4th ed., XXXI, 241.

74. Lenin to Danishevskii, August 11, 1920, Trotsky Archive, T. 562.

75. Rumbold to Curzon, August 11, 1920, *DBFP*, XI, 463.

76. *Ibid.*, XI, 523, 524.

77. See Morstin's report to Supreme Command, August 11, 1920, AGND, XXVII/4541.

78. See *Foreign Relations: 1920*, III, 463-468.

79. See appeals of the State Defense Council, Premier Witos, General Józef Haller, calls of the Polish episcopate, youth manifestoes, etc., in Kumaniecki, *Odbudowa państwowości*, pp. 284-290, 323, 329.

80. Wincenty Witos, *Moje wspomnienia* (3 vols.; Paris, 1964-1965), II, 310.

81. Józef Piłsudski, *Pisma zbiorowe* (10 vols.; Warsaw, 1937-1938), VII, 152-153.

82. See the letter in *Niepodległość*, n.s., 7 (1962), 123; reprinted in Witos, *Moje wspomnienia*, II, 290-292.

83. See *DBFP*, VIII, 734.

84. Still, Witos showed it to Rataj and perhaps other peasant leaders as well.

85. See Trotsky, *Kak vooruzhalas revoliutsiia*, II/2, 166.

86. Chicherin's telegraphic reply to questions by the Berlin correspondent of International News Service. See Kilmarnock to Curzon, Aug. 15, 1920, PRO, F.O. 371/3917, no. 211722.

87. The controversy about the plan of the Battle of Warsaw had been going on ever since the victory. For a summary of the literature

see my "Weygand and the Battle of Warsaw." According to Piłsudski, he used a plan prepared by General Rozwadowski which he himself greatly modified. See protocol of the State Defense Council, August 27, 1920, *Dokumenty i materiały*, III, 375. For a discussion among Soviet military leaders on the strategic errors of the 1920 campaign, see Erickson, *The Soviet High Command*, pp. 99-101.

88. Notes dated August 1920 (probably around the 18th), Trotsky Archive, T. 548, 549, 551. Underlining in text. Compare Lenin, *Polnoe sobranie sochinenii*, LI, 260.

89. Lenin to Smilga, August 18, 1920, Trotsky Archive, T. 568; also in *Leninskii Sbornik*, XXXIV (1942), 347, but without Smilga's name. According to Suslov the order was sent to the Western Front on August 19 (*Politicheskoe obespechenie*, p. 93).

90. Signed by Tukhachevskii and Smilga; text in Suslov, *Politicheskoe obespechenie*, pp. 92-93.

91. See "Theses of lectures, meetings and talks concerning failures at the western front," sent out by Smolensk gubernia committee for military affairs on August 25; Smolensk Archive: Kommunisticheskaia Partia Sovetskogo Soiuza, Partiinyi Archiv, WKP 119, Widener Library, Harvard University.

92. Suslov, *Politicheskoe obespechenie*, pp. 92-99.

93. Trotsky, *Kak vooruzhalas revoliutsiia*, III,/1, 91. Compare his telegram to Lenin, on August 17, 1920, Trotsky Archive, T. 566.

94. Excerpts from protocol, Trotsky Archive, T. 570; compare *Leninskii Sbornik*, XXXIV (1942), 348.

95. Lenin to Kamenev, August 20, 1920, in Lenin, *Polnoe sobranie sochinenii*, LI, 266.

96. See Lenin's remarks on October 15, 1920, *Sochineniia*, XXV, 426.

97. See Fedor G. Zuev, *Mezhdunarodnyi imperializm organizator napadenia panskoi Polshi na sovetskuiu Rossiiu 1919-1920* (Moscow, 1954), pp. 197-198. The Poles were badly informed about the divisions within the Central Committee and assumed that Trotsky, Radek, and Zinoviev favored war at all cost. See AGND, XXXI/5630.

98. Stanisław Mackiewicz, *Historia Polski od 11 listopada 1918 r. do 17 września 1939 r.* (London, 1941), p. 134.

99. Trąmpczyński, on September 24, 1920, *Sprawozdanie stenograficzne*, CLXVIII/4.

100. See "Protokoły Rady Obrony Państwa," p. 272, and an interview in *Kurjer Poranny*, August 29, 1920, reprinted in Piłsudski, *Pisma zbiorowe*, V, 167.

101. Skarbek on August 25, 1920, "Protokoły Rady Obrony Państwa," p. 267.

102. See Piotr S. Wandycz, *France and her Eastern Allies, 1919-1925* (Minneapolis, 1962), p. 175; full text of the note of August 23, 1920 in *Dokumenty i materiały*, III, 351-354.

103. See protocol of August 27, 1920, *Dokumenty i materiały*, III, 370-375; "Protokoły Rady Obrony Państwa," pp. 268-276.

104. See text in Kumaniecki, *Odbudowa państwowości*, p. 398, who gives the date of August 25; and *Dokumenty i materiały*, III, 368-369, which dates it August 26.

105. White to Secretary of State, August 24, 1920, RG. 59, 760c.61/-242, National Archives.

106. See protocol of the cabinet meeting of August 11, 1920, *Dokumenty i materiały*, III, 309-310.

107. See Witos, *Moje wspomnienia*, II, 285.

108. Lenin wired that to complain against the enemy's "treachery" while there was no armistice was "ridiculous." He ordered the chief delegate to be tough, and keep his *sang-froid*. See Lenin to Danishevskii, August 17, 1920, in Lenin, *Polnoe sobranie sochinenii*, LI, 261. Other delegates were Petr Smidovich and Nikolai Skrypnik.

109. Lenin to Chicherin, August 14, 1920, *Leninskii Sbornik*, XXXVI (1959), 118-119.

110. See Jan Dąbski, *Pokój ryski, wspomnienia, pertraktacje, tajne układy z Joffem, listy* (Warsaw, 1931), pp. 39-41; also Dąbski to Ministry of Foreign Affairs, August 17, 1920, AGND, XXVII/4671; compare telegram of Polish delegation no. 77, *ibid.*, XXVII/4672.

111. See *Dokumenty i materiały*, III, 327-330. Chicherin wired Danishevskii the official explanation of the relationship between the Ukraine and Russia, which was not too clear. Dąbski asked Sapieha for additional credentials. See *ibid.*, III, 331; Dąbski to Sapieha, August 20, 1920, AGND, XXVII/4668; and Polish delegation to Sapieha, August 22, 1920, *ibid.*, XXVII/4677. Interestingly enough Zatonskii admitted in 1921 that he could not tell what was really the relationship between Moscow and Kiev. See *Desiatyi sezd RKP(b)*, p. 205.

112. See Dąbski, *Pokój ryski*, pp. 42-44; Dąbski to Sapieha, August 20, 1920, AGND, XXVII/4674. English translation in Komarnicki, *Rebirth of the Polish Republic*, pp. 724-725.

113. For a convenient comparison of the two documents see Komarnicki, *Rebirth of the Polish Republic*, pp. 670-673. The difference between the 20 versts mentioned by Lloyd George and the 50 in the document at Minsk seems to have resulted from Lloyd George's mistake.

114. Polish translation in Dąbski, *Pokój ryski*, pp. 49-51, and Dąbski to Sapieha, August 24, 1920, AGND, XXVII/4674. Russian text in *DVP SSSR*, III 137-139, and *Dokumenty i materiały*, III, 340-342; English translation in Komarnicki, *Rebirth of the Polish Republic*, pp. 670-673, and Degras, *Soviet Documents*, I, 200-202. The Soviet publication and Degras give erroneously the date of August 17 instead of 19.

115. On September 10, 1920, *DBFP*, VIII, 789.

116. Dąbski to Ministry of Foreign Affairs, August 20, 1920, and Polish delegation to Warsaw, August 22, AGND, XXVII/4668, 4677.

117. Martov on October 15, 1920; see Unabhängige Sozialdemokratische Partei Deutschlands (USPD), *Protokoll*, p. 212.

118. Lenin to Smilga, August 20, 1920, Trotsky Archive, T. 571.

119. An intercepted message from Chicherin to Kamenev on August 11, 1920 contained the cryptic words: "General impression semi-official Poland will accept armistice terms which will be made public tomorrow"; PRO, F.O. 371/3917, no. 211450. Compare Karol Lapter, "Zarys stosunków polsko-radzieckich w latach 1917-1960" (mimeographed; Warsaw, 1961), p. 19; S. W. Page, *Lenin and World Revolution* (New York, 1959), p. 239.

120. Warsaw received the first direct wire from Minsk on August 24. See White to Secretary of State, August 24, 1920, RG 59, 760c.61/-249, National Archives.

121. See the somewhat embarrassed reply of Chicherin to Sapieha August 22, 1920, *DVP SSSR*, III, 142; also AGND, XXVII/4677.

122. See the messages in Trotsky Archive, T. 576, 577, 578. Witos wrote that Dąbski used the incident to drag the talks but it is not certain that this was necessary at this stage. See Witos, *Moje wspomnienia*, II, 367.

123. Dąbski, *Pokój ryski*, pp. 60-64; Dąbski to Sapieha, August 26, 1920, AGND, XXVII/4695; *Dokumenty i materiały*, III, 345-349.

124. Protocols of sessions of August 23 and 25, *Dokumenty i materiały*, III, 345-350, 355-365.

125. Dąbski to Ministry of Foreign Affairs, August 23 and 24, 1920, AGND, XXVII/4669 and 4682.

126. At the meeting with the Italian premier Giolitti on August 22-23. For British realization of the meaning of Soviet terms see especially Foreign Office comments on August 12, 15, PRO, F.O. 371/3917, nos. 211450, 211722.

127. See Stanisław Grabski, *The Polish-Soviet Frontier* (London, 1943), pp. 25-26; Dąbski's report in *Dokumenty i materiały*, III, 412-413; Sapieha's remarks in "Protokoły Rady Obrony Państwa," pp. 273-274; Komarnicki, *Rebirth of the Polish Republic*, p. 727.

Chapter 11.   The Peace Settlement

1. Chicherin to Sapieha, August 27, 1920, *Dokumenty vneshnei politiki SSSR* (Moscow, 1959—), III, 150-151 (cited as *DVP SSSR*).

2. Chicherin to Sapieha, August 29, 1920, *ibid.*, III, 156-159.

3. Sapieha to Chicherin, August 30, 1920, *Dokumenty i materiały do historii stosunków polsko-radzieckich* (Warsaw, 1962—), III, 380-381.

4. Chicherin and Rakovskii to Polish Government, September 1, and Chicherin to Sapieha, September 6, 1920, *DVP SSSR*, III, 159-160, 166.

5. Sapieha to Chicherin, September 9, 1920, *ibid.*, III, 167.

6. See the telegram of the Polish minister in Riga to Moscow, in Kazimierz W. Kumaniecki, ed., *Odbudowa państwowości polskiej: najważniejsze dokumenty* (Warsaw, 1924), p. 410.

7. Protocol of the fifth session, *Dokumenty i materiały*, III, 390-395.

8. Józef Piłsudski, *Pisma zbiorowe* (10 vols., Warsaw, 1937-1938), VI, 124.

9. Petliura to Livytskyi, November 28, 1920, in Simon Petliura, *Statti, lysty, dokumenty* (New York, 1956), pp. 391-392.

10. See Władysław Pobóg-Malinowski, *Najnowsza historia polityczna Polski, 1864-1945* (3 vols., Paris, 1953, London, 1956-1960), II, 374n.

11. White to Secretary of State, August 21, 1920, Record Group 59, "Political Relations between Poland and the Soviet Union," 760c.61/243, National Archives.

12. See Morstin to Supreme Command, September 4, 1920, Akta Adiutantury Generalnej Naczelnego Dowództwa, Piłsudski Institute, New York (cited as AGND), LXI/6251. Compare French analysis of the possibilities of a Polish-Wrangel front in *Dokumenty i materiały*, III, 422-425.

13. Askenazy to Piłsudski, September 2, 1920, AGND, X/4756.

14. See Gorlov to Giers, September 7, 21, October 4, 1920, Giers Archive, file 81, Hoover Institution, Stanford, Calif. Compare MS Zapiski. P. N. Shatilova, pp. 104-105, Archive of Russian and East European History and Culture, Columbia University (cited as AREEH). Zuev claims that Makhrov was willing to give up Belorussia with Minsk, but the above documents fail to confirm it. See Fedor G. Zuev, *Mezhdunarodnyi imperializm organizator napadenia panskoi Polshi na sovetskuiu Rossiu, 1917-1920* (Moscow, 1954), pp. 204-205. According to Makhrov himself (cited in George A. Brinkley, *The Volunteer Army and the Allied Intervention in South Russia 1917-1921* [Notre Dame, 1966], p. 265), he had authority to negotiate only on military cooperation. Sapieha mentioned that Wrangel would agree to a "liberal Polish boundary" in the Ukraine, but that was before the talks with Makhrov. See White to Secretary of State, August 21, 1920, RG 59, 760c.61/243, National Archives.

15. Gibson to Secretary of State, September 2, 1920, *Foreign Relations of the United States: 1920* (3 vols.; Washington, D.C., 1942-1947), III, 401.

16. For British views see *Documents on British Foreign Policy, 1918-1945*, ed. E. L. Woodward and R. Butler (1st series; London, 1947—), XI 532-537, 539-540, 542, 544-545, 571-572, 581 (cited as *DBFP*); Lord D'Abernon, *The Eighteenth Decisive Battle of the World* (London, 1931), p. 91; A. L. Kennedy, *Old Diplomacy and New: 1876-1922* (London, 1922), p. 332; also Titus Komarnicki, *Rebirth of the Polish Republic* (London, 1957), pp. 702-703. For the French see my *France and her Eastern Allies, 1919-1925* (Minneapolis, 1962), pp. 175-177; and Morstin's telegram in AGND, LIX/4650 and LXI/6251. For American views see Gibson's dispatches in *Foreign Relations: 1920*, III, *passim*.

17. See "Protokoły Rady Obrony Państwa," ed. Artur Leinwand and Jan Molenda, in *Z Dziejów Stosunków Polsko-Radzieckich: Studia*

i Materiały, I (1965), 288; Sapieha to Chicherin, September 11, and Chicherin to Sapieha, September 12, 1920, *DVP SSSR,* III, 178. The Polish text, dated September 10, not 11, is in AGND, XXVIII/4899. The same date appears in *Dokumenty i materiały,* III, 409.

18. In PRO, Cab. 21/179.

19. See Volodymyr Kedrovskyi, *Ryzhske Andrusovo: Spomyny pro rosiisko-polski myrovi perehovory v 1920 r.* (Winnipeg, 1936), p. 11.

20. Circular of Septembr 10, 1920, *Dokumenty i materiały,* III, 400-411.

21. In a draft report for the State Defense Council Rozwadowski said that "If the Soviets themselves really want peace there is no doubt that they ought to withdraw their armies not only along the Minsk-Ka-linkowicze-Korosten-Zmierzynka [Zhmerinka] railroad, but logically at once beyond the Dnieper and Dvina." See Akta Generała Rozwadow-skiego, I, no. 49, Piłsudski Institute. For the final border see map in Adam Rozwadowski, *Generał Rozwadowski* (Cracow, 1929), opposite p. 107.

22. See protocol of the State Defense Council session of September 11, 1920 which contains the text of instructions. *Dokumenty i materiały,* III, 412-422. The text is also in AGND, XXVIII/4931.

23. Aleksander Ładoś, "Wasilewski w rokowaniach ryskich," *Nie-podległość,* 16 (1937), 233.

24. One may note in passing that Lastouski, the "premier" of the Belorussian People's Republic, addressed a note to Poland and the RSFSR on August 21, 1920, demanding admission to the negotiations. It appears that both sides ignored it. See AGND, XXXIII/6382.

25. For a comparison of the views of *Gazeta Warszawska, Gazeta Poranna, Robotnik,* and *Rzeczpospolita* see a press report in "Wschod-nie granice Polski," Ciechanowski Deposit, Hoover Institution.

26. On September 8, 10, 11, 1920, Leon Trotsky, *Kak vooruzhalas revo!iutsiia* (3 vols. in 4, Moscow, 1923-1924), II/2, 170-171, 173-174, 175-176.

27. On the conditions of troops on the western front see protocol no. 35, September 3, 1920, of the Smolensk Gubernia Committee, Smolensk Archive, WKP 6, Widener Library, Harvard University.

28. Klara Zetkin, *Reminiscences of Lenin* (London, 1929), p. 20.

29. Chiang Kai-shek, *Soviet Russia in China* (New York, 1957), p. 22.

30. Lenin on December 22, 1920, *Sochineniia,* XXVI, 24; on March 8, 1921, *ibid.,* XXVI, 205; Trotsky, *Lenin* (New York, 1962), pp. 114-115, and *My Life* (New York, 1931), p. 459; J. V. Stalin, *Sochineniia* (13 vols.; Moscow, 1946-1951), V, 167; Boris M. Shaposhnikov, *Na Visle: k istorii kampanii 1920 g.* (Moscow, 1924), p. 22, 202; Krestinskii, on March 8, 1921, called the Warsaw battle a rout (*razgrom*): *Desiatyi sezd RKP(b), Mart 1921 g.* (Moscow, 1962), p. 41. Compare opinions of Danishevskii and Antonov-Ovseenko cited in P. V. Suslov, *Politicheskoe obespechenie sovetsko-po!skoi kampanii 1920 goda* (Moscow and Leningrad, 1930), pp. 155-156.

31. On September 8, 1920, *DVP SSSR,* III, 170; the translation

in Jane Degras, ed., *Soviet Documents on Foreign Policy, 1917-1941* (3 vols.; New York, 1951-1953), I, 206 is misdated.

32. Leon Trotsky, *Kak vooruzhalas revoliutsiia* (3 vols. in 4; Moscow, 1923-1924), II/2, 176. He repeated the same point on September 24, 1920, *Sochineniia*, XVII/2, 465-466.

33. Marchlewski (Markhlevskii), "Mir s Polshei," *Kommunisticheskii Internatsional*, no. 14 (1920), 2752-2753.

34. Lenin to Dzierżyński, August 28, and to Trotsky, September 9, 1920, in V. I. Lenin, *Polnoe sobranie sochinenii* (5th ed.; Moscow, 1958—), LI, 271, 277.

35. See Lenin to Ioffe, September 16, 1920, *Leninskii Sbornik* XXXIV, (1942), 359.

36. Compare draft and final text in *ibid.*, XXXVI (1959), 123-126 and *DVP SSSR*, III, 204-206.

37. See A. Bolotin, *Deviataia konferentsiia RKP(b)* (Moscow, 1956), p. 27. Compare the leading article in *Pravda*, September 24, 1920. According to an intercepted Soviet telegram the VTsIK adopted the declaration by a two-thirds majority. See AGND, XXXVIII/7612. Details concerning Bukharin and Radek were reported by a Farbman, a correspondent of the *Manchester Guardian*, who was present at the meeting. See Talents to Curzon, September 29, 1920, PRO, F.O. 371/3920, no. 215433.

38. This is what Rumbold learned from Sapieha. Rumbold to Curzon, September 10, 1920, PRO, F.O. 371/3920, no. 214697.

39. See S. Iu. Vygodskii, *V. I. Lenin: rukovoditel vneshnei politiki sovetskogo gosudarstva, 1917-1923* (Leningrad, 1960), pp. 142-143. Compare Georgii V. Chicherin, *Stati i rechi po voprosam mezhdunarodnoi politiki* (Moscow, 1961), p. 283.

40. See Jan Dąbski, *Pokój ryski, wspomnienia, pertraktacje, tajne układy z Joffem, listy* (Warsaw, 1931), pp. 76-78; Dąbski to Sapieha, September 19 and 20, 1920, AGND, XXVIII/4941, 4991, XXXIII/6228.

41. Leonhard Horst, "At the Riga Peace Conference," *Living Age*, 307 (November 20, 1920), 459.

42. See Kedrovskyi, *Ryzhske Andrusovo*, pp. 17-20.

43. See *Leninskii Sbornik*, XXXVI (1959), 123. Compare Lenin's remark scribbled on a Glavkom report on a strategic border: "this is the maximum frontier." September 23, 1920, *ibid.*, XXXV (1945), 152.

44. Lenin, *Sochineniia*, XXV, 379.

45. Trotsky's order in *Kak vooruzhalas revoliutsiia*, II/2, 177. Interview on September 24, 1920, Trotsky, *Sochineniia*, XVII/2, 467.

46. See Dąbski, *Pokój ryski*, pp. 83-86.

47. Dąbski wired Sapieha on September 26, 1920 that Ioffe said the offer contained a "desired time limit" but was not an ultimatum; AGND, XXVIII/4941.

48. Gibson to Secretary of State, September 18, 1920, *Foreign Relations: 1920*, III, 404. Rozwadowski kept in touch with Makhrov, and both Piłsudski and Sapieha told Wrangel's envoy they were doing

everything to prolong the negotiations. See Brinkley. *The Volunteer Army.* p. 226.

49. Gibson to Secretary of State, September 23, 1920, RG 59, 760c. 61/344, National Archives.

50. On Ioffe's views see Myszkowski's telegram of September 24, 1920, AGND, XXXVIII/7609.

51. See Dąbski to Sapieha on September 25 and 26, 1920, AGND, XXVIII/4941.

52. See Ładoś, "Wasilewski," pp. 232-235. Compare Stanisław Grabski, *Z codziennych walk i rozważań* (Poznan, 1923) pp. 104-105, and Stanisław Janikowski to Świtalski, September 26, 1920, AGND, XXVIII/4934.

53. See Dąbski, *Pokój ryski,* pp. 86-87.

54. See text in *Dokumenty i materiały,* III, 437-441 (in Russian); Dąbski, *Pokój ryski,* pp. 92-96. Also see Dąbski to Sapieha, September 28, 1920, AGND, XXVIII/4941, and Kuliński to Supreme Command, September 27 [*sic*], 1920, *ibid.,* XXVIII/4890.

55. For the sequel to the Soviet offer and Polish reaction see Dąbski to Sapieha, September 28 and two notes on September 29, in AGND, XXVIII/4941; Kedrovskyi, *Ryzhske Andrusovo,* pp. 33-35; note of press section of the Ministry of Foreign Affairs, October 4, 1920, "Pertraktacje pokojowe polsko-rosyjskie," Ciechanowski Deposit. Hoover Institution. For an idea of Soviet difficulties on the front see protocol 38, October 1, 1920 of Smolensk Gubernia Committee, Smolensk Archive, WKP 6.

56. Ioffe to Dąbski, September 30, 1920, *DVP SSSR,* III, 225-226. Dąbski *Pokój ryski,* p. 120, gives a brief summary only.

57. See Major Polakiewicz to Piłsudski, October 20, 1920, AGND, XI/5279. The idea of using Eastern Galicia as a trump in negotiations may have originated with Lenin. See his remarks on Galicia in a note to Trotsky, September 9, 1920, Trotsky Archive, T. 583, Houghton Library, Harvard University.

58. For the conversation, see Dąbski, *Pokój ryski,* pp. 104-109.

59. See "Protokoły Rady Obrony Państwa," pp. 312-317. Session of October 1, 1920. On Sapieha's plans to go to Riga see also Gibson to Secretary of State, September 18, 23, October 1, 1920, RG 59, 760c.61/ 322, 344, 357, National Archives.

60. See Dąbski, *Pokój ryski, p.* 110. Compare Karol Poznański, "Jak to naprawdę było w Rydze z Mińskiem?" *Tydzień Polski,* November 28, 1964.

61. See Dąbski, *Pokój ryski,* pp. 110-113; compare Dąbski to Sapieha (two messages) October 2, 1920, AGND, XXVIII/4941; Kuliński to Supreme Command, October 2, 1920, *ibid.,* XXVIII/4885.

62. Sapieha to Dąbski, October 2, 1920, *ibid.,* XXVIII/4941.

63. See Kuliński to Supreme Command, October 3, 1920, in which the general said that since only the government instructions were binding, the Supreme Command act via the government and not put pressure on him; *ibid.,* XXVIII/4941.

64. See Stanisław Grabski, *The Polish-Soviet Frontier* (London, 1943), pp. 34-35.

65. See Dąbski, *Pokój ryski*, pp. 113-116; compare Kuliński to Supreme Command, October 4, 1920, AGND, XXXII/6165. The general reported that Ioffe would agree to a frontier up to Mołodeczno.

66. See Dąbski, *Pokój ryski*, pp. 99-103.

67. For the meeting and text of protocol see *ibid.*, pp. 117-119; and Dąbski to Sapieha, October 6, 1920, AGND, XXVIII/4889. Also *Dokumenty i materiały*, III, 460. Contrary to Dąbski's testimony Major Polakiewicz wrote General Kuliński that news of the signing came at 5.00 P.M. See AGND, XI/5279. If one accepts Polakiewicz's report it would seem that Dąbski hurried matters and failed to consult all the delegates.

68. See Major Polakiewicz to General Kuliński, October 6, 1920 and to Piłsudski, October 20, 1920, AGND, XI/5279; Captain Myszkowski to Colonel Matuszewski, October 6, 1920, *ibid.*, XXXII/6007.

69. See AGND, XXX/5336.

70. Dąbski, *Pokój ryski*, p. 121.

71. See an account of a talk with Major Polakiewicz in Kedrovskyi, *Ryzhske Andrusovo*, p. 23, 39.

72. See a note for Matuszewski in *Dokumenty i materiały*, III, 460n.

73. See Kedrovskyi, *Ryzhske Andrusovo*, pp. 41-44.

74. Sapieha to Dąbski, October 10, 1920, *Dokumenty i materiały*, III, 462-463.

75. Piłsudski, wrote Witos in his memoirs, wanted a continuation of the war, and his officers were making Dąbski's life at Riga difficult. See Wincenty Witos, *Moje wspomnienia* (3 vols.; Paris, 1964-1965), II, 368ff. Compare Dąbski, *Pokój ryski*, p. 121ff; Gorlov to Giers, October 4, 1920, about Piłsudski's desire to break off the negotiations, *Giers Archive*, file 81. See a polemic concerning Piłsudski's intention between Adam Pragier and Juliusz Łukasiewicz in *Wiadomości Polskie* 42 (84), 1941 and following issues.

76. *Sprawozdanie stenograficzne*, CLXX/4, October 7, CLXXI/18-19, October 8, 1920.

77. Piłsudski later admitted his full responsibility. See his *Pisma zbiorowe*, VI, 124. For a recent detailed treatment of the Wilno affair, see Piotr Łossowski, *Stosunki polsko-litewskie w latach 1918-20* (Warsaw, 1966) pp. 264-304.

78. All contemporary observers and historians believed that Sapieha had nothing to do with the Wilno coup, but new documentary evidence proves the contrary. See Świtalski's report to Piłsudski, October 2, 1920, which says that Sapieha "has cold feet as far as the Wilno operation is concerned" and insists that the threads of the intrigue be woven in an "invisible" fashion (AGND, X/4922).

79. Pro-memoria by Juliusz Łukasiewicz and Roman Knoll (undated but probably around mid-October 1920), *ibid.*, XXX/5331.

80. Lorraine to Curzon, October 21, 1920, *DBFP*, XI, 630, and other dispatches, pp. 607, 642, 653.

81. See *Generał Rozwadowski*, p. 102. Compare memorandum of M. Świechowski in AGND, XXII/3204, and remarks in Tadeusz Katelbach, "Rola Piłsudskiego w sprawie polsko-litewskiej," *Niepodległość*, n.s., 1 (1948), *passim*.

82. Janikowski to Świtalski, October 10, 1920, AGND, XXIX/5330.

83. For these developments see Janikowski to Świtalski, October 10, 1920, AGND, XXIX/5330; Ładoś, "Wasilewski," p. 237; statements of Polakiewicz and other officers to Shelukhin and Kedrovskyi, in Kedrovskyi, *Ryzhske Andrusovo*, p. 39; Artur Leinwand, *Polska Partia Socjalistyczna wobec wojny polsko-radzieckiej 1919-1920* (Warsaw, 1964), p. 237; Michał Sokolnicki, "Józef Piłsudski a zagadnienie Rosji," *Niepodległość*, n.s., 2 (1950), 65; British report that Sapieha was "on the eve of his intended departure for Riga," Lorraine to Curzon, October 7, 1920, *DBFP*, XI, 589; Gorlov's report to Giers, October 11, 1920, according to which Sapieha said that Poland "was ready not to sign peace" (Giers Archive, file 81).

84. See Zetkin, *Reminiscences of Lenin*, pp. 21-22.

85. Report to the Eighth Congress of Soviets, December 23-29, 1920, *DVP SSSR*, II, 715.

86. *Leninskii Sbornik*, XXXVI (1959), 130.

87. Lenin to Trotsky, October 10, 1920, in Lenin, *Polnoe sobranie sochinenii*, LI, 298; Trotsky to Lenin, October 10, 1920, Trotsky Archive, T. 606.

88. See Dabski, *Pokój ryski*, pp. 123-125.

89. See Mikhail I. Kulichenko, *Borba kommunisticheskoi partii za reshenie natsionalnogo voprosa v 1918-1920 godakh* (Kharkov, 1963), p. 297.

90. Dąbski argued with those Poles who accused him of having been duped by Ioffe. See *Pokój ryski*, p. 126. For a criticism of Dąbski coming from his own party see Witos, *Moje wspomnienia*, II, 369, 371, and Maciej Rataj, *Pamiętniki, 1918-1927* (Warsaw, 1965), pp. 82, 90.

91. English and French translation in *League of Nations Treaty Series*, IV (Geneva, 1921), 32-40; Russian in *DVP SSSR*, III, 245-252; Polish in *Dokumenty i materiały*, III, 465-472; and Kumaniecki, *Odbudowa państwowości*, pp. 422-426. See also Dąbski to Sapieha, October 12, 1920, AGND, XXVIII/4941.

92. Text in *DVP SSSR*, III, 256-258, reprinted in *Dokumenty i materiały III*, 476-477. I was unable to locate the Polish text. According to Dąbski he agreed to the protocol on October 9, 1920. See Dąbski to Ministry of Foreign Affairs, October 9, 1920, AGND, XXVIII/4941.

93. Russian text in *DVP SSSR*, III, 253-256; Polish in *Dokumenty i materiały*, III, 472-475, and Kumaniecki, *Odbudowa państwowości*, pp. 426-428. English and French translation in *League of Nations Treaty Series*, IV (1921) pp. 40-44.

94. See Dąbski to Ministry of Foreign Affairs, October 9, 1920, AGND, XXVIII/4941.

95. Piłsudski, *Pisma zbiorowe*, V, 175-176.

96. Instruction of October 10, 1920, *Dokumenty i materiały*, III, 463-465.

97. *Ibid.*, III, 478.

98. For earlier British attempts to persuade Warsaw "not to hurt the respectable patriotism of the Russian people," see Derby to Curzon and Curzon to Derby, October 7, 1920, *DBFP*, XI, 584-585, 587. For the *démarche* of Britsh and French envoys and the Polish reply see AGND, XXIX/5147 and LXIX/5321. Compare Gibson to Department of State, October 11 and 14, 1920, RG 59, 760c.61/382 and 760c. 60m.48, National Archives.

99. On October 22, 1920, *Sprawozdanie stenograficzne*, CLXXVII/6.

100. Tadeusz Hołówko, "Skutki pokoju w Rydze," *Przymierze*, November 28, 1920.

101. See reports for the Supreme Command during October 1920, AGND, XXX/5526.

102. Grabski, *Z codziennych walk i rozważań*, p. 5.

103. Report no. 21, April 26, 1921, AGND, XXXVII/7275.

104. See Isaak Mazepa, *Ukraina v ohni i buri revo'iutsii 1917-1921* (3 vols.; Prague 1942-1943), pp. 55-56; Kedrovskyi, *Ryzhske Andrusovo*, pp. 41-42 and *passim*. Also Żaboklicki, "Kwestia białoruska," December 2, 1920, and the memorandum of the Polish Council of Grodno, December 20, 1920, AGND, XXXII/6121.

105. See B. A. Bakhmetev to Acting Secretary of State, October 14, 1920, *Foreign Relations: 1920*, III, 406-407.

106. See Trotsky "Mir s Polshei dostignut," October 13, 1920, *Kak vooruzhalas revo'iutsiia*, II/2, 178-180.

107. On October 15, 1920, *Sochineniia*, XXV, 420.

108. "Preliminarnyi mir Sovetskoi Rossii s Polshei," *Pravda*, October 15, 1920. Iurii Steklov commented on Riga in a similar vein in *Izvestia* on October 15. Compare Samuil E. Rabinovich, *Istoriia grazhdanskoi voiny* (Moscow, 1933), pp. 114-115.

109. See D. Z. Manuilskii, "O Rizhskikh peregovorakh," *Kommunisticheskii Internatsional*, no. 15 (1920), 3077-3082.

110. See "Wschodnie granice Polski na zasadzie pokoju ryskiego," *Komunistyczna Trybuna*, November 21, 1920 (cited from a copy in AGND, XXXIII/6314). Also "Mir s Polshei," *Kommunisticheskii Internatsional*, no. 14, (1920) 2754.

111. See *Dokumenty i materiały*, III, 500-504.

Chapter 12. Epilogue

1. See Savinkov to Wrangel, October 15, 1920, MS Boris Savinkov, Ts. Russia S.2672, Hoover Institution, Stanford, Calif. Compare Anatolii P. Velmin, "Russkaiia emigratsiia v Polshe v 1919-1921 gg.," Archive of Russian and East European History and Culture, Columbia University (cited as AREEH). Also Makhrov's account in George

Brinkley, *The Volunteer Army and the Allied Intervention in South Russia 1917-1921* (Notre Dame, 1966), p. 269.

2. On August 27, 1920, Polish intelligence began to promote recruitment for Balakhovich forces. See *Dokumenty i materiały do historii stosunków polsko-radzieckich* (Warsaw, 1962—), III, 377-378.

3. See the reports of Walery Sławek and others to Supreme Command, November 5 and 11, 1920, Akta Adiutantury Generalnej Naczelnego Dowództwa, XXXI/5636 and 5694. Piłsudski Institute, New York (cited as AGND). Compare British legation report of November 25, 1920, PRO, F.O. 371/5399, no. 4255.

4. Steklov, "Klochok bumagi?"*Izvestia*, November 4, 1920.

5. Text in *Dokumenty vneshnei politiki SSSR* (Moscow, 1959—), III, 328 (cited as *DVP SSSR*).

6. See Matuszewski's report, November 22, 1920, in AGND, XXXII/6122.

7. See Sapieha and Chicherin telegrams in *DVP SSSR*, III, 353-356.

8. Jan Dąbski, *Pokój ryski, wspomnienia, pertraktacje, tajne układy z Joffem, listy* (Warsaw, 1931), p. 173.

9. See texts in *DVP SSSR*, III, 531-534; *Dokumenty i materiały*, III, 551-565; Kazimierz W. Kumaniecki, ed., *Odbudowa państwowości polskiej: najważniejsze dokumenty* (Warsaw and Cracow, 1924), pp. 489-499.

10. On February 28, 1921, V. I. Lenin, *Sochineniia* (3rd. ed., 30 vols., Moscow, 1935-1937) XXVI, 187-193.

11. See Dąbski, *Pokój ryski*, pp. 190-192. English text in Jane Degras, ed., *Soviet Documents on Foreign Policy, 1917-1941* (3 vols.; New York, 1951-1953), I, 242-244.

12. Russian text with ten annexes in *DVP SSSR*, III, 618-658; Polish in *Dokumenty i materiały*, III, 572-609; and incomplete in Kumaniecki, *Odbudowa państwowości*, pp. 525-545. English and French translation in *League of Nations Treaty Series*, VI (Geneva, 1921), 122-169. Ukrainian text in *ibid.*, VI, 102-121.

13. Figure concerning Poles is by Marchlewski, who added that most of these people were peasants and workers. See his "Polskii vopros i oktiabrskaia revoliutsiia," *Zhizn Natsionalnostei*, 1 (1923), 230. According to the 1921 census there were nearly four million Ukrainians and over one million Belorussians in Poland.

14. Cited in the Archive of the Polish Government-in-Exile, Montreal, file 5.

15. Leon Trotsky, *Lenin* (New York, 1962), p. 115.

16. Alexander Dallin, "The Use of International Movements," in Ivo J. Lederer, ed., *Russian Foreign Policy* (New Haven, 1962), p. 346.

17. Maciej Rataj, *Pamiętniki, 1918-1927* (Warsaw, 1965), p. 48.

18. For a one-sided presentation of the elements which assured the victory of Soviet federalism see Mikhail I. Kulichenko, *Borba kommunisticheskoi partii za reshenie natsionalnogo voprosa v 1918-1920 godakh* (Kharkov, 1963), pp. 305-308.

19. Mikhail N. Pokrovskii, *Vneshniaia politika Rossii v XX veke*

(Moscow, 1926), p. 94. And Bruce Lockhard added that Chicherin "never took a decision without reference to Lenin'" (*Memoirs of a British Agent* [London, New York, 1932], p. 221).

20. Rumbold to Curzon, September 20, 1920, PRO, F.O. 371/3920, no. 214854.

21. Jędrzej Giertych, *Pół wieku polskiej polityki* (London, 1947), p. 59. Not a literal translation.

22. Two authors writing from opposite points of view agree on this. A Communist historian wrote: "Toward the end of 1919 and at the beginning of 1920 both sides prepared for military operations on a large scale." See Tadeusz Jędruszczak, "Stanowisko Polski i mocarstw Ententy w sprawie polskiej granicy wschodniej," *Sprawy Międzynarodowe*, 12, no. 6 (1959), 72. And General Julian Stachiewicz opined: "Toward the beginning of 1920 both belligerants, Poland and Soviet Russia were making large-scale preparations for a decisive military showdown which was to take place during 1920." See *Działania zaczepne 3 armii na Ukrainie* (Warsaw, 1925), p. 1.

Index

Russian Research Center Studies

* Out of print.

† Publications of the Harvard Project on the Soviet Social System.

‡ Published jointly with the Center for International Affairs, Harvard University.